TRAVELS
IN
SYRIA AND THE HOLY LAND

by
Johann Ludwig Burkhardt
(John Lewis Burckhardt)

Contents

EDITOR'S PREFACE

It is hoped that little apology is necessary for the publication of a volume of Travels in Asia, by a Society, whose sole professed object is the promotion of discoveries in the African continent.

The Association having had the good fortune to obtain the services of a person of Mr. Burckhardt's education and talents, resolved to spare neither time nor expense in enabling him to acquire the language and manners of an Arabian Musulman in such a degree of perfection, as should render the detection of his real character in the interior of Africa extremely difficult.

It was thought that a residence at Aleppo would afford him the most convenient means of study, while his intercourse with the natives of that city, together with his occasional tours in Syria, would supply him with a view of Arabian life and manners in every degree, from the Bedouin camp to the populous city. While thus preparing himself for the ultimate object of his mission, he was careful to direct his journeys through those parts of Syria which had been the least frequented by European travellers, and thus he had the opportunity of making some important additions to our knowledge of one of those countries of which the geography is not less interesting by its connection with ancient history, than it is imperfect, in consequence of the impediments which modern barbarism has opposed to scientific researches. After consuming near three years in Syria, Mr. Burckhardt, on his arrival in Egypt, found himself prevented from pursuing the execution of his instructions, by a suspension of the usual commercial intercourse with the interior of Africa, and was thus, during the ensuing five years, placed under the necessity of employing his time in Egypt and the adjacent countries in the same manner as he had done in Syria. After the journeys in Egypt, Nubia, Arabia, and Mount Sinai, which have been briefly described in the Memoir prefixed to the former volume of his travels, his death at Cairo, at the moment when he was preparing for immediate departure to Fezzan, left the Association in possession of a large collection of manuscripts concerning the countries visited by their traveller in these preparatory journeys, but of nothing more than oral information as to those to which he had been particularly sent. As his journals in Nubia, and in the regions adjacent to the Astaboras, although relating only to an incidental part of his mission to Africa, were descriptive of countries coming strictly within the scope of the African Association, these, together with all his collected information on the interior of Africa, were selected for earliest publication. The present volume contains his observations in Syria and Arabia Petraea; to which has been added his tour in the Peninsula of Mount Sinai, although the latest of all his travels in date, because it is immediately connected, by its subject, with his journey through the adjacent districts of the Holy Land. There still remain manuscripts sufficient to fill two volumes; one of these will consist of his travels in Arabia, which were confined to the Hedjaz, or Holy Land of the Musulmans, the part least accessible to Christians; the fourth volume will contain very copious remarks on the Arabs on the Desert, and particularly the Wahabys.

The two principal maps annexed to the present volume have been constructed under the continued inspection of the Editor, by Mr. John Walker, junior, by whom they have been delineated and engraved.

In the course of this process, it has been found, that our traveller's bearings by the compass are not always to be relied on. Those which were obviously incorrect, and useless for geographical purposes, have been omitted in the Journal; some instances of the same kind, which did not occur to the Editor until the sheets were printed, are noticed in the Errata, and if a few still remain, the reader is intreated not to consider them as proofs of negligence in the formation of the maps, which have been carefully constructed from Burckhardt's materials, occasionally assisted and corrected by other extant authorities. One cannot easily decide, whether the errors in our traveller's bearings are chiefly to be attributed to the variable nature of the instrument, or to the circumstances of haste and concealment under which he was often obliged to take his observations, though it is sufficiently evident that be fell into the error, not uncommon with unexperienced travellers, of multiplying bearings to an excessive degree, instead of verifying a smaller number, and measuring intermediate angles with a pocket sextant. However his mistakes may have arisen, the consequence has been, that some parts of the general map illustrative of his journeys in Syria and the Holy Land have been constructed less from his bearings than from his distances in time, combined with those of other travellers, and checked by some known points on the coast. Hence also a smaller scale has been chosen for that map than may be formed from the same materials when a few points in the interior are determined by celestial observations. In the mean time it is hoped, that the present sketch will be sufficient to enable the reader to pursue the narrative without much difficulty, especially as the part of Syria which the traveller examined with more minuteness than any other, the Haouran, is illustrated by a map upon a larger scale, which has been composed from two delineations made by him in his two journeys in that province.

It appears unnecessary to the Editor to enter into any lengthened discussion in justification of the ancient names which he has inserted in the maps; he thinks it sufficient to refer to the copious exposition of the evidences of Sacred Geography contained in the celebrated work of Reland. Much is still wanting to complete this most interesting geographical comparison; and as a great part of the country visited by Burckhardt has since his time been explored by a gentleman better qualified to illustrate its antiquities by his learning; who travelled under more favourable circumstances, and who was particuarly diligent in collecting those most faithful of all geographical evidences, ancient inscriptions, it may be left to Mr. W. Bankes, to illustrate more fully the ancient geography of the Decapolis and adjoining districts, and to remove some of the difficulties arising from the ambiguity of the ancient authorities.

It will be found, perhaps, that our traveller is incorrect in supposing, that the ruins at Omkeis are those of Gamala, for the situalion of Omkeis, the strength of its position, and the extent of the ruins, all favour the opinion that it was Gadara, the chief city of Peraea, the strongest place in this part of the country, and the situation of which, on a mountain over against Tiberias and Scythopolis, [Polyb.1.5.c.71. Joseph.de Bel. Jud.l.4.c.8. Euseb. Onomast.]. The distance of the ruins at Omkeis from the Hieromax and the hot baths seems to have been Burckhardt's objection to their being the remains of Gadara; but this distance is justified by St. Jerom, by Eusebius, and by a writer of the 5th century. According to the two former authors the hot baths were not at Gadara, but at a place near it called Aitham, or Aimath, or Emmatha; and the latter correctly states the distance at five miles. Reland Palaest. p.302, 775. Perhaps Gamala was at El Hosn; Gaulanitis, of which Gamala was the chief town, will then correspond very well with Djolan.] corresponds precisely with that of Omkeis. But it will probably be admitted, that our traveller has rightly placed several other cities, such as Scythopolis, Hippus, Abila, [There were two cities of this name. Abil on the Western borders of the Haouran appears to have been the Abila of Lysanias, which the Emperors

Claudius and Nero gave together with Batanaea and Trachonitis, to Herodes Agrippa. Joseph. Ant. Jud. l.19.c.5.--sl.20.c.7.] Gerasa, Amathus; and he has greatly improved our knowledge of Sacred Geography, by ascertaining many of the Hebrew sites in the once populous but now deserted region, formerly known by the names of Edom, Moab, Ammon, and the country of the Amorites.

The principal geographical discoveries of our traveller, are the nature of the country between the Dead Sea and the gulf of Aelana, now Akaba;-- the extent, conformation, and detailed topography of the Haouran;--the site of Apameia on the Orontes, one of the most important cities of Syria under the Macedonian Greeks;--the site of Petra, which, under the Romans, gave the name of Arabia Petraea to the surrounding territory;-- and the general structure of the peninsula of Mount Sinai; together with many new facts in its geography, one of the most important of which is the extent and form of the AElanitic gulf, hitherto so imperfectly known as either to be omitted in the maps, or marked with a bifurcation at the extremity, which is now found not to exist.

M. Seetzen, in the years 1805 and 1806, had traversed a part of the Haouran to Mezareib and Draa, had observed the Paneium at the source of the Jordan at Banias, had visited the ancient sites at Omkeis, Beit-er- Ras, Abil, Djerash and Amman, and had followed the route afterwards taken by Burckhardt through Rabbath Moab to Kerek, from whence he passed round the southern extremity of the Dead Sea to Jerusalem. The public, however, has never received any more than a very short account of these journeys, taken from the correspondence of M. Seetzen with M. de Zach, at Saxe-Gotha. [This correspondence having been communicated to the Palestine Association, was translated and printed by that Society in the year 1810, in a quarto of forty-seven pages.] He was quite unsuccessful in his inquiries for Petra, and having taken the road which leads to Mount Sinai from Hebron, he had no suspicion of the existence of the long valley known by the names of El Ghor, and El Araba.

This prolongation of the valley of the Jordan, which completes a longitudinal separation of Syria, extending for three hundred miles from the sources of that river to the eastern branch of the Red Sea, is a most important feature in the geography of the Holy Land,--indicating that the Jordan once discharged itself into the Red Sea, and confirming the truth of that great volcanic convulsion, described in the nineteenth chapter of Genesis, which interrupted the course of the river, which converted into a lake the fertile plain occupied by the cities of Adma, Zeboin, Sodom and

Gomorra, and which changed all the valley to the southward of that district into a sandy desert.

The part of the valley of the Orontes, below Hamah, in which stood the Greek cities of Larissa and Apameia, has now for the first time been examined by a scientific traveller, and the large lake together with the modern name of Famia, which have so long occupied a place in the maps of Syria, may henceforth be erased.

The country of the Nabataei, of which Petra was the chief town, is well characterized by Diodorus. [Diod. Sic.l.2,c.48.] as containing some fruitful spots, but as being for the greater part, desert and waterless. With equal accuracy, the combined information of Eratosthenes, [Eratosth. ap. Strab. p.767.] Strabo, [Strabo, p.779.] and Pliny, [Plin. Hist Nat.l.6,c.28.] describes Petra as falling in a line, drawn from the head of the Arabian gulf (Suez) to Babylon,--as being at the distance of three or four days from Jericho, and of four or five from Phoenicon, which was a place now called Moyeleh, on the Nabataean coast, near the entrance of the AElanitic gulf,--and as situated in a valley of about two miles in length surrounded with deserts, inclosed within precipices, and watered by a river. The latitude of 30 degrees 20 minutes ascribed by Ptolemy to Petra, agrees moreover very accurately with that which is the result of the geographical information of Burckhardt. The vestiges of opulence, and the apparent date of the architecture at Wady Mousa, are equally conformable with the remains of the history of Petra, found in Strabo, [P.781.] from whom it appears that previous to the reign of Augustus, or under the latter Ptolemies, a very large portion of the commerce of Arabia and India passed through Petra to the Mediterranean: and that ARMIES of camels were required to convey the merchandise from Leuce Come, on the Red Sea, [Leuce Come, on the coast of the Nabataei, was the place from whence AElius Gallus set out on his unsuccessful expedition into Arabia, (Strabo, ibid.) Its exact situation is unknown.] through Petra to Rhinocolura, now El Arish. But among the ancient authorities regarding Petra, none are more curious than those of Josephus, Eusebius, and Jerom, all persons well acquainted with these countries, and who agree in proving that the sepulchre of Aaron in Mount Hor, was near Petra. [Euseb. et Hieron. Onomast.]. Joseph. Ant. Jud.l.4.c.4.] For hence, it seems evident, that the present object of Musulman devotion, under the name of the tomb of Haroun, stands upon the same spot which has always been regarded as the burying-place of Aaron; and there remains little doubt, therefore, that the mountain to the west of Petra, is the Mount Hor of the Scriptures, Mousa being, perhaps, an Arabic corruption of Mosera, where Aaron is said to have died. [Deuter.c.x.v.6. In addition to the proofs of the site of Petra, just stated, it is worthy of remark that the distance of eighty-three Roman miles from Aila, or AElana, to Petra, in the Table (called Theodosian or Peutinger,) when compared with the distance on the map, gives a rate of about 7/10 of a Roman mile to the geographical mile in direct distance, which is not only a correct rate, but accords very accurately with that resulting from the other two routes leading from Aila in the Table, namely, from Aila to Clysma, near the modern Suez, and from Aila to Jerusalem. Szadeka, which Burckhardt visited to the south of Wady Mousa, agrees in distance and situation as well as in name with the Zadagasta of the Table, or Zodocatha of the Notitiae dignitatum Imperii. See Reland Palaest. p. 230. Most of the other places mentioned on the three roads of the Table are noticed by Ptolemy or in the Notitiae.

And here, the Editor may be permitted to add a few words on a third Roman route across these deserts, (having travelled the greater part of it three times,) namely, that from Gaza to Pelusium. In the Itinerary of Antoninus, the places, and their interjacent distances are stated as follows, Gaza, 22 M.P. Raphia, 22 M.P. Rhinocolura, 26 M.P. Ostracine, 26 M.P. Casium, 20 M.P. Pentaschoenus, 20 M.P. Pelusium. The Theodosian Table agrees with the Itinerary, but is defective in some of the names and distances; Gerrhae, placed by the Table at 8 M.P. eastward of Pelusium, is confirmed in this situation by Strabo and Ptolemy. Strabo confirms the Itinerary in regard to Raphia, omits to notice Ostracine, and in placing Casium at three hundred stades from Pelusium, differs not much from the 40 M.P. of the Itinerary, or the ten schoenes indicated by the word Pentaschoenus, midway.

The name of Rafa is still preserved near a well in the desert, at six hours march to the southward of Gaza, where among many remains of of ancient buildings, two erect granite columns are supposed by the natives to mark the division between Africa and Asia. Polybius remarks (l.5,c.80), that Raphia was the first town of Syria, coming from Rhinocolura, which was considered an Egyptian town. Between Raphia and the easternmost inundations of the Nile, the only two places at which there is moisture sufficient to produce a degree of vegetation useful to man, are El Arish and Katieh. The whole tract between these places, except where it has been encroached upon by moving sands, is a plain strongly impregnated with salt, terminatig towards the sea in a lagoon or irruption of the sea anciently called Sirbonis. As the name of Katieh, and its distance from Tineh or Pelusium, leave no doubt of its being the ancient Casium, the only remaining question is, whether El Arish is Rhinocolura, or Ostracine? A commentary of St. Jerom, on the nineteenth chapter of Isaiah, v.18, suggests the possibility that the modern name El Arish may be a corruption of the Hebrew Ares, which, as Jerom observes, alludes to Ostracine. Jerom was well acquainted with this country; but as the translators of Isaiah have supposed the word not to have been Ares, and as Jerom does not state that Ares was a name used in his time, the conjecture is not of much weight. It is impossible to reconcile the want of water so severely felt at Ostracine (Joseph. de Bel. Jud. 1.4, ad fin. Plutarch, in M. Anton. Gregor. Naz. ep. 46.), with El Arish, where there are occasional torrents, and seldom any scarcity of well water, either there or at Messudieh, two hours westward. Ostracine, therefore, was probably about mid-way between El Arish and Katieh, on the bank described by Strabo (p. 760), which separates the Sirbonis from the sea. This maritime position of Ostracine is confirmed by the march of Titus, (Joseph. ibid.) Leaving the limits of the Pelusiac territory, he moved across the desert on the first day, not to the modern Katieh, but to the temple of Jupiter, at Mount Casium, on the sea shore, at the Cape now called Ras Kasaroun; on the second day to Ostracine; on the third to Rhinocolura; on the fourth to Raphia; on the fifth to Gaza. It will be seen by the map that these positions, as now settled, furnished exactly five convenient marches, the two longest being naturally through the desert of total privation, which lies between El Arish and Katieh. As the modern route, instead of following the sea shore, passes to the southward of the lagoon, the site of Ostracine has not yet been explored.

It would seem, from the evidence regarding Petra which may be collected in ancient history, that neither in the ages prior to the commercial opulence of the Nabataei, nor after they were deprived of it, was Wady Mousa the position of their principal town.

When the Macedonian Greeks first became acquainted with this part of Syria by means of the expedition which Antigonus sent against the Nabataei, under the command of his son Demetrius, we are informed by Diodorus that these Arabs placed their old men, women, and children upon a certain rock, steep, unfortified by walls, admitting only of one access to the summit, and situated 300 stades beyond the lake Asphaltitis. [Diod. Sic. 1.19.c.95, 98.] As this interval agrees with that of Kerek from the southern extremity of the Dead Sea, and is not above half the distance of Wady Mousa from the same point; and as the other parts of the description are well adapted to Kerek, while they are inapplicable to Wady Mousa, we can hardly doubt that Kerek was at that time the fortress of the Nabataei; and that during the first ages of the intercourse of that people with the Greeks, it was known to the latter by the name Petra, so often applied by them to barbarian hill-posts.

When the effects of commerce required a situation better suited than Kerek to the collected population and increased opulence of the Nabataei, the appellation of Petra was transferred to the new city at Wady Mousa, which place had before been known to the Greeks by the name of Arce, a corruption perhaps of the Hebrew Rekem. [Joseph. Antiq. Jud. l.4,c.4.] To Wady Mousa, although of a very different aspect from Kerek, the name Petra was equally well adapted; and Kerek then became distinguished among the Greeks by its indigenous name, in the Greek form of Charax, to which the Romans added that of Omanorum, or Kerek of Ammon, [Plin. Hist. Nat. l.6,c.28.] to distinguish it from another Kerek, now called Kerek el Shobak. The former Kerek was afterwards restored by the Christians to the Jewish division of Moab, to which, being south of the river Arnon, it strictly belonged, and it was then called in Greek Charagmoba, under which name we find it mentioned as one of the cities and episcopal dioceses of the third Palestine. [Hierocl. Synecd. Notit. Episc. Graec.]

When the stream of commerce which had enriched the Nabataei had partly reverted to its old Egyptian channel, and had partly taken the new course, which created a Palmyra in the midst of a country still more destitute of the commonest gifts of nature, then Arabia Petraea, [A comparison of the architecture at Wady Mousa, and at Tedmour, strengthens the opinion, that Palmyra flourished at a period later than Petra.] Wady Mousa was gradually depopulated. Its river, however, and the intricate recesses of its rocky valleys, still attract and give security to a tribe of Arabs; but the place being defensible only by considerable numbers, and being situated in a less fertile country than Kerek, was less adapted to be the chief town of the Nabataei, when they had returned to their natural state of divided wanderers or small agricultural communities. The Greek bishopricks of the third Palestine were obliterated by the Musulman conquest, with the sole exception of the metropolitan Petra, whose titular bishop still resides at Jerusalem, and occasionally visits Kerek, as being the only place in his province which contains a Christian community. Hence Kerek has been considered the see of the bishoprick of Petra, and hence has arisen the erroneous opinion often adopted by travellers from the Christians of Jerusalem, that Kerek is the site of the ancient capital of Arabia Petraea.

The Haouran being only once mentioned in the Sacred Writings, [Ezekiel. c. xlvii v. 16.] was probably of inconsiderable extent under the

Jews, but enlarged its boundaries under the Greeks and Romans, by whom it was called Auranitis. It has been still farther increased since that time, and now includes not only Auranitis, but Ituraea also, or Ittur, of which Djedour is perhaps a corruption; together with the greater part of Basan, or Batanaea, and Trachonitis. Burckhardt seems not to have been aware of the important comment upon Trachonitis afforded by his description of the singular rocky wilderness of the Ledja, and by the inscriptions which he copied at Missema, in that district. It appears from these inscriptions, that Missema was anciently the town of the Phaenesii, and the metrocomia or chief place of Trachon, the descriptions of which district by Strabo and Josephus, [Strabo, 755, 756. Joseph. Antiq. Jud. l.15,c.13.] are in exact conformity with that which Burckhardt has given us of the Ledja.

From Strabo and Ptolemy, [Strabo, ibid. Ptolemy, l.5,c.15.] we learn that Trachonitis comprehended all the uneven country extending along the eastern side of the plain of Haouran, from near Damascus to Boszra. It was in consequence of the predatory incursions of the Arabs from the secure recesses of the Ledja into the neighbouring plains, that Augustus transferred the government of Trachonitis from Zenodorus, who was accused of encouraging them, to Herod, king of Judaea. [Joseph. Antiq. Jud.l.5,c.10. De Bell. Jud.l.1,c.20.] The two Trachones, into which Trachonitis was divided, agree with the two natural divisions of the Ledja and Djebel Haouran.

Oerman, an ancient ruin at the foot of the Djebel Haouran, to the east of Boszra, appears from an inscription copied there by Burckhardt, to be the site of Philippopolis, a town founded by Philip, emperor of Rome, who was a native of Boszra.

Another ancient name is found at Hebran, in the same mountains, to the N.E. of Boszra, where an inscription records the gratitude of the tribe of AEedeni to a Roman veteran. The Kelb Haouran, or summit of the Djebel Haouran, appears to be the Mount Alsadamum of Ptolemy. [Ptolem.l.5,c.15.]

Of the ancient towns just mentioned, Philippopolis alone is noticed in ancient history; and although the name of Phaeno occurs as a bishoprick of Palestine, and that the adjective Phaenesius is applied to some mines at that place, it seems evident that these Phaenesii were different from those of Trachon, and that they occupied a part of Idumaea, between Petra and the southern extremity of the Dead Sea. [Reland. Palaest. 1.3, voce Phaeno.]

9

Mezareib, a village and castle on the Hadj route, appears to be the site of Astaroth, the residence of Og, king of Bashan; [Deuter. c.l.v.4. Josh. c.ix.v.10.] for Eusebius [Euseb. Onomast.] places Astaroth at 6 miles from Adraa (or Edrei, now Draa,) between that place and Abila (now Abil), and at 25 miles from Bostra, a distance very nearly confirmed by the Theodosian Table, which gives 24 Roman miles between those two places. It will be seen by the map, that the position of Mezareib conforms to all these particulars. The unfailing pool of the clearest water, which now attracts the men and cattle of all the surrounding country to Mezareib in summer, must have made it a place of importance in ancient times, and therefore excited the wonder of our traveller at its having preserved only some very scanty relics of antiquity.

Although Mount Sinai, and the deserts lying between that peninsula and Judaea, have not, like the latter country, preserved many of the names of Holy Scripture, the new information of Burckhardt contains many facts in regard to their geography and natural history, which may be useful in tracing the progress of the Israelites from Egypt into Syria.

The bitter well of Howara, 15 hours southward of Ayoun Mousa, corresponds as well in situation as in the quality of its water, with the well of Marah, at which the Israelites arrived after passing through a desert of three days from the place near Suez where they had crossed the Red Sea. [Exodus, c.xiv. xv. Numbers. c.xxxiii.]

The Wady Gharendel, two hours beyond Howara, where are wells among date trees, seems evidently to be the station named Elim, which was next to Marah, and at which the Israelites found "twelve wells of water, and threescore and ten palm trees." [Exodus, c.xv. Numbers, c.xxxiii.] And it is remarkable, that the Wady el Sheikh, and the upper part of the Wady Feiran, the only places in the peninsula where manna is gathered from below the tamarisk trees, accord exactly with that part of the desert of Sin, in which Moses first gave his followers the sweet substance gathered in the morning, which was to serve them for bread during their long wandering; [Exodus, c.xvi.] for the route through Wady Taybe, Wady Feiran, and Wady el Sheikh, is the only open and easy passage to Mount Sinai from Wady Gharendel; and it requires the traveller to pass for some distance along the sea shore after leaving Gharendel, as we are informed that the Israelites actually did, on leaving Elim. [Numbers, c.xxxiii.v.10, 11.]

The upper region of Sinai, which forms an irregular circle of 30 or 40 miles in diameter, possessing numerous sources of water, a temperate climate, and a soil capable of supporting animal and vegetable nature, was the part of the peninsula best adapted to the residence of near a year, during which the Israelites were numbered and received their laws.

About the beginning of May, in the fourteenth month from the time of their departure from Egypt, the children of Israel quitted the vicinity of Mount Horeb, and under the guidance of Hohab, the Midianite, brother- in-law of Moses, marched to Kadesh, a place on the frontiers of Canaan, of Edom, and of the desert of Paran or Zin. [Numbers, c.x. et seq. and c.33. Deuter. c.i.] Not long after their arrival, "at the time of the 'first ripe grapes,'" or about the beginning of August, spies were sent into every part of the cultivated country, as far north as Hamah. [Numbers, c.xiii. Deuter. c.i.] The report which they brought back was no less favourable to the fertility of the land, than it was discouraging by its description of the warlike spirit and preparation of the inhabitants, and of the strength of the fortified places; and the Israelites having in consequence refused to follow their leaders into Canaan, were punished by that long wandering in the deserts lying between Egypt, Judaea, and Mount Sinai, of which the sacred historian has not left us any details, but the tradition of which is still preserved in the name of El Tyh, annexed to the whole country; both to the desert plains, and to the mountains lying between them and Mount Sinai.

In the course of their residence in the neighbourhood of Kadesh, the Israelites obtained some advantages over the neighbouring Canaanites, [Numbers, c.xxi.] but giving up at length all hope of penetrating by the frontier, which lies between Gaza and the Dead Sea, they turned to the eastward, with a view of making a circuit through the countries on the southern and eastern sides of the lake. [Numbers, c.xx, xxi.] Here however, they found the difficulty still greater; Mount Seir of Edom, which under the modern names of Djebal, Shera, and Hesma, forms a ridge of mountains, extending from the southern extremity of the Dead Sea to the gulf of Akaba, rises abruptly from the valleys El Ghor and El Araba, and is traversed from west to east by a few narrow Wadys only, among which the Ghoeyr alone furnishes an entrance that would not be extremely difficult to a hostile force. This perhaps was the "high way," by which Moses, aware of the difficulty of forcing a passage, and endeavouring to obtain his object by negotiation, requested the Edomites to let him pass, on the condition of his leaving the fields and vineyards untouched, and of purchasing provisions and water from the inhabitants. [Numbers, c.xx. Deuter, c.i.] But Edom "refused to give Israel passage through his border," and "came out against him with much people, and with a strong hand." [Numbers, c.xx.] The situation of the Israelites therefore, was very critical. Unable to force their way in either direction, and having enemies on three sides; (the Edomites in front, and the Canaanites, and Amalekites on their left flank and rear,) no alternative remained for them but to follow the valley El Araba southwards, towards the head of the Red Sea. At Mount Hor, which rises abruptly from that valley, "by the coast of the land of Edom," [Numbers, ibid.] Aaron died, and was buried in the conspicuous situation, which tradition has preserved as the site of his tomb to the present day. Israel then "journeyed from Mount Hor, by the way of the Red Sea, to compass the land of Edom," [Numbers, c.xxi.] "through the way of the plain from Elath, and from Eziongeber," until "they turned and passed by the way of the wilderness of Moab, and arrived at the brook Zered." [Deuter, c.ii.] It may be supposed that they crossed the ridge to the southward of Eziongeber, about the place where Burckhardt remarked, from the opposite coast, that the mountains were lower than to the northward, and it was in this part of their wandering that they suffered from the serpents, of which our traveller observed the traces of great numbers on the opposite shore of the AElanitic gulf. The Israelites then issued into the great elevated plains which are traversed by the Egyptian and Syrian pilgrims, on the way to Mekka, after they have passed the two Akabas. Having entered these plains, Moses received the divine command, "You have compassed this mountain long enough, turn you northward."--"Ye are to pass through the coast of your brethren the children of Esau, which dwell in Seir, and they shall be afraid of you." [Deuter, c.ii.] The same people who had successfully repelled the approach of the Israelites from the strong western frontier, was alarmed now that they had come round upon the weak side of the country. But Israel was ordered "not to meddle" with the children of Esau, but "to pass through their coast" and to "buy meat and water from them for money," in the same manner as the caravan of Mekka is now supplied by the people of the same mountains, who meet the pilgrims on the Hadj route. After traversing the wilderness on the eastern side of Moab, the Israelites at length entered that country, crossing the brook Zered in the thirty-eighth year, from their first arrival at Kadesh Barnea, "when all the generation of the men of war were wasted out from among the host." [Deuter, c.ii.] After passing through the centre of Moab, they crossed the Arnon, entered Ammon, and were at length permitted to begin the overthrow of the possessors of the promised land, by the destruction of Sihon the Amorite, who dwelt at Heshbon. [Numbers, c.xxi. Deuter, c.ii.] The preservation of the latter name, and of those of Diban, Medaba, Aroer, Amman, together with the other geographical facts derived from the journey of

Burckhardt through the countries beyond the Dead Sea, furnishes a most satisfactory illustration of the sacred historians.

It remains for the Editor only to add, that while correcting the foreign idiom of his Author, and making numerous alterations in the structure of the language, he has been as careful as posible not to injure the originality of the composition, stamped as it is with the simplicity, good sense, and candour, inseparable from the Author's character. In the Editor's wish, however, to preserve this originality, he cannot flatter himself that incorrect expressions may not sometimes have been left. In regard to the Greek inscriptions, he thinks it necessary only to remark, that although the propriety of furnishing the reader with fac-similes of all such interesting relicts of ancient history cannot in general be doubted, yet in the present instance, the trouble and expense which it would have occasioned, would hardly have been compensated by the importance of the monuments themselves, or by the degree of correctness with which they were copied by the traveller. They have therefore been printed in a type nearly resembling the Greek characters which were in use at the date of the inscriptions, and the Editor has taken the liberty of separating the words, and of supplying in the small cursive Greek character, the defective parts of the traveller's copies.

The Editor takes this opportunity of stating, that in consequence of some discoveries in African geography, which have been made known since the publication of Burckhardt's Travels in Nubia, he has made some alterations in the maps of the second edition of that work. The observations of Captain Lyon have proved Morzouk to be situated a degree and a half to the southward of the position formerly assigned to it, and his enquiries having at the same time confirmed the bearing and distance between Morzouk and Bornou, as reported by former travellers, a corresponding change will follow in the latitude of Bornou, as well as in the position of the places on the route leading to those two cities from the countries of the Nile.

A journey into Nubia, by the Earl of Belmore, and his brother, the Hon. Capt. Corry, has furnished some latitudes and longitudes, serving to correct the map of "the course of the Nile, from Assouan to the confines of Dongola", which the Editor constructed from the journals of Burckhardt, without the assistance of any celestial observations. The error in the map as to the most distant point observed by Lord Belmore is however so small, that it has not been thought necessary to make any alteration in that map for the second edition of Burckhardt's Journey in Nubia; but the whole delineation of this part of the Nile will be corrected from the recent observations, in a new edition of the Supplement to the Editor's general Map of Egypt.

Since the Journey of Lord Belmore, Mr. Waddington and Mr. Hanbury, taking advantage of an expedition sent into AEthiopia by the Viceroy of Egypt, have prolonged the examination of the Nile four hundred miles beyond the extreme point reached by Burckhardt; and some French gentlemen have continued to follow the army as far as Sennaar. The presence of a Turkish army in that country will probably furnish greater facilities for exploring the Bahr el Abiad, or western branch of the Nile, than have ever before been presented to travellers; there is reason to hope, that the opportunity will not be neglected, and thus a survey of this celebrated river from its sources to the Mediterranean, may, perhaps, at length be made, if not for the first time, for the first time at least since the extinction of Egyptian science.

The expedition of the Pasha of Egypt has already produced some important additions to African geography. By permission of Mr. Waddington, the Editor has corrected, from that gentleman's delineation, the parts of the Nile above Mahass, for the second edition of Burckhardt's Nubia, and from the information transmitted to England by Mr. Salt, he has been enabled to insert in the same map, the position of the ruins of an ancient city situated about 20 miles to the north-eastward of Shendy.

These ruins had already been partially seen by Bruce and Burckhardt, [Burckhardt passed through the vestiges of what seems to have been a dependency of this city on the Nile, at seven hours to the north of Shendy, and two hours to the south of Djebail; the latter name, which is applied by Burckhardt to a large village on a range of hills, is evidently the same as the Mount Gibbainy, where Bruce observed the same ruins, which have now been more completely explored by M. Cailliaud. See Travels in Nubia, p.275. Bruce's Travels, Vol. iv. p.538, 4to.] and there can be little doubt that Bruce was right in supposing them to be the remains of Meroe, the capital of the great peninsula of the same name, of which the general geography appears to have been known with considerable accuracy to men of science in the Augustan age, although it had not been visited by any of the writers whose works have reached us. For, assuming [To illustrate the following observations, as well as some of the preceding, a small drawing of the course of the Nile is inserted in the margin of the map of Syria which accompanies the present volume.] these ruins to mark the site of the city Meroe, and that the latitude and longitude of Shendy have been accurately determined by Bruce, whose instruments were good, and whose competency to the task of observation is undoubted, it will be found that Ptolemy is very nearly right in ascribing the latitude of 16.26 to the city Meroe. [Ptolem. 1.4,c.8.] Pliny [Plin. Hist. Nat. 1.2,c.73.] is equally correct in stating that the two points of the ecliptic, in which the sun is in the zenith at Meroe, are the 18th degree of Taurus, and the 14th degree of Leo. The 5000 stades which Strabo [Strabo, p. 113.] and Pliny [Plin. ibid.] We learn from another passage in Pliny, (l.6,c.29,) that the persons sent by Nero to explore the Nile, measured 884 miles, "by the river", from Syene to Meroe.] assert to be the distance between Meroe and Syene is correct, at a rate of between 11 and 12 stades to the geographical mile; if the line be taken in direct distance, as evidently appears to have been the intention of Strabo, by his thrice stating (upon the authority of Eratosthenes,) that the distance from Meroe to Alexandria was 10,000 stades. [Eratosth. ap. strab. p. 62. Strabo, p. 113, 825.] The latitudes of Ptolemy equally accord in shewing the equidistance of Syene from Meroe and from Alexandria; the latitude of Syene being stated by him at 23-50, [Ptolem. 1.4,c.6.] and that of Alexandria at 31-0. [Ptolem. ibid.] The description of the island of Meroe as being 3000 stades long, and 1000 broad, in form like a shield, and as formed by the confluence of the Astasobas, Astapus, and Astaboras, [Eratosth. ap. Strab. p.786. Strab. p.821. Diodor. Sic. l.l,c.33. Heliodor. AEthiop. l.10,c.5] is perfectly applicable to the great peninsula watered on the east by the Tacazze, and on the west by the Bahr el Abiad, after receiving the Bahr el Azrek. The position of the city Meroe is shewn by Artemidorus, Ptolemy, and Pliny, [Artemid. ap. Strab. p.771. Ptolem. 1.4,c.8. Plin. Hist. Nat. l.6,c.29.] to have been, like the ruins near Shendy, near the northern angle of the island, or the confluence of the rivers. The island between Djebail and Shendy which Bruce calls Kurgos, answers to that which Pliny describes as the port of Meroe; and finally, the distance of "15 days to a good walker," which Artemidorus [Artemid. ibid.] places between Meroe and the sea, giving a rate of about 16 English miles a-day, in direct distance, is a correct statement of the actual distance between the ruins near Shendy and Souakin. [It is fair to remark, that there are two authorities which tend to place the city of Meroe 30 or 40 miles to the southward of the ruins near Shendy. Eratosthenes states it to have been at 700 stades, and Pliny at 70 miles above the confluence. But it is rare indeed to find a coincidence of many ancient authorities in a question where numbers are concerned, unless one author has borrowed from another, which is probably the case in regard to the two just quoted.]

It will hardly be contested, that the modern name of Merawe, which is found attached to a town near the ruins of an ancient city, discovered by Messrs. Waddington and Hanbury in the country of the

Sheygya, is sufficient to overthrow the strong evidence just stated. It may rather be inferred, that the Greek Meroe was formed from a word signifying "city" in the ancient AEthiopic language, which has continued up to the present time, to be attached to the site of one of the chief cities on the banks of the Nile,--thus resembling in its origin many names of places in various countries, which from simple nouns expressive in the original language of objects or their qualities, such as city, mountain, river, sacred, white, blue, black, have been converted by foreigners into proper names.

The ruins near Merawe seem to those of Napata, the chief town of the country intermediate between Meroe and Egypt, and which was taken by the praefect Petronius, in the reign of Augustus, when it was the capital of Queen Candace; [Ptolem. l.4,c.7. Strabo, p.820. Plin. Hist. Nat.l.6,c.29.] for Pliny, on the authority of the persons sent by Nero to EXPLORE the river above Syene, states 524 Roman miles to have been the interval between Syene and Napata, and 360 miles to have been that between Napata and Meroe, which distances correspond more nearly than could have been expected with the real distances between Assouan, Merawe, and Shendy, taken along the general curve of the river, without considering the windings in detail. [We must not, however, too confidently pronounce on REAL distances until we possess a few more positions fixed by astronomical observations.]

The island of Argo, from its extent, its important ruins, its fertility, as well as from the similarity of name, seems to be the Gora, of Juba, [Ap. Plin. ibid.] or the Gagaudes, which the explorers of Nero reported to be situated at 133 miles below Napata.

In placing Napata at the ruins near Mérawe, it is necessary to abandon the evidence of Ptolemy, whose latitude of Napata is widely different from that of Merawe; and as we also find, that he is considerably in error, in regard to the only point between Syene and Meroe, hitherto ascertained, namely, the Great Cataract, which he places 37 minutes to the north of Wady Halfa, still less can we rely upon his authority for the position of the obscurer towns.

Although the extreme northern point to which the Nile descends below Berber, before it turns to the south, is not yet accurately determined in latitude, nor the degree of southern latitude which the river reaches before it finally takes the northern course, which it continues to the Mediterranean, we cannot doubt that Eratosthenes had received a tolerably correct account of its general course from the Egyptians, notwithstanding his incorrectness in regard to the proportionate length of the great turnings of the river.

"The Nile," he says "after having flowed to the north from Meroe for the space of 2700 stades, turns to the south and southwest for 3700 stades, entering very far into Lybia, until it arrives in the latitude of Meroe; then making a new turn, it flows to the north for the space of 5300 stades, to the great Cataract, whence inclining a little eastward, it traverses 1200 stades to the small Cataract of Syene, and then 5300 stades to the sea. [Ap. Strab. p.786. The only mode of reconciling these numbers to the truth, is to suppose the three first of them to have been taken with all the windings of the stream, the two last in a direct line, and even then they cannot be very accurate.] The Nile receives two rivers, which descending from certain lakes surround the great island of Meroe. That which flows on the eastern side is called Astaboras, the other is the Astapus, though some say it is the Astasobas," &c.

This ambiguity, it is hardly necessary to observe, was caused by the greater magnitude of the Astasobas, or Bahr el Abiad, or White River, which caused it to give name to the united stream after its junction with the Astapus, or Bahr el Azrek, or Blue River; and hence Pliny, [Plin. Hist. Nat. l.5,c.9.] in speaking of Meroe, does not say that it was formed by the Astapus, but by the Astasobas. In fact, the Astapus forms the boundary of the island, as it was called, on the S.W. the Astasobas, or united stream, on the N.W.

WILLIAM MARTIN LEAKE, Acting Secretary of the African Association.

JOURNAL OF A TOUR FROM DAMASCUS IN THE COUNTRIES OF THE LIBANUS, AND ANTI-LIBANUS.

September 22, 1810.--I Left Damascus at four o'clock P.M. with a small caravan destined for Tripoli; passed Salehíe, and beyond it a Kubbe, [Kubbe, a cupola supported by columns or walls; the sepulchre of a reputed saint.] from whence I had, near sun-set, a most beautiful view of the city of Damascus and its surrounding country. From the Kubbe, the road passes along the left side of the valley in which the Barrada runs, over uneven ground, which for the greater part is barren rock. After a ride of two hours and a quarter from Salehie, we descended to the river's side, and passed the Djissr [Djissr--Bridge.] Dumar; on the other side of which we encamped. It is a well-built bridge, with two archies, at twenty minutes distance from the village Dumar.

September 23.--We set off before daylight, crossing the mountains, in one of whose Wadys [Wady--Valley.] the Barrada winds along; we crossed it repeatedly, and after two hours arrived at the village Eld-jdide, built on the declivity of a hill near the source of one of the numerous rivulets that empty themselves into the Barrada. One hour and three quarters further, we descended into the Wady Barrada, near two villages, built on either side of the river, opposite to each other, called Souk Barrada. [Souk (market) is an appellation often added to villages, which have periodical markets.] The valley of the Barrada, up to Djissr Barrada, is full of fruit trees; and where its breadth permits, Dhourra and wheat are sown. Half an hour further, is Husseine, a small village in the lower part of the valley. Three-quarters of an hour, El Souk; here the Wady begins to be very narrow. A quarter of an hour beyond, turning round a steep rock, the valley presents a very wild and picturesque aspect. To the left, in the mountain, are six chambers cut in the rock; said to be the work of Christians, to whom the greater part of the ancient structures in Syria are ascribed. The river was not fordable here; and it would have taken me at least two hours to reach, by a circuitous route, the opposite mountains. A little way higher up is the Djissr el Souk, at the termination of the Wady; this bridge was built last year, as appears by an Arabic inscription on the rock near it. From the bridge the road leads up the side of the mountain, and enters, after half an hour's ride, upon a plain country. The river has a pretty cascade, near which are the remains of a bridge. The above mentioned plain is about three- quarters of an hour in breadth, and three hours in length; it is called Ard Zebdeni, or the district of Zebdeni; it is watered by the Barrada, one of whose sources is in the midst of it; and by the rivulet called Moiet [Moye--Water.] Zebdeni, whose source is in the mountain, behind the village of the same name. The latter river, which empties itself into the Barrada, has, besides the source in the Ard Zebdeni, another of an equal size near Fidji, in a side branch of the Wady Barrada, half an hour from the village Husseine. The fall of the river is very rapid. We followed the plain of Zebdeni from one end to the other: it is limited on one side by the eastern part of the Anti- Libanus, called here Djebel Zebdeni. Its cultivable ground is waste till near the village of Beroudj, where I saw plantations of mulberry trees, which seemed to be well taken care of. Half an hour from Beroudj is the village of Zebdeni, and between them the ruined Khan Benduk (the bastard Khan). Zebdeni is a considerable village; its inhabitants breed cattle, and the silk-worm, and have some dyeing houses. I had a letter for the Sheikh of Zebdeni from a Damascene; the Sheikh ordered me an Argile [Argile--A Persian pipe, in which the smoke passes through water.] and a cup of coffee, but went to supper with his household, without inviting me to join them. This being considered an insult, I left his house and went to sup with the muleteers, with whom I slept upon an open piece of ground before a ruined bath, in the midst of the village. The inhabitants of Zebdeni are three-fourths Turks, and the remainder Greek Catholics; it is a place much frequented by those passing from Damascus to the mountain.

September 24.--Left the village before day-light and crossed the Anti- Libanus, at the foot of which Zebdeni lies. This chain of mountains is, by the inhabitants of the Bekaa and the Belad [Belad--District, province.] Baalbec, called Djebel [Djebel--Mountain.] Essharki (or the eastern mountain), in opposition to Djebel el Gharbi, the western mountain, otherwise called Djebel Libnan (Libanus); but that part of it which lies nearer to Zebdeni than to the great valley, is called Djebel Zebdeni. We travelled for the greater part of the morning upon the mountain. Its rock is primitive calcareous, of a fine grain; upon the highest part I found a sandy slate: on the summit and on the eastern side of this part of the Anti-Libanus there are many spots, affording good pasturage, where a tribe of Turkmans sometimes feed their cattle. It abounds also in short oak trees, of which I saw none higher than twelve or fifteen feet. Our road lay N.W. Two hours and a half from Zebdeni we passed a spot with several wells, called Bir [Bir-- Well.] Anhaur, or Bekai. The western declivity of the mountain, towards the district of Baalbec, is completely barren, without pasture or trees. After five hours and three quarters riding we descended into the plain, near the half-ruined village of El Kanne, and passed the river of El Kanne, whose source is at three hours distance, in the mountain. It empties itself into the Liettani, in the plain, two hours below Kanne. I here left the caravan and took a guide to Zahle, where I meant to stay a few days. Our way lay W.b.N. across the plain; passed the village El Nahrien Haoush Hale, consisting of miserable mud cottages. The plain is almost totally uncultivated. Passed the Liettani at two hours from El Kanne. Half an hour, on the other side of it, is the village Kerak, at the foot of the Djebel Sannin; it consists of about one hundred and fifty-houses and has some gardens in the plain, which are watered by a branch of the Berdoun, or river of Zahle. Kerak is entirely inhabited by Turks; it belongs to: the dominions of the Emir of the Druses, who some years ago took it by force from the Emir of Baalbec. On the southern side of the village is a mosque, and adjoining to it a long building, on the eastern side of which are the ruins of another mosque, with a Kubbe still remaining. The long building contains, under a flat roof, the pretended tomb of Noah; it consists of a tomb-stone above ten feet long, three broad and two high, plastered all over; the direction of its length is S.E. and N.W. The Turks visit the grave, and pretend that Noah is really buried there. At half an hour from Kerak is the town of Zahle, built in an inlet of the mountain, on a steep ascent, surrounded with Kerums (vineyards). The river Berdoun here issues from a narrow valley into the plain and waters the gardens of

Zahle.

September 25th.--Took a walk through the town with Sheikh Hadj Farakh. There are eight or nine hundred houses, which daily increase, by fugitives from the oppressions of the Pashas of Damascus and of the neighbouring petty tyrants. Twenty-five years ago there were only two hundred houses at Zahle: it is now one of the principal towns in the territory of the Emir Beshir. It has its markets, which are supplied from Damascus and Beirout, and are visited by the neighbouring Fellahs, and the Arabs El Naim, and El Harb, and El Faddel, part of whom pass the winter months in the Bekaa, and exchange their butter against articles of dress, and tents, and horse and camel furniture. The inhabitants, who may amount to five thousand, are all Catholic Greeks, with the exception only of four or five Turkish families. The Christians have a bishop, five churches and a monastery, the Turks have no mosque. The town belongs to the territory of the Druses, and is under the authority of the Emir Beshir, but a part of it still belongs to the family of Aamara, whose influence, formerly very great in the Mountain, has lately been so much circumscribed by the Emir, that the latter is now absolute master of the town. The Emir receives the Miri, which is commonly the double of its original assessment (in Belad Baalbec it is the triple), and besides the Miri, he makes occasional demands upon the town at large. They had paid him forty-five purses a few weeks before my arrival. So far the Emir Beshir's government resembles perfectly that of the Osmanlys in the eastern part of Syria: but there is one great advantage which the people enjoy under his command--an almost complete exemption from all personal exactions, and the impartiality of justice, which is dealt out in the same manner to the Christian and to the Turk. It is curious, that the peace of so numerous a body should be maintained without any legal power whatsoever. There is neither Sheikh nor governor in the town; disputes are settled by the friends of the respective parties, or if the latter are obstinate, the decision is referred to the tribunal of the Emir Beshir, at Deir el Kammar. The inhabitants, though not rich, are, in general, in independent circumstances; each family occupies one, or at most two rooms. The houses are built of mud; the roofs are supported by one or two wooden posts in the midst of the principal room, over which beams of pine-wood are laid across each other; upon these are branches of oak trees, and then the earth, which forms the flat terrace of the house. In winter the deep snow would soon break through these feeble roofs, did not the inhabitants take care, every morning, to remove the snow that may have fallen during the night. The people gain their subsistence, partly by the cultivation of their vineyards and a few mulberry plantations, or of their fields in the Bekaa, and partly by their shops, by the commerce in Kourdine sheep, and their manufactures. Almost every family weaves cotton cloth, which is used as shirts by the inhabitants and Arabs, and when dyed blue, as Kombazes, or gowns, by the men. There are more than twenty dyeing houses in Zahle, in which indigo only is employed. The Pike [The Pike is a linear measure, equal to two feet English, when used for goods of home manufacture, and twenty-seven inches for foreign imported commodities.] of the best of this cotton cloth, a Pike and a half broad, costs fifty paras, (above 1s. 6d. English). The cotton is brought from Belad Safad and Nablous. They likewise fabricate Abbayes, or woollen mantles. There are above one hundred horsemen in the town. In June 1810, when the Emir Beshir joined with his corps the army of Soleiman Pasha, to depose Youssef Pasha, he took from Zahle 400 men, armed with firelocks.

On the west side of the town, in the bottom of the Wady, lies the monastery of Mar Elias, inhabited by a prior and twenty monks. It has extensive grape and mulberry plantations, and on the river side a well cultivated garden, the products of which are sold to the town's people. The prior received me with great arrogance, because I did not stoop to kiss his hands, a mark of respect which the ecclesiastics of this country are accustomed to receive. The river of Zahle, or Berdoun, forms the frontier of the Bekaa, which it separates from the territory belonging to the Emir of Baalbec, called Belad Baalbec; so that whatever is northward from the bridge of the Berdoun, situated in the valley, a quarter of an hour below Zahle, belongs to Belad Baalbec; and whatever is south-ward, to the Bekaa. Since Soleiman Pasha has governed Damascus, the authority of the Emir Beshir has been in some measure extended over the Bekaa, but I could not inform myself of the distinct laws by which it had been regulated. The Pashas of Damascus, and the Emir Beshirs, have for many years been in continual dispute about their rights over the villages of the Bekaa. Following up the Berdoun into the Mountain, are the villages of Atein, Heraike, and another in the vicinity of Zahle.

September 26.--On the night of the 25th to the 26th, was the Aid Essalib, or feast of the Cross, the approach of which was celebrated by repeated discharges of musquets and the lighting of numerous fires, which illuminated all the mountains around the town and the most conspicuous parts of the town itself.

I rode to Andjar, on the eastern side of the Bekaa, in a direction south-east by south, two hours and a half good walking from Zahle. I found several encampments of the Arabs Naim and Faddel in the plain. In one hour and a quarter, passed the Liettani, near an ancient arched bridge; it had very little water: not the sixth part of the plain is cultivated here. The place called Andjar lies near the Anti-Libanus, and consists of a ruined town-wall, inclosing an oblong square of half an hour in circumference; the greater part of the wall is in ruins. It was originally about twelve feet thick, and constructed with small unhewn stones, loosely cemented and covered by larger square stones, equally ill cemented. In the enclosed space are the ruins of habitations, of which the foundations alone remain. In one of these buildings are seen the remains of two columns of white marble, one foot and a quarter in diameter. The whole seems to have been constructed in modern times. Following the

Mountain to the southward of these ruins, for twenty minutes, I came to the place where the Moiet Andjar, or river of Andjar, has its source in several springs. This river had, when I saw it, more than triple the volume of water of the Liettani; but though it joins the latter in the Bekaa, near Djissr Temnin, the united stream retains the name Liettani. There are remains of ancient well-built walls round all the springs which constitute the source of the Andjar; one of the springs, in particular, which forms a small but very deep basin, has been lined to the bottom with large stones, and the wall round it has been constructed with large square stones, which have no traces of ever having been cemented together. In the wall of a mill, which has been built very near these springs, I saw a sculptured architrave. These remains appear to be much more ancient than those of Andjar, and are perhaps coeval with the buildings at Baalbec. I was told, by the people of the mill, that the water of the larger spring, in summer time, stops at certain periods and resumes its issue from under the rock, eight or ten times in a day. Further up in the mountain, above the spring, is a large cavern where the people sometimes collect saltpetre; but it is more abundant in a cavern still higher in the mountain.

Following the road northward on the chain of the Anti-Libanus, half an hour from these springs, I met with another copious spring; and a little higher, a third; one hour further, is a fourth, which I did not visit. Near the two former are traces of ancient walls. The waters of all these sources join in Moiet Andjar, and they are all comprised under the appellation of the Springs of Moiet Andjar. They are partly covered with rushes, and are much frequented by water fowls, and wild boars also resort to them in great numbers.

August 27th.--Being disappointed in my object of proceeding to Baalbec, I passed the day in the shop of one of the petty merchants of Zahle, and afterwards supped with him. The sales of the merchants are for the greater part upon credit; even those to the Arabs for the most trifling sums. The common interest of money is 30 percent.

August 28th.--Set out in the afternoon for Baalbec, with a native of that place, who had been established with his family at Zahle, for several years. Passed the villages of Kerak, Abla, Temnin, Beit Shaeme, Haoush el Rafka, Tel Hezin, and arrived, after seven hours, at Baalbec. [The following are the names of villages in Belad Baalbec, between Baalbec and Zahle. On the Libanus, or on the declivity near its foot; Kerak, Fursul, Nieha, Nebi Eily, Temnin foka (the upper Temnin) Bidneil, Smustar, Hadad Tareie, Nebi Ershaedi, Kefferdein Saide, Budei, Deir Akhmar, Deir Eliaout, Sulife, Btedai. In the plain; Abla, Temnin tahte (the lower

Temnin) Ksarnabe, Beit Shaeme, Gferdebesh, Haoush el Rafka, Haoush el Nebi, Haoush Esseneid, Telhezin (with a copious spring), Medjdeloun, Haoush Barada, Haoush Tel Safie, Tel Wardin, Sergin, Ain, Ouseie, Haoush Mesreie, Bahami, Duris, Yead. On the Anti-Libanus, or near its foot; Briteil, Tallie, Taibe, Khoreibe, El Aoueine, Nebi Shit, Marrabun, Mouze, Kanne, Deir el Ghazal, Reia, Hushmush. All these villages are inhabited by Turks or Metawelis; Abla and Fursul are the only Christian villages. I subjoin the villages in the plain to the N. of Baalbec, belonging to the territory of Baalbec. On the Libanus; Nebba, Essafire, Harbate. On the Plain; Tunin, Shaet, Ras el Haded, Leboue, El Kaa. Anti-Libanus, and at its foot: Nahle, El Ain, Nebi Oteman, Fiki, Erzel, Mukra, El Ras.]

The territory of Baalbec extends, as I have before mentioned, down to the Bekaa. On the eastern side it comprises the mountain of the Anti- Libanus, or Djebel Essharki, up to its top; and on the western side, the Libanus likewise, as far as its summits. In the plain it reaches as far as El Kaa, twelve hours from Baalbec and fourteen hours from Homs, where the Anti-Libanus terminates, and where the valley between the two moun- tains widens considerably, because the Anti-Libanus there takes a more eastern direction. This district is abundantly watered by rivulets; almost every village has its spring, all of which descend into the valley, where most of them lose themselves, or join the Liettani, whose source is be- tween Zahle and Baalbec, about two hours from the latter place, near a hill called Tel Hushben. The earth is extremely fertile, but is still less cul- tivated than in the Bekaa. Even so late as twelve years ago, the plain, and a part of the mountain, to the distance of a league and a half round the town, were covered with grape plantations; the oppressions of the gover- nors, and their satellites have now entirely destroyed them; and the inhabitants of Baalbec, instead of eating their own grapes, which were renowned for their superior flavour, are obliged to import them from Fursul and Zahle. The government of Baalbec has been for many years in the hands of the family of Harfush, the head family of the Metaweli of Syria. [The Metaweli are of the sect of Ali, like the Persians; they have more than 200 houses at Damascus, but they conform there to the rites of the orthodox Mohammedans.] In later times, two brothers, Djahdjah and Sultan, have disputed with each other the possession of the government; more than fifteen individuals of their own family have perished in these contests, and they have dispossessed each other by turns, according to the degree of friendship or enmity which the Pashas of Damascus bore to the one or the other. During the reign of Youssef Pasha, Sultan was Emir; as soon as Soleiman was in possession of Damascus, Sultan was obliged to fly, and in August, 1810, his brother Djahdjah returned to his seat, which he had already once occupied. He pays a certain annual sum to the Pasha, and extorts double its amount from the peasant. The Emir Beshir has, since the reign of Soleiman Pasha, likewise acquired a certain influence over Baalbec, and is now entitled to the yearly sum of fifteen purses from this district. The Emir Djahdjah resides at Baalbec, and keeps there about 200 Metaweli horsemen, whom he equips and feeds out of his own purse. He is well remembered by several Europeans, especially English travellers, for his rapacity, and inhospitable behaviour.

The first object which strikes the traveller arriving from the Bekaa, is a temple [This temple is not seen in approaching Baalbec from Damascus.] in the plain, about half an hour's walk from the town, which has received from the natives the appellation of Kubbet Duris. Volney has not described this temple. It is an octagon building supported by eight beautiful granite columns, which are all standing. They are of an order resembling the Doric; the capitals project very little over the shaft, which has no base. Over every two pillars lies one large stone, forming the architrave, over which the cornice is still visible, very little adorned with sculpture. The roof has fallen in. On the N.W. side, between two of the columns, is an insulated niche, of calcareous stone, projecting somewhat beyond the circumference of the octagon, and rising to about two feet below the roof. The granite of the columns is particularly beautiful, the feldspath and quartz being mixed with the hornblende in large masses. The red feldspath predominates. One of the columns is distinguished from the rest by its green quartz. We could not find any traces of inscriptions.

September 29th.--I took lodgings in a small room belonging to the catholic priest, who superintends a parish of twenty-five Christian families. This being near the great temple, I hastened to it in the morning, before any body was apprised of my arrival.

The work of Wood, who accompanied Dawkins to Baalbec in 1751, and the subsequent account of the place given by Volney, who visited Baalbec in 1784, render it unnecessary for me to enter into any description of these ruins. I shall only observe that Volney is incorrect in describing the rock of which the buildings are constructed as granite; it is of the primitive calcareous kind, but harder than the stone of Tedmor. There are, however, many remains of granite columns in different parts of the building.

Having seen, a few months before, the ruins of Tedmor, a comparison between these two renowned remains of antiquity naturally offered itself to my mind. The entire view of the ruins of Palmyra, when seen at a certain distance, is infinitely more striking than those of Baalbec, but there is not any one spot in the ruins of Tedmor so imposing as the interior view of the temple of Baalbec. The temple of the Sun at Tedmor is upon a grander scale than that of Baalbec, but it is choked up with Arab houses, which admit only of a view of the building in detail. The archilecture of Baalbec is richer than that of Tedmor.

The walls of the ancient city may still be traced, and include a larger space than the present town ever occupied, even in its most flourishing state. Its circuit may be between three and four miles. On the E. and N. sides the gates of the modern town, formed in the ancient wall, still remain entire, especially the northern gate; it is a narrow arch, and comparatively very small. I suppose it to be of Saracen origin. The women of Baalbec are esteemed the handsomest of the neighbouring country, and many Damascenes marry Baalbec girls. The air of Belad Baalbec and the Bekaa, however, is far from being healthy. The chain of the Libanus interrupts the course of the westerly winds, which are regular in Syria during the summer months; and the want of these winds renders the climate extremely hot and oppressive.

September 30th.--I again visited the ruins this morning. The Emir had been apprised of my arrival by his secretary, to whom I had a letter of recommendation. He sent the secretary to ask whether I had any presents for him; I answered in the negative, but delivered to him a letter, which the Jew bankers of the Pasha of Damascus had given me for him; these Jews being men of great influence. He contented himself with replying that as I had no presents for him, it was not necessary that I should pay him my respects; but he left me undisturbed in my pursuits, which was all I wanted.

Near a well, on the S. side of the town, between the temple and the mountain, I found upon a stone the following inscription;

C. CASSIVS ARRIANVS

MONVMENTVM SIBI

-OCO SVO VIVVS

FECIT

In the afternoon I made a tour in the invirons of Baalbec. At the foot of the Anti-Libanus, a quarter of an hour's walk from the town, to the south is a quarry, where the places are still visible from whence several of the large stones in the south wall of the castle were extracted; one large block is yet remaining, cut on three sides, ready to be transported to the building, but it must be done by other hands than those of the Metaweli.

Two other blocks, cut in like manner, are standing upright at a little distance from each other; and near them, in the rock, are two small excavated tombs, with three niches in each, for the dead, in a style of workmanship similar to what I saw to the north of Aleppo, in the Turkman mountains towards Deir Samaan. In the hills, to the S.W. of the town, just behind this quarry, are several tombs, excavated in the rock, like the former, but of larger dimensions. In following the quarry towards the village of Duris, numerous natural caverns are met with in the calcareous rocks; I entered more than a dozen of them, but found no traces of art, except a few seats or steps rudely cut out. These caverns serve at present as winter habitations for the Arabs who pasture their cattle in this district. The principal quarry was a full half hour to the southward of the town.

The mountains above Baalbec are quite uncultivated and barren, except at the Ras el Ain, or sources of the river of Baalbec, where a few trees only remain. This is a delightful place, and is famous amongst the inhahitants of the adjoining districts for the salubrity of its air and water. Near the Ain, are the ruins of a church and mosque.

The ruined town of Baalbec contains about seventy Metaweli families, and twenty-five of Catholic Christians. Amidst its ruins are two handsome mosques, and a fine bath. The Emir lives in a spacious building called the Serai. The inhabitants fabricate white cotton cloth like that of Zahle; they have some dyeing houses, and had, till within a few years, some tanneries. The men are the artizans here, and not the women. The property of the people consists chiefly of cows, of which every house has ten or fifteen, besides goats and sheep. The goats are of a species not common in other parts of Syria; they have very long ears, large horns, and long hair, but not silky like that of the goats of Anatolia.

The breed of Baalbec mules is much esteemed, and I have seen some of them worth on the spot £30 to £35. sterling.

October 1st.--After having again visited the ruins, I engaged a man in the forenoon, to shew me the way to the source of the rivulet called Djoush. It is in a Wady in the Anti-Libanus, three quarters of an hour distant from Baalbec. The rivulet was very small, owing to the remarkable dryness of the season, and was lost in the Wady before it reached the plain; at other times it flows down to Baalbec and joins the river, which, after irrigating the gardens and fields round the town, loses itself in the plain. A little higher in the mountain than the spot where the water of the Djoush first issues from the spring, is a small perpendicular hole, through which I descended, not without some danger, about sixteen

feet, into an aqueduct which conveys the water of the Djoush underground for upwards of one hundred paces. This aqueduct is six feet high
and three feet and a half wide, vaulted above, and covered with a thick
coat of plaister; it is in perfect preservation; the water in it was about ten
inches deep. In following up this aqueduct I came to a vaulted chamber
about ten feet square, built with large hewn stones, into which the water
falls through another walled passage, but which I did not enter, being
afraid that the water falling on all sides might extinguish the only candle
that I had with me. Below this upper passage, another dark one is visible
through the water as it falls down. The aqueduct continues beyond the
hole through which I descended, as far as the spot where the water issues
from under the earth. Above ground, at a small distance from the spring,
and open towards it, is a vaulted room, built in the rock, now half filled
with stones and rubbish.

Ten or twelve years ago, at the time when the plague visited these
countries and the town of Baalbec, all the Christian families quitted the
town, and encamped for six weeks around these springs.

From Djoush we crossed the northern mountain of the valley, and
came to Wady Nahle, near the village of Nahle, situated at the foot of the
mountain, and one hour and a half E.b.N. from Baalbec. There is nothing
remarkable in the village, except the ruins of an ancient building, consisting at present of the foundations only, which are strongly built; it
appeared to me to be of the same epoch as the ruins of Baalbec. The rivulet named Nahle rises at one hour's distance, in a narrow Wady in the
mountain. The neighbourhood of Baalbec abounds in walnut trees; the
nuts are exported to Zahle and the mountains, at two or two and a half
piastres per thousand.

In the evening we left Baalbec, and began to cross the plain in the
direction of the highest summit of Mount Libanus. We passed the village
of Yeid on the left, and a little farther on, an encampment of Turkmans.
During the winter, the territory of Baalbec is visited by a tribe of Turkmans called Suedie, by the Hadidein Akeidat, the Arabs Abid, whose
principal seat is near Hamil, between El Kaa and Homs; and the Arabs
Harb. The Suedie Turkmans remain the whole year in this district, and in
the valleys of the Anti-Libanus. All these tribes pay tribute to the Emir of
Baalbec, at the rate of twelve or fifteen pounds of butter for each tent, for
the summer pasture. At the end of three hours march we alighted at the
village Deir el Akhmar, two hours after sunset. This village stands just at
the foot of the mountain; it was at this time deserted, its inhabitants having quitted it a few weeks before to escape the extortions of Djahdjah, and

retired to Bshirrai. In one of the abandoned houses we found a shepherd who tended a flock belonging to the Emir; he treated us with some milk, and made a large fire, round which we lay down, and slept till day-break.

October 2d.--The tobacco of Deir el Akhmar is the finest in Syria. There is no water in the village, but at twenty minutes from it, towards the plain, is a copious well. After ascending the mountain for three hours and a half, we reached the village Ainnete: thus far the mountain is covered with low oak trees (the round-leaved, and common English kinds), and has but few steep passages. Nearly one hour from Ainnete begins a more level country, which divides the Upper from the Lower Libanus. This part was once well cultivated, but the Metaweli having driven the people to despair, the village is in consequence deserted and in ruins. A few fields are still cultivated by the inhabitants of Deir Eliaout and Btedai, who sow their seed in the autumn, and in the spring return, build a few huts, and watch the growing crop. The walnut tree abounds here.

There are three springs at Ainnete, one of which was dried up; another falls over the rock in a pretty cascade; they unite in a Wady which runs parallel with the upper mountain as far as the lake Liemoun, two hours west of Ainnete; at this time the lake was nearly dry, an extraordinary circumstance; I saw its bed a little higher up than Ainnete.

From Ainnete the ascent of the mountain is steep, and the vegetation is scanty; though it reaches to the summit. A few oaks and shrubs grow amongst the rocks. The road is practicable for loaded mules, and my horse ascended without difficulty. The honey of Ainnete, and of the whole of Libanus, is of a superior quality.

At the end of two hours and a half from Ainnete we reached the summit, from whence I enjoyed a magnificent view over the Bekaa, the Anti- Libanus, and Djebel Essheikh, on one side, and the sea, the sea shore near Tripoli, and the deep valley of Kadisha on the other. We were not quite upon the highest summit, which lay half an hour to the right. Baalbec bore from hence S. by E, and the summit of Djebel Essheikh S. by W. The whole of the rock is calcareous, and the surface towards the top is so splintered by the action of the atmosphere, as to have the appearance of layers of slates. Midway from Ainnete I found a small petrified shell, and on breaking a stone which I picked up on the summit, I discovered another similar petrifaction within it.

Having descended for two hours, we came to a small cultivated plain. On this side, as well as on the other, the higher Libanus may be distinguished from the lower; the former presenting on both sides a steep barren ascent of two to two hours and a half; the latter a more level wooded country, for the greater part fit for cultivation this difference of surface is observable throughout the Libanus, from the point where I crossed it, for eight hours, in a S. W. direction. The descent terminates in one of the numerous deep valleys which run towards the seashore.

I left my guide on the small plain, and proceeded to the right towards the Cedars, which are visible from the top of the mountain, standing half an hour from the direct line of the route to Bshirrai, at the foot of the steep declivities of the higher division of the mountain. They stand on uneven ground, and form a small wood. Of the oldest and best looking trees, I counted eleven or twelve; twenty-five very large ones; about fifty of middling size; and more than three hundred smaller and young ones. The oldest trees are distinguished by having the foliage and small branches at the top only, and by four, five, or even seven trunks springing from one base; the branches and foliage of the others were lower, but I saw none whose leaves touched the ground, like those in Kew Gardens. The trunks of the old trees are covered with the names of travellers and other persons, who have visited them: I saw a date of the seventeenth century. The trunks of the oldest trees seem to be quite dead; the wood is of a gray tint; I took off a piece of one of them; but it was afterwards stolen, together with several specimens of minerals, which I sent from Zahle to Damascus.

At an hour and a quarter from the Cedars, and considerably below them, on the edge of a rocky descent, lies the village of Bshirrai, on the right bank of the river Kadisha.

October 3d.--Bshirrai consists of about one hundred and twenty houses. Its inhabitants are all Maronites, and have seven churches. At half an hour from the village is the Carmelite convent of Deir Serkis (St. Sergius,) inhabited at present by a single monk, a very worthy old man, a native of Tuscany, who has been a missionary to Egypt, India, and Persia.

Nothing can be more striking than a comparison of the fertile but uncultivated districts of Bekaa and Baalbec, with the rocky mountains, in the opposite direction, where, notwithstanding that nature seems to afford nothing for the sustenance of the inhabitants, numerous villages flourish, and every inch of ground is cultivated. Bshirrai is surrounded with fruit trees, mulberry plantations, vineyards, fields of Dhourra, and other corn, though there is scarcely a natural plain twenty feet square. The inhabitants with great industry build terraces to level the ground and prevent the earth from being swept down by the winter rains, and at the same time to retain the water requisite for the irrigation of their crops. Water is very abundant, as streams from numerous springs descend on every side into the Kadisha, whose source is two hours distant from Bshirrai, in the direction of the mountain from whence I came.

Bshirrai belongs to the district of Tripoli, but is at present, with the whole of the mountains, in the hands of the Emir Beshir, or chief of the Druses. The inhabitants of the village rear the silk-worm, have excellent plantations of tobacco, and a few manufactories of cotton stuffs used by the mountaineers as shawls for girdles. Forty years ago the village was in the hands of the Metaweli, who were driven out by the Maronites.

In the morning I went to Kanobin; after walking for two hours and a half over the upper plain, I descended the precipitous side of a collateral branch of the valley Kadisha, and continued my way to the convent, which I reached in two hours and a half. It is built on a steep precipice on the right of the valley, at half an hour's walk from the river, and appears as if suspended in the air, being supported by a high wall, built against the side of the mountain. There is a spring close to it. The church, which is excavated in the rock, and dedicated to the Virgin, is decorated with the portraits of a great number of patriarchs. During the winter, the peasants suspend their silk-worms in bags, to the portrait of some favourite saint, and implore his influence for a plenteous harvest of silk; from this custom the convent derives a considerable income.

Kanobin is the seat of the patriarch of the Maronites, who is at the head of twelve Maronite bishops, and here in former times he generally passed the summer months, retiring in the winter to Mar Hanna; but the vexations and insults which the patriarchs were exposed to from the Metaweli, in their excursions to and from Baalbec, induced them for many years to abandon this residence. The present patriarch is the first who for a long time has resided in Kanobin. Though I had no letter of introduction to him, and was in the dress of a peasant, he invited me to dinner, and I met at his table his secretary, Bishop Stefano, who has been educated at Rome, and has some notions of Europe. While I was there, a rude peasant was ordained a priest. Kanobin had once a considerable library; but it has been gradually dispersed; and not a vestige of it now remains. The cells of the monks are, for the most part, in ruins.

Three hours distant from Kanobin, at the convent Kashheya, which is near the village Ehden, is a printing office, where prayer-books in the Syriac language are printed. This language is known and spoken by many Maronites, and in this district the greater part of them write Arabic in the Syriac characters. The names of the owners of the silk-worms were all written in this character in different hands, upon the bags suspended in the church.

I returned to Bshirrai by an easier road than that which I had travelled in the morning; at the end of three quarters of an hour I regained the upper plain, from whence I proceeded for two hours by a gentle ascent, through fields and orchards, up to the village. The potatoe succeeds here very well; a crop was growing in the garden of the Carmelite convent; it has also been cultivated for some time past in Kesrouan. In the mountains about Kanobin tigers are said to be frequently met with; I suppose ounces are meant.

October 4th.--I departed from Bshirrai with the intention of returning to Zahle over the higher range of the Libanus. We crossed the Kadisha, at a short distance from Bishirrai, above the place where it falls over the precipice: at one hour distant from Bshirrai, and opposite to it, we passed the village of Hosrun. The same cultivation prevails here as in the vicinity of Bshirrai; mulberry and walnut trees, and vines, are the chief productions. From Hosrun we continued our way along the foot of the highest barren part of Libanus. About two hours from its summit, the mountain affords pasturage, and is capable of cultivation, from the numerous springs which are everywhere met with. During the greater part of this day's journey I had a fine view of the sea shore between Tartous and Tripoli, and from thence downwards towards Jebail.

At three hours and a half from Hosrun, still following the foot of the upper chain of the Libanus, we entered the district of Tanurin (Ard Tanurin), so called from a village situated below in a valley. The spots in the mountain, proper for cultivation, are sown by the inhabitants of Tanurin; such as afford pasture only are visited by the Arabs El Haib. I was astonished at seeing so high in the mountain, numerous camels and Arab huts. These Arabs pass the winter months on the sea shore about Tripoli, Jebail, and Tartous. Though like the Bedouins, they have no fixed habitations, their features are not of the true Bedouin cast, and their dialect, though different from that of the peasants, is not a pure Bedouin dialect. They are tributary to the Turkish governors, and at peace with all the country people; but they have the character of having a great propensity to thieving. Their property, besides camels, consists in horses, cows, sheep, and goats. Their chief is Khuder el Aissy.

On leaving the district of Tanurin, I entered Ard Laklouk, which I cannot describe better, than by comparing it to one of the pasturages in the Alps. It is covered with grass, and its numerous springs, together with the heavy dews which fall during the summer months, have produced a verdure of a deeper tint than any I saw in the other parts of Syria which I visited. The Arabs El Haib come up hither also, and wander about the district for five months in the year; some of them even remain here the whole year; except that in winter they descend from the pastures, and pitch their tents round the villages of Tanurin and Akoura, which are situated in a valley, sheltered on every side by the perpendicular sides of the Upper Libanus. At Tanurin and Laklouk the winter corn was already above ground. The people water the fields for three or four days before they sow the seed.

Akoura has a bad name amongst the people of this country; its inhabitants, who are all Greek Catholics, are accused of avarice, and inhospitality. The mountaineers, when upon a journey, never think of spending a para, for their eating, drinking, or lodging. On arriving in the evening at a village, they alight at the house of some acquaintance, if they have any, which is generally the case, and say to the owner, "I am your guest," Djay deyfak. The host gives the traveller a supper, consisting of milk, bread, and Borgul, and if rich and liberal, feeds his mule or mare also. When the traveller has no acquaintance in the village, he alights at any house he pleases, ties up his beast, and smokes his pipe till he receives a welcome from the master of the house, who makes it a point of honour to receive him as a friend, and to give him a supper. In the morning he departs with a simple "Good bye." Such is the general custom in these parts; the inhabitants of Akoura, however, are noted for refusing to receive travellers, to whom they will neither give a supper, nor sell them provision for ready money; the consequence of which conduct is, that the Akourans, when travelling about, are obliged to conceal their origin, in order to obtain food on the road. My guide had a friend at Akoura, but he happened to be absent; we therefore alighted at another house, where we obtained with much difficulty a little barley for our horses; and we should have gone supperless to rest, had I not repaired to the Sheikh, and made him believe I was a Kourdine (my dress being somewhat like that of the Kourds) in the service of the

Pasha of Damascus, on my way to the Emir Beshir. As I spoke with confidence, the Sheikh became alarmed, and sent us a few loaves of bread, and some cheese; on my return, I found my guide in the midst of a large assembly of people, abusing them for their meanness.

The property of the inhabitants of this village consists of cows and other cattle, silkworms, and plantations of olive trees.

At Akoura Djebel Libnan terminates; and farther down towards Zahle and the Bekaa, the mountain is called Djebel Sannin. The Libanus is here more barren and wild than further to the north. The rocks are all in perfectly horizontal layers, some of which are thirty to forty yards in thickness, while others are only a few yards.

October 5th.--We left the inhospitable Akoura before day light, and reached, after one hour and three quarters, a village called Afka, situated in the bottom of a valley, near a spring, whose waters join those of Wady Akoura, and flow down towards Jebail.

The name Afka is found in the ancient geography of Syria. At Aphaca, according to Zosimus, was a temple of Venus, where the handsomest girls of Syria sacrificed to the goddess: it was situated near a small lake, between Heliopolis and the sea coast. [Zosim. l.i.c.58.] The lake Liemoun is at three hours distance from Afka. I could not hear of any remains of antiquity near Afka. All the inhabitants are Metaweli, under the government of Jebail. Near it, towards Jebail, are the Metaweli villages of Mghaiere, Meneitere, and Laese.

From Afka the road leads up a steep Wady. At half an hour from it is the spring called Ain Bahr; three quarters of an hour beyond it is a high level country, still on the western side of the summit of the mountain. This district is called Watty el Bordj, from a small ruined tower. It is three or four hours in length, and two in breadth. In the spring the Arabs Abid, Turkmans, and Kourdines, here pasture their cattle. These Kourdines bring annually into Syria from twenty to thirty thousand sheep, from the mountains of Kourdistan; the greater part of which are consumed by Aleppo, Damascus, and the mountains, as Syria does not produce a sufficient number for its inhabitants. The Kourd sheep are larger than those of Syria, but their flesh is less esteemed. The Kourd sheep-dealers first visit with their flocks Aleppo, then Hama, Homs, and Baalbec; and what they do not sell on the road, they bring to pasture at Watty el Bordj, whither the people of Zahle, Deir el Kammar, and other towns in the mountains repair, and buy up thousands of them, which they afterwards sell in retail to the peasants of the mountains.

They buy them for ready money at twenty to thirty piastres a head, and sell them two months afterwards at thirty to forty. The mountaineers of the Druse and Maronite districts breed very few sheep, and very seldom eat animal food. On the approach of their respective great festivals, (Christmas with the Maronites, and Ramadan with the Druses) each head of a family kills one or two sheep; during the rest of the year, he feeds his people on Borgul, with occasionally some old cow's, or goat's flesh. It is only in the largest of the mountain towns of the Druses and Maronites that flesh is brought daily to market.

There are no springs or water in the Watty el Bordj; but the melting of the snow in the spring affords drink for men and cattle, and snow water is often found during the greater part of the summer in some funnel-shaped holes formed in the ground by the snow. At the time I passed no water was any where to be found. In many places the snow remains throughout the year; but this year none was left, not even on the summits of the mountain, except in a few spots on the northern declivity of the Libanus towards the district of Akkar. Watty el Bordj affords excellent pasturage; in many spots it is overgrown with trees, mostly oaks, and the barbery is also very frequent. We started partridges at every step. Our route lay generally S.W. by S.

Four hours from Ain Bahr, we entered the mountain, a part of which is considered to belong to Kesrouan. It is completely stony and rocky, and I found some calcareous spath. I shall here remark that the whole of the mountain from Zahle to Belad Akkar is by the country people comprehended under the general name of Djurd Baalbec, Djurd meaning, in the northern Arabic dialect, a rocky mountain.

Crossing this part of the mountain Sannin for two hours, we came to a spring called Ain Naena, from whence another road leads down north- eastwards, into the territory of Baalbec. This route is much frequented by the people of Kesrouan, who bring this way the iron ore of Shouair, to the Mesbek or smelting furnaces at Nebae el Mauradj, two hours from hence to the north-east, Shouair, which is at least ten hours distance, affording no fuel for smelting. The iron ore is carried upon mules and asses, one day's journey and a half to the Mesbek, where the mountain abounds in oak. From Aine Naena we gradually descended, and in three hours reached Zahle.

October 6th.--At Zahle I found the Catholic bishop, who was absent on his episcopal tour during my first visit to this place. He is distinguished from his countrymen by the politeness of his manners, the liberality of his sentiments, his general information, and his desire of knowledge, though at a very advanced age. I had letters for him; and he recommended himself particularly to me by being the friend of Mr. Browne, the African traveller, who had lived with him a fortnight, and had visited Baalbec in his company. His diocese comprises the whole Christian community in the Bekaa, and the adjoining villages of the mountain. He is, with five other bishops, under the orders of the Patriarch at Mekhalis, and there are, besides, seven monasteries under this diocese in Syria. The Bishop's revenue arises from a yearly personal tax of half a piastre upon all the male adults in his diocese. He lives in a truly patriarchal manner, dressing in a simple black gown, and black Abbaye, and carries in his hand a long oaken stick, as an episcopal staff. He is adored by his parishioners, though they reproach him with a want of fervour in his intercourse with other Christian sects; by which they mean fanatism, which is a striking feature in the character of the Christians not only of the mountain, but also of the principal Syrian towns, and of the open country. This bigotry is not directed so much against the Mohammedans, as against their Christian brethren, whose creed at all differs from their own.

It need hardly be mentioned here, that many of those sects which tore Europe to pieces in the earlier ages of Christianity, still exist in these countries: Greeks, Catholics, Maronites, Syriacs, Chaldeans, and Jacobites, all have their respective parishes and churches. Unable to effect any thing against the religion of their haughty rulers the Turks, they turn the only weapons they possess, scandal and intrigue, with fury against each other, and each sect is mad enough to believe that its church would flourish on the ruins of those of their heretic brethren. The principal hatred subsists between the Catholics and the Greeks; of the latter, many thousands have been converted to Catholicism, so that in the northern parts of Syria all Catholics, the Maronites excepted, were formerly of the Greek church: this is the case in Aleppo, Damascus, and in all the intermediate country; communities of original Latin Christians being found only around Jerusalem and Nablous. The Greeks of course see with indignation the proselytism of their brethren, which is daily gaining ground, and avenge themselves upon the apostates with the most furious hatred. Nor are the Greek and original Latin Christians backward in cherishing similar feelings; and scenes most disgraceful to Christianity are frequently the consequence. In those parts where no Greeks live, as in the mountains of Libanus, the different sects of Catholics turn their hatred against each other, and the Maronites fight with the converted Greek Catholics, or the Latins, as they do at Aleppo with the followers of the Greek church. This system of intolerance, at which the Turkish governors smile, because they are constantly gainers by it, is carried so far that, in many places, the passing Catholic is obliged to practise the Greek rites, in order to escape the effects of the fanatism of the inhabitants. On my way from Zahle to Banias, we stopped one night at Hasbeya and another at Rasheya el Fukhar; at both of which places my guide went to the Greek church, and prayed according to its forms; in passing through Zahle, as he informed me, the Greeks found it equally necessary to conform with the rites of the Latin Catholics. The intrigues carried on at Jerusalem between the Greek and Latin monks contribute to increase these diputes, which would have long ago led to a Christian civil war in these countries, did not the iron rod of the Turkish government repress their religious fury.

The vineyards are estimated at the exact number of vines they contain, and each vine, if of good quality, is worth one piastre. The Miri or land tax of every hundred vines is ten paras. For many years past a double Miri has been levied upon Zahle.

October 7th.--Remained at Zahle, and enjoyed the instructive conversation of the Bishop Basilios.

October 8th.--I went to see the ruined temple called Heusn Nieha, two hours from Zahle, in the Djebel Sannin, and half an hour from the village of Fursul. These remains stand in a Wady, surrounded by barren rocks, having a spring near them to the eastward. The temple faced the west. A grand flight of steps, twelve paces broad, with a column three feet and a half in diameter at each end of the lower step, formed the approach to a spacious pronaos, in which are remains of columns: here a door six paces in width opens into the cella, the fallen roof of which now covers the floor, and the side walls to half their original height only remain. This chamber is thirty-five paces in length by fifteen in breadth. On each of the side walls stood six pilasters of a bad Ionic order. At the extremity of the chamber are steps leading to a platform, where the statue of the deity may, perhaps, have stood: the whole space is here filled up with fragments of columns and walls. The square stones used in the construction of the walls are in general about four or five cubic feet each, but I saw some twelve feet long, four feet high, and four feet in breadth. On the right side of the entrance door is a staircase in the wall, leading to the top of the building, and much resembling in its mode of construction the staircase in the principal temple of Baalbec. The remains of the capitals of columns betray a very corrupt taste, being badly sculptured, and without any elegance either in design or execution; and the temple seems to have been built in the latest times of paganism, and was perhaps subsequently repaired, and converted into a church. The stone with which it has been built is more decayed than that in the ruins at Baalbec, being here more exposed to the inclemency of the weather. No inscriptions were any where visible. Around the temple are some ruins of ancient and others of more modern habitations.

Above Fursul is a plain called Habis, in which are a number of grottos excavated in the rock, apparently tombs; but I did not visit them.

October 9th.--I was disappointed in my intention of proceeding, and passed the day in calling at several shops in the town, and conversing with the merchants and Arab traders.

October 10th.--I set out for Hasbeya, accompanied by the same guide with whom I had made the mountain tour. We crossed the Bekaa nearly in the direction of Andjar. [The following are the villages in the Bekaa, and at the foot of the western mountain, which from Zahle southward takes the name of Djebel Riehan; namely, Saad-Nayel, Talabaya, Djetye, Bouarish, Mekse, Kab Elias, Mezraat, Bemherye, Aamyk, Deir Tenhadish, Keferya, Khereyt Kena, Beit Far, Ain Zebde, Segbin, Deire el Djouze, Bab Mara, Aitenyt, El Kergoue, El Medjdel, Belhysz, Lala, Meshgara, Sahhar Wyhbar, Shedite, Nebi Zaour, Baaloul, Bedjat, Djub Djenin, Tel Danoub, El Khyare, El Djezyre, El Estabbel, El Merdj, Tel el Akhdar, Taanayl, Ber Elias, Deir Zeinoun.] The generality of the inhabitants of the Bekaa are Turks; one fifth, perhaps, are Catholic Christians. There are no Metaweli. The land is somewhat better cultivated than that of Belad Baalbec, but still five- sixths Of the soil is left in pasture for the Arabs. The Fellahs (peasant cultivators) are ruined by the exorbitant demands of the proprietors of the soil, who are, for the greater part, noble families of Damascus, or of the Druse mountains. The usual produce of the harvest is tenfold, and in fruitful years it is often twenty fold.

After two hours and three quarters brisk walking of our horses, we passed Medjdel to our right, near which, on the road, lies a piece of a large column of acalcareous and flinty breccia. Half an hour beyond Medjdel, we reached a spring called Ain Essouire. Above it in the hills which branch out of the Anti-Libanus, or Djurd Essharki, into the Bekaa, is the village Nebi Israi, and to the left, in the Anti-Libanus, is the Druse village of Souire. A little farther on we passed Hamara, a village on the Anti-Libanus. At one hour from Ain Essouire, is Sultan Yakoub, with the tomb of a saint, a place of holy resort of the Turks. Below it lies the Ain Sultan Yakoub. Half an hour farther is Nebae el Feludj, a spring. Our road lay S. by W. At the end of three hours and a half from Ain Essouire, we reached the village El Embeite, on the top of a hill, opposite to Djebel Essheikh. The route to this place, from Medjdel, lay through a valley of the Anti-Libanus, which, farther on, towards El Heimte, loses itself in the mountains comprised under the name of Djebel Essheikh. The summit of this mountain, which bears west from Damascus, is probably the highest in Syria, for snow was still lying upun it. The mountain belongs to the district of the Emir of the Druses, commanding at Rasheia, a Druse village at one hour and a half from El Heimte. We slept at El Heimte, in the house of the Druse Sheikh, and the Khatib, or Turkish priest of the village, gave us a plentiful supper. The Druses in this district affect to adhere strictly to the religious precepts of the Turks. The greater part of the inhabitants of El Heimte are Druses belonging to Rasheia. Near it are the villages of Biri and Refit.

October 11th.--We set out at day-break, and at the end of an hour passed on the left the Druse villages Deneibe and Mimis, and at two hours Sefa on our right, also a Druse village. Our road lay over an uneven plain, cultivated only in spots. After three hours and a half, we came to Ain Efdjur, direction S.W. by W.; from thence in two hours and a half we reached the Djissr-Moiet-Hasbeya, or bridge of the river of Hasbeya, whose source is hard by; the road lying the whole way over rocky ground little susceptible of culture. From the Djissr we turned up a steep Wady E. b. S. and arrived, in about three quarters of an hour, at Hasbeya, situated on the top of a mountain of no great height. I had letters from the Greek patriarch of Damascus to the Greek bishop of Hasbeya, in whose house, four years ago, Dr. Seetzen spent a week, having been prevented from proceeding by violent snow and rain. The bishop happened to be absent on my arrival, and I therefore took up my lodging in the house of a poor Greek priest, with whose behaviour towards me I had every reason to be satisfied.

October 12th.--The village or town of Hasbeya may contain seven hundred houses; half of which belong to Druse families; the other half are inhabited by Christians, principally Greeks, though there are also Catholics and Maronites here. There are only forty Turkish families, and twenty Enzairie. The inhabitants make cotton cloth for shirts and gowns, and have a few dyeing houses. The principal production of their fields is olives. The chief of the village is an Emir of the Druses, who is dependent both on the Pasha of Damascus and the Emir Beshir. He lives in a well-built Serai, which in time of war might serve as a castle. The following villages belong to the territory of Hasbeya: Ain Sharafe, El Kefeir, Ain Annia, Shoueia, Ain Tinte, El Kankabe, El Heberie, Rasheyat el Fukhar, Ferdis, Khereibe, El Merie, Shiba, Banias, Ain Fid, Zoura, Ain Kamed Banias, Djoubeta, Fershouba, Kefaer Hamam, El Waeshdal, El Zouye.

The neighbourhood of Hasbeya is interesting to the mineralogist. I was told by the priest that a metal was found near it, of which nobody knew the name, nor made any use. Having procured a labourer, I found after digging in the Wady a few hundred paces to the E. of the village, several small pieces of a metallic substance, which I took to be a native amalgam of mercury. According to the description given me, cinnabar is also found here, but we could discover no specimen of it after half an hour's digging. The ground all around, and the spring near the village, are strongly impregnated with iron; the rock is sandstone, of a dark red colour. The other mineral curiosities are, a number of wells of bitumen Judaicum, in the Wady at one hour below the village on the west side, after recrossing the bridge; they are situated upon the declivity of a chalky hill; the bitumen is found in large veins at about twenty feet below the surface. The pits are from six to twelve feet in diameter; the workmen descend by a rope and wheel, and in hewing out the bitumen, they leave columns of that substance at different intervals, as a support to the earth above; pieces of several Rotolas in weight each [The Rotola is about five pounds.] are brought up. There are upwards of twenty-five of these pits or wells, but the greater part of them are abandoned and overgrown with shrubs. I saw only one, that appeared to have been recently worked; they work only during the summer months. The bitumen is called Hommar, and the wells, Biar el Hommar. The Emir possesses the monopoly of the bitumen; he alone works the pits, and sells the produce to the merchants of Damascus, Beirout, and Aleppo. It was now at thirty-three paras the Rotola, or about two-pence-halfpenny the pound.

I left Hasbeya on the same day, and continued to descend the valley on the side of the river. Half an hour from the bridge, I arrived at Souk el Khan. In the hills to the right is the village Kankabe. Souk el Khan is a large ruined Khan, where the inhabitants, to the distance of one day's journey round, assemble every Tuesday to hold a market. In the summer they exhibit their merchandize in the open air; but in the winter they make use of some large rooms, still remaining within the Khan. The road to Banias leads along the valley, parallel with the course of the river; but as I had heard of some ruins in the mountain, at a village called Hereibe, to the east of the route, I turned in that direction, and reached the village in two hours after quitting Hasbeya. Between Souk el Khan and Hereibe lies the village Ferdous. Hereibe is considerably higher than the river. All this neighbourhood is planted with olive-trees; and olives, from hence to Damascus, are the most common food of the inhabitants, who put them into salt, but they do not thereby entirely remove the bitter taste. At Aleppo and Damascus, olives destined for the table are immersed for a fortnight in water, in which are dissolved one proportion of chalk and two proportions of alkali; this takes away all bitterness, but the fruit is at the same time deprived of a part of its flavour.

On the west side of the village of Hereibe stands a ruined temple, quite insulated; it is twenty paces in length, and thirteen in breadth; the entrance is towards the west, and it had a vestibule in front with two columns. On each side of the entrance are two niches one above the other, the upper one has small pilasters, the lower one is ornamented on the top by a shell, like the niches in the temple at Baalbec. The door- way, which has no decoration whatever, opens into a room ten paces square, in which no columns, sculpture, or Ornaments of any kind are visible; three of the walls only are standing. At the back of this chamber is a smaller, four paces and a half in breadth, by ten in length, in one corner of which is a half-ruined staircase, leading to the top of the building; in this smaller room are four pilasters in the four angles; under the large room are two spacious vaults. On the outside of the temple, at the east corners, are badly wrought pilasters of the Ionic order. The roof has fallen in, and fills up the interior. The stone employed is of the same quality as that used at Heusn Nieha and Baalbec.

From Hereibe I came to the spring Ain Ferkhan in one hour; and from thence, in three quarters of an hour, to the village Rasheyat-el-Fukhar, over mountainous ground. The village stands on a mountain which commands a beautiful view of the lake Houle, its plain, and the interjacent country. It contains about one hundred houses, three-fourths of which are inhabited by Turks and the remainder by Greeks. The inhabitants live by the manufacture of earthen pots, which they sell to the distance of four or five days journey around, especially in the Haouran and Djolan; they mould them in very elegant shapes, and paint them with a red-earth: almost every house has its pottery, and the ovens in which the pots are baked are common to all. The Houle bears from Rasheyat-el-Fukhar, between S. by E. and S.E. by S. Kalaat el Shkif, on the top of the mountain, towards Acre, E. by N. and Banias, though not visible, S.

October 13th.--We set out in a rainy morning from Rasheyat-el-Fukhar. I was told that in the mountain to the E. one hour and a half, were considerable ruins. The mountains of Hasbeya, or the chain of the Djebel Essheikh, divide, at five hours N. from the lake, into two branches. The western, a little farther to the south, takes the name of Djebel Safat, the eastern joins the Djebel Heish and its continuations, towards Banias. Between the two lie the lake of the Houle and the Ard el Houle, the latter from three to four hours in breadth. We descended from Rasheyat-el-Fukhar into the plain, in which we continued till we reached Banias, at the end of four hours, thoroughly drenched by a heavy shower of rain. We alighted at the Menzel or Medhaafe; this is a sort of Khan found in almost every village through which there is a frequented route. Strangers sleep in the Medhaafe, and the Sheikh of the village generally sends them their dinner or supper; for this he does not accept of any present, at least not of such as common travellers can offer; but it is custmary to give something to the servant or watchman (Natur) who brings the meal, and takes care that nothing is stolen from the strangers' baggage. The district of Banias is classic ground; it is the ancient Caesarea Philippi; the lake Houle is the Lacus Samachonitis.

My money being almost expended, I had no time to lose in gratifying my curiosity in the invirons of Banias. Immediately after my arrival I took a man of the village to shew me the way to the ruined castle of Banias, which bears E. by S. from it. It stands on the top of a mountain, which forms part of the mountain of Heish, at an hour and a quarter from Banias; it is now in complete ruins, but was once a very strong fortress. Its whole circumference is twenty-five minutes. It is surrounded by a wall ten feet thick, flanked with numerous round towers, built with equal blocks of stone, each about two feet square. The keep or citadel seems to have been on the highest summit, on the eastern side, where the walls are stronger than on the lower, or western side. The view from hence over the Houle and a part of its lake, the Djebel Safad, and the barren Heish, is magnificent. On the western side, within the precincts of the castle, are ruins of many private habitations. At both the western corners runs a succession of dark strongly built low apartments, like cells, vaulted, and with small narrow loop holes, as if for musquetry. On this side also is a well more than twenty feet square, walled in, with a vaulted roof at least twenty-five feet high; the well was, even in this dry season, full of water: there are three others in the castle. There are many apartments and recesses in the castle, which could only be exactly described by a plan of the whole building. It seems to have been erected during the period of the crusades, and must certainly have been a very strong hold to those who possessed it. I saw no inscriptions, though I was afterwards told that there are several both in Arabic and in Frank (Greek or Latin). The castle has but one gate, on the south side. I could discover no traces of a road or paved way leading up the mountain to it. The valley at its S.E. foot is called Wady Kyb, that on its western side Wady el Kashabe, and on the other side of the latter, Wady el Asal. In winter time the shepherds of the Felahs of the Heish, who encamp upon the mountain, pass the night in the castle with their cattle.

Banias is situated at the foot of the Heish, in the plain, which in the immediate vicinity of Banias is not called Ard Houle, but Ard Banias. It contains about one hundred and fifty houses, inhabited mostly by Turks: there are also Greeks, Druses, and Enzairie. It belongs to Hasbeya, whose Emir nominates the Sheikh. On the N.E. side of the village is the source of the river of Banias, which empties itself into the Jordan at the distance of an hour and a half, in the plain below. Over the source is a perpendicular rock, in which several niches have been cut to receive statues.

The largest niche is above a spacious cavern, under which the river rises. This niche is six feet broad and as much in depth, and has a smaller niche in the bottom of it. Immediately above it, in the perpendicular face of the rock, is another niche, adorned with pilasters, supporting a shell ornament like that of Hereibe.

There are two other niches near these, and twenty paces farther two more nearly buried in the ground at the foot of the rock. Each of these niches had an inscription annexed to it, but I could not decipher any thing.

In the middle niche of the three, which are represented in the engraving, the base of the statue is still visible. Banias, or Caesareia Philippi, was the Dan of the Jews. The name Paneas was derived from the worship of Pan. The niche in the cavern probably contained a statue of Pan, and the other niches similar dedications to the same or other deities. The cavern and sanctuary of Pan, are described by Josephus, from whom it appears also that the fountain was considered the source of the Jordan, and at the same time the outlet of a small lake called Phiala, which was situated 120 stades from Caesareia towards Trachonitis, or the north-east. The whole mountain had the name of Paneium. The hewn stones round the spring may have belonged, perhaps, to the temple of Augustus, built here by Herod. Joseph. de Bel. Jud. l.i,c.16. Antiq. Jud. l.3,c.10,-l.15,c.10. Euseb. Hist. Eccl. l.12,c.17. The inscription appears to have been annexed to a dedication by a priest of Pan, who had prefixed the usual pro salute for the reigning Emperors. Ed.]

Upon the top of the rock, to the left of the niches, is a mosque dedicated to Nebi Khouder, called by the Christians Mar Georgius, which is a place of devotion for Mohammedan strangers passing this way. Round the source of the river are a number of hewn stones. The stream flows on the north side of the village; where is a well built bridge and some remains of the ancient town, the principal part of which seems, however, to have been on the opposite side of the river, where the ruins extend for a quarter of an hour from the bridge. No walls remain, but great quantities of stones and architectural fragments are scattered about. I saw also an entire column, of small dimensions. In the village itself, on the left side of the river, lies a granite column of a light gray colour, one foot and a half in diameter.

October 15th.--It being Ramazan, we remained under a large tree before the Menzel, smoking and conversing till very late. The researches which Mr. Seetzen made here four years ago were the principal topic; he continued his tour from hence towards the lake of Tabaria, and the eastern borders of the Dead Sea. The Christians believe that he was sent by the Yellow King (Melek el Aszfar, a title which they give the Emperor of Russia) to examine the country preparatory to an invasion, to deliver it from the Turkish yoke. The Turks, on the contrary, believe, that, like all strangers who enquire after inscriptions, he was in search of treasure. When questioned on this subject at Baalbec, I answered, "The treasures of this country are not beneath the earth; they come from God, and are on the surface of the earth. Work your fields and sow them; and you will find the greatest treasure in an abundant harvest." "By your life (a common oath) truth comes from your lips," (is a common word used in Syria for which signifies "thy mouth."] Wuhiyatak, el hak fi tummak) was the reply.

On the south side of the village are the ruins of a strong castle, which, from its appearance and mode of construction, may be conjectured to be of the same age as the castle upon the mountain. It is surrounded by a broad ditch, and had a wall within the ditch. Several of its towers are still standing. A very solid bridge, which crosses the winter torrent, Wady el Kyd, leads to the entrance of the castle, over which is an Arabic inscription; but for want of a ladder, I could make out nothing of it but the date "600 and ... years (....)," taking the era of the Hedjra, it coincides with the epoch of the crusades. There are five or six granite columns built into the walls of the gateway.

I went to see the ruins of the ancient city of Bostra, of which the people spoke much, adding that Mousa (the name assumed by Mr. Seetzen) had offered thirty piastres to any one who would accompany him to the place, but that nobody had ventured, through fear of the Arabs. I found a good natured fellow, who for three piastres undertook to lead me to the spot. Bostra must not be confounded with Boszra, in the Haouran; both places are mentioned in the Books of Moses. The way to the ruins lies for an hour and a half in the road by which I came from Rasheyat- el-Fukhar, it then ascends for three quarters of an hour a steep mountain to the right, on the top of which is the city; it is divided into two parts, the largest being upon the very summit, the smaller at ten minutes walk lower down, and resembling a suburb to the upper part. Traces are still visible of a paved way that had connected the two divisions. There is scarcely any thing in the ruins worth notice; they consist of the foundations of private habitations, built of moderate sized square stones. The lower city is about twelve minutes walk in circumference; a part of the four walls of one building only remains entire; in the midst of the ruins was a well, at this time dried up. The circuit of the upper city may be about twenty minutes; in it are the remains of several buildings. In the highest part is a heap of wrought stones of larger dimensions than the rest, which seem to indicate that some public building had once stood on the spot. There are several fragments of columns of one foot and of one foot and a half in diameter. In two different places a short column was standing in the centre of a round paved area of about ten feet in diameter. There is likewise a deep well, walled in, but now dry.

The country around these ruins is very capable of cultivation. Near the lower city are groups of olive trees. Pieces of feldspath of various colours are scattered about in great quantities upon the chalky rock of this mountain. I found in going up a species of locust with six very long legs, and a slender body of about four inches in length. My guide told me that this insect was called [This is the abbreviation of -.] Salli al-nabi, i.e. "pray to the Prophet."

I descended the mountain in the direction towards the source of the Jordan, and passed, at the foot of it, the miserable village of Kerwaya. Behind the mountain of Bostra is another, still higher, called Djebel Meroura Djoubba. At one hour E. from Kerwaye, in the Houle, is the tomb of a Turkish Sheikh, with a few houses near it, called Kubbet el Arbai- in w-el-Ghadjar.

The greater part of the fertile plain of the Houle is uncultivated; the Arabs El Faddel, El Naim, and the Turkmans pasture their cattle here. It is watered by the river of Hasbeya, the Jordan, and the river of Banias, besides several rivulets which descend from the mountains on its eastern side. The source of the Jordan, or as it is here called, Dhan, is at an hour and a quarter N.E. from Banias. It is in the plain, near a hill called Tel-el-Kadi. There are two springs near each other, one smaller than the other, whose waters unite immediately below. Both sources are on level ground, amongst rocks of tufwacke. The larger source immediately forms a river twelve or fifteen yards across, which rushes rapidly over a stony bed into the lower plain. There are no ruins of any kind near the springs; but the hill over them seems to have been built upon, though nothing now is visible. At a quarter of an hour to the N. of the spring are ruins of ancient habitations, built of the black tufwacke, the principal rock found in the plain. The few houses at present inhabited on that spot are called Enkeil. I was told that the ancient name of the river of Banias was Djour, which added to the name of Dhan, made Jourdan; the more correct etymology is probably Or Dhan, in Hebrew the river of Dhan. Lower down, between the Houle and the lake Tabaria, it is called Orden by the inhabitants; to the southward of the lake of Tabaria it bears the name of Sherya, till it falls into the Dead Sea.

October 15th.--My guide returned to Zahle. It was my intention to take a view of the lake and its eastern borders; but a tumour, which threatened to prevent both riding and walking, obliged me to proceed immediately to Damascus. I had reason to congratulate myself on the determination, for if I had staid a day longer, I should have been compelled to await my recovery at some village on the road. Add to this, I had only the value of four shillings left, after paying my guide: this alone, however, should not have prevented me from proceeding, as I knew that two days were sufficient to enable me to gratify my curiosity, and a guide would have thought himself well paid at two shillings a day; as to the other expenses, travelling in the manner of the country people rendered money quite unnecessary.

There are two roads from Banias to Damascus: the one lies through the villages of Koneitza and Sasa; the other is more northly; I took the latter, though the former is most frequented, being the route followed by all the pilgrims from Damascus and Aleppo to Jerusalem; but it is less secure for a small caravan, owing to the incursions of the Arabs. The country which I had visited to the westward is perfectly secure to the stranger: I might have safely travelled it alone unarmed, and without a guide. The route through the district of the Houle and Banias, and from thence to Damascus, on the contrary, is very dangerous: the Arabs as well as the Felahs, are often known to attack unprotected strangers, and a small body of men was stripped at Koneitza during my stay at Banias.

As soon as I declared my wish to return to Damascus, I was advised by several people present to take a guard of armed men with me, but knowing that this was merely a pretext to extort money without at all ensuring my safety, I declined the proposal, and said I should wait for a Kaffle. It fortunately happened that the Sheikh of the village had business at Damascus, and we were glad of each other's company. We set out in the afternoon, accompanied by the Sheikh's servant. The direction of the route is E.b.S. up the mountain of the Heish, behind the castle of Banias. We passed several huts of Felahs, who live here the whole summer, and retire in winter to their villages. They make cheese for the Damascus market. At the end of an hour and a half we came to Ain el Hazouri, a spring, with the tomb of Sheikh Othman el Hazouri just over it; to the north of it one hour are the ruins of a city called Hazouri. The mountain here is overgrown with oaks, but contains good pasturage; I was told that in the Wady Kastebe, near the castle, there are oak trees more than sixty feet high. One hour more brought us to the village of Djoubeta, where we remained during the night at the house of some friends of the Sheikh of Banias. This village belongs to Hasbeya; it is inhabited by about fifty Turkish and ten Greek families; they subsist chiefly by the cultivation of olives, and by the rearing of cattle. I was well treated at the house where we alighted, and also at that of the Sheikh of the village, where I went to drink a cup of coffee. It being Ramadan, we passed the greater part of the night in conversation and smoking; the company grew merry, and knowing that I was curious about ruined places, began to enumerate all the villages and ruins in the neighbourhood, of which I subjoin the names. [The ruins of Dara, Bokatha, Bassisa, Alouba, Afkerdouva, Hauratha (this was described as being of great extent, with many walls and arches still remaining,) Enzouby, Hauarit, Kleile, Emteile, Mesherefe, Zar, Katloube in the Wady Asal, Kseire, Kafoua, Beit el Berek. The villages of Kfershouba, Maonyre in the district Kereimat, Ain el Kikan, Mezahlak, Merj el Rahel, Sheba, Zeneble, Zor or Afid, Merdj Zaa. In the Houle, Amerie, Nebi Djahutha, Sheheil.] The neighbouring mountains of the Heish abound in tigers (nimoura); their skins are much esteemed by the Arab Sheikhs as saddle cloths. There are also bears, wolves, and stags; the wild boar is met with in all the mountains which I visited in my tour.

October 16th.--The friends of the Sheikh of Banias having dissuaded him from proceeding, on account of the dangers of the road, his servant and myself set out early in the morning. In three quarters of an hour we reached the village of Medjel, inhabited by Druses, with four or five Christian families. The Druses who inhabit the country near Damascus are very punctual in observing the rites of the Mohammedan religion, and fast, or at least pretend to do so, during the Ramadan. In their own country, some profess Christianity, others Mohammedism. The chief, the Emir Beshir, keeps a Latin confessor in his house; yet all of them, when they visit Damascus, go to the mosque. Medjel is situated on a small plain high up in the mountain; half an hour further on is a spring; and at one hour and a quarter beyond, is a spacious plain. The mountain here is in most places capable of cultivation. In one hour more we reached the top. The oak tree is very frequent here as well as the bear's plum (Khoukh eddeb), the berries of which afford a very refreshing nourishment to the traveller. The rock is partly calcareous, and partly of a porous tufa, but softer than that which I saw in the Houle. At one hour and a quarter farther is the Beit el Djanne (the House of Paradise), in a narrow Wady, at a spot where the valley widens a little. On its western side are several se-pulchral caves hewn in the chalky rock. Another quarter of an hour brought us to the Ain Beit el Djanne, a copious spring, with a mill near it; and from thence, in half an hour, we reached the plain on the eastern side of the mountain. Our route now lay N.E. by E.; to the right was the open country adjoining the Haouran, to the left the chain of the Heish, at the foot of which we continued to travel for the remainder of the day. The villages on the eastern declivity of the Heish, between Beit el Djanne and Kferhauar are, Hyna, Um Esshara, Dourboul, Oerna, and Kalaat el Djendel.

At three hours and a half from the point where the Wady Beit el Djanne terminates in the plain is the village Kferhauar. Before we entered it I saw to the left of the road a tomb which attracted my attention by its size. I was told that it was the Kaber Nimroud (the tomb of Nimrod); it consists of a heap of stones about twenty feet in length, two feet high, and three feet broad, with a large stone at both extremities, similar to the tombs in Turkish cemeteries. This is probably the Kalat Nimroud laid down in maps, to the south of Damascus; at least I never heard of any Kalaat Nimroud in that direction.

To the right of our road, one hour and a half from Kferhauar, lay Sasa, and near it Ghaptata. Half an hour farther from Kferhauar we alighted at the village Beitima. On a slight eminence near Kferhauar stands a small tower, and there is another of the same size behind Beitima. The principal article of culture here is cotton: the crop was just ripe, and the inhabitants were occupied in collecting it. There are Druses at Kferhauar as well as at Beitima; at the latter village I passed an uncom-fortable rainy night, in the court-yard of a Felah's house.

October 17th.--We continued to follow the Djebel Heish (which however takes a more northern direction than the Damascus road for four hours, when we came to Katana, a considerable village, with good houses, and spacious gardens; the river, whose source is close to the village, emp-ties itself into the Merj of Damascus.

Three hours from Katana, passing over the district called Ard el Lauan, we came to Kfersousa. Beyond Katana begins the Djebel el Djou-she, which continues as far as the Djebel Salehie, near Damascus, uniting, on its western side, the lower ridge of mountains of the Djebel Essheikh. Kfersousa lies just within the limits of the gardens of the Merdj of Da-mascus. In one hour beyond it I re-entered Damascus, greatly fatigued, having suffered great pain.

BURCKHARDT

After returning to Damascus from my tour in the Haouran, I was desirous to see the ruins of Rahle and Bourkoush, in the Djebel Essheikh, which I had heard mentioned by several people of Rasheya during my stay at Shohba. On the 12th of December, I took a man with me, and rode to Katana, by a route different from that through the Ard el Lauan, by which I travelled from Katana to Damascus in October. It passes in a more southerly direction through the villages of Deir raye, one hour beyond Bonabet Ullah; and another hour Djedeide; one hour and a quarter from Djedeide is Artous, in which are many Druse families; in an hour from Artous we reached Katana. This is a very pleasant road, through well cultivated fields and groves. I here saw nurseries of apricot trees, which are transplanted into the gardens at Damascus. To the south of Artous three quarters of an hour, is the village of Kankab, situated upon a hill; below it is the village of Djoun, opposite to which, and near the village Sahnaya, lies the Megarat Mar Polous, or St. Paul's cavern, where the Apostle is related to have hidden himself from the pursuit of his enemies at Damascus. The monks of Terra Santa, who have a convent at Damascus, had formerly a chapel at Sahnaya, where one of their fraternity resided; but the Roman Catholic Christians of the village having become followers of the Greek church, the former abandoned their establishment. To the N.E. of Djedeide, and half an hour from it, is the village Maddharnie.

Katana is one of the chief villages in the neighbourhood of Damascus; it contains about one hundred and eighty Turkish families, and four or five of Christians. The Sheikh, to whom the village belongs, is of a very rich Damascus family, a descendant of a Santon, whose tomb is shewn in the mosque of the village. Adjoining to the tomb is a hole in the rocky ground, over which an apartment has been built for the reception of maniacs; they are put down into the hole, and a stone is placed over its mouth; here they remain for three or four days, after which, as the Turks pretend, they regain their senses. The Christians say that the Santon was a Patriarch of Damascus, who left his flock, and turned hermit, and that he gained great reputation amongst the Turks, because whenever he prostrated himself before the Deity, his sheep imitated his example. Katana has a bath, and near it the Sheikh has a good house. The villagers cultivate mulberry trees to feed their silk worms, and some cotton, besides corn. The day after my arrival I engaged two men to shew me the way to the ruins. We began to cross the lower branches of the Djebel Essheikh, at the foot of which Katana is situated, and after an hour and a quarter came to Bir Karme, likewise called El Redhouan, a spring in a narrow valley. We rode over mountainous ground in the road to Rasheya, passed another well of spring water, and at the end of four hours reached Rahle, a miserable Druse village, half an hour to the right of the road from Katana to Rasheia. The ruins are to the north of the village, in the narrow valley of Rahle, and consist principally of a ruined temple, built of large square stones, of the same calcareous rock used in the buildings of Baalbec: little else remains than the foundations, which are twenty paces in breadth, and thirty in length; within the area of the temple are the foundations of a circular building. Many fragments of columns are lying about, and a few extremely well formed capitals of the Ionic order. Upon two larger stones lying near the gate, which probably formed the architrave, is the figure of a bird with expanded wings, not inferior in execution to the bird over the architrave of the great temple at Baalbec; its head is broken off; in its claws is something of the annexed form, bearing no resemblance to the usual figure of the thunderbolt. On the exterior, wall, on the south side of the temple, is a large head, apparently of a female, three feet and a half high, and two feet and a half broad, sculptured upon one of the large square stones which form the wall: its features are perfectly regular, and are enclosed by locks of hair, terminating in thin tresses under the chin. This head seems never to have belonged to a whole length figure, as the stone on which it is sculptured touches the ground. Near the ruins is a deep well. A few hundred paces to the south, upon an eminence, are the ruins of another edifice, of which there remain the foundations of the walls, and a great quantity of broken columns of small size. Around these edifices are the remains of numerous private habitations; a short column is found standing in most of them, in the centre of the foundations of the building. In the neighbouring rocks about a dozen small cells are excavated, in some of which are cavities for bodies. I found no inscriptions. S.W. from Rahle, one hour and a half, are the ruins of the castle of Bourkush. We passed the spring called Ain Ward (the rose spring), near a plain in the midst of the mountains called Merdj Bourkush. The ruins stand upon a mountain, which appeared to me to be one of the highest of the lower chain of the Djebel Essherk. At the foot of the steep ascent leading up to the castle, on the N.W. side, is a copious spring, and another to the W. midway in the ascent. These ruins consist of the outer walls of the castle, built with large stones, some of which are eight feet long, and five broad. A part only of the walls are standing. In the interior are several apartments which have more the appearance of dungeons than of habitations. The rock, upon which the whole structure is erected, has been levelled so as to form an area within, round which ran a wall; a part of this wall is formed by the solid rock, upwards of eight feet high, and as many broad, the rock having been cut down on both sides.

To the E. of this castle are the ruins of a temple built much in the same style as that of Rahle, but of somewhat smaller dimensions, and constructed of smaller stones. The architrave of the door is supported by two Corinthian pilasters. A few Druse families reside at Bourkush, who cultivate the plain below. On the S.E. side of the ascent to the castle are small caverns cut in the rock. From this point Katana bore S.E.

We returned from Bourkush to Katana by Ain Embery, a rivulet whose source is hard by in the Wady, with some ruined habitations near it. The distance from Bourkush to Katana is two hours and a half brisk walking of a horse. The summit of the mountain was covered with snow. I heard of several other ruins, but had no time to visit them. There are several villages of Enzairie in the mountain. On the third day from my departure I returned to Damascus.

JOURNAL OF AN EXCURSION INTO THE HAOURAN IN THE AUTUMN AND WINTER OF 1810

November 8th.--On returning from the preceding tour, I was detained at Damascus for more than a fortnight by indisposition. As soon as I had recovered my health I began to prepare for a journey into the plain of the Haouran, and the mountains of the Druses of the Haouran, a country which, as well from the reports of natives, as from what I heard that Mr. Seetzen had said of it, on his return from visiting a part of it four years ago, I had reason to think was in many respects highly interesting. I requested of the Pasha the favour of a Bouyourdi, or general passport to his officers in the Haouran, which he readily granted, and on receiving it I found that I was recommended in very strong terms. Knowing that there were many Christians, chiefly of the Greek church, I thought it might be equally useful to procure from the Greek Patriarch of Damascus, with whom I was well acquainted, a letter to his flock in the Haouran. On communicating my wishes, he caused a circular letter to be written to all the priest, which I found of greater weight among the Greeks than the Bouyourdi was among the Turks.

Being thus furnished with what I considered most necessary, I assumed the dress of the Haouran people, with a Keffie, and a large sheepskin over my shoulders: in my saddle bag I put one spare shirt, one pound of coffee beans, two pounds of tobacco, and a day's provender of barley for my horse. I then joined a few Felahs of Ezra, of one of whom I hired an ass, though I had nothing to load it with but my small saddle-bag; but I knew this to be the best method of recommending myself to the protection of my fellow travellers; as the owner of the ass necessarily becomes the companion and protector of him who hires it. Had I offered to pay him before setting out merely for his company on the way, he would have asked triple the sum I gave him, without my deriving the smallest advantage from this increase, while he would have considered my conduct as extraordinary and suspicious. In my girdle I had eighty piastres, (about £4. sterling) and a few more in my pocket, together with a watch, a compass, a journal book, a pencil. a knife, and a tobacco purse. The coffee I knew would be very acceptable in the houses where I might alight; and throughout the journey I was enabled to treat all the company present with coffee.

My companions intending to leave Damascus very early the next morning, I quitted my lodgings in the evening, and went with them to sleep in a small Khan in the suburb of Damascus, at which the Haouaerne, or people of Haouran, generally alight.

November 9th.--We departed through this gate of the Meidhan, three hours before sun-rise, and took the road by which the Hadj annually commences its laborious journey; this gate is called Bab Ullah, the Gate of God, but might, with more propriety be named Bab-el-Maut, the Gate of Death; for scarcely a third ever returns of those whom a devout adherence to their religion, or the hope of gain impel to this journey. The approach to Damascus on this side is very grand: being formed by a road above one hundred and fifty paces broad, which is bordered on each side by a grove of olive trees, and continues in a straight line for upwards of an hour. A quarter of an hour from Bab Ullah, to the left, stands a mosque with a Kiosk, called Kubbet el Hadj, where the Pasha who conducts the Hadj passes the first night of his journey, which is invariably the fifteenth of the month Shauwal. On the other side of the road, and opposite to it, lies the village El Kadem (the foot), where Mohammed is said to have stopped, without entering Damascus, when coming from Mekka. Half an hour farther is a bridge over a small rivulet: to the left are the villages Zebeine and Zebeinat; to the right the village Deir raye. In another half hour we came to a slight ascent, called Mefakhar; at its foot is a bridge over the rivulet El Berde; to the right is the village El Sherafie: to the left, parallel with the road, extends a stony district called War- ed-djamous the Buffaloes War, War being an appellation given to all stony soils whether upon plains or mountains. Here the ground is very uneven; in traversing it we passed the Megharat el Haramie or Thief's Cavern, the nightly refuge of disorderly persons. On the other side of the War is a descent called Ard Shoket el Haik, which leads into the plain, and in half an hour to the village El Kessoue; distant from Damascus three hours and a quarter in a S.S.E. direction. El Kessoue is a considerable village, situated on the river Aawadj, or the crooked, which flows from the neighbourhood of Hasbeya, and waters the plain of Djolan; in front of the village a well paved bridge crosses the river, on each side of which, to the W. and E. appears a chain of low mountains; those to the east are called Djebel Manai, and contain large caverns; the summits of the two chains nearest the village are called by a collective name Mettall el Kessoue. I stopped for half an hour at Kessoue, at a coffee house by the road side. The village has a small castle, or fortified building, over the bridge.

From Kessoue a slight ascent leads up to a vast plain, called Ard Khiara, from a village named Khiara. In three quarters of an hour from Kessoue we reached Khan Danoun, a ruined building. Here, or at Kessoue, the pilgrim caravan passes the second night. Near Khan Danoun, a rivulet flows to the left. This Khan, which is now in ruins, was built in the usual style of all the large Khans in this country: consisting of an open square, surrounded with arcades, beneath which are small apartments for the accommodation of travellers; the beasts occupy the open square in the centre. From Khan Danoun the road continues over the plain, where few cultivated spots appear, for two hours and a quarter; we then reached a Tel, or high hill, the highest summit of the Djebel Khiara, a low mountain chain which commences here, and runs in a direction parallel with the Djebel Manai for about twenty miles. The mountains Khiara and Manai are sometimes comprised under the name of Djebel Kessoue, and so I find them laid down in D'Anville's map. The summit of Djebel Khiara is called Soubbet Faraoun. From thence begins a stony district, which extends to the village Ghabarib, one hour and a quarter from the Soubbet. Upon a hill to the W. of the road, stands a small building crowned with a cupola, to which the Turks resort, from a persuasion that the prayers there offered up are peculiarly acceptable to the deity. This building is called Meziar Eliasha, or the Meziar of Elisha. The Hadj route has been paved in several places for the distance of a hundred yards or more, in order to facilitate the passage of the pilgrims in years when the Hadj takes place during the rainy season. Ghabarib has a ruined castle, and on the side of the road is a Birket or reservoir, with a copious spring. These cisterns are met with at every station on the Hadj route as far as Mekka; some of them are filled by rain water; others by small streams, which if they were not thus collected into one body would be absorbed in the earth, and could not possibly afford water for the thousands of camels which pass, nor for the filling of the water-skins.

At one hour beyond Ghabarib is the village Didy, to the left of the road: one hour from Didy, Es-szanamein, the Two Idols; the bearing of the road from Kessoue is S.b.E. [The variation of the compass is not computed in any of the bearings of this journal.] Szanamein is a considerable village, with several ancientbuildings and towers; but as my companions were unwilling to stop, I could not examine them closely. I expected to revisit them on my return to Damascus, but I subsequently preferred taking the route of the Loehf. I was informed afterwards that many Greek inscriptions are to be found at Szanamein.

From Szanamein the Hadj route continues in the same direction as before to Tafar and Mezerib; we left it and took a route more easterly. That which we had hitherto travelled being the high road from the Haouran to Damascus, is perfectly secure, and we met with numerous parties of peasants going to and from the city; but we had scarcely passed Szanamein when we were apprised by some Felahs that a troop of Arabs Serdie had been for several days past plundering the passengers and villages in the neighbourhood. Afraid of being surprised, my companions halted and sewed their purses up in a camel's pack saddle; I followed their example. I was informed that these flying parties of Arabs very rarely drive away the cattle of the Haouran people, but are satisfied with stripping them of cash, or any new piece of dress which they may have purchased at Damascus, always however giving them a piece of old clothing of the same kind in return. The country from Szanamein to one hour's distance along our road is stony, and is thence called War Szanamein. After passing it, we met some other Haouran people, whose reports concerning the Arabs so terrified my companions, that they resolved to give up their intention of reaching Ezra the same day, and proceeded to seek shelter in a neighbouring village, there to wait for fresh news. We turned off a little to our left, and alighted at a village called Tebne, distant one hour and a half from Szanamein. We left our beasts in the court-yard of our host's house, and went to sup with the Sheikh, a Druse, at whose house strangers are freely admitted to partake of a plate of Burgoul. Tebne stands upon a low hill, on the limits of the stony district called the Ledja, of which I shall have occasion to speak hereafter. The village has no water but what it derives from its cisterns, which were at this time nearly dry. It consists wholly of ancient habitations, built of stone, of a kind which I shall describe in speaking of Ezra.

November 10th.--We quitted Tebne early in the morning, and passing the villages Medjidel, Mehadjer, Shekara, and Keratha, all on the left of the route, arrived, at the end of three hours and a quarter, at Ezra. Here commences the plain of the Haouran, which is interrupted by numerous insulated hills, on the declivities, or at the foot of which, most of the villages of the Haouran are seated. From Tebne the soil begins to be better cultivated, yet many parts of it are overgrown with weeds. On a hill opposite Manhadje, on the west side of the road, stands a Turkish Meziar, called Mekdad. In approaching Ezra we met a troop of about eighty of the Pasha's cavalry; they had, the preceding night, surprised the above- mentioned party of Arabs Serdie in the village of Walgha, and had killed Aerar, their chief, and six others, whose heads they were carrying with them in a sack. They had also taken thirty-one mares, of which the greater number were of the best Arabian breeds. Afraid of being pursued by the friends of the slain they were hastening back to Damascus, where, as I afterwards heard, the Pasha presented them with the captured mares, and distributed eight purses, or about £200. amongst them.

On reaching Ezra I went to the house of the Greek priest of the village, whom I had already seen at the Patriarch's at Damascus, and with whom I had partly concerted my tour in the Haouran. He had been the conductor of M. Seetzen, and seemed to be very ready to attend me also, for a trifling daily allowance, which he stipulated. Ezra is one of the principal villages of the Haouran; it contains about one hundred and fifty Turkish and Druse families, and about fifty of Greek Christians. It lies within the precincts of the Ledja, at half an hour from the arable ground: it has no spring water, but numerous cisterns. Its inhabitants make cotton stuffs, and a great number of millstones, the blocks for forming which, are brought from the interior of the Ledja; the stones are exported from hence, as well as from other villages in the Loehf, over the greater part of Syria, as far as Aleppo and Jerusalem. They vary in price, according to their size, from fifteen to sixty piastres, and are preferred to all others on account of the hardness of the stone, which is the black tufa rock spread over the whole of the Haouran, and the only species met with in this country.

Ezra was once a flourishing city; its ruins are between three and four miles in circumference. The present inhabitants continue to live in the ancient buildings, which, in consequence of the strength and solidity of their walls, are for the greater part in complete preservation

They are built of stone, as are all the houses of the villages in the Haouran and Djebel Haouran from Ghabarib to Boszra, as well as of those in the desert beyond the latter. In general each dwelling has a small entrance leading into a court-yard, round which are the apartments; of these the doors are usually very low. The interior of the rooms is constructed of large square stones; across the centre is a single arch, generally between two and three feet in breadth, which supports the roof; this arch springs from very low pilasters on each side of the room, and in some instances rises immediately from the floor: upon the arch is laid the roof, consisting of stone slabs one foot broad, two inches thick, and about half the length of the room, one end resting upon short projecting stones in the walls, and the other upon the top of the arch. The slabs are in general laid close to each other; but in some houses I observed that the roof was formed of two layers, the one next the arch having small intervals between each slab, and a second layer of similar dimensions was laid close together at right angles with the first. The rooms are seldom higher than nine or ten feet, and have no other opening than a low door, with sometimes a small window over it. In many places I saw two or three of these arched chambers one above the other, forming so many stories. This substantial mode of building prevails also in most of the ancient public edifices remaining in the Haouran, except that in the latter the arch, instead of springing from the walls or floor, rests upon two short columns. During the whole of my tour, I saw but one or two arches, whose curve was lofty; the generality of them, including those in the public buildings, are oppressively low. To complete the durability of these structures, most of the doors were anciently of stone, and of these many are still remaining; sometimes they are of one piece and sometimes they are folding doors; they turn upon hinges worked out of the stone, and are about four inches thick, and seldom higher than about four feet, though I met with some upwards of nine feet in height.

I remained at Ezra, in the priest's house, this and the following day, occupied in examining the antiquities of the village. The most considerable ruins stand to the S.E. of the present habitations; but few of the buildings on that side have resisted the destructive hand of time. The walls, however, of most of them yet remain, and there are the remains of a range of houses which, to judge from their size and solidity, seem to have been palaces. The Ezra people have given them the appellation of Seraye Malek el Aszfar, or the Palace of the Yellow King, a term given over all Syria, as I have observed in another place, to the Emperor of Russia. The aspect of these ruins, and of the surrounding rocky country of the Ledja, is far from being pleasing: the Ledja presents a level tract covered with heaps of black stones, and small irregular shaped rocks, without a single agreeable object for the eye to repose upon. On the west and north sides of the village are several public edifices, temples, churches, &c. The church of St. Elias, in which the Greeks celebrate divine service, is a round building, of which the roof is fallen in, and only the outer wall standing. On its S. side is a vestibule supported by three arches, the entrance to which is through a short arched dark passage.

On the south side of the village stands an edifice, dedicated to St. Georgius, or El Khouder, as the Mohammedans, and sometimes the

Christians, call that Saint. It is a square building of about eighty- five feet the side, with a semicircular projection on the E. side; the roof is vaulted, and is supported by eight square columns, which stand in a circle in the centre of the square, and are united to one another by arches. They are about two feet thick, and sixteen high, with a single groove on each side. Between the columns and the nearest part of the wall is a space of twelve feet. The niche on the east side contains the altar. The vaulted roof is of modern construction. The building had two entrances; of which the southern is entirely walled up; the western also is closed at the top, leaving a space below for a stone door of six feet high. over which is a broad stone with the Greek inscription upon it:

"A.D. 410. This was the third year of the Emperor Theodosius the younger, in whose reign the final decrees were issued against the Pagan worship. It appears from the inscription that the building upon which it is written was an ancient temple, converted into a church of St. George."

Before the temple is a small paved yard, now used as the exclusive burial ground of the Greek priests of Ezra.

In the midst of the present inhabited part of the village stand the ruins of another large edifice; it was formerly applied to Christian worship, and subsequently converted into a mosque: but it has long since been abandoned. It consists of a quadrangle, with two vaulted colonnades at the northern and southern ends, each consisting of a double row of five columns. In the middle of the area stood a parallel double range of columns of a larger size, forming a colonnade across the middle of the building; the columns are of the Doric order, and about sixteen feet high. The side arcades are still standing to half their height; those of the middle area are lying about in fragments; the E. and W. walls of the building are also in ruins. Over the entrance gate are three inscribed tablets.

Over an inner gate I saw an inscription, much defaced, which seemed to be in Syrian characters.

Adjoining this building stands a square tower, about fifty feet high; its base is somewhat broader than its top. I frequently saw similar structures in the Druse villages; and in Szannamein are two of the same form as the above: they all have windows near the summit; in some, there is one window on each side, in others there are two, as in this at Ezra. They have generally several stories of vaulted chambers, with a staircase to ascend into them.

To the E. of the village is the gateway of another public building, the interior of which has been converted into private dwellings; this building is in a better style than those above described, and has some trifling sculptured ornaments on its gate.

There are many private habitations, principally at the S. end of the town, with inscriptions over the doors; most of which are illegible. The following I found in different parts of the village, on stones lying on the ground, or built into the walls of houses.

I observed a great difference in the characters in which all the above inscriptions were engraved. That of S. Georgius is the best written.

In the evening I went to water my horse with the priest's cattle at the spring of Geratha, one hour distant from Ezra, N. by E. I met there a number of shepherds with theyr flocks; the rule is, that the first who arrives at the well, waters his cattle before the others; several were therefore obliged to wait till after sunset. There are always some stone basins round the wells, out of which the camels drink, the water being drawn up by leathern buckets, and poured into them: disputes frequently happen on these occasions. The well has a broad staircase leading down to it; just by it lies a stone with an inscription

This well is called Rauad.

November 12th.--I left Ezra with the Greek priest, to visit the villages towards the mountain of the Haouran. I had agreed to pay him by the day, but I soon had reason to repent of this arrangement. In order to protract my journey, and augment the number of days, he loaded his horse with all his church furniture, and at almost every village where we alighted he fitted up a room, and said mass; I was, in consequence, seldom able to leave my night's quarters before mid-day, and as the days were now short our day's journey was not more than four or five hours. His description of me to the natives varied with circumstances; sometimes I was a Greek lay brother, sent to him by the Patriarch, a deception which could not be detected by my dress, as the priesthood is not distinguished by any particular dress, unless it be the blue turban, which they generally wear; sometimes he described me as a physician who was in search of herbs; and occasionally he owned that my real object was to examine the country. Our road lay S.E. upon the borders of the stony district called Ledja; and at the end of two hours we passed the village of Bousser on our left, which is principally inhabited by Druses; it lies in the War, and contains the Turkish place of pilgrimage, called Meziar Eliashaa. Near it, to the S. is the small village Kherbet Hariri. In one hour we passed Baara, a village under the control of the Sheikh of Ezra; and at half an hour farther to our right, the village Eddour. The Wady Kanouat, a torrent which takes its rise in the mountain, passes Baara, where it turns several mills in the winter season; towards the end of May it is generally dried up. At one hour from Baara is the Ain Keratha, or Geratha, according to Bedouin and Haouran pronunciation. At the foot of a hill in the War are several wells; this hill is covered with the ruins of the ancient city of Keratha, of which the foundations only remain: there had been such a scarcity of water this year, that the people of Bousser were obliged to fetch it from these wells. A quarter of an hour E. of them is the village Nedjran, in the Ledja, in which are several ancient buildings inhabited by Druses. In the Ledja, in the neighbourhood of Keratha, are many spots of arable ground. Upon a low hill, in our route, at an hour and a quarter from the Ain or well, is Deir el Khouat, i.e. the Brothers' Monastery, a heap of ruins. From thence we travelled to the south-eastward for three quarters of an hour, to the village Sedjen, where we alighted, at the house of the only Christian family remaining among the Druses of the place. Sedjen is built, like all these ancient towns, entirely of the black stone peculiar to these mountains.

November 13th.--We left Sedjen about noon; and in half an hour came to the spring Mezra, the water of which is conducted near to Sedjen by an ancient canal, which empties itself in the summer time into a large pond; in the winter the stream is joined by a number of small torrents, which descend from the Djebel Haouran between Kanouat and Soueida; it empties itself farther to the west into the Wady Kanouat. Above the spring is a ruined castle, and near it several other large buildings, of which the walls only are standing; the castle was most probably built to protect the water. There is a tradition that Tamerlane filled up the well; and a similar story is repeated in many parts of the Haouran: it is said that he threw quick-silver into the springs, which prevented the water from rising to the surface; and that the water collecting under ground from several sources near Mezerib, at length burst forth, and formed the copious spring at that place, called Bushe. From Mezra to Medjel we travelled E.N.E. one hour. It rained the whole day. On arriving at Medjel I alighted to copy some inscriptions, when the Druse Sheikh immediately sent for me, to know what I was about. It is a general opinion with these people that inscriptions indicate hidden treasure; and that by reading or copying them a knowledge is obtained where the treasure lies. I often combated this opinion with success, by simply asking them, whether, if they chose to hide their money under ground, they would be so imprudent as to inform strangers where it lay? The opinion, however, is too strongly rooted in the minds of many of the country people, to yield to argument; and this was the case with the Sheikh of Medjel. Having asked me very rudely what business I had, I presented to him the Pasha's Bouyourdi; but of twenty people present no one could read it; and when I had read it to them, they refused to believe that it was genuine. While coffee was roasting I left the room, finished copying some inscriptions, and rode off in a torrent of rain.

There are two other buildings in the town, which I suppose to have been sepulchral. In one of them is a long inscription, but the rain had made it illegible. We rode on for three quarters of an hour farther to the village Kafer el Loehha, situated in the Wady Kanouat, on the borders of the Ledja. I here passed a comfortable evening, in the company of some Druses, who conversed freely with me, on their relations with their own Sheikhs, and with the surrounding Arabs.

November 14th.--The principal building of Kafer el Loehha is a church, whose roof is supported by three arches, which, like those in the private dwellings, spring from the floor of the building. Not far from the church, on its west side, is another large edifice, with a rotunda, and a paved terrace before it.

From Kafer el Loehha we rode N. forty minutes, to a village called Rima el Loehf, inhabited by only three or four Druse families. At the entrance of the village stands a building eight feet square and about twenty feet high, with a flat roof, and three receptacles for the dead; it has no windows; at its four corners are pilasters.

The walls of this apartment are hollow, as appears by several holes which have been made in them, in search of hidden treasure. Beneath it is a subterraneous apartment, in which is a double row of receptacles for the dead, three in each row, one above the other; each receptacle is two feet high, and five feet and a half long. The door is so low as hardly to allow a person to creep in.

This village has two Birkets, or reservoirs for water, which are filled in winter time by a branch of the Wady Kanouat; they were completely dried up this summer, a circumstance which rarely happens. Near both the Birkets are remains of strong walls. Upon an insulated hill three quarters of an hour S.E. from Rima, is Deir el Leben [Aarabic], i.e. Monastery of Milk; Rima is on the limits of the Ledja; Deir in the plain between it and the mountain Haouran. The Deir consists of the ruins of a square building seventy paces long, with small cells, each of which has a door; it contained also several larger apartments, of which the arches only remain. The roof of the whole building has fallen in.

Half an hour E. of Deir el Leben lies a ruined, uninhabited village upon a Tel, called Doubba it has a Birket and a spring. To the N.E. of it is the inhabited Druse village Bereike. We advanced half an hour E. to the village Mourdouk on the declivity of the Djebel Haouran; it has a spring, from whence the Druses of Rima and Bereike obtain their daily supply of water. From the spring we proceeded to the eastward on the side of the mountain. At our feet extended the Ledja from between N.E.b.N. where it terminates, near Tel Beidhan, to N.W. by N. its furthest western point, on the Haouran side. Between the mountain and the Ledja is an intermediate plain of about one hour in breadth, and for the greater part uncultivated. Before us lay three insulated hills, called Tel Shiehhan, Tel Esszoub, which is the highest, and Tel Shohba; they are distant from each other half an hour, the second in the middle. One hour and a half to the S.E. of Tel Shohba is one of the projecting summits of the mountain called Tel Abou Tomeir.

From Mourdouk our road lay for an hour and a half over stony ground, to Shohba the seat of the principal Druse Sheikhs, and containing also some Turkish and Christian families. It lies near the foot of Tel Sho-hba, between the latter and the mountain; it was formerly one of the chief cities in these districts, as is attested by its remaining town walls, and the loftiness of its public edifices. The walls may be traced all round the city, and are perfect in many places; there are eight gates, with a paved cause-way leading from each into the town. Each gate is formed of two arches, with a post in the centre. The eastern gate seems to have been the princi-pal one, and the street into which it opens leads in a straight line through the town; like the other streets facing the gates, it is paved with oblong flat stones, laid obliquely across it with great regularity. Following this street through a heap of ruined habitations on each side of it, where are many fragments of columns, I came to a place where four massy cubical structures formed a sort of square, through which the street runs; they are built with square stones, are twelve feet long by nine high, and, as appears by one of them, which is partly broken down, are quite solid, the centre being filled up with stones. Farther on to the right, upon a terrace, stand five Corinthian columns, two feet and a quarter in diameter, all quite en-tire. After passing these columns I came to the principal building in this part of the town; it is in the form of a crescent, fronting towards the east, without any exterior ornaments, but with several niches in the front. I did not venture to enter it, as I had a bad opinion of its present possessor, the chief of Shohba, who some years ago compelled M. Seetzen to turn back from hence towards Soueida. I remained unknown to the Druses during my stay at Shohba. Before the above mentioned building is a deep and large reservoir, lined with small stones. To the right of it stands another large edifice of a square shape, built of massy stones, with a spacious gate; its interior consists of a double range of vaults, one above the other, of which the lower one is choaked up as high as the capitals of the columns which support the arches.

Beyond and to the left of this last mentioned building, in the same street, is a vaulted passage with several niches on both sides of it, and dark apartments, destined probably for the reception of the bodies of the governors of the city. Farther on are the remaining walls of a large building.

To the west of the five Corinthian columns stands a small building, which has been converted into a mosque; it contains two columns about ten inches in diameter, and eight feet in height, of the same kind of fine grained gray granite, of which I had seen several columns at Banias in the Syrian mountains.

To the south of the crescent formed building, and its adjoining edifice, stands the principal curiosity of Shohba, a theatre, in good preservation. It is built on a sloping site, and the semicircle is enclosed by a wall nearly ten feet in thickness, in which are nine vaulted entrances into the interior. Between the wall and the seats runs a double row of vaulted chambers one over the other. Of these the upper chambers are boxes, opening towards the seats, and communicating behind with a passage which separates them from the outer wall. The lower chambers open into each other, those at the extremities of the semi- circle excepted, which have openings towards the area of the theatre. The entrance into the area is by three gates, one larger, with a smaller on either side; on each side of the two latter are niches for statues. The diameter of the area, near the entrance, is thirty paces; the circle round the upper row of seats is sixty-four paces; there are ten rows of seats. Outside the principal entrance is a wall, running parallel with it, close to which are several small apartments.

To the S.E. of Shohba are the remains of an aqueduct, which conveyed water into the town from a spring in the neighbouring mountain, now filled up. About six arches are left, some of which are at least forty feet in height. At the termination of this aqueduct, near the town, is a spacious building divided into several apartments, of which that nearest to the aqueduct is enclosed by a wall twelve feet thick, and about twenty-five feet high; with a vaulted roof, which has fallen in. It has two high vaulted entrances opposite to each other, with niches on each side. In the walls are several channels from the roof to the floor, down which the water from the aqueduct probably flowed. On one side of this room is an entrance into a circular chamber fourteen feet in diameter; and on the other is a similar apartment but of smaller dimensions, also with channels in its walls; adjoining to this is a room without any other opening than a very small door; its roof, which is still entire, is formed of small stones cemented together with mortar; all the walls are built of large square stones. The building seems evidently to have been a bath.

The inhabitants of Shohba fabricate cotton cloth for shirts and gowns. They grow cotton, but it is not reckoned of good quality. There are only three Christian families in the village. There are three large Birkets or wells, in two of which there was still some water. There is no spring near. Most of the doors of the houses, are formed of a single slab of stone, with stone hinges.

November 15th.--Our way lay over the fertile and cultivated plain at the foot of the Jebel Haouran, in a north-easterly direction. At a quarter of an hour from the town we passed the Wady Nimri w-el Heif, a torrent coming from the mountain to the S.E. In the winter it furnishes water to a great part of the Ledja, where it is collected in cisterns. There is a great number of ruined mills higher up the Wady. Three or four hours distant, we saw a high hill in the Djebel, called Um Zebeib. Three quarters of an hour from Shohba we passed the village Asalie, inhabited by a few families; near it is a small Birket. In one hour and three quarters we came to the village Shakka; on its eastern side stands an insulated building, consisting of a tower with two wings: it contains throughout a double row of arches and the tower has two stories, each of which forms a single chamber, without any opening but the door.

Adjoining the village, on the eastern side, are the ruins of a handsome edifice; it consists of an apartment fourteen paces square opening into an arcade, which leads into another apartment similar to the first. In the first, whose roof has fallen down, there are pedestals for statues all round the walls. On one side are three dark apartments, of which that in the centre is the largest; on the opposite side is a niche. The entrance is towards the east. To the south of these ruins stood another building, of which the front wall only is standing.

On the north side of the village are the ruins also of what was once an elegant structure; but nothing now remains except a part of the front, and some arches in the interior. It is thirty paces in length, with a flight of steps, of the whole length of the building, leading up to it. The entrance is through a large door whose sides and architrave are richly sculptured. On each side is a smaller door, between which and the great door are two niches supported by Ionic pilasters, the whole finely worked.

Within are three aisles or rows of arches, of which the central is much the largest; they rest upon short thick columns of the worst taste.

At some distance to the north of the village stands a small insulated tower There are several similar towers in the village, but without inscriptions.

The inhabitants of Shakka grow cotton; they are all Druses, except a single Greek family. To the S.E. of the village is the spring Aebenni with the ruined village Tefkha, about three quarters of an hour distant from Shakka. E.b.N. from Shakka one hour lies Djeneine, the last inhabited village on this side towards the desert. Its inhabitants are the shepherds of the people of El Hait. Half an hour to the north of Djeneine is Tel-Maaz, a hill on which is a ruined village. This is the N.E. limit of the mountain, which here turns off towards the S. behind Djeneine. At three quarters of an hour from Shakka, N.N.W. is El Hait, inhabited entirely by Catholic Christians. Here we slept.

East of El Hait three quarters of an hour lies the village Heitt.

November 16th.--We returned from Hait, directing our route towards Tel Shiehhan. In one hour we passed the village of Ammera.

From Ammera our way lay direct towards Tel Shiehhan. The village Um Ezzeitoun lay in the plain below, one hour distant, in the borders of the Ledja. Upon the top of Tel Shiehhan is a Meziar. Tel Szomeit, a hill in the Ledja, was seen to the N.W. about three hours distant; Tel Aahere, also in the Ledja, to the west, about four hours distant. The Tel Shiehhan is completely barren up to its top: near its eastern foot we passed the Wady Nimri w-el Heif, close to a mill which works in the winter time. From hence we passed between the Tel Shiehhan and Tel Es- Szoub; the ground is here covered with heaps of porous tufa and pumice stone. The western side of the Tel Shohba seems to have been the crater of a volcano, as well from the nature of the minerals which lie collected on that side of the hill, as from the form of a part of the hill itself, resembling a crater, while the neighbouring mountains have rounded tops, without any sharp angles.

We repassed Ain Mourdouk, and continued our way on the sloping side of the mountain to Saleim, a village one hour from the spring; it has been abandoned by its former inhabitants, and is now occupied only by a few poor Druses, who take refuge in such deserted places to avoid the oppressive taxes; and thus sometimes escape the Miri for one year. They here grow a little tobacco. In the village is a deep Birket. At the entrance of Saleim are the ruins of a handsome oblong building, with a rich entablature: its area is almost entirely filled up by its own ruins. Just by is a range of subterraneous vaults. The Wady Kanouat passes near the village. The day was now far gone, and as my priest was afraid of travelling by night, we quickened our pace, in order to reach Soueida before dark. From Saleim the road lies through a wood of stunted oaks, which continues till within one hour of Soueida. We had rode three quarters of an hour when I was shewn, E. from our road, up in the mountain, half an hour distant, the ruins of Aatin, with a Wady of the same name descending into the plain below. In the plain, to the westward, upon a hillock one hour distant, was the village Rima el Khalkhal, or Rima el Hezam (Hezam means girdle, and Khalkhal, the silver or glass rings which the children wear round their ankles.) Our road from Saleim lay S. by E. over a stony uncultivated ground, till within one hour of Soueida, where the wood of oaks terminates, and the fields begins, which extend up the slope of the mountain for half an hour to the left of the road. From Saleim to Soueida is a distance of two hours and three quarters.

Soueida is situated upon high ground, on a declivity of the Djebel Haouran; the Kelb Haouran, or highest summit of the mountain, bearing S.E. from it. It is considered as the first Druse village, and is the residence of the chief Sheikh. To the north, and close to it, descends the deep Wady Essoueida, coming from the mountain, where several other Wadys unite with it; it is crossed by a strong well built bridge, and it turns five or six mills near the village. Here, as in all their villages, the Druses grow a great deal of cotton, and the cultivation of tobacco is general all over the mountain. Soueida has no springs, but there are in and near it several Birkets, one of which, in the village, is more than three hundred paces in circuit, and at least thirty feet deep: a staircase leads down to the bottom, and it is entirely lined with squared stones. To the S. of the village is another of still larger circumference, but not so deep, also lined with stone, called Birket el Hadj, from the circumstance of its having, till within the last century, been a watering place for the Hadj, which used to pass here.

To the west of Soueida, on the other side of the Wady, stands a ruined building, which the country people call Doubeise: it is a perfect square of thirteen paces, with walls two feet thick, and ornamented on each side with six Doric pilasters, sixteen spans high, and reaching to within two feet of the roof, which has fallen down, and fills up the interior. No door or opening of any kind is visible. On the wall between the pilasters are some ornaments in bas-relief.

Soueida was formerly one of the largest cities of the Haouran; the circuit of its ruins is at least four miles: amongst them is a street running in a straight line, in which the houses on both sides are still standing; I was twelve minutes in walking from one end to other. Like the streets of modern cities in the East, this is so very narrow as to allow space only for one person or beast to pass. On both sides is a narrow pavement. The great variety seen in the the mode of construction of the houses seems to prove that the town has been inhabited by people of different nations. In several places, on both sides of the street, are small arched open rooms, which I supposed to have been shops. The street commences in the upper part of the town, at a large arched gate built across it; descending from thence I came to an elegant building, in the shape of a crescent, the whole of whose front forms a kind of niche, within which are three smaller niches. Continuing along the street I entered, on the left, an edifice with four rows of arches, built with very low pillars in the ugly style already described.

At the lower end of the street is a tower about thirty feet high, and eighteen square.

Turning from the beginning of the street, to the south, I met with a large building in ruins, with many broken pillars; it seems to have been a church; and it is joined to another building which has the appearance of having once been a monastery. In the paved area to the S. of it lies a water trough, formed of a single stone, two feet and a half in breadth, and seven feet in length, ornamented with four busts in relief, whose heads have been knocked off.

On the side of the pedestal is a figure of a bird with expanded wings, about one foot high, and below it is a man's hand grasping at something.

Near the Sheikh's house stands a colonnade of Corinthian columns, which surrounded a building, now entirely in ruins, but which appears to have been destined for sepulchres, as there are some small arched doors, quite choaked up, leading to subterraneous apartments.

November 17th.--We rode to the ruined city called Kanouat, two hours to the N.E. of Soueida; the road lying through a forest of stunted oaks and Zarour trees, with a few cultivated fields among them. Kanouat is situated upon a declivity, on the banks of the deep Wady Kanouat, which flows through the midst of the town, and whose steep banks are supported by walls in several places. To the S.W. of the town is a copious spring. On approaching Kanouat from the side of Soueida, the first object that struck my attention was a number of high columns, upon a terrace, at some distance from the town; they enclosed an oblong square fifteen paces in breadth, by twenty-nine in length. There were originally six columns on one side, and seven on the other, including the corner columns in both numbers; at present six only remain, and the bases of two others; they are formed of six pieces of stone, and measure from the top of the pedestal to the base of the capital twenty-six feet; the height of the pedestal is five feet; the circumference of the column six feet. The capitals are elegant, and well finished. On the northern side was an inner row of columns of somewhat smaller dimensions than the outer row; of these one only is standing. Within the square of columns is a row of subterraneous apartments. These ruins stand upon a terrace ten feet high, on the N. side of which is a broad flight of steps. The pedestals of all the columns had inscriptions upon them; but nothing can now be clearly distinguished.

Two divisions of the town may be distinguished, the upper, or principal, and the lower. The whole ground upon which the ruined habitations stand is overgrown with oak trees, which hide the ruins. In the lower town, over the door of an edifice which has some arches in its interior, and which has been converted in modern times into a Greek church, is an inscription.

A street leads up to this building, paved with oblong flat stones placed obliquely across the road in the same manner which I have described at Shohba. Here are several other buildings with pillars and arches: the principal of them has four small columns in front of the entrance and an anti-room leading to an inner apartment, which is supported by five arches. The door of the anti-room is of one stone, as usual in this country, but it is distinguished by its sculptured ornaments.

The principal building of Kanouat is in the upper part of the town, on the banks of the Wady. The street leading up to it lies along the deep bed of the Wady, and is paved throughout; on the side opposite to the precipice are several small vaulted apartments with doors. The entrance of the building is on the east side, through a wide door covered with a profusion of sculptured ornaments. In front of this door is a vestibule supported by five columns, whose capitals are of the annexed form. This vestibule joins, towards the north, several other apartments; their roofs, some of which were supported by pillars, have now all fallen down. The above-mentioned wide door opens into the principal apartment of the edifice, which is twenty-two paces in breadth by twenty-five in length. From each side of the entrance, through the middle of the room, runs a row of seven pillars, like those described above; at the further end, this colonnade is terminated by two Corinthian columns. All the sixteen columns are twenty spans high, with pedestals two feet and a half high. In the wall on the left side of this saloon are three niches, supported by short pillars. To the west is another vestibule, which was supported by five Corinthian columns, but four of them only are now standing. This vestibule communicates through an arched gate with an area, on the W. side of which are two Corinthian pillars with projecting bases for statues. On the S. side of the area is a large door, with a smaller one on each side. That in the centre is covered with sculptured vines and grapes, and over the entrance is the figure of the cross in the midst of a bunch of grapes. I observed similar ornaments on the great gate at Shakka, and I have often seen them since, over the entrances of public edifices. In the interior of the area, on the E. side, is a niche sixteen feet deep, arched at the bottom, with small vaulted rooms on both its sides, in which there is no other opening than the low door. On the S. and W. sides, the building is enclosed by a large paved area.

At a short distance from thence is another building, whose entrance is through a portico consisting of four columns in front and of two others behind, between two wings; on the inner sides of which are two niches above each other. The columns are about thirty-five feet high, and three feet and a half in diameter. Part of the walls only of the building are standing. In the wall opposite the entrance are two niches, one above the other. Not far from this building, toward its western side, I found, lying upon the ground, the trunk of a female statue of very inelegant form and coarse execution; my companion the priest spat upon it, when I told him that such idols were anciently objects of adoration; by its side lay a well executed female foot. I may here mention for the information of future travellers in these parts, that on my return to Soueida, I was told that there was a place near the source of spring water, where a great number of figures of men, women, beasts, and men riding naked on horses, &c. were lying upon the ground.

Besides the buildings just mentioned, there are several towers with two stories upon arches, standing insulated in different parts of the town; in one of them I observed a peculiarity in the structure of its walls, which I had already seen at Hait, and which I afterwards met with in several other places; the stones are cut so as to dovetail, and fit very closely.

The circuit of this ancient city may be about two miles and a half or three miles. From the spring there is a beautiful view into the plain of the Haouran, bounded on the opposite side by the mountain of the Heish, now covered with snow. There were only two Druse families at Kanouat, who were occupied in cultivating a few tobacco fields. I returned to Soueida by the same road which I had come.

November 18th.--After having made the tour of the city, I took coffee at the house of the Sheikh, whose brother and sons received me very politely, and I visited some sick people in the village,--for I was continually pressed, wherever I went, to write receipts for the sick,--I then left Soueida, with the intention of sleeping the following night in some Arab tent in the mountain, where I wished to see some ruined villages. The priest's fear of catching cold prevented me from proceeding according to my wishes. Passing the Birket el Hadj, we arrived in an hour and a quarter at a miserable village called Erraha; twenty minutes farther we passed the Wady el Thaleth, so called from three Wadys which, higher up, in the mountain unite into one. Here were pointed out to me, at half an hour to the N.E. on the side of the Wady in the mountain, the spring called Ain Kerashe, and at half an hour's distance, in the plain, the Druse village Resas. In a quarter of an hour from Thaleth, we reached Kherbet Rishe, a ruined village, and in one hour more Ezzehhoue, where my companion insisted upon taking shelter from the rain.

November 19th.--A rivulet passes Ezzehhoue, called Ain Ettouahein; i.e. the Source of the Mills, which comes down from Ain Mousa, the spring near Kuffer, and flows towards Aaere. Ezzehhoue is a Druse village, with a single Christian family. I was not well received by the Druse Sheikh, a boy of sixteen years, although he invited me to breakfast with him; but I was well treated by the poor Christian family. When I left the village there was a rumor amongst the Druses, that I should not be permitted to depart, or if I was, that I should be waylaid on the road, but neither happened. The people of the village make coffee mortars out of the trunks of oak trees, which they sell at twenty and twenty-five piastres each, and export them over the whole of the Haouran. At three quarters of an hour from Ezzehhoue, to the left of our route, is the Tel Ettouahein, an insulated hill in the plain, into which the road descends at a short distance from the village. Near the hill passes the Wady Ezzehhoue, a winter torrent which descends from the mountain. Two hours from Ezzehhoue is Aaere, a village standing upon a Tel in the plain.

Aaere is the seat of the second chief of the Druses in the Haouran: he is one of the most amiable men I have met with in the East, and what is still more extraordinary, he is extremely desirous to acquire knowledge. In the conversations I had with him during my repeated visits at Aaere, he was always most anxious to obtain information concerning European manners and institutions. He begged me one day to write down for him the Greek, English, and German alphabets, with the corresponding sound in Arabic beneath each letter; and on the following day he shewed me the

copy he had taken of them. His kindness towards me was the more remarkable, as he could not expect the smallest return for it. He admired my
lead pencils, of which I had two, but refused to accept one of them, on my
offering it to him. These Druses, as well as those of Kesrouan, firmly believe that there are a number of Druses in England; a belief originating in
the declaration of the Christians in these countries, that the English are
neither Greeks, nor Catholics, and therefore not Christians.

November 20th.--Being desirous of visiting the parts of the
Haouran bordering upon the desert, of crossing the Djebel Haouran, or
mountainous part of the district, and of exploring several ruined cities
which I had heard of in the desert, I engaged, with the Sheikh's permission, two Druses and a Christian, to act as guides. As there was
considerable risque of meeting with some hostile tribe of Arabs on the
road, I gave my purse to the Greek priest, who promised to wait for my
return; he did not keep his word, however, for he quitted Aaere, taking my
money with him, no doubt in the view of compelling me to follow him to
his village, from whence he might again have a chance of obtaining a
daily allowance, by accompanying me, though he well knew that it was
my intention to return to Damascus by a more western route; nor was this
all, he took twenty piastres out of my purse to buy straw for his camels.
On his repeatedly confessing to me, afterwards, his secret wishes that
some Frank nation would invade and take possession of the country, I told
him that he would by no means be a gainer by such an event, as a trick
such as that he had played me would expose him to be turned out of his
living and thrown into a prison. "You must imprison all the people of the
country then," was his reply; and he spoke the truth. I have often reflected
that if the English penal laws were suddenly promulgated in this country,
there is scarcely any man in business, or who, has money-dealings with
others, who would not be found liable to transportation before the end of
the first six months.

Our road lay over the plain, E.N.E. for three quarters of an hour;
we then began to mount by a slight ascent. In an hour and a quarter we
came to two hills, with the ruins of a village called Medjmar, on the right
of the road. At a quarter of an hour from thence is the village Afine, in
which are about twenty-five Druse families; it has a fine spring. Here the
ascent becomes more steep. At one hour from Afine, E.b.S. upon the
summit of the lower mountain, stands Hebran. Here is a spring and a ruined church, with the foundations of another building near it.

The mountain upon which Hebran stands is stony, but has places
fit for pasturage. The plain to the S. is called Amman, in which is a

spring. That to the E. is called Zauarat, and that to the S.W. Merdj el Dau-
let; all these plains are level grounds, with several hillocks, and are
surrounded by mountains.

There are a few families at Hebran.

Proceeding from Hebran towards the Kelb (dog), or, as the Arabs
here call it, Kelab Haouran, in one houre we came to Kuffer, once a considerable town. It is built in the usual style of this country, entirely of
stone; most of the houses are still entire; the doors are uniformly of stone,
and even the gates of the town, between nine and ten feet high, are of a
single piece of stone. On each side of the streets is a foot pavement two
feet and a half broad, and raised one foot above the level of the street itself, which is seldom more than one yard in width. The town is three
quarters of an hour in circumference, and being built upon a declivity, a
person may walk over it upon the flat roofs of the houses; in the court-
yards of the houses are many mulberry trees. Amongst several arched edifices is one of somewhat larger dimensions, with a steeple, resembling
that at Ezra; in the paved court-yard lies an urn of stone. In later times this
building had been a mosque, as is indicated by several Arabic inscriptions. In the wall within the arched colonnade is a niche elegantly adorned
with sculptured oak-leaves.

We dined in the church, upon the Kattas which my guides had
killed. These birds, which resemble pigeons, are in immense numbers
here; but I found none of them in the eastern parts of the Djebel Haouran.

To the N.E. of Kutfer is the copious spring already mentioned,
called Ain Mousa, the stream from which, we had passed at Ezzehhoue.
There is a small building over it.

We arrived, after sunset, in one hour from Kuffer, at an encampment of Arabs Rawafie, immediately at the foot of the Kelab; and there
took up our quarters for the night. The tent of our host was very neat, being formed with alternate white and black Shoukes, or cloth made of
goat's hair. I here found the Meharem to the right of the man's apartment.
We were treated as usual with coffee and Feita. I had been rather feverish
during the whole day, and in the evening the symptoms increased, but,
cold as the night was, and more especially on the approach of morning
when the fire which is kept up till midnight gradually dies out, I found
myself completely recovered the next day. This encampment consisted of
ten or twelve tents, in the midst of the forest which surrounds the Kelab.

November 21st.--The Kelab is a cone rising from the lower ridge
of the mountains; it is barren on the S. and E. sides, but covered on the N.

and W. with the trees common to these mountains. I was told that in clear weather the sea is visible from its top, the ascent to which, from the encampment, was said to be one hour. The morning was beautiful but very cold, the whole mountain being covered with hoar frost. We set off at sun-rise, and rode through the forest one hour, when we breakfasted at an encampment of Arabs Shennebele, in the midst of the wood. From thence I took two Arabs, who volunteered their services, to guide me over the mountains into the eastern plain. We soon reached the termination of the forest, and in half an hour passed the Merdj el Kenttare, a fine meadow (where the young grass had already made its appearance), in the midst of the rocky mountain, which has no wood here. A rivulet called El Keine, whose source is a little higher up in the mountain, flows through the meadow. Three quarters of an hour farther, and to the right of the road, upon a hill distant half an hour, are the ruins of the village El Djefne; to the left, at the same distance, is Tel Akrabe. We passed many excellent pasturing places, where the Arabs of the mountain feed their cattle in the spring; but the mountain is otherwise quite barren. Half an hour farther, descending the mountain, we passed Wady Awairid, whose torrent, in winter, flows as far as Rohba, a district so called, where is a ruined city of the same name, on the eastern limits of the Szaffa. [The Szaffa is a stony district, much resembling the Ledja, with this difference, that the rocks with which it is covered are considerably larger, although the whole may be said to be even ground. It is two or three days in circumference, and is the place of refuge of the Arabs who fly from the Pasha's troops, or from their enemies in the desert. The Szaffa has no springs; the rain water is collected in cisterns. The only entrance is through a narrow pass, called Bab el Szaffa, a cleft, between high perpendicular rocks, not more than two yards in breadth, which one ever dared to enter as an enemy. If a tribe of Arabs intend to remain a whole year in the Szaffa, they sow wheat and barley on the spots fit for cultivation on its precincts. On its E. limits are the ruined villages of Boreisie, Oedesie, and El Koneyse. On its western side this district is called El Harra, a term applied by the Arabs to all tracts which are covered with small stones, being derived from Harr, i.e. heat (reflected from the ground.)] Our route lay to the north-east; we descended by the banks of the Wady into the plain, and at a short distance from where the Wady enters it, arrived at Zaele in two hours and three quarters from the Arab encampment where we had breakfasted.

Zaele owes its origin to the copious spring which rises there, and which renders it, in summer time, a much frequented watering place of the Arabs. The ruined city which stands near the spring is half an hour in circuit; it is built like all those of the mountain, but I observed that the stone doors were particularly low, scarcely permitting one even to creep in. A cupola once stood over the spring, and its basin was paved.

The spring of Zaele flows to the S.E. and loses itself in the plain.

One hour and a half to the eastward of Zaele stands Tel Shaaf, with a ruined city. E. four hours, Melleh, a ruined city in the plain; and upon a Tel near it, Deir el Nuzrany. The plain, for two hours from Zaele, is called El Haoui. Towards the E. and S.E. of Zaele are the following ruined places: Boussan, at the foot of the mountain; Khadera; Aans, Om Ezzeneine; Kherbet Bousrek; Habake.

The great desert extends to the N.E.E., and S.E. of Zaele; to the distance of three days journey eastward, there is still a good arable soil, intersected by numerous Tels, and covered with the ruins of so many cities and villages, that, as I was informed, in whatever direction it is crossed, the traveller is sure to pass, in every day, five or six of these ruined places. They are all built of the same black rock of which the Djebel consists. The name of the desert changes in every district; and the whole is sometimes called Telloul, from its Tels or hillocks. Springs are no where met with in it, but water is easily found on digging to the depth of three or four feet. At the point where this desert terminates, begins the sandy desert called El Hammad, which extends on one side to the banks of the Euphrates, and on the other to the N. of Wady Serethan, as far as the Djof.

I wished to proceed to Melleh, but my Druse companions were not to be prevailed upon, through fear of the Arabs Sheraka, a tribe of the Arabs Djelaes, who were said to be in that neighbourhood. We herefore recrossed the mountain from Zaele, and passed its south-eastern corner, on which there are no trees, but many spots of excellent pasture. In two hours from Zaele we came to a spring called Ras el Beder, i.e. the Moon's Head, whose waters flow down into the plain as far as Boszra. From the spring we redescended, and reached Zahouet el Khudher, a ruined city, standing in a Wady, at a short distance from the plain. One hour from these ruins a rivulet called Moiet Maaz passes through the valley, whose source is to the N.W. up in the mountain, one hour distant, near a ruined place called Maaz. This is a very romantic, secluded spot; immediately behind the town the valley closes, and a row of willows, skirting both banks of the rivulet in its descent, agreeably surprise the traveller, who rarely meets in these districts with trees raised by the labour of man; but it is probable that these willows will not long withstand the destroying hands of the Arabs: fifteen years ago there was a larger plantation here, which was cut down for fire wood; and every summer many of the trees share the same fate.

Zahouet el Khudher was formerly visited by the Christians of the Haouran, for the purpose of offering up their prayers to the Khudher, or St. George, to whom a church in the bottom of the valley is dedicated. The Turks also pay great veneration to this Saint, so much so that a few goats-hair mats, worth five or six piastres, which are left on the floor of the sanctuary of the church, are safe from the robbers. My Druse guides carried them to a house in the town, to sleep upon; but returned them carefully on the following morning. The Arabs give the name of Abd Maaz to St. George. The church has a ruined cupola.

Upon elevated ground on the W. side of the Wady stands the small ruined town of Zahouet, with a castle on the summit of the hill. I could find no legible inscriptions there.

We had reached Zahouet after sunset; and the dread of Arabs, who very frequently visit this place, made us seek for a night's shelter in the upper part of the town, where we found a comfortable room, and lighted a still more comfortable fire. We had tasted nothing since our breakfast; and my guides, in the full confidence of meeting with plenty of Kattas and partridges on our road, had laid in a very small provision of bread on setting out, but had brought a sack of flour mixed with salt, after the Arab fashion. Unluckily, we had killed only two partridges during the day, and seen no Kattas; we therefore had but a scanty supper. Towards midnight we were alarmed by the sound of persons breaking up wood to make a fire, and we kept upon our guard till near sun-rise, when we proceeded, and saw upon the wet ground the traces of men and dogs, who had passed the night in the church, probably as much in fear of strangers as we were ourselves.

November 22d.--I took a view of the town, after which we descended into the plain, called here Ard Aaszaf, from a Tel named Aazaf, at half an hour from the Khudher. The abundant rains had already covered the plain with rich verdure. Our way lay S. At the end of an hour and a quarter we saw to our left, one mile distant from the road, a ruined castle upon a Tel called Keres; close to our road was a low Birket. To the right, three or four miles off, upon another Tel, stands the ruined castle El Koueires. From Keres to Ayoun, two hours distant from Zahouet el Khudher, the ground is covered with walls, which probably once enclosed orchards and well cultivated fields. At Ayoun are about four hundred houses without any inhabitants. On its west side are two walled-in springs, from whence the name is derived. It stands at the eastern foot of the Szfeikh a hill so called, one hour and a half in length. I saw in the town four public edifices, with arches in their interior; one of them is distinguished by the height and fine curve of the arches, as well as by the complete state of the whole building. Its stone roof has lost its original black colour, and now presents a variety of hues, which on my entering surprised me much, as I at first supposed it to be painted. The door is ornamented with grapes and vine leaves. There is another large building, in which are three doors, only three feet high.

From Ayoun ruined walls of the same kind as those we met with in approaching Ayoun extend as far as Oerman, distant one hour and a half, in the open plain. Oerman is an ancient city, somewhat larger than Ayoun. In it are three towers, or steeples, built in the usual mode, which I have described at Kuffer. On the walls of a miserable building adjoining the S. side of the town are the following six inscribed tablets, built into the wall; the second is inverted, a proof that they have been placed in this situation by modern barbarians as ornaments.

Oerman has a spring; but my guides, afraid of prolonging our stay in these desert parts, denied its existence when I enquired for it. I was informed afterwards that a large stone, on which is an inscription, lies near it. There are also several Birkets.

From Oerman we proceeded one hour and a quarter, to the town and castle called Szalkhat: the intermediate country is full of ruined walls. The soil of the desert, as well here as between Zahouet and Oerman, is black; and, notwithstanding the abundant rains, the ground was intersected in every direction by large fissures caused by the summer heat. The castle of Szalkhat is situated upon a hill at the southern foot of the Szfeikh. The town, which occupies the south and west foot of the castle hill, is now uninhabited; but fifteen years since a few Druse and Christian families were established here, as well as at Oerman: the latter retired to Khabeb, where I afterwards saw them, and where they are still called Szalkhalie. The town contains upwards of eight hundred houses, but presents nothing worthy of observation except a large mosque, with a handsome Madene or Minaret; the mosque was built in the year 620 of the Hedjra, or A.D. 1224, as appears from an inscription upon it; the Minaret is only two hundred years old. But even the mosque seems to have been nothing more than a repaired temple or church, as there are several well wrought niches in its outer walls: and the interior is vaulted, with arches supported by low pillars similar to those which have been before described. Several stones are lying about, with Greek inscriptions; but all so much defaced as to be no longer legible. Within the mosque lies a large stone with a fleur-de-lis cut upon it. In the court-yards of the houses of the town are a great number of fig and pomegranate trees; the former were covered with ripe fruit, and as we had tasted nothing this day but dry flour, we made a hearty dinner of the figs. There is no spring either in the castle or town of Szalkhat, but every house has a deep cistern lined with stone; there is also a large Birket.

The castle stands upon the very summit of the hill, and forms a complete circle; it is a very commanding position, and of the first importance as a defence of the Haouran against the Arabs. It is surrounded by a deep ditch, which separates the top of the hill from the part immediately below it. I walked round the outside of the ditch in twelve minutes. The upper hill, except in places where the rock is firm, is paved with large flat stones, similar to those of the castle of Aleppo: a number of these stones, as well as parts of the wall, have fallen down, and in many places have filled up the ditch to half its depth. I estimated the height of the paved upper hill to be sixty yards. A high arched bridge leads over the ditch into the castle. The wall of the castle is of moderate thickness, flanked all round by towers and turrets pierced with numerous loop holes, and is constructed of small square stones, like some of the eastern walls of Damascus. Most of the interior apartments of the castle are in complete ruins; in several of them are deep wells. On entering I observed over the gate a well sculptured eagle with expanded wings; hard by, on the left of the entrance, are two capitals of columns, placed one upon the other, each adorned with four busts in relief projecting from a cluster of palm leaves. The heads of the busts are wanting; the sculpture is indifferent. A covered way leads from the inside of the gateway into the interior; of this I took a very cursory view, as the day was near closing, and my companions pressed me very much to depart, that we might reach a village three hours distant; there being no water here for my horse, I the more readily complied with their wishes. Over the entrance of a tower in the interior I read these two lines: "In the name of God, the merciful and the munificent. During the reign of the equitable king Saad-eddin Abou-takmar, the Emir--- ordered the building of this castle;" which makes it probable that it was erected for the defence of the country against the Crusaders. In one of the apartments I found, just appearing above the earth, the upper part of a door built of calcareous stone, a material which I have not met with in any part of the Haouran.

The hill upon which the castle stands consists of alternate layers of the common black tufwacke of the country, and of a very porous deep red, and often rose-cloured, pumice-stone: in some caverns formed in the latter, salt-petre collects in great quantities. I met with the same substance at Shohba.

S.W. of Szalkhat one hour and a half, stands the high Tel Abd Maaz, with a ruined city of the same name; there still remain large plantations of vines and figs, the fruit of which is collected by the Arabs in autumn. Near Abd Maaz is another ruin called Deffen. S. one hour is Tel Mashkouk, towards which are the ruins Tehhoule, Kfer ezzeit, and Khererribe.

We left Szalkhat towards sunset, on a rainy evening, in order to reach Kereye, a village three good hours distant. In one hour we passed the ruined village Meneidhere, with a copious spring near it. Our route lay through a stony plain, and the night now becoming very dark, with incessant rain, my guides lost their way, and we continued for three hours uncertain whether we should not be obliged to take up our night's quarters in the open plain. At length, however, we came to the bed of a Wady called Hameka, which we ascended for a short distance, and in half an hour after crossing it reached Kereye, about ten at night; here we found a comfortable Fellah's house, and a copious dish of Bourgul.

November 23d.--Kereye is a city containing about five hundred houses, of which four only were at this time inhabited. It has several ancient towers, and public buildings; of the latter the principal has a portico consisting of a triple row of six columns in each, supporting a flat roof; seven steps, extending the whole breadth of the portico, lead from the first row up to the third; the capitals of the columns are of the annexed form; their base is like the capital inverted. Behind the colonnade is a Birket surrounded with a strong wall.

To the S. and E. of Kereye are the ruins called Ai-in, Barade, Nimri, Bakke, Hout, Souhab, Rumman, Szemad, and Rafka. Kelab Haouran bears from Kereye N.&E. Kereye is three hours distance from Boszra, the principal town in the Haouran, remarkable for the antiquity of its castle, and the ancient ruins and inscriptions to be found there. I wished very much to visit it, and might have done so in perfect safety, and without expense; but I knew that there was a garrison of between three and four hundred Moggrebyns in the town; a class of men which, from the circumstance of their passing from one service to another, I was particularly desirous of avoiding. It was very probable that I might afterwards meet with some of the individuals of this garrison in Egypt, where they would not have failed to recognize my person, in consequence of the remarkable circumstance of my visit to Boszra; but as I did not think proper to state these reasons to my guides, who of course expected me to examine the greatest curiosity in the Haouran, I told them that I had had a dream, which made it advisable for me not to visit this place. They greatly applauded my prudent determination, accustomed as they had been to look upon me as a person who had a secret to insure his safety, when travelling about in such dangerous places. We therefore left Kereye in the morning, and proceeding N.E. reached in three quarters of an hour Houshhoush, after having crossed the Wady Djaar, which descends from the mountain. Houshhoush is a heap of ruins, upon a Tel in the plain, and is famed over all the Haouran for the immense treasures said to be buried there. Whenever I was asked by the Fellahs where I had been, they never failed to enquire particularly whether I had seen Houshhoush. The small ancient village contains nothing remarkable except a church, supported by a single arch which rests on pillars much higher than those generally seen in this country. At the foot of the hill are several wells. We found here a great number of mushrooms; we had met with some at Szalkhat; my guides taught me to eat them raw, with a morsel of bread. The quantity of Kattas here was beyond description; the whole plain seemed sometimes to rise; and far off in the air they were seen like large moving clouds.

W. of Houshhoush half an hour, in the plain, are Tel Zakak and Deir Aboud; the latter is a building sixty feet square, of which the walls only are standing; they are built with small stones, and have a single low door. From this place W.S.W. three quarters of an hour is Tahoun el Abiad i.e. the White Mill, the ruins of a mill on the banks of the Wady Ras el Beder, which I noticed in speaking of Zahouet el Khuder. S.W. from Tahoun, three quarters of an hour, is the ruined village Kourd, and W. from it one hour, the village Tellafe. Our way from Deir Aboud lay W.S.W.; at one hour and a half from it is the considerable ruined village Keires, on the Wady Zedi, the largest of all the Wadys which descend from the mountain into the plain. The soil of this uncultivated district is of a red colour, and appears to be very fertile. From hence I proceeded towards Boszra, which I observed at the distance of half an hour, from the high ground above Keires. The castle of Boszra bore W.S.W. that of Szalkhat E.S.S., and the Kelab Haouran N.E.; I was near enough to distinguish the castle, and the mosque which is called by the Mohammedans El Mebrek, from the lying down of the Caliph Othman's camel.

Turning from hence, in a N.W. direction, we came to the ruined village Shmerrin, about three quarters of an hour from Keires.

Near the village stands an insulated tower, with an Arabic inscription, but so high that I could not copy it. The Wady Zedi passes close to this village, where a bridge of three arches is built over it; I was told that in winter the waters often rise over the bridge. Farther to the west this Wady joins that of Ghazale.

From Shmerrin we travelled to the northward; about an hour and a half to our left was the village Kharaba. We were now upon the Hadj route formerly pursued by the pilgrims from Damascus through the Ledja to Soueida and Boszra. The road is still marked by stones scattered over it, the remains, probably, of its pavement.

Thee quarters of an hour from Shmerrin, close to the right of the road, stands Deir Esszebeir, a ruined village with a building like a monastery. At sunset we reached Aaere, two hours and a quarter from Shmerrin.

November 24th and 25th.--I remained at Aaere these two days, during which the Sheikh continued his friendly behaviour towards me. It was my wish to make an excursion towards the western parts of the plain of the Haouran, in order to visit Draa, and the ruins of Om Edjemal and Om Ezzeroub, distant one day's journey from Draa, which, judging from all the information I had received, seemed to be well worth seeing. I offered to any person, or company of men, who would undertake to guide me to the spot, thirty piastres, a large sum in these parts, but nobody was to be found. The fact was that the road from Aaere to Draa, as well as that from thence to Om Edjemal, was infested by a party of Arabs Serdie, the brother of whose chief had recently been killed by the Pasha's troops; and besides these, it was known that numerous parties of Arabs Sheraka made incursions in the same direction I was therefore obliged to give up my project, but with the intention of executing it at a future period.

November 28th.--I left Aaere in the company of a Druse; at parting the Sheikh made me promise that I would again visit his village. The direction of our route was to the N.W. In an hour and a quarter, over a plain, in most parts cultivated, we reached El Kenneker, a solid building upon a hill, with a few habitations round it; all the villages in this part are inhabited; we saw the traces of the Wahabi in a burnt field. E. from hence one hour is Deir Ettereife. N.E. half an hour, the village Hadid; half an hour farther passed Ousserha, a village with a copious spring. One hour and a half E. we saw Walgha. Just before we reached Ousserha we passed the Wady El Thaleth, which I have mentioned between Soueida and Zahouet. Continuing on the side of the Wady for three quarters of an hour, we came to Thaale, where there is a Birket: here we stopped to breakfast. It is inhabited by Mohammedans only.

From Thaale one hour S.W. is Tel Sheikh Houssein, with the village Deir Ibn Kheleif; to the W. of which is El Kerak. We proceeded from Thaale in a W. direction, half an hour, to Daara, a village with a Birket.

One hour to the W. of the village is Rakham. Travelling from Daara N.W. we reached in one hour and a quarter the village Melihat Ali, to the S. of which, half an hour, stands Melihat el Ghazale. In one hour and a quarter from Melihat Ali we reached Nahita, where we slept. On the S. side of the village, near a well, now filled up, stands a small square tower, built with large stones; there is a long inscription over its entrance, but illegible.

This village has a large Birket, and contains a ruined tower, with vaulted buildings adjoining.

From thence, in one hour and a quarter, I reached Ezra, and alighted at the house of the priest. I again endeavoured to visit Draa, but no body would undertake to act as my guide except a peasant, in whose company I did not think that I should be sufficiently secure; for it had been a constant rule with me, during this tour, not to expose myself to any hazard, well knowing that this was not the place, where duty and honour obliged me to do so; on the contrary, I felt that I should not be justified in risking my life, in this quarter, destined as I am to other, and it is hoped, more important pursuits.

November 28th.--I left Ezra this morning with the priest, to visit some villages in the northern Loehf, and if possible to enter the Ledja. We rode one hour to Keratha, close to which is a spring. From Keratha, in an hour and a quarter, we came to Mehadje, whence I saw Tel Shiehhan bearing E.S.E. To the east of the road from Ezra to Mehadje on the Ledja are the ruins of Sour and Aazim. From Mehadje we entered the Ledja, and continued in it, at half an hour's distance from the cultivated plain, in the direction N.E., till we reached Khabeb at the end of two hours. Between Tebne and Khabeb lies the village Bossir. From Khabeb the Kelab Haouran bears S.S.E. This is a considerable village, inhabited for the greater part by Catholic Christians, who, as I have mentioned above, emigrated from Szalkhat. The Sheikh is a Druse. I met here a poor Arab, a native of the country three days journey from Mekka; he told me that the Wahabi had killed four of his brothers; that he fled from home, and established himself at Dael, a village in the Haouran, which was ransacked last summer by the same enemies, when he lost the whole of his property. This man corroborated what I have repeatedly been told, that a single person may travel over the Wahabi dominions with perfect safety.

November 29th.--I here took two Druses to conduct me into the interior of the Ledja. The Arabs who inhabit that district pay some deference to the Druses, but none whatever to the Turks or Christians of the neighbouring villages. In one hour we passed the two ruined cities Zebair and Zebir, close to each other. At the end of two hours and a quarter, our road lying in the direction of the Kelab Haouran, we came to the ruined village Djedel. Thus far the Ledja is a level country with a stony soil covered with heaps of rocks, amongst which are a number of small patches of meadow, which afford excellent pasture for the cattle of the Arabs who inhabit these parts. From Djedel the ground becomes uneven, the pasturing places less frequent, the rocks higher, and the road more difficult. I had intended to proceed to Aahere, where there is a fine spring; but evening coming on we stopped near Dhami, three hours and three quarters from Khabeb, and two hours distant from Aahere. It appears strange that a city should have been built by any people in a spot where there is neither water nor arable ground, and nothing but a little grass amidst the stones. Dhami may contain three hundred houses, most of which are still in good preservation. There is a large building whose gate is ornamented with sculptured vine leaves and grapes, like those at Kanouat.

Every house appears to have had its cistern; there are many also in the immediate vicinity of the town: they are formed by excavations in the rock, the surface of which is supported by props of loose stones. Some of them are arched and have narrow canals to conduct the water into them from the higher grounds. S.E. of Dhami half an hour is Deir Dhami, another ruined place, smaller than the former, and situated in a most dreary part of the Ledja, near which we found, after a good deal of search, an encampment of Arabs Medledj, where we passed the night.

November 30th.--These Arabs being of a doubtful character, and rendered independent by the very difficult access of their rocky abode, we did not think it prudent to tell them that I had come to look at their country; they were told, therefore, that I was a manufacturer of gunpowder, in search of saltpetre, for at Dhami, and in most of the ruined villages in the Ledja, the earth which is dug up in the court- yards of the houses, as well as in the immediate vicinity of them, contains saltpetre, or as it is called in Arabic, Melh Baroud, i.e. gunpowder salt.

The Ledja, which is from two to three days journey in length, by one in breadth, is inhabited by several tribes of Arabs; viz. Selman, Medledj, Szolout, Dhouhere, and Siale; of these the Szolout may have about one hundred tents, the Medledj one hundred and twenty, and the others fifty or sixty. They breed a vast number of goats, which easily find pasturage amongst the rocks; a few of them also keep sheep and cows, and cultivate the soil in some parts of the Ledja, where they sow wheat and barley. They possess few horses; the Medledj have about twenty, and the Szolout and Dhouhere each a dozen. But I shall have occasion to speak of these Arabs again in describing the people of the country.

The tent in which we slept was remarkably large, although it could not easily be perceived amidst the labyrinth of rocks where it was pitched; yet our host was kept awake the whole night by the fear of robbers, and the dogs barked incessantly. He told me next morning that the Szolout had lately been very successful in their nightly depredations upon the Medledj. Our host having no barley, gave my horse a part of some wheat which he had just brought from the plain, to bake into bread for his family.

December 1st.--We departed at sunrise, the night having been so cold that none of us was able to sleep. We found our way with great difficulty out of the labyrinth of rocks which form the inner Ledja, and through which the Arabs alone have the clue. Some of the rocks are twenty feet high, and the country is full of hills and Wadys. In the outer Ledja trees are less frequent than here, where they grow in great numbers among the rocks; the most common are the oak, the Malloula, and the Bouttan; the latter is the bitter almond, from the fruit of which an oil is extracted used by the people of the country to anoint their temples and forehead as a cure for colds; its branches are in great demand for pipe tubes. There are no springs in any part of this stony district, but water collects, in winter time, in great quantities in the Wadys, and in the cisterns and Birkets which are every where met with; in some of these it is kept the whole summer; when they are dried up the Arabs approach the borders of the Ledja, called the Loehf, to water their cattle at the springs in that district. The camel is met with throughout the Ledja, and walks with a firm step over the rocky surface. In summer he feeds on the flowers or dry grass of the pasturing places. In the interior parts of the Ledja the rocks are in many places cleft asunder, so that the whole hill appears shivered and in the act of falling down: the layers are generally horizontal, from six to eight feet, or more, in thickness, sometimes covering the hills, and inclining to their curve, as appears from the fissures, which often traverse the rock from top to bottom. In many places are ruined walls; from whence it may be conjectured that a stratum of soil of sufficient depth for cultivation had in ancient times covered the rock.

We had lost our road, when we met with a travelling encampment of Medledj, who guided us into a more open place, where their companions were pitching their tents. We breakfasted with them, and I was present during an interesting conversation between one of my Druse companions and an Arab. The wife of the latter, it appeared, had been carried off by another Arab, who fearing the vengeance of the injured husband, had gone to the Druse Sheikh of Khabeb, and having secured his Dakhil, or protection, returned to the woman in the Ledja. The Sheikh sent word to the husband, cautioning him against taking any violent measures against his enemy. The husband, whom we here met with, wished to persuade the Druses that the Dakhil of the Sheikh was unjust, and that the adulterer ought to be left to his punishment. The Druse not agreeing with him, he swore that nothing should prevent him from shedding the blood of the man who had bereft him of his own blood; but I was persuaded that he would not venture to carry his threat into effect; for should he kill his enemy, the Druses would not fail to be revenged upon the slayer or his family.

The outer Ledja is to be distinguished from the inner, on this side as well as on that by which we entered it, the former being much less rocky, and more fit for pasturage than the latter. On the borders of the inner Ledja we passed several places where the mill-stones are made, which I have mentioned in a former part of my journal. The stones are cut horizontally out of the rocks, leaving holes of four or five feet in depth, and as many in circumference; fifty or sixty of these excavations are often met with in the circumference of a mile. The stones are carried to be finished at Ezra, Mehadje, Aeib, Khabeb, and Shaara. In one hour and a half from the borders of the Ledja, we came to Kastal Kereim, a ruined village, with a Birket; half an hour from it, Kereim, a Druse village. Between Kereim and Khabeb in the Loehf, is Aeib, a Druse village, in which is a powder manufactory; there is another at Khabeb. Half an hour from Kereim is Kalaat Szamma, a ruined village, with several towers. One hour and a half, Shaara, a village inhabited by about one hundred Druse and Christian families. We travelled this day about eight hours and a half. Shaara was once a considerable city; it is built on both sides of a Wady, half an hour from the cultivated plain, and is surrounded by a most dreary barren War. It has several large solidly built structures, now in ruins, and amongst others a tower that must have been about forty-five feet high. In the upper town is an ancient edifice with arches, converted into a mosque.

There is a salt-petre manufactory in the town; the earth in which the salt-petre is found, is collected in great quantities in the ruined houses, and thrown into large wooden vessels perforated with small holes on one side near the bottom. Water is then poured in, which drains through the holes, into a lower vessel, from whence it is taken, and poured into large copper kettles; after boiling for twenty-four hours, it is left in the open air; the sides of the kettles then become covered with crystals, which are afterwards washed to free them from all impurities. One hundred Rotolas of saline earth give from one to one and a half Rotola of salt-petre. I was told by the Sheikh of the village, who is the manufacturer on his own account, that he sends yearly to Damascus as much as one hundred Kantars. Here is also a gunpowder manufactory.

December 2d.--The Greek priest, who had not ventured to accompany me into the Ledja, I found again at Shaara. I wished to see some parts of the northern Loehf, and particularly the ruins of Missema, of which I heard much from the country people. I therefore engaged a man at Shaara, to conduct me to the place, and from thence to Damascus. We set out in the morning, proceeded along the limits of the War, in an easterly direction, and in three quarters of an hour came to the sources of water called Sheraya; they are five or six in number, are situated just on the borders of the War, and extend as far as Missema, watering all the plain before them. Here, in the spring, the people of Shaara grow vegetables and water melons, and in summer the Arabs of the Ledja sometimes sow the neighbouring fields with wheat; but the frequent passage of the Bedouins renders the collection of the harvest somewhat precarious. Missemi, or Missema, is situated in the Ledja, at one hour and a half from Shaara; it is a ruined town of three miles in circuit

The principal ruin in the town is a temple, in tolerable preservation; it is one of the most elegant buildings which I have seen in the Haouran. The approach to it is over a broad paved area, which has once been surrounded by a row of short pillars; a flight of six steps, the whole length of the façade, leads up to the portico, which consists of seven Doric columns, but of which three only are now standing. The entrance to the temple is through a large door in the centre, on each side of which is a smaller door; over the latter are niches. There are no sculptured ornaments on any part of the great door: the temple is sixteen paces square within. Four Corinthian columns standing in a square in the centre of the chamber support the roof. About two feet and a half under their capitals is a ring; their pedestals are three feet and a half high. Opposite the entrance is a large semicircular niche, the top of which is elegantly sculptured so as to resemble a shell. On either side of the niche is a pilaster, standing opposite to one of the columns. At the door are two pilasters similarly placed, and two others upon each of the side walls. Projecting from the bottom of each of these side walls, are four pedestals for busts or statues. The roof is formed of several arches, which, like the walls, are constructed with large stones. On either side of the interior niche is a small dark room. The door of the temple faces the south, and is almost completely walled up with small stones.

There are several other public buildings at Missema; but in no way remarkable for their architecture. I had been told that in one of these buildings was a large stone covered with small Greek characters. I sought for it in vain. Missema has no inhabitants; we met with only a few workmen, digging the saline earth: there are no springs here, but a number of cisterns. E. of Missema are no inhabited villages, but the Loehf contains several in ruins. From Missema our way lay N.N.W. over the desert plain, towards Djebel Kessoue. This route is much frequented in the summer time by the Aeneze, who pass this way to and from the Haouran. The plain is intersected in every direction by paths formed by camels, called Daroub el aarb. At the end of two hours we saw to the left, in the mountains, the ruined village Om el Kezour; and one hour eastward from thence, in the plain, an insulated pillar called Amoud Esszoubh, i.e. the Column of the Morning, on which, as I was afterwards told, are several inscriptions. Our road now turned N. and we reached, after sunset, in three hours and a quarter from Missema, the ruined village Merdjan, where we found some men who had come to sow a few acres of ground, and partook of a frugal supper with them.

December 3d.--The small village of Merdjan is picturesquely situated on a gentle declivity near the foot of the mountain, and is surrounded by orchards, and poplar trees, which have escaped the rapacious hands of the Arabs: hard by flows a rivulet, which irrigates the adjacent grounds. We left Merdjan early in the morning. Twenty minutes north is Ain Toby, or the spring of the gazelle, consisting of several wells, round one of which are the remains of a well built wall. At one hour and a half is Soghba, a few houses surrounded by a wall; three quarters of an hour from thence is Deir Ali, a village at the western foot of Djebel Mane; before we came to the village we crossed the Moiet Deir Ali, a rivulet whose source is in the neighbourhood. Half an hour from Deir Ali is Meshdie, a small village, in the valley between Djebel Mane and Djebel Khiara, which is about three hours in breadth. The ground is here for the greater part cultivated. Our route was N.N.W. from Deir Ali, from whence, in two hours, we reached El Kessoue, and towards sunset we entered Damascus.

JOURNAL OF A TOUR FROM ALEPPO TO DAMASCUS, THROUGH THE VALLEY OF THE ORONTES AND MOUNT LIBANUS, IN FEBRUARY AND MARCH, 1812.

February 14th.--I LEFT Aleppo at mid-day; and in half an hour came to the miserable village Sheikh Anszary, where I took leave of my worthy friends Messieurs Barker and Van Masseyk, the English and Dutch Consuls, two men who do honour to their respective countries. I passed the two large cisterns called Djob Mehawad, and Djob Emballat, and reached, at the end of two hours and a half, the Khan called Touman, near a village of the same name, situated on the Koeyk, or river of Aleppo. The Khan is in a bad state; Pashas no longer think of repairing public edifices.

February 15th--After a march of ten hours and a half, I arrived at Sermein, having had some difficulty in crossing the muddy plain. The neighbourhood of Sermein is remarkable for great numbers of cisterns and wells hewn in the rock: in the town every house has a similar cistern; those in the plain serve to water the peasants' cattle in the summer, for there are no springs in these parts. On the S.E. side of Sermein is a large subterraneous vault, cut in the solid rock, divided into several apartments, and supported in various places by round pillars with coarsely wrought capitals; near this are several other excavations, all inhabited by the poor peasants. Sermein belongs to the family of Khodsy Effendy of Aleppo.

February 16th.--Half an hour to the left, near our road, is an insulated hill, with the tomb of a saint, called Kubbet Denneit; the plain is here well cultivated, but nothing is sown at present between Khan Touman and Sermein. To the right of the road, on a similar hill, stands Mezar

Kubbet Menebya; and one hour to the right, also upon a Tel, Mezar Tar. Half an hour S.E. from Denneit is the village Gemanas.

In two hours and a half from Sermein we reached the town of Edlip, the approach to which is very picturesque; it lies round the foot of a hill, which divides it into two parts; there is a smaller hill on the N. side: the town is surrounded by olive plantations, and the whole landscape put my companion, an English traveller, in mind of Athens and its vicinity. Here again are many wells cut in the rocky soil round the town. This place is called Little Edlip. Of Great Edlip, the name only remains: it stood at half an hour's distance from the present town, which is of modern date, or about the middle of the seventeenth century. I reckoned the number of its houses at about one thousand. The inhabitants are for the most part Turks; there are only eighty Greek Christian families, and three of Armenian Greeks. They have a church, and three priests, and are under the immediate jurisdiction of the Greek Patriarch of Damascus.

The principal trade of Edlip is in soap; there are some manufactories of cotton stuffs, and a few dyeing-houses. The Bazars are well built, some of them of stone. In the town are several Khans, two of which are destined for the reception of strangers; but the best edifice is the soap manufactory (El Meszbane), a large building. Edlip has no gardens, because there is no water but from wells and cisterns; there are a few orchards of pomegranate and fig trees, and some vine plantations. The place is supplied with vegetables from Rieha, and from Aere, a village two hours distant, lying between Darkoush and Djissr Shogher. There is a single spring in the town of brackish water, which is never used but in seasons of great drought; a man who had cleansed the bottom of the deep well in which the spring issues, told me that he found two openings in the rock, near each other, from the one of which flows sweet water, while that from the other is brackish. I made the tour of the town in thirty-seven minutes; the rocky ground is full of caverns, wells, and pits.

Edlip is held by the family of Kuperly Zaade of Constantinople; but a part of its revenue is a Wakf to the Harameyn, that is to say, it contributes to defray the expenses of the two holy cities Mekka and Medina. The town pays annually to the above family, twenty purses for themselves, and fifteen for the holy cities; the latter sum was formerly sent to Mekka every year with the pilgrim caravan; but it is now paid into the hands of the Kuperlys. The town of Djissr Shogher, distant six hours from Edlip, on the road to Ladikia, belongs to the same family, and is likewise a Wakf attached to the holy cities; it pays fifteen purses to the Kuperlys, and seven to the Harameyn. The revenue arising from thirteen or fourteen villages in the neighbourhood of Djissr Shogher has been assigned to the support of several hospitals which the Kuperlys have built in that town, where a number of poor people are fed daily gratis. Neither Edlip nor Shogher pays any land-tax or Miri, in consequence of their being attached to Mekka; but there is a custom-house at Edlip, where duties are levied on all kinds of provisions, as rice, coffee, oil, raisins, tobacco, &c. the proceeds of which amount to nearly one hundred purses; besides a house tax, which yields twenty purses. The duties levied on provisions at Djissr Shogher amount to twenty purses.

The government of Edlip is in the hands of a Mutsellim, named by the Porte; the real power had been for many years in the rich family of Ayash, till the present chief of that family, Mahmoud Ibn Ayash, a man famous for his hospitality and upright character, had the misfortune to lose all his influence. In 1810 his house became involved in a deadly quarrel with that of Djahya, in consequence of a game of Jerid, which took a serious turn, and in which much blood was shed. Djahya left Edlip, and went to Rieha and Djissr Shogher, where he succeeded in engaging in his interest Seyd Aga and Topal Aly, the rebel chiefs of those towns, who only wanted a pretext to fall upon Edlip; they accordingly stirred up the inhabitants against Mahmoud, who was obliged to fly to Aleppo, and having sent the Mutsellim, Moury Aga, back to Constantinople, they put Abou Shah, the brother-in-law of Topal Aly, in his place, and brought Djahya back to Edlip. After some months the two rebels came to a compromise with Mahmoud, who returned to Edlip, and Djahya, in turn, fled to Aleppo; Mahmoud's power, however, was now at an end: the two chiefs are at present masters of the town, and share its spoils; but its wealth has much decreased since these events took place. In eighteen months it has paid upwards of six hundred purses; and on the day before our arrival a new contribution of two hundred had spread despair among the inhabitants. A Kadhi is sent here early from Constantinople. Sermein bears from hence S.E. by E. There are no dependent villages in the territory of Edlip.

February 17th.--We left Edlip after mid-day. Our road lay through a wood of olive trees, in a fertile uneven plain of red argillaceous soil. In one hour we reached Sheikh Hassan, the tomb of a saint; in an hour and a quarter the insulated hill Tel Stommak, with the village Stommak on its west side. The direction from Edlip S. by W.: this hill seems to be an artificial mound of earth. The Wood of olive trees here terminates. In two hours and forty minutes we arrived at Rieha, which we did not enter, through fear of the rebel Seyd Aga, who occupies it. It contains about four or five hundred houses, is a much frequented market, and has two large soap manufactories. Rieha is situated on the northern declivity of the Djebel Erbayn, or the Mountain of the Forty; and belongs to the government of Aleppo; but since the expulsion of Mohammed Pasha, Seyd Aga has been in the possession of it, and governs also the whole mountain of Rieha, of which Djebel Erbayn forms a part. This man is a chief of that kind of cavalry which the Turks call Dehlys. He has about three hundred of them in his service, together with about one hundred Arnaouts; common interests have closely connected him with Topal Aly, the chief of the Dehlys at Djissr Shogher, who has about six hundred under his command, and with Milly Ismayl, another chief, who commands at Kalaat el Medyk. Unless the Porte finds means to disunite these three rebels, there is little probability of its reducing them. They at present tyrannize over the whole country from Edlip to Hamah.

About two hours to the S.E. of Rieha lies the village of Marszaf, and S. of the latter about one hour, the ruined town Benin. We ascended the mountain from Rieha, turned round its eastern corner, and in one hour from Rieha, reached the village of Kefr Lata. We were hospitably received at the house of the Sheikh of Kefr Lata, although his women only were at home. A wondering story-teller amused us in the evening with chanting the Bedouin history of the Beni Helal. Kefr Lata belongs to Ibn Szeyaf, one of the first families of Aleppo.

February 18th.--Kefr Lata is situated upon the mountain of Rieha, on the S. side of a narrow valley watered by a rivulet; it contains forty or fifty houses, all well built of square stones, which have been taken from the buildings of a town of the lower empire, which occupied the same site. The remains deserve notice, on account of the vast quantity of stone coffins and sepulchres. The mountain is a barren calcareous rock, of no great hardness. In some places are a few spots of arable ground, where the inhabitants of the village grow barley and Dhourra. On the side of the rivulet are some fruit trees. We were occupied the whole morning in visiting the neighbourhood of the village, which must have been anciently the burying place of all the great families of this district; the number of tombs being too considerable for so small a town as Kefr Lata appears to have been; no such sepulchres, or at least very few, are met with among the ruins of the large cities which we saw afterwards in the same mountain. Beginning on the west side of the village, I counted sixteen coffins and seven caves; the coffins are all excavated in the rock; the largest are nine feet long, and three feet and a half in breadth; the smaller seven feet long, and three feet broad; their depth is generally about five feet. In the greater part of them there is on one side a curved recess, cut in the rock, about four feet in length, and two feet in breadth. All these coffins had originally stone lids of a single block of stone, exactly covering the aperture of the coffin. Only a small proportion of these now remain entire, but there are some quite uninjured. I saw only two or three in which a sculptured frieze or cornice was carried along the whole length of the cover; the generality have only a few ornaments on the two ends; they are all of the annexed shape.

The apertures of the coffins are invariably even with the surface of the ground, and the lids only are seen from without, as if lying upon the surface.

The sepulchral caves vary in their sizes and construction; the entrance is generally through a low door, sometimes ornamented by short pilasters, into a vaulted room cut in the rock, the size of which varies from six to fifteen feet in length, and from four to ten feet in breadth; the height of the vault is about six feet; but sometimes the cave terminates in a flat roof. They all contain coffins, or receptacles for the dead; in the smaller chambers there is a coffin in each of the three sides: the larger contain four or six coffins, two opposite the entrance, and one on each side, or two on each of the three sides: the coffins in general are very rudely formed. Some of the natural caverns contain also artificial receptacles for the dead, similar to those already described; I have seen many of these caverns in different parts of Syria. The south side of the village being less rocky, there are neither caves nor coffins on that side. On the east side I counted twenty-one coffins, and five sepulchral caves; of the former, fourteen are within a very small space; the greater part of them are single, but in same places they have been formed in pairs, upon the same level, and almost touching each other.

Crossing to the N. side of the valley of Kefr Lata, I met with a long wall built with large blocks of stone; to the north of it is an oblong square, thirty-seven paces in length, and twenty-seven in breadth, cut out of the rock; in its walls are several niches. In the middle of it is a large coffin, with the remains of a wall which had enclosed it. To the E. of this is a similar square, but of smaller dimensions. I counted in this neighbourhood twenty coffins and four sepulchral caves, besides several open niches very neatly wrought in the side of the mountain, containing recesses for the dead.

Returning towards the village I passed the source of the rivulet which waters the valley. Over it stands an ancient building, which consists of a vaulted roof supported by four short columns, in a very bad heavy style; it is about thirieen feet in height.

We left the village about mid-day, and crossed the mountain in a northerly direction, by the short foot way to Rieha; in half an hour we reached the point of the mountain directly over Rieha. It is this part of the Djebel Rieha which is properly called Djebel Erbayn. In the last century a summer residence was built here just above the town; but it is now abandoned, although a most beautiful spot, surrounded by fruit trees of all sorts, with a copious spring, and presenting a magnificent view over the plains of Aleppo and Edlip. A spring, which here issues from under the rock, collects in front of the building into a large basin, from whence it flows down to Rieha. I here took the following bearings; Edlip N. by E.; Sermein N.E.b.N.; Mount St. Simon N.N.E.; Khan Touman E.N.E.; Djebel el Ala N.; Djebel Akra W.N.W. About one hour N.E. of Rieha lies the village Haleya.

From Djebel Erbayn we continued our road in a S.S.W. direction, on the declivity of the mountain of Rieha. In half an hour we passed a copious spring, enclosed by a square building, called El Monboaa. In the plain to the right we saw the village Kefrzebou, and half an hour to the west of it another, called Ourim. We met with several sepulchral caves on our road. Wherever, in these parts, the soil admits of culture, wheat and barley are sown among the rocks. If such spots are distant from a village, the cultivators pitch a few tents for the purpose of watching the seed and crop; such encampments are called Mezraa. In an hour and ten minutes we reached Nahle; two hours and forty minutes the village Meghara, with many remains of ancient buildings. Here I saw a neat sepulchral cave with a vaulted portico supported by two pillars. In three hours we reached the village Merayan; the direction of our route sometimes S.W. sometimes S.S.W. Just by Merayan is a large coffin, cut in the rocky ground, like those of Kefr Lata; and near it a spring, with ancient walls. In three hours and twenty minutes we came to Ahsin, half an hour to the west of which is the village Eblim. The principal produce of all these villages is grapes, which are carried to the Aleppo market, and there sold, in ordinary years, at about nine shillings per quintal; or else they are boiled to form the sweet glutinous extract called Debs, which is a substitute for sugar all over the East. At the end of four hours and a half we reached the village El Bara, where we finished our day's journey; but we met with a very cold reception, although I had taken the precaution of obtaining a letter of recommendation to the Sheikh of the village from the proprietor of it, Taleb

Effendi, of the family Tcheleby Effendi Toha Zade, the first house of Aleppo.

Half an hour N.W. of Bara lies the village Belyoum. A high hill, contiguous to the Djebel Rieha, called Neby Ayoub, bears N.W. from El Bara, distant about an hour and three quarters. On its summit is a Turkish chapel sacred to the memory of the prophet Ayoub (Job). Two hours distant from El Bara, S. by W. lies the village Kefr Nebyl.

February 20th.--The mountain of Rieha, of which El Bara forms a part, is full of the ruins of cities, which flourished in the times of the lower empire; [The following are the names of other villages and ruined towns, situated upon the mountain of Rieha from the information of a man or El Bara: viz. Medjellye, Betersa, Baouza, Has, El Rebeya, Serdjelle, El Djerada, Moarrat Houl, Moarrat Menhas, Beshelle, Babouza, El Deir, El Roweyha, with extensive ruins; Zer Szabber, Zer Louza, Moar Bellyt, Moar Szaf, Serdjeb Mantef, Nahle, El Rama, Kefr Rouma, Shennan, Ferkya, Belshou, Ahsarein, Moarrat Maater, Djebale, Kefrneba, Beskala, Moarrata, Djousef, El Fetteyry, El Ahmeyry, Erneba, El Arous, Kon Szafra, El Mezra, Aweyt, Kefr Shelaye, Szakhrein, Benames, Kefr Djennab, Szankoul.] those of El Bara are the most considerable of the whole, and as I had often heard the people of the country mention them, I thought it worth while to take this circuitous road to Hamah.

The ruins are about ten minutes walk to the west of the village. Directing our researches to that side we met with a sepulchral cave in the immediate vicinity of the town.

The following figure, in relief, was over it. We saw the same figure, with variations, over the gates of several buildings in these ruins; the episcopal staff is found in all of them. The best executed one that I saw was of this form. On the outside of the town are several sepulchral caves, and a few coffins.

The town walls on the E. side are yet standing; they are very neatly built with small stones, with a square pillar at every six or seven paces, about nine feet high. The ruins extend for about half an hour from south to north, and consist of a number of public buildings, churches, and private habitations, the walls and roofs of some of which are still standing. I found no inscriptions here. The stone with which the buildings are constructed is a soft calcareous rock, that speedily decays wherever it is exposed to the air; it is of the same description as that found in the buildings of the towns about the mountain of St. Simon, and in the ruins of St. Simon, where not a single legible inscription remains, though, as at Bara, traces of them are seen in many places. We surveyed the town in all directions, but saw no building worth noticing, except three tombs, which are plain square structures surmounted with pyramids. The pyramidal summit of one of them has fallen. The interior of these tombs is a square of six paces; on the side opposite the door is a stone coffin; and two others in each of the other two walls; the pyramidal roof is well constructed, being hollow to the top, with rounded angles, and without any interior support. On the outside the pyramid is covered with thin slabs, on each of which is a kind of knob, which gives the whole a very singular appearance. The height of the whole building may be about twenty-four feet. In one of the tombs is a window, the other is quite dark. Two of them stand near together; a third is in a different part of the town. The sides of one of the coffins is carved with a cross in the middle.

The mode of construction in all the private habitations is similar to that which I noticed in the ancient towns of the Haouran, and which, in fact, is still in use in most of the Arab villages in Syria, with this difference, that the latter build with timber and mud instead of stone.

On the N. side of El Bara stands a castle, built in the Saracen or Crusade style, with a spring near it, called Bir Alloun, the only one in the neighbourhood of the ancient town, and which apparently was insufficient to the inhabitants, as we found many cisterns cut very deep in the rock. Turning from the spring towards the present village, we passed the tomb of a Turkish saint, called Kubbet Ibn Imaum Abou Beker, where the son of Abou Beker is reported to have been killed: near it is a cave, with eight receptacles for the dead. I saw there some rocks of the same basaltic tufwacke which I met with in the Djebel el Hasz and in ome of the districts of Haouran.

The greater part of the villages of Djebel Rieha belong to the Dehly Bashi, at Rieha. Feteyry belongs to the district of Marra; its inhabitants have often been punished for their rebellious conduct, and their predatory incursions into the neighbouring districts; their spirit, however, is unbroken, and they still follow the same practices. The frontiers of the Pashaliks of Damascus and Aleppo run across the mountain of Rieha, which commences above Rieha, and extends to Kalaat el Medyk, varying in breadth from two to five hours: it is a low but very rocky chain, little fit for culture, except in the valleys; but it abounds in game, especially wild boars; and ounces have sometimes been killed in it.

We left the inhospitable Bara at mid-day, with two armed men, to escort us over the mountain into the valley of the Orontes. In half an hour we passed a ruined stone bridge across a narrow Wady; it rests upon piers, which are formed of immense blocks of stone piled upon one another. In one hour and twenty minutes we came to Kon Szafra, in a fertile valley on the top of the mountain, where a few families live in wretched huts amidst the ruins of an ancient town. N.W. about three quarters of an hour is the village of Mezraa. In an hour and forty minutes we reached the ruined town Djerada, and at the end of two hours and a half, Kefr Aweyt, a small village; Kefr, in the vulgar dialect, means ruins. Here the mountain is much less rocky, and more fit for culture. Our road lay S.W. b. S. The village of Feteyry, lies about one hour and a half south of Aweyt. After travelling three hours we came in sight of the Orontes, and then began to descend. The mountain on this side is rather steep, and its side is over-grown with herbs which afford an excellent pasturage. The plant asphodel (Siris) is very common; the inhabitants of Syria, by pulverising its dried roots, and mixing the powder with water, make a good glue, which is su-perior to that made with flour, as it is not attacked by worms. In the summer the inhabitants of the valley pasture their cattle in these moun-tains, as do likewise a few tribes of Arabs; among these are the Akeydat, of whom we passed a small encampment.

The part of Djebel Rieha which, beginning at Kon Szafra, extends to the valley of the Orontes, on the one side towards Kalaat el Medyk, on the other towards Djissr Shogher, bears the appellation of Djebel Shaehsabou. The continuation of the same mountain towards Rieha, be-sides its general name of Djebel Rieha, is likewise called Djebel Zaouy. In four hours and a quarter we reached the plain below, near an insulated hill, called Tel Aankye, which seems to be artificial.

The valley bordered on the E. side by Djebel Shaehsabou, and on the W. side by the mountains of the Anzeyry, is called El Ghab. It extends almost due north from three hours S. of Kalaat el Medyk to near Djissr Shogher: its breadth is about two hours, but becomes narrower towards the north; it is watered by the Aaszy, or Orontes, which flows near the foot of the western mountain, where it forms numerous marshes. The in-habitants of El Ghab are a mongrel race of Arabs and Fellahs, and are called Arab el Ghab. They live in winter time in a few villages dispersed over the valley, of which they cultivate only the land adjacent to their vil-lages; on the approach of hot weather they retire with their cattle to the eastern mountains, in search of pasture, and in order to escape the im-mense swarms of flies and gnats, which infest the Ghab in that season. In the winter the Aaszy inundates a part of the low grounds through which it flows, and leaves many small lakes and ponds; the valley is watered also by numerous springs and by rivulets, which descend from the mountains, especially from those on the east. To the N. of Tel Aankye, on the E. side towards Djissr Shogher, which is eight hours distant from Aankye, are the springs Ayn Bet Lyakhom, Ayn Keleydyn, Shaouryt, Kastal Hadj Assaf, Djob Soleyman, Djob el Nassouh, Djob Tel el Tyn.

Having passed to the left of Aankye, where is a small village, we continued our road up the valley due south; we passed near the spring Ayn el Aankye; in a quarter of an hour farther Ayn el Kherbe, and at the same distance farther south, the copious spring Ayn el Howash, from whence we turned to the right into the plain, and at the end of four hours and three quarters from El Bara, reached the village Howash, where we alighted at the Sheikh's house.

February 21st--Howash is the principal village of the Ghab; it is situated on the borders of a small lake, formed by the rivulet of Ayn el Howash. The surrounding country was at this time for the greater part inundated, and the Arabs passed in small boats from one village to an-other; in summer the inundation subsides, but the lakes remain, and to the quantity of stagnant water thus formed is owing the pest of flies and gnats abovementioned. There are about one hundred and forty huts at Howash, the walls of which are built of mud; the roofs are composed of the reeds which grow on the banks of the Orontes; the huts in which these people live in the mountain during the summer are formed also of reeds, which are tied together in bundles, and thus transported to the mountain, where they are put up so as to form a line of huts, in which the families within are separated from each other only by a thin partition of reeds.

The Arabs of Howash cultivate Dhourra and wheat, and, like all the Arabs of the Ghab, rear large herds of buffaloes, which are of a small kind, and much less spirited than those I saw in the plains of Tarsous. It is a common saying and belief among the Turks, that all the animal king-dom was converted by their Prophet to the true faith, except the wild boar and buffalo, which remained unbelievers; it is on this account that both these animals are often called Christians. We are not surprised that the boar should be so denominated; but as the flesh of the buffalo, as well as its Leben or sour milk, is much esteemed by the Turks, it is difficult to account for the disgrace into which that animal has fallen among them; the only reason I could learn for it, is that the buffalo, like the hog, has a habit of rolling in the mud, and of plunging into the muddy ponds in the summer time, up to the very nose, which alone remains visible above the surface.

The territory of Djissr Shogher extends as far as Howash; from thence, southward, begins the district of Kalaat el Medyk. The Sheikh of

Howash, called Mohammed el Cmar, is noted in the adjoining districts for his hospitality; but within bthese few years he has been reduced from great wealth to poverty by the extortions of Topal Aly of Djissr Shogher, and of Milly Ismayl of Kalaat el Medyk; the troops which are continually passing from one place to another are consuming the last remains of his property. The night we slept at his house, there were at least fifty people at supper, of whom about thirty were poor Arabs of his village; the others were all strangers.

We left Howash early in the morning, and rode along the eastern mountains, in this beautiful valley, which I can compare only to the valley of the Bekaa between the two Libani; the Ghab, however, has this great advantage over the Bekaa, that it is copiously watered by a large river and many rivulets, while the latter, in summer time, has little or no water. At half an hour from Howash we met with several fragments of shafts of columns, on the side of an ancient paved causeway. We followed this causeway for upwards of an hour, although in some places no remains of it were visible; at the distance of a quarter of an hour (at the rate of about three miles and a half an hour), from the first heap of fragments of columns, we met with a similar heap; then at an equal interval a third, and again a fourth; not more than four columns seemed to have stood together in any of these places. We conjectured that this had been a Roman road, and the columns its milliaria. The causeway was traced here and there farther to the south, but without any appearance of stations; it probably followed the whole length of the valley from Apamea to Djissr Shogher. One hour and a quarter from Howash is Ayn Houyeth, a copious spring. The Roman road is here about sixteen feet in breadth. To the right, in the plain, is the village of Houyeth, and near it another village, called Ain Uktol. On our right was a perpendicular rock, upon which were patches of rich verdure. Two hours and a quarter is Ayn el Taka, a large spring, issuing from near the foot of the mountain, and forming a small lake which communicates with the Orontes. Here are the remains of some ancient walls. The temperature of this spring, as well as of those which we passed on the way from Aankye, is like that of water which has been heated by the sun in the midst of summer: it is probably owing to this temperature, that we observed such vast numbers of fish in the lake, and that they resort here in the winter from the Orontes; it is principally the species called by the Arabs the Black Fish, on account of its ash- coloured flesh; its length varies from five to eight feet. The fishery is at present in the hands of the governor of Kalaat el Medyk, who carries it on, on his own account; the period is from November till the beginning of January. The fishermen, who are inhabitants of the village Sherya, situated on the borders of the lake, at half an hour's distance from Ayn el Taka, enjoy a partial exemption from the Miri, or land-tax; they fish with harpoons during the night, in small boats, which carry five or six men; and so numerous are the fish, that by throwing the harpoons at random, they fill their boats in the course of the night. The quantity taken might be doubled, if there were a ready market for them. The Kantar, of five hundred and eighty pounds weight, is sold at about four pounds sterling. The fish are salted on the spot, and carried all over Syria, and to Cyprus, for the use of the Christians during their long and rigid fasts. The income derived from this fishery by the governor of Kalaat el Medyk amounts to about one hundred and twenty purses, or three thousand pounds sterling. Besides the black fish, carp are also taken with nets, and carried to Hamah and Homs, where the Turks are very fond of them. The depth of the lake is about ten feet; its breadth is quite irregular, being seldom more than half an hour; its length is about one hour and a half.

One hour from Ayn el Taka, and the lake El Taka, we arrived at the foot of the hill upon which stands Kalaat el Medyk, or the castle of Medyk. It probably occupies the site of Apamea: for there can be little doubt that travellers have been wrong in placing that city at Hamah, the ancient Epiphania, or at some ruins situated at four hours distance from Hamah. Notwithstanding our desire to enter the castle, we could not venture to do so. The governor, Milly Ismayl, a man eighty-five years of age, and whose name has been well known in Syria for the last twenty years, was last year, when governor of Hamah, ordered by the Pasha of Damascus to march with his corps of Dehlys towards Ladakie, to join the Tripoli army, then fighting against the Anzeyrys, who inhabit the mountains between Ladakie and Antioch; in passing by Kalaat el Medyk, on his way to Djissr Shogher, he found the castle without a garrison, and took possession of it, thereby declaring himself a rebel. Orders have in consequence been given to strike off his head. Although his strong fortress enables him to defy these orders, his dread of being surprised induces him to try every means in his power to obtain his pardon from the Porte, and he has even sent considerable sums of money to Constantinople. [Damascus. April 28, 1812.--In the latter end of March, Milly Ismayl went to Hamah on some private business, and during his absence with his troops Topal Aly quietly seized upon the castle. The former now lives in retirement at Hamah, while the power and reputation of Topal have been thus considerably increased in the northern parts of Syria.] Under these circumstances my companion and myself were afraid that he might lay hold of us, in order to make our deliverance subservient to his purposes; we therefore passed by the foot of the hill, while we sent in our attendants to buy some provisions. The castle is built upon an almost insulated hill, communicating on its eastern side only with the mountain called Djebel.

Oerimy, the southernmost point of Djebel Shaehsabou, which turns off here towards the east, and continues for about three hours in an easterly direction. To the south of Oerimy the undulations of the mountain continue for about three hours, and terminate in the plain of Terimsy, of which I shall speak presently. The castle of Medyk is built of small stones, with several turrets, and is evidently of modern construction. On the E. side, close to the gate, are ruined habitations; and to the S. on the declivity of the hill, is a mosque enclosed by a wall, which forms a kind of out-work to the castle. Within the castle wall are thirty or forty houses, inhabited by Turks and Greek Christians. I was told that the only relic of antiquity is a wall in the governor's palace, built with large blocks of stone. At the western foot of the hill is a warm sulphureous spring, the water from which forms a pond; on the edge of the pond I found a fragment of a fine fluted Doric column. Near the spring is a large Khan for the accommodation of travellers. On the N. side of the hill are several columns scattered about.

As we wished to follow the valley of the Orontes as far as possible, we continued in the direction S. by W. along the plain, instead of taking the straight road towards Hamah. Half an hour from Kalaat el Medyk is Ayn Djoufar, a rivulet flowing down the eastern hills through Wady Djoufar; it runs towards the castle, and empties itself into the pond at the castle spring. Up in the hills, in the direction of Wady Djoufar, are the villages of Keframbouda, Kournas, Sheikh Hadid, and Djournye, a little beyond Ayn Djoufar we passed the spring Ayn Abou Attouf. In three quarters of an hour, another rivulet called Ayn el Sheikh Djouban, whose source is up in the hills. The valley El Ghab continues here of the same breadth as below. In the plain, about three quarters of an hour from Kalaat el Medyk, is a broad ditch, about fifteen feet deep, and forty in breadth, which may be traced for an hour and a half, towards the Orontes; near it is the village El Khandak (or the Ditch.) This ditch is not paved, and may formerly have served for the irrigation of the plain.

After proceeding for two hours from the castle, our two guides refused to go any farther, insisting that it would be impossible to continue longer in the valley; to say the truth, it was in many parts covered with water, or deep mud, for the rains had been incessant during several months, and the road we had already come, from the castle, was with difficulty passable; we were therefore obliged to yield, and turning to our left a little way up the hill, rested at the village of Sekeylebye, situated on one of the low hills, near a rivulet called Wady Sekeylebye. I may here observe that the springs coming from the eastern mountains of the Ghab never dry up, and scarcely even diminish during the height of summer.

From a point over the village, which belongs to Hamah, I took the following bearings: Tel Zeyn Abdein, near Hamah, S.E. Djebel Erbayn, between Hamah and Homs, S.S.E. The gap which separates the Anti-Libanus from the northern chain, to the W. of Homs and Hamah, S.by E. The highest point of Djebel Szoleyb, to the W. of Hamah and Homs, S. Tel Aasheyrne, in the plain, S. by W., Djebel Maszyad S.W. The eastern termination of Djebel Shaehsabou N.E. by E. To the S. and E. of Sekeylebye open the great plains which extend to the desert. To the S. distant one hour, near the borders of the hills which enclose the valley of the Ghab on this side, lies the Anzeyry village of Sherrar, a quarter of an hour from whence is an insulated hill called Tel Amouryn. Two hours southward of Sekeylebye is Tel Aasheyrne, and half an hour farther, Tel el Shehryh. In the valley, about one hour and a half S.W. of Sekeylebye, lies the village El Haourat, with a ford over the Orontes, where there is a great carp fishery. On the other side of the river is the insulated hillock Tel el Kottra. The highest point of the mountain of the Anzeyrys, on the W. side of the Orontes, appears to be opposite to Kalaat el Medyk; it is called Kubbet Neby Metta, and has a chapel upon it, dedicated to the saint Metta, who is held in great veneration by the Anzeyrys. The principal villages in this mountain, belonging to the Anzeyrys, who live there upon the produce of their excellent tobacco plantations, are the following: to the W. of Howash, El Shattha, to the S. of it, Merdadj, farther S. Aanab. To the W. of Kalaat el Medyk, Ayn el Keroum, a village whose inhabitants are rebels. To the W. of Ayn Djoban, Fakrou; above Tel el Kottra, Kalaat el Kebeys. The mountain belongs to the government of Ladakie, but is immediately under the Anzeyry chief, El Fakker, who resides in the castle of Szaffytta.

The inhabitants of the Ghab hold the Anzeyrys in contempt for their religion, and fear them, because they often descend from the mountains in the night, cross the Aaszy, and steal, or carry off by force, the cattle of the valley. [A peasant of Sekeylebye enumerated to me the following villages belonging to the government of Hamah, and situated to the N. and W. of that town. Beginning east-wards of his own village, he first mentioned El Sohhrye, then Setouhh, El Deyr, Kfer Djebein, Um Kaszr, Kassabye, Um el Aamed, Kferambouda, Kornas, El Djeleyme, El Mogheyer, El Habyt, Kefer Sedjen, Maar Zeyt, Maart Maater, Kefr Ayn, Kadhyb el Ban, Tel Aas, Kefr Zeyty, El Lattame, the principal village of the district of Hamah, Khan Shiehoun, Maryk, Howeyr, Tel Berran, Wady Edjfar, Wady Daurat, Maszyn Latmein, Tel Faes, Besseleya, Meskyn, Tayebe, Um Tennoura, El Hammamye, El Seyh, Seidjar, Khattab, Meharabe, Helfeya, Bellata, Kefr Behon, Zauran, Mardys, Maar Shour, El Djadjye, Zeyn Abdein, El Oesher. East and south-east of Hamah are the ruined villages: Kefr Houn, Ekfer Tab, Um Sedjra, Altouny, Kefr Eydoun, Sahyan, Marhatal, Heish, Moaka, Wady el Fathh,, Kefr Baesein, El Tahh, El Djofer Djerdjenaes, El Ghatfa, Mart Arab, Aar, Seker, Turky, Etleyl el Szauan, El Temaanaa, El Taamy, El Sheteyb, El Beleyl, Um Harteyn, El Zekeyat, El Hamra, Kfer Dadein, Maar Zelem, Naszab, Tel Faes, El Medjdel, Howeyr, Aatshan el Gebeybat, Sydy Aaly, Djaafar, Berdj el Abyadh, Berdj el Assuad, Kalaat el Ans, Stabelt Antar, Deh lubby.]

We passed the night in a half ruined house, without being able to get any refreshments, although the village belonged to a particular friend of mine at Hamah; indeed these peasants have scarcely any thing left to keep themselves from starving.

February 22d--Early this morning we set off in the direction of Hamah, and after a march of an hour and a half over the plain, reached Tel Szabba, an insulated hillock in the plain; half an hour from it lies a lake called Behirat Terimsy, or, simply El Terimsy. Its extent is from S.W. to N.E. about five to six miles long by two or three in breadth; its waters are scarcely any where deeper than five feet; but the depth of mud at the bottom is so great as to render it fatal for any one to enter the lake, at least so I was informed by several peasants who joined us. The water of the lake diminishes considerably in the summer time, but very seldom dries up entirely; the only instance upon record was during the great drought in 1810, when it is asserted that springs were discovered in the bed of the lake. I am not quite certain whether it communicates on the western side with the Orontes; our guides were not unanimous in their answers; the river, however, must at least pass very close to the lake. On the southern borders of the lake are the Tels or mounds of earth, called Telloul el Fedjera; on the E. side is the Tel Waoyat. The soil in the vicinity of the lake is a soft clay; and I had great difficulty in extricating my mare from the swamp as I approached to reconnoitre the lake, which our company had left to the right of the road. In the spring the earth hardens and is then covered with most luxuriant pasturage. In March the peasants and Arabs of all the neighbouring districts and villages, as well as the inhabitants of Hamah, send their horses and mules here to graze under the care of herdsmen, who regularly pitch their tents near the Waoyat, and each of whom receives a piastre a head from the owners. The cattle remain here till April. The best pasture seems to be on the S. and E. sides, the banks of the lake being there lower than on the opposite sides. It was here, perhaps, that the Seleucidae fed their herds of elephants.

Two hours and a half from Sekeylebye, to the left of the road, is a ruined mosque, called El Djelame; two hours and a half, Tel el Mellah, a hillock in the plain. Our road continued through fertile but uncultivated fields. E. of Tel Mellah about two hours is Tel Szeyad. After three hours and a half slow march we reached the Orontes, near a spot where a large wheel, of the same construction as those at Hamah, raises the water from the river, and empties it into a stone canal, by means of which the neighbouring fields are irrigated. At the end of four hours we came to a bridge over the river, on the other side of which the castle of Seidjar is situated. If I recollect rightly, the bridge rests upon thirteen arches; it is well built, but of modern construction. It is placed at the point where the Aaszy issues from between rugged mountains. On the summit of the range on the left bank stands the castle. To the S.E. of the castle, on the right bank of the river, is the tomb of a Sheikh called Aba Aabeyda el Djerrah, and to the S.E. of the latter, the Turkish chapel El Khudher. The windings of the river in the narrow rocky valley, where no space intervenes between the water and the base of the mountains, resemble those of the Wye in Monmouthshire. At the bridge of Seidjar, it is nearly as large as the Wye at Chepstow. Just by the bridge is a Khan of ancient construction; probably of the period of the crusades. A paved way leads up to the castle, which is at present inhabited by a few hundred families of peasants. It appears from the style of construction that the castle as it now stands, is of the time of the latter Califes; the walls, towers, and turrets, which surround it on the N., W. and S. sides, are evidently Saracen; but it should seem, from the many remains of Grecian architecture found in the castle, that a Greek town formerly stood here. Fragments of columns and elegant Corinthian and Doric capitals lie dispersed about it: amongst them is a coffin of fine marble, nine feet long, but I could find no remains of any ancient building. On the east side the river runs at the foot of a deep precipice. In the south wall a strong well built tower is still in perfect preservation; near it is a deep well, and a subterraneous passage, which, we were informed, leads down to the river side. We searched in vain for Greek inscriptions; on the above mentioned tower is a fine Arabic inscription, but too high to be copied by such short- sighted people as we both happened to be.

Part of the declivity of the hill upon which the castle is built is paved with flat stones, like the castle hills of Aleppo, El Hossn, and Szalkhat. In the plain to the S. and S.W. of the castle are the remains of ancient buildings, which indicate the site of a town; several fragments of columns, wrought stones, and a great deal of rubbish, are lying about.

To the S.W. of the bridge is the tomb of a saint named Sheikh Mahmoud, which is to the W. of a small village called Haourein. The rock of the hills, in the neighbourhood of Seidjar, is calcareous, of considerable hardness, and of a reddish yellow colour; on the S. side of the castle the rock seems to have been cut perpendicularly down almost as low as the river, either for the purpose of adding to the defence of the fortress on this side, or to facilitate the drawing up of water from the river.

We now crossed the low hills to the south of Seidjar, and entered the plain of Hamah, which is very little cultivated here. We proceeded in a south-easterly direction. In one hour and a half from Seidjar we passed a number of wells cut close to each other in the rocky ground. At one hour and three quarters is a small bridge over a torrent called El Saroudj, which empties itself into the Orontes. In two hours we saw to our left, about half an hour distant, the village Hedjam, on the right bank of the river; in two hours and three quarters, a small village called El Shyhy, was to our right; at three hours, we passed the village El Djadjye, distant from the left of the road a quarter of an hour; and near it the village El Kasa. The fertile soil now begins to be well cultivated. In four hours we reached Hamah, where we alighted, at the house of Selym Keblan, one of the Mutsellim's secretaries, the most gentlemanly Levantine I had yet known.

Hamah is situated on both sides of the Orontes; a part of it is built on the declivity of a hill, and a part in the plain; the quarters in the plain are called Hadher and El Djissr; those higher up El Aleyat, and El Medine. Medine is the abode of the Christians. The town is of considerable extent, and must contain at least thirty thousand inhabitants, of whom the Greek families, according to the Bishop's information, are about three hundred. In the middle of the city is a square mound of earth, upon which the castle formerly stood; the materials, as well as the stones with which it is probable that the hill was faced, have been carried away and used in the erection of modern buildings. There are four bridges over the Orontes in the town. The river supplies the upper town with water by means of buckets fixed to high wheels (Naoura), which empty themselves into stone canals, supported by lofty arches on a level with the upper parts of the town. There are about a dozen of the wheels; the largest of them, called Naoura el Mohammedye, is at least seventy feet in diameter. The town, for the greater part, is well built, although the walls of the dwellings, a few palaces excepted, are of mud; but their interior makes amends for the roughness of their external appearance. The Mutsellim resides in a seraglio, on the banks of the river. I enquired in vain for a piece of marble, with figures in relief, which La Roque saw; but in the corner of a house in the Bazar is a stone with a number of small figures and signs, which appears to be a kind of hieroglyphical writing, though it does not resemble that of Egypt. I counted thirteen mosques in the town, the largest of which has a very ancient Minaret.

The principal trade of Hamah is with the Arabs, who buy here their tent furniture and clothes. The Abbas, or woollen mantles made here, are much esteemed. Hamah forms a part of the province of Damascus, and is usually the station of three or four hundred horsemen, kept here by the Pasha to check the Arabs, who inundate the country in spring and summer. Few rich merchants are found in the town; but it is the residence of many opulent Turkish gentlemen, who find in it all the luxuries of the large towns, at the same time that they are in some measure removed from the extortions of the government. Naszyf Pasha, of the family of Adein, who has an annual income of about £8000. sterling, has built a very handsome house here. He is well known for his travels in Europe, and Barbary, and for his brave defence of Cairo, after the defeat of the Grand Vizir by General Kleber near Heliopolis. Being curious to see him, I waited upon him, notwithstanding the rule I had prescribed to myself of mixing as little as possible with Turkish grandees, and presented him a letter of recommendation. We conversed for about half an hour; he was very civil for a Pasha, and made many enquiries concerning Prince Augustus (the Duke of Sussex), whom he had known in Italy.

The government of Hamah comprises about one hundred and twenty inhabited villages, and seventy or eighty which have been abandoned. The western part of its territory is the granary of northern Syria, though the harvest never yields more than ten for one, chiefly in consequence of the immense numbers of mice, which sometimes wholly destroy the crops. I did not see any of these animals.

From a point on the cliff above the Orontes, called El Sherafe, the traveller enjoys a beautiful view over the town. At one hour and a half from it lies the Djebel Zeyn Aabdein in the direction N. by E.; this mountain has two prominent summits, called the Horns of Zeyn Aabdein; its continuation southward is called Djebel Keysoun, the highest point of which bears E. 1/2 N.; still farther south it protrudes in a point in the neighbourhood of Salamie, which bears S.E. and is called Djebel el Aala, upon which stands the castle called Kalaat Shemmasye. To the S. of Hamah, two hours distant, lies an insulated chalky mountain, two or three hours in length, from west to east, called Djebel Erbayn; its highest point bearing from Hamah S. 1/2 E. The Orontes flows on its E. side.

The Aaszy irrigates a great number of gardens belonging to Hamah, which in winter time are generally inundated. Whereever the gardens lie higher than the river, wheels like those already mentioned are met with in the narrow valley, for the purpose of raising up water to them. In summer the water of the river is quite clear.

February 27th.--We remained five days in the hospitable house of Selym, where a large company of Turks and Arabs assembled every evening; and it was with difficulty that we could prevail upon him to let us depart. The distance between Hamah and Tripoli, by the direct road, is four days, or three days by performing on the first a thirteen hours journey from Hamah to Hossn; but we wished to visit the castle of Maszyad, the seat of the Ismaylys, which is laid down upon most of the maps of Syria, but has rarely been visited by any travellers. We set out about mid-day, and travelling in a S.W. direction came in an hour and a half to the Christian village Kefrbehoun; and in two hours, to a hillock in the plain called Tel Afyoun, i.e. the opium-hill, with an ancient well. The number of these insulated mounds of earth in the eastern plain of Syria is very remarkable; their shape is sometimes so regular, that there can be no doubt of their being artificial; in several places there are two standing close together. It is a general remark that wherever there is such a mound, a village is found near it, and a spring, or at least an ancient well. At two hours and a half from Hamah is El Dobbe, a small village near the road: here the ground begins to be uneven, covered with rocks, and little fit for cultivation. At three hours and three quarters is Tel Mowah upon elevated ground, with the ruins of a considerable village; from hence Tel Afyoun bears W. 1/2 S., Hamah E.N.E., Homs S.S.E. In four hours and a half we came to considerable heaps of large hewn stones, and ruined habitations, called El Feiryouny, where a few families of Kurdines had pitched their tents. On the side of the road is a large and very neatly cut ancient well. The face of the country is hilly with a rocky soil, here and there cultivated. At the end of five hours and a half we reached Byszyn, a village inhabited by Anzeyrys, where we slept.

February 28th.--One hour and a half from Byszyn is the village of Shyghata The road ascends, through a rocky country, overgrown with shrubs and low trees. At two hours and a half is a ruined bridge over the winter torrent El Saroudj, which we had passed in the plain below, between Seidjar and Hamah; it was now so much swelled by the heavy rains, that we were trying in vain to cross it in different places, when a shepherd came to our assistance, and shewed us a ford. Considerable as the stream was, it is dried up in summer. We proceeded from the bridge in a W.N.W. direction, and, after a march of an hour and three quarters, during which we crossed several torrents, we reached the castle of Maszyad, or, as it is written in the books of the Miri, Meszyaf. The approach to the castle on two sides is across a large moor; to the N. of it are the highest points of the mountain of Maszyad, at the foot of which it stands, upon a high and almost perpendicular rock, commanding the wild moor in every direction, and presenting a gloomy romantic landscape. On the W. side is a valley, where the inhabitants cultivate wheat and barley. The town of Maszyad is built between the castle and the mountain, on the declivity of the mountain; it is upwards of half an hour in circumference, but the houses are in ruins, and there is not a single well built dwelling in the town, although stone is the only material used. The town is surrounded by a modern wall, and has three stone gates, of more ancient construction; on one of them I saw the following inscription:

.

The last line, as I was told by a man of Tripoli, contains the names of some of the deities of the Ismaylys. The mosque is now in ruins. There are several Arabic inscriptions in different parts of the town, which are all of the time of El Melek el Dhaher. The castle is surrounded by a wall of moderate thickness; and contains a few private habitations. Near the entrance, which is arched, stands a Corinthian capital, of indifferent workmanship, the only remain of Grecian architecture that I saw here. Within this gate is an arched passage, through which the road ascends to the inner and highest parts of the castle. Upon the vault I read the following inscription in large characters:-- "The deed (or fabric) of the Mamlouk Kosta." On the top of the rock are some apartments belonging to the castle; which appear to have had several floors. From a Kyosk, which the present governor has built here, there is a beautiful view down into the western valley. Maszyad is remarkable from being the chief seat of the religious sect called Ismayly. Enquiries have often been made concerning the religious doctrines of this sect, as well as those of the Anzeyrys and Druses. Not only European travellers, and Europeans resident in Syria, but many natives of influence, have endeavoured to penetrate the mysteries of these idolaters, without success, and several causes combine to make it probable, that their doctrines will long remain unknown. The principal reason is, that few individuals among them become acquainted

with the most important and secret tenets of their faith; the generality contenting themselves with the observance of some exterior practices, while
the arcana are possessed by the select few. It will be asked, perhaps,
whether their religious books would not unveil the mystery? It is true that
all the different sects possess books, which they regard as sacred, but they
are intelligible only to the initiated. A sacred book of the Anzeyrys fell
into the hands of a chief of the army of Youssef Pasha, which plundered
the castles of that sect in 1808; it came afterwards into the possession of
my friend Selym of Hamah, who had destined it as a present to me; but he
was prevailed upon to part with it to a travelling physician, and the book
is now in the possession of M. Rousseau, the French consul at Aleppo,
who has had it translated into French, and means to publish it; but it will
probably throw little light upon the question. Another difficulty arises
from the extreme caution of the Ismaylys upon this subject whenever they
are obliged to visit any part of the country under the Turkish government,
they assume the character of Mussulmans; being well aware that if they
should be detected in the practice of any rite contrary to the Turkish religion, their hypocrisy, in affecting to follow the latter, would no longer be
toleraled; and their being once clearly known to be pagans, which they are
only suspected to be at present, would expose them to the heaviest exactions, and might even be followed by their total expulsion or extirpation.
Christians and Jews are tolerated because Mohammed and his immediate
successors granted them protection, and because the Turks acknowledge
Christ and the prophets; but there is no instance whatever of pagans being
tolerated.

The Ismaylys are generally reported to adore the pudendum mu-
liebre, and to mix on certain days of the year in promiscuous debauchery.
When they go to Hamah they pray in the mosque, which they never do at
Kalaat Maszyad. This castle has been from ancient times their chief seat.
One of them asserted that his religion descended from Ismayl, the son of
Abraham, and that the Ismaylys had been possessed of the castle since the
time of El Melek el Dhaher, as acknowledged by the Firmahns of the
Porte. A few years since they were driven out of it by the Anzeyrys, in
consequence of a most daring act of treachery. The Anzeyrys and Ismaylys have always been at enmity, the consequence, perhaps, of some
religious differences. In 1807, a tribe of the former having quarrelled with
their chief, quitted their abode in their mountains, and applied to the Emir
of Maszyad for an asylum. The latter, glad of an opportunity to divide the
strength of his enemies, readily granted the request, and about three hundred, with their Sheikh Mahmoud, settled at Maszyad, the Emir carrying
his hospitality so far as to order several families to quit the place, for the

purpose of affording room for the new settlers. For several months all was tranquil, till one day, when the greater part of the people were at work in the fields, the Anzeyrys, at a given signal, killed the Emir and his son in the castle, and then fell upon the Ismaylys who had remained in their houses, sparing no one they could find, and plundering at the same time the whole town. On the following day the Anzeyrys were joined by great numbers of their countrymen, which proved that their pretended emigration had been a deep-laid plot; and the circumstance of its being kept secret for three months by so great a number of them, serves to shew the character of the people. About three hundred Ismaylys perished on this occasion; the families who had escaped in the sack of the town, fled to Hamah, Homs, and Tripoli, and their treacherous enemies successfully attacked three other Ismayly castles in the mountain. The Ismaylys then implored the protection of Youssef Pasha, at that time governor of Damascus, who marched with four or five thousand men against the Anzeyrys, retook the castles which had belonged to the Ismaylys, but kept the whole of the plunder of the Anzeyrys to himself. This castle of Maszyad, with a garrison of forty men, resisted his whole army for three months.

In 1810, after Youssef Pasha had been exiled by the Porte, the Ismaylys who had fled to Hamah, Homs, and Tripoli returned, and Maszyad is now inhabited by about two hundred and fifty Ismayly families, and by thirty of Christians. The chief, who resides in the castle, is styled Emir; his name is Zogheby, of the family of Soleiman; he informed me that his family had been possessors of the Emirship from remote times, and that they are recognised as such by express Firmahns from the Porte; Zogherby is a nephew of Mustafa, the Emir who was slain by the Anzeyrys. Some of his relations command in the Ismayly castles of El Kadmous, El Kohf, El Aleyka, and El Merkah, in the mountains towards Ladakie. After what has lately taken place, it extreme: they are, apparently, at peace, but many secret murders are committed: "Do you suppose," said a handsome young man to me, while his eyes flashed with anger, "that these whiskers shall turn gray before I shall have taken my revenge for a slaughtered wife and two infant children?" But the Ismaylys are weak; I do not think that they can muster eight hundred fire-locks, while the Anzeyrys are triple that number.

The principal produce of the neighbourhood of Maszyad is silk. They have large plantations of mulberry trees, which are watered by numerous rivulets descending on all sides from the mountain into the valley; and as few of them dry up in summer, this must be a delightful residence during the hot season. There are three or four Ismayly villages in the neighbourhood of Maszyad.

From the castle the ruins called Deir Szoleib bear W. distant about two hours and a half. I was told that there are large buildings at that place constructed with immense blocks of stone, and bearing infidel inscriptions; but the natives of these countries are unable to distinguish sculptured ornaments from letters in unknown languages, and travellers are often deceived by reports of long inscriptions, which prove to be nothing more than a few decorations of architecture.

February 29th.--Having been disappointed in our hopes of finding any thing remarkable at Kalaat el Maszyad, we directed our course to Tripoli. We began to fear that the incessant rains would make the torrents impassable, particularly the Saroudj, which we crossed yesterday. The Emir gave us one of his men to guide and protect us through his territories. After travelling for an hour and a half across the moor, along the side of the upper ridge of the mountains of Maszyad, we arrived at the village Soeida, near to which is the Mezar Sheikh Mohammed, with some plantations of mulberry trees. E. of it half an hour is Kherbet Maynye, a ruined village, with some ancient buildings; and in the mountain above it, the ruined castles Reszafa, and Kalaat el Kaher. There are several other ruined castles in this district, which appear to have been all built about the twelfth century. At two hours and a half is Beyadhein a village inhabited by Turkmans; to the E. of it, about half an hour, is a Tel in the plain, with an arched building upon it called Kubbet el Aadera, or the dome of the Virgin Mary, reported to be the work of the Empress Helena. On the summit of a mountain S. of the village, one hour, is the ruined castle Barein. Near Beyadhein we crossed the torrent Saroudj a second time; its different branches inundated the whole plain. Two hours and a half is the village Kortouman, inhabited by Turkmans, from whence Maszyad bears N. by W. Here we passed another torrent, near a mill, and in a storm of heavy rain and thunder reached Nyszaf, three hours and three quarters from Maszyad, the road from Kortouman lying S. by W. for the greater part in the plain.

Nyszaf is a considerable village, with large plantations of mulberry trees. It is inhabited by Turks and Anzeyrys. The mountain to the eastward, on the declivity of which it is built, is peopled by Turkmans, the greater part of whom do not speak Arabic. We dried our clothes at a fire in the Sheikh's house, and took some refreshment; we then ascended the mountain to the S. of the village, and my guides, who were afraid of the road through the upper part of the mountain, refusing to proceed, we halted for the night at Shennyn, an Anzeyry village halfway up the mountain. The declivity of the mountain is covered with vineyards, growing upon narrow terraces, constructed to prevent the rain from washing away the soil. From the grapes is extracted the Debs, which they sell at Hamah; three quintals of grapes are necessary to make one quintal of Debs, which was sold last year at the rate of £1. per quintal.

As our hosts appeared to be good natured people, I entered, after supper, into conversation with them, with a view to obtain some information upon their religious tenets; but they were extremely reserved upon this head. I had heard that the Anzeyrys maintained from time to time some communication with the East Indies, and that there was a temple there belonging to their sect, to which they occasionally sent messengers. In the course of our conversation I said that I knew there were some Anzeyrys in the East Indies; they were greatly amazed at this, and enquired how I had obtained my information: and their countenances seemed to indicate that there was some truth in my assertion. They are divided into different sects, of which nothing is known except the names, viz. Kelbye, Shamsye, and Mokladjye. Some are said to adore the sun and the stars, and others the pudendum muliebre. The Mokledjye wear in their girdle a small iron hook, which they use when making water; it is also said that they prostrate themselves every morning before their naked mothers, saying, and it is asserted that they have a promiscuous intercourse with their females in a dark apartment every Friday night; but these are mere reports. It is a fact, however, that they entertain the curious belief that the soul ought to quit the dying person's body by the mouth. And they are extremely cautious against any accident which they imagine may prevent it from taking that road. For this reason, whenever the government of Ladakie or Tripoli condemns an Anzeyry to death, his relations offer considerable sums, that he may be empaled instead of hanged. I can vouch for the truth of this belief, which proves at least that they have some idea of a future state. It appears that there are Anzeyrys in Anatolia and at Constantinople. Some years since a great man of this sect died in the mountain of Antioch, and the water with which his corpse had been washed was carefully put into bottles and sent to Constantinople and Asia Minor.

March 1st.--The weather having cleared up a little, we set out early, and in an hour and a half reached the top of the mountain, from whence we enjoyed a beautiful view to the east over the whole plain, and to the W. and S. towards Hossn and the Libanus. Hamah bore E.N.E. and Kalaat Maszyad N. by E. The castle of Hossn bore S.S.W. This part of the mountain is called Merdj el Dolb or Dhaheret Hadsour. On the top there is fine pasturage, with several springs. To the left, half an hour, is the high point called Dhaheret Koszeir, where is a ruined castle; this summit appears to be the highest point of the chain. The summit, on the western declivity, is the copious spring called Near Ayn Kydrih. In two hours we came to the village Hadsour, on the western side of the mountain, with the Mezar Sheikh Naszer. The country to the west of the summit belongs to the government of the district of Hossn. We now descended into the romantic valley Rowyd, full of mulberry and other fruit trees, with a torrent rolling in the bottom of it. At the end of two hours and three quarters is the village Doueyrellin, on the E. side of the Wady; on its W. side, in a higher situation, stands the village El Keyme; and one hour farther, to the S. of the latter, on the same side, is the village El Daghle. We crossed the Wady at the foot of the mountain, and continued along its right bank, on the slope of the mountain, through orchards and fields, till we arrived at the foot of the mountain upon which Kalaat el Hossn is built. Our horses being rather fatigued, we sent them on to Deir Djordjos, (the convent of St. George), where we intended to sleep, and walked up to the castle, which is distant six hours and a half from Shennyn. It is built upon the top of an insulated hill, which communicates on its western side only, with the chain of mountains we had passed. Below the walls of the castle, on the east side, is the town of Hossn, consisting of about one hundred and fifty houses. The castle is one of the finest buildings of the middle age I ever saw. It is evidently of European construction; the lions, which are carved over the gate, were the armorial bearings of the Counts of Thoulouse, whose name is often mentioned in the history of the crusades. It is surrounded by a deep paved ditch, on the outside of which runs a wall flanked with bastions and towers. The walls of the castle itself are very regularly constructed, and are ornamented in many places with high gothic arches, projecting several feet from the wall. The inner castle, which is seventy paces in breadth, and one hundred and twenty in length, is defended by bastions. A broad staircase, under a lofty arched passage, leads up from the gate into the castle, and was accessible to horsemen. In the interior we particularly admired a large saloon, of the best Gothic architecture, with arches intersecting each on the roof. In the middle of a court-yard we noticed a round pavement of stones elevated about a foot and a half above the ground, and eighteen paces in diameter; we could not account for its use; it is now called El Sofra, or the table. There are many smaller apartments in the castle, and several gothic chambers, most of which are in perfect preservation; outside the castle an aqueduct is still standing, into which the rain water from the neighbouring hills was conducted by various channels, and conveyed by the aqueduct into the castle ditch, which must have served as a reservoir for the use of the garrison, while it added at the same time to the strength of the fortress. Figures of lions are seen in various places on the outer wall, as well as Arabic inscriptions, which were too high to be legible from below. In other places, amidst half effaced inscriptions, the name of El Melek el Dhaher is distinguished. I saw no Greek inscriptions, nor any remains of Grecian architecture.

There are roses sculptured over the entrance of several apartments.

If Syria should ever again become the theatre of European warfare, this castle would be an important position; in its neighbourhood the Libanus terminates and the mountains of northern Syria begin; it therefore commands the communication from the eastern plains to the sea shore. El Hossn is the chief place of a district belonging to the government of Hamah; the Miri is rented of the Pasha of Damascus, by the Greek family of El Deib, who are the leading persons here. There is an Aga in the castle, with a few men for its defence. Having examined Hossn, we descended to the convent of Mar Djordjos (St. George), which lies half an hour to the N.W. and there passed the night. In the Wady towards the convent chestnut trees grow wild; I believe they are found in no other part of Syria. The Arabs call them Abou Feroue, i.e. "possessing a fur."

March 2d.--The Greek convent of St. George is famous throughout Syria, for the miracles which the saint is said to perform there. It is inhabited by a prior and three monks, who live in a state of affluence; the income of the convent being very considerable, passengers of all descriptions are fed gratis, and as it stands in the great road from Hamah to Tripoli, guests are never wanting. The common entertainment is Bourgul, with bread and olives; to Christians of respectability wine is added. The convent has large vine and olive plantations in its neighbourhood; it collects alms all over Syria, Anatolia, and the Greek islands, and by a Firmahn of the Porte, is declared to be free from all duties to the Pasha. Youssef Pasha of Damascus, however, made them pay forty thousand piastres, on the pretence that they had built a Khan for poor passengers without his permission. The prior, who is chosen by the brotherhood of the convent, is elected for life, and is under the immediate direction of the Patriarch of Damascus. Caravans generally stop at the Khan, while respectable travellers sleep in the convent itself. A spring near the convent is said to flow only at intervals of two or three days. The prior told me that the convent was built at the same time with the castle of Hossn.

We left Mar Djordjos in a heavy rain, descended into the Wady Mar Djordjos, and after two hours slight descent reached the plain near a spring called Neba el Khalife, round which are some ancient walls. A vast plain now opened before us, bordered on the west by the sea, which, however, was not yet distinguishable; on the N. by the mountains of Tartous, on the E. by the Anzeyrys mountains, and on the south by the Djebel Shara, which is the lower northern continuation of the Djebel Libnan and Djebel Akkar. To the right, distant about three hours, we saw the castle of Szaffytta, the principal seat of the Anzeyry, where their chief El Fakker resides. It is situated on the declivity of the Anzeyry mountains; near it stands an ancient tower, called Berdj Mar Mykhael, or St. Michael's Tower. About seven hours from Szaffytta, towards Kalaat Maszyadt, are the ruins of a temple now called Hassn Soleiman, which, according to all reports, is very deserving of the traveller's notice; as indeed are all the mountains of Szaffytta, and the whole Anzeyry territory, where are the castles of Merkab, Khowabe, Kadmous, El Aleyka, El Kohf, Berdj Tokhle, Yahmour, Berdj Miar, Areyme, and several others. It would take ten days to visit these places.

We continued along the foot of the hills which form the Djebel Shara; they are inhabited by Turkmans and Kurdines. We passed several torrents, and had great difficulty in getting through the swampy soil. After a march of five hours and a half, we came to a rivulet, which had swollen so much from the rain of last night and this day that we could not venture to pass it. We found several peasants who were as anxious to cross it as ourselves, but who could not get their mules over. As the rain had ceased, we waited on the banks for the decrease of the waters, which is usually as rapid as their rise, but it soon appeared that the rain still continued to fall in the mountains, for the stream, instead of decreasing, became much larger. In this difficulty we had to choose between returning to the convent and sleeping in the open air on the banks of the rivulet; we preferred the latter, and passed an uncomfortable night on the wet ground. By daylight the waters had so far decreased, that we passed over without any accident.

March 3rd.--On the opposite side we met with another and larger branch of the same stream, and at the end of an hour and a quarter reached the Nahr el Kebir (the ancient Eleutherus), near a ruined bridge. This is a large torrent, dangerous at this period of the year from its rapidity. The Hamah caravans have been known to remain encamped on its banks for weeks together, without being able to cross it. On the opposite side stands a Khan, called Ayash, with the tomb of the saint, Sheikh Ayash, which is usually the third day's station of the caravans from Hamah to Tripoli.

Having crossed the river we followed the northern swellings of the mountain Akkar in a S.W. direction, having the plain all the way on our right. In one hour and a quarter from the Khan, we passed at half an hour's distance to the S. an insulated hillock in the plain, on which are some ruined buildings called Kella, and to the east of it half an hour, another hillock called Tel Aarous; and at the same distance S.E. of the latter, the village Haytha.

At two hours and a quarter from the Khan Ayash we passed the torrent Khereybe, coming down the Wady of that name, on our left, and the castle and village Khereybe, at a quarter of an hour from the road. Two hours and three quarters, is the village Halbe, on the declivity of the mountain. Three hours and a half, an old mosque upon the mountain above the road, with a village called El Djamaa (the mosque). Near to it, and where the mountains runs out in a point towards the north, is a hill called Tel Arka, which appears by its regularly flattened conical form and smooth sides to be artificial. I was told that on its top are some ruins of habitations, and walls. Upon an elevation on its E. and S. sides, which commands a beautiful view over the plain, the sea, and the Anzeyry mountains, are large and extensive heaps of rubbish, traces of ancient dwellings, blocks of hewn stone, remains of walls, and fragments of granite columns; of the latter I counted eight, six of which were of gray, and the other two of fine red granite. Here then must have stood the ancient town of Arca, where Alexander Severus was born: the hill was probably the citadel, or a temple may have stood on its top. On the west side of the hill runs the deep valley Wady Akka, with a torrent of the same name, which we passed, over a bridge near a mill. From thence the direction of our road continued W.S.W. From an elevated spot, at four hours and a half, Sheikh Ayash bore N.E. b. N. In five hours we reached the seashore; the sea here forms a bay extending from the point of Tartous as far as Tripoli. We now turned round the mountains on our left, along the seabeach, and passed several tents of Turkmans. Five hours and a half, at a short distance to the left, is an ancient tower on the slope of the mountain, called Abou Hannein. Five hours and three quarters is Khan el Bered, with a bridge over the Nahr el Bered, or cold river. At six hours and a half is the village Menny, to the left, at the foot of the mountain, the road lying through a low plain half an hour in breadth, between the mountain called Torboul and the sea; that part only which is nearest to the mountain is cultivated. In nine hours we arrived at Tripoli, and alighted at the house of the English agent Mr. Catziflis.

This city, which is called Tarabolos by the Arabs, and Tripoli by the Greeks and Italians, is built on the declivity of the lowest hills of the Libanus, and is divided by the Nahr Kadisha [Kadisha, in the Syrian language, means the holy, the proper name of the river is Nahr Abou Ali.] into two parts, of which the southern is the most considerable. On the N. side of the river, upon the summit of the hill, stands the tomb of Sheikh Abou Naszer, and opposite to it, on the S. side, the castle, built in the time of the crusades; this castle has often been in a ruined state, but it has lately been put into complete repair by Berber Aga. Many parts of Tripoli bear marks of the ages of the crusades; amongst these are several high arcades of gothic architecture, under which the streets run. In general the town is well built, and is much embellished by the gardens, which are not only attached to the houses in the town, but cover likewise the whole triangular plain lying between it and the sea. Tripoli stands in one of the most favoured spots in all Syria; as the maritime plain and neighbouring mountains place every variety of climate within a short distance of the inhabitants. The Wady Kadisha, higher up than Tripoli, is one of the most picturesque valleys I ever saw. At half an hour from the town is an aqueduct across the Wady, built upon arches; the natives call it Kontaret el Brins, a corruption, perhaps, of Prince. It conveys the water used for drinking, into the town, by means of a canal along the left bank of the Kadisha. A few yards above the aqueduct is a bridge across the stream.

I estimate the inhabitants of Tripoli at about fifteen thousand; of these one-third are Greek Christians, over whom a bishop presides. I was told that the Greeks are authorized, by the Firmahns of the Porte, to prevent any schismatic Greek from entering the town. This may not be the fact;--it is however certain, that whenever a schismatic is discovered here, he is immediately thrown into prison, put in irons, and otherwise very ill-treated. Such a statement can be credited by those only who are acquainted with the fanatism of the eastern Christians. There is no public building in the town deserving of notice. The Serai was destroyed during the rebellion of Berber. The Khan of the soap manufacturers is a large well built edifice, with a water basin in the middle of it.

Ten minutes above the town, in the Wady Kadisha, is a convent of Derwishes, most picturesquely situated above the river, but at present uninhabited. At half an hour's walk below the town, at the extreme angle of the triangular plain, is El Myna, or the port of Tripoli, which is itself a small town; the interjacent plain was formerly covered with marshes, which greatly injured the air; but the greater part of them have been drained, and converted into gardens. The remains of a wall may still be traced across the triangular plain; from which it appears that the western point was the site of the ancient city; wherever the ground is dug in that direction the foundations of houses and walls are found; indeed it is with stones thus procured that the houses in the Myna are built.

From the Myna northward to the mouth of the Kadisha runs a chain of six towers, at about ten minutes walk from each other, evidently intended for the defence of the harbour; around the towers, on the shore, and in the sea, lie a great number of columns of gray granile; there are at least eighty of them, of about a foot and a quarter in diameter, lying in the sea; many others have been built into the walls of the towers as ornaments. To each of the towers the natives have given a name. The most northern is called Berdj Ras el Nahr, from its being near the Kadisha; those to the south are Berdj el Dekye, Berdj el Sebaa, or the lion's tower; [The natives say, that on the shield carved above The gateway of this tower two lions were formerly visible.--These were the arms of Count Raymond de Thoulouse. I saw at Tripoli a leaden seal of the Count, with a tower, meant probably for the Berdj el Sebaa, on the reverse.] Berdj el Kanatter; Berdj el Deyoun, and Berdj el Mogharabe.

The harbour of Tripoli is formed by a line of low rocks, stretching from the point of the Myna about two miles into the sea, towards the north; they are called by the natives Feitoun. On the north the point of Tartous in some measure breaks the impetuosity of the sea; but when the northern winds blow with violence, vessels are often driven on shore. In a N.N.W. direction from the harbour extends a line of small islands, the farthest of which is about ten miles distant from the main land. They are named as follow: El Bakar, which is nearest to the harbour, Billan, about half a mile in circumference, with remains of ancient habitations, and several deep wells; there are several smaller rocks, comprised under the general name of El Mekattya, whose respective appellations are,--next is Sennenye, Nakhle, or El Eraneb, with several palm trees, formerly inhabited by a great number of rabbits; El Ramkein, and Shayshet el Kadhi.

The inhabitants of the Myna are chiefly Greek sailors or shipwrights; I found here half a dozen small country ships building or repairing. There is also a good Khan. On the southern side of the triangular plain is a sandy beach, where the sand in some places has formed itself by concretion into rocks, in several of which are large cisterns. In the bottom of the bay formed by the plain and by the continuation of the shore to the south, is a spring of sweet water, and near it large hillocks of sand, driven up from the shore by the westerly winds. The sea abounds in fish and shell fish; the following are the names of the best, in French and Arabic;

they were given to me by a French merchant, who has long resided in Tripoli; Dorade, Rouget, Loupe, Severelle, Leeche, Mulaye, Maire noir, Maire blanc, Vieille; these are caught with small baskets into which bait is put; the orifice being so made that if the fish enters, he cannot get out again. It is said that no other fish are ever found in the baskets.

Half an hour north of Tripoli, on the road we came by, is the tomb of Sheikh El Bedawy, with a copious spring near it, enclosed by a wall; it contains a great quantity of fish, which are considered sacred by the Turks of Tripoli, and are fed daily by the guardians of the tomb, and by the Tripolitans; no person dares kill any of them; they are, as the Turks express it, a Wakf to the tomb. The same kind of fish is found in the Kadisha.

The commerce of Tripoli has decreased lately, in proportion with that of the entire commerce of Syria. There are no longer any Frank establishments, and the few Franks who still remain are in the greatest misery. A French consul, however, resides here, M. Guys, an able antiquary, and who was very liberal in his literary communications to us. He has a very interesting collection of Syrian medals. Mr. Catziflis, who is a Greek, is a very respectable man, and rendered considerable services to the English army during the war in Egypt. He is extremely attentive and hospitable to English travellers.

The principal commerce of Tripoli is in silk produced upon the mountain, of which it exports yearly about 800 quintals or cwt., at about £80. sterling per quintal. Formerly the French merchants used to take silk in return for their goods, as it was difficult to obtain money in the Levantine trade; it is true that they sold it to a disadvantage in France; yet not so great as they would have done had they insisted on being reimbursed ready money, upon which they must have paid the discount. The silk was bought up at Marseilles by the merchants of Barbary, who thus procured it at a lower rate than they could do at Tripoli. This intercourse however has ceased in consequence of the ruin of French trade, and the Moggrebyns now visit Tripoli themselves, in search of this article, bringing with them colonial produce, indigo, and tin, which they buy at Malta. The sale of West India coffee has of late increased greatly in Syria; the Turks have universally adopted the use of it, because it is not more than half the price of Mokha coffee; a considerable market is thus opened to the West India planters, which is not likely to be interrupted, until the Hadj is regularly re- established, the principal traffic of which was in coffee.

The next chief article of exportation is sponges; they are procured on the sea shore; but the best are found at a little depth in the sea. The demand for them during the last two years has been very trifling; but I was told that fifty bales of twelve thousand sponges each might be yearly furnished; their price is from twenty-five to forty piastres per thousand. Soap is exported to Tarsous, for Anatolia and the Greek islands, as well as alkali for its manufacture, which is procured in the eastern desert. It is a curious fact, that soap should also be imported into Tripoli from Candia; the reason is that the Cretan soap contains very little alkali; here one-fourth of its weight of alkali is added to it, and in this state it is sold to advantage. The other exports are about one hundred or one hundred and twenty quintals of galls from the Anzeyry mountains: of yellow wax, from Libanus, about one hundred and twenty quintals, at about one hundred and fifty piastres per quintal; of Rubia tinctorum, which grows in the plains of Homs and Hamah, about fourteen hundred quintals, at from twenty to twenty-four piastres per quintal; of scammony, very little; of tobacco, a few quintals, which are sent to Egypt.

The territory of Tripoli extends over the greater part of Mount Libanus. The Pashalik is divided into the following districts, or Mekatta, as they are called: viz. El Zawye, or the lower part of Mount Libanus to the right of the Kadisha,--Djebbet Bshirrai, which lies round the village of that name near the Cedars.--El Kella,--El Koura, or the lower part of Mount Libanus to the left of the Kadisha.--El Kattaa, or the mountains towards Batroun;--Batroun,--Djebail,--El Fetouh, over Djebail, as far as Kesrouan.--Akkar, the northern declivity of Mount Libanus, a district governed at present by Aly Beg, a man famous for his generosity, liberality, and knowledge of Arabian literature.--El Shara, also under the government of Aly Beg.--El Dhannye.--The mountains to the N. and N.W. of Bshirrai.--El Hermel, towards Baalbec, on the eastern declivity of the Libanus; Szaffeita, and Tartous. The greater part of the mountaineers are Christians; in Bshirrai they are all Christians; in Akkar, Shara, and Koura, three- fourths are Christians. The Metawelis have possessions at Djebail, Dhannye, and Hermel. About eighty years since the latter peopled the whole district of Bshirrai, El Zawye, Dhannye, and part of Akkar; but the Turk and Christian inhabitants, exasperated by their vexatious conduct, called in the Druses, and with their assistance drove out the Metawelis. Since that period, the Druses have been masters of the whole mountain, as well as of a part of the plain. The Emir Beshir pays to the Pasha of Tripoli, for the Miri of the mountain, one hundred and thirty purses, and collects for himself upwards of six hundred purses. The duties levied upon the peasants in this district are generally calculated by the number of Rotolas of silk which the peasant is estimated to get yearly from his worms; the taxes on the mulberry trees are calculated in proportion to those on the silk. The peasant who rears silk-worms is reckoned to pay about twenty or twenty-five per cent. on his income, while he who lives by the produce of his fields pays more than fifty per cent.

I obtained the following information respecting the modern history of the Pashas of Tripoli.

Fettah Pasha, of three tails, was driven out of Tripoli by the inhabitants, about 1768, after having governed a few years. He was succeeded by Abd-er-rahman Pasha, but the rebels still maintained their ascendancy in the town. He had formerly been Kapydji for the Djerde or caravan, which departs annually from Tripoli to meet the Mekka caravan on its return. He made Mustafa, the chief of the rebels, his Touenkdji, and submitted to his orders, till he found an opportunity of putting him to death at Ladakie, whither he had gone to collect the Miri. The town was at the same time surprised, the castle taken, and all the ring-leaders killed. Abd-er-rahman Pasha governed for about two years.

Youssef Pasha, the son of Othman Pasha of Damascus, of the family of Adm, governed for eight or ten years, and was succeeded by his brother,

Abdullah Pasha, who remained in the government upwards of five years, and was afterwards named Pasha of Damascus. He is at present Pasha of Orfa.

Hassan Pasha, of the family of Adm, remained two years in office.

Hosseyn Pasha was sent with the Djerde, to kill Djezzar, who was on his way back from Mekka; but Djezzar poisoned him, before he could execute his design.

Derwish Pasha governed two years. One of the chiefs of his troops, Hassan Youssef, usurped the greater part of the authority until he was killed by the Pasha's orders.

Soleiman Pasha, now Pasha of Acre, governed at Tripoli about 1792, while Djezzar was at Damascus.

Khalyl Pasha, son of Abdullah Pasha, was driven out by the rebellious inhabitants, during the invasion of Syria by the French. One of the ring-leaders, Mustara Dolby, took possession of the castle, and reigned for two years. He was succeeded by Ibrahim Sultan, who was driven away by Mustafa Aga Berber, a man of talents and of great energy of character. He refused to pay the Miri into the hands of Youssef Pasha of Damascus, who had also been invested with the Pashalik of Tripoli, and having fortified the castle, he boldly awaited with a few trusty adherents the arrival of Youssef, who approached the town with an army of five or six thousand men. All the inhabitants fled to the mountain, except the French consul, a secret enemy of Berber. The army of Youssef no sooner entered the city, than they began plundering it; and in the course of a few months they completely sacked it, leaving nothing but bare walls; every piece of iron was carried off, and even the marble pavements were torn up and sold. The son of the French consul gained considerable sums by buying up a part of the plunder. The castle was now besieged, and some French artillerymen having been brought from Cyprus, a breach was soon made, but though defended by only one hundred and fifty men, none had the courage to advance to the assault. After a siege of five months Soleiman Pasba of Acre interceded for Berber, and Youssef Pasha, glad of a pretext for retreating, granted the garrison every kind of military honours; the remaining provisions in the castle were sold to the Pasha for ready money, and in February, 1809, Berber, accompanied by the officers of Soleiman Pasha, left the castle and retired to Acre. He was again named governor of Tripoli, when Soleiman Pasha of Acre and Damascus was, in 1810, invested with the Pashalik of Tripoli.

Seid Soleiman, Pasha of Damascus, received the same charge in 1812.

During our stay at Tripoli, Berber was in the neigbbourhood of Ladakie, making war against some rebel Anzeyrys; the castle of Tripoli was intrusted to the command of an Aga of Arnaouts, without being under the orders of Berber. It is very probable that Berber may yet become a conspicuous character in Syrian affairs, being a man of great spirit, firmness, and justice. The town of Tripoli was never in a better state than when under his command.

March 12th.--Having spent ten days at Tripoli very pleasantly, I took leave of my companion, who went to Ladakie and Antioch, and set out with a guide towards Damascus, with the intention of visiting the Kesrouan, and paying my respects to the chief of the mountain, the Emir Beshir, at Deir el Kammar. On the way I wished to visit some ruins in the Koura, which I had heard of at Tripoli. I therefore turned out of the great road, which follows the sea shore as far as Beirout. We set out in the evening, ascended the castle hill to the S. of the town, and arrived after an hour and a half at Deir Keiftein, where I slept. The road lay through a wood of olive trees, on the left bank of the Kadisha; over the lowest declivities of the Libanus. It is a part of the district El Koura, the principal produce of which is oil. The Zawye, on the other side of the Kadisha, also produces oil, and at the same time more grain than the Koura. Every olive tree here is worth from fifteen to twenty piastres. The soil in which the trees grow is regularly ploughed, but nothing is sown between the trees, as it is found that any other vegetation diminishes the quantity of olives. The ground round the stem is covered to the height of two or three feet with earth, to prevent the sun from hurting the roots, and to give it the full benefit of the rains. We met with a few tents of Arabs Zereykat and El Hayb, who were pasturing their sheep upon the wild herbs by the road side.

At half an hour's distance to the right runs the Djebel Kella in a north-easterly direction towards the sea; this mountain is under the immediate government of Tripoli, the Emir Beshir, to whom the whole Libanus belongs, not having been yet able to gain possession of it. The following are the principal villages of the Kella: Deyr Sakoub, Diddy, Fya, Kelhat, Betouratydj, Ras Meskha, Bersa, Nakhle, Beterran, Besh, Mysyn, Afs Dyk.

Keiftein is a small Greek convent, with a prior and two monks only; a small village of the same name stands near it. In the burying ground of the convent is a fine marble sarcophagus, under which an English consul of Tripoli lies buried. A long English nscription, with a Latin translation, records the virtues of John Carew, Esq. of Pembrokeshire, who was fifty years consul at Tripoli, and died the 5th of May, 1747, seventy-seven years of age.

March 13th.--Our road lay through the olive plantations called El Bekeya, between the Upper Libanus and the Djebel Kella. Half an hour to the right of the road, upon the latter mountain, is the village Nakhle, below it, Betouratydj, farther up the hill Fya, then, more to the south, Bedobba, and lastly, Afs Dyk; these villages stand very near together, although the Kella is very rocky, and little fit for culture; the peasants, however, turn every inch of ground to advantage. Half an hour from Keiftein is the village Ferkahel, on the side of the river; we saw here a few old date trees, of which there are also some at Nakhle. The inhabitants of the Koura are for the greater part of the Greek church; in Zawye all the Christians are Maronites. At one hour from Keiftein is the village Beserma. One hour and three quarters, continuing in the valley between the Libanus and the Kella, is the village Kfer Akka; we here turned up the Libanus. Half an hour from the Kfer Akka, on the side of the mountain, is a considerable village called Kesba, with the convent of Hantoura. At the same distance S. of Akka, is the village Kfer Zeroun. Two hours and a quarter from Keiftein, on the declivity of the mountain, is the convent of

St. Demetrius, or Deir Demitry. I here left my mare, and walked up the mountain to see the ruins of which I had been informed at Tripoli. In twenty minutes I reached the remains of an ancient town, standing on a piece of level ground, but with few houses remaining. These ruins are called by the people of the country Naous or Namous, which name is supposed to be derived from the word, i.e. a burying-place; but I think its derivation from the Greek more probable. On the S. side stand the ruins of two temples, which are worth the traveller's attention. The smaller one is very much like the temple of Hossn el Forsul, near Zahle, which I had seen on my way to Baalbec; it is an oblong building of about the same size; and is built with large square stones. The entrance is to the east. The door remains, together with the southern wall and a part of the northern. The west wall and the roof are fallen. In the south wall are two niches. Before the entrance was a portico of four columns, with a flight of steps leading up to it. The bases of the columns and fragments of the shafts, which are three feet in diameter, still remain. At about forty paces from the temple is a gate, corresponding to the door of the temple; a broad staircase leads up from it to the temple. The two door-posts of this outer gate are still standing, each formed of a single stone about thirteen feet high, rudely adorned with sculpture. At about one hundred and fifty yards from this building is the other, of much larger dimensions; it stands in an area of fifty paces in breadth, and sixty in length, surrounded by a wall, of which the foundation, and some other parts, still remain. The entrance to this area is through a beautiful gate, still entire; it is fourteen feet high and ten feet wide, the two posts, and the soffit are each formed of a single stone; the posts are elegantly sculptured. At the west end of this area, and elevated four or five feet above its level, stood the temple, opposite to the great gate; it presents nothing now but a heap of ruins, among which it is impossible to trace the original distribution of the building. The ground is covered with columns, capitals, and friezes; I saw a fragment of a column, consisting of one piece of stone nine feet in length, and three feet and a half in diameter. The columns are Corinthian, but not of the best workmanship. Near the S.W. angle of the temple are the foundations of a small insulated building. In order to level the surface of the area, and to support the northern wall, a terrace was anciently raised, which is ten feet high in the north-west corner. The wall of the area is built with large blocks of well cut stone, some of which are upwards of twelve feet in length. It appears however to have undergone repairs, as several parts of the wall are evidently of modern construction; it has perhaps been used as a stronghold by the Arabs. The stone of the building is calcareous, but not so hard as the rock of Baalbec. I saw no kind of inscriptions. The Naous commands a most beautiful view over the Koura and the sea. Tripoli bears N.

I descended to the convent of Mar Demitry, in which there is at present but one monk; and turning from thence in a S.W. direction, reached in half an hour the wild torrent of Nahr Beshiza; which dries up in summer time, but in winter sometimes swells rapidly to a considerable size. When Youssef Pasha besieged Tripoli, intelligence was received at a village near it, that a party of his troops intended to plunder the village; the inhabitants in consequence fled with their most valuable moveables the same evening, and retired up the Wady Beshiza, where they passed the night. It had unfortunately rained in the mountains above, and during the night the torrent suddenly swelled, and carried away eight or ten families, who had encamped in its bed; about fifteen persons perished. On the right bank, near the stream, lies the village Beshiza, and at ten minutes from it to the S.E. the ruins of a small temple bearing the name at present of Kenyset el Awamyd, or the church of the columns. The principal building is ten paces in length on the inside, and eight paces in breadth. The S. and W. walls are standing, but the E. has fallen down; the S. wall has been thrown out of the perpendicular by an earthquake. The entrance is from the west, or rather from the N.W. for the temple does not face the four cardinal points; the northern wall, instead of completing the quadrangle, consists of two curves about twelve feet in depth, and both vaulted like niches, as high as the roof, which has fallen in. In the S. wall are several projecting bases for statues. The door and its soffit, which is formed of a single stone, are ornamented with beautiful sculptures, which are not inferior to those of Baalbec. Before the entrance was a portico of four Ionic columns, of which three are standing; they are about eighteen feet high, and of a single stone. Opposite to each of the exterior columns of this portico is a pilaster in the wall of the temple. There are also two other pilasters in the opposite or eastern wall. Between the two middle columns of the portico is a gate six feet high, formed of two posts, with a stone laid across them; this is probably of modern date, as the exterior of the northern wall also appears to be; instead of forming two semicircles, as within, it is polygonal. Between the door and the pilaster, to the northward of it, is a niche. The entablature of the portico is perfect. In the midst of the building stands a large old oak tree, whose branches overshadow the temple, and supply the place of the roof, rendering the ruin a highly picturesque object. I saw no inscriptions.

Half an hour to the west of Beshiza lies the village of Deir Bashtar. From the temple we turned N.-eastward, and at the end of half an hour passed the village Amyoun, the chief place in the district of El Koura, and the residence of Assaf Ibn Asar, the governor of that province; he is a Greek Christian, and a collector of the Miri, which he pays into the hands of the Emir Beshir. Many Christian families are governors of provinces and Sheikhs of villages in the mountains: in collecting the

Miri, and making the repartitions of the extraordinary demands made by the Emir, they always gain considerable sums; but whenever a Sheikh has filled his purse, he is sure to fall a victim to the avidity of the chief governor. These Sheikhs affect all the pomp of the Turks; surpass them in family pride, and equal them in avarice, low intrigue, and fanatism. The governor of the province of Zawye is also a Christian, of the family of Dhaher.

Instead of descending towards the sea shore, which is the usual route to Batroun, I preferred continuing in the mountain. At an hour and a quarter from Amyoun, after having twice passed the Beshiza, or, as it is also called, the Nahr Aszfour, which runs in a very narrow Wady descending from the district of Laklouk, we reached the village of Keftoun, where is a convent. Above it lies the village of Betaboura, and in its neighbourhood Dar Shemsin and Kferhata. West of Amyoun is the village of Kfer Hasir. The industry with which these mountaineers cultivate, upon the narrow terraces formed on the steep declivity of the mountain, their vines and mulberry trees, with a few acres of corn, is really admirable. At two hours the village of Kelbata was on our right; a little farther, to the right, Ras Enhash.; below on the sea shore, at the extremity of a point of land, is a large village called Amfy, and near it the convent Deir Natour. It is with great difficulty that a horse can travel through these mountains; the roads are abominable, and the inhabitants always keep them so, in order to render the invasion of their country more difficult. The direction of Batroun, from the point where the road begins to descend, is S.W.b.W.

We descended the mountain called Akabe el Meszabeha, near the Wady Djaous, which lower down takes the name of Nahr Meszabeha. Two hours and a half from Amyoun, on the descent, is a fine spring, with a vaulted covering over it, called Ayn el Khowadja. At the end of three hours we reached a narrow valley watered by the last mentioned river, and bounded on the right hand by Djebel Nourye, which advances towards the sea, and on the left by another mountain; upon the former stands the village Hammad, and on the point of it, over the sea, the convent of Mar Elias. At three hours and a quarter, and where the valley is scarcely ten minutes in breadth, a castle of modern construction stands upon an insulated rock; it is called Kalaat Meszabeha, its walls are very slight, but the rock upon which it stands is so steep, that no beast of bur-then can ascend it. This castle was once in possession of the Metaweli, who frequently attacked the passengers in the valley. Near it is a bridge over the Wady. At three hours and three quarters, where the valley opens towards the sea, is the village Kobba, at the foot of the Djebel Nourye, with an ancient tower near it. At the end of four hours and a quarter we reached Batroun, where I slept, in one of the small Khans which are built by the sea side.

Batroun, the ancient Bostrys, contains at present three or four hundred houses. Its inhabitants are, for the greater part, Maronites; the rest are Greeks and Turks. The town and its territory belong to the Emir Beshir; but it is under the immediate government of two of his relations, Emir Kadan and Emir Melhem. The principal man in the town is the Christian Sheikh, of the family of Khodher. The produce of Batroun consists chiefly in tobacco. There is no harbour, merely an inlet capable of admitting a couple of coasting boats. The whole coast from Tripoli to Beirout appears to be formed of sand, accumulated by the prevailing westerly winds, and hardened into rocks. An artificial shelter seems to have been anciently formed by excavating the rocks, and forming a part of them into a wall of moderate thickness for the length of one hundred paces, and to the height of twelve feet. It was probably behind this wall that the boats of Bostrys anciently found shelter from the westerly gales. I saw but one boat between the rocks of Batroun.

March 14th.--Our road lay along the rocky coast. In three quarters of an hour we came to a bridge, called Djissr Medfoun, which crosses a winter torrent. The territory of Batroun extends to this bridge; its northern limits begin at the village of Hammad, upon the Djebel Nourye, which terminates the district of Koura; beyond the bridge of Medfoun is the village Aabeidat to the left. The mountain reaches quite down to the sea shore. The direction of our road was S.b.W. At two hours, upon a hill to the left of the road, called Berdj Reihani, stands a ruined arched building; on the road below it are three columns of sand stone. Up in the mountain are the Greek villages of Manszef, Berbar, Gharsous, and Korne. In three hours and a quarter we passed a Wady, without water, called Halloue. At every three or four miles on this road small Khans are met with, where refreshments of bread, cheese, and brandy are sold. Close to the sea shore are many deep wells, with springs of fresh water at their bottom. Three hours and a half is Djebail, the ancient Byblus. Above it, in the mountain, is the convent Deir el Benat, with the village Aamsheit. I passed on the outside of Djebail without stopping. The town is enclosed by a wall, some parts of which appear to be of the time of the crusades. Upon a stone in the wall I saw a rose, with a smaller one on each side. There is a small castle here, in which the Emir Beshir keeps about forty men. A few years ago Djebail was the residence of the Christian Abd el Ahad; he and his brother Djordjos Bas were the head men of the Emir Beshir, and in fact were more potent than their master. Djordjos Bas resided at Deir el Kammar. The district of Djebail was under the command of Abd el Ahad, who built a very good house here; but the two brothers shared the fate of all Christians who attempt to rise above their sphere; they were both put to death in the same hour by the Emir's orders; indeed there is scarcely an instance in the modern history of Syria, of a Christian or Jew having long enjoyed the power or riches which he may have acquired: these persons are always taken off in the moment of their greatest apparent glory. Abd el Hak, at Antioch; Hanna Kubbe, at Ladakie; Karaly, at Aleppo; are all examples of this remark. But, as in the most trifling, so in the most serious concerns, the Levantine enjoys the present moment, without ever reflecting on future consequences. The house of Hayne, the Jew Seraf, or banker, at Damascus and Acre, whose family may be said to be the real governors of Syria, and whose property, at the most moderate calculation, amounts to three hundred thousand pounds sterling, are daily exposed to the same fate. The head of the family, a man of great talents, has lost his nose, his ears, and one of his eyes, in the service of Djezzar, yet his ambition is still unabated, and he prefers a most precarious existence, with power, in Syria, to the ease and security he might enjoy by emigrating to Europe. The Christian Sheikh Abou Nar commands at Djebail, his brother is governor or Sheikh of Bshirrai.

Many fragments of fine granite columns are lying about in the neighbourhood of Djebail. On the S. side of the town is a small Wady with a spring called Ayn el Yasemein. The shore is covered with deep sand. A quarter of an hour from Djebail is a bridge over a deep and narrow Wady; it is called Djissr el Tel; upon a slight elevation, on its S. side, are the ruins of a church, called Kenyset Seidet Martein. Up in the mountains are two convents and several Maronite villages, with the names of which my Greek guide was unacquainted. In half an hour we came to a pleasant grove of oaks skirting the road; and in three quarters of an hour to the Wady Feidar, with a bridge across it; this river does not dry up in summer time. A little farther to the right of the road is an ancient watchtower upon a rock over the sea; the natives call it Berdj um Heish from an echo which is heard here; if the name Um Heish be called aloud, the echo is the last syllable "Eish," which, in the vulgar dialect, means "what?" (for). Many names of places in these countries have trivial origins of this kind. At two hours and a half we crossed by a bridge the large stream of Nahr Ibrahim, the ancient Adonis. Above us in the mountain is the village El Djissr. The whole lower ridge of mount Libanus, from Wady Medfoun to beyond Nahr Ibrahim, composes the district of El Fetouh, which is at present under the control of Emir Kasim, son of the Emir Beshir, who resides at Ghadsir in Kesrouan; he commands also in Koura. At two hours and a half, and to the left of the road, which runs at a short distance from the sea, is the convent of Mar Domeitt, with the village of El Bouar. The soil is here cultivated in every part with the greatest care. In three hours and a quarter we came to a deep well cut in the rock, with a spring at the bottom, called Ayn Mahous. At three hours and a half is a small harbour called Meinet Berdja, with a few houses round it. Boats from Cyprus land here, loaded principally with wheat and salt. To the right of the road, between Meinet Berdja and the sea, extends a narrow plain, called Watta Sillan; its southern part terminates in a promontory, which forms the northern point of the Bay of Kesrouan. Near the promontory stands an ancient tower, called Berdj el Kosszeir. In four hours and a quarter we reached Djissr Maammiltein, an ancient bridge, falling into ruins, over a Wady of the same name. The banks of this Wady form the boundary of separation between the Pahaliks of Saida and Tripoli, and divide the district of Fetouh from that of Kesrouan.

The country of Kesrouan, which I now entered, presents a most interesting aspect; on the one hand are steep and lofty mountains, full of villages and convents, built on their rocky sides; and on the other a fine bay, and a plain of about a mile in breadth, extending from the mountains to the sea. There is hardly any place in Syria less fit for culture than the Kesrouan, yet it has become the most populous part of the country. The satisfaction of inhabiting the neighbourhood of places of sanctity, of hearing church bells, which are found in no other part of Syria, and of being able to give a loose to religious feelings and to rival the Mussulmans in fanatisim, are the chief attractions that have peopled Kesrouan with Catholic Christians, for the present state of this country offers no political advantages whatever; on the contrary, the extortions of the Druses have reduced the peasant to the most miserable state of poverty, more miserable even than that in the eastern plains of Syria; nothing, therefore, but religious freedom induces the Christians to submit to these extortions; added perhaps to the pleasure which the Catholics derive from persecuting their brethren of the Greek church, for the few Greeks who are settled here are not better treated by the Maronites, than a Damascene Christian might expect to be by a Turk. The plain between the mountain and the sea is a sandy soil; it is sown with wheat and barley, and is irrigated by water drawn from wells by means of wheels. At five hours and a quarter is Ghafer Djouni, a market place, with a number of shops, built on the sea side, where there is a landing place for small boats.

The Beirout road continues from hence along the sea coast, but I wished to visit some convents in Kesrouan, and therefore turned up the mountain to the left. At the end of five hours and three quarters I came to a wood of firs, which trees are very common in these parts; to the right is the village Haret el Bottne. Six hours and three quarters Zouk Mykayl, the principal village in Kesrouan, where resides the Sheikh Beshera, of the family of Khazen, who is at present the governor of the province. The inhabitants of Zouk consist, for the greater part, of the shopkeepers and artizans who furnish Kesrouan with articles of dress or of luxury. I observed in particular many makers of boots and shoes. Seven hours, is Deir Beshara; a convent of nuns. At the end of seven hours and a quarter, I arrived at Antoura, a village in a lofty situation, with a convent, which formerly belonged to the Jesuits, but which is now inhabited by a Lazarist, the Abbate Gandolfi, who is the Pope's delegate, for the affairs of the eastern church. I had letters for him, and met with a most friendly reception: his intimate acquaintance with the affairs of the mountain, and of the Druses, which his residence of upwards of twelve years, and a sound understanding, have enabled him to acquire, renders his conversation very instructive to the inquisitive traveller.

March 15th--I left Antoura in the evening, to visit some convents in a higher part of the mountains of Kesrouan. Passed Wady Kheredj, and at three quarters of an hour from Antoura, the ruined convent of Bekerke, once the residence of the famous Hindye, whose history Volney has given. Now that passions have cooled, and that the greater part of the persons concerned are dead, it is the general opinion that Hindye's only crime was her ambition to pass for a saint. The abominable acts of debauchery and cruelty of which she was accused, are probably imaginary: but it is certain that she rigorously punished the nuns of her convent who hesitated to believe in her sanctity, or who doubted the visits of Jesus Christ, of which she boasted. Hindye died about. ten years since in retirement, in the convent of Seidet el Hakle. At one hour and a half from Antoura, on the top of the mountain, is the convent of Harissa, belonging to the Franciscans of Terra Santa, and inhabited at present by a single Piedmontese monk. On the breaking out of the war between England and the Porte, Mr. Barker, the Consul at Aleppo, received from the Emir Beshir an offer of this convent as a place of refuge in his territory. Mr. Barker resided here for two years and a half, and his prudent and liberal conduct have done great credit to the English name in the mountain. The French consuls on the coast applied several times to the Emir Beshir, by express orders from the French government, to have Mr. Barker and his family removed; but the Emir twice tore their letters in pieces and returned them by the messenger as his only answer. Harissa is a well built, large convent, capable of receiving upwards of twenty monks. Near it is a miserable village of the same name. The view from the terrace of the convent over the bay of Kesrouan, and the country as far as Djebail, on one side, and down to Beirout on the other, is extremely beautiful. The convent is situated in the midst of Kesrouan, over the village Sahel Alma.

March 16.--I slept at Harissa, and left it early in the morning, to visit Ayn Warka. The roads in these mountains are bad beyond description, indeed I never before saw any inhabited country so entirely mountainous as the Kesrouan: there are no levels on the tops of the mountain; but the traveller no sooner arrives on the summit, than he immediately begins the descent; each hill is insulated, so that to reach a place not more than ten minutes distant in a straight line, one is obliged to travel three or four miles, by descending into the valley and ascending again the other side. From Harissa I went north half an hour to the village Ghosta, near which are two convents called Kereim and Baklous. Kereim is a rich Armenian monastery, in which are twenty monks. The silk of this place is esteemed the best in Kesrouan. A little farther down is the village El Basha. One hour and a quarter Ayn Warka, another Maronite convent. I wished to see this place, because I had heard that a school had lately been established here, and that the convent contained a good library of Syrian books; but I was not so fortunate as to see the library; the bishop, although he received me well, found a pretext for not opening the room in which the books are kept, fearing, probably, that if his treasures should be known, the convent might some day be deprived of them. I however saw a beautiful dictionary in large folio of the Syriac language, written in the Syriac character, which, I suppose, to be the only copy in Syria. Its author was Djorjios el Kerem Seddany, who composed it in the year 1619. Kerem Seddany is the name of a village near Bshirrai. This dictionary may be worth in Syria eight hundred or a thousand piastres; but the convent would certainly not sell it for less than two thousand, besides a present to the bishop.

The school of Ayn Warka was established fifteen years since by Youssef, the predecessor of the present bishop. It is destined to educate sixteen poor Maronite children, for the clerical profession; they remain here for six or eight years, during which they are fed and clothed at the expense of the convent, and are educated according to the literary taste of the country; that is to say, in addition to their religious duties, they are taught grammar, logic, and philosophy. The principal books of instruction are the Belough el Arab,, and the Behth el Mettalae, both composed by the bishop Djermanous. At present there is only one schoolmaster, but another is shortly expected, to teach philosophy. The boys have particular hours assigned to the different branches of their studies. I found them sitting or lying about in the court-yard, each reading a book, and the master, in a common peasant's dress, in the midst of them. Besides the Arabic language they are taught to speak, write, and read the Syriac. The principal Syriac authors, whose books are in the library, are Ibn el Ebre, or as the Latins call him, Berebreo, Obeyd Yeshoua, and Ibn el Aassal, their works are chiefly on divinity. The bishop is building a dormitory for the boys, in which each of them is to have his separate room; he has also begun to take in pupils from all parts of Syria, whose parents pay for their board and education. The convent has considerable landed property, and its income is increased by alms from the Catholic Syrians. The boys, on leaving the convent, are obliged to take orders.

From Ayn Warka I ascended to the convent of Bezommar, one hour and a quarter distant. It belongs to the Armenian Catholics, and is the seat of the Armenian patriarch, or spiritual head of all the Armenians in the East who have embraced the Catholic faith. Bezommar is built upon the highest summit of the mountain of Kesrouan, which is a lower branch of the southern Libanus. It is the finest and the richest convent in Kesrouan, and is at present inhabited by the old patriarch Youssef, four bishops, twelve monks, and seventeen priests. The patriarch himself built the convent, at an expense of upwards of fifteen thousand pounds sterling. Its income is considerable, and is derived partly from its great landed possessions, and partly from the benefactions of persons at Constantinople, in Asia Minor, and in Syria. The venerable patriarch received me in his bed, from which, I fear, he will never rise again. The Armenian priests of this convent are social and obliging, with little of the pride and hypocrisy of the Maronites. Several of them had studied at Rome. The convent educates an indefinite number of poor boys; at present there are eighteen, who are destined to take orders; they are clothed and fed gratis. Boys are sent here from all parts of the Levant. I enquired after Armenian manuscripts, but was told that the convent possessed only Armenian books, printed at Venice.

I left Bezommar to return to Antoura. Half an hour below Bezommar is the convent Essharfe, belonging to the true Syrian church. The rock in this part is a quartzose sand-stone, of a red and gray colour. To the left, still lower down, is the considerable village Deir Aoun, and above it the Maronite convent Mar Shalleitta. I again passed Mar Harissa on my descent to Antoura, which is two hours and a half distant from it.

March 17th.--The district of Kesrouan, which is about three hours and a half in length, from N. to S. and from two to three hours in breadth across the mountains, is exclusively inhabited by Christians: neither Turks nor Druses reside in it. The Sheikh Beshara collects the Miri, and a son of the Emir Beshir resides at Ghazir, to protect the country, and take care of his father's private property in the district. The principal and almost sole produce is silk; mulberry trees are consequently the chief growth of the soil; wheat and barley are sown, but not in sufficient quantity for the consumption of the people. The quantity of silk produced annually amounts to about sixty Kantars, or three hundred and thirty English quintals. A man's wealth is estimated by the number of Rotolas of silk which he makes, and the annual taxes paid to government are calculated and distributed in proportion to them. The Miri or land-tax is taken upon the mule loads of mulberry leaves, eight or ten trees, in common years, yielding one load; and as the income of the proprietors depends entirely upon the growth of these leaves, they suffer less from a bad crop, because their taxes are proportionally low. The extraordinary extortions of the government, however, are excessive: the Emir often exacts five or six Miris in the year, and one levy of money is no sooner paid, than orders are received for a fresh one of twenty or thirty purses upon the province. The village Sheikh fixes the contributions to be paid by each village, taking care to appropriate a part of them to himself. Last year many peasants were obliged to sell a part of their furniture, to defray the taxes; it may easily be conceived therefore in what misery they live: they eat scarcely any thing but the worst bread, and oil, or soups made of the wild herbs, of which tyranny cannot deprive them. Notwithstanding the wretchedness in which they are left by the government, they have still to satisfy the greediness of their priests, but these contributions they pay with cheerfulness. Many of the convents indeed are too rich to require their assistance, but those which are poor, together with all the parish priests and church officers, live upon the people. Such is the condition of this Christian commonwealth, which instead of deserving the envy of other Christians, living under the Turkish yoke, is in a more wretched state than any other part of Syria; but the predominance of their church consoles them under every affliction, and were the Druse governor to deprive them of the last para, they would still remain in the vicinity of their convent.

Contributions are never levied on the convents, though the landed property belonging to them pays duties like that of the peasant; their income from abroad is free from taxes. Loans are sometimes required of the convents; but they are regularly reimbursed in the time of the next harvest. The priests are the most happy part of the population of Kesrouan; they are under no anxiety for their own support; they are looked upon by the people assuperior beings, and their repose is interrupted only by the intrigues of the convents, and by the mutual hostilities of the bishops.

The principal villages in Kesrouan, beginning from the north, are Ghadsir, Djedeide, Aar Amoun, Shenanayr, Sahel Alma, Haret Szakher, Ghozta, Deir Aoun, Ghadir, Zouk Mikayl, Djouni, Zouk Meszbah, Zouk el Kherab, and Kornet el Khamra.

March 18th--I left my amiable host, the Abate Gandolfi, and proceeded on my road to Deir el Kammar, the residence of the Emir Beshir. One hour from Antoura is Deir Lowyz. Between it and the village Zouk Mikayl lies the village Zouk Meszbah, with Deir Mar Elias. South of Deir Lowyz half an hour is the village Zouk el Kharab; half an hour E. of the latter, Deir Tanneis, and about the same distance S.E. the village Kornet el Khamra. From Deir Lowyz I again descended into the plain on the sea shore. The narrow plain which I mentioned as beginning at Djissr Maammiltein, continues only as far as Djouni, where the country rises, and continues hilly, across the southern promontoy of the bay of Kesrouan, on the farther side of which the narrow plain again begins, and continues as far as the banks of the Nahr el Kelb. I reached this river in half an hour from Antoura, at the point of its junction with the sea, about ten minutes above which it is crossed by a fine stone bridge. From the bridge the road continues along the foot of the steep rocks, except where they overhang the sea, and there it has been cut through the rock for about a mile. This was a work, however, of no great labour, and hardly deserved the following magnificent inscription, which is engraved upon the rock, just over the sea, where the road turns southward:

IMP CAES M AVRELIVS ANTONINV S . PIVS . FELIX .
AVGVSTVS PART . MAX . BRIT . MAX . GERM . MAXIMVS
PONTIFEX . MAXIMVS MONTIBVS INMINENTIBVS LICO
FLVMINI CAESIS VIAM DELATAVIT PER

. . . .

ANTONINIANAM SVAM

BURCKHARDT

The last line but one has been purposely erazed. Below the frame in which the above is engraved, is this figure.

Higher up in the road are several other places in the rock, where inscriptions have been cut, but the following one only is legible:

INVICTIM ANTONIN FELIX AUG MV . . IS NISIM

[In the year 1697 Maundrell read this inscription as follows: Invicte Imp. Antonine P. Felix Aug. multis annis impera. Ed.]

According to the opinion of M. Guys, the French consul at Tripoli, which seems well founded, the Emperor mentioned in the above inscriptions is not Antoninus Pius, but Caracalla; as the epithet Britannus cannot be applied to the former, but very well to the latter. Opposite to the bridge is an Arabic inscription, but for the greater part illegible.

The road continues for about half an hour through the rock over the sea, above which it is no where higher than fifty feet. At the southern extremity is a square basin hewn in the rock close by the sea, called El Mellaha, in which the salt water is sometimes collected for the purpose of obtaining salt by evaporation. On the summit of the mountain, to the left of the rocky road, lies the Deir Youssef el Berdj; half an hour south of it, in the mountain, is the village Dhobbye, and behind the latter the village Soleima, with a convent of the Terra Santa. The road from El Mellaha continues for an hour and a half on the sandy beach; about three quarters of an hour from the basin we passed the rivulet Nahr Antoun Elias, so called from a village and convent of that name, to the left of the road. Near the latter lies the village of Abou Romman, in the narrow plain between the mountain and the sea, and a little farther south, El Zeleykat. The district of Kesrouan, extends, to the south, as far as a small Khan, which stands a little beyond the Mellaha; farther south commences the Druse country of Shouf. At the termination of the sandy beach are seen ruins of Saracen buildings, with a few houses called Aamaret Selhoub.

We now left the sea shore to our right, and rode across the riangular point of land on the western extremity of which the town of Beirout is situated. This point projects into the sea about four miles beyond the line of the coast, and there is about the same distance in following that line across the base of the triangle. The road we took was through the fine cultivated plain called El Boudjerye, in a direction S. by W. Two hours and three quarters from El Mellaha is the village Hadded. Before we came to it, we crossed the Nahr Beirout, at a place where I saw, for the first time, a grove of date trees. Beyond the river the country is called Ard el Beradjene, from a tower by the sea side called Berdj el Beradjene; the

133

surrounding country is all planted with olive trees. In three hours and a quarter we crossed the Wady Ghadiry, on the other side of which lies the village Kefr Shyna. Upon the hills about three quarters of an hour S.E. of the place where the Ghadiry falls into the sea, stands the convent Mar Hanna el Shoeyfat. At the end of three hours and a half, the road begins to ascend: the Emir Beshir has had a new road made the greater part of the way up to Deir el Kammar, to facilitate the communication between his residence and the provinces of Kesrouan and Djebail. At the end of four hours is a fine spring, with a basin shaded by some large oak trees; it is called Ayn Besaba. At four hours and a half, the road still ascending, is the village Ayn Aanab, remarkable for a number of palm trees growing here at a considerable elevation above the sea. The mountain is full of springs, some of which form pretty cascades. On the front of a small building which has been erected over the spring in the village, I observed on both sides two figures cut upon the wall, with open mouths, and having round their necks a chain by which they are fastened to the ground. Whether they are meant for lions or calves I could not satisfy myself, nor could I learn whether they have any relation to the religious mysteries of the Druses.

The country from Kefr Shyna is wholly inhabited by Druses. The village of Aanab is the hereditary seat of the family of Ibn Hamdan, who are the chiefs of the Druses in the Haouran. At five hours and a half is the village Ayn Aanoub; a little above it the road descends into the deep valley in which the Nahr el Kadhi flows. The mountain is here overgrown with fine firs. Six hours and a half, is a bridge (Djissr el Khadhi) under which the Nahr flows in a rocky bed. The Franks on the coast commonly give to the Nahr Kadhi the name of Damour, an appellation not unknown to the natives. On the other side of the bridge the road immediately ascends to the village Kefrnouta, on the N. side of the river, where it turns round the side of the mountain to Deir el Kammar, distant seven hours and a quarter from El Mellaha. I rode through El Kammar, without stopping, and proceeded to the village of Beteddein, where the Emir Beshir is building a new palace.

The town of Deir el Kammar is situated on the declivity of the mountain, at the head of a narrow valley descending towards the sea. It is inhabited by about nine hundred Maronite, three hundred Druse, and fifteen or twenty Turkish families, who cultivate mulberry and vine plantations, and manufacture all the articles of dress of the mountaineers. They are particularly skilful in working the rich Abbas or gowns of silk, interwoven with gold and silver, which are worn by the great Sheikhs of the Druses, and which are sold as high as eight hundred piastres a piece. The Emir Beshir has a serai here. The place seems to be tolerably well built, and has large Bazars. The tombs of the Christians deserve notice. Every family has a stone building, about forty feet square, in which they place their dead, the entrance being always walled up after each deposit: this mode of interment is peculiar to Deir el Kammar, and arose probably from the difficulty of excavating graves in the rocky soil on which it is built. The tombs of the richer Christian families have a small Kubbe on their summit. The name of this town, signifying the Monastery of the Moon, originates in a convent which formerly stood here, dedicated to the Virgin, who is generally represented in Syria with the moon beneath her feet. Half an hour from Deir el Kammar, on the other side of the valley, lies Beteddein, which in Syriac, means the two teats, and has received its name from the similarity of two neighbouring hills, upon one of which the village is built. Almost all the villages in this neighbourhood have Syriac names.

March 19th.--The Emir Beshir, to whom I had letters of recommendation, from Mr. Barker at Aleppo, received me very politely, and insisted upon my living at his house. His new palace is a very costly edifice; but at the present rate of its progress five more years will be required to finish it. The building consists of a large quadrangle, one on side of which are the

Emir's apartments and his harem, with a private court-yard; two other sides contain small apartments for his people, and the fourth is open towards the valley, and Deir el Kammar, commanding a distant view of the sea. In the neighbouring mountain is a spring, the waters from which have been conducted into the quadrangle; but the Emir wishes to have a more abundant supply of water, and intends to bring a branch of the Nahr el Kadhi thither; for this purpose the water must be diverted from the main stream at a distance of three hours, and the expense of the canal is calculated at three thousand pounds sterling.

The Emir Beshir is at present master of the whole mountain from Belad Akkar down to near Akka (Acre), including the valley of Bekaa, and part of the Anti-Libanus and Djebel Essheikh. The Bekaa, together with a present of one hundred purses, was given to him in 1810, by Soleiman Pasha of Acre, for his assistance against Youssef Pasha of Damascus. He pays for the possession of the whole country, five hundred and thirty purses, of which one hundred and thirty go to Tripoli and four hundred to Saida or Acre; this is exclusive of the extraordinary demands of the Pashas, which amount to at least three hundred purses more. These sums are paid in lieu of the Miri, which the Emir collects himself, without accounting for it. The power of the Emir, however, is a mere shadow, the real government being in the hands of the Druse chief, Sheikh Beshir. [Beshir is a proper name borne by many people in the mountain. The accent is on the last syllable: the sound would be expressed in English by Besheer.] I shall here briefly explain the political state of the mountain.

It is now about one hundred and twenty years since the government of the mountain has been always entrusted by the Pashas of Acre and Tripoli to an individual of the family of Shehab, to which the Emir Beshir belongs. This family derives its origin from Mekka, where its name is known, in the history of Mohammed and the first Califes; they are Mussulmans, and some of them pretend even to be Sherifs. About the time of the crusades, for I have been unable to ascertain the exact period, the Shehabs left the Hedjaz, and settled in a village of the Haouran, to which they gave their family name; [A branch of the family is said to inhabit some mountains in Mesopotamia, under the command of Emir Kasem.] it is still known by the appellation of Shohba; and is remarkable for its antiquities, of which I have given some account, in my journal of a tour in the Haouran. The family being noble, or of Emir origin, were considered proper persons to be governors of the mountain; for it was, and still is thought necessary that the government should not be in the hands of a Druse. The Druses being always divided into parties, a governor chosen from among them would have involved the country in the quarrels of his own party, and he would have been always endeavouring to exterminate his adversaries; whereas a Turk, by carefully managing both parties, maintains a balance between them, though he is never able to overpower them completely; he can oppose the Christian inhabitants to the Druses, who are in much smaller numbers than the former, and thus he is enabled to keep the country in a state of tranquillity and in subjection to the Pashas. This policy has long been successful, notwithstanding the turbulent spirit of the mountaineers, the continual party feuds, and the ambitious projects of many chiefs, as well of the Druses as of the reigning house; the Pashas were careful also not to permit any one to become too powerful; the princes of the reigning family were continually changed; and party spirit was revived in the mountain whenever the interests of the Porte required it. About eighty years ago the country was divided into the two great parties of Keisy, whose banner was red, and Yemeny, whose banner was white, and the whole Christian population ranged itself on the one side or the other. The Keisy gained at length the entire ascendancy, after which none but secret adherents of the Yemeny remained, and the name itself was forgotten. Then arose the three sects of Djonbelat, Yezbeky, and Neked. These still exist; thirty years ago the two first were equal, but the Djonbelat have now got the upper hand, and have succeeded in disuniting the Yezbeky and Neked.

The Djonbelat draw their origin from the Druse mountain of Djebel Aala, between Ladakie and Aleppo: they are an old and noble family, and, in the seventeenth century, one of their ancestors was Pasha of Aleppo; it forms at present the richest and most numerous family, and the strongest party in the mountain.

The Yezbeky, or as they are also called, El Aemad, are few in number, but are reputed men of great courage and enterprize. Their principal residence is in the district of El Barouk, between Deir el Kammar and Zahle.

The Neked, whose principal Sheikh is at present named Soleiman, inhabit, for the greater part, Deir el Kammar; seven of their principal chiefs were put to death thirteen years ago in the serai of the Emir Beshir, and a few only of their children escaped the massacre; these have now attained to years of manhood, and remain at Deir el Kammar, watched by the Djonbelaty and the Aemad, who are united against them.

The Djonbelat now carry every thing with a high hand; their chief, El Sheikh Beshir is the richest and the shrewdest man in the mountain; besides his personal property, which is very considerable, no affair of consequence is concluded without his interest being courted, and dearly paid for. His annual income amounts to about two thousand purses, or fifty thousand pounds sterling. The whole province of Shouf is under his command, and he is in partnership with almost all the Druses who possess landed property there. The greater part of the district of Djesn is his own property, and he permits no one to obtain possesions in that quarter, while he increases his own estates yearly, and thus continually augments his power. The Emir Beshir can do nothing important without the consent of the Sheikh Beshir, with whom he is obliged to share all the contributions which he extorts from the mountaineers. It is from this cause that while some parts of the mountain are very heavily taxed, in others little is paid. The Druses form the richest portion of the population, but they supply little to the public contributions, being protected by the Sheikh Beshir. It will be asked, perhaps, why the Sheikh does not set aside the Emir Beshir and take the ostensible power into his own hands? Many persons believe that he entertains some such design, while others, better informed perhaps, assert that the Sheikh will never make the attempt, because he knows that the mountaineers would never submit to a Druse chief. The Druses are certainly in a better condition at present than they would be under the absolute sway of the Sheikh, who would soon begin to oppress instead of protecting them, as he now does; and the Christians, who are a warlike people, detest the name of Druse too much ever to yield quietly to a chief of that community. It is, probably, in the view of attaching the Christians more closely to him, and to oppose them in some measure to the Druses, that the Emir Beshir, with his whole family, has secretly embraced the christian religion. The Shehab, as I have already mentioned, were formerly members of the true Mussulman faith, and they never have had among them any followers of the doctrines of the Druses. They still affect publicly to observe the Mohammedan rites, they profess to fast during the Ramadhan, and the Pashas still treat them as Turks; but it is no longer matter of doubt, that the greater part of the Shehab, with the Emir Beshir at their head, have really embraced that branch only of the family which governs at Rasheya and Hasbeya continue in the religion of their ancestors.

Although the Christians of the mountain have thus become more attached to their prince, their condition, on the whole, is not bettered, as the Emir scarcely dares do justice to a Christian against a Druse; still, however, the Christians rejoice in having a prince of their own faith, and whose counsellors and household are with few exceptions of the same religion. There are not more than forty or fifty persons about him who are not Christians. One of the prince's daughters lately married a Druse of an Emir family, who was not permitted to celebrate the nuptials till he had been instructed in the doctrines of Christianity, had been baptized, and had received the sacrament. How far the Shehab may be sincere in their professions, I am unable to decide; it is probable that if their interests should require it, they would again embrace the religion of their ancestors.

In order to strengthen his authority the Emir Beshir has formed a close alliance with Soleiman Pasha of Acre, thus abandoning the policy of his predecessors, who were generally the determined enemies of the Turkish governors; this alliance is very expensive to the Prince, though it serves in some degree to counterbalance the influence of the Sheikh Beshir. The Emir and the Sheikh are apparently on the best terms; the latter visits the Emir almost every week, attended by a small retinue of horsemen, and is always received with the greatest apparent cordiality. I saw him at Beteddein during my stay there. His usual residence is at the village of Mokhtar, three hours distant from Beteddein, where he has built a good house, and keeps an establishment of about two hundred men. His confidential attendants, and even the porters of his harem, are Christians;

but his bosom friend is Sheikh el Nedjem, a fanatical Druse, and one of the most respected of their Akals. The Sheikh Beshir has the reputation of being generous, and of faithfully defending those who have put themselves under his protection. The Emir Beshir, on the contrary, is said to be avaricious; but this may be a necessary consequence of the smallness of his income. He is an amiable man, and if any Levantine can be called the friend of an European nation, he certainly is the friend of the English. He dwells on no topic with so much satisfaction as upon that of his alliance with Sir Sidney Smith, during that officer's command upon this coast. His income amounts, at most, to four hundred purses, or about £10.000. sterling, after deducting from the revenue of the mountain the sums paid to the Pashas, to the Sheikh Beshir, and to the numerous branches of his family. His favourite expenditure seems to be in building. He keeps about fifty horses, of which a dozen are of prime quality; his only amusement is sporting with the hawk and the pointer. He lives on very bad terms with his family, who complain of his neglecting them; for the greater part of them are poor, and will become still poorer, till they are reduced to the state of Fellahs, because it is the custom with the sons, as soon as they attain the age of fifteen or sixteen, to demand the share of the family property, which is thus divided among them, the father retaining but one share for himself. Several princes of the family are thus reduced to an income of about one hundred and fifty pounds a year. It has constantly been the secret endeavour of the Emir Beshir to make himself directly dependent upon the Porte, and to throw off his allegiance to the Pasha; but he has never been able to succeed. The conduct of Djezzar Pasha was the cause of this policy. Djezzar, for reasons which have already been explained, was continually changing the governors of the mountain, and each new governor was obliged to promise him large sums for his investiture. Of these sums few were paid at the time of Djezzar's death, and bills to the amount of sixteen thousand purses were found in his treasury, secured upon the revenue of the mountain. At the intercession of Soleiman Pasha, who succeeded Djezzar at Akka, and of Gharib Effendi, the Porte's commissioner (now Pasha of Aleppo), this sum was reduced to four thousand purses, of which the Emir Beshir is now obliged to pay off a part annually.

By opposing the Druse parties to each other, and taking advantage of the Christian population, a man of genius and energy of the Shehab family might perhaps succeed in making himself the independent master of the mountain. Such an event would render this the most important government in Syria, and no military force the Turks could send would be able to overthrow it. But at present the Shehab appear to have no man of enterprise among them.

The Shehab marry only among themselves, or with two Druse families, the Merad, and Kaszbeya. These and the Reslan, are the only Emir families, or descendants of the Prophet, among the Druses. These Emirs inhabit the province called El Meten. Emir Manzour, the chief of the Merads, is a man of influence, with a private annual income of about one hundred and twenty purses.

I shall now subjoin such few notes on the Druses as I was able to collect during my short stay in the mountain; I believe them to be authentic, because I was very careful in selecting my authourities.

With respect to the true religion of the Druses, none but a learned Druse can satisfy the enquirer's curiosity. What I have already said of the Anzeyrys is equally applicable to the Druses; their religious opinions will remain for ever a secret, unless revealed by a Druse. Their customs, however, may be described; and, as far as they can tend to elucidate the mystery, the veil may be drawn aside by the researches of the traveller. It seems to be a maxim with them to adopt the religious practices of the country in which they reside, and to profess the creed of the strongest. Hence they all profess Islamism in Syria; and even those who have been baptised on account of their alliance with the Shehab family, still practise the exterior forms of the Mohammedan faith. There is no truth in the assertion that the Druses go one day to the mosque, and the next to the church. They all profess Islamism, and whenever they mix with Mohammedans they perform the rites prescribed by their religion. In private, however, they break the fast of Ramadhan, curse Mohammed, indulge in wine, and eat food forbidden by the Koran. They bear an inveterate hatred to all religions except their own, but more particularly to that of the Franks, chiefly in consequence of a tradition current among them that the Europeans will one day overthrow their commonwealth: this hatred has been increased since the invasion of the French, and the most unpardonable insult which one Druse can offer to another, is to say to him "May God put a hat on you!" Allah yelebesak borneita.

Nothing is more sacred with a Druse than his public reputation: he will overlook an insult if known only to him who has offered it; and will put up with blows where his interest is concerned, provided nobody is a witness; but the slightest abuse given in public he revenges with the greatest fury. This is the most remarkable feature of the national character: in public a Druse may appear honourable; but he is easily tempted to a contrary behaviour when he has reason to think that his conduct will remain undiscovered. The ties of blood and friendship have no power amongst them; the son no sooner attains the years of maturity than he begins to plot against his father. Examples are not wanting of their assailing the chastity of their mothers, and towards their sisters such conduct is so frequent, that a father never allows a full grown son to remain alone with any of the females of his family. Their own religion allows them to take their sisters in marriage; but they are restrained from indulging in this connexion, on account of its repugnance to the Mohammedan laws. A Druse seldom has more than one wife, but he divorces her under the slightest pretext; and it is a custom among them, that if a wife asks her husband's permission to go out, and he says to her "Go;" without adding "and come back," she is thereby divorced; nor can her husband recover her, even though it should be their mutual wish, till she is married again according to the Turkish forms, and divorced from her second husband. It is known that the Druses, like all Levantines, are very jealous of their wives; adultery, however, is rarely punished with death; if a wife is detected in it, she is divorced; but the husband is afraid to kill her seducer, because his death would be revenged, for the Druses are inexorable with respect to the law of retaliation of blood; they know too that if the affair were to become public, the governor would ruin both parties by his extortions. Unnatural propensities are very common amongst them.

The Akal are those who are supposed to know the doctrines of the Druse religion; they superintend divine worship in the chapels or, as they are called, Khaloue, and they instruct the children in a kind of catechism. They are obliged to abstain from swearing, and all abusive language, and dare not wear any article of gold or silk in their dress. Many of them make it a rule never to eat of any food, nor to receive any money, which they suspect to have been improperly acquired. For this reason, whenever they have to receive considerable sums of money, they take care that it shall be first exchanged for other coin. The Sheikh El Nedjem, who generally accompanies the Sheikh Beshir, in his visits to the Emir, never tastes food in the palace of the latter, nor even smokes a pipe there, always asserting that whatever the Emir possesses has been unlawfully obtained. There are different degrees of Akal, and women are also admitted into the order, a privilege which many avail themselves of, from parsimony, as they are thus exempted from wearing the expensive head-dress and rich silks fashionable among them.

A father cannot entirely disinherit his son, in that case his will would be set aside; but he may leave him a single mulberry tree for his portion. There is a Druse Kadhi at Deir el Kammar, who judges according to the Turkish laws, and the customs of the Druses; his office is hereditary in a Druse family; but he is held in little repute, as all causes of importance are carried before the Emir or the Sheikh Beshir.

The Druses do not circumcise their children; circumcision is practised only in the mountain by those members of the Shehab family who continue to be Mohammedans.

The best feature in the Druse character is that peculiar law of hospitality, which forbids them ever to betray a guest. I made particular enquiries on this subject, and I am satisfied that no consideration of interest or dread of power will induce a Druse to give up a person who has once placed himself under his protection. Persons from all parts of Syria are in the constant practice of taking refuge in the mountain, where they are in perfect security from the moment they enter upon the Emir's territory; should the prince ever be tempted by large offers to consent to give up a refugee, the whole country would rise, to prevent such a stain upon their national reputation. The mighty Djezzar, who had invested his own creatures with the government of the mountain, never could force them to give up a single individual of all those who fled thither from his tyranny. Whenever he became very urgent in his demands, the Emir informed the fugitive of his danger, and advised him to conceal himself for a time in some more distant part of his territory; an answer was then returned to Djezzar that the object of his resentment had fled. The asylum which is thus afforded by the mountain is one of the greatest advantages that the inhabitants of Syria enjoy over those in the other parts of the Turkish dominions.

The Druses are extremely fond of raw meat; whenever a sheep is killed, the raw liver, heart, &c. are considered dainties; the Christians follow their example, but with the addition of a glass of brandy with every slice of meat. In many parts of Syria I have seen the common people eat raw meat in their favourite dish the Kobbes; the women, especially, indulge in this luxury.

Mr. Barker told me that during his two years residence at Harissa and in the mountain, he never heard any kind of music. The Christians are too devout to occupy themselves with such worldly pleasures, and the Druses have no sort of musical instruments.

The Druses have a few historical books which mention their nation; Ibn Shebat, for instance, as I was told, gives in his history of the Califes, that of the Druses also, and of the family of Shehab. Emir Haidar, a relation of the Emir Beshir, has lately begun to compile a history of the Shehabs, which already forms a thick quarto volume.

I believe that the greatest amount of the military forces of the Druses is between ten and fifteen thousand firelocks; the Christians of the mountain may, perhaps, be double that number; but I conceive that the most potent Pasha or Emir would never be able to collect more than twenty thousand men from the mountain.

The districts inhabited by Druses in the Pashalik of Saida are the following. El Tefahh, of which one half belongs to the Pasha. El Shomar, belonging for the greater part to the Pasha. El Djessein, one half of which belongs to the Porte. Kesrouan. El Metten. El Gharb el Fokany. El Gharb el Tahtany; in which the principal family is that of Beit Telhouk. El Djord, the principal family there is Beit Abd el Melek. El Shehhar; the principal family Meby el Dein. El Menaszef, under Sheikh Soleiman of the family of Abou Neked. El Shouf, the residence of the Sheikh Beshir. El Aarkoub, or Ard Barouk, belonging to the family of Aemad; and El Kharroub, belonging to the Djorbelat.

In 1811, the Druses of Djebel Ala, between Ladakie and Antioch, were driven from their habitations by Topal Aly, the governor of Djissr Shogher, whose troops committed the most horrible cruelties. Upwards of fifteen hundred families fled to their countrymen in the Libanus, where they were received with great hospitality; upwards of two hundred purses were collected for their relief, and the Djonbelat assigned to them convenient dwellings in different parts of the mountain. Some of them retired into the Haouran.

March 21st.--It was with difficulty that I got away from Beteddein. The Emir seemed to take great pleasure in conversing with me, as we spoke in Arabic, which made him much freer than he would have been, had he had to converse through the medium of an interpreter. He wished me to stay a few days longer, and to go out a hunting with him; but I was anxious to reach Damascus, and feared that the rain and snow would make the road over the mountain impassable; in this I was not mistaken, having afterwards found that if I had tarried a single day longer I should have been obliged to return along the great road by the way of Beirout. The Emir sent one of his horsemen to accompany me, and we set out about mid-day. Half an hour from Beteddein is the village Ain el Maszer, with a spring and many large walnut trees. To the left, on the right bank of the Nahr el Kadhi, higher in the mountain, are the villages Medjelmoush and Reshmeyia. At one hour is the village Kefrnebra, belonging to the Yezdeky, under the command of Abou Salma, one of their principal Sheikhs. The road lies along the mountain, gradually ascending. At one hour and a quarter are the two villages Upper and Lower Beteloun One hour and three quarters, the village Barouk, and near it the village Ferideis; these are the chief residence of the Yezdeky, and the principal villages in the district of Barouk. They are situated on the wild banks of the torrent Barouk, whose source is about one hour and a half distant. The Sheikh Beshir has conducted a branch of it to his new palace at Mokhtar; the torrent falls into the sea near Saida. From Barouk the road ascends the steep side of the higher region of the mountain called Djebel Barouk; we were an hour and a half in ascending; the summit was covered with snow, and a thick fog rested upon it: and had it not been for the footsteps of a man who had passed a few hours before us we should not have been able to find our way. We several times sunk up to our waists in the snow, and on reaching the top we lost the footsteps, when discovering a small rivulet running beneath the snow, I took it as our guide, and although the Druse was in despair, and insisted on returning, I pushed on, and after many falls reached the plain of the Bekaa, at the end of two hours from the summit; I suppose the straight road to be not more than an hour and quarter. The rivulet by which we descended is called Wady Dhobbye. We had no sooner entered the plain than it began to snow again, and it continued to rain and snow for several days. Small caravans from Deir el Kammar to Damascus pass the mountain even in winter; but to prevent the sharp hoofs of the mules from sinking deep into the snow, the muleteers are accustomed in the difficult places to spread carpets before them as they pass.

We reached the plain near a small village, inhabited only during the seed time. From thence the village of Djob Djennein bore S. by E. and the village of Andjar, in the upper part of the Bekaa, which I visited in the year 1810, from Zahle, E.N.E. From the foot of the mountain we were one hour in reaching the bridge over the Liettani, which has been lately re-paired by the Emir Beshir, who has also built a Khan near it, for the accommodation of travellers. At twenty minutes from the bridge lies the village Djob Djennein, one of the principal villages of the Bekaa; it is situated on the declivity of the Anti-Libanus, where that mountain begins to form part of the Djebel Essheikh. The Anti- Libanus here advances a little into the valley, which from thence takes a more western course.

The Emir Beshir has seven or eight villages about Djob Djennein, which together with the latter are his own property; but the whole Bekaa, since Soleiman succeeded to the Pashalik of Damascus in 1810, is also under his command. The villages to the north of Djob Djennein will be found enumerated in another place; [See page 31.] those to the south of it, and farther down in the valley, are Balloula, El Medjdel, Hammara, Sultan Yakoub, El Beiry, El Refeidh, Kherbet Kanafat, Ain Arab, and Leila. Having one of the Emir Beshir's men with me, I was treated like a great man in the house of the Sheikh of Djob Djennein; this I may be allowed to mention, as it is the only instance of my receiving such honours during my travels in Syria.

March 22nd.--Caravans reckon two days journey between Djob Djennein and Damascus; but as I was tolerably well mounted, and my guide was on a good mare of the Emir Beshir's, I resolved on reaching it in one day; we therefore pursued our route at a brisk walk and sometimes at a trot. We crossed the plain obliquely, having the projection of the Anti-Libanus, which ends at Djob Djennein, on our right. At thirty-five minutes from Djob Djennein, to the right, is the village Kamel el Louz, where are many ancient caves in the rocky mountain which rises behind it. In three quarters of an hour we reached the foot of the Anti- Libanus. On the summit of the mountain on our left, I observed a singular rock called Shekeik el Donia, or Hadjar el Konttara; my guide told me that the time would certainly arrive when some Frank nation would invade this country, and that on reaching this rock they would be completely routed. After a short ascent the road lies through a narrow plain, and then up another Wady, in the midst of which is the village of Ayty, two hours distant from Djob Djennein; it belongs to Sheikh Hassan, the brother of Sheikh Beshir, a very rich Druse, who is as avaricious as the latter is generous; he has however built a Khan here for the accommodation of travellers. There is a fine spring in the village; the inhabitants manufacture coarse earthen ware, with which they supply Damascus.

At the end of two hours and three quarters we reached the summit of the Anti-Libanus, where the heavy rains had already melted the greater part of the snow; here are some stunted oaks, and numerous springs. In three hours and a quarter we descended into a fine plain watered by the Wady Halloue, which we followed into a narrow valley, and on issuing from it passed a ruined Khan, with a spring, called Khan Doumas, which is five hours and a quarter from Djob Djennein. We left the village Doumas, which is half an hour from the Khan on our right, and at the end of six hours reached a high uneven plain, situated between the Anti Libanus and the chain of hills which commence near Katana; the plain is called Szakhret el Sham. Seven hours and a half, the ruined Khan Meylesoun. Eight hours and a half brought us to the termination of the Szakhret, from which we descended into the Ghouta, or plain of Damascus. At nine hours, the village Mezze, among the gardens of Damascus; and at the end of nine hours and three quarters we entered the city, which is generally reckoned fourteen hours journey from Djob Djennein.

Note.

Between Kesrouan and Zahle, I am informed that in the mountain, about six hours from the latter, are the ruins of an ancient city called Fakkra or Mezza. Large blocks of stone, some remains of temples, and several Greek inscriptions are seen there.

Between Akoura and Baalbec is a road cut in the rock, with several long Greek inscriptions, and near the source of the rivulet of Afka, near Akoura, are the ruins of an ancient building, which I unfortunately did not see during my passage through that village in 1810, although I enquired for them.

JOURNAL OF A TOUR FROM DAMASCUS INTO THE HAOURAN, AND THE MOUNTAINS TO THE E. AND S.E. OF THE LAKE OF TIBERIAS. IN THE MONTHS OF APRIL AND MAY, 1812.

In returning to Damascus, it was my intention to obtain some further knowledge of the Haouran, and to extend my journey over the mountains to the south of Damascus, where I wished to explore the ruins of Djerash (Gerasa) and of Amman (Philadelphia) in the ancient Decapolis, which M. Seetzen had discovered in his journey from Damascus to Jerusalem. An unexpected change in the government of Damascus obliged me to protract my stay in that city for nearly a month. The news had just been received of the dismissal of Soleiman Pasha, and it was necessary for me, before I set off, to ascertain whether the country would yield quietly to the command of the new Pasha; for, if rebel parties started up, and submission became doubtful, the traveller would run great hazards, would be unable to derive any advantage from the protection of the government, and would be obliged to force his way by the means of endless presents to the provincial chiefs.

As soon as I was satisfied of the tranquil state of the Pashalik, I set out for the Haouran. I took with me a Damascene, who had been seventeen times to Mekka, who was well acquainted with the Bedouins, inured to fatigue, and not indisposed to favour my pursuits; I had indeed reason to be contented with my choice of this man, though he was of little further use to me than to take care of my horse, and to assist in intimidating the Arabs, by some additional fire- arms.

We left Damascus on the morning of the 21st of April, 1812; and as my first steps were directed towards those parts of the Ledja which I had not visited during my first tour, we took the road of El Kessoue, Deir Ali, and El Merdjan, to the description of which in my former journal I may here add the following particulars: The N.E. part of Djebel Kessoue is called Djebel Aadelye. From Kessoue our road bore S.S.E. In one hour and a quarter from that place we passed the small village called Hausch el Madjedye; Hausch being an appellation applied to small villages enclosed by a wall, or rather to those whose houses join, so as to present by their junction a defence against the Arab robbers. The entrance to the Hausch is generally through a strong wooden gate, which is carefully secured every evening.

At an hour and three quarters from Kessoue is Deir Ali, to the north of which, upon the summit of Djebel Kessoue, is situated the Mezar el Khaledye; Deir Ali is a village inhabited by Druses, who keep the Arabs in great awe, by the reputation for courage which they have acquired upon many occasions. It seems rather extraordinary that the Druses, the known enemies of the Mohammedan faith, should be allowed to inhabit the country so near to the gate of the holy city, as Damascus is called; for not only Deir Ali, but three or four villages, as Artous, Esshera, Fye, and others, at only three hours distant from Damascus, are for the greater part peopled by them. Numbers of them are even settled in the town; the quarters called Bab Mesalla and El Hakle, in the Meidhan, or suburbs of the city, contain more than one hundred Druse families, who are there called Teyamene. In another quarter, called El Khereb, live three or four hundred Metaweli families, or Shiytes, of the sect of Aly; of this sect is the present Mutsellim, Aly Aga. The religious creeds of all these people are publicly known; but the fanatism of the Damascenes, however violent, is easily made subservient to their fears or interests; every religious and moral duty being forgotten when the prospect of gain or the apprehension of danger presents itself.

At three hours and a quarter from Kessoue is the village El Merdjan. When I passed this place in 1810, I found a single Christian family in it; I now found eight or ten families, most of them Druses, who had emigrated hither from Shaara, a well peopled village in 1810, but now deserted. They had brought the fertile soil round El Merdjan into cultivation, and had this year sown eight Ghararas of wheat and barley, or about one hundred and twenty cwt. English. [The Gharara of Damascus is eighty Muds, at three and a half Rotola per Mud, or twenty pounds.] The taxes paid by the village amounted to a thousand piastres, or fifty pounds sterling, besides the tribute extorted by the Bedouins. The vicinity of the village is watered by several springs. I was obliged to remain at Merdjan the next day, because my mare fell ill, and was unable to proceed. As I did not like to return to Damascus, I bought a mare of the Sheikh of the village, a Christian of Mount Libanus, who knew me, and who took a bill upon Damascus in payment. This mare I afterwards bartered for a Bedouin horse.

April 23d.--I left Merdjan to examine the eastern limits of the Ledja. We passed the Aamoud Eszoubh, or Column of the Morning, an insulated pillar standing in the plain; it is formed of the black stone of the Ledja, about twenty-five or thirty feet high, of the Ionic order, and with a high pedestal. I had been told that there were some inscriptions upon it, but I did not find any. The column is half an hour distant from Merdjan, to the eastward of south. Round the column are fragments of three or four others, which appear to have formed a small temple. The remains of a subterraneous aqueduct, extending from the village towards the spot where the column stands, are yet visible. In one hour from thence we passed a ruined village called Beidhan, with a saltpetre manufactory. Two hours from Merdjan is Berak, bearing from it S.E.b.E. Our road lay over a low plain between the Djebel Kessoue and the Ledja, in which the Bedouins of the latter were pasturing their cattle. Berak is a ruined town, situated on the N.E. corner of the Ledja; there is no large building of any consequence here; but there are many private habitations. Here are two saltpetre manufactories, in which the saltpetre is procured by boiling the earth dug up among the ruins of the town; saline earth is also dug up in the neighbouring plain; in finding the productive spots, they are guided by the appearance of the ground in the morning before sunrise, and wherever it then appears most wet with dew the soil beneath is found impregnated with salt. The two manufactures produce about three Kantars, or fifteen or sixteen quintals per month of saltpetre, which is sold at about fifteen shillings per quintal. The boilers of these manufactories are heated by brushwood brought from the desert, as there is little wood in the Ledja, about Berak. The whole of the Loehf, or limits of the Ledja, is productive of saltpetre, which is sold at Damascus and Acre; I saw it sold near the lake of Tiberias for double the price which it costs in the Loehf. In the interior of a house among the ruins of Berak, I saw the following inscription:

"The tenth of Peritius of the eighth year." [Peritius was one of the Macedonian months, the use of which was introduced into Syria by the Seleucidae. It answered to the latter part of December and beginning of January. Ed.].

Berak, like most of the ancient towns of the Ledja, has a large stone reservoir of water. Between these ruins and Missema lies the ruined city Om Essoud, in the Loehf.

Djebel Kessoue runs out in a S.E. direction as far as the N.E. limits of the Ledja, and consists of the same kind of rock as that district. The other branch of it, or Djebel Khiara, extends towards Shaara. One hour S.W. from Berak, in the Ledja, are the ruins of a tower called Kaszr Seleitein, with a ruined village near it. An Arab enumerated to me the following names of ruined cities and villages in the Ledja, which may be added to those mentioned in my former journal: Emseyke, El Wyr, Djedl, Essemeyer, Szour, Aasem Ezzeitoun, Hamer, Djerrein, Dedjmere, El Aareis El Kastall, Bord, Kabbara, El Tof, Etteibe, Behadel, El Djadj, Szomeith, El Kharthe, Harran, Djeddye, Serakhed, Deir, Dami, Aahere, Om el Aalek, Moben el Beit, Deir Lesmar.

I engaged a man at Berak to conduct me along the Loehf, or limits of the Ledja; this eastern part is called El Lowa, from the Wady Lowa, a winter torrent which descends from Djebel Haouran, and flows along the borders of the Ledja, filling in its course the reservoirs of all the ancient towns situated there; it empties itself into the Bahret el Merdj, or marshy ground at seven or eight hours east of Damascus, where the rivers of Damascus also are lost. Our road was S.S.E. In one hour from Berak we passed the Lowa, near a ruined bridge, where the Wady takes a more eastern direction. Some water remained in pools in different places in the Wady, the rains having been very copious during the winter season. In an hour and a half we passed Essowara, a ruined town on our right; we travelled along the fertile plain that skirts the rocky surface of the Ledja, which at two hours took a more southern direction. On our right was El Hazzem, a ruined town; and a little farther, Meharetein, also in ruins. All these towns are on the borders of the Ledja. Their inhabitants formerly cultivated the fields watered by the Lowa, of which the stone enclosures are still visible in some places. At three hours is El Khelkhele, a ruined town, where we slept, in the house of the owner of a saltpetre manufactory.

The Wady Lowa in some places approaches close to the Ledja, and in others advances for a mile into the plain; its banks were covered with the most luxuriant herbage, of which little use is made; the Arabs of the Ledja being afraid to pass beyond its limits, from the almost continual state of warfare in which they live with the powerful tribe of Aeneze, and the government of Damascus; while the Aeneze, on the other hand, are shy of approaching too near the Ledja, from fear of the nightly robberies, and of the fire-arms of the Arabs who inhabit it. The labourers in the salt-petre manufactories are Druses, whose reputation for individual courage, and national spirit, keeps the Arabs at a respectful distance.

April 24th.--Khelkhele, like all the ancient towns in the Haouran, is built entirely with stone. I did not observe any public edifice of impor-tance in the towns of the Lowa; there are some towers of moderate height, which seem to have been the steeples of churches; and a few houses are distinguished from the rest by higher arches in the apartments, and a few rude carvings over their doors. From Khelkhele, S.E. about two hours dis-tant, is a high Tel in the plain, it is called Khaledie, and has the ruins of a town on its top; nearly joining to it are the most northern projections of Djebel Haouran, which are distinguished on this side by a chain of low hillocks. To the E. of Khelkhele, about four hours, stands the Tel el Aszfar, farther E. the ruined village of Djoh Ezzerobe, and still further E. about nine or ten hours, from Khelkhele, the ruined village El Kasem, near which is a small rivulet. In the direction of Tel el Khaledie, and to the S.E. of it, are the ruined villages of Bezeine, and Bezeinat.

The direction of our route from Khelkhele was sometimes S.E. sometimes S. following the windings of the Ledja and the Lowa. At half an hour is the ruined village Dsakeir, in the Ledja, which here turns to the E. in the direction of Tel Shiehhan. On its S.E. corner stands the ruined town Sowarat el Dsakeir, where we found a party of Arabs Szolout en-camped, with whom we breakfasted. In one hour and a quarter we passed Redheimy, where the ground was covered with remains of ancient enclo-sures. One hour and a half, El Hadher; one hour and three quarters, El Laheda; two hours, Omten; two hours and a half, Meraszrasz; three hours, Om Haretein; three hours and a half, Essammera. All the above villages and towns are in ruins, and prove the once-flourishing state of the Ledja. In four hours we reached Om Ezzeitoun, a village inhabited by Druses. The advantages of a Wady like the Lowa are incalculable in these coun-tries, where we always find that cultivation follows the direction of the winter torrents, as it follows the Nile in Egypt. There are not many Wadys in this country which inundate the land; but the inhabitants make the best use of the water to irrigate their fields after the great rains have ceased. Springs are scarce, and it is from the Wadys that the reservoirs are filled which supply both men and cattle with water, till the return of the rainy season. It is from the numerous Wadys which rise in the Djebel Haouran that the population of the Haouran derives its means of existence, and the success of its agriculture.

Om Ezzeitoun is inhabited by thirty or forty families. It appears, by the extent of its ruins, to have been formerly a town of some note. I here copied several inscriptions.

The only ancient building of any consequence is a small temple, of which an arch of the interior, and the gate, only remain; on each side of the latter are niches

I had intended to sleep at Om Ezzeitoun, but I found the Druses very ill-disposed towards me. It was generally reported that I had discovered a treasure in 1810 at Shohba, near this place, and it was supposed that I had now returned to carry off what I had then left behind. I had to combat against this story at almost every place, but I was nowhere so rudely received as at this village, where I escaped ill treatment only by assuming a very imposing air, and threatening with many oaths, that if I lost a single hair of my beard, the Pasha would levy an avania of many purses on the village. I had with me an old passport from Soleiman Pasha, who, though no longer governor of Damascus, had been charged pro tempore with the government till the arrival of the new Pasha, who was expected from Constantinople. Soleiman had retired to his former government at Acre, but his Mutsellim at Damascus very kindly granted me strong letters of recommendation to all the authorities of the country, which were of great use to me in the course of my journey.

I left Om Ezzeitoun late in the evening, to proceed toward the mountain of Haouran. Our road lay on the N. side of Tel Shiehhan, close to which runs the Ledja; and the Wady Lowa descends the mountain on the west side of it. We proceeded in the direction of Soueida, and in an hour and a quarter from the village stopped, after sunset, at an encampment of the Djebel Haouran Arabs. My companion, and a guide whom I had engaged at Om Ezzeitoun, persuaded me to appear before the Arabs as a soldier belonging to the government, in order to get a good supper, of which we were in great want, that of the preceding night, at the saltpetre works, having consisted of only a handful of dry biscuit. We were served with a dish of rice boiled in sour milk, and were much amused by the sports and songs of the young girls of the tribe, which they continued in the moonlight till near midnight. One of the young men had just returned to the encampment, who had been taken prisoner by the Aeneze during a nightly predatory expedition. He showed us the marks of his fetters, and enlarged upon the mode of treating the Rabiat, or prisoner, among the

Aeneze. A friend had paid thirty camels for his liberation. In spring the Arabs of the Djebel Haouran and the Ledja take advantage of the approach of the Aeneze, to plunder daily among their enemies; they are better acquainted with the ground than the latter, a part of whose horses and cattle are every spring carried off by these daring mountaineers.

April 25th.--At half an hour from the encampment is the hill called Tel Dobbe, consisting of a heap of ruins, with a spring. To the N.E. of it, a quarter of an hour, is the ruined village of Bereit, which was inhabited in 1810, but is now abandoned. The Haouran peasants wander from one village to another; in all of them they find commodious habitations in the ancient houses; a camel transports their family and baggage; and as they are not tied to any particular spot by private landed property, or plantations, and find every where large tracts to cultivate, they feel no repugnance at quitting the place of their birth. In one hour we passed Seleim, which in 1810 was inhabited by a few poor Druses, but is now abandoned. Here are the ruins of a temple, built with much smaller stones than any I had observed in the construction of buildings of a similar size in the Haouran. On the four outer corners were Corinthian pilasters. At one hour and a quarter, road S. we entered the wood of oak-trees, which is continued along the western declivity of the Djebel. One hour and a half, in the wood, we passed the Wady Dyab, coming from the mountain. One hour and three quarters, passed Wady Kefr el Laha. At the end of two hours we reached Aatyl, a small Druse village in the midst of the wood. Here are the remains of two handsome temples; that which is on the N. side, is in complete ruins; it consisted of a square building, with a high arch across its roof; two niches were on each side of the gate, and in front of it a portico of columns, the number of which it is impossible to determine, the ground being covered by a heap of fragments of columns, architraves, and large square stones. This temple is called El Kaszr.

On the S.E. side of Aatyl stands the other temple, which is of small dimensions but of elegant construction. It has a portico of two columns and two pilasters, each of which has a projecting base for a statue, elevated from the ground about one-third of the height of the column, like the pillars of the great colonnade at Palmyra. The columns are Corinthian, but not of the best time of that order. The interior of the temple consists of an apartment with several arches without any ornaments; but the gate is covered with sculpture. The two pilasters forming the portico have inscriptions on their bases.

Near the temple I saw a bas-relief about ten inches square, representing a female bust, with hair in ringlets, falling upon the shoulders; it was lying on the ground; but it was not of such workmanship as to tempt me to take it with me. Upon the wall of one of the largest houses in the village was a long inscription; but too high for me to read.

N.E. of Aatyl, about one hour, up in the mountain, is a ruined tower called Berdj Mabroum.

The tobacco of Aatyl is preferred to that of any other part of the Haouran. I here saw a public woman, a Kahirene, who seemed to be kept at the expense of the whole village; I was surprised at this, for manners in the Haouran are generally almost as pure as among the Bedouins: public women are not suffered, and adultery is punished by the death of the woman, while the man is ruined by the heavy penalties exacted by the government in expiation of his guilt. Last year a married Turkish woman at Mohadje, a village in the Loehf, was caught in the embraces of a young Christian; her three brothers hastened to the spot, dragged her to the market place, and there in the presence of the whole community, cut her in pieces with their swords, loading her at the same time with the most horrible imprecations. The lover was fined ten purses.

From Aatyl I pursued my way one hour and a quarter S.S.E. to Soueida, at a short distance from which are the remains of an ancient road. As I had examined the antiquities of this village in 1810, and did not wish to be seen here a second time, I passed on without stopping, in the direction of Aaere, which is two hours and a half distant in a southwesterly direction. In the plain, and at a quarter of an hour to the west of Soueida, is the ruined convent Deir Senan. There is only a small Kurdine village in the road between Soueida and Aaere.

April 26th.--I remained this day at Aaere, in the house of the Druse chief the Sheikh Shybely Ibn Hamdan, where I alighted. The Sheikh appeared to be greatly pleased at my reappearance. Since my former visit, I had cultivated his friendship by letters and presents, which I had sent to him from Aleppo, and by which he was so much gratified, that he would have loaded me with presents in return, had I not thought proper to decline every thing of that kind, contenting myself with some very strong letters of recommendation from him to the authorities in those places which I intended to visit. Shybely is the kindest and most generous Turk I have known in Syria: and his reputation for these qualities has become so general, that peasants from all parts of the Haouran settle in his village. The whole of the Christian community of Soueida, with the Greek priest at their head, had lately arrived, so that Aaere has now become one of the most populous villages in this district. The high estimation in which the Sheikh is held arises from his great hospitality, and the justice and mildness with which he treats the peasants, upwards of forty of whom he feeds daily, besides strangers, who are continually passing here in their way to the Bedouin encampments; the coffee pot is always boiling in the Menzoul or stranger's room. He may now, in fact, be called the Druse chief of the Haouran, though that title belongs in strictness to his father-in-law, Hossein Ibn Hamdan, the Sheikh of Soueida.

April 27th.--I now thought that I might visit Boszra, which I had found it prudent to avoid in my former tour. Shybely gave me one of his men as a guide, and we followed the road which I have already described, as far as Shmerrin. At a quarter of an hour beyond Shmerrin, we passed the Wady Rakeik.

Boszra, is situated in the open plain, two hours distant from Aaere and is at present the last inhabited place in the south-east extremity of the Haouran; it was formerly the capital of Arabia Provincia, and is now, including its ruins, the largest town in the Haouran. It is of an oval shape, its greatest length being from E. to W.; its circumference is three quarters of an hour. It was anciently enclosed by a thick wall, which gave it the reputation of a place of great strength. Many parts of this wall, especially on the W. side, still remain; it was constructed with stones of a moderate size, strongly cemented together. The principal buildings in Boszra were on the E. side, and in a direction from thence towards the middle of the town. The S. and S.E. quarters are covered with ruins of private dwellings, the walls of many of which are still standing, but most of the roofs have fallen in. The style of building seems to have been similar to that observed in all the other ancient towns of the Haouran. On the W. side are springs of fresh water, of which I counted five beyond the precincts of the town, and six within the walls; their waters unite with a rivulet whose source is on the N.W. side, within the town, and which loses itself in the southern plain at several hours distance: it is called by the Arabs El Djeheir.

The Nahr el Ghazel, which in most maps, and even by D'Anville, is laid down in the immediate vicinity of Boszra, is unknown to the natives; but I was afterwards informed that there is a Wady Ghazel in the direction of Amman (Philadelphia), in the Djebel Belka, which descends from the mountain, and flows into the eastern plains, to the S. of Kalaat el Belka.

The principal ruins of Boszra are the following: a square building, which within is circular, and has many arches and niches in the wall: on either side of the door within are two larger niches, and opposite to the door on the east side of the circle is the sanctuary, formed of low arches supported by Corinthian pillars, without pedestals. Several beautiful sculptured friezes are inserted in the wall, but I was unable to discover from whence they had been taken; in front of the door stand four columns. The diameter of the rotunda is four paces; its roof has fallen in, but the walls are entire, without any ornaments. It appears to have been a Greek church. Over the gate is a long inscription, but it was illegible to my sight.

At a short distance to the west of this edifice is an oblong square building, called by the natives Deir Boheiry, or the Monastery of the priest Boheiry. On the top of the walls is a row of windows; on the north side is a high vaulted niche; the roof has fallen in; I observed no ornaments about it. On the side of its low gate is the following inscription in bad characters:

AEL AVREL THEONI LEG AVGG PR PR COS DESIG OPTIONES
[xx] LEG III KVRENAICAE VENERIANAE GALLIANAE RARISI--
MO ET PER OMNIA IUSTISSIMO SOCIO

Between these two buildings stands the gate of an ancient house, communicating with the ruins of an edifice, the only remains of which is a large semi-circular vault, with neat decorations and four small niches in its interior; before it lie a heap of stones and broken columns.

The natives have given to this house the name of Dar Boheiry, or the house of Boheiry. This Boheiry is a personage well known to the biographers of Mohammed, and many strange stories are related of him, by the Mohammedans, in honour of their Prophet, or by the eastern Christians, in derision of the Impostor. He is said to have been a rich Greek priest, settled at Boszra, and to have predicted the prophetic vocation of Mohammed, whom he saw when a boy passing with a caravan from Mekka to Damascus. Abou el Feradj, one of the earliest Arabic historians, relates this anecdote. According to the traditions of the Christians, he was a confidential counsellor of Mohammed, in the compilation of the Koran.

To the west of the abovementioned buildings stands the great mosque of Boszra, which is certainly coeval with the first aera of Mohammedanism, and is commonly ascribed to Omar el Khattab. Part of its roof has fallen in. On two sides of the square building runs a double row of columns, transported hither from the ruins of some Christian temple in the town. Those which are formed of the common Haouran stone are badly wrought in the coarse heavy style of the lower empire; but among them are sixteen fine variegated marble columns, distinguished both by the beauty of the material, and of the execution: fourteen are Co-rinthian, and two Ionic; they are each about sixteen or eighteen feet in height, of a single block, and well polished.

The walls of the mosque are covered with a coat of fine plaster, upon which were many Cufic inscriptions in bas-relief, running all round the wall, which was embellished also by numerous elegant Arabesque ornaments; a few traces of these, as well as of the inscriptions, still re-main. The interior court-yard of the mosque is covered with the ruins of the roof, and with fragments of columns, among which I observed a bro-ken shaft of an octagonal pillar, two feet in diameter; there are also several stones with Cufic inscriptions upon them.

Passing from the great mosque, southwards, we came to the prin-cipal ruin of Boszra, the remains of a temple, situated on the side of a long street, which runs across the whole town, and terminates at the west-ern gate. Of this temple nothing remains but the back wall, with two pilasters, and a column, joined by its entablature to the main wall; they are all of the Corinthian order, and both capitals and architraves are richly adorned with sculpture. In the wall of the temple are three rows of niches, one over the other. Behind this is another wall, half ruined. In front of the temple, but standing in an oblique direction towards it, are four large Co-rinthian Columns, equalling in beauty of execution the finest of those at Baalbec or Palmyra (those in the temple of the Sun at the latter place ex-cepted): they are quite perfect, are six spans in diameter, and somewhat more than forty-five feet in height; they are composed of many pieces of different sizes, the smallest being towards the top, and they do not appear to have been united by an entablature. They are not at equal distances, the space between the two middle ones being greater than the two other inter-vals. About thirty paces distant stands another column, of smaller dimensions, and of more elaborate but less elegant execution. I endeav-oured in vain to trace the plan of the edifice to which these columns belonged, for they correspond in no way with the neighbouring temple; it appeared that the main building had been destroyed, and its site built upon; nothing whatever of it remaining but these columns, the immediate vicinity of which is covered with the ruins of private houses. These four large columns, and those of Kanouat, are the finest remains of antiquity in the Haouran.

The ruin of the temple just described is in the upper part of the town, which slopes gently towards the west; not far from it, in descending the principal street, is a triumphal arch, almost entire, but presenting noth-ing very striking in its appearance, from the circumstance of the approach to it being choked with private houses, as is the case with all the public buildings in Boszra, except the church first mentioned. The arch consists of a high central arch, with two lower side arches; between these are Corinthian pilasters, with projecting bases for statues. On the inside of the arch were several large niches, now choked up by heaps of broken stones. On one of the pilasters is this inscription:

VLIO IVLIA . . . . . NAR PRAEF LEG. p ARTHICAE . . . . . . PPIANAE
DVCI DEVOTI S . MO . TREBICIVS CAVOINUS PRAEF ALAE
NOV. EFIRME CATAPRACTO PHILIPPIAN . PRAEPOSITO
OPTIMO

Among the ruins in the N.W. part of the town is an insulated mosque, and another stands near the above mentioned Deir Boheiry; in its court-yard is a stone covered with a long and beautiful Cufic inscription, which is well worth transporting to Europe; the characters being very small it would have required a whole day to copy it.

Not far from the great mosque is another triumphal arch, of smaller dimensions than the former, but remarkable for the thickness of its walls: it forms the entrance to an arched passage, through which one of the principal streets passed: two Doric columns are standing before it.

In the eastern quarter of the town is a large Birket or reservoir, almost perfect, one hundred and ninety paces in length, one hundred and fifty three in breadth, and enclosed by a wall seven feet in thickness, built of large square stones; its depth maybe about twenty feet. A staircase leads down to the water, as the basin is never completely filled. This reservoir is a work of the Saracens; made for watering the pilgrim caravan to Mekka, which as late as the seventeenth century passed by Boszra. A branch of the Wady Zeid [See p. 105.]empties itself in winter into the Birket. On the south side it is flanked by a row of houses, by some public edifices, and a mosque; and on the west side by an ancient cemetery; the other sides are open.

Upon a broken stone, in the middle of the town, is the following inscription, in characters similar to those which I met with at Hebron, Kanouat, and Aaere.

I now quitted the precincts of the town, and just beyond the walls, on the S. side came to a large castle of Saracen origin, probably of the time of the Crusades: it is one of the best built castles in Syria, and is sur-

BURCKHARDT

rounded by a deep ditch. Its walls are very thick, and in the interior are
alleys, dark vaults, subterraneous passages, &c. of the most solid construction. What distinguishes it from other Syrian castles, is that on the
top of it there is a gallery of short pillars, on three sides, and on the fourth
side are several niches in the wall, without any decorations; many of the
pillars are still standing. The castle was garrisoned, at the time of my visit,
by six Moggrebyns only. There is a well in the interior.

The castle of Boszra is a most important post to protect the harvests of the Haouran against the hungry Bedouins; but it is much
neglected by the Pashas of Damascus, and this year the crops of the inhabitants of Boszra have been almost entirely consumed by the horses of
the Aeneze, who were encamped on the E. side of the Djebel Haouran.

In proceeding from the castle westwards, I arrived, in a quarter of
an hour, at the western gate of the town, where the long street terminates.
The gate is a fine arch, with niches on each side, in perfect preservation:
the people of Boszra call it Bab el Haoua, or the Wind gate, probably because the prevailing or summer breezes blow from that point. A broad
paved causeway, of which some traces yet remain, led into the town; vestiges of the ancient pavement are also seen in many of the streets, with a
paved footway on each side; but the streets are all narrow, just permitting
a loaded camel to pass.

Near the Bab el Haoua are the springs above mentioned, called
Ayoun el Merdj; with some remains of walls near them. The late Youssef
Pasha of Damascus built here a small watch-tower, or barrack, for thirty
men, to keep the hostile Arabs at a distance from the water. The town
walls are almost perfect in this part, and the whole ground is covered with
ruins, although there is no appearance of any large public building. Upon
an altar near one of the springs was the following inscription:

ANTONIAE FORTVNATAE ANTONIVS. V
. . CES CONIVGI PIISIMAE

Near it is another altar, with a defaced inscription.

In going northward from the springs, I passed the rivulet Djeheir,
whose source is at a short distance, within the precincts of the town. It
issues from a stone basin, and was conducted anciently in a canal. Over it
seems to have stood a small temple, to judge by the remains of several

159

columns that are lying about. The source is full of small fish. Youssef Pasha built a barrack here also; but it was destroyed by the Wahabi who made an incursion into the Haouran in 1810, headed by their chief Ibn Saoud, who encamped for two days near this spot, without being able to take the castle, though garrisoned by only seven Moggrebyns. The banks of the Djeheir are a favourite encampment of the Bedouins, and especially of the Aeneze.

Beyond the town walls, and at some distance to the north of the Djeheir, stands the famous mosque El Mebrak; and near it is the cemetery of the town. Ibn Affan, who first collected the scattered leaves of the Koran into a book, relates that when Othman, in coming from the Hedjaz, approached the neighbourhood of Boszra with his army, he orderd his people to build a mosque on the spot where the camel which bore the Koran should lie down; such was the origin of the mosque El Mebrak. [Mebrak means the spot where a camel couches down, or a halting-place.] It is of no great size; its interior was embellished, like that of the great mosque, with Cufic inscriptions, of which a few specimens yet remain over the Mehrab, or niche towards which the face of the Imam is turned in praying. The dome or Kubbe which covered its summit has been recently destroyed by the Wahabi.

The above description comprises all the principal antiquities of Boszra. A great number of pillars lie dispersed in all directions in the town; but I observed no remains of granite. Its immediate invirons are also covered with ruins, principally on the W. and N.W. sides, where the suburbs may have formerly stood.

Of the vineyards, for which Boszra was celebrated, even in the days of Moses, and which are commemorated by the Greek medals, not a vestige remains. There is scarcely a tree in the neighbourhood of the town, and the twelve or fifteen families who now inhabit it cultivate nothing but wheat, barley, horse-beans, and a little Dhourra. A number of fine rose trees grow wild among the ruins of the town, and were just beginning to open their buds.

April 28th.--I was greatly annoyed during my stay at Boszra, by the curiosity of the Aeneze, who were continually passing through the place. It had been my wish to visit the ruined city of Om El Djemal, which is eight hours distant from Boszra, to the S.; but the demands of the Arabs for conducting me thither were so exorbitant, exceeding even the sum which I had thought necessary to bring with me from Damascus to defray the expenses of my whole journey, that I was obliged to return to Aaere towards mid-day, after having offered thirty piastres for a guide, which no one would accept. None but Aeneze could have served me, and with them there was no reasoning; they believed that I was going in search of treasure, and that I should willingly give any sum to reach the spot where it was hid.

April 29th.--I took leave of my worthy friend Shybely, who would not let us depart alone, but engaged a Bedouin to accompany us towards the western parts of the Haouran; this man was a Bedouin of Sayd, or Upper Egypt, of the tribe of Khelafye, who inhabit to the west of Girge; he had entered the service of the Mamelouks, and had been with one of them to Mekka, from whence he returned to Damascus, where he entered into the Pasha's cavalry; here he had the misfortune to kill one of his comrades, which obliging him to fly, he repaired to the Aeneze, with whom he found security and protection.

Half an hour from Aaere we passed Wady Ghothe, with the village of Ghothe to our left; route N.W.b.N. One hour and a half, the village Om Waled, one hour and three quarters, the village El Esleha, inhabited principally by Christians. Two hours and a quarter, passed Wady Soueida. Two hours and a half the village Thale, to the west of which, one hour, is Tel Hossein, with the village Kheraba. At three hours and a quarter is the village El Daara, with Wady Daara; here we dined at an encampment of Arabs of Djebel Haouran, who are in the habit of descending into the plain to pasture their cattle, as soon as the country is evacuated by the Aeneze. At four hours and three quarters is Melieha el Aattash, in a direction N.W. from Daara; from thence our route lay W. by N. Not more than one-third of the plain was cultivated, though the peasants had sown more grain this year, than they had done for many years back. S. of Melieha half an hour lies the village Rakham. Five hours and a half the village El Herak. Five hours and three quarters, the village El Hereyek. In all these villages are several reservoirs of water, for the supply of the inhabitants during summer, and which are filled either by the winter torrents descending from the Djebel Haouran, or by rain water, which is conducted into them from every side by narrow channels: they are all of ancient date, and built entirely with the black Haouran stone; but I saw in none of the villages any edifice of magnitude. Near Hereyek we fell in with the encampment of the Damascus beggars, who make an excursion every spring to the Haouran, to collect alms from the peasants and Arabs; these contributions are principally in butter and wool, which they sell on their return to Damascus. They had about a dozen tents, and as many asses, and I saw a good mare tied before the tent of the Sheikh, who is a man of consequence among the thieves and vagabonds of Damascus. His name is El

Shuhadein: he invited us to drink a cup of coffee, and take some refreshment; but my companions, who knew him, advised me to keep clear of him. At six hours and a quarter, we passed at a short distance to our left, the village Olma, our route being N.W. About one hour S.W. of Olma lies the village El Kerek. Eight hours and twenty-five minutes, the village Naeme. Most of these villages stand upon, or near, low hillocks or Tels, the only objects which break the monotony of the plain.

It was at Naeme that I saw, for the first time, a swarm of locusts; they so completely covered the surface of the ground, that my horse killed numbers of them at every step, whilst I had the greatest difficulty in keeping from my face those which rose up and flew about. This species is called in Syria, Djerad Nedjdyat or Djerad Teyar, i.e. the flying locusts, being thus distinguished from the other species, called Djerad Dsahhaf, or devouring locusts. The former have a yellow body; a gray breast, and wings of a dirty white, with gray spots. The latter, I was told, have a whitish gray body, and white wings. The Nedjdyat are much less dreaded than the others, because they feed only upon the leaves of trees and vegetables, sparing the wheat and barley. The Dsahhaf, on the contrary, devour whatever vegetation they meet with, and are the terror of the husbandmen; the Nedjdyat attack only the produce of the gardener, or the wild herbs of the desert. I was told, however, that the offspring of the Nedjdyat produced in Syria partake of the voracity of the Dsahhaf, and like them prey upon the crops of grain.

Those which I saw in the Haouran, and afterwards in the gardens of Damascus, fly in separate bodies, and do not spread over a whole district. The young of this species are quite black until a certain age.

The Bedouins eat locusts, which are collected in great quantities in the beginning of April, when the sexes cohabit, and they are easily caught; after having been roasted a little upon the iron plate, on which bread is baked, they are dried in the sun, and then put into large sacks, with the mixture of a little salt. They are never served up as a dish, but every one takes a handful of them when hungry. The peasants of Syria do not eat locusts, nor have I myself ever had an opportunity of tasting them: there are a few poor Fellahs in the Haouran, however, who sometimes pressed by hunger, make a meal of them; but they break off the head and take out the entrails before they dry them in the sun. The Bedouins swallow them entire. The natural enemy of the locust is the bird Semermar; which is of the size of a swallow, and devours vast numbers of them; it is even said that the locusts take flight at the cry of the bird. But if the whole feathered tribe of the districts visited by locusts were to unite their efforts, it would avail little, so immense are the numbers of these dreadful insects.

At eight hours and three quarters from Aaere, and at a short distance to the right, is the village Obta; our route N.W. by N. Nine hours and a quarter, we saw, at one hour to the left, the village El Kherbe. Nine hours and three quarters, Shemskein, one of the principal villages in the Haouran. As we had rode at a very brisk pace, the above distance of nine hours and three quarters may be computed at nearly twelve hours of the common travelling. Shemskein, a village containing upwards of one hundred families, is situated on the Hadj road, on the side of Wady

Hareir, over which a solid bridge has been built on one side of the village: this Wady comes from the north-east at four or six hours distance, and flows south-west. It is one of the largest torrents of Haouran, and was at this moment full of water, while most of the other Wadys were nearly dried up. The Sheikh of Shemskein has the title of Sheikh el Haouran, and holds the first rank among the village Sheikhs of the country. In the time of Hadj he collects from the Haouran and Djolan about fifteen hundred camels, and accompanies them to Mekka. His income is considerable, as the peasants of the different villages of the Haouran, when engaged in disputes with neighbouring villagers, or with their Sheikhs, generally apply in the first instance to his tribunal.

We alighted at the Sheikh's house, in the court-yard of which we found almost the whole population of the village assembled: there had been a nuptial feast in the village, and the Nowars or gypsies, were playing music. These Nowar, who are called Korbatt at Aleppo, are dispersed over the whole of Syria; they are divided into two principal bodies, viz. the Damascenes, whose district extends as far as Hassia, on the Aleppo road; and the Aleppines, who occupy the country to the north of that line. They never dare go beyond the limits which they have allotted to each other by mutual consent: both bodies have an Aga, who pays to the Grand Signior about five hundred piastres per annum, and collects the tribute from his subjects, which in the Damascus territory amounts annually to twenty piastres a head for every full grown male.

April 30th.--As I wished to visit from Shemskein the Mezareib, and to ascend from thence the mountains of Adjeloun, I set out in the company of an old acquaintance of Aleppo, a Janissary, who had entered into the service of the Pasha of Damascus, and was now stationed at Mezareib. Following the Hadj road, in a S.S.E. direction, in an hour and a quarter from Shemskein we crossed the Wady Aar, coming from the east. Half an hour to the left of the road is Daal, a considerable village; and between Daal and Mezareib, but more to the eastward, lies the village of Draa, the ancient Edrei. Two hours, Tefas, with a well built mosque.

At the end of three hours, we arrived at El Mezareib, El Mezareib is the first castle on the Hadj road from Damascus, and was built by the great Sultan Selym, three hundred and eight years ago. It is the usual residence of the Aga of the Haouran; but that office is now vacant, the late Aga having been deposed, and no one has yet been appointed to succeed him. The garrison of the castle consisted of a dozen Moggrebyns, whose chief, a young black, was extremely civil to me. The castle is of a square form, each side being, as well as I can recollect, about one hundred and twenty paces in length. The entrance is through an iron gate, which is regularly shut after sunset. The interior presents nothing but an empty yard enclosed by the castle wall, within which are ranges of warehouses, where the provisions for the Hadj are deposited; their flat roofs form a platform behind the parapet of the castle wall, where sixteen or eighteen mud huts have been built on the top of the warehouses, as habitations for the peasants who cultivate the neighbouring grounds. On the east side two miserable guns are planted. Within the castle is a small mosque. There are no houses, beyond its precincts. Close by it, on the N. and E. sides, are a great number of springs, whose waters collect, at a short distance, into a large pond or lake, of nearly half an hour in circumference, in the midst of which is an island. On an elevated spot at the extremity of a promontory, advancing into the lake, stands a chapel, around which are many ruins of ancient buildings. The water of the lake is as clear as crystal, neither weeds nor grass growing in it; its depth in the middle is much more than the heighth of a man; the bottom is sand, and gravel of the black Haouran stone. It abounds with fish, particularly carp, and a species called Emshatt. In summer time, after the harvests of the Haouran have been gathered in, when the Aeneze approach the more populous parts of the country, the borders of the lake are crowded every evening with thousands of camels, belonging to these Arabs, who prefer filling their water skins here, as they say that the water keeps better than any other. The water of the springs is slightly tepid, and nearly of the same temperature as that of the springs near Kalaat el Medyk, in the valley of the Orontes. According to the Arabs the springs emit a copious steam in the winter mornings. An ancient mill stands near one of them, with a few broken stones around it; but it does not appear that any village or city of note stood here, though the quantity of water seems inviting to settlers. The springs as well as the lake are known by the name of El Budje.

The pilgrim caravan to Mekka collects at the Mezareib, where the Pasha, or Emir el Hadj, remains encamped for ten days, in order to collect the stragglers, and to pay to the different Arab tribes the accustomed tribute for the passage of the caravan through the desert. The warehouses of the castle are annually well stocked with wheat, barley, biscuit, rice, tobacco, tent and horse equipage, camel saddles, ropes, ammunition, &c. each of which has its particular warehouse. These stores are exclusively for the Pasha's suite, and for the army which accompanies the Hadj; and are chiefly consumed on their return. It is only in cases of great abundance, and by particular favour, that the Pasha permits any articles to be sold to the pilgrims. At every station, as far as Medina, is a castle, but generally smaller than this, filled with similar stores.

The Haouran alone is required to deliver every year into the store houses of the Mezareib, two thousand Gharara of barley, or about twenty or twenty-five thousand cwt. English. The town of Damascus has been fed for the last three months with the biscuit stored in the Mezareib for the Hadj.

As far as the Pasha was concerned, the affairs of the great Caravan were generally well managed; but there still reigned a great want of economy, and the expenses of the Hadjis increased every year. Of late years, the hire of a single camel from Damascus to Mekka has been seven hundred and fifty piastres; as much, and often more, was to be paid on coming back; and the expenses on the road, and at Mekka, amounted at least to one thousand piastres, so that in the most humble way, the journey could not be performed at less than two thousand five hundred piastres, or £125. sterling. A camel with a litter cost fifteen hundred in going, and as much in coming back. Of the whole caravan not above one-tenth part were real pilgrims, the rest consisted of soldiers, the servants of soldiers, people attached to the Pasha's suite, merchants, pedlars, camel-drivers, coffee and pipe waiters, a swarm of Bedouins, together with several tents of public women from Damascus, who were so far encouraged, that, whenever they were unable to obtain from their lovers the daily food for their horses or mules, they obtained a supply from the Pasha's stores.

The greater part of the pilgrims usually contract for the journey with one of the great undertakers, or Mekouam, as they are called; this agreement is only for a beast of transport and for water; as to eating, the pilgrims generally mess together at their own expense, in bodies of about half a dozen. The Mekouam, on agreeing to furnish a beast of burthen, are bound to replace whatever may die on the road, and are therefore obliged to carry with them at least one unloaded camel for every loaded one. It is a general practice with the Mekouam to obtain as large sums as possible on account from the pilgrims who engage with them for the journey; they generally agree among each other upon the sum to be demanded, as well as the moment at which it is to be called for: so that if the pilgrims resist the imposition, the Hadj sometimes remains encamped on the same spot for several days, the Mekouam all refusing to proceed, and feeing the Pasha for his connivance at their injustice. On their return to Damascus, if they have already extorted from the pilgrims in the course of the journey more than the amount of their contract, as often happens, they generally declare themselves to be bankrupts, and then the value of a few camels is all that remains to pay their debts to the pilgrims.

Those pilgrims who do not engage with the Mekouam, as is generally the case with those who come from Armenia and the borders of the Black sea, perform the journey somewhat cheaper upon their own beasts; but they are ill-treated on the road by the Mekouam, are obliged to march the last in the caravan, to encamp on the worst ground, to fill their water skins the last, and are often even avanized by the Pasha. It is difficult to conceive the wretched condition of the greater part of the Hadjis, and the bad conduct of the troops and Arabs. Thieving and robbery have become general among them, and it is more the want of sleep from fear of being plundered, which causes the death of so many pilgrims, than the fatigues of the journey. The Pasha's troops, particularly those called Howara, which bring up the rear of the caravan, are frequently known to kill the stragglers during the night, in order to strip them of their property. The Pasha, it is true, often punishes such delinquents, and scarcely a day passes without some one being empaled alive; the caravan moves on, and the malefactor is left to be devoured by the birds of prey. The Bedouins are particularly dexterous in pilfering; at night they sometimes assume the dress of the Pasha's infantry, and thus introduce themselves unnoticed amongst the camels of the rich Hadjis, when they throw the sleeping owner from his mule or camel, and in the confusion occasioned by the cries of the fallen rider, drive off the beast.

The caravan marches daily from Asser, or about three hours after mid- day, during the whole of the night, and till the followingmorning, when the tents are pitched. It never stops but during prayers. The Arabs of Sokhne, Tedmor, and Haouran, together with the Bedouins who let out their camels, precede or follow the caravan at the distance of one day's march. They transport the provisions for the Pasha's troops, of which they steal, and publicly sell at least two-thirds. They march during the day, and encamp in the evening. Their caravan is called El Selma. It passes the great caravan once every two or three days, and then encamps till the latter comes up, when they supply the Pasha's suite with provisions. The cheapest mode of performing the pilgrimage is to agree for a camel with one of those Arabs; but the fatigue is much greater in following the Selma.

The last year in which the Hadj quitted Damascus, the pilgrims reached the gates of Medina, but they were not permitted to enter the town, nor to proceed to Mekka; and after an unsuccessful negotiation of seven days, they were obliged to return to Damascus. About two hundred Persian Hadjis only, who were with the caravan, were allowed to pass on paying a large sum of money. Ibn Saoud, the Wahabi chief, had one interview with Abdullah Pasha, accompanied by the whole of his retinue, at Djebel Arafat, near Mekka; they exchanged presents, and parted as friends.

Of the seven different pilgrim caravans which unite at Mekka, two only bear the Mahmal, the Egyptian and Syrian; the latter is the first in rank.

We left Mezareib towards the evening, and were obliged to proceed alone along the Hadj route, the fear of the Aeneze rendering every one unwilling to accompany us. In a quarter of an hour we came to a bridge over the Wady Mezareib, called Djissr Kherreyan; to the left, near the road, is the ruined village Kherbet el Ghazale, where the Hadj sometimes encamps. It often happens that the caravan does not encamp upon the usual spots, owing to a wish either to accelerate or to prolong the journey. Past the Akabe, near the head of the Red Sea, beyond which the bones of dead camels are the only guides of the pilgrim through the waste of sand, the caravan often loses its way, and overshoots the day's station; in such cases the water-skins are sometimes exhausted, and many pilgrims perish through fatigue and thirst.

At one hour from the Mezareib, following the river that issues from the small lake, are several mills: from thence, south-west, begins the district called Ollad Erbed. Half an hour to the right, at some distance from the road, is the village Tel el Shehab; forty minutes, Wady Om El Dhan, coming from the eastward, with a bridge over it, built by Djezzar Pasha. In winter this generally proves a very difficult passage to the Hadj, on account of the swampy ground, and the peasants of the adjacent villages are, in consequence, obliged to cover the road with a thick layer of straw. At one hour to the right of the road is the village El Torra, on the top of a low chain of hills, forming a circle, through the centre of which lies the road. Here, as in so many other parts of the Haouran, I saw the most luxuriant wild herbage, through which my horse with difficulty made his way. Artificial meadows can hardly be finer than these desert fields: and it is this which renders the Haouran so favourite an abode of the Bedouins. The peasants of Syria are ignorant of the advantages of feeding their cattle with hay; they suffer the superfluous grass to wither away, and in summer and winter feed them on cut straw. In one hour and a quarter we passed Wady Torra; our road lying S.S.E. One hour and three quarters, we came to Wady Shelale, a torrent descending from the southern hills, and flowing in a deep bed, along which the road continues for some time. In two hours and three quarters quick walking, we came to Remtha, a station of the Hadj; which encamps near two Birkets or reservoirs formed in the bed of the Wady by means of three high walls built across it. A large tribe of Aeneze were watering their cattle as we passed. The surrounding country is hilly: the village is built upon the summits of several hills, and contains about one hundred families. In its neighbourhood are a number of wells of fresh water. We met with a very indifferent reception at the Sheikh's house, for the inhabitants of the villages on the Hadj route exceed all others in fanatism: an old man was particularly severe in his animadversions on Kafers treading the sacred earth which leads to the Kaabe, and the youngsters echoed his insulting language. I found means, however, to show the old man a penknife which I carried in my pocket, and made him a present of it, before he could ask it of me; we then became as great friends as we had been enemies, and his behaviour induced a like change in the others towards me. A penknife worth two shillings overcomes the fanatism of a peasant; increase the present and it will have equal effect upon a townsman; make it a considerable sum, and the Mufti himself will wave all religious scruples. Remtha is the last inhabited village on this side of the Haoun: the greater part of its houses are built against the caverns, with which this calcareous country abounds; so that the rock forms the back of the house, while the other sides are enclosed by a semicircular mud wall whose extremities touch the rock.

May 1st.--From Remtha I wished to cross the mountains directly to Djerash, which, I had reason to believe, was not more than seven or eight hours distant. It was with difficulty that I found a guide, because I refused to be answerable for the value of the man's horse and gun, in case we should be plundered by Arab robbers. A sum of twelve piastres, however, at last tempted one of the Fellahs, and we rode off late in the morning, our road lying toward the southern mountains, in a direction S. by W. Remtha is on the boundary line of the Haouran; which to the south-eastward runs by Om el Djemal and Szamma, two ruined towns. The district bordering upon the Haouran in this part is called Ezzoueit, and

stretches across the mountain nearly as far as Djerash. To the E. of Remtha runs a chain of low hills, called Ezzemle, extending towards the S.E.
nearly to Kalaat Mefrek, a ruined castle situated on the eastern extremity
of Djebel Zoueit. At one hour and a quarter, brisk walking of our horses,
we saw to the right, or west, about one hour distant, the ruins of a town
called Eszereikh, at the foot of Djebel Beni Obeyd. From thence the village of Hossn bore W. by S. The Kalaat el Mefrek, or, as the Arabs call it,
El Ferka, lay in a S.E. direction, distant about three hours. About one hour
and a half distant, in a S.W. direction, is the ruined village of Remeith,
with several large columns lying on the ground. At two hours and a half
from Remtha we passed a Tel, with the ruined village Dehama, on its top;
near the foot-way lay several broken shafts of columns. At three hours, on
reaching the Wady Warran, our route began to ascend. The Wady, which
descends from the mountain Zoueit, was at this time dry. Three hours and
a quarter brought us to three fine Doric columns lying on the ground. We
met several Arabs, but they did not venture to attack three men armed
with musquets, and gave us a friendly Salam Aleykum. We now ascended
the mountain, which is calcareous with flint, in following the windings of
the Wady. Wild pistachio trees abound; higher up oaks become more frequent, and the forest thickens; near the top, which we reached in five
hours and a quarter from Remtha, are some remains of the foundations of
ancient buildings. The Djebel Kafkafa, as this summit is called, commands a beautiful view over the plain of Djerash and the neighbouring
mountains of Zerka and Belka. The ruins of Djerash, which were distinctly seen, and the highest points of Djebel Belka behind them, bore
S.S.W.; the highest points of Djebel Zerka S. The district of Zoueit terminates at Djebel Kafkafa; and the country called El Moerad, lying S.W.
and W. commences: to the S. the Zoueit runs parallel with the Moerad as
far as Wady Zerka.

On gaining Djebel Kafkafa, our guide discovered that he had
gone astray, for it was not our intention, on setting out, to make directly
for Djerash, but to rest for the night in the village of Souf, and from
thence to visit the ruins on the following morning. We therefore turned
more to the westward on quitting the Djebel, and fell in with the road,
which continued through a thick wood, till we saw Souf, an hour and a
half distant before us, bearing W.S.W. At the end of seven hours and a
quarter from Remtha, we reached the spring of Souf, and allayed our
thirst, for we had been without water the whole day; there being very few
springs in the Djebel Zoueit; though it abounds in luxuriant pasture, and is
full of hares and partridges. In seven hours and a half we reached the vil-

lage of Souf, where I alighted, at the house of the Sheikh El Dendel, an honest and hospitable man.

Souf is situated on the declivity of the mountain, on the western side of a Wady called El Deir, the stream of which, called also El Ker-ouan, is supplied from three copious springs that issue from under a rock near the village, at a short distance from each other. They bear the names of Ain el Faouar, Ain el Meghaseb, and Ain el Keykabe, and with their united waters the narrow plain of Djerash is irrigated. Souf is a village with about forty families, whose principal riches are some olive planta-tions on the sides of Wady Deir: it is the chief village in the country called Moerad, in which the following are also situated: Ettekitte, one hour distant from Djerash, and abandoned last year; Bourma; Hamtha; Djezaze; and Debein. It is customary in these mountains for every house to manufacture gunpowder as well for its own consumption, as for sale to the neighbouring Arabs. In every house which I entered I saw a large mortar, which was continually in motion, even when a fire was kindled in the midst of the room: the powder is formed of one part of sulphur, five and a half parts of saltpetre, and one part of the charcoal of the poplar tree; it is not very good, but serves very well the purposes of this people.

I passed a most unpleasant night here. It is the custom, for the sake of saving lamp-oil, to light every evening a large fire, for the supply of which, there is plenty of dry wood in the neighbouring mountain. The room where I lodged was thus soon filled with smoke, which had no other issue than a small door, and even this was shut to keep out the cattle. The peasants seemed to delight in the heat thus occasioned; they took off all their clothes except the Abba, and sat smoking and laughing till mid-night; I wished to imitate them, but did not dare to strip, for fear of shewing the leathern girdle containing my money, which I wore under my clothes. Towards the morning the fire went out, and the company was asleep: I then opened the door to let the smoke out, and slept a few hours under the influence of the morning breeze.

There is an ancient ruined square building at Souf, with several broken columns. Near the sources are numerous caverns, in which the poor families of Souf reside.

May 2d.--Being impatient to reach Djerash, I left Souf early in the morning, taking with me a guide, who was afterwards to have con-ducted me towards Szalt, in the Djebel Belka. Our road lay along the mountain on the west side of Wady Deir. On the E. side of the wady, half an hour from Souf, is the ruined place called Kherbet Mekbela. Three quarters of an hour from Souf, in our road, and just over the ruined city of

Djerash, are the ruins called Kherbet el Deir, with a Turkish chapel named Mezar Abou Beker. Our road lay S.S.E. In one hour we passed, n the declivity of the mountain, descending towards Djerash, a place which I supposed to have been the burying place of Djerash. I counted upwards of fifty sarcophagi, and there were many more; they are formed of the calcareous stone with which the Zoueit and Moerad mountains are composed. Some of them are sunk to a level with the surface of the ground, which is very rocky; others appear to have been removed from their original position. The largest was ten spans in length, and three and a half in breadth; but the greater part are much smaller, and are not even large enough to contain the corpse of a full grown person. On the sides of a few of them are sculptured ornaments in bas-relief, as festoons, genii, &c. but in a mutilated state, and not remarkable for beauty of execution; I saw only one that was elegantly wrought. The whole of these sarcophagi had flat covers, a few of which still remain. Upon one of the largest of the sarcophagi, and which is one of those first met with in going from Souf, is a long inscription, but so mutilated as to be almost wholly illegible. In the neighbourhood are several heaps of large square stones, the remains of some building.

In an hour and a half from Souf we reached the city walls of Djerash, or Kerash,, the Dj being the Bedouin pronunciation of the letter, which in the language of the city corresponds with our K. Djerash was built upon an elevated plain in the mountains of Moerad, on uneven ground, on both sides of Wady Deir, which, besides the name of Kerouan, bears also that of Seil Djerash, or the river of Djerash. This river empties itself, at a short distance from the town, into the Wady Zerka, probably the Jabock of the ancients. The principal part of the city stands on the right bank of the river, where the surface is more level than on the opposite side, although the right bank is steeper than the other. The present ruins prove the magnitude and importance of the ancient city; and the modern name leads to the belief that it was the ancient Gerasa, one of the principal towns of the Decapolis, although this position does not at all agree with that given to Gerasa from the ancient authorities by D'Anville, who places it to the north-east of the lake of Tiberias, forty miles to the north-westward of this place. The ruins are nearly an hour and a quarter in circumference, following insulated fragments of the walls, which were upwards of eight feet in thickness, and built of square hewn stones of middling size; I could not judge of their original heighth, as the upper parts were every where demolished.

I shall now enumerate the principal curiosities of Djerash, agreeably to the annexed plan, which may give a general idea of the whole; for its accuracy in regard to distances I do not mean to vouch, as I had, at most, only four hours to make my survey, and it was with great difficulty that I could persuade my three companions to wait so long for me. None of them would accompany me through the ruins, on account of their fear of the Bedouins, who are in the habit of visiting this Wady, they therefore concealed themselves beneath the trees that overshade the river. The first object that strikes the attention in coming from Souf, after passing the town-wall, is a temple (a). Its main body consists of an oblong square, the interior of which is about twenty-five paces in length, and eighteen in breadth. A double row, of six columns in each row, adorned the front of the temple; of the first row five columns are yet standing, of the second, four; and on each side of the temple there remains one column belonging to the single row of pillars that surrounded the temple on every side except the front. Of these eleven columns nine are entire, and two are without capitals. Their style of architecture is much superior to that of the great colonnade hereafter to be mentioned, and seems to belong to the best period of the Corinthian order, their capitals being beautifully ornamented with the acanthus leaves. The shafts are composed of five or six pieces, and are seven spans and a half in diameter, and thirty-five to forty feet in heighth. I was unable to ascertain the number of columns in the flanks of the peristyle. The temple stands upon an artificial terrace elevated five or six feet above the ground. The interior of the temple is choaked with the ruins of the roof; a part of the front wall of the cella has fallen down; but the three other sides are entire. The walls are wthout ornament; on the interior of each of the two side walls, and about mid-way from the floor, are six niches, of an oblong shape, and quite plain: in the back wall, opposite to the door, is a vaulted recess, with a small dark chamber on each side. The upper part of a niche is visible on the exterior of the remains of the front wall, with some trifling but elegantly sculptured ornaments. This ruin stands within a peribolus or large area surrounded by a double row of columns. The whole edifice seems to have been superior in taste and magnificence to every public building of this kind in Syria, the temple of the Sun at Palmyra excepted. On the two sides marked (x) of the colonnade of the peribolus many bases and broken shafts of the inner row of columns are yet standing; on the two other sides there are but few; these columns are three spans and a half in diameter. On the long side (x) forty columns may be traced to have stood, at only three paces distant from each other; on the opposite long side one perfect column is yet standing; on the short side (x) are three in the outer row without their capitals. The corner columns of this peribolus were double, and in the shape of a heart, as in the annexed figure. Of the outer row of the peribolus very little remains; indeed it may be doubted whether any outer row ever existed opposite to the back of the temple, where the ground is rocky and uneven. The number of columns which originally adorned the temple and its area was not less than two hundred or two hundred and fifty.

Proceeding westwards from the above described ruin, through the remains of private habitations, at about two hundred yards distant from it are the remains of a small temple (b), with three Corinthian pillars still standing. A street, still paved in some places, leads from thence south-westwards, to a spot where several small broken columns are lying. Turning from thence to the south-east, I entered a street (c) adorned with a colonnade on either side; about thirty broken shafts are yet standing, and two entire columns, but without their capitals. On the other side of the street, opposite to them, are five columns, with their capitals and entablatures. These columns are rather small, without pedestals, of different sizes, the highest being about fifteen feet, and in a bad taste.

Originally there must have been about fifty pillars in this street; a little farther on to the south-east this street crosses the principal street of the town; and where the two streets meet, are four large cubical masses of stone (d), each occupying one of the angles of the intersection, similar to those which I saw at Shohba, and intended, perhaps, to imitate the beautiful pedestals in the middle of the great portico at Palmyra. These cubes are about seven feet high, and about eighteen spans broad; on each side of them is a small niche; three are entire, and the fourth is in ruins. They may have served as pedestals for statues, or, like those at Palmyra, may have supported a small dome upon columns, under which stood a statue. I endeavoured to examine the tops of the cubes, but they are all thickly overgrown with shrubs, which it was not in my power to clear away. There were no traces whatever of statues having stood upon those which I saw at Shohba.

Following the great street, marked (e), south-westwards, I came again to the remains of columns on both sides: these were much larger than the former, and the street, of which some parts of the pavement yet remain, was much broader than that marked (c). On the right hand side of the street stand seventeen Corinthian columns, sixteen of which are united by their entablature; they vary in size, and do not correspond in height either with those opposite to them or with those in the same line; a circumstance which, added to the style of the capitals, seems to prove that

the long street is a patch-work, built at different periods, and of less ancient construction than the temple. Some of the columns are as high as
thirty feet, others twenty-five; the shortest I estimated at twenty feet.
Their entablatures are slightly ornamented with sculptured bas-reliefs.
Where a high column stands near a shorter one the architrave over the
latter reposes upon a projecting bracket worked into the shaft of the
higher one. Next comes, following the street in the same S.W. direction,
on the right, one insulated column; and three large columns with their entablature, joined to four shorter ones, in the way just described; then two
columns, and five, and two, all with their entablatures; making, in the
whole, on the right side of the street, counting from the cubes, thirty-four
columns, yet standing. On the left, opposite the three large ones joined to
the four smaller, are five columns of middling size, with their entablatures, and a single large one; but the greater number of the columns on
this side have fallen, and are lying on the ground. In some places behind
the colonnade on the right, are low apartments, some of which are
vaulted, and appear to have been shops. They are similar to those which I
saw in the long street at Soueida, in the mountain of the Druses.

The long street just described terminates in a large open space (f)
enclosed by a magnificent semicircle of columns in a single row; fifty-
seven columns are yet standing; originally there may have been about
eighty. To the right, on entering the forum, are four, and then twenty- one,
united by their entablatures. To the left, five, seven, and twenty, also with
entablatures; the latter twenty are taller than the others, the lower ground
on which they stand having required an increased height of column in
order to place the whole entablature of the semicircle on the same level.
The pillars near the entrance are about fifteen feet in height, and one foot
and a half in diameter: they are all of the Ionic order, and thus they differ
from all the other columns remaining in the city. The radius of the semicircle, in following the direction of the long street, was one hundred and
five paces.

At the end of the semicircle, opposite to the long street, are several basins, which seem to have been reservoirs of water, and remains of
an aqueduct are still visible, which probably supplied them. To the right
and left are some low arched chambers. From this spot the ground rises,
and on mounting a low but steep hill before me, I found on its top the remains of a beautiful temple (g), commanding a view over the greater part
of the town. The front of the temple does not stand directly opposite to the
long street and the forum, but declines somewhat to the northward. Like
the temple first described, it was adorned with a Corinthian peristyle, of

which one column only remains, at the south angle. In front was a double row of columns, with eight, as I conjecture, in each row. They seem to have been thrown down by an earthquake, and many of them are now lying on the declivity of the hill, in the same order in which they originally stood. They are six spans and a half in diameter, and their capitals appeared to me of a still finer execution than those of the great temple. I am unable to judge of the number of columns on the long sides of the peristyle: their broken shafts lie about in immense heaps. On every side of the temple except the front, there appears to have been a large ditch round the temple. Of the cella the walls only remain, the roof, entrance, and back wall having fallen down. The interior of the cella is thirty paces in length, and twenty-four in breadth; the walls within are in a better state than those of the temple (a), which are much impaired. On the outside of each of the two long walls, was a row of six niches, similar to those within the temple (a).

On entering the temple by the front door, I found on the right a side door, leading towards a large theatre (h), on the side of the hill, and at about sixty paces distant from the temple. It fronts the town, so that the spectators seated upon the highest row of benches, enjoyed the prospect of all its principal buildings and quarters. There are twenty- eight rows of seats, upwards of two feet in breadth: between the sixteenth and seventeenth rows, reckoning from the top, a tier of eight boxes or small apartments intervenes, each separated from the other by a thick wall. The uppermost row of benches is about one hundred and twenty paces in circuit. In three different places are small narrow staircases opening into the rows, to facilitate the ingress or egress of the spectators. In front, the theatre is closed by a proscenium or wall, about forty paces in length, embellished within by five richly decorated niches, connected with each other by a line of middling sized columns; of which two remain with their entablatures, and six without their capitals. Within these was another parallel range of columns, of which five are yet standing, with their entablatures. The entrance to the theatre, was by steps between the two ends of the proscenium and the two extremities of the semicircle. Near the proscenium the steps on both sides are ruined, but in the other parts they are perfect. The town wall runs very near the back of the theatre.

On this side of the town there are no other ruins of any consequence, excepting the south-west gate, which is about five minutes walk from the semicircle of columns: it is a fine arch, and, apparently, in perfect preservation, with a smaller one on each side adorned with several pilasters. I did not examine it closely; meaning to return to it in taking a review of what I had already seen, but my guides were so tired with wait-ing, that they positively refused to expose their persons longer to danger, and walked off, leaving me the alternative of remaining alone in this desolate spot, or of abandoning the hope of correcting my notes by a sec-ond examination of the ruins.

Returning from the theatre, through the long street, towards the four cubic pedestals, I continued from thence in a straight line along the main street (l), the pavement of which is preserved in several places. On the right hand, were first seven columns, having their entablatures; and farther on, to the left, seven others, also with their entablatures; then, on the right, three large columns without entablatures, but with pedestals, which none of those already mentioned have; opposite to the latter, on the left hand side of the street, are two insulated columns. The three large columns are equal in size to those of the peristyle of the temple (a); they stand in the same line with the colonnade of the street, and belonged to a small building (m), of the body of which nothing remains except the cir-cular back wall, containing several niches, almost in complete ruins.

There is another stone with an inscription upon it; but I could make nothing of it. The street is here choaked up with fragments of col-umns. Close to the three columns stands a single one, and at a short distance further, to the left, is a large gateway (n), leading up to the tem-ple (a), which is situated on considerably higher ground, and is not visible from the street. On either side of the gateway are niches; and a wall, built of middling sized square stones, which runs for some distance, parallel with the street.

Continuing along the main street, I came at (q), to a single col-umn, and then to two with entablatures, on the right; opposite to them, on the left, are three single columns. Beyond the latter, for one hundred paces, all the columns have fallen; I then came to an open rotunda (r), with four entrances; around the inside of its wall are projecting pedestals for statues; the entraces on the right and left, conduct into a street running at right angles to the main street. I followed this cross street to my left, and found on the right hand side of it three short Ionic pillars with their entablatures, close to the rotunda. Proceeding in the same direction I soon reached a quadrangle (s) of fine large Corinthian columns, the handsom-est in the town, next to those of the temple. To the right stand four with their entablatures, and one single; formerly they were six in number, the fifth is the deficient one: the first and sixth are heart-shaped, like those in the area of the temple (a.) They are composed of more than a dozen frusta, and what is remarkable in a place where stone is so abundant, each frustum consists of two pieces; opposite to the two first columns of the row just described are two columns with their entablatures.

This colonnade stands in front of a theatre (t), to which it evidently formed an appendage. This theatre is not calculated to hold so many spectators as the one already described though its area is considerably larger, being from forty-five to fifty paces in diameter. It has sixteen rows of benches, with a tier of six boxes intervening between the tenth and eleventh rows, reckoning from the top. Between every two boxes is a niche, forming a very elegant ornament. This theatre was evidently destined for purposes different from the other, probably for combats of wild beasts, &c.; The area below the benches is more extensive, and there is a suite of dark arched chambers under the lowest row of seats, opening into the area near the chief entrance of the theatre, which is from the southeast, in the direction by which I entered the colonnade in front of the theatre. There seems formerly to have been a wall across the diameter of the semi-circle, and between this wall and the colonnade there is on both sides a short wall, with a large niche or apartment in it; the colonnade stands upon lower ground than the theatre. Having returned from hence to the rotunda in the long street, I followed it along the colonnade (v) and found the greater number of the columns to have Ionic capitals. On the right side are only two small columns, with their entablatures; to the left, are eight, two, three, two, four, and again three, each set with their entablatures; close to the ruined town-gate (w), near the bank of the river, is a single column.

I shall now describe the ancient buildings, which I observed on the south-west side of the long street. The street which leads from the theatre across the rotunda (r) is prolonged from thence towards the side of the river: it was lined with columns, of which two only, with their entablatures, remain, and it terminates at a vast edifice (u), situated over the river, and extending along its banks forty or fifty paces; it is divided into many apartments, the greater part of which have arched roofs; some of them are very lofty.

I now returned towards the gateway (n), and found, opposite to it, and to the great temple (a), a second cross street running towards the river; it had originally a colonnade, but none of the columns are now standing; it terminates, at about thirty paces from the main street, in a gate, through which I entered into a long quadrangle of columns, where, on the right hand, four, and then three columns, with their entablatures, are still standing. At the end of this place, are the remains of a circular building fronting a bridge (p) across the river: this bridge is of steep ascent, owing to the northern banks being considerably higher than the southern, and it is no longer passable.

Having returned to the four cubical pedestals (d), I followed to the left the continuation of the street (c), by which I had first approached those pedestals, and which having crossed the main street at the pedestals, leads south-westward to the river, where it terminated at a broad flight of steps, leading down to the bridge (k); of the colonnade of this street (i), some broken shafts only are standing. The bridge is fourteen feet wide, with a high centre arch and two lower ones; it is built with great solidity, and its pavement is exactly of the same construction as that which I observed in the streets of Shohba; [See page 70.] its centre is broken down. An aqueduct is traced from the side of the building (u), passing near the two bridges, towards the southern gate of the town. Such weremy observations of the ruins on the right bank of the Wady.

On the left bank little else remains than heaps of ruins of private habitations, and numerous fragments of columns. I must confess, however, that I did not examine the part of the town towards the south gate; but I have reason to believe, from the view which I had of it while on the temple hill, that nothing of consequence, either as to buildings or columns, is there to be met with. The only buildings which I observed to the left of the river are near to it, upon a narrow plain which stretches along its banks. Nearly opposite to the temple (m), are the remains of a building (y) similar in construction to that marked (u), on the right bank. I supposed it to be a bath; a stream of water descends from a spring in the mountain, and after flowing through this division of the town, passes this building, and empties itself into the river. The arched rooms of the building (y) are loftier than those in (u). Near the former stand four columns; two insulated, and two with entablatures; also two broken shafts, the only fluted ones that I saw in the city. On the left bank of the river, nearly opposite to the town-gate (w), is a ruined building (x), which appears to have been a small temple; a single column is standing amidst a heap of broken ones.

Between this spot and the building (y) are the remains of an aqueduct.

Besides the one hundred and ninety columns, or thereabouts, which I have enumerated in the above description, there are upwards of one hundred half columns also standing. I did not see any marks of the frusta of the columns having been joined by iron hooks, as at Palmyra. Of the private habitations of the city there is none in a state of preservation, but the whole of the area within the walls is covered with their ruins.

The stone with which Djerash is built is calcareous, of considerable hardness, and the same as the rock of the neighbouring mountains; I did not observe any other stone to have been employed, and it is matter of surprise that no granite columns should be found here, as they abound in Syrian cities of much less note and magnificence than Djerash.

It had been my intention to proceed from Djerash to the village of Djezaze, in my way to the castle of Szalt in the mountains of Belka, from whence I hoped to be able to visit Amman. After many fruitless enquiries for a guide, a man of Souf at last offered to conduct me to Szalt, and he had accompanied us as far as Djerash; but when, after having surveyed the ruins, I rejoined my companions, he had changed his mind, and insisted on returning immediately to Souf; this was occasioned by his fear of the Arabs Beni Szakher, who had for sometime past been at war with the Arabs of Djebel Belka and the government of Damascus, and who were now extending their plundering incursions all over the mountain. The name of the Beni Szakher is generally dreaded in these parts; and the greater or less facility with which the traveller can visit them, depends entirely upon the good or bad terms existing between those Arabs and the Pasha; if they are friends, one of the tribe may easily be found to serve as a guide; but when they are enemies, the traveller is exposed to the danger of being stripped; and, if the animosity of the two parties is very great, of even being murdered. The Mutsellim of Damascus had given me letters to the chief of the Arabs El Belka, and to the commander of the Pasha's cavalry, who had been sent to assist them against the Beni Szakher. The allies were encamped in the neighbourhood of Kalaat el Zerka, while the Beni Szakher had collected their forces at Amman itself, a place still famous for the abundance of its waters. Under these circumstances, I determined to proceed first to Szalt, hoping that I might from thence attain Amman more easily, as the inhabitants of Szalt, who are always more or less rebellious towards the government of Damascus, are generally on friendly terms with the Bedouins. The fears of my guide, however, prevented me from executing this plan, and I was most reluctantly obliged to return to Souf, for it would have been madness to proceed alone.

We returned to Souf, not by the road over the mountain, but in following the course of the rivulet in the valley El Deir, which we reascended up to the village: we found the greater part of the narrow plain in the valley sown with wheat and barley by the people of Souf. Half an hour from the town, in the Wady, are the remains of a large reservoir for water, with some ruined buildings near it. This is a most romantic spot; large oak and walnut trees overshade the stream, which higher up flows over a rocky bed; nearer the village are some olive plantations in the Wady. We reached Souf in two hours from Djerash. I enquired in vain for a guide to Szalt; the return of the man who had engaged to conduct me made the others equally cautious, and nobody would accept of the fifteen piastres which I offered. I thought in unnecessary, therefore, to stop any longer at Souf, and left it the same evening, in order to visit Djebel Adjeloun. Our road lay W.N.W. up a mountain, through a thick forest of oak trees. In three quarters of an hour from Souf we reached the summit of the mountain, which forms the frontier between the district of Moerad and the Djebel Adjeloun. This is the thickest forest I had yet seen in Syria, where the term forest (or) is often applied to places in which the trees grow at twenty paces from each other. In an hour and a half we came to the village Ain Djenne, in a fertile valley called Wady Djenne, at the extremity of which several springs issue from under the rock.

May 3d.--There are several christian families at Ain Djenne. In the neighbouring mountain are numerous caverns; and distant half an hour, is the ruined village of Mar Elias. When enquiring for ruins, which might answer to those of Capitolias, I had been referred to this place, no person in these mountains having knowledge of any other ruins. An olive plantation furnishes the principal means of subsistence to the eighty families who inhabit the village of Ain Djenne.

We set out early in the morning, and descended the valley towards Adjeloun, which has given its name to the district: it is built in a narrow passage on both sides of the rivulet of Djenne, and contains nothing remarkable except a fine ancient mosque. I left my horse here, and took a man of the village to accompany me to the castle of Rabbad, which stands on the top of a mountain three quarters of an hour distant from Adjeloun. To the left of the road, at a short distance, is the village Kefrandjy. From Ain Djenne Kalaat el Rabbad bears W. by N.; it is the residence of the chief of the district of Adjeloun. The house of Barekat, in whom this authority has for many years resided, had lately been quarrelling about it among themselves; the chief, Youssef el Barekat, had been besieged for several months in the castle; he was now gone to the Aga of Tabaria, to engage him in his interests; and his family were left in the castle with strict orders not to let any unknown persons enter it, and to keep the gate secured. I had letters of recommendation to Youssef from the Mutsellim of Damascus; when I arrived at the castle-gate, all the inhabitants assembled upon the wall, to enquire who I was, and what I wanted. I explained to them the nature of my visit, and shewed them the Mutsellim's letter, upon which they opened the iron gate, but continued to entertain great suspicions of me until a man who could read having been sent for, my letter was read aloud; all the family then vied in civilities towards me, especially when I told them that I intended to proceed to Tabaria.

Kalaat Er-Rabbad is very strong, and, as appears from several Arabic inscriptions, was built by Sultan Szelah-eddyn; its date is, therefore, that of the Crusades, and the same as that of many castles in other parts of Syria, which owe their origin to the vigilance, and prudence of that monarch; I saw nothing particularly worth notice in it; its thick walls, arched passages, and small bastions, are common to all the castles of the middle ages. It has several wells; but on the outside, it is distinguished by the deep and broad ditch which surrounds it, and which has been excavated at immense labour in the rock itself upon which the castle stands. Rabbad is two hours distant from the Ghor, or valley of the river Jordan, over which, as well as the neighbouring mountains, it commands a fine prospect. It is now inhabited by about forty persons, of the great family of El Barekat.

I returned from Kalaat Rabbad to Adjeloun, where I rejoined my companions, and after mid-day set out for El Hossn, the principal village in the district of Beni Obeid. Our road lay up the mountain, in the narrow Wady Teis. At half an hour from Adjeloun we passed the spring called Ain Teis. At two hours the district of Djebel Adjeloun terminates, and that of Obeid begins. The country is for the greater part woody, and here the inhabitants collect considerable quantities of galls. Our road lay N.E.; the summits of the mountain bear the name El Meseidjed. At three hours and a half is a Birket of rain-water, from whence the road descends over barren hills towards El Hossn, distant five hours and a quarter from Adjeloun.

El Hossn is the principal village of the district called Beni Obeid; it stands on the declivity of the mountain, and is inhabited by upwards of one hundred families, of which about twenty-five are Greek Christians, under the jurisdiction of the patriarch of Jerusalem. I saw nothing remarkable here but a number of wells cut out of the rock. I happened to alight at the same house where M. Seetzen had been detained for eleven days, by bad weather; his hospitable old landlord, Abdullah el Ghanem, made many enquiries after him.

May 4th.--I found very bad company at El Hossn. It is usual for the Pasha of Damascus to send annually one of the principal officers of his government to visit the southern provinces of the Pashalik, to exact the arrears of the Miri, and to levy new extortions. The Aga of Tabaria, who was invested this year with the office, had just arrived in the village with a suite of one hundred and fifty horsemen, whom he had quartered upon the peasants; my landlord had seven men and fifteen horses for his share, and although he killed a sheep, and boiled about twenty pounds of rice, for supper, yet the two officers of the party in his house were continually asking for more, spoiled all his furniture, and, in fact, acted worse than an enemy would have done. It is to avoid vexations of this kind that the peasants abandon the villages most exposed to such visits.

We left Hossn late in the morning and proceeded to Erbad, one hour and a quarter N.N.E. from the former. Our road lay over the plain. Erbad is the chief place in the district of that name, likewise called the district of Beni Djohma, or of Bottein, from the Sheikh's being of the family of Bottein. The names of Beni Obeid, and Beni Djohma, are probably derived from Arab tribes which anciently settled here; but nobody could tell me the origin of these appellations. The inhabitants do not pretend to be descendants of those tribes, but say that these were their dwelling places from time immemorial.

The castle of Erbad stands upon a low hill, at the foot of which lies the village. The calcareous rock which extends through Zoueit, Moerad, Adjeloun, and Beni Obeid, begins here to give way to the black Haouran stone, with which all the houses of Erbad are built, as well as the miserable modern walls of the castle. A large ancient well built reservoir is the only curiosity of this place; around it lay several handsome sarcophagi, of the same kind of rock, with some sculptured bas- reliefs upon them. Part of the suite of the Aga of Tabaria, consisting of Moggrebyns, was quartered at Erbad. From hence I wished to visit the ruins of Beit el Ras, which are upon a hill at about one hour and a half distant. I was told that the ruins were of large extent, that there were no columns standing, but that large ones were lying upon the ground. From Beit el Ras I intended again to cross the mountain in order to see the ruins of Om Keis, and from thence to visit the Djolan.

We were shewn the road from Erbad, but went astray, and did not reach Beit el Ras. One hour and a half N. by W. of Erbad we passed the village Merou; from thence we travelled W.N.W. to El Hereimy, two hours from Erbad; and from El Hereimy N.N.W. to Hebras, three hours from Erbad. Hebras is the principal village in the district of Kefarat, and one of the largest in these countries. It is inhabited by many Greek Christian families. One hour and a half to the N.E. of it are the ruins of Abil, the ancient Abila, one of the towns of the Decapolis; neither buildings nor columns remain standing; but I was told that there are fragments of columns of a very large size.

May 5th.--I took a guide from hence to shew me to Om Keis, which, I was told, was inhabited by several families. I there intended to pass the night, and to proceed the next day to Feik, a village on the E. side of the lake of Tabaria In half an hour from Hebras we passed the spring Ain el Terab, in a Wady, which farther to the north-westward joins the Wady Szamma, and still lower down unites with the Wady Sheriat el Mandhour. At one hour and a quarter to our right was the village Obder, on the banks of Wady Szamma, which runs in a deep ravine, and half an hour farther north-west, the village Szamma. The inhabitants of the above villages cultivate gardens of fruit trees and all kinds of vegetables on the side of the rivulet. The villages belong to the district of Kefarat. To the left of our route extends a country full of Wadys, called the district of Serou, to the southward of which begins that of Wostye. At one hour and a half to our left, distant half an hour, we saw, in the Serou, the village Faour. Between Hebras and Szamma begins the Wady el Arab, which continued to the left parallel with our route; it is a fertile valley, in which the Arabs Kelab and others cultivate a few fields. There are several mills on the water-side. Our route lay W. by N. and W.N.W. across the Kefarat, which is uneven ground, rising towards the west, and is intersected by many Wadys. At the end of three hours and a quarter we reached Om Keis.

Om Keis is the last village to the west, in the district of Kefarat; it is situated near the crest of the chain of mountains, which bound the valley of the lake of Tabaria and Jordan on the east. The S. end of the lake bears N.W. To the N. of it, one hour, is the deep Wady called Sheriat el Mandhour, which is, beyond a doubt, the Hieromax of the Greeks and Jarmouk of the Israelites.

To the south, at the same distance, flows the Wady el Arab, which joins the Sheriat in the valley of El Ghor , not far from the junction of the latter with the Jordan. I am doubtful to what ancient city the ruins of Om Keis are to be ascribed. [It was probably Gamala, which Josephus describes as standing upon a mountain bordered by precipices. Gadara appears from the authorities of Pliny and Jerom to have been at the warm baths, mentioned below, on the north side of the Sheriat el Mandhour; Gadara Hieromiace praefluente. Plin. Nat. Hist. l.i.c.18. Gadara, urbs trans Jordanem contra Scythopolin et Tiberiadem, ad orientalem plagam, sita in monte, ad cujns radices aquae calidae erumpunt, balneis super aedificatis,--Hieron. in Topicis]

At Om Keis the remains of antiquity are very mutilated. The ancient town was situated round a hill, which is the highest point in the neighbourhood. To the east of the hill are a great number of caverns in the calcareous rock, some of which have been enlarged and rendered habitable. Others have been used as sepulchral caves. Great numbers of sarcophagi are lying about in this direction: they are all of black stone, which must have been transported from the banks of the river below: the dimensions of the largest are nine spans in length by three in breadth; they are ornamented with bas-reliefs of genii, festoons, wreaths of flowers, and some with busts, but very few of them are of elegant wor [k]manship. I counted upwards of seventy on the declivity of the hill. On the summit of the hill are heaps of wrought stones, but no remains of any important building: on its west and north sides are the remains of two large theatres, built entirely of black stone. That on the W. side is in better preservation than the other, although more ruined than the theatres at Djerash. The walls and the greater part of the seats yet remain; a tier of boxes intervenes between the rows of seats, as at Djerash, and there are deep vaulted apartments beneath the seats. There are no remains of columns in front of either theatre. The theatre on the north side of the hill, which is in a very dilapidated state, is remarkable for its great depth, caused by its being built on a part of the steepest declivity of the hill; its uppermost row of seats is at least forty feet higher than the lowest; the area below the seats is comparatively very small. From these two theatres the principal part of the town appears to have extended westwards, over an even piece of ground at the foot of the hill; its length from the hill was at least half an hour. Nothing is at present standing; but there are immense heaps of cut stones, columns, &c. dispersed over the plain. A long street, running westward, of which the ancient pavement still exists in most parts, seems to have been the principal street of the town. On both sides there are vast quantities of shafts of columns. At a spot where a heap of large Corinthian pillars lay, a temple appears to have stood. I here saw the base of a large column of gray granite. The town terminates in a narrow point, where a large solid building with many columns seems to have stood.

With the exception of the theatres, the buildings of the city were all constructed of the calcareous stone which constitutes the rock of every part of the country which I saw between Wady Zerka and Wady Sheriat. In Djebel Adjeloun, Moerad, and Beni Obeid, none of the basalt or black stone is met with; but in some parts of El Kefarat, in our way from Hebras to Om Keis, I saw alternate layers of calcareous and basaltic rock, with thin strata of flint. The habitations of Om Keis are, for the greater part, caverns. There is no water but what is collected in reservoirs during rains; these were quite dried up, which was the occasion, perhaps, of the place having been abandoned, for we found not a single inhabitant.

My guide being ignorant of the road to Feik, wished to return to Hebras; and I was hesitating what to do, when we were met by some peasants of Remtha, in the Haouran, who were in their way to the Ghor, to purchase new barley, of which grain the harvest had already begun in the hot climate of that valley. I joined their little caravan. We continued, for about half an hour from Om Keis, upon the high plain, and then descended the mountains, the western declivity of which is entirely basaltic. At the end of two hours from Om Keis, we reached the banks of the Sheriat el Mandhour, or Sheriat el Menadhere which we passed at a ford. This river takes the additional name of the Arabs who live upon its banks, to distinguish it from the Sheriat el Kebir (Great Sheriat), by which the Jordan is known. The Sheriat el Menadhere is formed by the united streams of the Nahr Rokad, which flows from near Ain Shakhab, through the eastern parts of Djolan; of the Hereir, whose source is in the swampy ground near Tel Dilly, on the Hadj route, between Shemskein and El Szannamein: of the Budje, which comes from Mezareib, and after its junction with the Hereir, is called Aweired, and of the Wady Hamy Sakkar, besides several other smaller Wadys. The name of Sheriat, is first applied to the united streams near Szamme. From thence it flows in a deep bed of tufwacke; and its banks are cultivated by the Arabs Menadhere (sing. Mandhour), who live under tents, and remove from place to place, but without quitting the banks of the river. They sow wheat and barley, and cultivate pomegranates, lemons, grapes, and many kinds of fruit and vegetables, which they sell in the villages of the Haouran and Djolan. Further to the west the Wady becomes so narrow as to leave no space between the edge of the stream, and the precipices on both sides. It issues from the mountain not far from the south end of the lake of Tabaria, and about one hour lower down is joined by the Wady el Arab; it then empties itself into the Jordan, called Sheriat el Kebir, at two hours distant from the lake; D'Anville is therefore wrong in making it flow into the lake itself. The river is full of fish, and in the Wady its course is very rapid. The shrub called by the Arabs Defle, grows on its banks; it has a red flower, and according to the Arabs is poisonous to cattle. The breadth of the stream, where it issues from the mountains, is about thirty-five paces, its depth (in the month of May) between four and five feet.

We had now entered the valley of the Ghor, which may be compared to the valley of the Bekaa, between the Libanus and Anti- Libanus, and the valley El Ghab of the Orontes. The mountains which enclose it are not to be compared in magnitude with those of the Bekaa; but the abundance of its waters renders its aspect more pleasing to the eye, and may make its soil more productive. It is one of the lowest levels in Syria;

lower than the Haouran and Djolan, by nearly the whole height of the eastern mountains; its temperature is hotter than I had experienced in any other part of Syria: the rocky mountains concentrating the heat, and preventing the air from being cooled by the westerly winds in summer. In consequence of this higher degree of heat, the productions of the Ghor ripen long before those of the Haouran. The barley harvest, which does not begin in the upper plain till fifteen days later we here found nearly finished. The Haouran, on the other hand, was every where covered with the richest verdure of wild herbage, while every plant in the Ghor was already dried up, and the whole country appeared as if in the midst of summer. Volney has justly remarked that there are few countries where the changes from one climate to another are so sudden as in Syria; and I was never more convinced of it than in this valley. To the north was the Djebel El Sheikh, covered with snow; to the east the fertile plainsof Djolan clothed in the blossoms of spring; while to the south, the withered vegetation of the Ghor seemed the effect of a tropical sun. The breadth of the valley is about an hour and a half, or two hours.

From the ford over the Sheriat we proceeded across the plain in a N.W. direction; it was covered with low shrubs and a tree bearing a fruit like a small apple, very agreeable to the taste; Zaarour is the name given to it by the inhabitants of Mount Libanus; those of Damascus call it Zaaboub; and the Arabs have also another name for it, which I forget. In an hour and upwards, from the ford, we reached the village Szammagh, situated on the most southern extremity of the lake of Tabaria; it contains thirty or forty poor mud houses, and a few built with black stone. The Jordan issues out of the lake about a quarter of an hour to the westward of the village, where the lake ends in a straight line, extending for about forty minutes in a direction nearly east and west. From hence the highest point of Djebel el Sheikh bears N.N.W.; the town of Szaffad N. by E. Between the lake and the first bridge over the Jordan, called Djissr el Medjami, at about two hours and a half from hence, are two fordable passages across the river.

Excepting about one hundred Fedhans around Szammagh, no part of the valley is cultivated in this neighbourhood. Somewhat lower down begin the corn fields of the Arabs el Ghor, who are the principal inhabitants of the valley: those living near Szammagh are the Arabs el Sekhour, and the Beshaatoue. The only villages met with from hence as far as Beysan (the ancient Scythopolis), are to the left of the Jordan, Maad, at the foot of Djebel Wostye, and El Erbayn. From Szammagh to Beysan the valley is called Ghor Tabaria. I swam to a considerable distance in the lake, without seeing a single fish; I was told, however, that there were privileged fishermen at Tabaria, who monopolize the entire fishery. The beach on this side is a fine gravel of quartz, flint, and tufwacke. There is no shallow water, the lake being of considerable depth close in shore. The only species of shell which I saw on the beach was of the smallest kind, white and about an inch and a half long. There are no kinds of rushes or reeds on the shores in this neighbourhood.

May 6th.--The quantities of mosquitos and other vermin which always by preference attack the stranger accustomed to more northern climates, made me pass a most uncomfortable night at Szammagh. We departed early in the morning, in order to visit the hot wells at the foot of the mountain of Om Keis, the situation of which had been pointed out to me on the preceding day. Returning towards the place where the Sheriat issues from the Wady, we followed up the river from thence and in one hour and three quarters from Szammagh, we reached the first hot-well. The river flows in a deep bed, being confined in some places on both sides by precipices of upwards of one hundred feet in height, whose black rocks present a most striking contrast with the verdure on their summits. For several hundred yards before we arrived at the hot-well, I perceived a strong sulphureous smell in the air. The spring is situated in a very narrow plain, in the valley, between the river and the northern cliffs, which we descended. The plain had been covered with rich herbage, but it was now dried up; a great variety of shrubs and some old palm trees also grow here: the heat in the midst of the summer must be suffocating. The spring bubbles up from a basin about forty feet in circumference, and five feet in depth, which is enclosed by ruins of walls and buildings, and forms below a small rivulet which falls at a short distance into the river. The water is so hot, that I found it difficult to keep my hand in it; it deposits upon the stones over which it flows a thick yellow sulphureous crust, which the neighbouring Arabs collect, to rub their camels with, when diseased. Just above the basin, which has originally been paved, is an open arched building, with the broken shaft of a column still standing; and behind it are several others, also arched, which may have been apartments for the accommodation of strangers: the large stones forming these structures are much decayed, from the influence of the exhalations. This spring is called Hammet el Sheikh, and is the hottest of them all. At five minutes distance, ascending the Wady, is a second of the same kind, but considerably cooler; it issues out of a basin covered with weeds, and surrounded with reeds, and has some remains of ancient buildings about it; it is called Hammet Errih, and joins the waters from the first source. Following the course of the river, up the Wady, eight more hot springs are met with; I shall here mention their names, though I did not see them. 1. Hammet aand Ettowahein, near some mills; 2. Hammet beit Seraye; 3. Hammet Essowanye; 4. Hammet Dser Aryshe; 5. Hammet Zour Eddyk; 6. Hammet Erremlye; 7. Hammet Messaoud; 8. Hammet Om Selym; this last is distant from that of El Sheikh two hours and a half. These eight springs are on both sides of the Wady, and have remains of ancient buildings near them. I conceive that a naturalist would find it well worth his time to examine the productions of this Wady, hitherto almost unknown. In the month of April the Hammet el Sheikh is visited by great numbers both of sick and healthy people, from the neighbourhood of Nablous and Nazaret, who prefer it to the bath of Tabaria; they usually remain about a fortnight.

We returned from the Hamme by the same road we came; on reaching the plain of El Ghor we turned to our right up the mountain. We here met a wild boar of great size; these animals are very numerous in the Ghor, and my companions told me that the Arabs of the valley are unable to cultivate the common barley, called here Shayr Araby, on account of the eagerness with which the wild swine feed upon it, they are therefore obliged to grow a less esteemed sort, with six rows of grains, called Shayr Kheshaby, which the swine do not touch. At three quarters of an hour from the spot where we began to ascend, we came to a spring called Ain el Khan, near a Khan called El Akabe, where caravans sometimes alight; this being the great road from the Djolan and the northern parts of the Haouran to the Ghor. Akabe is a general term for a steep descent. In one hour we passed a spring called Ain el Akabe, more copious than the former. From thence we reached the summit of the mountain, one hour and a quarter distant from its foot, where the plain commences; and in one hour and three quarters more, entered the village of Feik, distant about four hours and a half from Szammagh, by the road we travelled.

One hour to the E. of Szammagh, on the shore of the lake, lies the village Kherbet Szammera, with some ancient buildings: it is the only inhabited village on the E. side of the lake, its site seems to correspond with that of the ancient Hippos. Farther north, near the shore, are the ruined places called Doeyrayan, and Telhoun. Three quarters of an hour to the N. of Khan el Akabe, near the summit of the mountain, lies, the half ruined, but still inhabited village of Kefer Hareb.

The country to the north of the Sheriat, in the direction of Feik, is, for a short distance, intersected by Wadys, a plain then commences, extending northwards towards the Djebel Heish el Kanneytra, and eastwards towards the Haouran.

Feik is a considerable village, inhabited by more than two hundred families. It is situated at the head of the Wady of the same name, on the ridge of a part of the mountain which incloses the E. shore of the lake of Tabaria, and it enjoys a fine view over the middle part of the lake. The rivulet of Feik has three sources, issuing from beneath a precipice, round the summit of which the village is built in the shape of a crescent. Having descended the hill for three quarters of an hour, a steep insulated hill is met with, having extensive ruins of buildings, walls, and columns on its top; they are called El Hossn, and are, perhaps, the remains of the ancient town of Regaba or Argob.

Feik, although situated in the plain of Djolan, does not actually belong to that district, but constitutes a territory of itself; it forms part of the government of Akka, and is, I believe, the only place belonging to that Pashalik on the E. side of the Jordan; it was separated from the Pashalik of Damascus by Djezzar Pasha. There being a constant passage through Feik from the Haouran to Tabaria and Akka, more than thirty houses in the town have open Menzels for the entertainment of strangers of every description, and supply their cattle, gratis. The landlords have an allowance from the government for their expenses, which is made by a deduction from the customary taxes; and if the Menzel is much frequented, as in the case of that of the Sheikh, no Miri at all is collected from the landlord, and the Pasha makes him also an yearly allowance in money, out of the Miri of the village. The establishment of these public Menzels, which are general over the whole country to the S. of Damascus, does great honour to the hospitable spirit of the Turks; but it is, in fact, the only expense that the government thinks itself obliged to incur for the benefit of the people of the country. A peasant can travel for a whole month without expending a para; but people of any distinction give a few paras on the morning of their departure to the waiter or watchman. If the traveller does not choose to alight at a public Menzel, he may go to any private house, where he will find a hospitable landlord, and as good a supper as the circumstances of his host can afford.

I observed upon the terraces of all the houses of Feik, a small apartment called Hersh, formed of branches of trees, covered with mats; to this cool abode the family retires during the mid-day heats of summer. There are a few remains of ancient buildings at Feik; amongst others, two small towers on the two extremities of the cliff. The village has large olive plantations.

May 7th.--Our way over the plain was in the direction N.E. by E. Beyond the fields of Feik, the district of Djolan begins, the southern limits of which are the Wady Hamy Sakker, and the Sheriat. Djolan appears to be the same name as the Greek Gaulanitis; but its present limits do not quite correspond with those of the ancient province, which was confined to a narrow strip of land along the lake, and the eastern shore of the Jordan. The territory of Feik must have formed part of Hippene; the mountain in front of it was mount Hippos, and the district of Argob appears to have been that part of the plain (making part of Djolan), which extends from Feik northwards for three or four hours, and which is enclosed on the east by the Djebel Heish, and on the west by the descent leading down to the banks of the lake.

Half an hour from Feik we passed, on our left, a heap of ruins called Radjam el Abhar. To the S.E. at about one hour distant, is the village Djeibein; to the left, at three quarters of an hour, is the ruined village El Aal, on the side of the Wady Semak, which descended from the Djebel Heish: there is a rivulet of spring-water in the Wady, which empties itself into the lake near the ruined city of Medjeifera, in this part the Wady is full of reeds, of which the people make mats. On the other side of the Wady, about half an hour distant from it, upon a Tel, is the ruined city called Kaszr Berdoweil (Castle of Baldwin). The plain here is wholly uncultivated, and is overgrown with a wild herb called Khob, which camels and cows feed upon. At one hour and three quarters is a Birket of rain water, called Nam, with a spring near it. At two hours and a quarter are the extensive ruins of a city, called Khastein, built with the black stone of the country, but preserving no remains of any considerable building. Two hours and three quarters, on our left, is Tel Zeky, to the left of which, about one hour and a half, is the southern extremity of the Djebel Heish, where stands a Tel called El Faras. The Djebel Heish is separated from the plain bya stony district, of one hour in breadth, where the Arabs of the country often take refuge from the extortions of the Pasha. In three hours we passed Wady Moakkar, flowing from the mountain into the Sheriat. Here the direction of our road was E.S.E. The Arab who accompanied me presented me with a fruit which grows wild in these parts, and is unknown in the northern parts of Syria, and even at Damascus; it is of the size of a small egg, of the colour of the Tomato or love-apple, of a sweet agreeable taste, and full of juice. It grows upon a shrub about six inches high, which I did not see, but was told that its roots were three or four feet in length, and presented the figure of a man in all its parts. The fruit is called by the Arabs Djerabouh.

At three hours and a quarter, at a short distance to our left, was the ruined village Om el Kebcur. In three hours and a half we passed Wady Seide; and at the end of three hours and three quarters reached the bridge of Wady Hamy Sakker We met all the way Arabs and peasants going to the Ghor to purchase barley.

The bridge of Hamy Sakker is situated near the commencement of the Wady , where it is of very little depth; lower down it has a rapid fall, and runs between precipices of perpendicular rocks of great height, until it joins the Sheriat, about two hours and a half from the bridge. The bridge is well built upon seven arches. At four hours we reached a spring called Ain Keir, and a little farther another called Ain Deker. The rocky district at the foot of Djebel Heish extends on this side as far as these springs. In five hours we passed Wady Aallan, a considerable torrent flowing towards the Sheriat, with a ruined bridge; and in five hours and a half Tseil,, an inhabited village. Here the plain begins to be cultivated. There are no villages excepting Djeibein to the south of the road by which we had travelled, as far as the banks of the Sheriat. The inhabitants of the country are Bedouins, several of whose encampments we passed. Tseil is one of the principal villages of Djolan, and contains about eighty or one hundred families, who live in the ancient buildings of the ruined town; there are three Birkets of rain water belonging to it. The only building of any size is a ruined mosque, which seems to have been a church. In coming from Feik the soil of the plain is black, or gray; at Tseil it begins to be of the same red colour as the Haouran earth.

After dinner we continued our route. In half an hour from Tseil we passed on our left Tel Djemoua. The greater part of the plain was covered with a fine crop of wheat and barley. During the years 1810 and 1811, the crops were very bad all over Syria; the rains of last winter, however, having been very abundant, the peasants are every where consoled with the hopes of a good harvest. It was expected that the Haouran and Djolan would yield twenty-five times the quantity of the seed sown, which is reckoned an excellent crop. Half an hour north of Tel Djemoua lies Tel Djabye, with a village. At one hour and three quarters from Tseil is the village Nowa, where we slept. This is the principal village in the Djolan, and was formerly a town of half an hour in circumference. Its situation corresponds with that in D'Anville's map of Neve. There are a number of ruined private dwellings, and the remains of some public edifices. A temple, of which one column with its entablature remains, has been converted into a mosque. At the S. end of the village is a small square solid building, probably a mausoleum; it has no other opening than the door. Beyond the precincts of the village, on the N. side, are the ruins of a large square building, of which the sculptured entrance only remains, with heaps of broken columns before it. The village has several springs, as well as cisterns. The Turks revere the tomb of a Santon buried here, called Mehy eddyn el Nowawy.

May 8th.--Our route lay N.E. At two hours from Nowa is the village Kasem, which forms the southern limits of the district of Djedour, and the northern frontier of Djolan; some people, however, reckon Djolan the limits of Nowa. One hour E.b.S. of Kasem stands the village Om el Mezabel; one hour and a half E.N.E. of Kasem. the great village Onhol. In two hours and a half from Nowa we passed, to the left, distant about half an hour, the Tel el Hara, with the village of the same name at its foot; this is the highest Tel in the plains of Haouran and Djolan. Three hours and a quarter is the village Semnein; and three hours and three quarters, the village Djedye. The plain was badly cultivated in these parts. From hence our road turned N.N.E. At five hours is Kefer Shams, with some ancient buildings; all these villages have large Birkets. At five hours and three quarters is Deir e Aades, a ruined village in a stony district, intersected by several Wadys. Six hours and a quarter, Tel Moerad; eight hours Tel Shak-hab, a village with a small castle, and copious springs; it lies about an hour and a half to the west of Soubbet Faraoun. The cattle of a large encampment of Naym wa spread over the whole plain near Shak-hab. At eight hours and three quarters, there was on our left a rocky country resembling the Ledja; it is called War Ezzaky, and has a ruined Khan called Ezzeiat; the millstones for the supply of Damascus are hewn in this War, which consists of the black Haouran stone. In ten hours we reached Khan Denoun; and in ten hours and three quarters, long after sun-set, the village El Kessoue.

May 9th.--We arrived early in the morning at Damascus.

POLITICAL DIVISIONS OF THE COUNTRY TO THE
SOUTHWARD OF DAMASCUS
WITH
REMARKS ON THE INHABITANTS OF THE HAOURAN.

Before I submit to the reader, a few general remarks upon the inhabitants of the Haouran, I shall briefly recapitulate the political divisions of the country which extends to the southward of Damascus, as far as Wady Zerka.

1. El Ghoutta. Under this name is comprehended the immediate neighhourhood of Damascus, limited on the north by Djebel Szalehie, on the west by the Djebel el Sheikh, on the south by Djebel Kessoue, and on the east by the plain El Merdj. It is under the immediate government of the Mutsellim of Damascus. All the gardens of Damascus are reckoned in the Ghoutta, which contains upwards of eighty villages, and is one of the most fertile districts in Syria.

2. Belad Haouran. To the south of Djebel Kessoue and Djebel Khiara begins the country of Haouran. It is bordered on the east by the rocky district El Ledja, and by the Djebel Haouran, both of which are sometimes comprised within the Haouran; and in this case the Djebel el Drouz, or mountain of the Druses, whose chief resides at Soueida, may be considered another subdivision of the Haouran. To the S.E. where Boszra and El Remtha are the farthest inhahited villages, the Haouran borders upon the desert. Its western limits are the chain of villages on the Hadj road, from Ghebarib as far south as Remtha. The greater part of its villages will he found enumerated in the two Journals.

POLITICAL DIVISIONS OF THE COUNTRY

The Haouran comprises therefore part of Trachonitis and Ituraea, the whole of Auranitis, and the northern districts of Batanaea. Edrei, now Draa, was situated in Batanaea.

3. Djedour. The flat country south of Djebel Kessoue, east of Djebel el Sheikh, and west of the Hadj road, as far as Kasem or Nowa, is called Djedour. It contains about twenty villages.

The following are the names of the inhabited villages of the country called Djedour; El Kenneya, Sheriat el Ghoufa, Sheriat el Tahna, Deir Maket,, Um el Mezabel, El Nakhal, El Szannamein, Teil Kefrein, Merkasem, Nawa, where are considerable ruins; Heitt, El Hara, Akrebbe eddjedour, Essbebhara, Djelein, Namr, Essalemie,, El Nebhanie, Deir el Ades, Deir el Bokht,, Kafershamy, Keitta, Semlein, Djedeie, Thereya, Um Ezzeijtoun.

The greater part of Ituraea appears to be comprised within the limits of Djedour. The governor of Djolan usually commands also in Djedour.

4. Djolan, which comprises the plain to the south of Djedour, and to the west of Haouran. Its southern frontier is the Nahr Aweired by which it is separated from the district of Erbad, and the Sheriat el Mandhour, which separates it from the district El Kefarat. On the west it is limited by the territory of Feik, and on the northwest by the southern extremity of Djebel Heish. Part of Batanaea, Argob, Hippene, and perhaps Gaulanitis, is comprised within this district. The maps of Syria are in general incorrect with regard to the mountains of Djolan. The mountain El Heish, which is the southern extremity of Djebel el Sheikh, terminates (as I have mentioned before) at Tel el Faras, which is about three hours and a half to the north of the Sheriat or Hieromax; and the mountains begin again at about the same distance to the south of the same river, in the district of Wostye; leaving an open country between them, which extends towards the west as far as Akabe Feik, and Akabe Om Keis, which are the steep descents forming the approaches to the lake of Tabaria, and to the Ghor of Tabaria from the east. The maps, on the contrary, make the Djebel Heish join the southern chain of Wostye, instead of leaving an open country of near eight hours between them. The principal villages of Djolan, beginning from the south, are the following: Aabedein, Moarrye, Shedjara, Beiterren, Sahhem, Seisoun, Kefr Essamer, Seiatein, Beit Akkar, Djomra, Sheikh Saad, near Tel Sheikh Saad, Ayoub, Deir Ellebou, Kefr Maszer, Adouan, Tel el Ashaara, Tseil, El Djabye, Esszefeire, Djernein, El Kebbash, Nowa. The Aga of Haouran is generally at the same time governor of Djolan.

5. El Kanneytra comprises the mountain El Heish, from the neighbourhood of Banias to its southern extremity. It is the Mount Hermon of the ancients. Its chief place is Kanneytra (perhaps the ancient Canatha), where the Aga el Kanneytra resides.

6. Belad Erbad, or Belad Beni Djohma, likewise called El Bottein, which name it derives from the family of Bottein, who are the principal men of the country. It is limited on the north by the Aweired, which separates it from the Djolan, on the east by the Hadj route, on the south by the territory of Beni Obeid, and on the west, by the rising ground and the many Wadys which compose the territory of El Kefarat. The greater part of Batanaea is comprised within its limits; and it is remarkable that the name of Bottein has some affinity with that of Batanaea. Its principal villages are: Erbad (the Sheikh's residence), El Bareha, Kefr Djayz, Tokbol, El Aaal (by some reckoned in Djolan), Kefr Youba, Djemha. The ruined villages and cities of Belad Erbad are as follows: Djerye, Zebde, Hanneine, Beit el Ras, Ain ed Djemel.

7. El Kefarat, a narrow strip of land, running along the south borders of the Wady Sheriat el Mandhour from the frontiers of Belad Erbad to Om Keis. Its principal village is Hebras.

8. Esserou. This district lies parallel to El Kefarat, and extends from Belad Erbad to the Ghor. It is watered by Wady el Arab. Its principal village is Fowar.

The Kefarat as well as the Serou are situated between the Sheriat and the mountains of Wostye. They may be called flat countries in comparison with Wostye and Adjeloun; and they appear still more so from a distance; but if examined near, they are found to be intersected by numerous deep valleys. There seems, however, a gradual ascent of the ground towards the west. The valleys are inhabited for the greater part by Bedouins.

9. Belad Beni Obeid is on the eastern declivity of the mountains of Adjeloun. It is bordered on the north by Erbad, on the west by the mountain Adjeloun, on the east and south by the district Ezzoueit. The southern parts of Batanaea are comprised within these limits. Its principal village is El Hossn, where the Sheikh resides. Its other villages are: Haoufa, Szammad, Natefa, El Mezar, Ham, Djehfye, Erreikh, Habdje, Edoun. In the mountain near the summit of Djebel Adjeloun, in that part of the forest which is called El Meseidjed, are the following ruined places: Nahra, Kefr Khal, Hattein, Aablein, Keferye, Kherbat, Esshaara, Aabbein, Sameta, Aabeda, Aafne, Deir Laouz.

11. El Koura Is separated from Adjeloun on the S.W. side by Wady Yabes, which empties itself into the Jordan, in the neighbourhood of Beysan. To the west and north-west it borders on Wostye, to the east on Belad Beni Obeid. It is a mountainous country which comprizes the northern parts of the ancient Galaaditis. Its principal villages are, Tobne, where resides the Sheikh or el Hakem, who exercises his influence likewise over the villages of Omba, Szammoua,, Deir Abou Seid, Hannein, Zemmal, Kefer Aabeid, Kefer Awan, Beit Edes, Khanzyre, Kefer Radjeb, Kefer Elma.

12. El Wostye. To the south of Serou, and east of the Ghor Beysan.

13. Djebel Adjeloun. On the north-east and east, it borders on Beni Obeid, on the south and south-east on the district of Moerad; on the west on the Ghor, and on the north on the Koura. It is throughout a mountainous country, and for the greater part woody. Part of the ancient Galaaditis is comprised within its limits. Its principal place is Kalaat Rab-

bad, where the Sheikh resides. It contains besides the following villages: Ain Djenne, Adjeloun, Ain Horra, Ardjan, Rasoun, Baoun, Ousera, Halawe, Khara, El Kherbe, Kefrendjy. The principal ruined places in this district are, Rostem, Seleim, Kefer Eddorra, Szoan, Deir Adjeloun.

14. Moerad, is limited on the north by Djebel Adjeloun, on the east by Ezzoueit, on the south by Wady Zerka, on the west by the Ghor. It forms part of Galaaditis, and is in every part mountainous. Its principal village, where the Sheikh lives, is Souf; its other villages are Borma, Ettekitte, at present abandoned; Debein, Djezaze, Hamthe. The summits of the mountain of Adjeloun, which mark the limits between Adjeloun and Moerad, are called Oeraboun. Half of it belongs to Adjeloun, the other to Moerad. It contains the following ruined places; Szafszaf, El Hezar, Om Eddjeloud, Om Djoze, El Haneik, Eshkara,, Oeraboun, El Ehsenye, Serabeis, Nedjde.

15. Ezzoueit lies to the east of Beni Obeid and Moerad, being separated from the latter by the Wady Deir and Seil Djerash; it is situated to the north of Wady Zerka, and extends eastwards beyond the Hadj route to the southward of the ruined city of Om Eddjemal, between Remtha and El Fedhein. Part of it is mountainous, the remainder a flat country. There are at present no inhabited villages in the Zoueit. Its ruined places are Erhab, Eydoun, Dadjemye, Djebe, Kafkafa, Mytwarnol, Boeidha, Khereysan, Kherbet, Szamara, Khenezein, Remeith, Abou Ayad, El Matouye, Essaherye, Ain Aby, Eddhaleil, Ayoun. It forms the southern parts of the Galaaditis.

Beyond the Zerka the chain of mountains increases in breadth, and the Belka begins; it is divided into different districts, of which I may be able to give some account hereafter.

The whole country, from Kanneytra (exclusive) to the Zerka, is at present in the government of the Aga of Tabaria; but this can only happen when the Pasha of Acre is at the same time Pasha of Damascus.

Remarks on the Inhabitants of the Haouran.

The Haouran is inhabited by Turks, Druses, Christians, and Arabs, and is visited in spring and summer by several Arab tribes from the desert. The whole country is under the government of the Pasha of Damascus, who generally sends a governor to Mezareib, intituled Agat el Haouran.

The Pasha appoints also the Sheikh of every village, who collects the Miri from both Turks and Christians. The Druses are not under the control of the Agat el Haouran, but correspond directly with the Pasha. They have a head Sheikh, whose office, though subject to the confirmation of the Pasha, has been hereditary from a remote period, in the family of Hamdan. The head Sheikh of the Druses nominates the Sheikh of each village, and of these upwards of eight are his own relations: the others are members of the great Druse families. The Pasha constantly maintains a force in the Haouran of between five and six hundred men; three hundred and fifty or four hundred of whom are at Boszra, and the remainder at Mezareib, or patrolling the country. The Moggrebyns are generally employed in this service. I compute the population of the Haouran, exclusive of the Arabs who frequent the plain, the mountain (Djebel Haouran), and the Ledja, at about fifty or sixty thousand, of whom six or seven thousand are Druses; and about three thousand Christians. The Turks and Christians have exactly the same modes of life; but the Druses are distinguished from them in many respects. The two former very nearly resemble the Arabs in their customs and manners; their ordinary dress is precisely that of the Arabs; a coarse white cotton stuff forms their Kombaz or gown, the Keffie round the head is tied with a rope of camel's hair, they wear the Abba over the shoulder, and have the breast and feet naked; they have also adopted, for the greater part, the Bedouin dialect, gestures, and phraseology; according to which most articles of household furniture have names different from those in the towns; it requires little experience however to distinguish the adults of the two nations from one another. The Arabs are generally of short stature, with thin visage, scanty beard, and brilliant black eyes; while the Fellahs are taller and stouter, with a strong beard, and a less piercing look; but the difference seems chiefly to arise from their mode of life; for the youth of both nations, to the age of sixteen, have precisely the same appearance. The Turks and Christians of the Haouran live and dress alike, and religion seems to occasion very little difference in their respective conditions. When quarrels happen the Christian fears not to strike the Turk, or to execrate his religion, a liberty which in every town of Syria would expose the Christian to the penalty of death, or to a very heavy pecuniary fine. Common sufferings and dangers in the defence of their property may have given rise to the toleration which the Christians enjoy from the Turks in the Haouran; and which is further strengthened by the Druses, who shew equal respect to both religions. Of the Christians four-fifths are Greeks; and the only religious animosities which I witnessed during my tour, were between them and the Catholics.

Among the Fellahs of the Haouran, the richest lives like the poorest, and displays his superior wealth only on the arrival of strangers. The ancient buildings afford spacious and convenient dwellings to many of the modern inhabitants, and those who occupy them may have three or four rooms for each family; but in newly built villages, the whole family, with all its household furniture, cooking utensils, and provision chests, is commonly huddled together in one apartment. Here also they keep their wheat and barley in reservoirs formed of clay, called Kawara, which are about five feet high and two feet in diameter. The chief articles of furniture are, a handmill, which is used in summer, when there is no water in the Wadys to drive the mills; some copper kettles; and a few mats; in the richer houses some woollen Lebaet are met with, which are coarse woollen stuffs used for carpets, and in winter for horse- cloths: real carpets or mattrasses are seldom seen, unless it be upon the arrival of strangers of consequence. Their goat's hair sacks, and horse and camel equipments, are of the same kind as those used by the Bedouins, and are known by the same names. Each family has a large earthen jar, of the manufacture of Rasheiat el Fukhar, which is filled every morning by the females, from the Birket or spring, with water for the day's consumption. In every house there is a room for the reception of strangers, called from this circumstance Medhafe; it is usually that in which the male part of the family sleeps; in the midst of it is a fire place to boil coffee.

The most common dishes of these people are Burgoul and Keshk; in summer they supply the place of the latter by milk, Leben, and fresh butter. Of the Burgoul I have spoken on other occasions; there are two kinds of Keshk, Keshk-hammer and Keskh-leben; the first is prepared by putting leaven into the Burgoul, and pouring water over it; it is then left until almost putrid, and afterwards spread out in the sun, to dry; after which it is pounded, and when called for, served up mixed with oil, or butter. The Keskh-leben is prepared by putting Leben into the Burgoul, instead of leaven; in other respects the process is the same. Keskh and bread are the common breakfast, and towards sunset a plate of Burgoul, or some Arab dish, forms the dinner; in honour of strangers, it is usual to serve up at breakfast melted butter and bread, or fried eggs, and in the evening a fowl boiled in Burgoul, or a kid or lamb; but this does not very often happen. The women and children eat up whatever the men have left on their plates. The women dress in the Bedouin manner; they have a veil over the head, but seldom veil their faces.

Hospitality to strangers is another characteristic common to the Arabs, and to the people of Haouran. A traveller may alight at any house he pleases; a mat will be immediately spread for him, coffee made, and a breakfast or dinner set before him. In entering a village it has often happened to me, that several persons presented themselves, each begging that I would lodge at his house; and this hospitality is not confined to the traveller himself, his horse or his camel is also fed, the first with half or three quarters of a Moud [The Moud is about nineteen pounds English.] of barley, the second with straw; with this part of their hospitality, however, I had often reason to be dissatisfied, less than a Moud being insufficient upon a journey for a horse, which is fed only in the evening, according to the custom of these countries. As it would be considered an affront to buy any corn, the horse must remain ill-fed, unless the traveller has the precaution to carry a little barley in his saddle-bag, to make up the deficiency in the host's allowance. On returning to Aaere to the house of the Sheikh, after my tour through the desert, one of my Druse guides insisted upon taking my horse to his stables, instead of the Sheikh's; when I was about to depart, the Druse brought my horse to the door, and when I complained that he had fallen off greatly in the few days I had remained in the village, the Sheikh said to me in the presence of several persons, "You are ignorant of the ways of this country; if you see that your host does not feed your horse, insist upon his giving him a Moud of barley daily; he dares not refuse it." It is a point of honour with the host never to accept of the smallest return from a guest; I once only ventured to give a few piastres to the child of a very poor family at Zahouet, by whom we had been most hospitably treated, and rode off without attending to the cries of the mother, who insisted upon my taking back the money.

Besides the private habitations, which offer to every traveller a secure night's shelter, there is in every village the Medhafe of the Sheikh, where all strangers of decent appearance are received and entertained. It is the duty of the Sheikh to maintain this Medhafe, which is like a tavern, with the difference that the host himself pays the bill: the Sheikh has a public allowance to defray these expenses, &c. and hence a man of the Haouran, intending to travel about for a fortnight, never thinks of putting a single para in his pocket; he is sure of being every where well received, and of living better perhaps than at his own home. A man remarkable for his hospitality and generosity enjoys the highest consideration among them.

The inhabitant of the Haouran estimates his wealth by the number of Fedhans, [The word Fedhan is applied both to the yoke of oxen and to the quantity of land cultivated by them, which varies according to circumstances. In some parts of Syria, chiefly about Homs, the Fedhan el

Roumy, or Greek Fedhan, is used, which means two pair of oxen.] or pairs of cows or oxen which he employs in the cultivation of his fields. If it is asked, whether such a one has piastres (Illou gheroush), a common mode of speaking, the answer is, "A great deal; he drives six pair of oxen," (Kethiar bimashi sette fedhadhin); there are but few, however, who have six pair of oxen; a man with two or three is esteemed wealthy: and such a one has probably two camels, perhaps a mare, or at least a Gedish (a gelding), or a couple of asses: and forty or fifty sheep or goats.

The fertility of the soil in the Haouran depends entirely upon the water applied to it. In districts where there is plenty of water for irrigation, the peasants sow winter and summer seeds; but where they have to depend entirely upon the rainy season for a supply, nothing can be cultivated in summer. The harvest in the latter districts, therefore, is in proportion to the abundance of the winter rains. The first harvest is that of horse-beans at the end of April: of these there are vast tracts sown, the produce of which serve as food for the cows and sheep. Camels are fed with the flour made from these beans, mixed with barley meal, and made into a paste. Next comes the barley harvest, and towards the end of May, the wheat: in the interval between the two last, the peasants eat barley bread. In abundant years, wheat sells at fifty piastres the Gharara, [Three Rotola and a half make a Moud, and eighty Moud a Gharara. A Rotola is equal to about five and a halfpounds English.] or about two pounds ten shillings for fifteen cwt. English. In 1811, the Gharara rose as high as to one hundred and ninety piastres. The wheat of the Haouran is considered equal, if not superior to any other in Syria. Barley is generally not more than half the price of wheat. When I was in the Haouran, the price of an ox or cow was about seventy piastres, that of a camel about one hundred and fifty piastres.

The lands which are not capable of artificial irrigation are generally suffered to lie fallow one year; a part of them is sometimes sown in spring with sesamum, cucumbers, melons, and pulse. But a large part of the fruit and vegetables consumed in the Haouran is brought from Damascus, or from the Arabs Menadhere, who cultivate gardens on the banks of the Sheriat el Mandhour.

The peasants of Haouran are extremely shy in speaking of the produce of their land, from an apprehension that the stranger's enquiries may lead to new extortions. I have reason to believe, however, that in middling years wheat yields twenty-five fold; in some parts of the Haouran, this year, the barley has yielded fifty-fold, and even in some instances eighty. A Sheikh, who formerly inhabited the small village of

Boreika, on the southern borders of the Ledja, assured me that from twenty Mouds of wheat-seed he once obtained thirty Ghararas, or one hundred and twenty fold. Fields watered by rain (the Arabs call them Boal,), yield more in proportion to the seed sown, than those which are artificially watered; this is owing to the seed being sown thinner in the former. The Haouran crops are sometimes destroyed by mice, though not so frequently as in the neighbourhood of Homs and Hamah. Where abundance of water may be conducted into the fields from neighbouring springs, the soil is again sown, after the grain harvests, with vegetables, lentils, peas, sesamums, &c.

The Fellahs who own Fedhans often cultivate one another's fields in company: a Turk living in a Druse village often wishes to have a Druse for his companion, to escape in some degree the vexations of the Druse Sheikh. At the Druse Sheikhs, black slaves are frequently met with; but the Turk and Christian proprietors cultivate their lands by hired native labourers. Sometimes the labourer contracts with a townsman, and receives from him oxen, ploughs, and seed. A labourer who has one Fedhan or two oxen under his charge, usually receives at the time of sowing one Gharara of corn. After the harvest he takes one-third of the produce of the field; but among the Druses only a fourth. The master pays to the government the tax called Miri, and the labourer pays ten piastres annually. The rest of the agricultural population of the Haouran consists of those who subsist by daily labour. They in general earn their living very hardly. I once met with a young man who had served eight years for his food only at the expiration of that period he obtained in marriage the daughter of his master, for whom he would, otherwise, have had to pay seven or eight hundred piastres. When I saw him he had been married three years; but he complained bitterly of his father-in-law, who continued to require of him the performance of the most servile offices, without paying him any thing; and thus prevented him from setting up for himself and family.

Daughters are paid for according to the respectability of their father, sometimes as high as fifteen hundred piastres, and this custom prevails amongst Druses, Turks, and Christians. If her family is rich the girl is fitted out with clothes, and a string of zequins or of silver coin, to tie round her head; after which she is delivered to her husband. I had an opportunity of witnessing an espousal of two Christians at Aaere, in the house of a Christian: the bride was brought with her female friends and relations, from her native village, one day's journey distant, with two camels decorated with tassels, bells, &c., and was lodged with her relations in Aaere. They entered the village preceded by women beating the tamborine, and by the village youths, firing off their musquets. Soon afterwards the bridegroom retired to the spring, which was in a field ten minutes from the village, where he washed, and dressed himself in new clothes. He then entered the village mounted on a caparisoned horse, surrounded by young men, two of whom beat tamborines, and the others fired musquets. He alighted before the Sheikh's house, and was carried for about a quarter of an hour by two men, on their arms, amidst continued singing and huzzaing: the Sheikh then exclaimed, "Mebarek el Aris", Blessed be the bridegroom! which was repeated by all present, after which he was set down, and remained till sunset, exposed to the jests of his friends; after this he was carried to the church, where the Greek priest performed the marriage ceremony, and the young couple retired to their dwelling. The bridegroom's father had slaughtered several lambs and kids, a part of which was devoured by mid- day; but the best pieces were brought in three enormous dishes of Bourgul to the Sheikh's Medhafe; two being for the mob, and the third for the Sheikh, and principal men of the village. In the evening paras were collected by one of the bridegroom's friends, who sung verses in praise of all his acquaintance, every one of whom, when named, was expected to make a present.

The oppressions of the government on one side, and those of the Bedouins on the other, have reduced the Fellah of the Haouran to a state little better than that of the wandering Arab. Few individuals either among the Druses or Christians die in the same village in which they were born. Families are continually moving from one place to another; in the first year of their new settlement the Sheikh acts with moderation towards them; but his vexations becoming in a few years insupportable, they fly to some other place, where they have heard that their brethren are better treated, but they soon find that the same system prevails over the whole country. Sometimes it is not merely the pecuniary extortion, but the personal enmity of the Sheikh, or of some of the head men of the village, which drives a family from their home, for they are always permitted to depart. This continued wandering is one of the principal reasons why no village in the Haouran has either orchards, or fruit- trees, or gardens for the growth of vegetables. "Shall we sow for strangers?" was the answer of a Fellah, to whom I once spoke on the subject, and who by the word strangers meant both the succeeding inhabitants, and the Arabs who visit the Haouran in the spring and summer.

The taxes which all classes of Fellahs in the Haouran pay, may be classed under four heads: the Miri; the expense of feeding soldiers on the march; the tribute to the Arabs; and extraordinary contributions. The Miri is levied upon the Fedhan; thus if a village pay twelve purses to the Miri, and there are thirty pair of oxen in it, the master of each pair pays a thirtieth. Every village being rated for the Miri in the land-tax book of the Pasha, at a fixed sum, that sum is levied as long as the village is at all inhabited, however few may be its inhabitants. In the spring of every year, or, if no strangers have arrived and settled, in every second or third spring, the ground of the village is measured by long cords, when every Fellah occupies as much of it as he pleases, there being always more than sufficient; the amount of his tax is then fixed by the Sheikh, at the ratio which his number of Fedhans bears to the whole number of Fedhans cultivated that year. Whether the oxen be strong or weak, or whether the quantity of seed sown or of land cultivated by the owner of the oxen be more or less, is not taken into consideration; the Fellah is supposed to keep strong cattle, and plough as much land as possible. Some sow six Gharara of wheat or barley in the Fedhan, others five, and others seven. The boundaries of the respective fields are marked by large stones. The Miri is paid in kind, or in money, at the will of the Pasha; the Fellahs prefer the latter, by which they are always trifling gainers.

From what has been said, it is evidently impossible for the Fellah to foresee the amount of Miri which he shall have to pay in any year; and in addition to this vexation, the Miri for each village, though it is never diminished upon a loss of inhabitants, is sometimes raised upon a supposed increase of population, or upon some other pretext. It may, generally, be remarked, that the villages inhabited by the Druses usually pay more Miri than those in the plain, because some allowance is made to the latter, in consideration of the tribute which they are obliged to pay to the Arabs, and from which the former are exempt. At Aaere, the year before my first visit, the Fedhan had paid one hundred and fifty piastres, at Ezra, one hundred and eighty, and at some villages in the plain, one hundred and twenty. In the year 1812, the Miri, including some extra demands, amounted in general to five hundred piastres the Fedhan.

The second tax upon the Fellahs is the expense of feeding soldiers on the march; if the number is small they go to the Sheikh's Medhafe; but if they are numerous, they are quartered, or rather quarter themselves, upon the Fellahs: in the former case, barley only for their horses is supplied by the peasant, while the Sheikh furnishes provisions for the men, but the peasant is not much benefited by this regulation, for the soldiers are in general little disposed to be satisfied with the frugal fare of the Sheikh, and demand fowls, or butcher's meat; which must be supplied by the village. On their departure, they often steal some article belonging to the house. The proportion of barley to be furnished by each individual to the soldiers horses, depends of course upon the number of horses to be fed, and of Fedhans in the village: at Aaere, in the year 1809, it amounted to fifty piastres per Fedhan. The Sheikh of Aaere has six pair of oxen, for which he pays no taxes, but the presence of strangers and troops is so frequent at his Medhafe, that this exemption had not been thought a sufficient remuneration, and he is entitled to levy, in addition, every year, two or three Gharara of corn, each Gharara being in common years, worth eighty or one hundred piastres. Some Sheikhs levy as much as ten Gharara, besides being exempted from taxation for eight, ten, or twelve pair of oxen.

The third and most heavy contribution paid by the peasants, is the tribute to the Arabs. The Fahely, Serdie, Beni Szakher, Serhhan, who are constant residents in the Haouran, as well as most of the numerous tribes of Aeneze, who visit the country only in the summer, are, from remote times, entitled to certain tributes called Khone (brotherbood), from every village in the Haouran. In return for this Khone, the Arabs abstain from touching the harvest of the village, and from driving off its cattle and camels, when they meet them in their way. Each village pays Khone to one Sheikh in every tribe; the village is then known as his Ukhta or Sister, as the Arabs term it, and he protects the inhabitants against all the members of his own tribe. It may easily be imagined, however, that depredations are often committed, without the possibility of redress, the depredator being unknown, or flying immediately towards the desert. The amount of the Khone is continually increasing; for the Arab Sheikh is not always contented with the quantity of corn he received in the preceding year, but asks something additional, as a present, which soon becomes a part of his accustomed dues.

If the Pasha of Damascus were guided by sound policy, and a right view of his own interests, he might soon put an end to the exactions of the Arabs, by keeping a few thousand men, well paid, in garrison in the principal places of the Haouran; but instead of this, his object is to make the Khone an immediate source of income to himself; the chief Sheikhs of the Fehely and Serdie receive yearly from the Pasha a present of a pelisse, which entitles them to the tribute of the villages, out of which the Fehely pays about twenty purses, and the Serdie twelve purses into the Pasha's treasury. The Serdie generally regulate the amount of the Khone which they levy, by that which the Fehely receive; and take half as much; but the Khone paid to the Aeneze chiefs is quite arbitrary, and the sum paid to a single Sheikh varies according to his avidity; or the wealth of the Fellahs, from thirty and forty piastres up to four hundred, which are generally paid in corn.

These various oppressive taxes, under which the poor Fellah groans, are looked upon as things of course, and just contributions; and he considers himself fortunate, if they form the whole of his sufferings: but it too often happens that the Pasha is a man who sets no bounds to his rapacity, and extraordinary sums are levied upon the village, by the simple command issued from the Hakim el Haouran to the village Sheikh to levy three or four hundred piastres upon the peasants of the place. On these occasions the women are sometimes obliged to sell their ear-rings and bracelets, and the men their cattle, to satisfy the demand, and have no other hope than that a rich harvest in the following year shall make amends for their loss. The receipt of the Miri of the whole Pashalik of Damascus is in the hands of the Jew bankers, or Serafs of the Pasha, who have two and a half per cent. upon his revenue, and as much upon his expenditure. They usually distribute the villages amongst their creatures, who repair thither at the time of harvest, to receive the Miri; and who generally extort, besides, something for themselves.

The Druses who inhabit the villages in the Loehf, and those on the sides of the Djebel Haouran, are to be classed with the Fellahs of the plain with regard to their mode of living and their relations with the government. Their dress is the same as that of the Fellahs to the W. of Damascus; they seldom wear the Keffie, and the grown up men do not go barefoot like the other Fellahs of the Haouran. I have already mentioned that their chief resides at Soueida, of which village he is also the Sheikh. On the death of the chief, the individual in his family who is in the highest estimation from wealth or personal character succeeds to the title, and is confirmed by the Pasha. It is known that on the death of Wehebi el Hamdan, the present chief, who is upwards of eighty, Shybely el Hamdan, the Sheikh of Aaere, will succeed him. The chief has no income as such, it being derived from the village of which he is Sheikh; and his authority over the others goes no further than to communicate to them the orders of the Pasha. In manners these Druses very much resemble those of the mountains of Kesrouan.

The families form clans almost independent of each other; and among whom there are frequent quarrels. Insults are studiously avenged by the respective families, and the law of blood-revenge is in full force among them, without being mitigated by the admission of any pecuniary commutation. They all go armed, as do the Turks and Christians of the

Haouran in general. Few Druses have more than one wife; but she may be divorced on very slight pretexts.

With respect to their religion, the Druses of the Haouran, like those in Mount Libanus, have the class of men called Akoul (sing. Aakel), who are distinguished from the rest by a white turban, and the peculiarity of the folds in which they wear it. The Akoul are not permitted to smoke tobacco; they never swear, and are very reserved in their manners and conversation. I was informed that these were their only obligations; and it appears probable, for I observed Akoul boys of eight or ten years of age, from whom nothing more difficult could well be expected, and to whom it is not likely that any important secret would be imparted. I have seen Akouls of that age, whose fathers were not of the order, because, as they told me, they could not abstain from smoking and swearing. The Sheikhs are for the greater part Akouls. The Druses pray in their chapels, but not at stated periods; these chapels are called Khalawe, i.e. an insulated place, and none but Druses are allowed to enter them. They affect to follow the doctrines of Mohammed, but few of them pray according to the Turkish forms: they fast during Ramadan in the presence of strangers, but eat at their own homes, and even of the flesh of the wild boar, which is frequently met with in these districts. It is a singular belief both among the western Druses, and those of the Haouran, that there are a great number of Druses in England; an opinion founded perhaps upon the fanatical opinions of the Christians of Syria, who deny the English to be followers of Christ, because they neither confess nor fast. When I first arrived at the Druse village of Aaere there was a large company in the Medhafe, and the Sheikh had no opportunity of speaking to me in private; he therefore called for his inkstand, and wrote upon a piece of paper the following questions, which I answered as well as I could, and returned him the paper: "Where do the five Wadys flow to, in your country?--Do you know the grain of the plant Leiledj; and where is it sown?--What is the name of the Sultan of China?--Are the towns of Hadjar and Nedjran in the Yemen known to you?--Is Hadjar in ruins? and who will rebuild it?--Is the Moehdy (the Saviour) yet come, or is he now upon the earth?".

I have not been able to obtain any information concerning the period at which the Druses first settled in these parts. Min Kadim, a long time ago, was the general answer of all those whom I questioned on the subject. During my stay at Aaere news arrived there, that a body of one hundred and twenty Druses had left the western mountains, and were coming to settle in Haouran.

The Pasha of Damascus has entrusted to the Druses of the Haouran, the defence of the neighbouring villages against such of the Arabs as may be at war with him; but the Druses perform this service very badly: they are the secret friends of all the Arabs, to whom they abandon the villages of the plain, on the condition that their own brethren are not to be molested; and their Sheikhs receive from the Arabs presents in horses, cattle, and butter. While at Aaere I witnessed an instance of the good understanding between the Druses and the Arabs Serdie, whom I have already mentioned as having been at war with the Pasha, at the time of my visit to the Haouran: seeing in the evening some Arabs stealing into the court-yard of the Sheikh's house, I enquired who they were, and was told that they were Serdie, come in search of information, whether any more troops were likely to be sent against them from Damascus. It is for this kind of treachery that the Fellahs in the Haouran hate the Druses.

The authority both of the Druse and Turkish village Sheikh is very limited, in consequence of the facility with which the Fellahs can transport themselves and families to another village. I was present during a dispute between a Christian Fellah and a Druse chief, who wished to make the former pay for the ensuing year at the rate of the same number of Fedhans that he had paid for the preceding year, though he had now one pair of oxen less. After much wrangling, and high words on both sides, the Christian said, "Very well, I shall not sow a single grain, but retire to another village;" and by the next morning he had made preparation for his departure; when the Sheikh having called upon him, the affair was amicably settled, and a large dish of rice was dressed in token of reconciliation. When disputes happen between Druses, they are generally settled by the interference of mutual friends, or by the Sheikhs or their respective families, or by the great chiefs; or failing these, the two families of the two parties come to blows rather than bring their differences before the court of justice at Damascus. Among the Turks litigations are, in the last extremity, decided by the Kadhi of Damascus, or by the Pasha in person. The Christians often bring their differences before the tribunal of priests or that of the Patriarch of Damascus, and before the Kadhi in times when it is known that Christians can obtain justice, which is not the case under every governor.

The Bedouins of the Haouran are of two classes; those who are resident, and those who visit it in the spring and summer only. The resident Arabs are the Fehily, Serdie, Beni Szakher, Serhhan; the Arabs of the mountain Haouran, or Ahl el Djebel, and those of the Ledja. By resident, I do not mean a fixed residence in villages, but that their wanderings are confined to the Haouran, or to some particular districts of it. Thus the four first mentioned move through every part of the country from Zerka up to the plains of Ard

Zeikal, according to their relations with other tribes, their own affairs, and the state of pasturage in the different districts. The Beni Szakher generally encamp at the foot of the western mountains of Belka and the Heish, the Serhhan near them, and the Fehily and Serdie in the midst of the cultivated districts, or at a short distance from them, according to the terms they are upon with the Pasha. [When I was in the Haouran the Fehliy were encamped near the Szaffa, the Beni Szakher near Fedhein, the Serhhan at the foot of the Belka, and the Serdie near Om Eddjemal.] The Ahl el Djebel move about in the mountain; those of the Ledja seldom venture to encamp beyond their usual limits in that district. But I have spoken more largely of these tribes and their mutual interests in another place. The Fehily and Serdie are called Ahl el Dyrel, or national Arabs, and pay tribute to the Pasha, who, however, is often at war with them for withholding it, or for plundering his troops or the Fellahs.

If the Pasha happens to be at war with other tribes, they are bound to join his troops; but in this they are guided entirely by the advantage which they are likely to derive from the contest. They receive Khone from all the villages of the Haouran, the Djolan, and many of those in the Djebel Adjeloun.

The Ahl el Djebel and the Arabs el Ledja are kept in more strict dependence upon the Pasha than the other tribes; both are subject to an annual tribute, which is levied on each tent according to the wealth of its owner; this is collected from the Arabs el Ledja by the Sheikh of the Fellahs, and ascends from ten to sixty piastres for each tent. It seldom happens that the Arabs el Djebel prove rebels, but those of the Ledja often with-hold the tribute, in the confidence that the recesses of their abode cannot he forced; in this case nothing makes them yield but want of water, when their own springs failing, they are obliged to approach the perennial sources of the Loehf.

The Arabs of the Djebel Haouran are the shepherds of the people of the plains, who entrust to them in summer and winter their flocks of goats and sheep, which they pasture during the latter season amongst the rocks of the mountains. In spring the Arabs return the flocks to their owners, who sell a part of them at Damascus, or make butter from the milk during the spring months. The Arabs receive for their trouble one-fourth of the lambs and kids, and a like proportion of the butter. Casual losses in the flocks are borne equally by both parties.

The following are the different tribes of the Ahl el Djebel; Esshenabele, El Hassan, El Haddie, Ghiath, Essherefat, Mezaid, El Kerad, Beni Adhan, and Szammeral. Of those of the Ledja I have already spoken. The Ahl el Djebel are always at peace with the other Arabs; but those of the Ledja are often at war with the Fehily and Serdie. I come now to the second class, or wandering Arabs.

In May the whole Haouran is coverered with swarms of wanderers from the desert, who remain there till after September; these are at present almost exclusively of the tribe of Aeneze. Formerly the Haouran was often visited by the Sherarat, from the Mekka road, at fifteen stations from Damascus; by the Shammor, from Djebel Shammor, and by the Dhofir from the Irak country. On the arrival of the Aeneze, the resident Arabs who may happen to be at war with them, conceal themselves in the neighbourhood of the western mountain or in the Szaffa, or they retire towards Mezareib and Szannamein. The Aeneze come for a two-fold purpose, water and pasturage for the summer, and a provision of corn for the winter. If they are at peace with the Pasha they encamp quietly among the villages, near the springs or wells if at war with him, for their relations with the government of Damascus are as uncertain as their own with each other, they keep in the district to the S. of Boszra, towards Om Eddjemal and Fedhein, extending their limits south as far as El Zerka. The Pasha generally permits them to purchase corn from the Haouran, but in years when a scarcity is apprehended, a restriction is put upon them.

Till within a few years the Aeneze were the constant carriers of the Hadj, and made yearly contracts with the Pasha for several thousand camels, by which they were considerable gainers, as well as by the fixed tribute which many of their Sheikhs had made themselves entitled to from the pilgrim caravan; and by their nightly plunder of stragglers, and loaded camels during the march. These advantages have made the Aeneze inclined to preserve friendly terms with the Pashalik of Damascus, and to break allegiance to the Wahabi chief, notwithstanding they have been for twelve years converts to his religious doctrines. If, however, they shall become convinced that the Hadj is no longer practicable, they will soon turn their arms against their former friends, an event which is justly dreaded by the people of the Haouran.

The tribe of Aeneze which most usually visits the Haouran is the Would Ali, under their chiefs Etteiar and Ibn Ismayr; the latter has at present more interest than any other Arab Sheikh, with the Pasha, from whom he occasionally receives considerable presents, as an indemnification for his losses by the suspension of the Hadj, as well as to induce him to keep his Arabs on good terms with the Turkish governors of the Pashalik.

DESCRIPTION OF A JOURNEY FROM DAMASCUS THROUGH THE MOUNTAINS OF ARABIA PETRAEA, AND THE DESERT EL TY, TO CAIRO; IN THE SUMMER OF 1812.

WISHING to obtain a further knowledge of the mountains to the east of the Jordan, and being still more desirous of visiting the almost unknown districts to the east of the Dead sea, as well as of exploring the country which lies between the latter and the Red sea, I resolved to pursue that route from Damascus to Cairo, in preference to the direct road through Jerusalem and Ghaza, where I could not expect to collect much information important for its novelty. Knowing that my intended way led through a diversity of Bedouin tribes, I thought it advisable to equip myself in the simplest manner. I assumed the most common Bedouin dress, took no baggage with me, and mounted a mare that was not likely to excite the cupidity of the Arabs. After sun-set, on the 18th of June, 1812, I left Damascus, and slept that night at Kefer Souse, a considerable village, at a short distance from the city-gate, in the house of the guide whom I had hired to conduct me to Tabaria.

Kefer Souse is noted for its olive plantations; and the oil which they produce is esteemed the best in the vicinity of Damascus.

June 19th.--In one hour we passed the village Dareya; where terminate the gardens and orchards which surround Damascus on all sides to a distance of from six to ten miles. We found the peasants occupied with the corn harvest, and with the irrigation of the cotton fields, in which the plants had just made their appearance above ground. The plain is every where cultivated. In two hours and three quarters we passed Kokab, a small village on the western extremity of the chain of low hills known by the appellation of Djebel Kessoue. To the left of the road from Dareya to Kokab are the villages Moattamye, Djedeide and Artous; and to the right of it, El Ashrafe, and Szahhnaya. The direction of our route was W.S.W. Beyond Kokab, a small part only of the plain is cultivated. At three hours and three quarters, to our left, was the village Wadhye, and a little farther the village Zaky. Route S.W. b. W. Four hours and a half, Khan el Sheikh, a house for the accommodation of travellers, this being the great road from Akka to Damascus. The Khan is inhabited by a few families, and stands near the river Seybarany, which flows towards the Ghoutta of Damascus. We followed the banks of the river over a stony desert; on the opposite bank extends the rocky district called War Ezzaky, mentioned in my former Journal. In five hours and three quarters we passed a rocky tract called Om el Sheratytt. Several heaps of stones indicate the graves of travellers murdered in this place by the Druses, who, during their wars with Djezzar Pasha, were in the habit of descending from the neighbouring mountain, Djebel el Sheikh, in order to waylay the caravans. The Seybarany runs here in a deep bed of the Haouran black stone. In six hours and a quarter we passed the river, over a solid bridge. At six hours and three quarters is the village Sasa, at the foot of an insulated hill; it is well built, and contains a large Khan, with a good mosque. The former was full of travellers. We slept here till midnight, and then joined a small caravan destined for Akka.

June 20th.--Our road lay over a rocky plain, called Nakker Sasa, slightly ascending. In one hour we passed a bridge over the river Meghannye. At the end of three hours we issued from the rocks, and entered into a forest of low straggling oak-trees, called Heish Shakkara. Three hours and a half, we passed to the right of an insulated hill, called Tel Djobba. The whole country is uncultivated. In four hours we saw, at about half an hour to our right, the ruined Khan of Kereymbe; the road still ascending. Near Kereymbe begins the mountain called Heish el Kanneytra, a lower ridge of Djebel el Sheikh, (the Mount Hermon of the Scriptures), from which it branches out southwards. At five hours Tel Hara was about one hour and a half to the S. of the road, which from Sasa followed the direction of S.W. and sometimes that of S.W. by W. At seven hours is the village of Kanneytra; from Kereymbe to this place is an open country, with a fertile soil, and several springs.

Kanneytra is now in ruins, having been deserted by its inhabitants since the period of the passage of the Visier's troops into Egypt. It is enclosed by a strong wall, which contains within its circuit a good Khan, a fine mosque with several short columns of gray granite, and a copious spring; there are other springs also near it. On the north side of the village are the remains of a small ancient city, perhaps Canatha; these ruins consist of little more than the foundations of habitations. The caravans coming from Akka generally halt for the night at Kanneytra. We reposed here a few hours, and then continued our journey, over ground which still continues to rise, until we reached the chain of hills, which form the most conspicuous part of the mountain Heish. The ground being here considerably elevated above the plain of Damascus and the Djolan, these hills, when seen from afar, appear like mountains, although, when viewed from their foot, they are of very moderate height. They are insulated, and terminate, as I have already mentioned, at the hill called Tel Faras, towards the plain of Djolan. The Bedouins who pasture their cattle in these mountains retire in the hot season towards the Djebel el Sheikh. The governor of the Heish el Kanneytra, who receives his charge every year from the Pasha, used formerly to reside at Kanneytra; but since that place has been deserted, he usually encamps with the Turkmans of the Heish, and goes from one encampment to another, to collect the Miri from these Arabs.

At the end of seven hours and a half we passed Tel Abou Nedy, with the tomb of the Sheikh Abou Nedy. At eight hours is a reservoir of water, a few hundred paces to the S. of the road, which the Bedouins call Birket el Ram, and the peasants Birket Abou Ermeil; it lies near the foot of Tel Abou Nedy, is about one hundred and twenty paces in circumference, and is supplied by two springs which are never dry; one of them is in the bottom of a deep well in the midst of the Birket. Just by this reservoir are the ruins of an ancient town, about a quarter of an hour in circuit, of which nothing remains but large heaps of stones. Five minutes farther is another Birket, which is filled by rain water only. The neighbourhood of these reservoirs is covered with a forest of short oak trees. The rock of the mountain consists of sand-stone, and the basalt of Haouran. Beyond the Birkets the road begins to descend gently, and at nine hours and a half, just by the road, on the left, is a large pond called Birket Nefah or Tefah (I am uncertain which), about two hundred paces in circumference: there are remains of a stone channel communicating with the Birket. Some of my companions asserted that the pond contained a spring, while others denied it; from which I inferred that the water never dries up completely. I take this to be the Lake Phiala, laid down in the maps of Syria, as there is no other lake or pond in the neighbourhood. From hence towards Feik, upon the mountains to the E. of the lake of Tiberias, is an open country intersected by many Wadys. At ten hours we passed a large hill to the left, called Tel el Khanzyr, the boar's hill. The ground was here covered with the finest pasturage; the dry grass was as high as a horse, and so thick, that we passed through it with difficulty. At ten hours and a half are several springs by the side of the road, called Ayoun Essemmam. Eleven hours and a quarter, are the ruins of a city called Noworan, with a copious spring near it. Some walls yet remain, and large hewn stones are lying about. At thirteen hours is the bridge over the Jordan, called Djissr Beni Yakoub; the road continues in an easy slope till a quarter of an hour above the bridge, where it becomes a steep descent. The river flows in a narrow bed, and with a rapid stream; for the lake Houle, whose southern extremity is about three quarters of an hour north of the bridge, is upon a level considerably higher than that of the lake of Tiberias. The bridge is of a solid construction, with four arches: on its E. side is a Khan, much frequented by travellers, in the middle of which are the ruins of an ancient square building constructed with basalt, and having columns in its four angles. The Khan contains also a spring. The Pasha of Damascus here keeps a guard of a few men, principally for the purpose of collecting the Ghaffer, or tax paid by all Christians who cross the bridge. The ordinary Ghaffer is about nine-pence a head, but the pilgrims who pass here about Easter, in their way to Jerusalem, pay seven shillings. The bridge divides the Pashaliks of Damascus and Akka. On the west of it is a guard-house belonging to the latter. Banias (Caesarea Philippi) bears from a point above the bridge N. by E.

The lake of Houle, or Samachonitis, is inhabited only on the eastern borders; there we find the villages of Esseira and Eddeir; and between them a ruined place called Kherbet Eddaherye complete. The south-west shore bears the name of Melaha, from the ground being covered with a saline crust. The fisheries of the lake are rented of the Mutsellim of Szaffad by some fishermen of that town. The narrow valley of the Jordan continues for about two hours S. of the bridge, at which distance the river falls into the lake of Tiberias. About an hour and a quarter from the bridge, on the E. side of the river, is the village Battykha; its inhabitants cultivate large quantities of cucumbers and gourds, which they carry to the market of Damascus, three weeks before the same fruits ripen there; the village is also noted for its excellent honey. June 21st.--We ascended the western banks of the valley of the Jordan, and then continued upon a plain, called Ard Aaseifera, a small part of which is cultivated by the inhabitants of Szaffad. There are several springs in the plain. In an hour and a quarter, we began to ascend the chain of mountains known by the name of Djebel Szaffad, which begin on the N.W. side of the lake of Houle, being a southern branch of the Djebel el Sheikh, or rather of the Anti-

Libanus. On the steep acclivity of this mountain we passed to the left of the village Feraab. The road ascends through a narrow valley, called Akabet Feraein, and passes by the spring of Feraein. In two hours and three quarters from the bridge, we reached the summit of the mountain, from whence the Djebel el Sheik bears N.E. The whole is calcareous, with very little basalt or tufwacke. At the end of three hours and a half, after a short descent, we reached Szaffad, the ancient Japhet; it is a neatly built town, situated round a hill, on the top of which is a castle of Saracen structure. The castle appears to have undergone a thorough repair in the course of the last century, it has a good wall, and is surrounded by a broad ditch. It commands an extensive view over the country towards Akka, and in clear weather the sea is visible from it. There is another but smaller castle, of modern date, with half ruined walls, at the foot of the hill. The town is built upon several low hills, which divide it into different quarters; of these the largest is inhabited exclusively by Jews, who esteem Szaffad as a sacred place. The whole may contain six hundred houses, of which one hundred and fifty belong to the Jews, and from eighty to one hundred to the Christians. In 1799 the Jews quarter was completely sacked by the Turks, after the retreat of the French from Akka; the French had occupied Szaffad with a garrison of about four hundred men, whose outposts were advanced as far as the bridge of Beni Yakoub. The town is governed by a Mutsellim, whose district comprises about a dozen villages. The garrison consists of Moggrebyns, the greater part of whom have married here, and cultivate a part of the neighbouring lands. The town is surrounded with large olive plantations and vineyards, but the principal occupations of the inhabitants are indigo dyeing, and the manufacture of cotton cloth. On every Friday a market is held, to which all the peasants of the neighbourhood resort. Mount Tabor bears from Szaffad S.S.W.

June 22d.--As there is no Khan for travellers at Szaffad, and I had no letters to any person in the town, I was obliged to lodge at the public coffee house. We left the town early in the morning, and descended the side of the mountain towards the lake; here the ground is for the greater part uncultivated and without trees. At two hours and a quarter is Khan Djob Yousef, or the Khan of Joseph's Well, situated in a narrow plain. The Khan is falling rapidly into ruin; near it is a large Birket. Here is shewn the well into which Joseph was let down by his brothers; it is in a small court-yard by the side of the Khan, is about three feet in diameter, and at least thirty feet deep. I was told that the bottom is hewn in the rock: its sides were well lined with masonry as far as I could see into it, and the water never dries up, a circumstance which makes it difficult to believe that this was the well into which Joseph was thrown. The whole of the mountain in the vicinity is covered with large pieces of black stone; but the main body of the rock is calcareous. The country people relate that the tears of Jacob dropping upon the ground while he was in search of his son turned the white stones black, and they in consequence call these stones Jacob's tears. Joseph's well is held in veneration by Turks as well as Christians; the former have a small chapel just by it, and caravan travellers seldom pass here without saying a few prayers in honour of Yousef. The Khan is on the great road from Akka to Damascus. It is inhabited by a dozen Moggrebyn soldiers, with their families, who cultivate the fields near it.

We continued to descend from Djob Yousef; the district is here called Koua el Kerd, and a little lower down Redjel el Kaa. At one hour and a half from the Djob Yousef we came to the borders of the lake of Tiberias. At a short distance to the E. of the spot where we reached the plain, is a spring near the border of the lake, called Ain Tabegha, with a few houses and a mill; but the water is so strongly impregnated with salt as not to be drinkable. The few inhabitants of this miserable place live by fishing. To the N.E. of Tabegha, between it and the Jordan, are the ruins called Tel Houm, which are generally supposed to be those of Capernaum. Here is a well of salt water, called Tennour Ayoub. The rivulet El Eshe empties itself into the lake just by. Beyond Tabegha we came to a ruined Khan, near the borders of the lake, called Mennye, a large and well constructed building. Here begins a plain of about twenty minutes in breadth, to the north of which the mountain stretches down close to the lake. That plain is covered with the tree called Doum or Theder, which bears a small yellow fruit like the Zaarour. It was now about mid-day, and the sun intensely hot, we therefore looked out for a shady spot, and reposed under a very large fig-tree, at the foot of which a rivulet of sweet water gushes out from beneath the rocks, and falls into the lake at a few hundred paces distant. The tree has given its name to the spring, Ain-et-Tin; near it are several other springs, which occasion a very luxuriant herbage along the borders of the lake. The pastures of Mennye are proverbial for their richness among the inhabitants of the neighbouring countries. High reeds grow along the shore, but I found none of the aromatic reeds and rushes mentioned by Strabo. [Greek. 1.16, p.755] The N.W. and S. shores are generally sandy, without reeds, but large quantities grow at the mouths of the Wadys on the E. side.

In thirty-eight minutes from Khan Mennye we passed a small rivulet, which waters Wady Lymoun. At about one hour's distance from our road, up in the mountain, we saw the village Sendjol, about half an hour to the west of which lies the village Hottein. In forty-five minutes we passed the large branch of the Wady Lymoun. The mountains which border the lake here terminate in a perpendicular cliff, which is basaltish with an upper stratum of calcareous rock; and the shore changes from the direction S.W. by S. to that of S. by E. In the angle stands the miserable village El Medjdel, one hour distant from Ain-et-Tin, and agreeing both in name and position with the ancient Magdala. The Wady Hammam, in which stands the Kalaat ibn-Maan, branches off from Medjdel. Proceeding from hence the shore of the lake is overgrown with Defle (Solanum furiosum), and there are several springs close to the water's side. At the end of two hours and a quarter from Ain-et-Tin, we reached Tabaria.

June 23d.--There being no Khan for travellers at Tabaria I went to the Catholic priest, and desired him to let me have the keys of the church, that I might take up my quarters there; he gave them to me, but finding the place swarming with vermin, I removed into the open churchyard.

Tabaria, the ancient Tiberias, [Tel el Faras, the southern extremity of Djebel Heish, bears from a point above Tabaria N.E. by E.] stands close to the lake, upon a small plain, surrounded by mountains. Its situation is extremely hot and unhealthy, as the mountain impedes the free course of the westerly winds which prevail throughout Syria during the summer. Hence intermittent fevers, especially those of the quartan form, are very common in the town in that season. Little rain falls in winter, snow is almost unknown on the borders of the lake, and the temperature, on the whole, appears to be very nearly the same as that of the Dead sea. The town is surrounded towards the land by a thick and well built wall, about twenty feet in height, with a high parapet and loop-holes. It surrounds the city on three sides, and touches the water at its two extremities; but there are some remains on the shore of the lake, which seem to indicate that the town was once inclosed on this side also. I observed, likewise, some broken columns of granite in the water close to the shore. The town wall is flanked by twenty round towers standing at unequal distances. Both towers and walls are built with black stones of moderate size, and seem to be the work of not very remote times; the whole being in a good state of repair, the place may be considered as almost impregnable to Syrian soldiers.

Tabaria, with its district of ten or twelve villages, forms a part of the Pashalik of Akka. Being considered one of the principal points of defence of the Pashalik, a garrison of two or three hundred men is constantly kept here, the greater part of whom are married, and settled. During the reign of Djezzar a colony of two hundred Afghan soldiers were persuaded by the Pasha to establish themselves at Tabaria; many of them were natives of Kashmir: and among others their Aga, who was sent for expressly by Djezzar. After the Pasha's death they dispersed over Syria, but I found two Kashmirines still remaining, who gave me the history of their colony in broken Arabic.

The Christian church is dedicated to St. Peter, and is said to have been founded on the spot where St. Peter threw his net. It belongs to the community of Terra Santa and is visited annually on St. Peter's day by the Frank missionaries of Nazaret, who celebrate mass in it on this occasion. In the street, not far from the church, is a large stone, formerly the architrave of some building; upon which are sculptured in bas-relief two lions seizing two sheep.

There are about four thousand inhabitants in Tabaria, one-fourth of whom are Jews. The Christian community consists only of a few families, but they enjoy great liberty, and are on a footing of equality with the Turks. The difference of treatment which the Christians experience from the Turks in different parts of Syria is very remarkable. In some places a Christian would be deprived of his last farthing, if not of his life, were he to curse the Mohammedan religion when quarrelling with a Turk; while in others but a few hours distant, he retorts with impunity upon the Mohammedan, every invective which he may utter against the Christian religion. At Szaffad, where is a small Christian community, the Turks are extremely intolerant; at Tiberias, on the contrary, I have seen Christians beating Turks in the public Bazar. This difference seems chiefly to depend upon the character of the local government. That of Soleiman Pasha of Akka, the successor of Djezzar, is distinguished for its religious tolerance; while Damascus still continues to be the seat of fanatism, and will remain so as long as there are no Frank establishments or European agents in that city.

A Bazar has lately been built at Tabaria, in which I counted about a dozen retail shops. The traffic of the inhabitants is principally with the Bedouins of the Ghor, and of the district of Szaffad. The shopkeepers repair every Monday to the Khan at the foot of Mount Tabor, where a market, called Souk el Khan is held, and where the merchandize of the town is bartered chiefly for cattle. The far greater part of the inhabitants of Tabaria cultivate the soil; they sow the narrow plain to the west of the town, and the declivity of the western mountain, which they irrigate artificially by means of several springs. The heat of the climate would enable them to grow almost any tropical plant, but the only produce of their fields are wheat, barley, Dhourra, tobacco, melons, grapes, and a few vegetables. The melons are of the finest quality, and are in great demand at Akka and Damascus, where that fruit is nearly a month later in ripening. Knowing how fond the Syrians in general are of the early fruits, I sent to my friends at Damascus a mule load of these melons, which, according to eastern fashion, is a very acceptable and polite present. About three hundred and fifty pounds weight English of melons sell at Tabaria for about eight shillings. I was informed that the shrub which produces the balm of Mecca succeeds very well here, and that several people have it in their gardens. It was described to me as a low shrub, with leaves resembling those of the vine, the fruit about three inches long and in the form of a cucumber, changing from green to a yellow colour when ripe; it is gathered in June, oil is then poured over it, and in this state it is exposed to the sun, after which the juic [e] forming the balm is expressed from it.

The Jews of Tiberias occupy a quarter on the shore of the lake in the middle of the town, which has lately been considerably enlarged by the purchase of several streets: it is separated from the rest of the town by a high wall, and has only one gate of entrance, which is regularly shut at sunset, after which no person is allowed to pass. There are one hundred and sixty, or two hundred families, of which forty or fifty are of Polish origin, the rest are Jews from Spain, Barbary, and different parts of Syria. Tiberias is one of the four holy cities of the Talmud; the other three being Szaffad, Jerusalem, and Hebron. It is esteemed holy ground, because Jacob is supposed to have resided here, and because it is situated on the lake Genasereth, from which, according to the most generally received opinion of the Talmud, the Messiah is to rise. The greater part of the Jews who reside in these holy places do not engage in mercantile pursuits; but are a society of religious persons occupied solely with their sacred duties. There are among them only two who are merchants, and men of property, and these are styled Kafers or unbelievers by the others, who do nothing but read and pray. Jewish devotees from all parts of the globe flock to the four holy cities, in order to pass their days in praying for their own salvation, and that of their brethren, who remain occupied in worldly pursuits. But the offering up of prayers by these devotees is rendered still more indispensible by a dogma contained in the Talmud, that the world will return to its primitive chaos, if prayers are not addressed to the God of Israel at least twice a week in these four cities; this belief produces considerable pecuniary advantage to the supplicants, as the missionaries sent abroad to collect alms for the support of these religious fraternities plead the danger of the threatened chaos, to induce the rich Jews to send supplies of money, in order that the prayers may be constantly offered up. Three or four missionaries are sent out every year; one to the coasts of Africa from Damietta to Mogadore, another to the coasts of Europe from Venice to Gibraltar, a third to the Archipelago, Constantinople, and Anatolia; and a fourth through Syria. The charity of the Jews of London is appealed to from time to time; but the Jews of Gibraltar have the reputation of being more liberal than any others, and, from four to five thousand Spanish dollars are received annually from them. The Polish Jews settled at Tabaria send several collectors regularly into Bohemia and Poland, and the rich Jewish merchants in those countries have their pensioners in the Holy Land, to whom they regularly transmit sums of money. Great jealousy seems to prevail between the Syrian and Polish Jews. The former being in possession of the place, oblige the foreighers to pay excessively high for their lodgings; and compel them also to contribute considerable sums towards the relief of the indigent Syrians, while they themselves never give the smallest trifle to the poor from Poland.

The pilgrim Jews, who repair to Tiberias, are of all ages from twelve to sixty. If they bring a little money with them the cunning of their brethren here soon deprives them of it; for as they arrive with the most extravagant ideas, of the holy cities, they are easily imposed upon before their enthusiasm begins to cool. To rent a house in which some learned Rabbin or saint died, to visit the tombs of the most renowned devotees, to have the sacred books opened in their presence, and public prayers read for the salvation of the new-comers, all these inestimable advantages, together with various other minor religious tricks, soon strip the stranger of his last farthing; he then becomes dependent upon the charity of his nation, upon foreign subsidies, or upon the fervour of some inexperienced pilgrim. Those who go abroad as missionaries generally realise some property, as they are allowed ten per cent. upon all alms collected, besides their travelling expenses. The Jewish devotees pass the whole day in the schools or the synagogue, reciting the Old Testament and the Talmud, both of which many of them know entirely by heart. They all write Hebrew; but I did not see any fine hand-writing amongst them; their learning, seems to be on the same level as that of the Turks, among whom an Olema thinks he has attained the pinnacle of knowledge if he can recite all the Koran together with some thousand of Hadeath, or sentences of the Prophet, and traditions concerning him; but neither Jews, nor Turks, nor Christians, in these countries, have the slightest idea of that criticism, which might guide them to a rational explanation or emendation of their sacred books. It was in vain that I put questions to several of the first Rabbins, concerning the desert in which the children of Israel sojourned for forty years; I found that my own scanty knowledge of the geography of Palestine, and of its partition amongst the twelve tribes, was superior to theirs.

There are some beautiful copies of the books of Moses in the Syrian synagogue, written upon a long roll of leather, not parchment, but no one could tell me when or where they were made; I suspect, however, that they came from Bagdad, where the best Hebrew scribes live, and of whose writings I had seen many fine specimens at Aleppo and Damascus. The libraries of the two schools at Tiberias are moderately stocked with Hebrew books, most of which have been printed at Vienna and Venice. Except some copies of the Old Testament and the Talmud, they have no manuscripts.

They observe a singular custom here in praying; while the Rabbin recites the Psalms of David, or the prayers extracted from them, the congregation frequently imitate by their voice or gestures, the meaning of some remarkable passages; for example, when the Rabbin pronounces the words, "Praise the Lord with the sound of the trumpet," they imitate the sound of the trumpet through their closed fists. When "a horrible tempest" occurs, they puff and blow to represent a storm; or should he mention "the cries of the righteous in distress," they all set up a loud screaming; and it not unfrequently happens that while some are still blowing the storm, others have already begun the cries of the righteous, thus forming a concert which it is difficult for any but a zealous Hebrew to hear with gravity.

The Jews enjoy here perfect religious freedom, more particularly since Soleiman, whose principal minister, Haym Farkhy, is a Jew, has succeeded to the Pashalik of Akka. During the life of Djezzar Pasha they were often obliged to pay heavy fines; at present they merely pay the Kharadj. Their conduct, however, is not so prudent as it ought to be, in a country where the Turks are always watching for a pretext to extort money; they sell wine and brandy to the soldiers of the town, almost publicly, and at their weddings they make a very dangerous display of their wealth. On these occasions they traverse the city in pompous procession, carrying before the bride the plate of almost the whole community, consisting of large dishes, coffee pots, coffee cups, &c., and they feast in the house of the bridegroom for seven successive days and nights. The wedding feast of a man who has about fifty pounds a year, and no Jew can live with his family on less, will often cost more than sixty pounds. They marry at a very early age, it being not uncommon to see mothers of eleven and fathers of thirteen years. The Rabbin of Tiberias is under the great

Rabbin of Szaffad, who pronounces final judgment on all contested points of law and religion.

I found amongst the Polish Jews, one from Bohemia, an honest German, who was overjoyed on hearing me speak his own language, and who carried me through the quarter, introducing me to all his acquaintance. In every house I was offered brandy, and the women appeared to be much less shy than they are in other parts of Syria. It may easily be supposed that many of these Jews are discontented with their lot. Led by the stories of the missionaries to conceive the most exalted ideas of the land of promise, as they still call it, several of them have absconded from their parents, to beg their way to Palestine, but no sooner do they arrive in one or other of the four holy cities, than they find by the aspect of all around them, that they have been deceived. A few find their way back to their native country, but the greater number remain, and look forward to the inestimable advantage of having their bones laid in the holy land. The cemetery of the Jews of Tiberias is on the declivity of the mountain, about half an hour from the town; where the tombs of their most renowed persons are visited much in the same manner as are the sepulchres of Mussulman saints. I was informed that a great Rabbin lay buried there, with fourteen thousand of his scholars around him.

The ancient town of Tiberias does not seem to have occupied any part of the present limits of Tabaria, but was probably situated at a short distance farther to the south, near the borders of the lake. Its ruins begin at about five minutes walk from the wall of the present town, on the road to the hot-wells. The only remains of antiquity are a few columns, heaps of stones, and some half ruined walls and foundations of houses. On the sea-side, close to the water, are the ruins of a long thick wall or mole, with a few columns of gray granite, lying in the sea. About mid-way between the town and the hot-wells, in the midst of the plain, I saw seven columns, of which two only are standing upright; and there may probably be more lying on the ground, hid among the high grass with which the plain is covered; they are of gray granite, about twelve or fourteen feet long, and fifteen inches in diameter; at a short distance from them is the fragment of a beautiful column of red Egyptian granite, of more than two feet in diameter. These ruins stretch along the sea-shore, as far as the hot springs, and extend to about three hundred yards inland. The springs are at thirty-five minutes from the modern town, and twenty paces from the water's edge; they were probably very near the gate of the ancient town. No vestiges of buildings of any size are visible here; nothing being seen but the ruins of small arched buildings, and heaps of stone.

There are some other remains of ancient habitations on the north side of the town, upon a hill close to the sea, which is connected with the mountain; here are also some thick walls which indicate that this point, which commands the town, was anciently fortified. None of the ruined buildings in Tiberias or the neighbourhood are constructed with large stones, denoting a remote age; all the walls, of which any fragments yet remain, being of small black stones cemented together by a very thick cement. Upon a low hill on the S.W. side of the town stands a well built mosque, and the chapel of a female saint.

The present hot-bath is built over the spring nearest the town, and consists of two double rooms, the men's apartment being separated from that of the women. The former is a square vaulted chamber, with a large stone basin in the centre, surrounded by broad stone benches; the spring issues from the wall, and flows into the basin or bath. After remaining in the water for about ten minutes, the bathers seat themselves naked upon the stone benches, where they remain for an hour. With this chamber a coffee room cummunicates. in which a waiter lives during the bathing season, and where visitors from a distance may lodge. The spring which has thus been appropriated to bathing, is the largest of four hot sources; the volume of its water is very considerable, and would be sufficient to turn a mill. Continuing along the shore for about two hundred paces, the three other hot-springs are met with, or four, if we count separately two small ones close together. The most southern spring seems to be the hottest of all; the hand cannot be held in it. The water deposits upon the stones over which it flows in its way towards the sea, a thick crust, but the colour of the deposit is not the same from all the springs; in some it is white, in the others it is of a red yellowish hue, a circumstance which seems to indicate that the nature of the water is not the same in all the sources. There are no remains whatever of ancient buildings near the hottest spring.

People from all parts of Syria resort to these baths, which are reckoned most efficacious in July; they are recommended principally for rheumatic complaints, and cases of premature debility. Two patients only were present when I visited them. Some public women of Damascus, who were kept by the garrison of Tabaria, had established themselves in the ruined vaults and caverns near the baths.

In the fourteenth century, according to the testimony of the Arabian geographers, the tomb of Lokman the philosopher was shewn at Tiberias. Not having been immediately able to find a guide to accompany me along the valley of the Jordan, I visited a fortress in the mountain near

Medjdel, [See page 320.] of which I had heard much at Tabaria. It is called Kalaat Ibn Maan, the castle of the son of Maan, or Kalaat Hamam, the Pigeon's castle, on account of the vast quantity of wild pigeons that breed there. It is situated half An hour to the west of Medjdel, on the cliff which borders the Wady Hamam. In the calcareous mountain are many natural caverns, which have been united together by passages cut in the rock, and enlarged, in order to render them more commodious for habitation; walls have also been built across the natural openings, so that no person could enter them except through the narrow communicating passages; and wherever the nature of the almost perpendicular cliff permitted it, small bastions were built, to defend the entrance of the castle, which has been thus rendered almost impregnable. The perpendicular cliff forms its protection above, and the access from below is by a narrow path, so steep as not to allow of a horse mounting it. In the midst of the caverns several deep cisterns have been hewn. The whole might afford refuge to about six hundred men; but the walls are now much damaged. The place was probably the work of some powerful robber, about the time of the Crusades; a few vaults of communication, with pointed arches, denote Gothic architecture. Below in the valley runs a small rivulet, which empties itself into the Wady Lymoun. Here the peasants of Medjdel cultivate some gardens.

In returning from the Kalaat Hamam I was several times reprimanded by my guide, for not taking proper care of the lighted tobacco that fell from my pipe. The whole of the mountain is thickly covered with dry grass, which readily takes fire, and the slightest breath of air instantly spreads the conflagration far over the country, to the great risk of the peasant's harvest. The Arabs who inhabit the valley of the Jordan invariably put to death any person who is known to have been even the innocent cause of firing the grass, and they have made it a public law among themselves, that even in the height of intestine warfare, no one shall attempt to set his enemy's harvest on fire. One evening, while at Tabaria, I saw a large fire on the opposite side of the lake, which spread with great velocity for two days, till its progress was checked by the Wady Feik.

The water of the lake of Tiberias along its shores from Medjdel to the hot-wells, is of considerable depth, with no shallows. I was told that the water rises during the rainy season, three or four feet above its ordinary level, which seems not at all improbable, considering the great number of winter torrents which empty themselves into the lake. The northern part is full of fish, but I did not see a single one at Szammagh at the southern extremity. The most common species are the Binni, or carp, and the Mesht, which is about a foot long, and five inches broad, with a flat body, like the sole. The fishery of the lake is rented at seven hundred piastres per annum: but the only boat that was employed on it by the fishermen fell to pieces last year, and such is the indolence of these people, that they have not yet supplied its loss. The lake furnishes the inhabitants of Tiberias with water, there being no spring of sweet water near the town. Several houses have salt wells.

June 26th.—I took a guide to Mount Tabor. The whole of this country, even to the gates of Damascus, is in a state of insecurity, which renders it very imprudent to travel alone. Merchants go only in large caravans. We ascended the mountain to the west of the town, and in thirty-five minutes passed the ruined vil [lage] of Szermedein, on the declivity of the mountain, where is a fine spring, and the tomb of a celebrated saint. The people of Tabaria here cultivate Dhourra, melons, and tobacco. At the end of one hour we reached the top of the steep mountain, from whence Mount Tabor, or Djebel Tor, as the natives call it, bears S.W. by S. From hence the road continues on a gentle declivity, in the midst of well cultivated Dhourra fields, as far as a low tract called Ardh el Hamma. The whole district is covered with the thorny shrub Merar. On the west side of Ardh el Hamma we again ascended, and reached the village of Kefer Sebt, distant two hours and a half from Tabaria, and situated on the top of a range of hills which run parallel to those of Tabaria. About half an hour to the N.E. is the spring Ain Dhamy, in a deep valley. From hence a wide plain extends to the foot of Djebel Tor; in crossing it, we saw on our right, about three quarters of an hour from the road, the village Louby, and a little farther on, the village Shedjare. The plain was covered with the wild artichoke, called Khob; it bears a thorny violet coloured flower, in the shape of an artichoke, upon a stem five feet in height. In three hours and a quarter, we arrived at the Khan of Djebel Tor, a large ruinous building, inhabited by a few families. On the opposite side of the road is a half ruined fort. A large fair is held here every Monday. Though the Khan is at no great distance from the foot of Mount Tabor, the people could not inform us whether or not the Mount was inhabited at present; nor were they hospitable enough either to lend or sell us the little provision we might want, should there be no inhabitants. At a quarter of an hour from the Khan is a fine spring, where we found an encampment of Bedouins of the tribe of Szefeyh, whose principal riches consist in cows. My guide went astray in the valleys which surround the lower parts of Djebel Tor, and we were nearly three hours, from our departure from the Khan, in reaching the top of the Mount.

Mount Tabor is almost insulated, and overtops all the neighbouring summits. On its south and west sides extends a large plain, known by the name of Merdj Ibn Aamer, the Plain of Esdrelon of the Scriptures. To the S. of the plain are the mountains of Nablous, and to the N. of it, those of Nazareth, which reach to the foot of Mount Tabor, terminating at the village of Daboury. The plain of Esdrelon is about eight hours in length and four in breadth, it is very fertile, but at present almost entirely deserted. The shape of Mount Tabor is that of a truncated cone; its sides are covered to the top with a forest of oak and wild pistachio trees; its top is about half an hour in circuit. The mountain is entirely calcareous. We found on the top a single family of Greek Christians, refugees from Ezra, a village in the Haouran, where I had known them during my stay there in November, 1810. They had retired to this remote spot, to avoid paying taxes to the government, and expected to remain unnoticed; they rented the upper plain at the rate of fifty piastres per annum from the Sheikh of Daboury, to which village the mountain belongs; the harvest, which they were now gathering in, was worth about twelve hundred piastres, and they had had the good fortune not to be disturbed by any tax-gatherers, which will certainly not be the case next year, should they remain here.

On the top of Mount Tabor are found the remains of a large fortress. A thick wall, constructed with large stones, may be traced quite round the summit, close to the edge of the precipice; on several parts of it are the remains of bastions. On the west side a high arched gate, called Bab el Haoua, or the gate of the winds, is shewn, which appears to have been the principal entrance. The area is overspread with the ruins of private dwellings, built of stone with great solidity. There are no springs, but a great number of reservoirs have been cut in the rock, two of which are still of service in supplying water. The Christians consider Mount Tabor a holy place, in honour of the Transfiguration, but the exact spot at which it took place is not known; and the Latins and Greeks are at variance upon the subject. The Latins celebrate the sacred event in a small cavern, where they have formed a chapel; at about five minutes walk from which, the Greeks have built a low circular wall, with an altar before it, for the same purpose. The Latin missionaries of the Frank convent of Nazareth send annually two fathers to celebrate a mass in their chapel; they generally choose St. Peter's day for making this visit, and arrive here in the morning, in order that they may read the evening mass in the church of St. Peter at Tabaria. The Greek priests of Nazareth visit their chapel of Mount Tabor on the festival of the Virgin, on which occasion several thousand pilgrims repair to the mountain, where they pass the night under tents with their families, in mirth and feasting.

During the greater part of the summer Mount Tabor is covered in the morning with thick clouds, which disperse towards mid-day. A strong wind blows the whole of the day, and in the night dews fall, more copious than any I had seen in Syria. In the wooded parts of the mountain are wild boars and ounces. I lodged with my old acquaintance the Arab of Ezra, who had taken up his quarters in one of the ruined habitations.

June 27th.—After mid-day we returned to Tabaria by the same road. On entering the church-yard of St. Peter's, my old lodgings, I was not a little surprised to find it full of strangers. Mr. Bruce, an English traveller, had arrived from Nazareth, in company with several priests of the Frank convent, who intended to celebrate mass at night, this being St. Peter's day. I was easily prevailed on by Mr. Bruce to accompany him on his return to Nazareth the following morning, the more so, as I there hoped to find a guide for the valley of the Jordan; for no person at Tabaria seemed to be inclined to undertake the journey, except in the company of an armed caravan.

June 28th.—We left Tabaria two hours before sun-rise. There are two direct roads to Nazareth; one by Kefer Sebt and El Khan, the other by Louby. We took a third, that we might visit some spots recorded in the New Testament. In one hour from Tabaria we passed a spring called Ain el Rahham. At two hours and a half, the road leads over a high uncultivated plain, to Hedjar el Noszara, the Stones of the Christians, four or five blocks of black stone, upon which Christ is said to have reclined while addressing the people who flocked around him. The priests of Nazareth stopped to read some prayers over the stones. Below this place, towards the N.E. extends a small plain, called Sahel Hottein. The country is intersected by Wadys. About one hour distant from the stones, upon the same level, stands a hill of an oblong shape, with two projecting summits on one of its extremities; the natives call it Keroun Hottein, the Horns of Hottein. The Christians have given it the appellation of Mons Beatitudinis, and pretend that the five thousand were there fed. We travelled over an uneven, uncultivated ground, until we arrived at Kefer Kenna, four hours and a quarter from Tabaria, a neat village with a copious spring surrounded by plantations of olive and other fruit trees, and chiefly inhabited by Catholic Christians. This is the Cana celebrated in the New Testament for the miracle at the marriage feast; and the house is shewn in which Our Saviour performed it. We rested under an immense fig-tree, which afforded shelter from the sun to a dozen men and as many horses and mules. From hence the road ascends, and continues across chalky hills, overgrown with low shrubs, as far as Naszera or Nazareth, eight hours from Tabaria, by the road we travelled. I alighted at the convent belonging to the missionaries of Terra Santa. Here Mr. Bruce introduced me to Lady Hester Stanhope, who had arrived a few days before from Jerusalem and Akka, and was preparing to visit the northern parts of Syria, and among other places Palmyra. The manly spirit and enlightened curiosity of this lady ought to make many modern travellers ashamed of the indolent indifference with which they hurry over foreign countries. She sees a great deal, and carefully examines what she sees; but it is to be hoped that the polite and distinguished manner in which she is every where received by the governors of the country, will not impress her with too favourable an opinion of the Turks in general, and of their disposition towards the nations of Europe.

Naszera is one of the principal towns of the Pashalik of Akka; its inhabitants are industrious, because they are treated with less severity than those of the country towns in general; two-thirds of them are Turks, and one-third Christians; there are about ninety Latin families; together with a congregation of Greek Catholics and another of Maronites. The house of Joseph is shewn to pilgrims and travellers; but the principal curiosity of Nazareth is the convent of the Latin friars, a very spacious and commodious building, which was thoroughly repaired, and considerably enlarged in 1730. Within it is the church of the Annunciation, in which the spot is shewn where the angel stood, when he announced to the Virgin Mary the tidings of the Messiah; behind the altar is a subterraneous cavern divided into small grottos, where the Virgin is said to have lived: her kitchen, parlour, and bedroom, are shewn, and a narrow hole in the rock, in which the child Jesus once hid himself from his persecutors; for the Syrian Christians have a plentiful stock of such traditions, unfounded upon any authority of Scripture. The pilgrims who visit these holy spots are in the habit of knocking off small pieces of stone from the walls of the grottos, which are thus continually enlarging. In the church a miracle is still exhibited to the faithful; a fine granite column, the base and upper part of which remain, has lost the middle part of its shaft. According to the tradition, it was destroyed by the Saracens, ever since which time, the upper part has been miraculously suspended from the roof, as if attracted by a load-stone. All the Christians of Nazareth, with the friars of course at their head, affect to believe in this miracle, although it is perfectly evident that the upper part of the column is connected with the roof. The church is the finest in Syria, next to that of the Holy Sepulchre at Jerusalem, and contains two tolerably good organs. Within the walls of the convent are two gardens, and a small burying ground; the walls are very thick, and serve occasionally as a fortress to all the Christians of the town. There are at present eleven friars in the convent.

The yearly expenses of the establishment amount to upwards of £900. sterling, a small part of which is defrayed by the rent of a few houses in the town, and by the produce of some acres of corn land; the rest is remitted from Jerusalem. The whole annual expenses of the Terra Santa convents are about £15,000. They have felt very sensibly the occupation of Spain by the French, and little has been received from Europe for the last four years; while the Turkish authorities exact the same yearly tribute and extraordinary contributions, as formerly; [The Terra Santa pays to the Pasha of Damascus about £12000. a year; the Greek convent of Jerusalem pays much more, as well to maintain its own privileges, as with a view to encroach upon those of the Latins.] so that if Spain be not speedily liberated, it is to be feared that the whole establishment of the Terra Santa must be abandoned. This would be a great calamity, for it cannot be doubted that they have done honour to the European name in the Levant, and have been very beneficial to the cause of Christianity under the actual circumstances of the East.

The friars are chiefly Spanjards; they are exasperated against France, for pretending to protect them, without affording them the smallest relief from the Pasha's oppressions: [I understood from the Spanish consul at Cairo, that when the news of the capture of Madrid, in August, 1812, reached Jerusalem, the Spanish priests celebrated a public Te Deum, and took the oaths prescribed by the new constitution of the Cortes.] but they are obliged to accept this protection, as the Spanish ambassador at Constantinople is not yet acknowledged by the Porte. They are well worth the attention of any ambassador at the Porte, whose government is desirous of maintaining an influence in Syria, for they command the consciences of upwards of eighty thousand souls.

When the French invaded Syria, Nazareth was occupied by six or eight hundred men, whose advanced posts were at Tabaria and Szaffad. Two hours from hence, General Kleber sustained with a corps not exceeding fifteen hundred men, the attack of the whole Syrian army, amounting to at least twenty-five thousand. He was posted in the plain of Esdrelon, near the village of Foule, where he formed his battalion into a square, which continued fighting from sun-rise to mid-day, until they had expended almost all their ammunition. Bonaparte, informed of Kleber's perilous situation, advanced to his support with six hundred men. No sooner had he come in sight of the enemy and fired a shot over the plain, than the Turks, supposing that a large force was advancing, took precipitately to flight, during which several thousands were killed, and many drowned in the river Daboury, which then inundated a part of the plain. Bonaparte dined at Nazareth, the most northern point that he reached in Syria, and returned the same day to Akka.

After the retreat of the French from Akka, Djezzar Pasha resolved on causing all the Christians in his Pashalik to be massacred, and had already sent orders to that effect to Jerusalem and Nazareth; but Sir Sidney Smith being apprized of his intentions reproached him for his cruelty in the severest terms, and threatened that if a single Christian head should fall, he would bombard Akka and set it on fire. Djezzar was thus obliged to send counter orders, but Sir Sidney's interference is still remembered with heartfelt gratitude by all the Christians, who look upon him as their deliverer. "His word," I have often heard both Turks and Christians exclaim, "was like God's word, it never failed." The same cannot be said of his antagonist at Akka, who maliciously impressed the Christians, certainly much inclined in his favour, with the idea of his speedy return from Egypt. On retreating from Akka he sent word to his partizans at Szaffad and Nazareth, exhorting them to bear up resolutely against the Turks but for three months, when, he assured them upon his honour, and with many oaths, that he would return with a much stronger force, and deliver them from their oppressors.

The inhabitants of Nazareth differ somewhat in features and colour from the northern Syrians; their physiognomy approaches that of the Egyptians, while their dialect and pronunciation differ widely from those of Damascus. In western Palestine, especially on the coast, the inhabitants, seem in general, to bear more resemblance to the natives of Egypt, than to those of northern Syria. Towards the east of Palestine, on the contrary, especially in the villages about Nablous, Jerusalem, and Hebron, they are evidently of the true Syrian stock, in features, though not in language. It would be an interesting subject for an artist to pourtray accurately the different character of features of the Syrian nations; the Aleppine, the Turkman, the native of Mount Libanus, the Damascene, the inhabitant of the sea-coast from Beirout to Akka, and the Bedouin, although all inhabiting the same country, have distict national physiognomies, and a slight acquaintance with them enables one to determine the native district of a Syrian, with almost as much certainty as an Englishman may be distinguished at first sight from an Italian or an inhabitant of the south of France.

The Christians of Nazareth enjoy great liberty. The fathers go a shooting alone in their monastic habits to several hours distance from the convent, without ever being insulted by the Turks. I was told that about thirty years ago the padre guardiano of the convent was also Sheikh or chief justice of the town, an office for which he paid a certain yearly sum to the Pasha of Akka; the police of the place was consequently in his hands, and when any disturbance happened, the reverend father used to take his stick, repair to the spot, and lay about him freely, no matter whether upon Turks or Christians. The guardian has still much influence in the town, because he is supposed, as usual, to be on good terms with the Pasha, but at present the chief man at Nazareth is M. Catafago, a merchant of Frank origin, born at Aleppo. He has rented from the Pasha about twelve villages situated in the neighbourhood of Nazareth and the plain of Esdrelon, for which he pays yearly upwards of £3000. [The villages in the Pashalik of Akka are all of the description which the Turkish law calls Melk. They are all assessed at certain yearly sums, which each is obliged to pay, whatever may be the number of its inhabitants. This is one of the chief causes of the depopulation of many parts of Syria.] His profits are very considerable, and as he meddles much in the politics and intrigues of the country, he has become a person of great consequence. His influence and recommendations may prove very useful to travellers in Palestine, especially to those who visit the dangerous districts of Nablous. It happened luckily during my stay at Nazareth, that two petty merchants arrived there from Szalt, to take up some merchandize which they sell at Szalt on account of their principals at this place. Szalt was precisely the point I wished to reach, not having been able to visit it during my late tour in the mountains of Moerad; on their return therefore I gladly joined their little carayan, and we left Nazareth at midnight, on the 1st of July.

July 2d.—Our road lay over a mountainous country. In two hours from Nazareth we passed a small rivulet. Two hours and a half, the village Denouny, and near it the ruins of Endor, where the witch's grotto is shewn. From hence the direction of our route was S.S.E. Leaving Mount Tabor to the left we passed along the plain of Esdrelon: meeting with several springs in our road; but the country is a complete desert, although the soil is fertile. At five hours and a half is the village of Om el Taybe, belonging to the district of Djebel Nablous, or as it is also called Belad Harthe. The inhabitants of Nablous are governed by their own chiefs, who are invested by the Pasha. It is said that the villages belonging to the district can raise an army of five thousand men. They are a restless people, continually in dispute with each other, and frequently in insurrection against the Pasha. Djezzar never succeeded in completely subduing them, and Junot, with a corps of fifteen hundred French soldiers, was defeated by them. The principal chief of Nablous at present is of the family of

Shadely. In six hours and three quarters we passed the village of Merasz-rasz, upon the summit of a chain of hills on the side of Wady Oeshe, which falls into the Jordan. At about half an hour to the north of this Wady runs another, called Wady Byre, likewise falling into that river. Between these two valleys are situated the villages of Denna and Kokab. Beyond Meraszrasz we began to descend, and reached the bottom of the valley El Ghor in seven hours and three quarters from our departure from Nazareth. We now turned more southward, and followed the valley as far as Bysan, distant eight hours and a quarter from Nazareth.

The two merchants and myself had left the caravan at Meraszrasz, and proceeded to Bysan, there to repose till the camels came up: but the drivers missed the road, and we continued almost the whole day in search of them. Bysan (Bethsan, Scythopolis) is situated upon rising ground, on the west side of the Ghor, where the chain of mountains bordering the valley declins considerably in height, and presents merely elevated ground, quite open towards the west. At one hour distant, to the south, the mountains begin again. The ancient town was watered by a river, now called Moiet Bysan, or the water of Bysan, which flows in different branches towards the plain. The ruins of Scythopolis are of considerable extent, and the town, built along the banks of the rivulet and in the valleys formed by its several branches, must have been nearly three miles in circuit. The only remains are large heaps of black hewn stones, many foundations of houses, and the fragments of a few columns. I saw only a single shaft of a column standing. In one of the valleys is a large mound of earth, which appeared to me to be artificial; it was the site perhaps of a castle for the defence of the town. On the left bank of the stream is a large Khan, where the caravans repose which take the shortest road from Jerusalem to Damascus.

The present village of Bysan contains seventy or eighty houses; its inhabitants are in a miserable condition, from being exposed to the depredations of the Bedouins of the Ghor, to whom they also pay a heavy tribute. After waiting here some time for the arrival of the caravan, we rode across the valley, till we reached the banks of the Jordan, about two hours distant from Bysan, which bore N.N.W. from us. We here crossed the river at a ford, where our companions arrived soon afterwards.

The valley of the Jordan, or El Ghor, which may be said to begin at the northern extremity of the lake of Tiberias, has near Bysan a direction of N. by E. and S. by W. Its breadth is about two hours. The great number of rivulets which descend from the mountains on both sides, and form numerous pools of stagnant water, produce in many places a pleasing verdure, and a luxuriant growth of wild herbage and grass; but the greater part of the ground is a parched desert, of which a few spots only are cultivated by the Bedouins. In the neighbourhood of Bysan the soil is entirely of marle; there are very few trees; but wherever there is water high reeds are found. The river Jordan, on issuing from the lake of Tiberias, flows for about three hours near the western hills, and then turns towards the eastern, on which side it continues its course for several hours. The river flows in a valley of about a quarter of an hour in breadth, which is considerably lower than the rest of the plain of Ghor; this lower valley is covered with high trees and a luxuriant verdure, which affords a striking contrast with the sandy slopes that border it on both sides. The trees most frequently met with on the banks of the Jordan are of the species called by the Arabs Gharab and Kottab [The following are the names or the rivulets which descend from the western mountains into the Ghor, to the north or Bysan. Beginning at the southern extremity of the lake of Tiberias are Wady Fedjaz, Ain el Szammera, Wady Djaloud, Wady el Byre, and Wady el Oeshe. To the south of Bysan are Wady el Maleh, Wady Medjedda, with a ruined town so called, Wady el Beydhan, coming from the neighbourhood of Nablous, and Wady el Farah. On the east side of the Jordan, beginning at the Sheriat el Mandhour, and continuing to the place where we crossed the river, the following Wadys empty themselves into it: Wady el Arab, Wady el Koszeir, Wady el Taybe, Wady el Seklab, which last falls into the Jordan near the village Erbayn, about one hour's distance north of the place where we crossed. This Wady forms the boundary between the districts; called El Koura and El Wostye.

On the west side of the river, to the north of Bysan, are the following ruined places in the Ghor: beginning at the lake, Faszayl, El Odja, Ayn Sultan. Near where we crossed, to the south, are the ruins of Sukkot. On the western banks of the river, farther south than Ayn Sultan, which is about one hour distant from Bysan, there are no ruins, as far as Rieha, or Jericho, the yalley in that direction being full of rocks, and little susceptible of cultivation.].

The river, where we passed it, was about eighty paces broad, and about three feet deep; this, it must be recollected, was in the midst of summer. In the winter it inundates the plain in the bottom of the narrow valley, but never rises to the level of the upper plain of the Ghor, which is at least forty feet above the level of the river. The river is fordable in many places during summer, but the few spots where it may be crossed in the rainy season are known only to the Arabs.

After passing the river we continued our route close to the foot of the eastern mountain. In half an hour from the ford we crossed Wady Mous, coming from the mountains of Adjeloun. In one hour and a quarter we passed Wady Yabes, and near it, the Mezar, or saint's tomb called Sherhabeib. In two hours we came to a stony and hilly district, intersected by several deep but dry Wadys, called Korn el Hemar, the Ass's Horn. Our direction was alternately S. and S. by W. Here the Jordan returns to the western side of the valley. The Korn el Hemar projects into the Ghor about four miles, so that when seen from the north the valley seems to be completely shut up by these hills. From thence a fertile tract commences, overgrown with many Bouttom or wild pistachio trees. Large tracts of ground were burnt, owing probably to the negligence of travellers who had set the dry grass on fire. At the end of six hours, and late at night, we passed to the right, the ruins of an ancient city standing on the declivity of the mountain and still bearing its original name Amata. My companions told me that several columns remain standing, and also some large buildings. A small rivulet here descends into the plain. In six hours and a half we reached the Mezar Abou Obeida, where we rested for two hours. The tomb of the Sheikh is surrounded by a few peasant's houses; but there are no inhabitants at present, except the keeper of the tomb and his wife, who live upon the charity of the Bedouins. It appears from the account given by the great Barbary traveller, Ibn Batouta, that in the sixteenth century this part of the Ghor was well cultivated, and full of villages.

The valley of the Jordan affords pasturage to numerous tribes of Bedouins. Some of them remain here the whole year, considering it as their patrimony; others visit it only in winter; of the latter description are the Bedouins who belong to the districts of Naszera and Nablous, as well as those of the eastern mountains. We met with several encampments of stationary Bedouins, who cultivate a few fields of wheat, barley, and Dhourra. They are at peace with the people of Szalt, to many of whom the greater part of them are personally known; we therefore passed unmolested; but a stranger who should venture to travel here unaccompanied by a guide of the country would most certainly be stripped. [For the names of the Bedouin tribes see the classification, in the Appendix.] July 3d.— We departed from Abou Obeida long before sun-rise, proceeding from thence in a more western direction. In a quarter of an hour we passed the northern branch of the river El Zerka, near a mill, which was at work. In one hour we passed the principal stream, a small river, which empties itself into the Jordan about one hour and a half to the S.W. of the spot where it issues from the mountain. Its banks are overgrown with Defle (Solanum furiosum). On the other side of the Zerka we ascended the mountain by a steep acclivity, but the road, from being much frequented, is tolerably good. The mountain consists of calcareous rock, with layers of various coloured sand-stone, and large blocks of the black Haouran stone, or basalt, which forms a principal feature in the mineralogy of Eastern Syria. In two hours and three quarters we arrived at the top of the mountain, from whence Abou Obeida bore N.N.W. Here we had a fine view over the valley below.

On the west side of the Jordan, between the river and the mountains of Nablous, I remarked a chain of low calcareous rocky heights which begin at about three hours north of Abou Obeida, and continue for several hours distance to the S. of that place on the opposite side of the river. The highest point of Djebel Nablous bore N.W.; the direction of Nablous itself was pointed out to me as W.N.W. On the summit where we stood are some large heaps of hewn stones, and several ruined walls, with the fragments of three large columns. The Arabs call the spot El Meysera. The Zerka, or Jabock of the Scriptures, divides the district of Moerad from the country called El Belka. The highest summit of the mountains of Moerad seems to be considerably higher than any part of the mountains of Belka. From Meysera the road continues over an uneven tract, along the summit of the lower ridge of mountains which form the northern limits of the Belka. We had now entered a climate quite different from that of the Ghor. During the whole of yesterday we had been much oppressed by heat, which was never lessened by the slightest breeze; in the Belka mountains, on the contrary, we were refreshed by cool winds, and every where found a grateful shade of fine oak and wild pistachio trees, with a scenery more like that of Europe than any I had yet seen in Syria. In three quarters of an hour from Meysera we passed a spring. I was told that in the valley of the Zerka, at about one hour above its issue from the mountains into the plain, are several hills, called Telloul el Dahab (the Hills of Gold), so called, as the Arabs affirm, from their containing a gold mine. In one hour and a quarter we passed the ruined place called El Herath. The Arabs cultivate here several fields of Dhourra and cucumbers. My companions seeing no keepers in the neighbouring wood carried off more than a quintal of cucumbers. About one hour to the S.E. of Herath are the ruined places called Allan, and Syhhan. At the end of two hours we reached the foot of the mountain called Djebel Djelaad and Djebel Djelaoud, the Gilead of the Scriptures, which runs from east to west, and is about two hours and a half in length. Upon it are the ruined towns of Djelaad and Djelaoud. We ascended the western extremity of the mountain, and then reached the lofty mountain called Djebel Osha, whose summit overtops the whole of the Belka. In three hours and a quarter from Meysera we passed near the top of Mount Osha, our general direction being still S.S.E. The forest here grows thicker; it consists of oak, Bouttom, and Balout trees. The Keykab is also very common. In three hours and three quarters we descended the southern side of the mountain, near the tomb of Osha, and reached Szalt, four hours and a half distant from Meysera. Near the tomb of Osha was an encampment of about sixty tents of the tribe of Abad; they had lately been robbed of almost all their cattle by the Beni Szakher, and were reduced to such misery that they could not afford to give us a little sour milk which we begged of them. They were still at war with the Beni Szakher, and were in hopes of recovering a part of their property; but as they were too weak to act openly, they had encamped, for protection, in the neighbourhood of their friends the inhabitants of Szalt. They intended to make from hence some plundering excursions against their enemies, for they had now hardly any thing more to lose in continuing at war with them. I alighted at Szalt at the house of one of my companions, where I was hospitably entertained during the whole of my stay at this place.

The town of Szalt is situated on the declivity of a hill, crowned by a castle, and is surrounded on all sides by steep mountains. It is the only inhabited place in the province of Belka, and its inhabitants are quite independent. The Pashas of Damascus have several times endeavoured in vain to subdue them. Abdulla Pasha, the late governor, besieged the town for three months, without success. The population consists of about four hundred Musulman and eighty Christian families of the Greek church, who live in perfect amity and equality together: the Musulmans are composed of three tribes, the Beni Kerad, the Owamele, and the Kteyshat, each of which has its separate quarter in the town; the principal Sheikhs, at present two in number, live in the castle; but they have no other authority over the rest than such as a Bedouin Sheikh exercises over his tribe. The castle was almost wholly rebuilt by the famous Dhaher el Omar, [See the history of Sheikh Dhaher, the predecessor of Djezzar Pasha in the government of Akka, in Volney. Voyage en Egypte et en Syrie, vol. ii. chap. 25. Ed.] who resided here several years. He obtained possession by the assistance of the weakest of the two parties into which the place was divided, but he was finally driven out by the united efforts of both parties.

The castle is well built, has a few old guns, and is surrounded by a wide ditch. In the midst of the town is a fine spring, to which there is a secret subterraneous passage from the castle, still made use of in times of siege. In a narrow valley about ten minutes walk from the town, is another spring called Ain Djedour, the waters of both serve to irrigate the gardens and orchards which lie along the valley. Opposite to Ain Djedour is a spacious sepulchral cave cut in the rock, which the people affirm to have been a church. In the town, an old mosque is the only object that presents itself to the antiquary. The Christians have a small church, dedicated to the Virgin, where divine service is performed by two priests, who each receive annually from their community about £4. They are not very rigid observers either of their prayers or fasts; and although it was now the time of Lent with the Greeks, I daily saw the most respectable Christians eating flesh and butter.

The greater part of the population of Szalt is agricultural, a few are weavers, and there are about twenty shops, which sell on commission for the merchants of Nazareth, Damascus, Nablous, and Jerusalem, and furnish the Bedouins with articles of dress and furniture. The prices are at least fifty per cent. higher than at Damascus. The culture consists of wheat and barley, the superfluous produce of which is sold to the Bedouins; vast quantities of grapes are also grown, which are dried and sold at Jerusalem. The arable fields are at least eight miles distant from Szalt, in the low grounds of the neighbouring mountains, where they take advantage of the winter torrents. In the time of harvest the Szaltese transport their families thither, where they live for several months under tents, like true Bedouins. The principal encampment is at a place called Feheis, about one bour and a half to the S.E. of Szalt.

In addition to the means of subsistence just mentioned the inhabitants of Szalt have several others: in July and August they collect, in the mountains of the Belka the leaves of the Sumach, which they dry and carry to the market at Jerusalem, for the use of the tanneries; upwards of five hundred camel loads are yearly exported, at the rate of fifteen to eighteen piastres the cwt. The merchants also buy up ostrich feathers from the Bedouins, which they sell to great advantage at Damascus.

The food and clothing of the Szaltese are inferior in quality to those of the peasants of northern Syria. Their dress, especially the women's approaches to that of the Bedouins: their language is the true Bedouin dialect. The only public expense incurred by them is that of entertaining travellers: for this purpose there are four public taverns (Menzel, or Medhafe), three belonging to the Turks and one to the Christians; and whoever enters there is maintained as long as he chooses, provided his stay be not prolonged to an unreasonable period, without reasons being assigned for such delay. Breakfast, dinner, and supper, with a proportionate number of cups of coffee, are served up to the stranger, whoever he may be. For guests of respectability a goat or lamb is slaughtered, and some of the inhabitants then partake of the supper. The expenses incurred by these Menzels are shared among the heads of families, according to their respective wealth, and every tavern has a kind of landlord, who keeps the accounts, and provides the kitchen out of the common stock. I was told that every respectable family paid about fifty piastres per annum into the hands of the master of the Menzels, which makes altogether a sum of about £1000. spent in the entertainment of strangers. Were the place dependent on any Turkish government, more than triple that sum would be extorted from its inhabitants for the support of passengers. Besides the Menzels every family is always ready to receive any acquaintances who may prefer their house to the public inn. It will readily be conceived, that upon these terms the people of Szalt are friends of the neighbouring Bedouins; who moreover fear them because they have a secure retreat, and can muster about four hundred fire-locks, and from forty to fifty horses. The powerful tribe of Beni Szakher alone is fearless of the people of Szalt; on the contrary, they exact a small yearly tribute from the town, which is willingly paid, in order to secure the harvest against the depredations of these formidable neighbours; disputes nevertheless arise, and Szalt is often at war with the Beni Szakher.

While I remained at Szalt I was told of a traveller of whom I had also heard in the Haouran; he was a Christian of Abyssinia, whose desire it was to end his days at Jerusalem; he first sailed from Massoua to Djidda, where he was seized by the Wahabi, and carried to their chief Ibn Saoud at Deraye, where he remained two years. From Deraye he crossed the desert with the encampments of wandering Bedouins, in the direction of Damascus, and last year he reached Boszra in the Haouran, from whence he was sent by the Christians to Szalt, where he remained a few days, and then proceeded for Jerusalem. When he arrived at the Jordan, he declared to his companions that he was a priest, a circumstance which he had always kept secret; he continued two days on the banks of the river fasting and praying, and from thence made his way alone to Jerusalem. He never tasted animal food, and although he had experienced no sickness on the road, he died soon after his arrival in the holy city.

It was not my intention to tarry at Szalt; I wished to proceed by the first opportunity to Kerek, a town on the eastern side of the Dead sea; but the communications in these deserted countries are far from being regular, and the want of a proper guide obliged me to delay my departure for ten days; during this delay I had the good fortune to see the ruins of Amman, which I had not been able to visit in the course of my late tour in the Decapolis. But before I describe Amman I shall subjoin some notes on the neighbourhood of Szalt.

A narrow valley leads up from Szalt towards the Mezar Osha, which I have already mentioned. Half way up, the valley is planted with vines, which are grown upon terraces as in Mount Libanus, to prevent their being washed away by the winter torrents. The Mezar Osha is supposed to contain the tomb of Neby Osha, or the prophet Hosea, equally revered by Turks and Christians, and to whom the followers of both religions are in the habit of offering prayers and sacrifices. The latter consist generally of a sheep, to be slain in honour of the saint, or of some perfumes to be burnt over his tomb. I was invited to partake of a sheep presented by a suppliant, to whose prayers the saint had been favourable. There was a large party, and we spent a very pleasant day under a fine oak-tree just by the tomb. The wives and daughters of those who were invited were present, and mixed freely in the conversation. The tomb is covered by a vaulted building, one end of which serves as a mosque; the tomb itself, in the form of a coffin, is thirty-six feet long, three feet broad, and three feet and a half in height, being thus constructed in conformity with the notion of the Turks, who suppose that all our forefathers were giants, and especially the prophets before Mohammed. The tomb of Noah in the valley of Coelo-Syria is still longer. The coffin of Osha is covered with silk stuffs of different colours, which have been presented to him as votive offerings. Visitors generally throw a couple of paras upon the tomb. These are collected by the guardian, and pay the expenses of illuminating the apartment during the summer months; for in the winter season hardly any body seeks favours at the shrine of the saint. In one corner stands a small plate, upon which some of the most devout visitors place a piece of incense. A wooden partition separates the tomb from the mosque, where the Turks generally say a few prayers before they enter the inner apartment. On the outside of the building is a very large and deep cistern much frequented by the Bedouins. Here is a fine view over the Ghor. Rieha, or Jericho, is visible at a great distance to the southward. About half an hour to the N.W. of Osha, on the lower part of the mountain, is the ruined place called Kafer Houda.

As pilgrimage in the east is generally coupled with mercantile speculations, Osha's tomb is much resorted to for commercial purposes, and like Mekka and Jerusalem, is transformed into a fair at the time of the visit of the pilgrims. The Araps of the Belka, especially the Beni Szakher, bring here Kelly or soap-ashes, which they burn during the summer in large quantities: these are bought up by a merchant of Nablous, who has for many years monopolized the trade in this article. The soap-ashes obtained from the herb Shiman, of the Belka, are esteemed the best in the country, to the S. of Damascus, as those of Palmyra are reckoned the best in northern Syria. They are sold by the Arabs for about half a crown the English cwt., but the purchaser is obliged to pay heavy duties upon them. The chief of the Arabs of El Adouan, who is looked upon as the lord of the Belka, although his tribe is at present considerably weakened, exacts for himself five piastres from every camel load, two piastres for his writer, and two piastres for his slave. The town of Szalt takes one piastre for every load, the produce of which duty is divided among the public taverns of the town. The quantity of soap-ashes brought to the Osha market amounts, one year with another, to about three thousand camel loads. The Nablous merchant is obliged to come in person to Szalt in autumn. According to old customs, he alights at a private house, all the expenses of which he pays during his stay; he is bound also to feed all strangers who arrive during the same period at Szalt; in consequence of which the Menzels remain shut; and he makes considerable presents on quitting the place. In order that all the inhabitants may share in the advantages arising from his visits, he alights at a different house every year.

In descending the narrow valley to the south of Szalt, the ruins of a considerable town are met with, consisting of foundations of buildings and heaps of stones. The Arabs call the place Kherbet el Souk. Near it is a fine spring called Ain Hazeir (perhaps the ancient Jazer), which turns several mills, and empties itself into the Wady Shoeb. The latter joins the Jordan near the ruined city of Nymrein. In a S.W. direction from Szalt, distant about two hours and a half, are the ruined places called Kherbet Ayoub, Heremmela, Ayra, one of the towns built by the tribe of Gad, and Yerka. East of Szalt, about one hour, are the ruins called El Deir.

I found it impossible at Szalt to procure a guide to Amman; the country was in a state which rendered it very dangerous to travel through it: the Beni Szakher were at war with the Arabs of Adouan, with the government of Damascus, and with the Rowalla, a branch of the Aeneze; and we heard daily of skirmishes taking place between the contending parties, principally near the river Zerka. Amman being a noted spring, was frequented by both the hostile parties; and although, the people of Szalt were now at peace with the Beni Szakher, having concluded it on the day of my arrival, yet they were upon very indifferent terms with the Adouan and Rowalla. I had once engaged four armed men to accompany me on foot to the place, but when we were just setting out, after sunset, their wives came crying to my lodging, and upbraided their husbands with madness in exposing their lives for a couple of piastres. Being equally unsuccessful in several other attempts, and tired of the exaggerations of my land-lord, who pretended that I should be in danger of being stripped, and even killed, I at length became impatient, and quitting Szalt in the evening of the 6th, I rode over to Feheis, where the greater part of the Szaltese were encamped, for the labours of the harvest, and where it was more likely that I should meet with a guide. On my way I passed the deep Wady Ezrak, where is a rivulet and several mills.

El Feheis is a ruined city, with a spring near it; here are the remains of an arched building, in which the Christians sometimes perform divine service. Below Feheis, upon the top of a lower mountain, is the ruined place called El Khandok, which appears to have been a fort; it is surrounded with a wall of large stones, and the remains of several bastions are visible. From a point near Khandok, the Dead sea, which I saw for the first time, bears S.W. b. W.

At Feheis I was so fortunate as to find a guide who five years ago had served in the same capacity to Mousa, the name assumed by M. Seetzen. As he was well acquainted with all the Bedouins, and on friendly terms with them, he engaged to take me to Amman, in company with another horseman.

July 7th.—We set off before sunrise. On leaving Feheis we crossed a mountainous country, passed through a thick forest of oak trees, and in three quarters of an hour reached the Ardh el Hemar, which is the name of a district extending north and south for about two hours. Here are a number of springs, which have rendered it a favourite place of resort of the Bedouins: the valley was covered with a fine coat of verdant pasture. From hence the road ascended through oak woods and pleasant hills, over flinty ground, till we reached, after a march of two hours and a half, an elevated plain, from whence we had an extensive view towards the east. The plain, which in this part is called El Ahma, is a fertile tract, interspersed with low hills; these are for the greater part crowned with ruins, but they are of irregular forms, unlike the Tels or artificial heights of the Haouran, and of northern Syria. Just by the road, at the end of three hours, are the ruins called El Kholda. To the left are the ruins of Kherbet Karakagheish; and to the right, at half an hour's distance, the ruins of Sar, and Fokhara. At about one hour south of Sar begins the district called Kattar or Marka. The ruins which we passed here, as well as all those before mentioned in the mountains of Belka, present no objects of any interest. They consist of a few walls of dwelling houses, heaps of stones, the foundations of some public edifices, and a few cisterns now filled up;

there is nothing entire, but it appears that the mode of building was very solid, all the remains being formed of large stones. It is evident also, that the whole of the country must have been extremely well cultivated, in order to have afforded subsistence to the inhabitants of so many towns. At the end of three hours and a half we entered a broad valley, which brought us in half an hour to the ruins of Amman, which lies about nineteen English miles to the S.E. by E. of Szalt. The annexed plan [not included] will give an idea of the situation and ruins of Amman, one of the most ancient of the cities recorded in Jewish history. The town lies along the banks of a river called Moiet Amman, which has its source in a pond (a), at a few hundred paces from the south-western end of the town; I was informed that this river is lost in the earth one hour below the pond, that it issues again, and takes the name of Ain Ghazale; then disappears a second time and rises again near a ruined place called Reszeyfa; beyond which it is said to be lost for a third time, till it reappears about an hour to the west of Kalaat Zerka, otherwise called Kaszr Shebeib, near the river Zerka, into which it empties itself. Ain Ghazale is about one hour and a half distant from Amman, Kalaat Zerka is four hours distant. The river of Amman runs in a valley bordered on both sides by barren hills of flint, which advance on the south side close to the edge of the stream.

The edifices which still remain to attest the former splendour of Amman are the following: a spacious church (b), built with large stones, and having a steeple of the shape of those which I saw in several ruined towns in the Haouran. There are wide arches in the walls of the church.— A small building (c), with niches, probably a temple.—A temple (d), of which a part of the side walls, and a niche in the back wall are remaining; there are no ornaments either on the walls, or about the niche.——A curved wall (e) along the water side, with many niches: before it was a row of large columns, of which four remain, but without capitals, I conjecture this to have been a kind of stoa, or public walk; it does not communicate with any other edifice.—A high arched bridge (f) over the river; this appears to have been the only bridge in the town, although the river is not fordable in the winter. The banks of the river, as well as its bed, are paved, but the pavement has been in most places carried away by the violence of the winter torrent. The stream is full of small fish. On the south side of the river is a fine theatre, the largest that I have seen in Syria. It has forty rows of seats; between the tenth and eleventh from the bottom occurs a row of eight boxes or small apartments, capable of holding about twelve spectators each; fourteen rows higher, a similar row of boxes occupies the place of the middle seats, and at the top of all there is a third tier of boxes excavated in the rocky side of the hill, upon the declivity of which the theatre is built. On both wings of the theatre are vaults. In front was a colonnade, of which eight Corinthian columns yet remain, besides four fragments of shafts; they are about fifteen feet high, surmounted by an entablature still entire. This colonnade must have had at least fifty columns; the workmanship is not of the best Roman times. Near this theatre is a building (h), the details of which I was not able to make out exactly; its front is built irregularly, without columns, or ornaments of any kind. On entering I found a semi-circular area, enclosed by a high wall in which narrow steps were formed, running all round from bottom to top. The inside of the front wall, as well as the round wall of the area, is richly ornamented with sculptured ornaments. The roof, which once covered the whole building, has fallen down, and choaks up the interior in such a way as to render it difficult to determine whether the edifice has been a palace, or destined for public amusements. Nearly opposite the theatre, to the northward of the river, are the remains of a temple (k), the posterior wall of which only remains, having an entablature, and several niches highly adorned with sculpture. Before this building stand the shafts of several columns three feet in diameter. Its date appears to be anterior to that of all the other buildings of Amman, and its style of architecture is much superior. At some distance farther down the Wady, stand a few small columns (i), probably the remains of a temple. The plain between the river and the northern hills is covered with ruins of private buildings, extending from the church (c) down to the columns (i); but nothing of them remains, except the foundations and some of the door posts. On the top of the highest of the northern hills stands the castle of Amman, a very extensive building; it was an oblong square, filled with buildings, of which, about as much remains as there does of the private dwellings in the lower town. The castle walls are thick, and denote a remote antiquity: large blocks of stone are piled up without cement, and still hold together as well as if they had been recently placed; the greater part of the wall is entire, it is placed a little below the crest of the hill, and appears not to have risen much above the level of its summit. Within the castle are several deep cisterns. At (m) is a square building, in complete preservation, constructed in the same manner as the castle wall; it is without ornaments, and the only opening into it is a low door, over which was an inscription now defaced. Near this building are the traces of a large temple (n); several of its broken columns are lying on the ground; they are the largest I saw at Amman, some of them being three feet and a half in diameter; their capitals are of the Corinthian order. On the north side of the castle is a ditch cut in the rock, for the better defence of this side of the hill, which is less steep than the others.

The ruins of Amman being, with the exception of a few walls of flint, of calcareous stone of moderate hardness, have not resisted the ravages of time so well as those of Djerash. The buildings exposed to the atmosphere are all in decay, so that there is little hope of finding any inscriptions here, which might illustrate the history of the place. The construction shews that the edifices were of different ages, as in the other cities of the Decapolis, which I have examined.

I am sensible that the above description of Amman, though it notices all the principal remains, is still very imperfect; but a traveller who is not accompanied with an armed force can never hope to give very satisfactory accounts of the antiquities of these deserted countries. My guides had observed some fresh horse-dung near the water's side, which greatly alarmed them, as it was a proof that some Bedouins were hovering about. They insisted upon my returning immediately, and refusing to wait for me a moment, rode off while I was still occupied in writing a few notes upon the theatre. I hastily mounted the castle hill, ran over its ruins, and galloping after my guides, joined them at half an hour from the town. When I reproached them for their cowardice, they replied that I certainly could not suppose that, for the twelve piastres I had agreed to give them, they should expose themselves to the danger of being stripped and of losing their horses, from a mere foolish caprice of mine to write down the stones. I have often been obliged to yield to similar reasoning. A true Bedouin, however, never abandons his companion in this manner; whoever, therefore, wishes to travel in these parts, and to make accurate observations, will do well to take with him as many horsemen as may secure him against any strolling party of robbers.

About four or five bours S.S.W. from Amman are the ruins called El Kohf, with a large temple, and many columns. About eight hours S.S.E. is the ruined city of Om el Reszasz, i.e. the Mother of Lead, which, according to all accounts, is of great extent, and contains large buildings. In my present situation it was impossible for me to visit these two places. I hope that some future traveller will be more fortunate.

We returned from Amman by a more northern route. At one hour and three quarters, we passed the ruined place called Djebeyha; in two hours the ruins of Meraze. The hills which rise over the plain are covered to their tops with thick heath. At two hours and a half are the ruins of Om Djouze, with a spring. Sources of water are seldom met with in this upper plain of the Belka, a circumstance that greatly enhances the importance of the situation of Amman. At three hours and a half is Szafout, where are ruins of some extent, with a spring; the gate of a public edifice is still standing. To the north and north- east of this place, at the foot of the mountain on which it stands, extends a broad valley called El Bekka; it is extremely fertile, and is in part cultivated by the people of Szalt, and the Arabs of the Belka. The Beni Szakher had burnt up the whole of the crops before they concluded peace with Szalt. In the Bekka is a ruined place called Ain el Basha, with a spring.

From Szafout we returned by Ardh el Hemar to Feheis, which we reached in four hours and a half from Szafout. Near the springs of Hemar we found a cow that had gone astray from some Bedouin encampment; my guides immediately declared her to be a fair prize, and drove her off before them to Feheis, where she was killed, to prevent the owner from claiming her, and the encampment feasted upon the flesh for two days. N.E. from Szafout, distant about two hours, is a ruined city, with several edifices still standing, called Yadjoush. N. of Amman, two hours, is a ruined building called El Nowakys, on the interior wall of which are some busts in relief, according to the report of one who had seen them, but whose veracity was rather doubtful.

On my return to Szalt I was obliged to remain there several days longer, for want of a guide; for the road to Kerek is a complete desert, and much exposed to the inroads of the Arabs. At last I found a man who engaged to serve me, but his demands were so exorbitant, that I was several days in bargaining with him. Mousa, (M. Seetzen), he said, had paid his guide twenty-five piastres for the trip from hence to Kerek, and he would not, therefore, go the same road for less than twenty- three; this was an enormous sum for a journey of two days, in a country where an Arab will toil for a fortnight without obtaining so great a sum. My principal objection to paying so much was, that it would become known at Kerek, which, besides other difficulties it might bring me into, would have obliged me to pay all my future guides in the same proportion. My landlord, however, removed this objection by making the guide take a solemn oath that he would never confess to having received more than six piastres for his trouble. There was no other proper guide to be got, and I began to be tired of Szalt, for I saw that my landlord was very earnest in his endeavours to get me away; I resolved therefore to trust to my good fortune, and to set out with no other company than that of an armed horseman. In the evening I returned to Feheis, from whence we departed early the next morning.

July 13th.—We passed Ardh el Hemar, in the neighbourhood of which are the ruined places El Ryhha, Shakour, Meghanny, and Mekabbely; and at a short distance farther on in the wood, we met two men quite naked. Whenever the Bedouins meet any other Arabs in the desert, of inferior force, and who are unknown to them, they level their lances, and stop their horses within about ten yards of the strangers, to enquire whether they are friends or not. My guide had seen the two men at a great distance among the trees; be called to me to get my gun ready, and we galloped towards them; but they no sooner saw us than they stopped, and cried out, "We are under your protection!" They then told us that they were peasants of a village near Rieha or Jericho; that they had been carried away from their own fields by a party of Beni Szakher, with whom their village happened to be at war, as far as Yadjoush, where the latter had encampments; that after being required to pay the price of blood of one of the tribe slain by the inhabitants of their village, they had been beaten, and stripped naked; but that at last they had found means to escape. Their bruises and sores bore testimony to the truth of their story; instances of such acts of violence frequently occur in the desert. In one hour and three quarters we came to the ruins of Kherbet Tabouk, which seems to have been a place of some importance. Many wild fig-trees grow here. The direction of our road was S. b. E. Here the woody country terminates, and we found ourselves again upon the high plain called El Ahma, which has fertile ground, but no trees. At two hours and a quarter is a ruined Birket, or reservoir of rain water, called Om Aamoud, from some fragments of columns, which are found here. In two hours and a half we passed, on our right, the Wady Szyr, which has its source near the road, und falls below into the Jordan. Above the source, on the declivity of the valley, are the ruins called Szyr. We continued to travel along a well trodden road for the greater part of the day. At three hours were the ruins of Szar, to our left. At three hours and a half, and about half an hour west of the road, are the ruins of Fokhara, on the side of the Wady Eshta, which empties itself into the Jordan. Here are a number of wild fig-trees. The whole of the country to the right of the road is intersected with deep Wadys and precipices, and is overgrown in many parts with fine woods. We had at intervals a view of the Ghor below. To the left of the road is the great plain, with many insulated hillocks. In three hours and a half we passed a hill called Dhaheret el Hemar, or the Ass's Back. At three hours and three quarters, to the right, are the ruins of Meraszas, with a heap of stones called Redjem Abd Reshyd, where, according to Bedouin tradition, a wonderful battle took place between a slave of an Arab called Reshyd, and a whole party of his master's enemies. Here terminates the district El Ahma. To the left are the ruins called Merdj Ekke. The soil in this vicinity is chalky. Last year a battle was fought here between the troops of the Pasha of Damascus, and the Beni Szakher, in which the former were routed. At four hours and a half, and about three quarters of an hour to our right, we saw the ruins of Naour on the side of a rivulet of that name, which falls into the Jordan opposite Rieha, or Jericho, driving in its course several mills, where the Bedouins of the Belka grind their corn. On both sides of the road are many vestiges of ancient field-enclosures. From Naour our road lay S. At five hours and three quarters are the ruins of El Aal, probably the Eleale of the Scriptures: it stands upon the summit of a hill, and takes its name from its situation, Aal meaning "the high." It commands the whole plain; and the view from the top of the hill is very extensive, comprehending the whole of the southern Belka. From hence the mountain of Shyhhan, behind which lies Kerek, bears S. by W. El Aal was surrounded by a well built wall, of which some parts yet remain. Among the ruins are a number of large cisterns, fragments of walls, and the foundations of houses; but nothing worth particular notice. The plain around is alternately chalk and flint. At six hours and a quarter is Hesban, upon a hill, bearing S.W. from El Aal. Here are the ruins of a large ancient town, together with the remains of some edifices built with small stones; a few broken shafts of columns are still standing, a number of deep wells cut in the rock, and a large reservoir of water for the summer supply of the inhabitants. At about three quarters of an hour S.E. of Hesban are the ruins of Myoun, the ancient Baal Meon, of the tribe of Ruben.

In order to see Medaba, I left the great road at Hesban, and proceeded in a more eastern direction. At six hours and three quarters, about one hour distant from the road, I saw the ruins of Djeloul, at a short distance to the east of which, are the ruined places called El Samek, El Mesouh, and Om el Aamed, situated close together upon low elevations. At about four hours distant, to the east of our road, I observed a chain of hills, which begins near Kalaat Zerka, passes to the east of Amman, near the Kalaat el Belka, (a station of the Syrian Hadj, called by the Bedouins Kalaat Remeydan), and continues as far as Wady Modjeb. The mountains bear the name of El Zoble; the Hadj route to Mekka lies along their western side. At seven hours and a quarter is El Kefeyrat, a ruined town of some extent. In seven hours and a half we came to the remains of a well paved ancient causeway; my guide told me that this had been formerly the route of the Hadj, and that the pavement was made by the Mohammedans; but it appeared to me to be a Roman work. At the end of eight hours we reached Madeba, built upon a round hill; this is the ancient Medaba, but there is no river near it. It is at least half an hour in circumference; I observed many remains of the walls of private houses, constructed with blocks of silex; but not a single edifice is standing. There is a large Birket, which, as there is no spring at Madeba might still be of use to the Bedouins, were the surrounding ground cleared of the rubbish, to allow the water to flow into it; but such an undertaking is far beyond the views of the wandering Arab. On the west side of the town are the foundations of a temple, built with large stones, and apparently of great antiquity. The annexed is its form and dimensions. A part of its eastern wall remains, constructed in the same style as the castle wall at Amman. At the entrance of one of the courts stand two columns of the Doric order, each of two pieces, without bases, and thicker in the centre than at either extremity, a peculiarity of which this is the only instance I have seen in Syria. More modern capitals have been added, one of which is Corinthian and the other Doric, and an equally coarse architrave has been laid upon them. In the centre of one of the courts is a large well.

About half an hour west of Madeba, are the ruins of El Teym, perhaps the Kerjathaim of the Scripture, where, according to my guide, a very large Birket is cut entirely in the rock, and is still filled in the winter with rain water. As there are no springs in this part of the upper plain of the Belka, the inha [bi]tants were obliged to provide by cisterns for their supply of water during the summer months. We returned from Madeba towards the great road, where we fell in with a large party of Bedouins, on foot, who were going to rob by night an encampment of Beni Szakher, at least fourteen hours distant from hence. Each of them had a small bag of flower on his back, some were armed with guns and others with sticks. I was afterwards informed that they drove off above a dozen camels belonging to the Beni Szakher. They pointed out to us the place where their tribe was encamped, and as we were then looking out for some place where we might get a supper, of which we stood in great need, we followed the direction they gave us. In turning a little westwards we entered the mountainous country which forms the eastern border of the valley of the Jordan, and descending in a S.W. direction along the windings of a Wady, we arrived at a large encampment of Bedouins, at the end of ten hours and a half from our setting out in the morning. The upper part of the mountains consists entirely of siliceous rock. We passed on the road several spots where the Bedouins cultivate Dhourra.

We were well received by the Bedouins of the encampment; who are on good terms with the people of Szalt: one of the principal Sheikhs of which place is married to the daughter of the chief of this tribe. They belong to the Ghanemat, whose Sheikh, called Abd el Mohsen, is one of the first men in the Belka. The chief tribe in this province, for many years, was the Adouan, but they are now reduced to the lowest condition by their inveterate enemies the Beni Szakher. The latter, whose abode had for a long space of time been on the Hadj road, near Oella, were obliged, by the increasing power of the Wahabi, to retire towards the north. They approached the Belka, and obtained from the Adouan, who were then in possession of the excellent pasturage of this country, permission to feed their cattle here, on paying a small annual tribute. They soon proved, however, to be dangerous neighbours; having detached the greater part of the other tribes of the Belka from their alliance with the Adouan, they have finally succeeded in driving the latter across the Zerka, notwithstanding the assistance which they received from the Pasha of Damascus. Peace had been made in 1810, and both tribes had encamped together near Amman, when Hamoud el Szaleh, chief of the Adouan, made a secret arrangement with the Pasha's troops, and the tribe of Rowalla, who were at war with the Beni Szakher to make a united attack upon them. The plot was well laid, but the valour of the Beni Szakher proved a match for the united forces of their enemies; they lost only about a dozen of their horsemen, and about two thousand sheep, and since that time an inveterate enmity has existed between the Beni Szakher and the Adouan. The second chief of Adouan, an old man with thirteen sons, who always accompany him to the field, joined the Beni Szakher, as did also the greater part of the Arabs of the Belka. In 1812, the Adouan were driven into the mountains of Adjeloun, and to all appearance will never be able to reenter the Belka. [For the enumeration of the Belka Arabs, see the classification of Syrian Bedouins, in the Appendix.]

The superiority of the pasturage of the Belka over that of all southern Syria, is the cause of its possession being thus contested. The Bedouins have this saying, "Thou canst not find a country like the Belka."—Methel el Belka ma teltaka; the beef and mutton of this district are preferred to those of all others. The Bedouins of the Belka are nominally subject to an annual tribute to the Pasha of Damascus; but they are very frequently in rebellion, and pay only when threatened by a superior force. For the last two years Abd el Mohsen has not paid any thing. The contribution of the Adouan is one- tenth of the produce of their camels, sheep, goats, and cows, besides ten pounds of butter for every hundred sheep. [The hundred of any kind of cattle is here called Shilleie.] The Arabs of the Belka have few camels; but their herds of cows, sheep, and goats are large; and whenever they have a prospect of being able to secure the harvest against the incursions of enemies, they cultivate patches of the best soil in their territory. In summer they remain in the valleys on the side of the Ghor, in the winter a part of them descend into the Ghor itself, while the others encamp upon the upper plain of the Belka.

July 14th.—We left the encampment of Abd el Mohsen early in the morning, and at one hour from it, descending along a winding valley, we reached the banks of the rivulet Zerka Mayn, which is not to be confounded with the northern Zerka. Its source is not far from hence; it flows in a deep and barren valley through a wood of Defle trees, which form a canopy over the rivulet impenetrable to the meridian sun. The red flowers of these trees reflected in the river gave it the appearance of a bed of roses, and presented a singular contrast with the whitish gray rocks which border the wood on either side. All these mountains are calcareous, mixed with some flint. The water of the Zerka Mayn is almost warm, and has a disagreeable taste, occasioned probably by the quantity of Defle flowers that fall into it. Having crossed the river we ascended the steep side of the mountain Houma, at the top of which we saw the summit of Djebel Attarous, about half an hour distant to our right; this is the highest point in the neighbourhood, and seems to be the Mount Nebo of the Scripture. On its summit is a heap of stones overshaded by a very large wild pistachio tree. At a short distance below, to the S.W. is the ruined place called Kereyat. The part of the mountain over which we rode was completely barren, with an uneven plain on its top. In two hours and a half we saw at about half an hour to our right, the ruins of a place called Lob, which are of some extent. We passed an encampment of Arabs Ghanamat. At the end of three hours and three quarters, after an hour's steep descent, we reached Wady Wale; the stream contains a little more water than the Zerka Mayn; it runs in a rocky bed, in the holes of which innumerable fish were playing; I killed several by merely throwing stones into the water. The banks of the rivulet are overgrown with willows, Defle, and tamarisks, and I saw large petrifactions of shells in the valley. About one hour to the west of the spot where we passed the Wale are the ruins of a small castle, situated on the summit of a lower ridge of mountains; the Arabs call it Keraoum Abou el Hossein.

In the valley of Wale a large party of Arabs Sherarat was encamped, Bedouins of the Arabian desert, who resort hither in summer for pasturage. They are a tribe of upwards of five thousand tents; but not having been able to possess themselves of a district fertile in pasturage, and being hemmed in by the northern Aeneze, the Aeneze of the Nedjed, the Howeytat, and Beni Szakher, they wander about in misery, have very few horses, and are not able to feed any flocks of sheep or goats. They live principally on the Hadj route, towards Maan, and in summer approach the Belka, pushing northward sometimes as far as Haouran. They are obliged to content themselves with encamping on spots where the Beni Szakher and the Aeneze, with whom they always endeavour to live at peace, do not choose to pasture their cattle. The only wealth of the Sherarat consists in camels. Their tents are very miserable; both men and women go almost naked, the former being only covered round the waist, and the women wearing nothing but a loose shirt hanging in rags about them. These Arabs are much leaner than the Aeneze, and of a browner complexion. They have the reputation of being very sly and enterprising thieves, a title by which they think themselves greatly honoured.

In four hours and a half, after having ascended the mountain on the S. side of the Wale, we reached a fine plain on its summit. All the country to the southward of the Wale, as far as the Wady Modjeb, is comprised under the appellation of El Koura, a term often applied in Syria to plains: El Koura is the "Plains of Moab" of the Scripture; the soil is very sandy, and not fertile. The Haouran black stone, or basalt, if it may be so called, is again met with here. The river El Wale rises at about three hours distance to the E. of the spot where we passed it, near which it takes a winding course to the south until it approaches the Modjeb, where it again turns westwards. The lower part of the river changes its name into that of Seyl Heydan, which empties itself into the Modjeb at about two hours distant from the Dead sea, near the ruined place called Dar el Ryashe. The Wale seems to be the same called Nahaliel in D'Anville's map, but this name is unknown to the Arabs; its source is not so far northward as in the map. Between the Wady Zerka Mayn and the Wale is another small rivulet called Wady el Djebel. At the end of six hours and a half we reached the banks of the Wady Modjeb, the Arnon of the Scriptures, which divides the province of Belka from that of Kerek, as it formerly divided the small kingdoms of the Moabites and the Amorites. When at about one hour's distance short of the Modjeb I was shewn to the N.E. of us, the ruins of Diban, the ancient Dibon, situated in a low ground of the Koura.

On the spot where we reached the high banks of the Modjeb are the ruins of a place called Akeb el Debs. We followed, from thence, the top of the precipice at the foot of which the river flows, in an eastern direction, for a quarter of an hour, when we reached the ruins of Araayr, the Aroer of the Scriptures, standing on the edge of the precipice; from hence a foot-path leads down to the river. In the Koura, about one hour to the west of Araayr, are some hillocks called Keszour el Besheir. The view which the Modjeb presents is very striking: from the bottom, where the river runs through a narrow stripe of verdant level about forty yards across, the steep and barren banks arise to a great height, covered with immense blocks of stone which have rolled down from the upper strata, so that when viewed from above, the valley looks like a deep chasm, formed by some tremendous convulsion of the earth, into which there seems no possibility of descending to the bottom; the distance from the edge of one precipice to that of the opposite one, is about two miles in a straight line.

We descended the northern bank of the Wady by a foot-path which winds among the masses of rock, dismounting on account of the steepness of the road, as we had been obliged to do in the two former valleys which we had passed in this day's march; this is a very dangerous pass, as robbers often waylay travellers here, concealing themselves behind the rocks, until their prey is close to them. Upon many large blocks by the side of the path I saw heaps of small stones, placed there as a sort of weapon for the traveller, in case of need. No Arab passes without adding a few stones to these heaps. There are three fords across the Modjeb, of which we took that most frequented. I had never felt such suffocating heat as I experienced in this valley, from the concentrated rays of the sun and their reflection from the rocks. We were thirty-five minutes in reaching the bottom. About twelve minutes above the river I saw on the road side a heap of fragments of columns, which had been about eight feet in height. A bridge has been thrown across the stream in this place, of one high arch, and well built; but it is now no longer of any use, though evidently of modern date. At a short distance from the bridge are the ruins of a mill. The river, which flows in a rocky bed, was almost dried up, having less water than the Zerka Mayn and Wale, but its bed bears evident marks of its impetuosity during the rainy season, the shattered fragments of large pieces of rock which had been broken from the banks nearest the river, and carried along by the torrent, being deposited at a considerable height above the present channel of the stream. A few Defle and willow trees grow on its banks.

The principal source of the Modjeb is at a short distance to the N.E. of Katrane, a station of the Syrian Hadj; there the river is called Seyl Sayde [Seyl means rivulet in this country.], lower down it changes its name to Efm el Kereim, or, as it is also called, Szefye. At about one hour east of the bridge it receives the waters of the Ledjoum, which flow from the N.E. in a deep bed; the Ledjoum receives a rivulet caled Seyl el Mekhreys, and then the Baloua, after which it takes the name of Enkheyle. Near the source of the Ledjoum is the ruined place called Tedoun ; and near the source of the Baloua is a small ruined castle called Kalaat Baloua. The rivulet Salyhha, coming from the south, empties itself into the Modjeb below the bridge.

Near the confluence of the Ledjoum and the Modjeb there seemed to be a fine verdant pasture ground, in the midst of which stands a hill with some ruins upon it, and by the side of the river are several ruined mills. In mounting the southern ascent from the Modjeb, we passed, upon a narrow level at about five minutes from the bridge, the ruins of a small castle, of which nothing but the foundations remains: it is called Mehatet el Hadj, from the supposition that the pilgrim route to Mekka formerly passed here, and that this was a station of the Hadj. Near the ruin is a Birket, which was filled by a canal from the Ledjoum, the remains of which are still visible. This may, perhaps, be the site of Areopolis. My guide told me that M. Seetzen had been partly stripped at this place, by some Arabs. We did not meet with any living being in crossing the Wady. Near the ruins is another heap of broken columns, like those on the opposite bank of the river; I conjecture that the columns were Roman milliaria, because a causeway begins here, and runs all the way up the mountain, and from thence as far as Rabba; it is about fifteen feet broad, and was well paved, though at present in a bad state, owing to a torrent which rushes along it from the mountain in winter time. At twenty-eight minutes from the Mehatet el Hadj are three similar columns, entire, but lying on the ground. We were an hour and three quarters in ascending from the bridge to the top; on this side the road might easily be made passable for horses. In several places the rock has been cut through to form the path. The lower part of the mountains is calcareous; I found great numbers of small petrified shells, and small pieces of mica are likewise met with. Towards the upper part of the mountain the ground is covered with large blocks of the black Haouran stone, [It is from this black and heavy stone, (which M. Seetzen calls basalt, but which I rather conceive to belong to the species called tufwacke by the Germans), that the ancient opinion of there having been mountains of iron on the east side of the Jordan appears to have arisen. Even now the Arabs believe that these stones consist chiefly of iron, and I was often asked if I did not know how to extract it.] which I found to be more porous than any specimens of it which I had seen further northward. On the summit of this steep southern ascent are the ruins of a large square building, of which the foundations only remain, covered with heaps of stone; they are directly opposite Araayr, and the ruins above mentioned are also called Mehatet el Hadj. I believe them to be of modern date.

We had now again reached a high plain. To our right, about three quarters of an hour, was the Djebel Shyhhan, an insulated mountain, with the ruined village of that name on its summit. To our left, on the E. side of the Ledjoum, about two or three hours distant, is a chain of low mountains, called El Ghoweythe, running from N. to S. about three or four hours. To the south of El Ghoweythe begins a chain of low hills, called El Tarfouye, which farther south takes the name of Orokaraye; it then turns westward, and terminates to the south-west of Kerek. From the Mehatet el Hadj we followed the paved road which leads in a straight line towards Rabba, in a S.W. direction; in half an hour, we met some shepherds with a flock of sheep, who led us to the tents of their people behind a hill near the side of the road. We were much fatigued, but the kindness of our hosts soon made us forget our laborious day's march. We alighted under the tent of the Sheikh, who was dying of a wound he had received a few days before from a thrust of a lance; but such is the hospitality of these people, and their attention to the comforts of the traveller, that we did not learn the Sheikh's misfortune till the following day. He was in the women's apartment, and we did not hear him utter any complaints. They supposed, with reason, that if we were informed of his situation it would prevent us from enjoying our supper. A lamb was killed, and a friend of the family did the honours of the table: we should have enjoyed our repast had there not been an absolute want of water, but there was none nearer than the Modjeb, and the daily supply which, according to the custom of the Arabs, had been brought in before sun-rise, was, as often happens, exhausted before night; our own water skins too, which we had filled at the Modjeb, had been emptied by the shepherds before we reached the encampment. This loss was the more sensible to me, as in desert countries where water seldom occurs, not feeling great thirst during the heat of the day, I was seldom in the habit of drinking much at that time; but in the evening, and the early part of the night, I always drank with great eagerness.

July 15th.—We left our kind hosts, who belonged to the Arabs Hamaide, early in the morning, and continued our route along the ancient road. At half an hour from the encampment we passed the ruined village El Ryhha, in one hour and a half we arrived at the ruins of an ancient city called Beit Kerm, belonging to which, on the side of the road, are the remains of a temple of remote antiquity. Its shape is an oblong square, one of the long sides forming the front, where was a portica of eight columns in antis: the columns, three feet in diameter, are lying on the ground. Within the temple, a great part of the walls of which are fallen, there are fragments of smaller columns. The stones used in the construction of the walls are about five feet long, and two feet broad. At one hour and three quarters is the ruined village of Hemeymat. This district, which is an even plain, is very fertile, and large tracts are here cultivated by the inhabitants of Kerek, and the Arabs Hamaide. At two hours and a half is Rabba, probably the ancient Rabbath Moab, where the ancient causeway terminates. The ruins of Rabba are about half an hour in circuit, and are situated upon a low hill, which commands the whole plain. I examined a part of them only, but the rest seemed to contain nothing remarkable. On the west side is a temple, of which one wall and several niches remain, by no means distinguished for elegance. Near them is a gate belonging to another building, which stood on the edge of a Birket. Distant from these ruins about thirty yards stand two Corinthian columns of middling size, one higher than the other. In the plain, to the west of the Birket, stands an insulated altar. In the town many fragments are lying about; the walls of the larger edifices are built like those of Heit Kerm. There are many remains of private habitations, but none entire. There being no springs in this spot, the town had two Birkets, the largest of which is cut entirely out of the rocky ground, together with several cisterns. About three quarters of an hour to the S.E. of Rabba, are two copious springs, called El Djebeyba, and El Yaroud. From Rabba our road lay S. by E. At four hours are the ruins of Kereythela. At the end of five hours we entered a mountainous district, full of Wadys; and after a march of six hours we reached the town of Kerek.

I hesitated where I should alight at Kerek, and whether I should announce myself as a Turk or a Christian, for I knew that the success of my progress southward depended upon the good will of the people of this place. I had a letter of recommendation to the Sheikh of the town, given to me by a Turkish gentleman of Damascus, whose wife was a native of Kerek, and he had mentioned me in such terms as led me to anticipate a good reception; but as I knew that I should be much harassed by inquisitive visitors, were I to take up my lodgings at the Sheikh's house, I determined to alight at some Christian's, and then consult upon my future proceeding with the Greek priest, whom I knew by report. I no sooner entered the north gate of the town, where is the quarter of the Christians, than I was surrounded by several of these hospitable people, who took hold of the bridle of my horse, every one insisting upon my repairing to his dwelling; I followed one, and the whole neighbourhood was soon assembled, to partake of the sheep that was slaughtered in honour of my arrival; still no one had asked me who I was, or whither I was going. After some conversation with the priest, I thought it expedient to pay a visit of ceremony to the Sheikh, in order to deliver my letter; I soon however had reason to repent: he received me very politely; but when he heard of my intention of proceeding southward, he told me that he could not allow of my going forward with one guide only, and that as he was preparing to visit the southern districts himself, in a few days, I should wait for him or his people to conduct me. His secretary then informed me, that it was expected I should make some present to the Sheikh, and pay him, besides, the sum which I must have given for a guide. The present I flatly refused to make, saying that it was rather the Sheikh's duty to make a present to the guest recommended to him by such a person as my Damascene friend was. With respect to the second demand, I answered that I had no more money with me than was absolutely necessary for my journey. Our negotiations on this point lasted for several days; when seeing that I could obtain no guide without an order from the Sheikh, I at last agreed to pay fifteen piastres for his company as far as Djebel Sherah. If I had shewn a disposition to pay this sum immediately, every body would have thought that I had plenty of money, and more considerable sums would have been extorted; in every part of Turkey it is a prudent rule not to grant the Turks their demands immediately, because they soon return to the charge. Had I not shewn my letter to the Sheikh, I should have procured a guide with little trouble, I should have had it in my power to see the borders of the Dead sea, and should have been enabled to depart sooner; but having once made my agreement with him, I was obliged to wait for his departure, which was put off from day to day, and thus I was prevented from going to any distance from the town, from the fear of being left behind. I remained therefore at Kerek for twenty successive days, changing my lodgings almost every day, in order to comply with the pressing invitations of its hospitable inhabitants.

The town of Kerek, a common name in Syria, is built upon the top of a steep hill, surrounded on all sides by a deep and narrow valley, the mountains beyond which command the town. In the valley, on the west and north sides, are several copious springs, on the borders of which the inhabitants cultivate some vegetables, and considerable plantations of olive trees. The principal of these sources are, Ain Sara, which issues from the rock in a very romantic spot, where a mosque has been built, now in ruins; this rivulet turns three mills: the other sources are Ain Szafszaf, Ain Kobeyshe, and Ain Frandjy, or the European spring, in the rock near which, as some persons told me, is an inscription in Frank characters, but no one ever would, or could, shew it me.

The town is surrounded by a wall, which has fallen down in several places; it is defended by six or seven large towers, of which the northern is almost perfect, and has a long Arabic inscription on its wall, but too high to be legible from the ground; on each side of the inscription is a lion in bas-relief, similar to those seen on the walls of Aleppo and Damascus. The town had originally only two entrances, one to the south and the other to the north; they are dark passages, forty paces in length, cut through the rock. An inscription on the northern gate ascribes its formation to Sultan Seyf- eddin. Besides these two gates, two other entrances have been formed, leading over the ruins of the town wall. At the west end of the town stands a castle, on the edge of a deep precipice over the Wady Kobeysha. It is built in the style of most of the Syrian castles, with thick walls and parapets, large arched apartments, dark passages with loop-holes, and subterraneous vaults; and it probably owes its origin, like most of these castles, to the prudent system of defence adopted by the Saracens against the Franks during the Crusades. In a large Gothic hall are the remains of paintings in fresco, but so much defaced that nothing can be clearly distinguished. Kerek having been for some time in the hands of the Franks, this hall may have been built at that time for a church, and decorated with paintings. Upon an uncouth figure of a man bearing a large chain I read the letters IONI, painted in large characters; the rest of the inscription was effaced. On the side towards the town the castle is defended by a deep fosse cut in the rock; near which are seen several remains of columns of gray and red granite. On the south side the castle hill is faced with stone in the same manner as at Aleppo, El Hossn, Szalkhat, &c. On the west side a wall has been thrown across the Wady, to some high rocks, which project from the opposite side; a kind of Birket has thus been formed, which formerly supplied the garrison with water. In the castle is a deep well, and many of the private houses also have wells, but their water is brackish; others have cisterns, which save the inhabitants the trouble of fetching their water from the Wady below. There are no antiquities in the town, excepting a few fragments of granite columns. A good mosque, built by Melek el Dhaher, is now in ruins. The Christians have a church, dedicated to St. George, or El Khuder, which has been lately repaired. On the declivity of the Wady to the south of the town are some ancient sepulchral caves, of coarse workmanship, cut in the chalky rock.

Kerek is inhabited by about four hundred Turkish, and one hundred and fifty Christian families; the former can furnish upwards of eight hundred firelocks, the latter about two hundred and fifty. The Turks are composed of settlers from all parts of southern Syria, but principally from the mountains about Hebron and Nablous. The Christians are, for the greater part, descendants of refugees from Jerusalem, Bethlehem, and Beit Djade. They are free from all exactions, and enjoy the same rights with the Turks. Thirty or forty years ago Kerek was in the hands of the Bedouin tribe called Beni Ammer, who were accustomed to encamp around the town and to torment the inhabitants with their extortions. It may be remarked generally of the Bedouins, that wherever they are the masters of the cultivators, the latter are soon reduced to beggary, by their unceasing demands. The uncle of the present Sheikh of Kerek, who was then head of the town, exasperated at their conduct, came to an understanding with the Arabs Howeytat, and in junction with these, falling suddenly upon the Beni Ammer, completely defeated them in two encounters. The Ammer were obliged to take refuge in the Belka, where they joined the Adouan, but were again driven from thence, and obliged to fly towards Jerusalem. For many years afterwards they led a miserable life, from not being suffi-ciently strong to secure to their cattle good pasturing places. About six years ago they determined to return to Kerek, whatever might be their fate; in their way round the southern extremity of the Dead sea they lost two thirds of their cattle by the attacks of their inveterate enemies, the Terabein. When, at last, they arrived in the neighbourhood of Kerek, they threw themselves upon the mercy of the present Sheikh of the town, Youssef Medjaby, who granted them permission to remain in his district, provided they would obey his commands. They were now reduced, from upwards of one thousand tents, to about two hundred, and they may at present be considered as the advanced guard of the Sheikh of Kerek, who employs them against his own enemies, and makes them encamp wher-ever he thinks proper. The inhabitants of Kerek have thus become formidable to all the neighbouring Arabs; they are complete masters of the district of Kerek, and have great influence over the affairs of the Belka.

The Christians of Kerek are renowned for their courage, and more especially so, since an action which lately took place between them and the Rowalla, a tribe of Aeneze; a party of the latter had on a Sunday, when the men were absent, robbed the Christian encampment, which was at about an hour from the town, of all its cattle. On the first alarm given by the women, twenty-seven young men immediately pursued the enemy, whom they overtook at a short distance, and had the courage to attack, though upwards of four hundred men mounted on camels, and many of them armed with firelocks. After a battle of two hours the Rowalla gave way, with the loss of forty-three killed, a great many wounded, and one hundred and twenty camels, together with the whole booty which they had carried off. The Christians had only four men killed. To account for the success of this heroic enterprise, I must mention that the people of Kerek are excellent marksmen; there is not a boy among them who does not know how to use a firelock by the time he is ten years of age.

The Sheikh of Kerek has no greater authority over his people than a Bedouin Sheikh has over his tribe. In every thing which regards the

Bedouins, he governs with the advice of the most respectable individuals of the town; and his power is not absolute enough to deprive the meanest of his subjects of the smallest part that prevails prevents the increase of wealth, and the richest man in the town is not worth more than about £1000. sterling. Their custom of entertaining strangers is much the same as at Szalt; they have eight Menzels, or Medhafe, for the reception of guests, six of which belong to the Turks, and two to the Christians; their expenses are not defrayed by a common purse: but whenever a stranger takes up his lodging at one of the Medhafes, one of the people present declares that he intends to furnish that day's entertainment, and it is then his duty to provide a dinner or supper, which he sends to the Medhafe, and which is always in sufficient quantity for a large company. A goat or a lamb is generally killed on the occasion, and barley for the guest's horse is also furnished. When a stranger enters the town the people almost come to blows with one another in their eagerness to have him for their guest, and there are Turks who every other day kill a goat for this hospitable purpose. Indeed it is a custom here, even with respect to their own neighbours, that whenever a visitor enters a house, dinner or supper is to be immediately set before him. Their love of entertaining strangers is carried to such a length, that not long ago, when a Christian silversmith, who came from Jerusalem to work for the ladies, and who, being an industrious man, seldom stirred out of his shop, was on the point of departure after a two months residence, each of the principal families of the town sent him a lamb, saying that it was not just that he should lose his due, though he did not choose to come and dine with them. The more a man expends upon his guests, the greater is his reputation and influence; and the few families who pursue an opposite conduct are despised by all the others.

Kerek is filled with guests every evening; for the Bedouins, knowing that they are here sure of a good supper for themselves and their horses, visit it as often as they can; they alight at one Medhafe, go the next morning to another, and often visit the whole before they depart. The following remarkable custom furnishes another example of their hospitable manners: it is considered at Kerek an unpardonable meanness to sell butter or to exchange it for any necessary or convenience of life; so that, as the property of the people chiefly consists in cattle, and every family possesses large flocks of goats and sheep, which produce great quantities of butter, they supply this article very liberally to their guests. Besides other modes of consuming butter in their cookery, the most common dish at breakfast or dinner, is Fetyte, a sort of pudding made with sour milk, and a large quantity of butter. There are families who thus consume in the course of a year, upwards of ten quintals of butter. If a man is known to have sold or exchanged this article, his daughters or sisters remain unmarried, for no one would dare to connect himself with the family of a Baya el Samin, or seller of butter, the most insulting epithet that can be applied to a man of Kerek. This custom is peculiar to the place, and unknown to the Bedouins.

The people of Kerek, intermarry with the Bedouins; and the Aeneze even give the Kerekein their girls in marriage. The sum paid to the father of the bride is generally between six and eighthundred piastres; young men without property are obliged to serve the father five or six years, as menial servants, in compensation for the price of the girl. The Kerekein do not treat their wives so affectionately as the Bedouins; if one of them falls sick, and her sickness is likely to prevent her for some time from taking care of the family affairs, the husband sends her back to her father's house, with a message that "he must cure her;" for, as he says, "I bought a healthy wife of you, and it is not just that I should be at the trouble and expense of curing her." This is a rule with both Mohammedans and Christians. It is not the custom for the husband to buy clothes or articles of dress for his wife; she is, in consequence, obliged to apply to her own family, in order to appear decently in public, or to rob her husband of his wheal and barley, and sell it clandestinely in small quantities; nor does she inherit the smallest trifle of her husband's property. The Kerekein never sleep under the same blanket with their wives; and to be accused of doing so, is considered as great an insult as to be called a coward.

The domestic manners of the Christians of Kerek are the same as those of the Turks; their laws are also the same, excepting those relating to marriage; and in cases of litigation, even amongst themselves, they repair to the tribunal of the Kadhy, or judge of the town, instead of submitting their differences to their own Sheikhs. The Kadhy is elected by the Sheikhs. With respect to their religious duties, they observe them much less than any other Greeks in Syria; few of them frequent the church, alleging, not without reason, that it is of no use to them, because they do not understand one word of the Greek forms of prayer. Neither are they rigid observers of Lent, which is natural enough, as they would be obliged to live almost entirely on dry bread, were they to abstain wholly from animal food. Though so intimately united with the Turks both by common interests and manners, as to be considered the same tribe, yet there exists much jealousy among the adherents of the two religions, which is farther increased by the Sheikh's predilection for the Christians. The Turks seeing that the latter prosper, have devised a curious method of participating in the favours which Providence may bestow on the Christians on account of their religion: many of them baptise their male children in the church of St. George, and take Christian godfathers for their sons. There is neither Mollah nor fanatic Kadhy to prevent this practice, and the Greek priest, who is handsomely paid for baptising, reconciles his conscientious scruples by the hope that the boy so baptized may perhaps die a Christian; added to this, he does not give the child entire baptism, but dips the hands and feet only in the water, while the Christian child receives total immersion, and this pious fraud sets all his doubts at rest as to the legality of the act. The priests pretend nevertheless that such is the efficacy of the baptism that these baptised Turks have never been known to die otherwise than by old age.

Kerek is the see of a Greek bishop, who generally resides at Jerusalem. The diocese is called Battra in Arabic, and [Greek] in Greek; and it is the general opinion among the clergy of Jerusalem, that Kerek is the ancient Petra; [The Greek bishops belonging to the Patriarchal see of Jerusalem are: 1. Kaisaryet Filistin; 2. Bysan: 3. Battra; 4. Akka; 5. Bethlehem; 6. Nazareth. The Greek bishops in partibus are; 1. Lyd; 2. Gaza; 3. Syna; 4. Yaffa; 5. Nablous; 6. Shabashye; 7. Tor Thabour: 8. Djebel Adjeloun.] but it will be seen in the sequel of this journal that there is good reason to think they are mistaken; Kerek therefore is probably the Charax Omanorum of Pliny. The bishop's revenue is about six pounds sterling per annum; he visits his diocese every five or six years. During my stay, a Greek priest arrived from Jerusalem, to collect for his convent, which had been at a great expense in rebuilding the church of the Holy Sepulchre. The Greeks delivered to him in sheep to the value of about fifteen pounds sterling.

The Kerekein cultivate the plains in the neighbouring mountains and feed their cattle on the uncultivated parts. One-third of the people remain encamped the whole year at two or three hours distant from the town, to superintend the cattle; the rest encamp in the harvest time only. During the latter period the Christians have two large camps or Douars, and the Turks five. Here they live like Bedouins, whom they exactly resemble, in dress, food, and language. The produce of their fields is purchased by the Bedouins, or exchanged for cattle. The only other commercial intercourse carried on by them is with Jerusalem, for which place a caravan departs every two months, travelling either by the route round the southern extremity of the Dead sea, which takes three days and a half, or by crossing the Jordan, a journey of three days. At Jerusalem they sell their sheep and goats, a few mules, of which they have an excellent breed, hides, wool, and a little Fowa or madder (Rubia tinctorum), which they cultivate in small quantities; in return they take coffee, rice, tobacco, and all kinds of articles of dress, and of household furniture. This journey, however, is undertaken by few of the natives of Kerek, the trade being almost wholly in the hands of a few merchants of Hebron, who keep shops at Kerek, and thus derive large profits from the indolence or ignorance of the Kerekein. I have seen the most common articles sold at two hundred per cent. profit. The trade is carried on chiefly by barter: and every thing is valued in measures of corn, this being the readiest representative of exchange in the possession of the town's-people; hence the merchants, make their returns chiefly in corn and partly in wool. The only artizans in Kerek who keep shops are a blacksmith, a shoemaker, and a silversmith. When the Mekka caravan passes, the Kerekein sell provisions of all kinds to the Hadj, which they meet at the castle of Katrana. Many Turks, as well as Christians, in the town, have negro slaves, whom they buy from the Bedouins, who bring them from Djidda and Mekka: there are also several families of blacks in Kerek, who have obtained their liberty, and have married free black women.

The houses of Kerek have only one floor, and three or four are generally built in the same court-yard. The roof of the apartment is supported by two arches, much in the same way as in the ancient buildings of the Haouran, which latter however have generally but one arch. Over the arches thick branches of trees are laid, and over the latter a thin layer of rushes. Along the wall at the extremity of the room, opposite to the entrance, are large earthen reservoirs of wheat (Kowari Arabic). There is generally no other aperture in these rooms than the door, a circumstance that renders them excessively disagreeable in the winter evenings, when the door is shut and a large fire is kindled in the middle of the floor.

Some of the Arab tribes in the territory of Kerek pay a small annual tribute to the Sheikh of Kerek, as do likewise the peasants who cultivate the shores of the Dead sea. In order, however, to secure their harvests against any casualties, the Kerekein have deemed it expedient to pay, on their, part, a tribute to the Southern Arabs called El Howeytat, who are continually passing this way in their expeditions against the Beni Szakher. The Christians pay to one of the Howeytat Sheikhs one Spanish dollar per family, and the Turks send them annually about fifteen mule loads of carpets which are manufacured at Kerek. Whenever the Sheikhs of the Beni Szakher visit the town, they receive considerable presents by way of a friendly tribute.

The district of Kerek comprises three other villages, which are under the orders of the Sheikh of Kerek: viz. Ketherabba, Oerak, and Khanzyre. There are besides a great number of ruined places in the district, the principal of which are the following; Addar, Hedjfa, Hadada, Thenye, three quarters of an hour to the S. of the town; Meddyn, Mouthe, Djeldjoun, Djefeiras, Datras, about an hour and a half S.E. of the town, where some walls of houses remain; Medjdelein, Yarouk, Seraf , Meraa, and Betra, where is a heap of stones on the foot of a high hill, distant from Kerek to the southward and westward about five hours.

Several Wadys descend from the mountains of Kerek into the plain on the shore of the Dead sea, and are there lost, either in the sands or in the fields of the peasants who cultivate the plain, none of them reaching the lake itself in the summer. To the S. of Modjeb is the Seyl Djerra, and farther south, Wady Beni Hammad. In the valley of this river, perhaps the Zared of Scripture, are hot-wells, with some ruined buildings near them, about five hours from Kerek, in a northern direction. Next follow Seyl el Kerek, Wady el Draah, Seyl Assal, perhaps Assan, which rises nearer Ketherabba; El Nemeyra, coming from Oerak; Wady Khanzyre, and El Ahhsa, a river which divides the territory of Kerek from the district to the S. of it, called El Djebel.

Not having had an opportunity of descending to the borders of the Dead sea, I shall subjoin here a few notes which I collected from the people of Kerek. I have since been informed that M. Seetzen, the most indefatigable traveller that ever visited Syria, has made the complete tour of the Dead sea; I doubt not that he has made many interesting discoveries in natural history.

The mountains which inclose the Ghor, or valley of the Jordan, open considerably at the northern extremity of the Dead sea, and encompassing it on the W. and E. sides approach again at its S. extremity, leaving only a narrow plain between them. The plain on the west side, between the sea and the mountains, is covered with sand, and is unfit for cultivation; but on the E. side, and especially towards the S. extremity, where it continues to bear the appellation of El Ghor, the plain is in many places very fertile. Its breadth varies from one to four and five miles; it is covered with forests, in the midst of which the miserable peasants build their huts of rushes, and cultivate their Dhourra and tobacco fields. These peasants are called El Ghowárene, and amount to about three hundred families; they live very poorly, owing to the continual exactions of the neighbouring Bedouins, who descend in winter from the mountains of Belka and Kerek, and pasture their cattle amidst the fields. The heat of the climate of this low valley, during the summer, renders it almost uninhabitable; the people then go nearly naked; but their low huts, instead of affording shelter from the mid-day heat rather increase it. At this period violent intermittent fevers prevail, to which, however, they are so much accustomed, that they labour in the fields during the intervals of the paroxysms of the disease.

The principal settlement of the Ghowárene is at the southern extremity of the sea, near the embouchure of the Wady el Ahhsa; their village is called Ghor Szafye, and is the winter rendezvous of more than ten large tribes of Bedouins. Its situation corresponds with that of Zoar. The spots not cultivated being for the greater part sandy, there is little pasturage, and the camels, in consequence, feed principally upon the leaves of the trees.

About eight hours to the N. of Szafye is the Ghor el Mezra, a village much frequented by the people of Kerek, who there buy the tobacco which they smoak. About the middle of the lake on the same eastern shore, are some ruins of an ancient city, called Towahein el Sukkar i.e. the Sugar Mills. Farther north the mountains run down to the lake, and a steep cliff overhangs the sea for about an hour, shutting out all passage along the shore. Still farther to the north are the ruined places called Kafreyn, and Rama, and in the valley of the Jordan, south of Abou Obeida, are the ruins of Nemrin, probably the Bethnimra of the Scriptures. In the vegetable productions of this plain the botanist would perhaps discover several unknown species of trees and plants; the reports of the Arabs on this subject are so vague and incoherent, that it is almost impossible to obtain any precise information from them; they speak, for instance, of the spurious pomegranate tree, producing a fruit exactly like that of the pomegranate, but which, on being opened, is found to contain nothing but a dusty powder; this, they pretend, is the Sodom apple-tree; other persons however deny its existence. The tree Asheyr, is very common in the Ghor. It bears a fruit of a reddish yellow colour, about three inches in diameter, which contains a white substance, resembling the finest silk, and enveloping some seeds. The Arabs collect the silk, and twist it into matches for their fire-locks, preferring it to the common match, because it ignites more readily. More than twenty camel loads might be annually procured, and it might perhaps be found useful in the silk and cotton manufactories of Europe. At present the greater part of the fruit rots on the trees. On making an incision into the thick branches of the Asheyr a white juice exsudes, which is collected by putting a hollow reed into the incision; the Arabs sell the juice to the druggists at Jerusalem, who are said to use it in medicine as a strong cathartic. [It is the same plant called Oshour by the people of Upper Egypt and Nubia. Norden, who has given a drawing of it, as found by him near the first cataract of the Nile, improperly denominates it Oshar.]

Indigo is a very common production of the Ghor; the Ghowárene sell it to the merchants of Jerusalem and Hebron, where it is worth twenty per cent. more than Egyptian indigo. One of the most interesting productions of this valley is the Beyrouk honey, or as the Arabs call it, Assal Beyrouk. I suppose it to be the manna, but I never had an opportunity of seeing it myself. It was described to me, as a juice dropping from the leaves and twigs of a tree called Gharrab, of the size of an olive tree, with leaves like those of the poplar, but somewhat broader. The honey collects upon the leaves like dew, and is gathered from them, or from the ground under the tree, which is often found completely covered with it. According to some its colour is brownish; others said it was of a grayish hue; it is very sweet when fresh, but turns sour after being kept two days. The Arabs eat it like honey, with butter, they also put it into their gruel, and use it in rubbing their water skins, in order to exclude the air. I enquired whether it was a laxative, but was answered in the negative. The Beyrouk honey is collected only in the months of May and June. Some persons assured me that the same substance was likewise produced by the thorny tree Tereshresh, and collected at the same time as that from the Gharrab.

In the mountains of Shera grows a tree called Arar, from the fruit of which the Bedouins extract a juice, which is extremely nutritive. The tree Talh, which produces the gum arabic, is very common in the Ghor; but the Arabs do not take the trouble to collect the gum. Among other vegetable productions there is a species of tobacco, called Merdiny, which has a most disagreeable taste; but, for want of a better kind, it is cultivated in great quantity, and all the Bedouins on the borders of the Dead sea are supplied with it. The coloquintida (Arabic or Arabic), grows wild every where in great quantities. The tree Szadder, which is a species of the cochineal tree, is also very common.

As to the mineral productions of the borders of the Dead sea, it appears that the southern mountains are full of rock salt, which is washed off by the winter rains, and carried down into the lake. In the northern Ghor pieces of native sulphur are found at a small depth beneath the surface, and are used by the Arabs to cure diseases in their camels. The asphaltum, Hommar, which is collected by the Arabs of the western shore, is said to come from a mountain which blocks up the passage along the eastern Ghor, and which is situated at about two hours south of wady

Modjeb. The Arabs pretend that it oozes from the fissures in the cliff, and collects in large pieces on the rock below, where the mass gradually increases and hardens, until it is rent asunder by the heat of the sun, with a loud explosion, and falling into the sea, is carried by the waves in considerable quantities to the opposite shores. At the northern extremity of the sea the stink-stone is found; its combustible properties are ascribed, by the Arabs, to the magic rod of Moses, whose tomb is not far from thence. The stones are thrown into the fires made of camel's dung, to encrease the heat.

Concerning the lake itself, I was informed that no visible increase of its waters takes place in winter time, as the greater part of the torrents which descend from the eastern mountains do not reach the lake, but are lost in the sandy plain. About three hours north of Szaffye is a ford, by which the lake is crossed in three hours and a half. Some Arabs assured me that there are spots in this ford where the water is quite hot, and where the bottom is of red earth. It is probable that there are hot springs in the bottom of the lake, which near the ford is nowhere deeper than three or four feet; and generally only two feet. The water is so strongly impregnated with salt, that the skin of the legs of those who wade across it soon afterwards peels entirely off.

The mountains about Kerek are all calcareous, with flint; they abound with petrified shells, and some of the rocks consist entirely of small shells. Fine specimens of calcareous spath, called by the Arabs Hadjar Ain el Shems, the Sun's eye, are found here. Ancient coins of copper, silver, and even of gold are found in the fields near Kerek; in general they are bought by the silversmiths, and immediately melted.

The direction of Jerusalem from Kerek, as pointed out to me several times, is N. by W. The direction of Katrane, a station of the pilgrim caravan to Mekka, is E.S.E. distant about eight hours. That of Szaffye, or the S. point of the Dead sea, is W. by S. distant about twelve hours. The Dead sea is here called Bahret Lout, the Sea of Lot. August   4th.—After having remained nearly three weeks at Kerek, waiting from day to day for the departure of the Sheikh, he at last set out, accompanied by about forty horsemen. The inhabitants of Kerek muster about one hundred horsemen, and have excellent horses; the Sheikh himself possessed the finest horse I had seen in Syria; it was a gray Saklawy, famous all over the desert.

We descended into the valley of Ain Frandjy, and ascended the mountain on the other side, our road lying nearly S.S.W. In one hour and a half from Kerek we reached the top of the mountain, from whence we had a fine view of the southern extremity of the Dead sea, which presented the appearance of a lake, with many islands or shoals covered with a white saline crust. The water is very shallow for about three hours from its south end. Where narrowest, it may be about six miles across. The mountain which we had passed was a barren rock of flint and chalk. We met with an encampment of Beni Hamyde, where we breakfasted. At the end of two hours and a half we reached, on the descent of the mountain, Ain Terayn, a fine spring, with the ruins of a city near it. The rivulet which takes its rise here joins that of Ketherabba, and descends along a narrow valley into the Ghor, which it reaches near the ruined place called Assal, from which it takes the name of Wady Assal. Near the rivulet are some olive plantations. At two hours and three quarters is Ketherabba, a village with about eighty houses. Many of its inhabitants live under tents pitched in the square open spaces left among the houses of the village. The gardens contain great numbers of large fig trees. The mountains in the neighbourhood are cultivated in some parts by the Beni Ammer. The village of Szaffye in the Ghor bears from hence W.

August 5th.—We left Ketherabba early in the morning. Our road lay through a wild and entirely barren rocky country, ascending and descending several Wadys. In one hour and a quarter we came to Oerak, a village of the same size as the former, very picturesquely situated; it is built at the foot of a high perpendicular cliff, down which a rivulet rushes into the Wady below. Many immense fragments have separated from the cliff, and fallen down; and amongst these rocks the houses of the village are built. Its inhabitants cultivate, besides wheat, barley, and dhourra, olives, figs, and tobacco, which they sell to advantage. We rested here the greater part of the day, under a large Kharnoub tree. Our Sheikh had no pressing business, but like all Arabs, fond of idleness, and of living well at other people's expense, he by no means hastened his journey, but easily found a pretext for stopping; wherever we alighted a couple of sheep or goats were immediately killed, and the best fruits, together with plenty of tobacco, were presented to us. Our company increased at every village, as all those Arabs who had horses followed us, in order to partake of our good fare, so that our party amounted at last to eighty men. At two hours and a quarter is a fine spring; two hours and a half, the village Khanzyre, which is larger than Oerak and Ketherabba. Here we stopped a whole day, our Sheikh having a house in the village, and a wife, whom he dared not carry to Kerek, having another family there. In the evening he held a court of justice, as he had done at Ketherabba, and decided a number of disputes between the peasants; the greater part of these were concerning money transactions between husbands and the families of their wives; or

267

related to the mixed property of the Arabs in mares, in consequence of the Bedouin custom of selling only one-half, or one-third of those animals.

August 6th.————Khanzyre is built on the declivity of one of the highest mountains on the eastern side of the Dead sea; in its neighbourhood are a number of springs whose united waters form a rivulet which irrigates the fields belonging to the village, and an extensive tract of gardens. The villages of this country are each governed by its own Sheikh, and the peasants are little better than Bedouins; their manners, dress, and mode of living are exactly the same. In the harvest time they live in the mountains under tents, and their cattle is entrusted during the whole year to a small encampment of their own shepherds. In the afternoon of this day we were alarmed by loud cries in the direction of the opposite mountain. The whole of our party immediately mounted, and I also followed. On reaching the spot from whence the cries came, we found two shepherds of Khanzyre quite naked; they had been stripped by a party of the Arabs Terabein, who live in the mountains of Hebron, and each of the robbers had carried off a fat sheep upon his mare. They were now too far off to be overtaken; and our people, not being able to engage the enemy, amused themselves with a sham-fight in their return home. They displayed superior strength and agility in handling the lance, and great boldness in riding at full speed over rugged and rocky ground. In the exercise with the lance the rider endeavours to put the point of it upon the shoulder of his adversary, thus showing that his life is in his power. When the parties become heated, they often bear off upon their lances the turbands of their adversaries, and carry them about with insolent vociferation. Our Sheikh of Kerek, a man of sixty, far excelled all his people in these youthful, exercises; indeed he seemed to be an accomplished Bedouin Sheikh; though he proved to be a treacherous friend to me. As I thought that I had settled matters with him, to his entire satisfaction, I was not a little astonished, when he took me aside in the evening to announce to me, that unless he received twenty piastres more, he would not take charge of me any farther. Although I knew it was not in his power to hinder me from following him, and that he could not proceed to violence without entirely losing his reputation among the Arabs, for ill-treating his guest, yet I had acquired sufficient knowledge of the Sheikh's character to be persuaded that if I did not acquiesce in his demand, he would devise some means to get me into a situation which it would have perhaps cost me double the sum to escape from; I therefore began to bargain with him; and brought him down to fifteen piastres. I then endeavoured to bind him by the most solemn oath used by the Bedouins; laying his hand upon the head of his little boy, and on the fore feet of his mare, he swore that he would, for that sum, conduct me himself, or cause me to be conducted, to the Arabs Howeytat, from whence I might hope to find a mode of proceeding in safety to Egypt. My precautions, however, were all in vain. Being satisfied that my cash was reduced to a few piastres, he began his plans for stripping me of every other part of my property which had excited his wishes. The day after his oath, when we were about to depart from Ayme, he addressed me in the presence of the whole company, saying that his saddle would fit my horse better than my own did, and that he would therefore change saddles with me. Mine was worth nearly forty piastres, his was not worth more than ten. I objected to the exchange, pretending that I was not accustomed to ride upon the low Bedouin saddle; he replied, by assuring me that I should soon find it much more agreeable than the town saddle; moreover, said he, you may depend upon it that the Sheikh of the Howeytat will take your saddle from you, if you do not give it to me. I did not dare to put the Sheikh in mind of his oath, for had I betrayed to the company his having extorted from me so much, merely for the sake of his company, he would certainly have been severely reprimanded by the Bedouins present, and I should thus have exposed myself to the effects of his revenge. All the bye-standers at the same time pressed me to comply with his request: "Is he not your brother?" said they. "Are not the best morsels of his dish always for you? Does he not continually fill your pipe with his own tobacco? Fie upon your stinginess." But they did not know that I had calculated upon paying part of the hire of a guide to Egypt with the value of the saddle, nor that I had already handsomely paid for my brotherhood. I at last reluctantly complied; but the Sheikh was not yet satisfied: the stirrups he had given me, although much inferior to those he had taken from me, were too good in his eyes, to form part of my equipment. In the evening his son came to me to propose an exchange of these stirrups against a pair of his own almost unfit for use, and which I knew would wound my ankles, as I did not wear boots; but it was in vain to resist. The pressing intreaties of all my companions in favour of the Sheikh's son lasted for two whole days; until tired at length with their importunity, I yielded, and, as had expected, my feet were soon wounded. I have entered into these details in order to shew what Arab cupidity is: an article of dress, or of equipment, which the poorest townsman would be ashamed to wear, is still a covetable object with the Bedouins; they set no bounds to their demands, delicacy is unknown amongst them, nor have they any word to express it; if indeed one persists in refusing, they never take the thing by force; but it is extremely difficult to resist their eternal supplications and compliments without yielding at last. With regard to my behaviour towards the Bedouins, I always endeavoured, by every possible means, to be upon good terms with my companions, whoever they were, and I seldom failed in my endeavours. I found, by experience, that putting on a grave face, and talking wisely among them was little calculated to further the traveller's views. On the contrary, I aspired to the title of a merry fellow; I joked with them whenever I could, and found that by a little attention to their ways of thinking and reasoning, they are easily put into good humour. This kind of behaviour, however, is to be observed only in places where one makes a stay of several days, or towards fellow travellers: in passing rapidly through Arab encampments, it is better for the traveller not to be too talkative in the tents where he alights, but to put on a stern countenance.

We left Khanzyre late in the evening, that we might enjoy the coolness of the night air. We ascended for a short time, and then began to descend into the valley called Wady el Ahsa. It had now become dark, and this was, without exception, the most dangerous route I ever travelled in my life. The descent is steep, and there is no regular road over the smooth rocks, where the foot slips at every step. We had missed our way, and were obliged to alight from our horses, after many of us had suffered severe falls. Our Sheikh was the only horseman who would not alight from his mare, whose step, he declared, was as secure as his own. After a march of two hours and a half, we halted upon a narrow plain, on the declivity of the Wady, called El Derredje, where we lighted a fire, and remained till day-break.

August 7th.—In three quarters of an hour from Derredje, we reached the bottom of the valley. The Wady el Ahsa, which takes its rise near the castle El Ahsa, or El Hassa, on the Syrian Hadj road, runs here in a deep and narrow bed of rocks, the banks of which are overgrown with Defle. There was more water in the rivulet than in any of those I had passed south of Zerka; the water was quite tepid, caused by a hot spring, which empties itself into the Ahsa from a side valley higher up the Wady. This forms the third hot spring on the east of the Dead sea, one being in the Wady Zerka Mayn, and another in the Wady Hammad. The valley of El Ahsa divides the district of Kerek from that of Djebal (plur. of Djebel), the ancient Gebalene. In the Ghor the river changes its name into that of Kerahy, and is likewise called Szafye. This name is found in all the maps of Arabia Petræa, but the course of the river is not from the south, as there laid down; Djebal also, instead of being laid down at the S.E. extremity of the lake, is improperly placed as beginning on the S.W. of it. The rock of the Wady el Ahsa is chiefly sand-stone, which is seldom met with to the N. of this valley; but it is very common in the southern mountains.

We ascended the southern side of the valley, which is less steep and rocky than the northern, and in an hour and a half reached a fine spring called El Kaszrein surrounded by verdant ground and tall reeds. The Bedouins of the tribe of Beni Naym, here cultivate some Dhourra fields and there are some remains of ancient habitations. In two hours and a quarter we arrived at the top of the mountain, when we entered upon an extensive plain, and passed the ruins of an ancient city of considerable extent called El Kerr, perhaps the ancient Kara, a bishopric belonging to the diocese of Rabba Moabitis; [See Reland. Palæst. Vol. i. p. 226.] nothing remains but heaps of stones. The plain, which we crossed in a S.W. by S. direction, consists of a fertile soil, and contains the ruins of several villages. At the end of two hours and three quarters we descended by a steep road, into a Wady, and in three hours reached the village of Ayme, situated upon a narrow plain at the foot of high cliffs. In its neighbourhood are several springs, and wherever these are met with, vegetation readily takes place, even among barren sandrocks. Ayme is no longer in the district of Kerek, its Sheikh being now under the command of the Sheikh of Djebal, whose residence is at Tafyle. One half of the inhabitants live under tents, and every house has a tent pitched upon its terrace, where the people pass the mornings and evenings, and sleep. The climate of all these mountains, to the southward of the Belka, is extremely agreeable; the air is pure, and although the heat is very great in summer, and is still further increased by the reflexion of the sun's rays from the rocky sides of the mountains, yet the temperature never becomes suffocating, owing to the refreshing breeze which generally prevails. I have seen no part of Syria in which there are so few invalids. The properties of the climate seem to have been well known to the ancients, who gave this district the appellation of Palæstina tertia, sive salutaris. The winter is very cold; deep snow falls, and the frosts sometimes continue till the middle of March. This severe weather is doubly felt by the inhabitants, as their dress is little fitted to protect them from it. During my stay in Gebalene, we had every morning a fog which did not disperse till mid-day. I could perceive the vapours collecting in the Ghor below, which, after sun-set, was completely enveloped in them. During the night they ascend the sides of the mountains, and in general are not entirely dissipated until near mid-day. From Khanzyre we had the Ghor all the way on our right, about eight or ten hours distant; but, in a straight line, not more than six hours.

August 8th.—At one hour and a quarter from Ayme, route S. b. W. we reached Tafyle, built on the declivity of a mountain, at the foot of which is Wady Tafyle. This name bears some resemblance to that of Phanon or Phynon, which, according to Eusebius, was situated between

Petra and Zoara. [Euseb. de nom. S.S.] Tafyle contains about six hundred houses; its Sheikh is the nominal chief of Djebal, but in reality the Arabs Howeytat govern the whole district, and their Sheikh has lately constructed a small castle at Tafyle at his own expense. Numerous springs and rivulets (ninety-nine according to the Arabs), the waters of which unite below and flow into the Ghor, render the vicinity of this town very agreeable. It is surrounded by large plantations of fruit trees: apples, apricots, figs, pomegranates, and olive and peach trees of a large species are cultivated in great numbers. The fruit is chiefly consumed by the inhabitants and their guests, or exchanged with the Bedouin women for butter; the figs are dried and pressed together in large lumps, and are thus exported to Ghaza, two long days journey from hence.

The inhabitants of Djebal are not so independent as the Kerekein, because they have not been able to inspire the neighbouring Bedouins with a dread of their name. They pay a regular tribute to the Beni Hadjaya, to the Szaleyt, but chiefly to the Howeytat, who often exact also extraordinary donations. Wars frequently happen between the people of Djebal and of Kerek, principally on account of persons who having committed some offence, fly from one town to seek an asylum in the other. At the time of my visit a coolness had existed between the two districts for several months, on account of a man of Tafyle, who having eloped with the wife of another, had taken refuge at Kerek; and one of the principal reasons which had induced our Sheikh to undertake this journey, was the hope of being able to bring the affair to an amicable termination. Hence we were obliged to remain three days at Tafyle, tumultuous assemblies were held daily, upon the subject, and the meanest Arab might give his opinion, though in direct opposition to that of his Sheikh. The father of the young man who had eloped had come with us from Kerek, for the whole family had been obliged to fly, the Bedouin laws entitling an injured husband to kill any of the offender's relations, in retaliation for the loss of his wife. The husband began by demanding from the young man's father two wives in return for the one carried off, and the greater part of the property which the emigrant family possessed in Tafyle. The father of the wife and her first cousin also made demands of compensation for the insult which their family had received by her elopement. Our Sheikh, however, by his eloquence and address, at last got the better of them all: indeed it must in justice be said that Youssef Medjaly was not more superior to the other mountaineers in the strength of his arm, and the excellence of his horsemanship, than he was by his natural talents. The affair was settled by the offender's father placing his four infant daughters, the youngest of whom was not yet weaned, at the disposal of the husband and his father-in-law, who might betrothe them to whomsoever they chose, and receive themselves the money which is usually paid for girls. The four daughters were estimated at about three thousand piastres, and both parties seemed to be content. In testimony of peace being concluded between the two families, and of the price of blood being paid, the young man's father, who had not yet shewn himself publickly, came to shake hands with the injured husband, a white flag was suspended at the top of the tent in which we sat, a sheep was killed, and we passed the whole night in feasting and conversation.

The women of Tafyle are much more shy before strangers than those of Kerek. The latter never, or at least very seldom, veil themselves, and they discourse freely with all strangers; the former, on the contrary, imitate the city ladies in their pride, and reserved manners. The inhabitants of Tafyle, who are of the tribe of Djowabere, supply the Syrian Hadj with a great quantity of provisions, which they sell to the caravan at the castle El Ahsa; and the profits which they derive from this trade are sometimes very great. It is much to be doubted whether the peasants of Djebal and Shera will be able to continue their field-labour, if the Syrian pilgrim caravan be not soon re-established. The produce of their soil hardly enables them to pay their heavy tribute to the Bedouins, besides feeding the strangers who alight at their Menzels: for all the villages in this part of the country treat their guests in the manner, which has already been described. The people of Djebal sell their wool, butter, and hides at Ghaza, where they buy all the little luxuries which they stand in need of; there are, besides, in every village, a few shopkeepers from El Khalyl or Hebron, who make large profits. The people of Hebron have the reputation of being enterprising merchants, and not so dishonest as their neighbours of Palestine: their pedlars penetrate far into the desert of Arabia, and a few of them remain the whole year round at Khaibar in the Nedjed.

The fields of Tafyle are frequented by immense numbers of crows; the eagle Rakham is very common in the mountains, as are also wild boars. In all the Wadys south of the Modjeb, and particularly in those of Modjeb and El Ahsa, large herds of mountain goats, called by the Arabs Beden, are met with. This is the Steinbock, or Bouquetin of the Swiss and Tyrol Alps they pasture in flocks of forty or fifty together; great numbers of them are killed by the people of Kerek and Tafyle, who hold their flesh in high estimation. They sell the large knotty horns to the Hebron merchants, who carry them to Jerusalem, where they are worked into handles for knives and daggers. I saw a pair of these horns at Kerek three feet and a half in length. The Arabs told me that it is very difficult to get a shot at them, and that the hunters hide themselves among the reeds on the banks of streams where the animals resort in the evening to drink; they also asserted, that when pursued, they will throw themselves from a height of fifty feet and more upon their heads without receiving any injury. The same thing is asserted by the hunters in the Alps. In the mountains of Belka, Kerek, Djebal, and Shera, the bird Katta [This bird is a species of partridge, Tetrao Alkatta, and is found in large flocks in May and June in every part of Syria. It has been particularly described in Russel's Aleppo, vol. ii. p. 194.] is met with in immense numbers; they fly in such large flocks that the Arab boys often kill two and three at a time, merely by throwing a stick amongst them. Their eggs, which they lay in the rocky ground, are collected by the Arabs. It is not improbable that this bird is the Seloua, or quail, of the children of Israel.

The peasants of Tafyle have but few camels; they till the ground with oxen and cows, and use mules for the transport of their provisions. At half an hour south of Tafyle is the valley of Szolfehe. From a point above Tafyle the mountains of Dhana (which I shall have occasion to mention hereafter) bore S.S.W.

August 11th.—During our stay at Tafyle we changed our lodgings twice every day, dining at one public house and supping at another. We were well treated, and had every evening a musical party, consisting of Bedouins famous for their performance upon the Rababa, or guitar of the desert, and who knew all the new Bedouin poetry by heart. I here met a man from Aintab, near Aleppo, who hearing me talk of his native town, took a great liking to me, and shewed me every civility.

We left Tafyle on the morning of the 11th. In one hour we reached a spring, where a party of Beni Szaleyt was encamped. At two hours was a ruined village, with a fine spring, at the head of a Wady. Two hours and three quarters, the village Beszeyra. Our road lay S.W. along the western declivity of the mountains, having the Ghor continually in view. The Wadys which descend the mountains of Djebal south of Tafyle do not reach the lowest part of the plain in the summer, but are lost in the gravelly soil of the valley. Beszeyra is a village of about fifty houses. It stands upon an elevation, on the summit of which a small castle has been built, where the peasants place their provisions in times of hostile invasion. It is a square building of stone, with strong walls. The villages of Beszeyra, Szolfehe, and Dhana are inhabited by descendants of the Beni Hamyde, a part of whom have thus become Fellahein, or cultivators, while the greater number still remain in a nomadic state. Those of

Beszeyra lived formerly at Omteda, now a ruined village three or four hours to the north of it. At that time the Arabs Howeytat were at war with the Djowabere, whose Sheikh was an ally of the Hamyde. The Howeytat defeated the Djowabere, and took Tafyle, where they constructed a castle, and established a Sheikh of their own election; they also built, at the same time, the tower of Beszeyra. The Hamyde of Omteda then emigrated to this place, which appears to have been, in ancient times, a considerable city, if we may judge from the ruins which surround the village. It was probably the ancient Psora, a bishopric of Palaestina tertia. [See Reland. Palæst. vol i. p. 218.] The women of Beszeyra were the first whom I saw wearing the Berkoa, or Egyptian veil, over their faces.

The Sheikh of Kerek had come thus far, in order to settle a dispute concerning a colt which one of the Hamyde of Beszeyra demanded of him. We found here a small encampment of Howeytat Arabs, to one of whom the Sheikh recommended me: he professed to know the man well, and assured me that he was a proper guide. We settled the price of his hire to Cairo, at eighty piastres; and he was to provide me with a camel for myself and baggage. This was the last friendly service of Sheikh Youssef towards me, but I afterwards learnt, that he received for his interest in making the bargain, fifteen piastres from the Arab, who, instead of eighty, would have been content with forty piastres. After the Sheikh had departed on his return, my new guide told me that his camels were at another encampment, one day's distance to the south, and that he had but one with him, which was necessary for the transport of his tent. This avowal was sufficient to make me understand the character of the man, but I still relied on the Sheikh's recommendation. In order to settle with the guide I sold my mare for four goats and for thirty-five piastres worth of corn, a part of which I delivered to him, and I had the remainder ground into flour, for our provision during the journey; he took the goats in payment of his services, and it was agreed that I should give him twenty piastres more on reaching Cairo. I had still about eighty piastres in gold, but kept them carefully concealed in case of some great emergency; for I knew that if I were to shew a single sequin, the Arabs would suppose that I possessed several hundreds, and would either have robbed me of them, or prevented me from proceeding on my journey by the most exorbitant demands.

August 13th.—I remained two days at Beszeyra, and then set out with the family of my guide, consisting of his wife, two children, and a servant girl. We were on foot, and drove before us the loaded camel and a few sheep and goats. Our road ascended; at three quarters of an hour, we came to a spring in the mountain. The rock is here calcareous, with basalt. At two hours and a half was Ain Djedolat, a spring of excellent water; here the mountain is overgrown with short Balout trees. At the end of two hours and three quarters, direction S. we reached the top of the mountain, which is covered with large blocks of basalt. Here a fine view opened upon us; to our right we had the deep valley of Wady Dhana, with the village of the same name on its S. side; farther west, about four hours from Dhana, we saw the great valley of the Ghor, and towards the E. and S. extended the wide Arabian desert, which the Syrian pilgrims cross in their way to Medina. In three hours and a quarter, after a slight descent, we reached the plain, here consisting of arable ground covered with flints. We passed the ruins of an ancient town or large village, called El Dhahel. The castle of Aaneiza, with an insulated hillock near it, a station of the pilgrims, bore S.S.E. distant about five hours; the town of Maan, S. distant ten or twelve hours; and the castle El Shobak, S.S.W. East of Aaneiza runs a chain of hills called Teloul Djaafar. Proceeding a little farther, we came to the high borders of a broad valley, called El Ghoeyr, (diminutive of Arabic El Ghor) to the S. of Wady Dhana. Looking down into this valley, we saw at a distance a troop of horsemen encamped near a spring; they had espied us, and immediately mounted their horses in pursuit of us. Although several people had joined our little caravan on the road, there was only one armed man amongst us, except myself. The general opinion was that the horsemen belonged to the Beni Szakher, the enemies of the Howeytat, who often make inroads into this district; there was therefore no time to lose; we drove the cattle hastily back, about a quarter of an hour, and hid them, with the women and baggage, behind some rocks near the road, and we then took to our heels towards the village of Dhana, which we reached in about three quarters of an hour, extremely exhausted, for it was about two o'clock in the afternoon and the heat was excessive. In order to run more nimbly over the rocks, I took off my heavy Arab shoes, and thus I was the first to reach the village; but the sharp flints of the mountain wounded my feet so much, that after reposing a little I could hardly stand upon my legs. This was the first time I had ever felt fear during my travels in the desert; for I knew that if I fell in with the Beni Szakher, without any body to protect me, they would certainly kill me, as they did all persons whom they supposed to belong to their inveterate enemy, the Pasha of Damascus, and my appearance was very much that of a Damascene. Our fears however were unfounded; the party that pursued us proved to be Howeytat, who were coming to pay a visit to the Sheikh at Tafyle; the consequence was that two of our companions, who had staid behind, because being inhabitants of Maan, and friends of the Beni Szakher, they conceived themselves secure, were stripped by the pursuers, whose tribe was at war with the people of Maan. Dhana, which I suppose to be the ancient Thoana, is prettily situated, on the declivity of Tor Dhana, the highest mountain of Djebal, and has fine gardens and very extensive tobacco plantations. The Howeytat have built a tower in the village. The inhabitants were now at war with those of Beszeyra, but both parties respect the lives of their enemies, and their hostile expeditions are directed against the cattle only. Having reposed at Dhana we returned in the evening to the spot where we had left the women and the baggage, and rested for the night at about a quarter of an hour beyond it.

August 14th.—We skirted, for about an hour, the eastern borders of Wady Ghoeyr, when we descended into the valley, and reached its bottom at the end of three hours and a half, travelling at a slow pace. This Wady divides the district of Djebal from that of Djebal Shera, or the mountains of Shera, which continue southwards towards the Akaba. These are the mountains called in the Scriptures Mount Seir, the territory of the Edomites. The valley of Ghoeyr is a large rocky and uneven basin, considerably lower than the eastern plain, upwards of twelve miles across at its eastern extremity, but narrowing towards the west. It is intersected by numerous Wadys of winter torrents, and by three or four valleys watered by rivulets which unite below and flow into the Ghor. The Ghoeyr is famous for the excellent pasturage, produced by its numerous springs, and it has, in consequence, become a favourite place of encampment for all the Bedouins of Djebal and Shera. The borders of the rivulets are overgrown with Defle and the shrub Rethem. The rock is principally calcareous; and there are detached pieces of basalt and large tracts of brescia formed of sand, flint, and pieces of calcareous stone. In the bottom of the valley we passed two rivulets, one of which is called Seil Megharye, where we arrived at the end of a four hours walk, and found some Bedouin women washing their blue gowns, and the wide shirts of their husbands. I had taken the lead of our party, accompanied by my guide's little boy, with whom I reached an encampment, on the southern side of the valley, to which these women belonged. This was the encampment to which my guide belonged, and where he assured me that I should find his camels. I was astonished to see nobody but women in the tents, but was told that the greater part of the men had gone to Ghaza to sell the soap-ashes which these Arabs collect in the mountains of Shera. The ladies being thus left to themselves, had no impediment to the satisfying of their curiosity, which was very great at seeing a townsman, and what was still more extraordinary, a man of Damascus (for so I was called), under their tents. They crowded about me, and were incessant in their inquiries respecting my affairs, the goods I had to sell, the dress of the town ladies, &c. &c. When they found that I had nothing to sell, nor any thing to present to them, they soon retired; they however informed me that my guide had no other camels in his possession than the one we had brought with us, which was already lame. He soon afterwards arrived, and when I began to expostulate with him on his conduct, he assured me that his camel would be able to carry us all the way to Egypt, but begged me to wait a few days longer, until he should be well enough to walk by its side; for, since we left Beszeyra he had been constantly complaining of rheumatic pains in his legs. I saw that all this was done to gain time, and to put me out of patience, in order to cheat me of the wages he had already received; but, as we were to proceed on the following day to another encampment at a few hours distance, I did not choose to say any thing more to him on the subject in a place where I had nobody but women to take my part; hoping to be able to attack him more effectually in the presence of his own tribe'smen.

August 15th.—We remained this day at the women's tents, and I amused myself with visiting almost every tent in the encampment, these women being accustomed to receive strangers in the absence of their husbands. The Howeytat Arabs resemble the Egyptians in their features; they are much leaner and taller than the northern Arabs; the skin of many of them is almost black, and their features are much less regular than those of the northern Bedouins, especially the Aeneze. The women are tall and well made, but too lean; and even the handsomest among them are disfigured by broad cheek bones.

The Howeytat occupy the whole of the Shera, as far as Akaba, and south of it to Moyeleh, five days from Akaba, on the Egyptian Hadj road. To the east they encamp as far as Akaba el Shamy, or the Akaba on the Syrian pilgrim route; while the northern Howeytat take up their winter quarters in the Ghor. The strength of their position in these mountains renders them secure from the attacks of the numerous hordes of Bedouins who encamp in the eastern Arabian desert; they are, however, in continual warfare with them, and sometimes undertake expeditions of twenty days journey, in order to surprise some encampment of their enemies in the plains of the Nedjed. The Beni Szakher are most dreaded by them, on account of their acquaintance with the country, and peace seldom lasts long between the two tribes. The encampment where I spent this day was robbed of all its camels last winter by the Beni Szakher, who drove off, in one morning, upwards of twelve hundred belonging to their enemies. The

Howeytat receive considerable sums of money as a tribute from the Egyptian pilgrim caravan; they also levy certain contributions upon the castles on the Syrian Hadj route, situated between Maan and Tebouk, which they consider as forming a part of their territory. They have become the carriers of the Egyptian Hadj, in the same manner, as the Aeneze transport with their camels the Syrian pilgrims and their baggage. When at variance with the Pashas of Egypt, the Howeytat have been known to plunder the caravan; a case of this kind happened about ten years ago, when the Hadj was returning from Mekka; the principal booty consisted of several thousand camel loads of Mocha coffee, an article which the pilgrims are in the constant habit of bringing for sale to Cairo; the Bedouins not knowing what to do with so large a quantity, sold the greater part of it at Hebron, Tafyle, and Kerek, and that year happening to be a year of dearth, they gave for every measure of corn an equal measure of coffee. The Howeytat became Wahabis; but they paid tribute only for one year, and have now joined their forces with those of Mohammed Aly, against Ibn Saoud.

August 16th.—We set out for the encampment of the Sheikh of the northern Howeytat, with the tent and family of my guide: who was afraid of leaving them in this place where be thought himself too much exposed to the incursions of the Beni Szakher. We ascended on foot, through many Wadys of winter torrents, up the southern mountains of the Ghoeyr; we passed several springs, and the ruined place called Szyhhan, and at the end of three hours walk arrived at a large encampment of the Howeytat, situated near the summit of the basin of the Ghoeyr. It is usual, when an Arab with his tent reaches an encampment placed in a Douar, or circle, that some of the families strike their tents, and pitch them again in such a way as to widen the circle for the admission of the stranger's tent; but the character of my guide did not appear to be sufficiently respectable to entitle him to this compliment, for not a tent was moved, and he was obliged to encamp alone out of the circle, in the hope that they would soon break up for some other spot where he might obtain a place in the Douar. These Arabs are much poorer than the Aeneze, and consequently live much worse. Had it not been for the supply of butter which I bought at Beszeyra, I should have had nothing but dry bread to eat; there was not a drop of milk to be got, for at this time of the year the ewes are dry; of camels there was but about half a dozen in the whole encampment.

I here came to an explanation with my guide, who, I saw, was determined to cheat me out of the wages he had already received. I told him that I was tired of his subterfuges, and was resolved to travel with him no longer, and I insisted upon his returning me the goats, or hiring me an-

279

other guide in his stead. He offered me only one of the goats; after a sharp dispute therefore I arose, took my gun, and swore that I would never re-enter his tent, accompanying my oath with a malediction upon him, and upon those who should receive him into their encampment, for I had been previously informed that he was not a real Howeytat, but of the tribe of Billy, the individuals of which are dispersed over the whole desert. On quitting his tent, I was surrounded by the Bedouins of the encampment, who told me that they had been silent till now, because it was not their affair to interfere between a host and his guest, but that they never would permit a stranger to depart in that way; that I ought to declare myself to be under the Sheikh's protection, who would do me justice. This being what I had anticipated, I immediately entered the tent of the Sheikh, who hap-pened to be absent; my guide now changed his tone, and began by offering me two goats to settle our differences. In the evening the Sheikh arrived, and after a long debate I got back my four goats, but the wheat which I had received at Beszeyra, as the remaining part of the payment for my mare, was left to the guide. In return for his good offices, the Sheikh begged me to let him have my gun, which was worth about fifteen piastres; I presented it to him, and he acknowledged the favour, by telling me that he knew an honest man in a neighbouring encampment, who had a strong camel, and would be ready to serve me as a guide.

August 18th.—I took a boy to shew me the way to this person, and driving my little flock before us, we reached the encampment, which was about one hour to the westward. The boy told the Bedouin that I had become the Sheikh's brother, I was therefore well received, and soon formed a favourable opinion of this Arab, who engaged to take me to Cairo for the four goats, which I was to deliver to him now, and twenty piastres (about one pound sterling) to be paid on my arrival in Egypt. This will be considered a very small sum for a journey of nearly four hundred miles; but a Bedouin puts very little value upon time, fatigue, and labour; while I am writing this, many hundred loaded camels, belonging to Bed-ouins, depart every week from Cairo for Akaba, a journey of ten days, for which they receive twenty-five piastres per camel. Had I been known to be an European, I certainly should not have been able to move without promising at least a thousand piastres to my guide. The excursion of M. Boutin, a French traveller, from Cairo to the Oasis of Jupiter Ammon, a journey of twelve days, undertaken in the summer of 1812, cost for guides only, four thousand piastres.

August 19th.—In the morning I went to the castle of Shobak, where I wished to purchase some provisions. It was distant one hour and a quarter from the encampment, in a S.E. direction. Shobak, also called Kerek el Shobak, perhaps the ancient Carcaria, [Euseb. de locis S.S.] is the principal place in Djebel Shera; it is situated about one hour to the south of the Ghoeyr, upon the top of a hill in the midst of low mountains, which bears some resemblance to Kerek, but is better adapted for a fortress, as it is not commanded by any higher mountains. At the foot of the hill are two springs, surrounded by gardens and olive plantations. The castle is of Saracen construction, and is one of the largest to the south of Damascus; but it is not so solidly built as the castle of Kerek. The greater part of the wall and several of the bastions and towers are still entire. The ruins of a well built vaulted church are now transformed into a public inn or Medhafe. Upon the architraves of several gates I saw mystical symbols, belonging to the ecclesiastical architecture of the lower empire. In several Arabic inscriptions I distinguished the name of Melek el Dhaher. Where the hill does not consist of precipitous rock, the surface of the slope is covered with a pavement. Within the area of the castle a party of about one hundred families of the Arabs Mellahein have built their houses or pitched their tents. They cultivate the neighbouring grounds, under the protection of the Howeytat, to whom they pay tribute. The horsemen of the latter who happen to encamp near the castle, call regularly every morning at one of the Medhafes of Shobak, in order to have their mares fed; if the barley is refused, they next day kill one of the sheep belonging to the town.

At one hour and a half north of Shobak, on the side of the Ghoeyr, lies the village of Shkerye. From Shobak the direction of Wady Mousa is S.S.W. Maan bears S.S.E. The mountain over Dhana, N.N.E. To the east of the castle is an encampment of Bedouin peasants, of the tribe of Hababene, who cultivate the ground. As I had no cash in silver, and did not wish to shew my sequins, I was obliged to give in exchange for the provisions which I procured at Shobak my only spare shirt, together with my red cap, and half my turban. The provisions consisted of flour, butter, and dried Leben, or sour milk mixed with flour and hardened in the sun, which makes a most refreshing drink when dissolved in water. There are several Hebron merchants at Shobak.

August 20th.—I remained in the tent of my new guide, who delayed his departure, in order to obtain from his friends some commissions for Cairo, upon which he might gain a few piastres. In the afternoon of this day we had a shower of rain, with so violent a gust of wind, that all the tents of the encampment were thrown down at the same moment, for the poles are fastened in the ground very carelessly during the summer months.

August 21st.—The whole encampment broke up in the morning, some Bedouins having brought intelligence that a strong party of Beni Szakher had been seen in the district of Djebal. The greater part of the males of the Howeytat together with their principal Sheikh Ibn Rashyd, were gone to Egypt, in order to transport the Pasha's army across the desert to Akaba and Yambo; we had therefore no means of defence against these formidable enemies, and were obliged to take refuge in the neighbourhood of Shobak, where they would not dare to attack the encampment. When the Bedouins encamp in small numbers, they choose a spot surrounded by high ground, to prevent their tents from being seen at a distance. The camp is, however, not unfrequently betrayed by the camels which pasture in the vicinity.

In the evening we took our final departure, crossing an uneven plain, covered with flints and the ruins of several villages, and then descended into the Wady Nedjed; the rivulet, whose source is in a large paved basin in the valley, joins that of Shobak. Upon the hills which border this pleasant valley are the ruins of a large town of the same name, of which nothing remains but broken walls and heaps of stones. In one hour and a quarter from our encampment, and about as far from Shobak, we reached the camp of another tribe of Fellahein Bedouins, called Refaya, where we slept. They are people of good property, for which they are indebted to their courage in opposing the extortions of the Howeytat. Here were about sixty tents and one hundred firelocks. Their herds of cows, sheep, and goats are very numerous, but they have few camels. Besides corn fields they have extensive vineyards, and sell great quantities of dried grapes at Ghaza, and to the Syrian pilgrims of the Hadj. They have the reputation of being very daring thieves.

August 22nd.—I was particularly desirous of visiting Wady Mousa, of the antiquities of which I had heard the country people speak in terms of great admiration; and from thence I had hoped to cross the desert in a straight line to Cairo; but my guide was afraid of the hazards of a journey through the desert, and insisted upon my taking the road by Akaba, the ancient Eziongeber, at the extremity of the eastern branch of the Red sea, where he said that we might join some caravans, and continue our route towards Egypt. I wished, on the contrary, to avoid Akaba, as I knew that the Pasha of Egypt kept there a numerous garrison to watch the movements of the Wahabi and of his rival the Pasha of Damascus; a person therefore like myself, coming from the latter place, without any papers to shew who I was, or why I had taken that circuitous route, would certainly have roused the suspicions of the officer commanding at Akaba, and the consequences might have been dangerous to me among the savage soldiery of that garrison. The road from Shobak to Akaba, which is tolerably good, and might easily be rendered practicable even to artillery, lies to the E. of Wady Mousa; and to have quitted it, out of mere curiosity to see the Wady, would have looked very suspicious in the eyes of the Arabs; I therefore pretended to have made a vow to slaughter a goat in honour of Haroun (Aaron), whose tomb I knew was situated at the extremity of the valley, and by this stratagem I thought that I should have the means of seeing the valley in my way to the tomb. To this my guide had nothing to oppose; the dread of drawing upon himself, by resistance, the wrath of Haroun, completely silenced him.

We left the Refaya early in the morning, and travelled over hilly ground. At the end of two hours we reached an encampment of Arabs Saoudye, who are also Fellahein or cultivators, and the strongest of the peasant tribes, though they pay tribute to the Howeytat. Like the Refaya they dry large quantities of grapes. They lay up the produce of their harvest in a kind of fortress called Oerak, not far from their camp, where are a few houses surrounded by a stone wall. They have upwards of one hundred and twenty tents. We breakfasted with the Saoudye, and then pursued the windings of a valley, where I saw many vestiges of former cultivation, and here and there some remains of walls and paved roads, all constructed of flints. The country hereabouts is woody. In three hours and a half we passed a spring, from whence we ascended a mountain, and travelled for some time along its barren summit, in a S.W. direction, when we again descended, and reached Ain Mousa, distant five hours and a half from where we had set out in the morning. Upon the summit of the mountain near the spot where the road to Wady Mousa diverges from the great road to Akaba, are a number of small heaps of stones, indicating so many sacrifices to Haroun. The Arabs who make vows to slaughter a victim to Haroun, think it sufficient to proceed as far as this place, from whence the dome of the tomb is visible in the distance; and after killing the animal they throw a heap of stones over the blood which flows to the ground. Here my guide pressed me to slaughter the goat which I had brought with me from Shobak, for the purpose, but I pretended that I had vowed to immolate it at the tomb itself. Upon a hill over the Ain Mousa the Arabs Lyathene were encamped, who cultivate the valley of Mousa. We repaired to their encampment, but were not so hospitably received as we had been the night before.

Ain Mousa is a copious spring, rushing from under a rock at the eastern extremity of Wady Mousa. There are no ruins near the spring; a little lower down in the valley is a mill, and above it is the village of Bad-abde, now abandoned. It was inhabited till within a few years by about twenty families of Greek Christians, who subsequently retired to Kerek. Proceeding from the spring along the rivulet for about twenty minutes, the valley opens, and leads into a plain about a quarter of an hour in length and ten minutes in breadth, in which the rivulet joins with another descending from the mountain to the southward. Upon the declivity of the mountain, in the angle formed by the junction of the two rivulets, stands Eldjy, the principal village of Wady Mousa. This place contains between two and three hundred houses, and is enclosed by a stone wall with three regular gates. It is most picturesquely situated, and is inhabited by the Lyathene abovementioned, a part of whom encamp during the whole year in the neighbouring mountains. The slopes of the mountain near the town are formed into artificial terraces, covered with corn fields and plantations of fruit trees. They are irrigated by the waters of the two rivulets and of many smaller springs which descend into the valley below Eldjy, where the soil is also well cultivated. A few large hewn stones dispersed over the present town indicate the former existence of an ancient city in this spot, the happy situation of which must in all ages have attracted inhabitants. I saw here some large pieces of beautiful saline marble, but nobody could tell me from whence they had come, or whether there were any rocks of this stone in the mountains of Shera.

I hired a guide at Eldjy, to conduct me to Haroun's tomb, and paid him with a pair of old horse-shoes. He carried the goat, and gave me a skin of water to carry, as he knew that there was no water in the Wady below.

In following the rivulet of Eldjy westwards the valley soon narrows again; and it is here that the antiquities of Wady Mousa begin. Of these I regret that I am not able to give a very complete account: but I knew well the character of the people around me; I was without protection in the midst of a desert where no traveller had ever before been seen; and a close examination of these works of the infidels, as they are called, would have excited suspicions that I was a magician in search of treasures; I should at least have been detained and prevented from prosecuting my journey to Egypt, and in all probability should have been stripped of the little money which I possessed, and what was infinitely more valuable to me, of my journal book. Future travellers may visit the spot under the protection of an armed force; the inhabitants will become more accustomed to the researches of strangers; and the antiquities of Wady Mousa will then be found to rank amongst the most curious remains of ancient art.

At the point where the valley becomes narrow is a large sepulchral vault, with a handsome door hewn in the rock on the slope of the hill which rises from the right bank of the torrent: on the same side of the rivulet, a little farther on, I saw some other sepulchres with singular ornaments. Here a mass of rock has been insulated from the mountain by an excavation, which leaves a passage five or six paces in breadth between it and the mountain. It forms nearly a cube of sixteen feet, the top being a little narrower than the base, the lower part is hollowed into a small sepulchral cave with a low door; but the upper part of the mass is solid. There are three of these mausolea at a short distance from each other. A few paces lower, on the left side of the stream, is a larger mausoleum similarly formed, which appears from its decayed state, and the style of its architecture, to be of more ancient date than the others. Over its entrance are four obelisks, about ten feet in height, cut out of the same piece of rock; below is a projecting ornament, but so much defaced by time that I was unable to discover what it had originally represented; it had, however, nothing of the Egyptian style.

Continuing for about three hundred paces farther along the valley, which is in this part about one hundred and fifty feet in breadth; several small tombs are met with on both sides of the rivulet, excavated in the rock, without any ornaments. Beyond these is a spot where the valley seemed to be entirely closed by high rocks; but upon a nearer approach, I perceived a chasm about fifteen or twenty feet in breadth, through which the rivulet flows westwards in winter; in summer its waters are lost in the sand and gravel before they reach the opening, which is called El Syk. The precipices on either side of the torrent are about eighty-feet in height; in many places the opening between them at top is less than at bottom, and the sky is not visible from below. As the rivulet of Wady Mousa must have been of the greatest importance to the inhabitants of the valley, and more particularly of the city, which was entirely situated on the west side of the Syk, great pains seem to have been taken by the ancients to regulate its course. Its bed appears to have been covered with a stone pavement, of which many vestiges yet remain, and in several places stone walls were constructed on both sides, to give the water its proper direction, and to check the violence of the torrent. A channel was likewise cut on each side of the Syk, on a higher level than the river, to convey a constant supply of water into the city in all seasons, and to prevent all the water from being absorbed in summer by the broad torrent bed, or by the irrigation of the fields in the valley above the Syk.

About fifty paces below the entrance of the Syk a bridge of one arch thrown over the top of the chasm is still entire; immediately below it, on both sides, are large niches worked in the rock, with elegant sculptures, destined probably for the reception of statues. Some remains of antiquities might perhaps be found on the top of the rocks near the bridge; but my guide assured me, that notwithstanding repeated endeavours had been made, nobody had ever been able to climb up the rocks to the bridge, which was therefore unanimously declared to be the work of the Djan, or evil genii. In continuing along the winding passage of the Syk, I saw in several places small niches cut in the rock, some of which were single; in other places there were three or four together, without any regularity; some are mere holes, others have short pilasters on both sides; they vary in size from ten inches to four or five feet in height; and in some of them the bases of statues are still visible. We passed several collateral chasms between perpendicular rocks, by which some tributary torrents from the south side of the Syk empty themselves into the river. I did not enter any of them, but I saw that they were thickly overgrown with Defle trees. My guide told me that no antiquities existed in these valleys, but the testimony of these people on such subjects is little to be relied on. The bottom of the Syk itself is at present covered with large stones, brought down by the torrent, and it appears to be several feet higher than its ancient level, at least towards its western extremity. After proceeding for twenty-five minutes between the rocks, we came to a place where the passage opens, and where the bed of another stream coming from the south joins the Syk. On the side of the perpendicular rock, directly opposite to the issue of the main valley, an excavated mausoleum came in view, the situation and beauty of which are calculated to make an extraordinary impression upon the traveller, after having traversed for nearly half an hour such a gloomy and almost subterraneous passage as I have described. It is one of the most elegant remains of antiquity existing in Syria; its state of preservation resembles that of a building recently finished, and on a closer examination I found it to be a work of immense labour.

The principal part is a chamber sixteen paces square, and about twenty- five feet high. There is not the smallest ornament on the walls, which are quite smooth, as well as the roof, but the outside of the entrance door is richly embellished with architectural decorations. Several broad steps lead up to the entrance, and in front of all is a colonnade of four columns, standing between two pilasters. On each of the three sides of the great chamber is an apartment for the reception of the dead. A similar excavation, but larger, opens into each end of the vestibule, the length of which latter is not equal to that of the colonnade as it appears in front, but terminates at either end between the pilaster and the neighbouring column. The doors of the two apartments opening into the vestibule are covered with carvings richer and more beautiful than those on the door of the principal chamber. The colonnade is about thirty-five feet high, and the columns are about three feet in diameter with Corinthian capitals. The pilasters at the two extremities of the colonnade, and the two columns nearest to them, are formed out of the solid rock, like all the rest of the monument, but the two centre columns, one of which has fallen, were constructed separately, and were composed of three pieces each. The colonnade is crowned with a pediment, above which are other ornaments, which, if I distinguished them correctly, consisted of an insulated cylinder crowned with a vase, standing between two other structures in the shape of small temples, supported by short pillars. The entire front, from the base of the columns to the top of the ornaments, may be sixty or sixty-five feet. The architrave of the colonnade is adorned with vases, connected together with festoons. The exterior wall of the chamber at each end of the vestibule, which presents itself to the front between the pilaster and the neighbouring column, was ornamented with colossal figures in basrelief; but I could not make out what they represented. One of them appears to have been a female mounted upon an animal, which, from the tail and hind leg, appears to have been a camel. All the other ornaments sculptured on the monument are in perfect preservation.

The natives call this monument Kaszr Faraoun, or Pharaoh's castle; and pretend that it was the residence of a prince. But it was rather the sepulchre of a prince, and great must have been the opulence of a city, which could dedicate such monuments to the memory of its rulers.

From this place, as I before observed, the Syk widens, and the road continues for a few hundred paces lower down through a spacious passage between the two cliffs. Several very large sepulchres are excavated in the rocks on both sides; they consist generally of a single lofty apartment with a flat roof: some of them are larger than the principal chamber in the Kaszr Faraoun. Of those which I entered, the walls were quite plain and unornamented; in some of them are small side rooms, with excavations and recesses in the rock for the reception of the dead; in others I found the floor itself irregularly excavated for the same purpose, in compartments six to eight feet deep, and of the shape of a coffin; in the floor of one sepulchre I counted as many as twelve cavities of this kind, besides a deep niche in the wall, where the bodies of the principal members of the family, to whom the sepulchre belonged, were probably deposited.

On the outside of these sepulchres, the rock is cut away perpendicularly above and on both sides of the door, so as to make the exterior facade larger in general than the interior apartment. Their most common form is that of a truncated pyramid, and as they are made to project one or two feet from the body of the rock they have the appearance, when seen at a distance, of insulated structures. On each side of the front is generally a pilaster, and the door is seldom without some elegant ornaments.

These fronts resemble those of several of the tombs of Palmyra, but the latter are not excavated in the rock, but constructed with hewn stones. I do not think, however, that there are two sepulchres in Wady Mousa perfectly alike; on the contrary, they vary greatly in size, shape, and embellishments. In some places, three sepulchres are excavated one over the other, and the side of the mountain is so perpendicular that it seems impossible to approach the uppermost, no path whatever being visible; some of the lower have a few steps before their entrance.

In continuing a little farther among the sepulchres, the valley widens to about one hundred and fifty yards in breadth. Here to the left is a theatre cut entirely out of the rock, with all its benches. It may be capable of containing about three thousand spectators: its area is now filled up with gravel, which the winter torrent brings down. The entrance of many of the sepulchres is in like manner almost choked up. There are no remains of columns near the theatre. Following the stream about one hundred and fifty paces further, the rocks open still farther, and I issued upon a plain two hundred and fifty or three hundred yards across, bordered by heights of more gradual ascent than before. Here the ground is covered with heaps of hewn stones, foundations of buildings, fragments of columns, and vestiges of paved streets; all clearly indicating that a large city once existed here; on the left side of the river is a rising ground extending westwards for nearly a quarter of an hour, entirely covered with similar remains. On the right bank, where the ground is more elevated, ruins of the same description are also seen. In the valley near the river, the buildings have probably been swept away by the impetuosity of the winter torrent; but even here are still seen the foundations of a temple, and a heap of broken columns; close to which is a large Birket, or reservoir of water, still serving for the supply of the inhabitants during the summer. The finest sepulchres in Wady Mousa are in the eastern cliff, in front of this open space, where I counted upwards of fifty close to each other.

High up in the cliff I particularly observed one large sepulchre, adorned with Corinthian pilasters.

Farther to the west the valley is shut in by the rocks, which extend in a northern direction; the river has worked a passage through them, and runs underground, as I was told, for about a quarter of an hour. Near the west end of Wady Mousa are the remains of a stately edifice, of which part of the wall is still standing; the inhabitants call it Kaszr Bent Faraoun, or the palace of Pharaoh's daughter. In my way I had entered several sepulchres, to the surprise of my guide, but when he saw me turn out of the footpath towards the Kaszr, he exclaimed: "I see now clearly that you are an infidel, who have some particular business amongst the ruins of the city of your forefathers; but depend upon it that we shall not suffer you to take out a single para of all the treasures hidden therein, for they are in our territory, and belong to us." I replied that it was mere curiosity, which prompted me to look at the ancient works, and that I had no other view in coming here, than to sacrifice to Haroun; but he was not easily persuaded, and I did not think it prudent to irritate him by too close an inspection of the palace, as it might have led him to declare, on our return, his belief that I had found treasures, which might have led to a search of my person and to the detection of my journal, which would most certainly have been taken from me, as a book of magic. It is very unfortunate for European travellers that the idea of treasures being hidden in ancient edifices is so strongly rooted in the minds of the Arabs and Turks; nor are they satisfied with watching all the stranger's steps; they believe that it is sufficient for a true magician to have seen and observed the spot where treasures are hidden (of which he is supposed to be already informed by the old books of the infidels who lived on the spot) in order to be able afterwards, at his ease, to command the guardian of the treasure to set the whole before him. It was of no avail to tell them to follow me and see whether I searched for money. Their reply was, "of course you will not dare to take it out before us, but we know that if you are a skilful magician you will order it to follow you through the air to whatever place you please." If the traveller takes the dimensions of a building or a column, they are persuaded that it is a magical proceeding. Even the most liberal minded Turks of Syria reason in the same manner, and the more travellers they see, the stronger is their conviction that their object is to search for treasures, "Maou delayl", "he has indications of treasure with him," is an expression I have heard a hundred times.

On the rising ground to the left of the rivulet, just opposite to the Kaszr Bent Faraoun, are the ruins of a temple, with one column yet standing to which the Arabs have given the name of Zob Faraoun, i.e. hasta virilis Pharaonis; it is about thirty feet high and composed of more than a dozen pieces. From thence we descended amidst the ruins of private habitations, into a narrow lateral valley, on the other side of which we began to ascend the mountain, upon which stands the tomb of Aaron. There are remains of an ancient road cut in the rock, on both sides of which are a few tombs. After ascending the bed of a torrent for about half an hour, I saw on each side of the road a large excavated cube, or rather truncated pyramid, with the entrance of a tomb in the bottom of each. Here the number of sepulchres increases, and there are also excavations for the dead in several natural caverns. A little farther on, we reached a high plain called Szetouh Haroun, or Aaron's terrace, at the foot of the mountain upon which his tomb is situated. There are several subterranean sepulchres in the plain, with an avenue leading to them, which is cut out of the rocky surface.

The sun had already set when we arrived on the plain; it was too late to reach the tomb, and I was excessively fatigued; I therefore hastened to kill the goat, in sight of the tomb, at a spot where I found a number of heaps of stones, placed there in token of as many sacrifices in honour of the saint. While I was in the act of slaying the animal, my guide exclaimed aloud, "O Haroun, look upon us! it is for you we slaughter this victim. O Haroun, protect us and forgive us! O Haroun, be content with our good intentions, for it is but a lean goat! O Haroun, smooth our paths; and praise be to the Lord of all creatures!". This he repeated several times, after which he covered the blood that had fallen on the ground with a heap of stones; we then dressed the best part of the flesh for our supper, as expeditiously as possible, for the guide was afraid of the fire being seen, and of its attracting hither some robbers.

August 23d.—The plain of Haroun and the neighbouring mountlains have no springs: but the rain water collects in low grounds, and in natural hollows in the rocks, where it partly remains the whole year round, even on the top of the mountain; but this year had been remarkable for its drought. Juniper trees grow here in considerable numbers. I had no great desire to see the tomb of Haroun, which stands on the summit of the mountain that was opposite to us, for I had been informed by several persons who had visited it, that it contained nothing worth seeing except a large coffin, like that of Osha in the vicinity of Szalt. My guide, moreover, insisted upon my speedy return, as he was to set out the same day with a small caravan for Maan; I therefore complied with his wishes, and we returned by the same road we had come. I regretted afterwards, that I had not visited Haroun's tomb, as I was told that there are several large and handsome sepulchres in the rock near it. A traveller ought, if possible, to see every thing with his own eyes, for the reports of the Arabs are little to be depended on, with regard to what may be interesting, in point of antiquity: they often extol things which upon examination, prove to be of no kind of interest, and speak with indifference of those which are curious and important. In a room adjoining the apartment, in which is the tomb of Haroun, there are three copper vessels for the use of those who slaughter the victims at the tomb: one is very large, and destined for the boiling of the flesh of the slaughtered camel. Although there is at present no guardian at the tomb, yet the Arabs venerate the Sheikh too highly, to rob him of any of his kitchen utensils. The road from Maan and from Wady Mousa to Ghaza, leads by the tomb, and is much frequented by the people of Maan and the Bedouins; on the other side of Haroun the road descends into the great valley.

In comparing the testimonies of the authors cited in Reland's Palaestina, it appears very probable that the ruins in Wady Mousa are those of the ancient Petra, and it is remarkable that Eusebius says the tomb of Aaron was shewn near Petra. Of this at least I am persuaded, from all the information I procured, that there is no other ruin between the extremities of the Dead sea and Red sea, of sufficient importance to answer to that city. Whether or not I have discovered the remains of the capital of Arabia Petræa, I leave to the decision of Greek scholars, and shall only subjoin a few notes on these ruins.

The rocks, through which the river of Wady Mousa has worked its extraordinary passage, and in which all the tombs and mausolea of the city have been excavated, as high as the tomb of Haroun, are sand-stone of a reddish colour. The rocks above Eldjy are calcareous, and the sandstone does not begin until the point where the first tombs are excavated. To the southward the sandstone follows the whole extent of the great valley, which is a continuation of the Ghor. The forms of the summits of these rocks are so irregular and grotesque, that when seen from afar, they have the appearance of volcanic mountains. The softness of the stone afforded great facilities to those who excavated the sides of the mountains; but, unfortunately, from the same cause it is in vain to look for inscriptions: I saw several spots where they had existed, but they are all now obliterated. The position of this town was well-chosen, in point of security; as a few hundred men might defend the entrance to it against a large army; but the communication with the neighbourhood must have been subjected to great inconveniences. I am not certain whether the passage of the Syk was made use of as a road, or whether the road from the town towards Eldjy was formed through one of the side valleys of the Syk. The road westwards towards Haroun, and the valley below, is very difficult for beasts of burthen. The summer heats must have been excessive, the situation being surrounded on all sides by high barren cliffs, which concentrate the reflection of the sun, while they prevent the westerly winds from cooling the air. I saw nothing in the position that could have compensated the inhabitants for these disadvantages, except the river, the benefit of which might have been equally enjoyed had the town been built below Eldjy. Security therefore was probably the only object which induced the people to overlook such objections, and to select such a singular position for a city. The architecture of the sepulchres, of which there are at least two hundred and fifty in the vicinity of the ruins, are of very different periods.

On our return I stopped a few hours at Eldjy. The town is surrounded with fruit-trees of all kinds, the produce of which is of the finest quality. Great quantities of the grapes are sold at Ghaza, and to the Bedouins. The Lyathene cultivate the valley as far as the first sepulchres of the ancient city; in their townhouses they work at the loom. They pay tribute to the Howeytat and carry provisions to the Syrian pilgrims at Maan, and to the Egyptian pilgrims at Akaba. They have three encampments of about eighty tents each. Like the Bedouins and other inhabitants of Shera they have become Wahabis, but do not at present pay any tribute to the Wahabi chief.

Wady Mousa is comprised within the territory of Damascus, as are the entire districts of Shera and Djebal. The most southern frontiers of the Pashalik are Tor Hesma, a high mountain so called at one day's journey north of Akaba; from thence northward to Kerek, the whole country belongs to the same Pashalik, and consequently to Syria; but it may easily be conceived that the Pasha has little authority in these parts. In the time of Djezzar, the Arabs of Wady Mousa paid their annual land- tax into his treasury, but no other Pasha has been able to exact it.

I returned from Eldjy to the encampment above Ain Mousa, which is considerably higher than the town, and set out from thence immediately, for I very much disliked the people, who are less civil to strangers than any other Arabs in Shera. We travelled in a southern direction along the windings of a broad valley which ascends from Ain Mousa, and reached its summit at the end of two hours and a quarter. The soil, though flinty, is very capable of cultivation.

This valley is comprised within the appellation of Wady Mousa, because the rain water which collects here joins, in the winter, the torrent below Eldjy. The water was anciently conducted through this valley in an artificial channel, of which the stone walls remain in several places. At the extremity of the Wady are the ruins of an ancient city, called Betahy, consisting of large heaps of hewn blocks of silicious stone; the trees on this mountain are thinly scattered. At a quarter of an hour from Betahy we reached an encampment, composed of Lyathene and Naymat, where we alighted, and rested for the night.

August 24th.—Our road lay S.S.W.; in one hour we came to Ain Mefrak, where are some ruins. From thence we ascended a mountain, and continued along the upper ridge of Djebel Shera. To our right was a tremendous precipice, on the other side of which runs the chain of sand-rocks which begin near Wady Mousa. To the west of these rocks we saw the great valley forming the continuation of the Ghor. At the end of three hours, after having turned a little more southward, we arrived at a small encampment of Djaylat where we stopped to breakfast. The Bedouin tents which composed a great part of this encampment were the smallest I had ever seen; they were about four feet high, and ten in length. The inhabitants were very poor, and could not afford to give us coffee; our breakfast or dinner therefore consisted of dry barley cakes, which we dipped in melted goat's grease. The intelligence which I learnt here was extremely agreeable; our landlord told us that a caravan was to set out in a few days for Cairo, from a neighbouring encampment of Howeytat, and that they intended to proceed straight across the desert. This was exactly what I wished, for I could not divest myself of apprehensions of danger in being exposed to the undisciplined soldiers of Akaba. It had been our intention to reach Akaba from hence in two days, by way of the mountainous district of Reszeyfa (a part of Shera so called) and Djebel Hesma; but we now gladly changed our route, and departed for the encampment of the Howeytat. We turned to the S.E. and in half an hour from the Djeylat passed the fine spring called El Szadeke, near which is a hill with extensive ruins of an ancient town consisting of heaps of hewn stones. From thence we descended by a slight declivity into the eastern plain, and reached the encampment, distant one hour and a half from Szadeke. The same immense plain which we had entered in coming from Beszeyra, on the eastern borders of the Ghoeyr, here presented itself to our view. We were about six hours S. of Maan, whose two hills, upon which the two divisions of the town are situated, were distinctly visible. The Syrian Hadj route passes at about one hour to the east of the encampment. About eight hours S. of Maan, a branch of the Shera extends for three or four hours in an eastern direction across the plain; it is a low hilly chain.

The mountains of Shera are considerably elevated above the level of the Ghor, but they appear only as low hills, when seen from the eastern plain, which is upon a much higher level than the Ghor. I have already noticed the same peculiarity with regard to the upper plains of El Kerek and the Belka: and it is observable also in the plain of Djolan relatively to the level of the lake of Tiberias. The valley of the Ghor, which has a rapid slope southward, from the lake of Tiberias to the Dead sea, appears to continue descending from the southern extremity of the latter as far as the Red sea, for the mountains on the E. of it appear to increase in height the farther we proceed southward, while the upper plain, apparently continues upon the same level. This plain terminates to the S. near Akaba, on the Syrian Hadj route, by a steep rocky descent, at the bottom of which begins the desert of Nedjed, covered, for the greater part, with flints. The same descent, or cliff, continues westward towards Akaba on the Egyptian Hadj road, where it joins the Djebel Hesma (a prolongation of Shera), about eight hours to the N. of the Red sea. We have thus a natural division of the country, which appears to have been well known to the ancients, for it is probably to a part of this upper plain, together with the mountains of Shera, Djebal, Kerek, and Belka, that the name of Arabia Petræa was applied, the western limits of which must have been the great valley or Ghor. It might with truth be called Petræa, not only on account of its rocky mountains, but also of the elevated plain already described, which is so much covered with stones, especially flints, that it may with great propriety be called a stony desert, although susceptible of culture: in many places it is overgrown with wild herbs, and must once have been thickly inhabited, for the traces of many ruined towns and villages are met with on both sides of the Hadj road between Maan and Akaba, as well as between Maan and the plains of Haouran, in which direction are also many springs. At present all this country is a desert, and Maan is the only inhabited place in it. All the castles on the Syrian Hadj route from Fedhein to Medina are deserted. At Maan are several springs, to which the town owes its origin, and these, together with the circumstance of its being a station of the Syrian Hadj, are the cause of its still existing. The inhabitants have scarcely any other means of subsistence than the profits which they gain from the pilgrims in their way to and from Mekka, by buying up all kinds of provisions at Hebron and Ghaza, and selling them with great profit to the weary pilgrims; to whom the gardens and vineyards of Maan are no less agreeable, than the wild herbs collected by the people of Maan are to their camels. The pomgranates, apricots, and peaches of Maan are of the finest quality. In years when a very numerous caravan passes, pomgranates are sold at one piastre each, and every thing in the same proportion. During the two days stay of the pilgrims, in going, and as many in returning, the people of Maan earn as much as keeps them the whole year.

Maan is situated in the midst of a rocky country, not capable of cultivation; the inhabitants therefore depend upon their neighbours of Djebal and Shera for their provision of wheat and barley. At present, owing to the discontinuance of the Syrian Hadj, they are scarcely able to obtain money to purchase it. Many of them have commenced pedlars among the Bedouins, and fabricators of different articles for their use, especially sheep-skin furs, while others have emigrated to Tafyle and Kerek. The Barbary pilgrims who were permitted by the Wahabi chief to perform their pilgrimage in 1810, and 1811, returned from Medina by the way of Maan and Shobak to Hebron, Jerusalem, and Yaffa, where they embarked for their own country, having taken this circuitous route on account of the hostile demonstrations of Mohammed Ali Pasha on the Egyptian road. Several thousands of them died of fatigue before they reached Maan. The people of this town derived large profits from the survivors, and for the transport of their effects; but it is probable that if the Syrian Hadj is not soon reestablished, the place will in a few years be abandoned. The inhabitants considering their town as an advanced post to the sacred city of Medina, apply themselves with great eagerness to the study of the Koran. The greater part of them read and write, and many serve in the capacity of Imams or secretaries to the great Bedouin Sheikhs. The two hills upon which the town is built, divide the inhabitants into two parties, almost incessantly engaged in quarrels which are often sanguinary; no individual of one party even marries into a family belonging to the other.

On arriving at the encampment of the Howeytat, we were informed that the caravan was to set out on the second day; I had the advantage, therefore, of one day's repose. I was now reduced to that state which can alone ensure tranquillity to the traveller in the desert; having nothing with me that could attract the notice or excite the cupidity of the Bedouins; my clothes and linen were torn to rags; a dirty Keffye, or yellow handkerchief, covered my head; my leathern girdle and shoes had long been exchanged, by way of present, against similar articles of an inferior kind, so that those I now wore were of the very worst sort. The tube of my pipe was reduced from two yards to a span, for I had been obliged to cut off from it as much as would make two pipes for my friends at

Kerek; and the last article of my baggage, a pocket handkerchief, had fallen to the lot of the Sheikh of Eldjy. Having thus nothing more to give, I expected to be freed from all further demands: but I was mistaken: I had forgotten some rags torn from my shirt, which were tied round my ancles, wounded by the stirrups which I had received in exchange from the Sheikh of Kerek. These rags happening to be of white linen, some of the ladies of the Howeytat thought they might serve to make a Berkoa, or face veil, and whenever I stepped out of the tent I found myself surrounded by half a dozen of them, begging for the rags. In vain I represented that they were absolutely necessary to me in the wounded state of my ancles: their answer was, "you will soon reach Cairo, where you may get as much linen as you like." By thus incessantly teazing me they at last obtained their wishes; but in my anger I gave the rags to an ugly old woman, to the no slight disappointment of the young ones.

August 26th.—We broke up in the morning, our caravan consisting of nine persons, including myself, and of about twenty camels, part of which were for sale at Cairo; with the rest the Arabs expected to be able to transport, on their return home, some provisions and army-baggage to Akaba, where Mohammed Ali Pasha had established a depot for his Arabian expedition. The provisions of my companions consisted only of flour; besides flour, I carried some butter and dried Leben (sour milk), which when dissolved in water, forms not only a refreshing beverage, but is much to be recommended as a preservative of health when travelling in summer. These were our only provisions. During the journey we did not sup till after sunset, and we breakfasted in the morning upon a piece of dry bread, which we had baked in the ashes the preceding evening, without either salt or leven. The frugality of these Bedouins is indeed without example; my companions, who walked at least five hours every day, supported themselves for four and twenty hours with a piece of dry black bread of about a pound and a half weight, without any other kind of nourishment. I endeavoured, as much as possible to imitate their abstemiousness, being already convinced from experience that it is the best preservative against the effects of the fatigues of such a journey. My companions proved to be very good natured people: and not a single quarrel happened during our route, except between myself and my guide. He too was an honest, good tempered man, but I suffered from his negligence, and rather from his ignorance of my wants, as an European. He had brought only one water-skin with him, which was to serve us both for drinking and cooking; and as we had several intervals of three days without meeting with water, I found myself on very short allowance, and could not receive any assistance from my companions, who had scarcely enough for themselves. But these people think nothing of hardships and privations, and take it for granted, that other people's constitutions are hardened to the same aptitude of enduring thirst and fatigue, as their own.

We returned to Szadeke, where we filled our water-skins, and proceeded from thence in a W.S.W. direction, ascending the eastern hills of Djebel Shera. After two hours march we began to descend, in following the course of a Wady. At the end of four hours is a spring called Ibn Reszeysz. The highest point of Djebel Hesma, in the direction of Akaba, bears from hence S.W. Hesma is higher than any part of Shera. In five hours we reached Ain Daleghe, a spring in a fertile valley, where the Howeytat have built a few huts, and cultivate some Dhourra fields. We continued descending Wady Daleghe, which in winter is an impetuous torrent. The mountains are quite barren here; calcareous rock predominates, with some flint. At the end of seven hours we left the Wady, which takes a more northern direction, and ascended a steep mountain. At eight hours and a half we alighted on the declivity of the mountain, which is called Djebel Koula, and which appears to be the highest summit of Djebel Shera. Our road was tolerably good all the way.

August 27th.—After one hour's march we reached the summit of Djebel Koula, which is covered with a chalky surface. The descent on the other side is very wild, the road lying along the edges of almost perpendicular precipices amidst large blocks of detached rocks, down a mountain entirely destitute of vegetation, and composed of calcareous rocks, sand-stone, and flint, lying over each other in horizontal layers. At the end of three hours we came to a number of tombs on the road side, where the Howeytat and other Bedouins who encamp in these mountains bury their dead. In three hours and a half we reached the bottom of the mountain, and entered the bed of a winter torrent, which like Wady Mousa has worked its passage through the chain of sand-stone rocks that form a continuation of the Syk. These rocks extend southwards as far as Djebel Hesma. The narrow bed is enclosed by perpendicular cliffs, which, at the entrance of the Wady, are about fifteen or twenty yards distant from each other, but wider lower down. We continued in a western direction for an hour and a half, in this Wady, which is called Gharendel. At five hours the valley opens, and we found ourselves upon a sandy plain, interspersed with rocks; the bed of the Wady was covered with white sand. A few trees of the species called by the Arabs Talh, Tarfa, and Adha, grow in the midst of the sand, but their withered leaves cannot divert the traveller's eye from the dreary scene around him. At six hours the valley again becomes narrower; here are some more tombs of Bedouins on the side of the road. At the end of six hours and a half we came to the mouth of the Wady, where it joins the great lower valley, issuing from the mountainous country into the plain by a narrow passage, formed by the approaching rocks. These rocks are of sand-stone and contain many natural caverns. A few hundred paces above the issue of the Wady are several springs, called Ayoun Gharendel, surrounded by a few date trees, and some verdant pasture ground. The water has a sulphureous taste, but these being the only springs on the borders of the great valley within one day's journey to the N. and S. the Bedouins are obliged to resort to them. The wells are full of leeches, some of which fixed themselves to the palates of several of our camels whilst drinking, and it was with difficulty that we could remove them. The name of Arindela, an ancient town of Palæstina Tertia, bears great resemblance to that of Gharendel.

On issuing from this rocky country, which terminates the Djebel Shera, on its western side, the Wady Gharendel empties itself into the valley El Araba, in whose sands its waters are lost. This valley is a continuation of the Ghor, which may be said to extend from the Red sea to the sources of the Jordan. The valley of that river widens about Jericho, and its inclosing hills are united to a chain of mountains which open and enclose the Dead sea. At the southern extremity of the sea they again approach, and leave between them a valley similar to the northern Ghor, in shape; but which the want of water makes a desert, while the Jordan and its numerous tributary streams render the other a fertile plain. In the southern Ghor the rivulets which descend from the eastern mountains, to the S. of Wady Szafye, or El Karahy, are lost amidst the gravel in their winter beds, before they reach the valley below, and there are no springs whatever in the western mountain; the lower plain, therefore, in summer is entirely without water, which alone can produce verdure in the Arabian deserts, and render them habitable. The general direction of the southern Ghor is parallel to the road which I took in coming from Khanzyre to Wady Mousa. At the point where we crossed it, near Gharendel, its direction was from N.N.E. to S.S.W. From Gharendel it extends southwards for fifteen or twenty hours, till it joins the sandy plain which separates the mountains of Hesma from the eastern branch of the Red sea. It continues to bear the appellation of El Ghor as far as the latitude of Beszeyra, to the S. of which place, as the Arabs informed me, it is interrupted for a short space by rocky ground and Wadys, and takes the name of Araba, which it retains till its termination near the Red sea. Near Gharendel, where I saw it, the whole plain presented to the view an expanse of shifting sands whose surface was broken by innumerable undulations, and low hills. The sand appears to have been brought from the shores of the Red sea by the

southerly winds; and the Arabs told me that the valley continued to present the same appearance beyond the latitude of Wady Mousa. A few
Talh trees (the acacia which produces the gum arable), Tarfa (tamarisk),
Adha, and Rethem, grow among the sand hills; but the depth of sand pre-
cludes all vegetation of herbage. Numerous Bedouin tribes encamp here
in the winter, when the torrents produce a copious supply of water, and a
few shrubs spring up upon their banks, affording pasturage to the sheep
and goats; but the camels prefer the leaves of the trees, especially the
thorny Talh.

The existence of the valley El Araba, the Kadesh Barnea, perhaps, of the Scriptures, appears to have been unknown both to ancient and
modern geographers, although it forms a prominent feature in the topography of Syria and Arabia Petræa. It deserves to be thoroughly
investigated, and travellers might proceed along it in winter time, accompanied by two or three Bedouin guides of the tribes of Howeytat and
Terabein, who could be procured at Hebron. Akaba, or Eziongeber, might
be reached in eight days by the same road by which the communication
was anciently kept up between Jerusalem and her dependencies on the
Red sea, for this is both the nearest and the most commodious route, and
it was by this valley that the treasures of Ophir were probably transported
to the warehouses of Solomon.

Of the towns which I find laid down in D'Anville's maps, between Zoara and Aelana, no traces remain, Thoana excepted, which is the
present Dhana. The name of Zoar is unknown to the Arabs, but the village
of Szafye is near that point; the river which is made by D'Anville to fall
into the Dead sea near Zoara, is the Wady El Ahhsa; but it will have been
seen in the above pages, [t]hat the course of that Wady is rather from the
east than south. I enquired in vain among the Arabs for the names of those
places where the Israelites had sojourned during their progress through
the desert; none of them are known to the present inhabitants. The country, about Akaba, and to the W.N.W. of it, might, perhaps, furnish some
data for the illustration of the Jewish history. I understand that M. Seetzen
went in a straight line from Hebron to Akaba, across the desert El Ty; he
may perhaps, have collected some interesting information on the subject.

The following ruined places are situated in Djebal Shera, to the
S. and S.S.W. of Wady Mousa; Kalaat Beni Madha, Atrah, a ruined
tower, with water near it, Djerba, Basta, Eyl, Ferdakh, with a spring;
Anyk, Bir el Beytar, a number of wells upon a plain surrounded by high
cliffs, in the midst of Tor Hesma. The caravans from Wady Mousa to
Akaba make these wells their first station, and reach Akaba on the eve-

ning of the second day; but they are two long days journeys of ten or twelve hours each. At the foot of Hanoun are the ruins of Wayra, and the two deserted villages of Beydha and Heysha. West of Hanoun is the spring Dhahel, with some ruins. In that neighbourhood are the ruined places Shemakh and Syk.

We were one hour and a half in crossing the Araba, direction W. by N. In some places the sand is very deep, but it is firm, and the camels walk over it without sinking. The heat was suffocating, and it was increased by a hot wind from the S.E. There is not the slightest appearance of a road, or of any other work of human art in this part of the valley. On the other side we ascended the western chain of mountains. The mountain opposite to us appeared to be the highest point of the whole chain, as far as I could see N. and S.; it is called Djebel Beyane; the height of this chain, however, is not half that of the eastern mountains. It is intersected by numerous broad Wadys, in which the Talh tree grows; the rock is entirely silicious, of the same species as that of the desert which extends from hence to Suez. I saw some large pieces of flint perfectly oval, three to four feet in length, and about a foot and a half in breadth.

After an hour and a half of gentle ascent we arrived at the summit of the hills, and then descended by a short and very gradual declivity into the western plain, the level of which although higher than that of the Araba, is perhaps one thousand feet lower than the eastern desert. We had now before us an immense expanse of dreary country entirely covered with black flints, with here and there some hilly chains rising from the plain. About six hours distant, to our right, were the hills near Wady Szays. The horizon being very clear near sunset, my companions pointed out to me the mountains of Kerek, which bore N.E. by N. Djebel Dhana bore N.E. by F., and Djebel Hesma S.S.E. I must here observe, that during all my journeys in the deserts I never allowed the Arabs to get a sight of my compass, as it would certainly have been considered by them as an instrument of magic. When on horseback I took the bearings, unseen, beneath my wide Arab cloak; under such circumstances it is an advantage to ride a mare, as she may easily be taught to stand quite still. When mounted on, a camel, which can never be stopped while its companions are moving on, I was obliged to jump off when I wished to take a bearing, and to couch down in the oriental manner, as if answering a call of nature. The Arabs are highly pleased with a traveller who jumps off his beast and remounts without stopping it, as the act of kneeling down is troublesome and fatiguing to the loaded camel, and before it can rise again, the caravan is considerably ahead. From Djebel Beyane we continued in the plain for upwards of an hour; and stopped for the night in a Wady which contains Talh trees, and extends across the plain for about half an hour. We had this day marched eleven hours.

August 28th.—In the morning we passed two broad Wadys full of tamarisks and of Talh trees, which have given to them the name of Abou Talhha. At the end of four hours we reached Wady el Lahyane. In this desert the water collects in a number of low bottoms and Wadys, where it produces verdure in winter time: and an abundance of trees with green leaves are found throughout the year. In the winter some of the Arabs of Ghaza, Khalyl, as well as those from the shores of the Red sea, encamp here. The Wady Lahyane [The road from Akaba to Ghaza passes here. It is a journey of eight long days. The watering places on it are, El Themmed, Mayeyu, and Berein. The distance from Akaba to Hebron is nine days. The springs on the road are: El Ghadyan, El Ghammer, and Weyba.] is several hours in extent; its bottom is full of gravel. We met with a few families of Arabs Heywat, who had chosen this place, that their camels might feed upon the thorny branches of the gum arabic tree, of which they are extremely fond. These poor people had no tents with them; and their only shelter from the burning rays of the sun, and the heavy dews of night, were the scanty branches of the Talh trees. The ground was covered with the large thorns of these trees, which are a great annoyance to the Bedouins and their cattle. Each Bedouin carries in his girdle a pair of small pincers, to extract the thorns from his feet, for they have no shoes, and use only a sort of sandal made of a piece of camel's skin, tied on with leathern thongs. In the summer they collect the gum arabic, which they sell at Cairo for thirty and forty patacks the camel load, or about twelve or fifteen shillings per cwt. English; but the gum is of a very inferior quality to that of Sennaar. My companions eat up all the small pieces that had been left upon the trees by the road side. I found it to be quite tasteless, but I was assured that it was very nutritive.

We breakfasted with the Arabs Heywat, and our people were extremely angry, and even insolent, at not having been treated with a roasted lamb, according to the promise of the Sheikh, who had invited us to alight. His excuse was that he had found none at hand; but one of our young men had overheard his wife scolding him, and declaring that she would not permit a lamb to be slaughtered for such miserable ill-looking strangers! The Bedouin women, in general, are much less generous and hospitable than their husbands, over whom they often use their influence, to curtail the allowance to guests and strangers.

At the end of five hours we issued from the head of Wady Lahyane again into the plain. The hill on the top of this Wady is called Ras el Kaa, and is the termination of a chain of hills which stretch across the plain in a northern direction for six or eight hours: it projects like a promontory, and serves as a land-mark to travellers; its rock is calcareous. The plain which we now entered was a perfect flat covered with black pebbles. The high insulated mountain behind which Ghaza is situated, bore from hence N. by W. distant three long days journey. At the end of seven hours, there was an insulated hill to the left of our road two hours distant, called Szoeyka; we here turned off to the left of the great road, in order to find water. In eight hours, and late at night, we reached several wells, called Biar Omshash, is where we found an encampment of Heywat, with whom we wished to take our supper after having filled our water skins; but they assured us that they had nothing except dry bread to give us. On hearing this my companions began to reproach them with want of hospitality, and an altercation ensued, which I was afraid would lead to blows; I therefore mounted my camel, and was soon followed by the rest. We continued our route during the night, but lost our road in the dark, and were obliged to alight in a Wady full of moving sands, about half an hour from the wells.

August 29th.—This day we passed several Wadys of Talh and tamarisk trees intermixed with low shrubs. Direction W. by S. The plain is for the greater part covered with flints; in some places it is chalky. Wherever the rain collects in winter, vegetation of trees and shrubs is produced. In the midst of this desert we met a poor Bedouin woman, who begged some water of us; she was going to Akaba, where the tents of her family were, but had neither provisions nor water with her, relying entirely on the hospitality of the Arabs she might meet on the road. We directed her to the Heywat at Omshash and in Wady Lahyane. She seemed to be as unconcerned, as if she were merely taking a walk for pleasure. After an uninterrupted march of nine hours and a half, we reached a mountain called Dharf el Rokob. It extends for about eight hours in a direction from N.W. to S.E. At its foot we crossed the Egyptian Hadj road; it passes along the mountain towards Akaba, which is distant from hence fifteen or eighteen hours. We ascended the northern extremity of the mountain by a broad road, and after a march of eleven hours reached, on the other side, a well called El Themmed, whose waters are impregnated with sulphur. The pilgrim caravan passes to the N. of the mountain and well, but the Arabs who have the conduct of the caravan repair to the well to fill the water skins for the supply of the Hadjis. The well is in a sandy soil, surrounded by calcareous rocks, and notwithstanding its importance, nothing has been done to secure it from being choaked up by the sand and gravel which every gust of wind drives into it. Its sides are not lined, and the Arabs take so little care in descending into it, that every caravan which arrives renders it immediately turbid.

The level plain over which we had travelled from Ras el Kaa terminates at Dharf el Rokob. Westward of it the ground is more intersected by hills and Wadys, and here begins the Desert El Ty, in which, according to tradition, both Jewish and Mohammedan, the Israelites wandered for several years, and from which belief the desert takes its name. We went this evening two hours farther than the Themmed, and alighted in the Wady Ghoreyr, after a day's march of thirteen hours and a half. The Bedouins, when travelling in small numbers, seldom alight at a well or spring, in the evening, for the purpose of there passing the night; they only fill their water-skins as quickly as possible, and then proceed on their way, for the neighbourhood of watering places is dangerous to travellers, especially in deserts where there are few of them, because they then become the rendezvous of all strolling parties.

August 30th.—On issuing from the Wady Ghoreyr we passed a chain of hills called Odjme, running almost parallel with the Dharf el Rokob. We had now re-entered the Hadj route, a broad well trodden road, strewn with the whitened bones of animals that have died by the way. The soil is chalky, and overspread with black pebbles. At the end of five hours and a half we reached Wady Rouak; here the term Wady is applied to a narrow strip of ground, the bed of a winter torrent, not more than one foot lower than the level of the plain, where the rain water from the inequalities of the surface collects, and produces a vegetation of low shrubs, and a few Talh trees. The greater part of the Wadys from hence to Egypt are of this description. The coloquintida grows in great abundance in all of them, it is used by the Arabs to make tinder, by the following process: after roasting the root in the ashes, they wrap it in a wetted rag of cotton cloth, they then beat it between two stones, by which means the juice of the fruit is expressed and absorbed by the rag, which is dyed by it of a dirty blue; the rag is then dried in the sun, and ignites with the slightest spark of fire. The Arabs nearest to Egypt use the coloquint in venereal complaints; they fill the fruit with camel's milk, roast it over the fire, and then give to the patient the milk thus impregnated with the essence of the fruit.

In nine hours and a half we passed a chain of low chalky hills called Ammayre. On several parts of the road were holes, out of which rock salt had been dug. At the end of ten hours and a half we arrived in the vicinity of Nakhel (i.e. date-tree), a fortified station of the Egyptian Hadj, situated about half an hour to the N. of the pilgrim's road. Our direction was still W. by N. Nakhel stands in a plain, which extends to an immense distance southward, but which terminates to the N. at about one hour's distance from Nakhel, in a low chain of mountains. The fortress is a large square building, with stone walls, without any habitations round it. There is a well of brackish water, and a large Birket, which is filled from the well, in the time of the Hadj. The Pasha of Egypt keeps a garrison in Nakhel of about fifty soldiers, and uses it as a magazine for the provisions of his army in his expedition against the Wahabi. The appellation Nakhel was probably given to this castle at a time when the adjacent country was covered with palm trees, none of which are now to be seen here. At Akaba, on the contrary, are large forests of them, belonging for the greater part to the Arabs Heywat. The ground about Nakhel is chalky or sandy, and is covered with loose pebbles.

We passed along the road as quickly as we could, for my companions were afraid lest their camels should be stopped by the Aga of Nakhel, to transport provisions to Akaba. The Arabs Heywat and Sowadye, who encamp in this district, style themselves masters of Akaba and Nakhel, and exact yearly from the Pasha certain sums for permitting him to occupy them; for though they are totally unable to oppose his troops, yet the tribute is paid, in order to take from them all pretext for plundering small caravans. About six hours to the S.W. of Nakhel is a chain of mountains called Szadder, extending in a S. E. direction.

Near Nakhel my Arab companions fell in with an acquaintance, who was burning charcoal for the Cairo market. He informed us that a large party of Arabs Sowaleha, with whom my Howeytats were at war, was encamped in this vicinity; it was, in consequence, determined to travel by night, until we should be out of their reach, and we stopped at sunset, about one hour west of Nakhel, after a day's march of eleven hours and a half, merely for the purpose of allowing the camels to eat. Being ourselves afraid to light a fire, lest it should be descried by the Sowaleha, we were obliged to take a supper of dry flour mixed with a little salt. During the whole of the journey the camels had no other provender than the withered shrubs of the desert, my dromedary excepted, to which I gave a few handfuls of barley every evening. Loaded camels are scarcely able to perform such a journey without a daily allowance of beans and barley.

August 31st—We set out before midnight, and continued at a quick rate the whole night. In these northern districts of Arabia the Bedouins, in general, are not fond of proceeding by night; they seldom travel at that time, even in the hottest season, if they are not in very large numbers, because, as they say, during the night nobody can distinguish the face of his friend, from that of his enemy. Another reason is, that camels on the march never feed at their ease in the day time, and nature seems to require that they should have their principal meal and a few hours rest in the evening. The favourite mode of travelling in these parts is, to set out about two hours before sun-rise, to stop two hours at noon, when every one endeavours to sleep under his mantle, and to alight for the evening at about one hour before sunset. We always sat round the fire, in conversation, for two or three hours after supper. During this night's march my companions frequently alluded to a superstitious belief among the Bedouins, that the desert is inhabited by invisible female demons, who carry off travellers tarrying in the rear of the caravans, in order to enjoy their embraces. They call them Om Megheylan, from Ghoul. The frequent loss of men who, exhausted by fatigue, loiter behind the great pilgrim caravans, and are cut off, stripped, and abandoned, by Bedouin robbers, may have given rise to this fable, which afforded my companions a subject of numerous jokes against me. "You townsmen," said they, "would be exquisite morsels for these ladies, who are accustomed only to the food of the desert."

We marched for four hours over uneven ground, and then reached a level plain, consisting of rich red earth fit for culture, and similar to that of the northern Syrian desert. We crossed several Wadys, in which we started a number of hares. At every twenty yards lay heaps of bones of camels, horses, and asses, by the side of the road. At six hours was a chain of low hills to the S. of the road, and running parallel with it. In seven hours we crossed Wady Nesyl, overgrown with green shrubs, but without trees. At the end of ten hours and a half we reached the mountainous country called El Theghar, or the mouths, which forms a boundary of the Desert El Ty, and separates it from the peninsula of Mount Sinai. We ascended for half an hour by a well formed road, cut in several places in the rock, and then followed the windings of a valley, in the bed of a winter torrent, gradually descending. On both sides of the Hadj road we saw numerous heaps of stones, the tombs of pilgrims who had died of fatigue; among others is shewn that of a woman who here died in labour, and whose infant was carried the whole way to Mekka, and back to Cairo in good health. At the end of fifteen hours we alighted in a valley of the Theghar, where we found an abundance of shrubs and trees.

September 1st.—We continued descending among the windings of the Wady, turning a little to the southward of the Hadj route. Among the calcareous hills of the Wady deep sands have accumulated, which have been blown thither from the shores of the Red sea; and in several parts there are large insulated rocks of porous tufwacke. After a march of four hours and a half we had a fine view of the sea, and gained the plain which extends to its shores, and which is apparently much below the level of the desert El Ty; it is covered with moving sands, among which a few low shrubs grow. The direction of our route was W.S.W. In seven hours we reached the wells of Mabouk, to our great satisfaction, as we had not a drop of water left in our skins. These wells are in the open plain, at the foot of some rocks. Good water, but in small quantities, is found every where on digging to the depth of ten or twelve feet. There were about half a dozen holes, five or six feet in circumference, with a foot of water in each; on drawing up the water the holes fill again immediately. We here met some shepherds of the Maazye, a tribe of Bedouins of the desert between Egypt and the Red sea, who were busy in watering a large herd of camels. They were so kind as to make room for us, in consideration of our being strangers and travellers; and we were occupied several hours in drawing up water. These wells were filled up last year by the Moggrebyn Hadj, on its passage, to revenge themselves upon Mohammed Ali, with whose treatment they were dissatisfied. The Egyptian pilgrims take a more northern route, but the Arabs who accompany them fill the water skins for the use of the caravan at these wells, and rejoin the Hadj by the route we travelled this morning. Near the wells are the ruins of a small building, with strong walls, which was probably constructed for the defence of the water, when the Hadj was still in its ancient splendour. On quitting the wells we turned off in the direction of Suez, our route lying W.N.W. There are no traces of a road here, for the track of caravans is immediately filled up by the moving sands, which covered the plain as far as I could discern, and in some places had collected into hills thirty or forty feet in height. At ten hours from our setting out in the morning we entered a plain covered with flints, and again fell in with the Hadj road. Here we took a W. by N. direction. At the end of eleven hours the plain was covered with a saline crust, and we crossed a tract of ground, about five minutes in breadth, covered with such a quantity of small white shells, that it appeared at a distance like a strip of salt. Shells of the same species are found on the shores of the lake of Tiberias. Once probably the sea covered the whole of this ground. At twelve hours and a half Suez bore S. about an hour and an half distant from us. To our right we saw marshy ground extending northwards, which the people informed me was full of salt; it is called, like all salt marshes, Szabegha. At the end of thirteen hours we crossed a low and narrow Wady, perhaps the remains of the canal of Ptolemy; and at fourteen hours and a half, alighted in Wady Redjel, where there were many Talh trees, and plenty of food for our camels.

September 2d.—We continued to travel over the plain, route W. by N. In two hours we reached Adjeroud, an ancient castle, which has lately been completely repaired by Mohammed Ali, who keeps a garrison here. There are two separate buildings, the largest of which is occupied by the soldiers, and the smaller contains a mosque with the tomb of a saint; they are both defended by strong walls against any attack of the Arabs. Here is also a copious well, but the water is very bitter, and can be used only for watering camels. The garrison is supplied from the wells of Mousa, opposite to Suez. Our road was full of the aromatic herb Baytheran, which is sold by the Arabs at Ghaza and Hebron.

Beyond Adjeroud many Wadys cross the plain. To the left we had the chain of mountains called Attaka. At the end of five hours, and about one hour to the right of the road, begins the chain of low mountains called Oweybe, running parallel with the Attaka. Our route lay W. by N. At eight hours the Attaka terminated on our left, and was succeeded by a ridge of low hills. The plain here is sandy, covered with black flints. We again passed several Wadys, and met two large caravans, transporting a corps of infantry to Suez. At the end of ten hours and a half we stopped in Wady Djaafar, which is full of low trees, shrubs, and dry herbs. From hence a hilly chain extends north-eastwards.

September 3d.—After a march of six hours along the plain, the ground began to be overspread with Egyptian pebbles. Route W. We passed several Wadys, similar to those mentioned above when describing Wady Rowak. At nine hours, we descried the Nile, with its beautiful verdant shores; at eleven hours began a hilly tract, the last undulations of Djebel Makattam; and in thirteen hours and a half we reached the vicinity of Cairo. Here my Arab companions left me, and proceeded to Belbeis, where, they were informed, their principal men were encamped, waiting for orders to proceed to Akaba. I discharged my honest guide, Hamd Ibn Hamdan, who was not a little astonished to see me take some sequins out of the skirts of my gown. As it was too late to enter the town, I went to some Bedouin tents which I saw at a distance, and entered one of them, in which, for the first time, I drank of the sweet water of the Nile. Here I remained all night. A great number of Bedouins were at this time collected near Cairo, to accompany the troops which were to be sent into Arabia after the Ramadhan.

CAIRO

September 4th.—I entered Cairo before sunrise; and thus concluded my journey, by the blessing of God, without either loss of health, or exposure to any imminent danger.

JOURNAL OF A TOUR IN THE PENINSULA OF MOUNT SINAI, IN THE SPRING OF 1816.

ABOUT the beginning of April 1816 Cairo was again visited by the plague. The Franks and most of the Christians shut themselves up; but as I neither wished to follow their example nor to expose myself unnecessarily in the town, I determined to pass my time, during the prevalence of the disease, among the Bedouins of Mount Sinai, to visit the gulf of Akaba, and, if possible, the castle of Akaba, to which, as far as I know, no traveller has ever penetrated. Intending to pass some days at the convent of Mount Sinai, I procured a letter of introduction to the monks from their brethren at Cairo; for without this passport no stranger is ever permitted to enter the convent; I was also desirous of having a letter from the Pasha of Egypt to the principal Sheikh of the tribes of Tor, over whom, as I knew by former experience, he exercises more than a nominal authority. With the assistance of this paper, I hoped to be able to see a good deal of the Bedouins of the peninsula in safety, and to travel in their company to Akaba. Such letters of recommendation are in general easily procured in Syria and Egypt, though they are often useless, as I found on several occasions during my first journey into Nubia, as well as in my travels in Syria, where the orders of the Pasha of Damascus were much slighted in several of the districts under his dominion.

A fortnight before I set out for Mount Sinai I had applied to the Pasha through his Dragoman, for a letter to the Bedouin Sheikh; but I was kept waiting for it day after day, and after thus delaying my departure a whole week, I was at last obliged to set off without it. The want of it was the cause of some embarrassment to me, and prevented me from reaching Akaba. It is not improbable that on being applied to for the letter, the Pasha gave the same answer as he gave at Tayf, when I asked him for a

Firmahn, namely, that as I was sufficiently acquainted with the language and manners of the Arabs, I needed no further recommendation.

The Arabs of Mount Sinai usually alight at Cairo in the quarter called El Djemelye, where some of them are almost constantly to be found. Having gone thither, I met with the same Bedouin with whom I had come last year from Tor to Cairo; I hired two camels from him for myself and servant, and laid in provisions for about six weeks consumption. We left Cairo on the evening of the 20th of April, and slept that night among the ruined tombs of the village called Kayt Beg, a mile from the city. From this village, at which the Bedouins usually alight, the caravans for Suez often depart; it is also the resort of smugglers from Suez and Syria.

April 21st.—We set out from Kayt Beg in the course of the morning, in the company of a caravan bound for Suez, comprising about twenty camels, some of which belonged to Moggrebyn pilgrims, who had come by sea from Tunis to Alexandria; the others to a Hedjaz merchant, and to the Bedouins of Mount Sinai, who had brought passengers from Suez to Cairo, and were now returning with corn to their mountains. As I knew the character of these Bedouins by former experience, and that the road was perfectly safe, at least as far as the convent, I did not think it necessary this time to travel in the disguise of a pauper. Some few comforts may be enjoyed in the desert even by those who do not travel with tents and servants; and whenever these comforts must be relinquished, it becomes a very irksome task to cross a desert, as I fully experienced during several of my preceding journeys.

The Bedouins of Sinai, or, as they are more usually denominated, the Towara, or Bedouins of Tor, formerly enjoyed the exclusive privilege of transporting goods, provisions, and passengers, from Cairo to Suez, and the route was wholly under their protection. Since the increased power of the Pasha of Egypt, it has been thrown open to camel-drivers of all descriptions, Egyptian peasants, as well as Syrian and Arabian Bedouins; and as the Egyptian camels are much stronger, for a short journey, than those of the desert, the Bedouins of Mount Sinai have lost the greater part of their custom, and the transport trade in this route is now almost wholly in the hands of the Egyptian carriers. The hire of a strong camel, from Cairo to Suez, was at this time about six or eight Patacks, from one and a half to two Spanish dollars.

The desert from Cairo to Suez is crossed by different routes; we followed that generally taken by the Towara, which lies mid-way between the great Hadj route, and the more southern one close along the mountains: the latter is pursued only by the Arabs Terabein, and other Syrian Bedouins. The route we took is called Derb el Ankabye.

We proceeded on a gentle ascent from Kayt Beg, and passed on the right several low quarries in the horizontal layers of soft calcareous stone of which the mountain of Mokattam, in the neighbourhood of Cairo, is composed; it is with this stone that the splendid Mamelouk tombs of Kayt Beg are built. At the end of an hour, the limestone terminated, and the road was covered with flints, petrosilex, and Egyptian pebbles; here are also found specimens of petrified wood, the largest about a foot in length. We now travelled eastward, and after a march of three hours halted upon a part of the plain, called El Mogawa, where we rested during the mid-day heat. Beyond this spot, to the distance of five hours from Cairo, we met with great quantities of petrified wood. Large pieces of the trunks of trees, three or four feet in length, and eight or ten inches in diameter, lay about the plain, and close to the road was an entire trunk of a tree at least twenty feet in length, half buried in sand. These petrifactions are generally found in low grounds, but I saw several also on the top of the low hills of gravel and sand over which the road lies. Several travellers have expressed doubts of their being really petrified wood, and some have crossed the desert without meeting with any of them. The latter circumstance is easily accounted for; the route we were travelling is not that usually taken to Suez. I have crossed this desert repeatedly in other directions, and never saw any of the petrifactions except in this part of it. As to its really being petrified wood there cannot be any reason to doubt it, after an inspection of the substance, in which the texture and fibres of the wood are clearly distinguishable, and perfectly resemble those of the date tree. I think it not improbable, that before Nechos dug the canal between the Nile and the Red sea, the communication between Arsinoe or Clysma and Memphis, may have been carried on this way; and stations may have been established on the spots now covered by these petrified trees; the water requisite to produce and maintain vegetation might have been procured from deep wells, or from reservoirs of rain water, as is done in the equally barren desert between Djidda and Mekka. After the completion of the canal, this route was perhaps neglected, the trees, left without a regular supply of water, dried up and fell, and the sands, with the winter rains and torrents, gradually effected the petrifaction. I have seen specimens of the petrified wood of date trees found in the Libyan desert, beyond the Bahr bala ma, where they were observed by Horneman in 1798, and in 1812, by M. Boutin, a French officer, who brought several of them to Cairo. They resemble precisely those which I saw on the Suez road, in colour, substance, and texture. Some of them are of silex, in others the substance seems to approach to hornblende.

We continued our route E. by S. over an uneven and somewhat hilly country covered with black petrosilex; and after a day's march of eight hours and a quarter, we halted in a valley of little depth, called Wady Onszary, where our camels found good pasture. Close by are some low hills, where the sands are seen in the state of formation into sand-rock, and presenting all the different gradations between their loose state and the solid stone. I saw a great quantity of petrified wood upon one of these hills, amongst which was the entire trunk of a date tree.

April 22d.—From Onszary we travelled E. by S. for one hour, and then E. At the end of three hours, the hilly country terminates, beyond which, in this route, no petrified wood is met with; we then entered upon a widely extended and entirely level plain, called by the Bedouins El Mograh, upon which we rested after a march of five hours and a half. While we were preparing our dinner two ostriches approached near enough to be distinctly seen. A shot fired by one of the Arabs frightened them, and in an instant they were out of sight. These birds come into this plain, from the eastward, from the desert of Tyh; but I never heard that the Bedouins of this country take the trouble of hunting them. The plain of Mograh is famous for the skirmishes which have taken place there, for the caravans that have been plundered in crossing it, and for the number of travellers that have been murdered on it. In former times, when this desert was constantly over- run by parties of robbers, the Mograh was always chosen by them as their point of attack, because, in the event of success, no one could escape them on a plain where objects can be distinguished in every direction to the distance of several hours. Even at present, since the route has been made more secure by the vigilance of the Pasha of Cairo, robberies sometimes happen, and in the autumn of 1815 a rich caravan was plundered by the Arabs Terabein. [These Arabs, under their Sheikh Abou Djehame, made an excursion about the same time over the mountains towards Cosseir, and plundered a caravan of pilgrims and merchants who were going to Kenne. The Sheikh was seized on his return by the Maazy tribe and carried to Cairo, where he remained a year in close confinement, and after having delivered part of his booty into the treasury of the Pasha, was released a few days before I set out.]

The desert of Suez is never inhabited by Bedouin encampments, though it is full of rich pasture and pools of water during winter and spring. No strong tribes frequent the eastern borders of Egypt, and a weak insulated encampment would soon be stripped of its property by nightly robbers. The ground itself is the patrimony of no tribe, but is common to all, which is contrary to the general practice of the desert, where every district has its acknowledged owners, with its limits of separation from those of the neighbouring tribes, although it is not always occupied by them.

In the afternoon we proceeded over the plain, and in eight hours and three quarters arrived opposite to the station of the Hadj, called Dar el Hamra which we left about three miles to the north of us, and which is distinguished by a large acacia tree, the only one in this plain. At the end of nine hours and a half, and about half an hour from the road, we saw a mound of earth, which, the Arabs told me, was thrown up about fifty years ago, by workmen employed by Ali Beg, then governor of Egypt, in digging a well there. The ground was dug to the depth of about eighty feet, when no water appearing the work was abandoned. At eleven hours and a quarter, our road joined the great Hadj route, which passes in a more northerly direction from Dar el Hamra to the Birket el Hadj, or inundation to the eastward of Heliopolis, four hours distant from Cairo, upon the banks of which the pilgrims encamp, previous to their setting out for Mekka. Between this road, and that by which we had travelled, lies another, also terminating at Kayt Beg. The southernmost route, which, as I have already mentioned, is frequented only by the Arabs Terabein, branches off from this common route at about six hours distant from Suez, and is called Harb bela ma (the road without water); it is very seldom frequented by regular caravans, being hilly and longer than the others, but I was told that notwithstanding its name, water is frequently met with in the low grounds, even in summer. Just beyond where we fell in with the Hadj route, we rested in the bed of a torrent called Wady Hafeiry, at the foot of a chain of hills which begin there, and extend to the N. of the route, and parallel with it towards Adjeroud. Our camels found abundance of pasture on the odoriferous herb Obeitheran, Santolina fragrantissima of Forskal, which grew here in great plenty.

April 23d.—Our road lay between the southern mountain and the abovementioned chain of hills to the north, called Djebel Uweybe, direction E.S.E. In three hours we passed the bed of a torrent called Seil Abou Zeid, where some acacia trees grow. The road is here encompassed on every side by hills. In four hours and a half we reached, in the direction E. by S. Wady Emshash, a torrent like the former, which in winter is filled by a stream of several feet in depth. Rains are much more frequent in this desert than in the valley of Egypt, and the same remark may be made in regard to all the mountains to the southward, where a regular, though not uninterrupted rainy season sets in, while in the valley of the Nile, as is well known, rain seldom falls even in winter. The soil and hills are here entirely calcareous.

We had been for the whole morning somewhat alarmed by the appearance of some suspicious looking men on camels at a distance in our rear, and our Bedouins had, in consequence, prepared their matchlocks. When we halted during the mid-day hours, they also alighted upon a hill at a little distance; but seeing us in good order, and with no heavy loads to excite their cupidity, they did not approach us. They, however, this evening, fell upon a small party of unarmed Egyptian peasants who were carrying corn to Suez, stripped them, took away their camels and loads, and the poor owners fled naked into Suez. It was afterwards learnt that they belonged to the tribe of Omran, who live on the eastern shore of the gulf of Akaba. Without establishing regular patrols of the Bedouins themselves on this road, it will never be possible to keep it free from robbers.

At six hours and a half begins a hilly country, with a slight descent through a narrow pass between hills, called El Montala, a favourite spot for robbers. At seven hours and a half we passed Adjeroud, about half an hour to our left; about two miles west of it is a well in the Wady Emshash, called Bir Emshash, which yields a copious supply of water in the winter, but dries up in the middle of summer if rains have not been abundant; the garrison of Adjeroud, where is a well so bitter that even camels will not drink the water, draws its supply of drinking water from the Bir Emshash. From hence the road turns S.E. over a slightly descending plain. At ten hours and a half is the well called Bir Suez, a copious spring enclosed by a massive building, from whence the water is drawn up by wheels turned by oxen, and emptied into a large stone tank on the outside of the building. The men who take care of the wheels and the oxen remain constantly shut up in the building for fear of the Bedouins. The water is brackish, but it serves for drinking, and the Arabs and Egyptian peasants travelling between Cairo and Suez, who do not choose to pay a higher price for the sweet water of the latter place, are in the habit of filling their water skins here, as do the people of Suez for their cooking provision. From an inscription on the building, it appears that it was erected in the year of the Hedjra 1018. We reached Suez about sunset, at the end of eleven hours and a half. I alighted with the Bedouins upon an open place between the western wall of the town, and its houses.

April 24th. In the time of Niebuhr Suez was not enclosed; there is now a wall on the west and south-west, which is rapidly falling to decay. The town is in a ruinous state; and neither merchants nor artisans live in it. Its population consists only of about a dozen agents, who receive goods from the ports of the Red sea, and forward them to their correspondents at Cairo, together with some shop-keepers who deal chiefly in provisions. The Pasha keeps a garrison here of about fifty horsemen, with an officer who commands the town, the neighbouring Arabs, and the shipping in the harbour. As Suez is one of the few harbours in the Red sea where ships can be repaired, some vessels are constantly seen at the wharf; the repairs are carried on by Greek shipwrights and smiths, in the service of the Pasha, who are let out to the shipowners by the commanding officer. Suez has of late become a harbour of secondary importance, the supplies of provisions, &c. for the Hedjaz being collected principally at Cosseir, and shipped from thence to Yembo and Djidda: but the trade in coffee and India goods still passes this way to Cairo. I saw numerous bales of spices and coffee lying near the shore, and a large heap of iron, together with packages of small wares, antimony, and Egyptian goods for exportation to Djidda, and ultimately to Yemen and India. The merchants complained of the want of camels to transport their goods to Cairo. The Pasha, who owns a considerable part of the imports of coffee, has fixed the carriage across the desert at a low price, and none of the agents venture to offer more to the camel drivers; the consequence of which is, that few are encouraged to come to Suez beyond the number required for the Pasha's merchandize. A caravan consisting of five or six hundred camels leaves Suez for Cairo on the 10th of each lunar month, accompanied by guards and two field-pieces; while smaller ones, composed of twenty or thirty beasts, depart almost every four or five days; but to these the merchants are shy of trusting their goods, because they can never depend on the safety of the road; accidents however seldom happen at present, so formidable is the name of Mohammed Ali.

Before the power of this Pasha was established in Egypt, and during the whole period of the Mamelouk government, the Bedouins might be called complete masters of Suez. Every inhabitant was obliged t [o] have his protector, Ghafyr, among the Bedouins of Mount Sinai, to whom he made annual presents of money, corn, and clothes, and who ensured to him the safe passage of his goods and person through the desert, and the recovery of whatever was plundered by the others. At that time the rate of freight was fixed by the Bedouins, and camels were in plenty; but, whenever the governors of Cairo quarrelled with the Bedouins, or ill- treated any of them at Cairo, the road was immediately interrupted, and the Bedouins placed guards over the well of Naba, two hours distant from Suez, in the hills on the eastern side of the gulf, to prevent the people of the town from drawing from thence their daily supply of sweet water. The difference was always settled by presents to the Bedouins, who, however, as may readily be conceived, often abused their power; and it not unfrequently happened that, even in time of peace, a Bedouin girl would be found, in the morning, sitting on the well, who refused permission to the water carriers of Suez to draw water unless they paid her with a new shirt, which they were obliged to do; for to strike her, or even to remove her by force, would have brought on a war with her tribe. The authority of the Bedouins is now at an end, though their Sheikhs receive from the Turkish governors of Suez a yearly tribute, under the name of presents, in clothes and money; the Pasha himself has become the Ghafyr of the people of Suez, and exacts from every camel load that passes through the gates from two to four dollars, for which he engages to ensure the passage through the desert; when the caravan however was plundered in 1815, he never returned the value of the goods to the owners.

The Arabs Terabein are the conductors of the caravans to Ghaza, and Khalyl (Hebron), the latter of which is eight days distant. At this time the freight per camel's load was eighteen Patacks, or four dollars and a half. These caravans bring the manufactures of Damascus, soap, glassware, tobacco, and dried fruits, which are shipped at Suez for the Hedjaz and Yemen.

The eastern part of the town of Suez is completely in ruins, but near the shore are some well built Khans, and in the inhabited part of the town are several good private houses. The aspect of Suez is that of an Arabian, and not an Egyptian town, and even in the barren waste, which surrounds it, it resembles Yembo and Djidda; the same motley crowds are met with in the streets, and the greater part of the shop-keepers are from Arabia or Syria. The air is bad, occasioned by the saline nature of the earth, and the extensive low grounds on the north and north-east sides, which are filled with stagnant waters by the tides. The inhabitants endeavour to counteract the influence of this bad atmosphere by drinking brandy freely; the mortality is not diminished by such a remedy, and fevers of a malignant kind prevail during the spring and summer.

The water of the well of Naba, though called sweet, has a very indifferent taste, and becomes putrid in a few days if kept in skins. The government has made a sort of monopoly of it; but its distribution is very irregular, and affrays often happen at the well, particularly when ships are on the point of sailing. In general, however, they touch at Tor, for a supply; those lying in the harbour might fill their casks at the well of Abou Szoueyra, about seven hours to the south of Ayoun Mousa, and about half an hour from the sea shore, where the water is good; but Arabs will seldom give themselves so much trouble for water, and will rather drink what is at hand, though bad, than go to a distance for good.

Ships, after delivering their cargoes at Suez, frequently proceed to Cosseir, to take in corn for the Hedjaz. They first touch at Tor for water, and then stand over to the western coast, anchoring in the creeks every evening till they reach their destination. The coast they sail along is barren, and without water, and no Arabs are seen. At one or two days sail from Suez is an ancient Coptic convent, now abandoned, called Deir Zafaran or Deir El Araba; it stands on the declivity of the mountain, at about one hour from the sea. Some wild date-trees grow there. At the foot of the mountain are several wells three or four feet deep, upon the surface of whose waters naphtha or petroleum is sometimes found in the month of November, which is skimmed off by the hand; it is of a deep brownish black colour, and of the same fluidity as turpentine, which it resembles in smell. This substance, which is known under the name of Zeit el Djebel, mountain oil, is collected principally by the Christians of Tor, and by the Arabs Heteim, of the eastern shore of the Red sea; it is greatly esteemed in Egypt as a cure for sores and rheumatism, and is sold at Suez and Tor, at from one to two dollars per pound.

Niebuhr, travelling in 1762, says that Suez derives its provisions in great part from Mount Sinai and Ghaza: this is not the case now. From Mount Sinai it obtains nothing but charcoal, and a few fruits and dates in the autumn; dried fruits of the growth of Damascus are the only import from Ghaza. The town is supplied with provisions from Cairo; vegetables are found only at the time of the arrival of the caravan. Every article is of the worst quality, and twenty-five per cent. dearer than at Cairo. Syrian, Turkish, and Moggrebyn pilgrims are constantly seen here, waiting for the departure of ships to the Hedjaz. I found three vessels in the harbour, and it may be calculated that one sails to the southward every fortnight. No Europeans are settled here; but an English agent is expected next year, to meet the ships from Bombay, according to a treaty made with the Pasha, by several English houses, who wished to open a direct communication between India and Egypt. [In May, 1817, a small fleet arrived at Suez direct from Bombay, which was composed of English ships, and of others belonging to Mohammed Ali Pasha: among the articles imported were two elephants destined by the Pasha as presents to the Porte. This has been the first attempt within the last forty years to open a direct trade between India and Egypt, and will be as profitable to the Pasha as it must be ruinous to his subjects. The cargoes of these ships and the coffee which he imports from Yemen, are distributed by him among the merchants of

Cairo, in proportion to their supposed capital in trade, and they are obliged to take the articles off his hands at the highest prices which they bear in the Bazar. If this trade is encreased by the Pasha, it will entirely prevent the merchants from importing goods on their own account from Djidda, the quantity they are thus obliged to take from the Pasha being fully sufficient for the consumption of Egypt.]

April 15th.—As the small caravan with which I had come to Suez remained there, I set out accompanied only by my guide and another Arab, whom he had engaged, and who afterwards proved through the whole journey a most serviceable, courageous, and honest companion. We left Suez early in the morning: the tide was then at flood, and we were obliged to make the tour of the whole creek to the N. of the town, which at low water can be forded. In winter time, and immediately after the rainy season, this circuit is rendered still greater, because the low grounds to the northward of the creek are then inundated, and become so swampy that the camels cannot pass them. We rode one hour and three quarters in a straight line northwards, after passing, close by the town, several mounds of rubbish, which afford no object of curiosity except a few large stones, supposed to be the ruins of Clysma or Arsinoë. We then turned eastwards, just at the point where the remains of the ancient canal are very distinctly visible: two swellings of the ground, of which the eastern is about eight or ten feet high, and the western somewhat less, run in a straight line northwards, parallel with each other, at the distance of about twenty-five feet. They begin at a few hundred paces to the N.W. of high-water mark, from whence northwards the ground is covered by a saline crust. We turned the point of this inlet, and halted for a short time at the wells of Ayoun Mousa, under the date trees. The water of these wells is copious, but one only affords sweet water, and this is so often rendered muddy by the passage of Arabs, whose camels descend into the wells, that it is seldom fit to supply a provision to the traveller, much less for shipping. We rested, at two hours and three quarters from the wells, in the plain called El Kordhye.

April 26th.—We proceeded over a barren sandy and gravelly plain, called El Ahtha, direction S. by E. For about an hour the plain was uneven; we then entered upon a widely-extended flat, in which we continued S.S.E. Low mountains, the commencement of the chain of Tyh, run parallel with the road, to the left, about eight miles distant; they are inhabited by Terabein. At the end of four hours and a half we halted for a few hours in Wady Seder which takes its name of Wady only, from being overflown with water when the rains are very copious, which, however, does not happen every year. Its natural formation by no means entitles it to be called a valley, its level being only a few feet lower than that of the desert on both sides. Some thorny trees grow in it, but no herbs for pasture. We continued our way S. b. E. over the plain, which was alternately gravelly, stony, and sandy. At the end of seven hours and a half we reached Wady Wardan, a valley or bed of a torrent, similar in nature to the former, but broader. Near its extremity, at the sea side, it is several miles in breadth; and here is the well of Abou Szoueyra, which I have already mentioned. The Arabs of Tor seldom encamp in this place, but the Terabein Arabs are sometimes attracted by the well. During the war which happened about eight years ago between the Towara and the Maazy Bedouins, who live in the mountains between Cairo and Cosseir, a party of the former happened to be stationed here with their families. They were surprised one morning by a troop of their enemies, while assembled in the Sheikh's tent to drink coffee. Seven or eight of them were cut down: the Sheikh himself, an old man, seeing escape impossible, sat down by the fire, when the leader of the Maazy came up, and cried out to him to throw down his turban and his life should be spared. The generous Sheikh, rather than do what, according to Bedouin notions, would have stained his reputation ever after, exclaimed, "I shall not uncover my head before my enemies;" and was immediately killed with the thrust of a lance. A low chain of sand-hills begins here to the west, near the sea; and the eastern mountains approach the road. At nine hours and a half, S.S.E. the eastern mountains form a junction with the western hills. At ten hours we entered a hilly country; at ten hours and three quarters we rested for the night in a barren valley among the hills, called Wady Amara. We met with nobody in this route except a party of Yembo merchants, who had landed at Tor, and were travelling to Cairo. The hills consist of chalk and silex in very irregular strata: the silex is sometimes quite black; at other times it takes a lustre and transparency much resembling agate.

April 27th.—We travelled over uneven hilly ground, gravelly and flinty. At one hour and three quarters we passed the well of Howara, round which a few date trees grow. Niebuhr travelled the same route, but his guides probably did not lead him to this well, which lies among hills about two hundred paces out of the road. He mentions a rock called Hadj er Rakkabe, as one German mile short of Gharendel; I remember to have halted under a large rock, close by the road side, a very short distance before we reached Howara, but I did not learn its name. The water of the well of Howara is so bitter, that men cannot drink it; and even camels, if not very thirsty, refuse to taste it.

From Ayoun Mousa to the well of Howara we had travelled fifteen hours and a quarter. Referring to this distance, it appears probable that this is the desert of three days mentioned in the Scriptures to have been crossed by the Israelites immediately after their passing the Red sea, and at the end of which they arrived at Marah.   In moving with a whole nation, the march may well be supposed to have occupied three days; and the bitter well at Marah, which was sweetened by Moses, corresponds exactly with that of Howara. This is the usual route to Mount Sinai, and was probably therefore that which the Israelites took on their escape from Egypt, provided it be admitted that they crossed the sea near Suez, as Niebuhr, with good reason, conjectures. There is no other road of three days march in the way from Suez towards Sinai, nor is there any other well absolutely bitter on the whole of this coast, as far as Ras Mohammed. The complaints of the bitterness of the water by the children of Israel, who had been accustomed to the sweet water of the Nile, are such as may daily be heard from the Egyptian servants and peasants who travel in Arabia. Accustomed from their youth to the excellent water of the Nile, there is nothing which they so much regret in countries distant from Egypt; nor is there any eastern people who feel so keenly the want of good water as the present natives of Egypt. With respect to the means employed by Moses to render the waters of the well sweet, I have frequently enquired among the Bedouins in different parts of Arabia whether they possessed any means of effecting such a change, by throwing wood into it, or by any other process; but I never could learn that such an art was known.

At the end of three hours we reached Wady Gharendel which extends to the N.E. and is almost a mile in breadth, and full of trees. The Arabs told me that it may be traced through the whole desert, and that it begins at no great distance from El Arysh, on the Mediterranean, but I had no means of ascertaining the truth of this statement. About half an hour from the place where we halted, in a southern direction, is a copious spring, with a small rivulet, which renders the valley the principal station on this route. The water is disagreeable, and if kept for a night in the water skins, it turns bitter and spoils, as I have myself experienced, having passed this way three times.

If we admit Bir Howara to be the Marah [Morra in Arabic means "bitter." Marah in Hebrew is "bitterness."] of Exodus (xv. 23), then Wady Gharendel is probably Elim, with its wells and date trees, an opinion entertained by Niebuhr, who, however, did not see the bitter well of Howara on the road to Gharendel. The nonexistence, at present, of twelve wells at Gharendel must not be considered as evidence against the just-stated conjecture; for Niebuhr says that his companions obtained water here by digging to a very small depth, and there was a great plenty of it, when I passed; water, in fact, is readily found by digging, in every fertile valley in Arabia, and wells are thus easily formed, which are quickly filled up again by the sands.

The Wady Gharendel contains date trees, tamarisks, acacias of different species, and the thorny shrub Gharkad, the Peganum retusum of Forskal, which is extremely common in this peninsula, and is also met with in the sands of the Delta on the coast of the Mediterranean. Its small red berry, of the size of a grain of the pomegranate, is very juicy and re-freshing, much resembling a ripe gooseberry in taste, but not so sweet. The Arabs are very fond of it, and I was told that in years when the shrub produces large crops, they make a conserve of the berries. The Gharkad, which from the colour of its fruit is also called by the Arabs Homra de-lights in a sandy soil, and reaches its maturity in the height of summer when the ground is parched up, exciting an agreeable surprise in the trav-eller, at finding so juicy a berry produced in the driest soil and season. [Might not the berry of this shrub have been used by Moses to sweeten the waters of Marah? The words in Exodus, xv. 25, are: "And the Lord shewed him a tree, which when he had cast into the waters, the waters were made sweet." The Arabic translation of this passage gives a differ-ent, and, perhaps, more correct reading: "And the Lord guided him to a tree, of which he threw something into the water, which then became sweet." I do not remember, to have seen any Gharkad in the neighbour-hood of Howara, but Wady Gharendel is full of this shrub. As these conjectures did not occur to me when I was on the spot, I did not enquire of the Bedouins whether they ever sweetened the water with the juice of the berries, which would probably effect this change in the same manner as the juice of pomegranate grains expressed into it.] The bottom of the valley of Gharendel swarms with ticks, which are extremely distressing both to men and beasts, and on this account the caravans usually encamp on the sides of the hills which border the valley.

We continued in a S.E. 1/2 E. direction, passing over hills, and at the end of four hours from our starting in the morning, we came to an open, though hilly country, still slightly ascending, S.S.E. and then reached by a similar descent, in five hours and a half, Wady Oszaita, en-closed by chalk hills. Here is another bitter well which never yields a copious supply, and sometimes is completely dried up. A few date trees stand near it. From hence we rode over a wide plain S.E. b. S. and at the end of seven hours and three quarters came to Wady Thale. Rock salt is found here as well as in Gharendel; date, acacia, and tamarisks grow in the valley; but they were now all withered. To our right was a chain of mountains, which extend towards Gharendel. Proceeding from hence south, we turned the point of the mountain, and then passed the rudely constructed tomb of a female saint, called Arys Themman, or the bridegroom of Themman, where the Arabs are in the habit of saying a short prayer, and suspending some rags of clothing upon some poles planted round the tomb. After having doubled the mountain we entered the valley called Wady Taybe, which descends rapidly to the sea. At the end of eight hours and a half we turned out of Wady Taybe into a branch of it, called Wady Shebeyke, in which we continued E.S.E. and halted for the night, after a day's march of nine hours and a quarter. This is a broad valley, with steep though not high cliffs on both sides. The rock is calcareous, and runs in even horizontal layers. Just over the road, a place was shewn to me from whence, some years since, a Bedouin of the Arabs of Tor precipitated his son, bound hands and feet, because he had stolen corn out of a magazine belonging to a friend of the family. In the great eastern desert the Aeneze Bedouins are not so severe in such instances; but they would punish a Bedouin who should pilfer any thing from his guest's baggage.

April 28th.—We set out before dawn, and continued for three quarters of an hour in the Wady, after which we ascended E. b. S. and came upon a high plain, surrounded by rocks, with a towering mountain on the N. side, called Sarbout el Djemel. We crossed the plain at sun rise; and the fresh air of the morning was extremely agreeable. There is nothing which so much compensates for the miseries of travelling in the Arabian deserts, as the pleasure of enjoying every morning the sublime spectacle of the break of day and of the rising of the sun, which is always accompanied, even in the hottest season, with a refreshing breeze. It was an invariable custom with me, at setting out early in the morning, to walk on foot for a few hours in advance of the caravan; and as enjoyments are comparative, I believe that I derived from this practice greater pleasure than any which the arts of the most luxurious capitals can afford. At two hours and a half the plain terminated; we then turned the point of the above-mentioned mountain, and entered the valley called Wady Hommar, in which we continued E. b. N. This valley, in which a few acacia trees grow, has no perceptible slope on either side; its rocks are all calcareous, with flint upon some of them; by the road side, I observed a few scratchings of the figures of camels, done in the same style as those in Wady Mokatteb copied by M. Niebuhr and M. Seetzen, but without any inscriptions. At four hours we issued from this valley where the southern rocks which enclose it terminate, and we travelled over a wide, slightly ascending plain of deep sand, called El Debbe, a name given by the Towara Bedouins to several other sandy districts of the same kind. The direction of our road across it was S. E. by S. At six hours and a half we entered a mountainous country, much devastated by torrents, which have given the mountains a very wild appearance. Here sand-stone rocks begin. We followed the windings of a valley, and in seven hours and a quarter reached the Wady el Naszeb, where we rested, under the shade of a large impending rock, which for ages, probably, has afforded shelter to travellers; it is I believe the same represented by Niebuhr in vol. i. pl. 48. He calls the valley Warsan, which is, no doubt, its true name, but the Arabs comprise all the contiguous valleys under the general name of Naszeb. Shady spots like this are well known to the Arabs, and as the scanty foliage of the acacia, the only tree in which these valleys abound, affords no shade, they take advantage of such rocks, and regulate the day's journey in such a way, as to be able to reach them at noon, there to take the siesta.

The main branch of the Wady Naszeb continues farther up to the S.E. and contains, at about half an hour from the place where we rested, a well of excellent water; as I was fatigued, and the sun was very hot, I neglected to go there, though I am sensible that travellers ought particularly to visit wells in the desert, because it is at these natural stations that traces of former inhabitants are more likely to be found than any where else. The Wady Naszeb empties its waters in the rainy season into the gulf of Suez, at a short distance from the Birket Faraoun.

While my guides and servant lay asleep under the rock, and one of the Arabs had gone to the well to water the camels and fill the skins, I walked round the rock, and was surprised to find inscriptions similar in form to those which have been copied by travellers in Wady Mokatteb. They are upon the surface of blocks which have fallen down from the cliff, and some of them appear to have been engraved while the pieces still formed a part of the main rock. There is a great number of them, but few can be distinctly made out. I copied the following from some rocks which are lying near the resting-place, at about an hundred paces from the spot where travellers usually alight. [not included] The fallen blocks must be closely examined in order to discover the inscriptions; in some places they are still to be seen on the rock above. They have evidently been done in great haste, and very rudely, sometimes with large letters, at others with small, and seldom with straight lines. The characters appear to be written from right to left, and although mere scratches, an instrument of metal must have been required, for the rock, though of sandstone, is of considerable hardness. Some of the letters are not higher than half an inch; but they are generally about fifteen lines in height, and four lines in breadth; the annexed figure, (as M. Seetzen has already observed in his publication upon these inscriptions in the Mines de l'Orient) is seen at the beginning of almost every line. Hence it appears that none of the inscriptions are of any length, but that they consist merely of short phrases, all similar to each other, in the beginning at least. They are perhaps prayers, or the names of pilgrims, on their way to Mount Sinai, who had rested under this rock. A few drawings of camels and goats, done in the coarsest manner, are likewise seen. M. Niebuhr (vol. i. pl. 50) has given some sketches of them.

Some Syale trees, a species of the mimosa, grow in this valley. The pod which they produce, together with the tenderest shoots of the branches, serve as fodder to the camels; the bark of the tree is used by the Arabs to tan leather. The rocks round the resting-place of Naszeb are much shattered and broken, evidently by torrents; yet no torrents within the memory of man have ever rushed down the valley.

In the afternoon we entered a lateral branch of the Naszeb, more northerly than the main branch which contains the well, and we gradually ascended it. We had been joined at the Ayoun Mousa by an Egyptian Bedouin, belonging to the Arabs of the province of Sherkyeh, who was married to a girl of the Towara Arabs; last night, being in the vicinity of the place where he knew his wife to be, he put spurs to the ass on which he was mounted, and thinking that he knew the road, he quitted the Wady Shebeyke two hours before we did, and without any provision of water. He missed his way on the sandy plain of Debbe, and instead of reaching the spring of Naszeb, where he intended to allay his thirst, he rode the whole of this morning and afternoon about the mountain in different directions, in fruitless search after the shady and conspicuous rock of Naszeb. Towards the evening we met him, so much exhausted with thirst, that his eyes had become dim, and he could scarcely recognise us; had he not fallen in with us he would probably have perished. My companions laughed at the effeminate Egyptian, as they called him, and his presumption in travelling alone in districts with which he was unacquainted. At the end of eight hours and three quarters, in a general direction of. E. by S. we passed a small inlet in the northern chain, where, at a short distance from the road, is said to be a well of tolerable water, called El Maleha, or the saltish. We then ascended with difficulty a steep mountain, composed to the top of moving sands, with a very few rocks appearing above the surface. We reached the summit after a day's march of nine hours and three quarters, and rested upon a high plain, called Raml el Morak. From hence we had an extensive view to the north, bounded by the chain of mountains called El Tyh; this range begins near the abovementioned mountain of Sarbout el Djemel, and extends in a curve eastwards twenty or twenty-five miles, from the termination of the Wady Hommar. At the eastern extremity lies a high mountain called Djebel Odjme, to the north of which begins another chain, likewise running eastwards towards the gulf of Akaba. The name of El Tyh is applied to this ridge as well as to the former, but it is specifically called El Dhelel. These chains form the northern boundaries of the Sinai mountains, and are the pasturing places of the Sinai Bedouins. They are the most regular ranges of the peninsula, being almost throughout of equal height, without any prominent peaks, and extending in an uninterrupted line eastwards. They are inhabited by the tribes of Terabein and Tyaha, the latter of whom are richer in camels and flocks than any other of the Towara tribes. The valleys of these mountains are said to afford excellent pasturage, and fine springs, though not in great numbers. The Terabein frequently visit Cairo and Suez; but the Tyaha have more intercourse with Ghaza, and Khalyl, and are a very bold, independent people, often at war with their neighbours, and, even now, caring little for the authority of the Pasha of Egypt. At the southern foot of the mountain Tyh extends a broad sandy plain, called El Seyh, which begins at the Debbe, and continues for two days journey eastwards. It affords good pasturage in spring, but has no water, and is therefore little frequented by Bedouins.

April 29th.—We crossed the plain of Raml Morak in a S. by E. direction. From hence the high peak of Serbal bore S. In an hour and a quarter we reached the upper chain of the mountains of Sinai, where grünstein begins, mixed in places with layers of granite, and we entered the valley called Wady Khamyle. At the end of two hours we passed in the valley a projecting rock, like that of Naszeb, serving for a resting-place to travellers: here I observed several inscriptions similar to those of Naszeb, but much effaced, together with rude drawings of mountain goats. As I did not wish to betray too much curiosity, until I could ascertain what conduct I ought to pursue in order to attain my chief object of penetrating to Akaba, I did not stop to copy these monuments. At the end of two hours and a half in the Wady Khamyle we came to the first Bedouin encampment which I had seen since leaving Suez. It belonged to the tribe of Szowaleha. On the approach of summer all the Bedouins leave the lower country, where the herbage is dried up, and retire towards the higher parts of the peninsula, where, owing to the comparatively cooler climate, the pasture preserves its freshness much longer. Ascending gently through the valley, we passed at three hours a place of burial called Mokbera, one of the places of interment of the tribe of Szowaleha. It seems to be a custom prevalent with the Arabs in every part of the desert, to have regular burial-grounds, whither they carry their dead, sometimes from the distance of several days journey. The burying ground seen by Niebuhr [Voyage, vol. i. p. 189] near Naszeb, which, as I have already mentioned, I passed without visiting, and missed in my way back, by taking a more southern road, appears to have been an ancient cemetery of the same kind, formed at a time when hieroglyphical characters were in use among all the nations under Egyptian influence. As there are no countries where ancient manners are so permanent as in the desert, it is probable that the same customs of sepulture then prevailed which still exist, and that the burying ground described by Niebuhr by no means proves the former existence of a city. Among the rude tombs of Mokbera, which consist, for the most part, of mere heaps of earth covered with loose stones, the tomb of Sheikh Hamyd, a Bedouin saint, is distinguished; the Szowaleha keep it always carefully covered with fresh herbs.

At the end of three hours and a half we entered another valley, called Wady Barak, where the ascent becomes more steep. Here the rock changes to porphyry, with strata of grünstein; the surface of the former is in most places completely black. The mountains on both sides of the valley are much shattered: detached blocks and loose stones covered their sides, and the bottom of the valley was filled, in many places to the depth of ten feet, with a layer of stones that had fallen down. The Wady becomes narrower towards the upper end, and the camels ascended with difficulty. At the end of six hours and a quarter we reached the extremity, to which the Bedouins apply the name of Djebel Leboua, the mountain of the lioness, a name indicating, perhaps, that lions existed at one period in the peninsula of Mount Sinai, though no longer to be found here. In ascending Wady Barak, I saw upon several blocks lying by the road side short inscriptions, generally of one line only, all of which began with the remarkable character already represented.

From the top of Djebel Leboua we descended a little, and entered the Wady Genne, a fine valley, several miles in breadth, and covered with pasturage. It lay in a straight line before us, and presented much of Alpine scenery. We here found several Bedouins occupied in collecting brushwood, which they burn into charcoal for the Cairo market; they prefer for this purpose the thick roots of the shrub Rethem, Genista raetam of Forskal, which grows here in abundance. Of the herbs which grow in this valley many were odoriferous, as the Obeytheran, Sille, perhaps the Zilla

Myagrum of Forskal; and the Shyh, or Artemisia. The Bedouins collect also the herb Adjrem, which they dry, break in pieces and pound between stones, and then use as a substitute for soap to wash their linen with. I was told that very good water is found at about two miles to the E. of this valley.

We gained the upper extremity of Wady Genne at the end of nine hours. The ranges of mountains in this country differ in their formation from all the other Arabian chains which I have seen, the valleys reaching to the very summits, where they form a plain, and thence descend on the other side. A very pointed peak of rocks, near the left of the summit of Wady Genne, is known by the appellation of Zob el Bahry. After crossing a short plain, we again descended S.E. by S. and entered the valley called Wady Berah, where I saw another block with inscriptions. Near it were many others, but effaced. The following was more regularly and clearly written than any I have seen: [not included] We descended slowly through this valley, which is covered with sand, till, at the end of ten hours, we entered a side valley called Wady Osh, and at ten hours and a half alighted at an encampment of Bedouins, pitched at no great distance from a burial ground similar to that which we had passed in the morning.

This encampment belonged to the Oulad Said, a branch of the Szowaleha tribe, and one of their Sheikhs, Hassan, had his tent here; this we entered, though he was absent, and the Arabs had a long and fierce dispute among themselves to decide who should have the honour of furnishing us a supper, and a breakfast the next morning. He who first sees the stranger from afar, and exclaims: "There comes my guest," has the right of entertaining him, whatever tent he may alight at. A lamb was killed for me, which was an act of great hospitality; for these Bedouins are poor, and a lamb was worth upwards of a Spanish dollar, a sum that would afford a supply of butter and bread to the family for a whole week. I found the same custom to prevail here, which I observed in my journey through the northern parts of Arabia Petraea; when meat is served up, it is the duty of one of the guests to demand a portion for the women, by calling out " Lahm el Ferash," i.e. "the meat for the apartment of the women;" and a part of it is then either set aside, or he is answered that this has been already done. In the evening we joined in some of the popular songs, of which a description will be found in my illustration of Bedouin manners. [This will form part of a subsequent volume. Ed]

I was naturally asked for what object I had come to these mountains. As the passage of Greeks on their way to visit the convent of Sinai is frequent, I might have answered that I was a Greek; but I thought it better to adhere to what I had already told my guides, that I had left Cairo, in order not to expose myself to the plague, that I wished to pass my time among the Bedouins while the disease prevailed, and that I intended to visit the convent. Other Moslems would have considered it impious to fly from the infection; but I knew that all these Bedouins entertain as great a dread of the plague as Europeans themselves. During the spring, when the disease usually prevails in Egypt, no prospect of gain can induce them to expose themselves to infection, by a journey to the banks of the Nile; the Bedouins with whom I left Cairo were the last who had remained there. Had the Pasha granted me a Firmahn to the great Sheikh of the Towara Arabs, I should have gone directly to his tent, and in virtue of it I should have taken guides to conduct me to Akaba; but being without the Firmahn, I thought it more prudent to visit the convent in the first instance, and to depart from thence for Akaba, in order to take advantage of such influence as the Prior might possess over the Bedouins, for though they pay little respect to the priests, yet they have some fear of being excluded from the gains accruing from the transport of visitors to the convent. As every white-skinned person, who makes his appearance in the desert, is supposed by the Arabs to be attached to the Turkish army, or the government of Cairo, my going to Akaba without any recommendations would have given rise to much suspicion, and I should probably have been supposed to be a deserter from the Turkish army, attempting to escape by that circuitous route to Syria; a practice which is sometimes resorted to by the soldiers, to whom, without the Pasha's passport, Egypt is closed both by sea and land.

In the Wady Osh there is a well of sweet water. From hence upwards, and throughout the primitive chain of Mount Sinai, the water is generally excellent, while in the lower chalky mountains all round the peninsula, it is brackish, or bitter, except in one or two places. The Wady Osh and Wady Berah empty their waters in the rainy season into Wady el Sheikh, above Feiran.

April 30th.—We did not leave our kind hosts till the afternoon, for they insisted on my taking a dinner before I set out. I gave to their children, who accompanied me a little way, some coffee beans to carry to their mothers, and some Kammereddein, a sweetmeat made at Damascus from apricots, of which I had laid in a large stock, and which is very acceptable to all the Bedouins of Syria, Egypt, and the Hedjaz. The offer of any reward to a Bedouin host is generally offensive to his pride; but some little presents may be given to the women and children. Trinkets and similar articles are little esteemed by the Bedouins; but coffee is in great request all over the desert; and sweetmeats and sugar are preferred to money, which, though it will sometimes be accepted, always creates a sense of humiliation, and consequently of dislike towards the giver. For my own part, being convinced that the hospitality of the Bedouin is afforded with disinterested cordiality, I was in general averse to making the slightest return. Few travellers perhaps will agree with me on this head; but will treat the Bedouins in the same manner as the Turks, and other inhabitants of the towns, who never proffer their services or hospitality without expecting a reward; the feelings of Bedouins, however, are very different from those of townsmen, and a Bedouin will praise the guest who departs from him without making any other remuneration than that of bestowing a blessing upon them and their encampment, much more than him who thinks to redeem all obligations by payment.

We returned from Wady Osh towards Wady Berah; but leaving the latter, which here takes a direction towards Wady Feiran, we ascended by a narrow valley called Wady Akhdhar. Here I again saw some inscriptions on blocks of stone lying by the road side. A few hours to the N.E. of Wady Osh is a mountain called Sheyger, where native cinnabar is collected; it is called Rasokht by the Arabs, and is usually found in small pieces about the size of a pigeon's egg. It is very seldom crystallized; but there are sometimes nodules on the surface; it stains the fingers of a dark colour, and its fracture is in perpendicular fibres. I did not hear that the Arabs traded at all in this metal. In Wady Osh are rocks of gneiss mixed with granite. Gneiss is found in many parts of the peninsula.

After one hour we came to a steep ascent, and descent, called El Szaleib, which occupied two hours. We then continued our descent into the great valley called Wady el Sheikh, one of the principal valleys of the peninsula. The rocks of Szaleib consist throughout of granite, on the upper strata of which run layers of red feldspath, some of which has fallen down and covers the valley in broken fragments. The Wady el Sheikh is broad, and has a very slight acclivity; it is much frequented by Bedouins for its pasturage. Whenever rain falls in the mountains, a stream of water flows through this Wady, and from thence through Wady Feiran, into the sea. We rode in a S.E. direction along the Wady el Sheikh for two hours, and then halted in it for the night, after an afternoon's march of four hours. Several Arabs of the encampment where we slept the preceding night had joined our party, to go to the convent, for no other reason, I believe, than to get a good dinner and supper on the road. This evening eight persons kneeled down round a dish of rice, cooked with milk which I had brought from Wady Osh, and the coffee-pot being kept on the fire, we sat in conversation till near midnight.

May 1st.—We continued in a S.E. direction, ascending slightly: the valley then becomes narrower. At two hours we came to a thick wood of tamarisk or Tarfa, and found many camels feeding upon their thorny shoots. It is from this evergreen tamarisk, which grows abundantly in no other part of the peninsula, that the manna is collected. We now approached the central summits of Mount Sinai, which we had had in view for several days. Abrupt cliffs of granite from six to eight hundred feet in height, whose surface is blackened by the sun, surround the avenues leading to the elevated platform, to which the name of Sinai is specifically applied. These cliffs enclose the holy mountain on three sides, leaving the E. and N.E. sides only, towards the gulf of Akaba, more open to the view. On both sides of the wood of Tarfa trees extends a range of low hills of a substance called by the Arabs Tafal, which I believe to be principally a detritus of the feldspar of granite, but which, at first sight, has all the appearance of pipe-clay; it is brittle, crumbles easily between the fingers, and leaves upon them its colour, which is a pale yellow. The Arabs sell it at Cairo, where it is in request for taking stains out of cloth, and where it serves the poor instead of soap, for washing their hands; but it is chiefly used to rub the skins of asses during summer, being supposed to refresh them, and to defend them against the heat of the sun.

At the end of three hours we entered the above-mentioned cliffs by a narrow defile about forty feet in breadth, with perpendicular granite rocks on both sides. The ground is covered with sand and pebbles, brought down by the torrent which rushes from the upper region in the winter time. In a broader part of the pass an insulated rock, about five feet high, with a kind of naturally formed seat, is shewn as a place upon which Moses once reposed, whence it has the name of Mokad Seidna Mousa; the Bedouins keep it covered with green or dry herbs, and some of them kiss it, or touch it with their hands, in passing by. Beyond it the valley opens, the mountains on both sides diverge from the road, and the Wady el Sheikh continues in a S. direction with a slight ascent. A little to the east, from hence, is the well called Bir Mohsen. After continuing in the Wady for an hour beyond the defile, we entered a narrow inlet in the eastern chain, and rested near a spring called Abou Szoueyr. At four hours and a half was a small walled plantation of tobacco, with some fruit trees, and onions, cultivated by some of the Bedouins Oulad Said. In the afternoon we crossed the mountain by a by-path, fell again into the Wady el Sheikh, and at the end of eight hours from our setting out in the morning reached the tomb of Sheikh Szaleh, from which the whole valley takes its name. The coffin of the Sheikh is deposited in a small rude stone building; and is surrounded by a thin partition of wood, hung with green cloth, upon which several prayers are embroidered. On the walls are suspended silk tassels, handkerchiefs, ostrich eggs, camel halters, bridles, &c. the offerings of the Bedouins who visit this tomb. I could not learn exactly the history of this Sheikh Szaleh: some said that he was the forefather of the tribe of Szowaleha; others, the great Moslem prophet Szaleh, sent to the tribe of Thamoud, and who is mentioned in the Koran; and others, again, that he was a local saint, which I believe to be the truth. Among the Bedouins, this tomb is the most revered spot in the peninsula, next to the mountain of Moses; they make frequent vows to kill a sheep in honour of the Sheikh should a wished-for event take place; and if this happens, the votary repairs to the tomb with his family and friends, and there passes a day of conviviality. Once in every year all the tribes of the To-wara repair hither in pilgrimage, and remain encamped in the valley round the tomb for three days. Many sheep are then killed, camel races are run, and the whole night is passed in dancing and singing. The men and women are dressed in their best attire. The festival, which is the greatest among these people, usually takes place in the latter part of June, when the Nile begins to rise in Egypt, and the plague subsides; and a caravan leaves Sinai immediately afterwards for Cairo. It is just at this period too that the dates ripen in the valleys of the lower chain of Sinai, and the pilgrimage to Sheikh Szaleh thus becomes the most remarkable period in the Bedouin year.

In the western mountain opposite Sheikh Szaleh, and about one hour and a half distant, is a fruitful pasturing place, upon a high mountain, with many fields, and plantations of trees, called El Fereya, where once a convent stood. It is in possession of the Oulad Said.

We continued from Sheikh Szaleh farther S. till at the end of six hours and a half we turned to our right into a broad valley, at the termination of which I was agreeably surprised by the beautiful verdure of a garden of almond trees belonging to the convent. From thence, by another short turn to the left, we reached the convent, in seven hours and a half. We alighted under a window, by which the priests communicate with the Arabs below. The letter of recommendation which I had with me was drawn up by a cord, and when the prior had read it, a stick tied across a rope was let down, upon which I placed myself, and was hoisted up. Like all travellers I received a cordial reception and was shewn into the same neatly furnished room in which all preceding Europeans had taken up their abode.

I rested in the convent three days. When I told the monks that I intended to go to Akaba, they gave me very little encouragement, particularly when they learnt that I had no Firmahn from the Pasha; but finding that I was firmly resolved, they sent for the chief Ghafyr, or protector of the convent, and recommended me strongly to him. The monks live in such constant dread of the Bedouins, who knowing very well their timid disposition, take every opportunity to strengthen their fears, that they believe a person is going to certain destruction who trusts himself to the guidance of these Bedouins any where but on the great road to Suez or to Tor. I had been particularly pleased with the character and behaviour of Hamd Ibn Zoheyr, the Bedouin who had joined us at Suez; and not being equally satisfied with the guide who had brought me from Cairo, I discharged him, and engaged Hamd for the journey to Akaba; he did not know the road himself, but one of his uncles who had been there assured us that he was well acquainted with the tribe of Heywat, which we should meet on the road, and with all the passages of the country; I therefore engaged him together with Hamd.

As no visitor of the convent is permitted to leave it without the knowledge of one of the Ghafyrs, who has a right to share in the profits of the escort, I was obliged to give a few piastres to him who is at present the director of the affairs of the convent in the desert. The Arabs have established here the same custom which I remarked in my journey from Tor to Cairo. Every one who is present at the departure of a stranger or of a loaded camel from the convent is entitled to a fee, provided the traveller has not passed a line, which is about one mile from the convent. To avoid this unnecessary company and expense, I stole out of the convent by night, as secretly as possible; but we were overtaken within the limits by a Bedouin, and my guides were obliged to give him six piastres, to make him desist from farther claims. I left my servant and unnecessary baggage at the convent, and mounted a camel, for the hire of which I gave five dollars, and I paid as much to each of my guides, who were also mounted, and were to conduct me to Akaba and back again.

May 4th.—I left the convent before day light, but travelled no farther to day than to the well of Abou Szoueyr, where we had rested on the first of May, and where a large company of Arabs assembled when they heard of our arrival. They quarrelled long with my guides for having taken me clandestinely from the convent, but were at last pacified by a lamb which I bought, and partook of with them. In the evening we heard from afar the songs of an encampment, to which my guides went, to join in the dance. I remained with the baggage, in conversation with an Arab who had lately come from Khalyl or Hebron, and who much dissuaded me from going to Akaba. He assured me that the uncle of Hamd my guide knew nothing of the Arabs of those parts, nor even the paths through the country; but I slighted his advice, because I believed that it was dictated by envy, and that he wished himself to be one of the party. The result shewed, however, that he was right.

May 5th.—At sunrise we left Abou Szoueyr, and ascended a hilly country for half an hour. After a short descent, which on this side terminates the district of Sinai, properly so called, we continued over a wide open plain, with low hills, called Szoueyry, direction N.E. b. E. In an hour and a half we entered a narrow valley called Wady Sal, formed by the lower ridges of the primitive mountains, in the windings of which we descended slightly E. b. N. and E.N.E. On the top I found the rock to be granite; somewhat lower down grünstein, and porphyry began to appear; farther on granite and porphyry cease entirely, and the rock consists solely of grünstein, which in many places takes the nature of slate. Some of the layers of porphyry are very striking; they run perpendicularly from the very summit of the mountain to the base, in a band of about twelve feet in width, and projecting somewhat from the other rocks on the mountain's side. I had observed similar strata in Wady Genne, but running horizontally along the whole chain of mountains, and dividing it, as it were, into two equal parts. The porphyry I have met with in Sinai is usually a red indurated argillaceous substance; in some specimens it had the appearance of red feldspath. In the argil are imbedded small crystals of hornblende, or of mica, and thin pieces of quartz at most two lines square. I never saw any large fragments of quartz in it. Its universal colour is red. The lower mountains of Sinai are much more regularly shaped than the upper ones: they are less rugged, have no insulated peaks, and their summits fall off in smooth curves.

The Wady Sal is extremely barren: we found no pasture for our camels, as no rain had fallen during the two last years, in the whole of this eastern part of the peninsula. A few acacia trees grew in different places; we rested at noon under one of them while a cup of coffee was prepared, and then pursued the Wady downwards until, at the end of seven hours, we issued from it into a small plain, which we soon crossed, and at seven hours and a half entered another valley, similar to the former, where I again saw some granite, of the gray, small-grained species [.] Our descent was here very rapid, and at the end of nine hours and a half we reached a lower level, in a broad valley running southwards. From hence the summit of Mount St. Catherine, behind the convent, bore S.W. by W. Calcareous and sand rocks begin here, and the bottom of the valley is deep sand. We rode in it in the direction N.E. by N. and after a march of eleven hours alighted in a plain, at a spot which afforded some shrubs for our camels to feed upon. The elder of my two guides, by name Szaleh, soon proved himself to be ignorant of the road. He might have passed this way in his youth, and have had a recollection of the general direction of the valleys; but when we arrived in the plain, he proceeded in various directions, in search of a road from the east. We had now, about six or eight miles to our left, a long and straight chain of mountains, the continuation, I believe, of that of Tyh or Dhelel, mentioned above, and running almost parallel with our route. The northern side of these mountains is inhabited by the tribe of Tyaha. Here passes the road which leads straight from the convent to Akaba, while the one we took descended to the sea, and had been chosen by my guides for greater security. The upper road passes by the watering places Zelka, El Ain (the Well), a place much frequented by Bedouins, and where many date-trees grow, and lastly by El Hossey. It is the common route from the convent to Khalyl and Jerusalem.

May 6th.—We started early, and continued our way over the plain, which is called Haydar. It appears to follow the mountain of Tyh as far as its western extremity, and there to join the Seyh, of which I have already spoken, thus forming the northern sandy boundary of the lower Sinai chain. As we proceeded, we approached nearer to the mountain, and at length fell in with the looked for road. The ground is gravelly but covered with moving sands which are raised by the slightest wind. To the east the country was open, with low hills, as far as I could see. Our road lay N.E.1/2 N. At one hour and a half Mount St. Catharine bore S.W. by W. We now descended into a valley of deep sand covered with blocks of chalk rock. At one hour and three quarters the valley is contracted into a narrow pass, between low hills of sand-stone, bearing traces of very violent torrents. At the end of two hours, route east by north, we quitted the valley, and crossed a rough rocky plain, intersected on every side by beds of torrents; and at two hours and three quarters halted near a rock. One of the guides went with the camels up a side valley, to bring water from the well Hadhra, (perhaps the Hazeroth [Hebrew] mentioned in Numbers xxxiii. 17), distant about two miles from the halting place. Near the well are said to be some date trees, and the remains of walls which formerly enclosed a few plantations.

We here met some Towara Bedouins on their way to Cairo with charcoal. After employing a considerable time in collecting the wood and burning it into coal they carry it to Cairo, a journey at least of ten days, and there sell it for three or four dollars per load: so cheap do they hold their labour, and so limited are their means of subsistence. In return, they bring home corn and clothes to their women and children.

We started again as soon as the camels returned from the well, but should probably have gone astray had not the Bedouins above mentioned pointed out the road we ought to take; for Szaleh, the uncle of Hamd, although he pretended to be quite at home in this district, gave evident proofs of being but very slightly acquainted with it. We made many windings between sand-stone rocks, which presented their smooth perpendicular sides to the road; some of them are of a red, others of a white colour; the ground was deeply covered with sand. The traces of torrents were observable on the rocks as high as three and four feet above the present level of the plain. Our main direction was E.N.E. At four hours and three quarters from the time we set out in the morning, we entered Wady Rahab, a fine valley with many Syale trees, where the sands terminate. Route E. At five hours and a half we entered another valley, broader than the former, where I again found an alternation of sand-stone and granite. The barrenness of this district was greater than I had yet witnessed in my travels, excepting perhaps some parts of the desert El Tyh; the Nubian valleys might be called pleasure grounds in comparison. Not the smallest green leaf could be discovered; and the thorny mimosa, which retains its verdure in the tropical deserts of Nubia, with very little supply of moisture, was here entirely withered, and so dry that it caught fire from the lighted cinders which fell from our pipes as we passed. We continued to descend by a gentle slope, and at six hours and a half entered Wady Samghy, coming from the south, in which we descended N.E. At the end of eight hours and a half we left this valley and turned E. into a side one, called Boszeyra; where we halted for the night, at eight hours and three quarters.

We had met in Wady Samghy two old Bedouins of the Mezeine tribe, who belong to the Towara nation: they were fishermen, on their way to the sea to exercise their profession. One of them carried in a small sack a measure of meal which was to serve for their food on shore, the other had a skin of water upon his shoulder; they were both half naked, and both approaching to seventy years of age. One of them was deaf, but so intelligent that it was easy to talk with him by signs; he had established a vocabulary of gestures with his companion, who had been his fishing partner for ten years, and who was one of the shrewdest and hardiest Bedouins I had ever seen; in his younger days he had been a noted robber, and in attempting to carry off the baggage of a French officer in the Sherkyeh province in Egypt, he was seized, laid under the stick, and so severely beaten, that his back had from that time become bent; but notwithstanding this misfortune and his age, he had lost none of his spirits, and his robust constitution still enabled him to cross these mountains on foot, and to exert his activity whenever it was required. These two men partook this evening of my supper; they of course asked me where I was going, and shook their heads when I told them I was bound for Akaba. None of my guides knew what business I had there, but they supposed that I had some verbal message to deliver to the Turkish Aga, who was at the head of the garrison. Ayd es Szaheny, the old robber, soon found out that my guide Szaleh knew little of the road, and still less of the Arab tribes before us. He plainly told him that he would not be able to ensure either my safety or his own, in passing through their districts, and reproached him for having deluded me with false assurances. There appeared to be so much good faith and sense in all the old man said, and I found him so well informed respecting the country, that I soon determined to engage him to join us; but as we were to descend the next morning by the same road to the sea-shore, I deferred making him any overtures till we should arrive there.

The Wady Boszeyra is enclosed by gray granite rocks, out of which the Towara Arabs sometimes hew stones for hand mills, which they dispose of to the northern Arabs, and transport for sale as far as Khalyl. It is very seldom that any Arabs pasture in the district we had traversed, from Wady Sal. The Towara find better pasturage in the southern and south-western parts of the peninsula, and as its whole population is very small, the more barren parts of it are abandoned, and especially this side, where very few wells are found.

May 7th.—From Boszeyra we crossed a short ridge of mountains, and then entered a narrow valley, the bed of a torrent, called Saada, in the windings of which we descended by a steeper slope than any of the former; our main direction E. The mountains on both sides were of moderate height and with gentle slopes, till after an hour and a half, when we reached a chain of high and perpendicular grünstein rocks, which hemmed in the valley so closely as to leave in several places a passage of only ten feet across. After proceeding for a mile in this very striking and majestic defile, I caught the first glimpse of the gulf of Akaba; the valley then widens and descends to the sea, and after two hours and a quarter we alighted upon the sandy beach, which is here several hundred paces in breadth; the grünstein and granite rocks reach all the way down; but at the very foot of the mountain a thin layer of chalk appeared just above the surface of the ground. The valley opens directly upon the sea, into which it empties its torrent when heavy rains fall. Some groves of date-trees stand close by the shore, among which is a well of brackish but drinkable water; the place is called El Noweyba. We now followed the coast in a direction N.N.E. and at the end of three hours and a quarter halted at a grove of date-trees, intermixed with a few tamarisks, called Wasta, close by the sea. Here is a small spring at a distance of fifty yards from the sea, and not more than eight feet above the level of the water; it was choked with sand, which we removed, and on digging a hole about three feet deep and one foot in diameter, it filled in half an hour with very tolerable water. The shore is covered with weeds brought hither by the tide.

Here the two Bedouins intended to take up their quarters for fishing, but I easily prevailed upon Ayd to accompany us farther on. He promised to conduct us as far as Taba, a valley in sight of Akaba, but declared that he should not be justified in holding out to me promises of safety beyond that point. This was all that I wished, for the present, thinking that when we arrived thither, I should be able to prevail on him to continue farther. Szaleh now gave me reason to suspect that, from the moment of our setting out, he had had treacherous intentions. He secretly endeavoured to persuade Hamd to return, and finding the latter resolved to fulfil his engagements, he declared that he had now shown us enough of the way, that we had only to follow the shore to reach Akaba, and that the weakness of his camel would not allow it to proceed farther. I replied that he was at liberty to take himself off, but that, on my return to the convent, I should pay him only for the three days he had travelled with me. This was not to his liking, and he therefore preferred going on. Before we left this place Ayd told me that as I had treated him with a supper last night, it was his duty to give me a breakfast this morning. While he kneaded a loaf of flour, and baked it in the ashes, his companion caught some fish, which we boiled, and made a soup of the broth mixed with bread. The deaf man was made to understand by signs that he was to wait for the return of Ayd, and we set out together before mid-day. Before us lay a small bay, which we skirted; the sands on the shore every where bore the impression of the passage of serpents, crossing each other in many directions, and some of them appeared to be made by animals whose bodies could not be less than two inches in diameter. Ayd told me that serpents were very common in these parts; that the fishermen were much afraid of them, and extinguished their fires in the evening before they went to sleep, because the light was known to attract them. As serpents are so numerous on this side, they are probably not deficient towards the head of the gulf on its opposite shore, where it appears that the Israelites passed, when they journeyed from mount Hor, by the way of the Red sea, to compass the land of Edom," and when the "Lord sent fiery serpents among the people." [Numbers c. xxi, v. 4, 6. The following passage of Deuteronomy (viii. 15) in giving a general description of this country, alludes to the serpents: "Who led thee through that great and terrible wilderness wherein were fiery serpents, and scorpions, and drought, where there was no water; who brought thee forth water out of the rock of flint. Who fed thee in the wilderness with manna," &c. Scorpions are numerous in all the adjacent parts of Palestine and the desert. The Author observes in a note in another place, that the Arabic translation of the Pentateuch has "serpents of burning bites," instead of "fiery serpents." Note of the Editor.]

On the opposite side of the gulf the mountains appeared to reach down to the sea-side. In the direction S.S.E. and S.E. they are high; to the northward the chain lowers, and from the point E.S.E. towards Akaba the level is still lower. We saw at a distance several Gazelles, which, my guides told me, descend at mid-day to the sea to bathe. At one hour from Wasta we reached near the sea another collection of palm trees, larger than the former, and having a well, which was completely choaked up. These trees receive no other irrigation than the winter rains; each tree has its acknowledged owner among some of the Towara tribes: those which I have just noticed belong to some persons of the tribe of Aleygat. Not the smallest attention is paid to the trees till the period of the date harvest, when the owners encamp under them with their families for about a week while the fruit is gathered. The shrub Gharkad also grows here in large quantities. At one hour and three quarters we came to another small bay, round which lay the road, the main direction of the shore being N.E. by N. The mountains approach very near to the water, leaving only a narrow sloping plain covered with loose stones, washed down from above by the torrents. The road was profusely strewed with shells of different species, all of which were empty. The fishermen collect the shells, take out the animals, and dry them in the sun, particularly that of the species called Zorombat, which I have also seen in plenty on the African coast of the Red sea, north of Souakin, and at Djidda, where they are much esteemed by the mariners, and are sold by the fishermen at Tor and Suez. I here made a rough measurement of the breadth of the gulf: having assumed a base of seven hundred paces along the beach, and then measured with my compass the angles formed at either extremity of it, with a prominent point of the opposite mountain, the result gave a breadth of about twelve miles. The vegetation appeared to be much less impregnated with saline particles than I had found it on other parts of the coast of the Red sea.

At two hours and three quarters we had to pass round the bottom of another bay, of red and white sand-stone, where steep rocks advance so close to the water as to leave only a narrow path. At three hours and three quarters we passed an opening into the mountain, called Wady Om Hash, from whence a torrent descends, which, after its issue from the mountain, spreads to a considerable distance along the shore, and produces verdure. The shrub Doeyny grows here in abundance; it is almost a foot in height, and continues green the whole year. The Arabs collect and burn it, and sell the ashes at Khalyl, where they are used in the glass manufactories. We passed on our left several similar inlets into the mountain, the beds of torrents, but my guides could not, or would not, tell their names.

The Bedouins are generally averse to satisfying the traveller's curiosity on such subjects; not being able to conceive what interest he has in informing himself of mere names, they ascribe to repeated questions of this nature improper motives. Some cunning is often required to get proper answers, and they frequently give false names, for no other reason than to have the pleasure of deluding the enquirer, and laughing at him among themselves behind his back. At four hours and a quarter we passed Wady Mowaleh; and at the end of five hours and three quarters reached the northern point of the last mentioned bay, formed by a projecting part of the mountain, or promontory, called Abou Burko, which means "he who wears a face veil," because on the top of it is a white rock, which is thought to resemble the white Berkoa, or face veil of the Arab women, and renders it a conspicuous object from afar. Noweyba, where we had first reached the shore, bore from hence S.S.W. We rested for the night in a pasturing place near the mountain, on the south side of the promontory. Old Ayd, who carried his net with him, brought us some fish. His dog eat the raw fish, and his master told me that the dog sometimes passed several months without any other food.

May 8th.—We set out long before day-break. None of our party was ever more ready to alight, or to take his supper, than Szaleh, and none more averse to start. During the whole way he was continually grumbling, and endeavouring to persuade the others to turn back. We were one hour in doubling the Abou Burko, a chalky rock, whose base is washed by the waves. On the other side we passed, at two hours, in the bottom of a small bay, Wady Zoara, where a few date trees grow, and a well of saltish water is found, unfit to drink. The maritime plain was here nearly two miles in breadth. Having made the tour of another bay from Abou Burko, we reached, at three hours and a half, a promontory forming its northern boundary, and called Ras Om Haye, a name derived from the great quantity of serpents found there, some of which, Ayd told me, were venemous; we however saw none of any kind. The whole coast of the AElanitic gulf, from Ras Abou Mohammed to Akaba, consists of a succession of bays separated from such other by head lands. The Ras Om Haye forms the western extremity of the mountain of Tyh, whose straight and regular ridge runs quite across the peninsula, and is easily distinguished from the surrounding mountains. We halted at the end of five hours in a rocky valley at the foot of Ras Om Haye, where acacia trees and some grass grow. Ayd assured us that in the mountain, at some distance, was a reservoir of rain water, called Om Hadjydjein, but he could not answer for its containing water at this time. He described to Hamd its situation, and the way to it, with a view of persuading him to go and fetch some water for us; but his description was so confused, and I thought contradictory in several circumstances, and withal so pompous, that I concluded it to be all a story, and told him he was a babbler. "A babbler!" he exclaimed; "min Allah, no body in my whole life ever called me thus before. A babbler! I shall presently shew you, which of us two deserves that name." He then seized one of the large water skins, and barefooted as he was, began ascending the mountain, which was covered with loose and sharp stones. We soon lost sight of him, but saw him again, farther on, climbing up an almost perpendicular path. An hour and a half after, he returned by the same path, carrying on his bent back the skin full of water, which could not weigh less than one hundred pounds, and putting it down before us said, "There! take it from the babbler!" I was so overcome with shame, that I knew not how to apologize for my inconsiderate language; but when he saw that I really felt myself in the wrong, he was easily pacified, and said nothing more about it till night, when seeing me take a hearty draught of the water, and hearing me praise its sweetness, compared with the brackish water of the coast, he stopped me, and said, "Young man, for the future never call an old Bedouin a babbler."

On the opposite side of the gulf the mountains recede somewhat from the shore, leaving at their feet a sloping plain. A place on the coast, called Hagol, bore from hence E. b. S; it is a fruitful valley by the water side, with large date plantations, which were clearly discernible. It is in possession of the tribe of Arabs called Akraba. Behind them, in the mountains, dwells the strong and warlike tribe of Omran. Hagol is one long day's journey from Akaba; to the south of it about four hours is a similar cluster of date trees, called El Hamyde, which bore from us S.E. b. E. The mountains on that coast are steep, with many peaks.

No Arabs live on the western coast, owing to the scanty pasturage; it is occasionally visited by fishermen and others, who come to collect the herb from which the soda ashes are obtained, or to cut wood and burn it into charcoal. The fishermen are very poor and visit the coast only during the summer months; they cure their fish with the salt which they collect on the southern part of the coast, and when they have thus prepared a sufficient quantity of fish, they fetch a camel and transport it to Tor or Suez. At Tor a camel's load of the fish, or about four hundred pounds, may be had for three dollars. The fishermen prepare also a sort of lard by cutting out the fat adhering to the fish and melting it, they then mix it with salt, preserve it in skins, and use it all the year round instead of butter, both for cookery and for anointing their bodies. Its taste is not disagreeable. As the Bedouins prefer the upper road, this road along the coast is seldom visited, except by poor pilgrims who have been cut off from the caravan, or robbed by Bedouins, and who being ignorant of the road across the desert to Cairo, sometimes make the tour of the whole peninsula by the sea side, as they are thus sure not to lose their way, and in winter-time seldom fail in finding pools of water. Ayd told me that he had frequently met with stragglers of this description, worn out with fatigue and hunger.

From hence northwards the shore runs N.E. 1/2 N. Having doubled the point of Om Haye, we found on the other side, after again passing round a small bay, at five hours and three quarters, a bank of sand running into the sea to a considerable distance, and several miles in breadth; it is called Wady Mokabelat, and is the termination of a narrow Wady in the mountains to our left, from whence issues a torrent which spreads in time of rain over a wide extent of ground, partly rocky and partly sandy, where it produces good pasturage, and irrigates many acacia trees. The view up this Wady or inlet of the mountain is very curious: at its mouth it is nearly two miles wide, and it narrows gradually upwards with the most perfect regularity, so that the eye can trace it for five or six miles, when it becomes so narrow as to present only the appearance of a perpendicular black line. At six hours and a half we came again to a mountain forming a promontory, called Djebel Sherafe. The mountains from Om Haye northward decline considerably in height. The highest point of the chain appears to be the summit above Noweyba, where we had descended to the shore.

Beyond Djebel Sherafe we found the road along the shore ob-
structed by high cliffs, and were obliged to make a detour by entering a
valley to the west, called Wady Mezeiryk. We ascended through many
windings, entered several lateral valleys, and descended again to the shore
at the end of eight hours and a half, at a point not more than half an hour
distant from where we had turned out of the road. We found the valley
Mezeiryk full of excellent pasture; many sweet-scented herbs were growing in it, and the acacia trees were all green. Upon enquiry I learnt that to
the north of Djebel Tyh copious rains had fallen during the winter, while
to the south of it there had been very little for the last two years, and in
the eastern parts none.

In the whole way from the convent I had not met with the smallest trace of antiquity, either inscriptions upon the rocks by the road-side
or any other labour of man, until we reached the summit of Wady
Mezeiryk, where, close to the road, is a large sand-stone rock, which
seems, for a small space, to have received an artificial surface. Upon it I
found rude drawings of camels, and of mountain and other goats, resembling those which I had before seen, and those which I saw afterwards in
the Wady Mokatteb. No inscriptions were visible, but the annexed figures
were drawn between the animals. These were the only drawings or inscriptions that I met with in the mountains to the E. of the convent,
although I passed many flat rocks, well suited to them. I am inclined to
think that the inscriptions have been written by pilgrims proceeding to
Mount Sinai, and that the drawings of animals which are executed in a
ruder manner and with a less steady hand, are the work of the shepherds
of the peninsula. We find only those animals represented which are natives of these mountains, such as camels, mountain and other goats, and
gazelles, but principally the two first, [It may be worthy of mention in this
place that among the innumerable paintings and sculptures in the temples,
and tombs of Egypt, I never met with a single instance of the representa-
tion of a camel. At Thebes, in the highest of the tombs on the side of the
Djebel Habou, called Abd el Gorne, which has not, I believe, been noticed
by former travellers, or even by the French in their great work, I found all
the domestic animals of the Egyptians represented together in one large
painting upon a wall, forming the most elaborate and interesting work of
the kind, which I saw in Egypt. A shepherd conducts the whole herd into
the presence of his master, who inspects them, while a slave is noting
them down. Yet even here I looked in vain for the camel.] and I had occasion to remark in the course of my tour, that the present Bedouins of Sinai
are in the habit of carving the figures of goats upon rocks and in grottos.
Niebuhr observes, that in the hieroglyphic inscriptions which he saw in

342

the ancient burying ground not far distant from Naszeb, he found figures of goats upon almost every inscribed tomb-stone; this animal is not very frequent in the hieroglyphic inscriptions of Egypt.

From the point where we descended again to the shore, we followed a range of black basaltic cliffs, into which the sea has worked several creeks, appearing like so many small lakes, with very narrow openings towards the sea; they are full of fish and shells. At the end of nine hours and a half we had passed these cliffs, and reached the plain beyond, upon which we continued our route near the shore, and rested for the night at ten hours and a quarter, under a palm-tree, in the vicinity of a deep brackish well, which we were obliged to excavate, in order to procure some water for our camels, they having drank none since we quitted Wasta. From hence the promontory of Om Haye bore S.W. b. S. This plain, which is the extremity of a valley descending from the western mountain, is called Wady Taba. Ayd had promised to conduct me to this spot, but no farther; nor would the new offers which I now made induce hire to advance. We had already passed beyond the limits of the Arabs Towara, which terminate on this side of Wady Mokabelat, and we were now in the territory of the Heywat, who have a very bad reputation. We had met with nobody on the road, but in Wady Mezeiryk, as well as in Wady Taba, we saw footsteps, which shewed that some persons must have passed there a short time before. None of my guides were acquainted with the tribe of Heywat; had we therefore met any strong party of them, they would certainly have stripped us, although not at war with the Towara, for it is a universal practice among Bedouins to plunder all passengers who are unknown to them, and not attended by guides of their own tribe, provided they possess any thing worth seizing. Szaleh had completely deluded both myself and his own nephew Hamd: he had confidently asserted that he knew the Heywat well, and that the first individual of them whom we should meet would easily be prevailed upon to join our party, and to serve as an additional protector. About one hour before us was another promontory, beyond which we knew that the country was well peopled by two other tribes, the Alowein and Omran, who are the masters of the district of Akaba, intrepid robbers, and allies of the Heywat, and who are to this day quite independent of the government of Egypt. Through them we must unavoidably pass to reach Akaba, and Ayd could not give me the smallest hope of being able to cross their valleys without being attacked. Had I been furnished with a Firmahn from Mohammed Ali Pasha, I should have repaired at once to the great Sheikh of the Towara, and obliged him to send for some Heywat or Omran guides, who might have ensured my safety. But having been disappointed in this respect, I had no alternative but to turn back. Hamd, it is true, bravely offered to accompany me wherever I chose to go, though he knew nothing of the road before us, or the Arabs upon it; but I saw little chance of success, and knew, from what I had heard during my journey from Kerek to Cairo, that the Omran not only rob but murder passengers. Ayd had seen on the shore the footsteps of a man, which he knew to be those of a fisherman, a friend of his who had probably passed in the course of this day. Had we met with him he might have served as our guide, but not a soul was any where to be seen. Under these circumstances I reluctantly determined to retrace my steps the next day, but, instead of proceeding by the shore, to turn off into the mountains, and return to the convent by a more western route.

Akaba was not far distant from the spot from whence we returned. Before sun-set I could distinguish a black line in the plain, where my sharp-sighted guides clearly saw the date-trees surrounding the castle, which bore N.E. 1 E.; it could not be more than five or six hours distant. Before us was a promontory called Ras Koreye, and behind this, as I was told, there is another, beyond which begins the plain of Akaba. The castle is situated at an hour and a half or two hours from the western chain, down which the Hadj route leads, and about the same distance from the eastern chain, or lower continuation of Tor Hesma, a mountain which I have mentioned in my journey through the northern parts of Arabia Petraea. The descent of the western mountain is very steep, and has probably given to the place its name of Akaba, which in Arabic means a cliff or a steep declivity; it is probably the Akabet Aila of the Arabian geographers; Makrizi says that the village Besak stands upon its summit. In Numbers, xxxiv. 4, the "ascent of Akrabbim" is mentioned, which appears to correspond very accurately to this ascent of the western mountain from the plain of Akaba. Into this plain, which surrounds the castle on every side except the sea, issues the Wady el Araba, the broad sandy valley which leads towards the Dead sea, and which I crossed in 1812, at a day and a half, or two days journey from Akaba. At about two hours to the south of the castle the eastern range of mountains approaches the sea. The plain of Akaba, which is from three to four hours in length, from west to east, and, I believe, not much less in breadth northward, is very fertile in pasturage. To the distance of about one hour from the sea it is strongly impregnated with salt, but farther north sands prevail. The castle itself stands at a few hundred paces from the sea, and is surrounded with large groves of date-trees. It is a square building, with strong walls, erected, as it now stands, by Sultan el Ghoury of Egypt, in the sixteenth century. In its interior are many Arab huts; a market is held there, which is frequented by Hedjaz and Syrian Arabs; and small caravans arrive sometimes from Khalyl. The castle has tolerably good water in deep wells. The Pasha of Egypt, keeps here a garrison of about thirty soldiers, to guard the provisions deposited for the supply of the Hadj, and for the use of the cavalry on their passage by this route to join the army in the Hedjaz. Cut off from Cairo, the soldiers of the garrison often turn rebellious; three years ago an Aga made himself independent, and whenever a corps of troops passed he shut the gates of the castle, and prepared to defend it. He had married a daughter of the chief of the Omran, and thus secured the assistance of that tribe. Being at last attacked by some troops sent against him from Cairo he fled to his wife's tribe, and escaped into Syria.

It appears that the gulf extends very little farther east than the castle, distant from which one hour, in a southern direction, and on the eastern shore of the gulf, lies a smaller and half-ruined castle, inhabited by Bedouins only, called Kaszer el Bedawy. At about three quarters of an hour from Akaba, and the same distance from Kaszer el Bedawy, are ruins in the sea, which are visible only at low water: they are said to consist of walls, houses, and columns, but cannot easily be approached, on account of the shallows. This information was not given to me by my guides, but after my return to Cairo, by some French Mamelouks, in the army of Mohammed Ali Pasha, who had formerly been for several weeks in garrison at Akaba; they, however, had never seen the ruins except from a distance. I enquired particularly whether the gulf did not form two branches at this extremity, as it has always been laid down in the maps, but I was assured that it had only a single ending, at which the castle is situated.

To the north of Akaba, in the mountain leading up to Tor Hesma, is a Wady known by the name of Wady Ithem. I was told that at a certain spot this valley is shut up by an ancient wall, the construction of which is ascribed by the Arabs to a king named Hadeid, whose intention in erecting it was to prevent the tribe of Beni Helal of Nedjed from making incursions into the plain. By this valley a road leads eastwards towards Nedjed, following, probably, a branch of the mountain which extends towards the Akaba of the Syrian Hadj route, where the pilgrims coming from Damascus descend by a steep and difficult pass into the lower plains of Arabia. I believe this chain of mountains continues in a direct and uninterrupted line from the eastern shore of the Dead sea to the eastern shore of the Red sea, and from thence to Yemen. Makrizi, the Egyptian historian, says, in his chapter on Aila (Akaba); "It is from hence that the Hedjaz begins; in former times it was the frontier place of the Greeks; at one mile from it, is a triumphal arch of the Caesars. In the time of the Islam it was a fine town, inhabited by the Beni Omeya. Ibn Ahmed Ibn Touloun (a Sultan of Egypt), made the road over the Akaba or steep mountain before Aila. There were many mosques at Aila, and many Jews lived there; it was taken by the Franks during the Crusades; but in 566, Salaheddyn transported ships upon camels from Cairo to this place, and recovered it from them. Near Aila was formerly situated a large and handsome town, called Aszyoun," (Eziongeber.)

My guides told me, that in the sea opposite to the above mentioned promontory of Ras Koreye, there is a small island; they affirmed that they saw it distinctly, but I could not, for it was already dusk when they pointed it out, and the next morning a thick fog covered the gulf. Upon this island, according to their statement, are ruins of infidels, but as no vessels are kept in these parts, Ayd, who had been here several times, had never been able to take any close view of them; they are described as extensive, and built of hard stone, and are called El Deir, "the convent," a word often applied by Arabs to any ruined building in which they suppose that the priests of the infidels once resided.

The Bedouins in the neighbourhood of Akaba, as I have already observed, are the Alouein, Omran, and Heywat. They are all three entitled to a passage duty from the Hadj caravan; the Alouein exact it as owners of the district extending from the western mountain, across the plain to Akaba; the Heywat, as the possessors of the country from the well of Themmed, to the summit of the same mountain; and the Omran as masters of the desert from Akaba southward as far as the vicinity of Moeleh. Caravans of these tribes come occasionally to Cairo in search of corn, but they are independent of the Pasha of Egypt, of which they give proofs, by continually plundering the loads of the Hadj caravans, and of all those who pass the great Hadj route through their districts. Their intercourse with Syria, especially with Khalyl, is much more frequent than with Cairo.

We had had through the whole of this day a very intense Simoum, or hot- wind, which continued also during the night. In the evening I bathed in the sea, but found myself immediately afterwards as much heated as I had been before. After retiring to sleep we were awakened by the barking of Ayd's dog, upon which Ayd springing up said he was sure that some people were in the neighbourhood. We therefore got our guns ready, and sat by the fire the whole night, for whatever may be the heat of the season, the Bedouin must have his fire at night. Szaleh gave evident signs of fear, but happily the morning came without realizing his apprehensions.

May 9th.—Ayd still expressed his certainty that somebody had approached us last night, so much confidence did he place in the barking of his dog; he therefore advised me to hasten my way back, as some Arabs might see our footsteps in the sand, and pursue us in quest of a booty. On departing, Ayd, who was barefooted, and whose feet had become sore with walking, took from under the date-bush round which we had passed the night, a pair of leathern sandals, which he knew belonged to his Heywat friend, the fisherman, and which the latter had hidden here till his return. In order to inform the owner that it was he who had taken the sandals, he impressed his footstep in the sand just by, which he knew the other would immediately recognise, and he turned the toes towards the south, to indicate that he had proceeded with the sandals in that direction.

We now returned across the plain to the before mentioned basalt cliffs, passed the different small bays, and turned up into Wady Mezeiryk. We had descended from our camels, which Szaleh was driving before him, about fifty paces in advance; I followed, and about the same distance behind me walked Hamd and Ayd. As we had seen nobody during the whole journey, and were now returning into the friendly districts of the Towara, we had ceased to entertain any fears from enemies, and were laughing at Ayd for recommending us to cross the valleys as quickly as possible. My gun was upon my camel, and I had just turned leisurely round an angle of the valley, when I heard Ayd cry out with all his might, "Get your arms! Here they are!" I immediately ran up to the camels, to take my gun, but the cowardly Szaleh, instead of stopping to assist his companions, made the camels gallop off at full speed up the valley.   I, however, overtook them, and seized my gun, but before I could return to Hamd, I heard two shots fired, and Ayd's war-hoop, "Have at him! are we not Towara?" Immediately afterwards I saw Hamd spring round the angle, his eyes flashing with rage, his shirt sprinkled with blood, his gun in one hand, and in the other his knife covered with blood; his foot was bleeding, he had lost his turban, and his long black hair hung down over his shoulders. "I have done for him!" he exclaimed, as he wiped his knife; "but let us fly." "Not without Ayd," said I: "No indeed," he replied; "without him we should all be lost."   We returned round the corner, and saw Ayd exerting his utmost agility to come up with us. At forty paces distance an Arab lay on the ground, and three others were standing over him. We took hold of Ayd's arm and hastened to our camels, though we knew not where to find them. Szaleh had frightened them so greatly by striking them with his gun, that they went off at full-gallop, and it was half an hour before we reached them; one of them had burst its girths, and thrown off its saddle and load. We replaced the load, mounted Ayd, and hastened to pass the rocks of Djebel Sherafe. We then found ourselves in a more open country, less liable to be waylaid amongst rocks, and better able to defend ourselves. Hamd now told me that Ayd had first seen four Bedouins running down upon us; they had evidently intended to waylay us from behind the corner, but came a little too late. When he heard Ayd cry out, he had just time to strike fire and to light the match of his gun, when the boldest of the assailants approached within twenty paces of him and fired; the ball passed through his shirt; he returned the fire but missed his aim; while his opponent was coolly reloading his piece, before his companions had joined him, Ayd cried out to Hamd, to attack the robber with his knife, and advanced to his support with a short spear which he carried; Haind drew his knife, rushed upon the adversary, and after re-ceiving a wound in the foot, brought him to the ground, but left him immediately, on seeing his companions hastening to his relief. Ayd now said that if the man was killed, we should certainly be pursued, but that if he was only wounded the others would remain with him, and give up the pursuit. We travelled with all possible haste, not knowing whether more enemies might not be behind, or whether the encampment of the wounded man might not be in the vicinity, from whence his friends might collect to revenge his blood.

Ayd had certainly not been mistaken last night; these robbers had no doubt seen our fire, and had approached us, but were frightened by the barking of the dog. Uncertain whether we were proceeding northward or southward, they had waited till they saw us set out, and then by a circui-tous route in the mountains had endeavoured, unseen, to get the start of us in order to waylay us in the passes of the Wady Mezeiryk. If they had reached the spot where we were attacked two or three minutes sooner, and had been able to take aim at us from behind the rock, we must all have inevitably perished. That they intended to murder us, contrary to the usual practice of Bedouins, is easily accounted for they knew from the situation of the place, where they discovered us, as well as from the dress and ap-pearance of my guides, that they were Towara Bedouins; but though I was poorly dressed, they must have recognized me to be a townsman, and a townsman is always supposed by Bedouins to carry money with him. To rob us without resistance was impossible, their number being too small; or supposing this had succeeded, and any of the guides had escaped, they knew that they would sooner or later be obliged to restore the property taken, and to pay the fine of blood and wounds, because the Towara were then at peace with all their neighbours. For these reasons they had no doubt resolved to kill the whole party, as the only effectual mode of avoiding all disclosures as to the real perpetrators of the murder. I do not believe that such atrocities often occur in the eastern desert, among the great Aeneze tribe; at least I never heard of any; but these Heywat Arabs are notorious for their bad faith, and never hesitate to kill those who do not travel under the protection of their own people, or their well known friends. Scarcely any other Bedouin robbers would have fired till they had summoned us to give up our baggage, and had received a shot for answer.

I had at first intended to visit, on my return, the upper mountains, to which there is a road leading through the Wady Mokabelat; but Ayd dissuaded me. He said that if the party from which we had just escaped meant to pursue us, they would probably lay in wait for us in some of the passes in that direction; as he did not doubt that it would be their belief, that we were bound for Tor or Suez, the nearest road to which places lies through the Wady Mokabelat. I yielded to his opinion, and we returned along the coast by the same road we had come. Hamd's wound was not dangerous; I dressed it as well as I could, and four days afterwards it was nearly healed. We travelled a part of the night.

May 10th,—early the next morning we again reached Noweyba, the place where we had first reached the coast. We here met Ayd's deaf friend. Szaleh had all the way, betrayed the most timorous disposition; in excuse for running away when we were attacked, he said that he intended to halt farther on in the Wady, in order to cover our retreat, and that he had been obliged to run after the camels, which were frightened by the firing; but the truth was, that his terrors deprived him of all power of reflection, otherwise he must have known that the only course, to be pursued in the desert, when suddenly attacked, is to fight for life, as escape is almost impossible.

Having been foiled in my hopes of visiting Akaba, I now wished to follow the shore of the gulf to the southward; but Szaleh would not hear of any farther progress in that direction, and insisted upon my going back to the convent. I told him that his company had been of too little use to me, to make me desirous of keeping him any longer; he therefore returned, no doubt in great haste, by the same route we had come, accompanied by the deaf man; I engaged Ayd to conduct us along the coast, Hamd being very ignorant of this part of the peninsula, where his tribe, the Oulad Sayd, never encamp.

The date trees of Noweyba belong to the tribe of Mezeine; here were several huts built of stones and branches of the trees, in which the owners live with their families during the date-harvest. The narrow plain which rises here from the sea to the mountain, is covered with sand and loose stones. Ayd told me that in summer, when the wind is strong, a hollow sound is sometimes heard here, as if coming from the upper country; the Arabs say that the spirit of Moses then descends from Mount Sinai, and in flying across the sea bids a farewell to his beloved mountains.

We rode from Noweyba round a bay, the southern point of which bore from thence S. by W. In two hours and three quarters from Noweyba we doubled the point, and rested for the night in a valley just behind it, called Wady Djereimele, thickly overgrown with the shrub Gharkad, the berries of which are gathered in great abundance. Red coral is very common on this part of the coast. In the evening I saw a great number of shellfish leave the water, and crawl to one hundred or two hundred paces inland, where they passed the night, and at sun-rise returned to the sea.

During the last two days of our return from the northward I had found no opportunity to take notes. I had never permitted my companions to see me write, because I knew that if their suspicions were once raised, it would at least render them much less open in their communications to me. It has indeed been a constant maxim with me never to write before Arabs on the road; at least I have departed from it in a very few instances only, in Syria; and on the Nile, in my first journey into Nubia; but never in the interior of Nubia, or in the Hedjaz. Had I visited the convent of Mount Sinai in the character of a Frank, with the Pasha's Firmahn, and had returned, as travellers usually do, from thence to Cairo, I should not have hesitated to take notes openly, because the Towara Arabs dread the Pasha, and dare not insult or molest any one under his protection. But wishing to penetrate into a part of the country occupied by other tribes, it became of importance to conceal my pursuits, lest I should be thought a necromancer, or in search of treasures. In such cases many little stratagems must be resorted to by the traveller, not to lose entirely the advantage of making memoranda on the spot. I had accustomed myself to write when mounted on my camel, and proceeding at an easy walk; throwing the wide Arab mantle over my head, as if to protect myself from the sun, as the Arabs do, I could write under it unobserved, even if another person rode close by me; my journal books being about four inches long and three broad, were easily carried in a waistcoat pocket, and when taken out could be concealed in the palm of the hand; sometimes I descended from my camel, and walking a little in front of my companions, wrote down a few words without stopping. When halting I lay down as if to sleep, threw my mantle over me, and could thus write unseen under it.

At other times I feigned to go aside to answer a call of nature, and then couched down, in the Arab manner, hidden under my cloak. This evening I had recourse to the last method; but having many observations to note, I remained so long absent from my companions that Ayd's curiosity was roused. He came to look after me, and perceiving me immoveable on the spot, approached on tip-toe, and came close behind me without my perceiving him. I do not know how long he had remained there, but suddenly lifting up my cloak, he detected me with the book in my hand. "What is this?" he exclaimed. "What are you doing? I shall not make you answerable for it at present, because I am your companion; but I shall talk further to you about it when we are at the convent." I made no answer, till we returned to the halting-place, when I requested him to tell me what further he had to say. "You write down our country," he replied, in a passionate tone, "our mountains, our pasturing places, and the rain which falls from heaven; other people have done this before you, but I at least will never become instrumental to the ruin of my country." I assured him that I had no bad intentions towards the Bedouins, and told him he must be convinced that I liked them too well for that; "on the contrary," I added, "had I not occasionally written down some prayers ever since we left Taba, we should most certainly have been all killed; and it is very wrong in you to accuse me of that, which if I had omitted, would have cost us our lives." He was startled at this reply, and seemed nearly satisfied. "Perhaps you say the truth," he observed; "but we all know that some years since several men, God knows who they were, came to this country, visited the mountains, wrote down every thing, stones, plants, animals, even serpents and spiders, and since then little rain has fallen, and the game has greatly decreased." The same opinions prevail in these mountains, which I have already mentioned to be current among the Bedouins of Nubia; they believe that a sorcerer, by writing down certain charms, can stop the rains and transfer them to his own country. The travellers to whom Ayd alluded were M. Seetzen, who visited Mount Sinai eight years since, and M. Agnelli, who ten years ago travelled for the Emperor of Austria, collecting specimens of natural history, and who made some stay at Tor, from whence he sent Arabs to hunt for all kinds of animals.

M. Seetzen traversed the peninsula in several directions, and followed a part of the eastern gulf as far northward, I believe, as Noweyba. This learned and indefatigable traveller made it a rule not to be intimidated by the suspicions and prejudices of the Bedouins; beyond the Jordan, on the shores of the Dead sea, in the desert of Tyh, in this peninsula, as well as in Arabia, he openly followed his pursuits, never attempting to hide his papers and pencils from the natives, but avowing

---

his object to be that of collecting precious herbs and curious stones, in the character of a Christian physician in the Holy Land, and in that of a Moslim physician in the Hedjaz. If the knowledge of the natural history of Syria and Arabia was the principal object of M. Seetzen's researches, he was perfectly right in the course which he adopted, but if he considered these countries only as intermediate steps towards the exploring of others, he placed his ultimate success in the utmost peril; and though he may have succeeded in elucidating the history of the brute creation, he had little chance of obtaining much information on the human character, which can only be done by gaining the confidence of the inhabitants, and by accommodating our notions, views, and manners, to their own. When M. Seetzen visited these mountains, the Towaras were not yet reduced to subjection by Mohammed Ali; he was obliged, on several occasions, to pay large sums for his passage through their country, and the Mezeine would probably have executed a plot which they had laid to kill him, had not his guides been informed of it, and prevented him from passing through their territory.

I had much difficulty in soothing Ayd; he remained quiet during the rest of the journey, but after our return to the convent, the report spread among the Arabs that I was a writer like those who had preceded me, and I thus completely lost their confidence.

May 11th.—We continued along the coast S.S.W. and at four hours passed a promontory, called Djebel Abou Ma, consisting of granite. From hence we proceeded S.W. by S. and at seven hours came to a sandy plain, on the edge of a large sheltered bay. We found here some Bedouin girls, in charge of a few goats; they told us that their parents lived not far off in the valley Omyle. We went there, and found two small tents, where three or four women and as many little children were occupied in spinning, and in collecting herbs to feed the lambs and kids, which were frisking about them. Ayd knew the women, who belonged to his own tribe of Mezeine. Their husbands were fishermen, and were then at the seashore. They brought us some milk, and I bought a kid of them, which we intended to dress in the evening. The women were not at all bashful; I freely talked and laughed with them, but they remained at several yards distance from me. Ayd shook them by the hand, and kissed the children; but Hamd, who did not know them, kept at the same distance as myself. Higher up in the Wady is a well of good water, called Tereibe.

From hence we went S.W. by S. and at eight hours came to Ras Methna, a promontory whose cliffs continue for upwards of a mile close by the water side. Granite and red porphyry here cross each other in irregular layers, in some places horizontally, in others perpendicularly. The granite of this peninsula presents the same numberless varieties as that above the cataract of the Nile, and near Assouan; and the same beautiful specimens of red, rose-coloured, and almost purple may be collected here, as in that part of Egypt. The transition from primitive to secondary rocks, partaking of the nature of grünstein or grauwacke, or hornstein and trap, presents also an endless variety in every part of the peninsula, so that were I even possessed of the requisite knowledge accurately to describe them, it would tire the patience of the reader. Masses of black trap, much resembling basalt, compose several insulated peaks and rocks. On the shore the granite sand carried down from the upper mountains has been formed into cement by the action of the water, and mixed with fragments of the other rocks already mentioned, has become a very beautiful breccia.

At the end of eight hours and three quarters we rested for the night, to the south of this promontory, in a valley still called Wady Methna. From some fishermen whom we met I bought some excellent fish, of a species resembling the turbot, and very common on this coast. These with our kid furnished an abundant repast to ourselves as well as to the fishermen. The love of good and plentiful fare was one of Ayd's foibles; and he often related with pride that in his younger days he had once eaten at a meal, with three other Bedouins, the whole of a mountain goat; although his companions, as he observed, were moderate eaters. Bedouins, in general, have voracious appetites, and whoever travels with them cannot adopt any better mode of attaching them to his interests than by feeding them abundantly, and inviting all strangers met with on the road to partake in the repast. Pounds given as presents in money have less effect than shillings spent in victuals; and the reputation of hospitality which the traveller thus gains facilitates his progress on every occasion. My practice was to leave the provision sack open, and at the disposal of my guides, not to eat but when they did, not to take the choice morsels to myself, to share in the cooking, and not to give any orders, but to ask for whatever I wanted, as a favour. By pursuing this method I continued during the remainder of the journey to be on the best terms with my companions, and had not the slightest altercation either with Hamd or Ayd.

On the eastern shore of the gulf, opposite the place where we rested, lies a valley called Mekna, inhabited by the tribe of Omran. Close to the shore are plantations of date and other fruittrees. The inhabitants of Mekna cross the gulf in small boats, and bring to this side sheep and goats for sale, of which they possess large flocks, and which are thus more plentiful in this part of the peninsula than in any other. The mountains behind Mekna recede from the sea, and further to the south take a more eastern direction, so as to leave a chain of hills between them and the shore, rising immediately from the water-side. The appearance of this gulf, with the mountains enclosing it on both sides, reminded me of the lake of Tiberias and of the Dead sea; and the general resemblance was still further heightened by the hot season in which I had visited all these places.

May 12th.—Our road lay S.S.W. along a narrow sandy plain by the sea side. In one hour and a half we reached Dahab, a more extensive cluster of date trees than I had before seen on this coast; it extends into the sea upon a tongue of land, about two miles beyond the line of the shore; to the north of it is a bay, which affords anchorage, but it is without protection against northerly winds. Dahab is, probably, the Dizahab mentioned in Deut. i. 1. There are some low hummocks covered with sand close to the shore of the low promontory, probably occasioned by the ruins of buildings. The plantations of date trees ar [e] here enclosed by low walls, within many of which are wells of indifferent water; but in one of them, about twenty-five feet deep, and fifty yards from the sea, we found the best water I had met with on any part of this coast in the immediate vicinity of the sea. About two miles to the south of the date groves are a number of shallow ponds into which the sea flows at hightide; here the salt is made which supplies all the peninsula, as well as the fishermen for curing their fish; the openings of the ponds being closed with sand, the water is left to evaporate, when a thick crust of salt is left, which is collected by the Bedouins. Dahab is a favourite resort of the fishermen, who here catch the fish called Boury in great quantities.

The date trees of Dahab, which belong to the tribe of Mezeine and Aleygat, presented a very different appearance to those of Egypt and the Hedjaz, where the cultivators always take off the lower branches which dry up annually; here they are suffered to remain, and hang down to the ground, forming an almost impenetrable barrier round the tree, the top of which only is crowned with green leaves. Very few trees had any fruit upon them; indeed date trees, in general, yield a very uncertain produce, and even in years, when every other kind of fruit is abundant, they are sometimes quite barren. We met here several families of Arabs, who had come to look after their trees, and to collect salt. In the midst of the small peninsula of Dahab are about a dozen heaps of stones irregularly piled together, but shewing traces of having once been united; none of them is higher than five feet. The Arabs call them Kobour el Noszara, or the tombs of the Christians, a name given by them to all the nations which peopled their country before the introduction of the Islam.

We remained several hours under the refreshing shade of the palm trees, and there continued our road. In crossing the tongue of land I observed the remains of what I conceived to be a road or causeway, which began at the mountain and ran out towards the point of the peninsula; the stones which had formed it were now separated from each other, but lay in a straight line, so as to afford sufficient proof of their having been placed here by the labour of man. To the south of Dahab the camel road along the shore is shut up by cliffs which form a promontory called El Shedjeir; we were therefore obliged to take a circuitous route through the mountains, and directed our road by that way straight towards Sherm, the most southern harbour on this coast. We ascended a broad sandy valley in the direction S.W.; this is the same Wady Sal in which we had already travelled in our way from the convent, and which empties itself into the sea. In the rocky sides of this valley I observed several small grottos, apparently receptacles for the dead, which were just large enough to receive one corpse; I at first supposed them to have been natural erosions of the sand-stone rock; but as there were at least a dozen of them, and as I had not seen any thing similar in other sand- rocks, I concluded that they had been originally formed by man, and that time had worn them away to the appearance of natural cavities.

We left the valley and continued to ascend slightly through windings of the Wady Beney and Wady Ghayb, two broad barren sandy valleys, till, at the end of four hours, we reached the well of Moayen el Kelab, at the extremity of Wady Ghayb, where it is shut up by a cliff. Here is a small pond of water under the shade of an impending rock, and a large wild fig-tree. On the top of a neighbouring part of the granite cliff, is a similar pond with reeds growing in it. The water, which is never known to dry up, is excellent, and acquires still greater value from being in the vicinity of a spacious cavern, which affords shade to the traveller. This well is much visited by the Mezeine tribe; on several trees in the valley leading to it, we found suspended different articles of Bedouin tent furniture, and also entire tent coverings. My guides told me that the owners left them here during their absence, in order not to have the trouble of carrying them about; and such is the confidence which these people have in one another, that no instance is known of any of the articles so left having ever been stolen: the same practice prevails in other parts of the peninsula. The cavern is formed by nature in a beautiful granite rock; its interior is covered on all sides with figures of mountain goats drawn with charcoal in the rudest manner; they are done by the shepherd boys and girls of the Towaras.

The heat being intense we reposed in the cavern till the evening, when, after retracing our road for a short distance, we turned into the Wady Kenney, which we ascended; at its extremity we began to descend in a Wady called Molahdje, a narrow, steep, and rocky valley of difficult passage. Ayd's dog started a mountain goat, but was unable to come up with it. We slept in this Wady, at one hour and a half from Moayen el Kelab.

May 13th.—Farther down the Wady widens and is enclosed by high granite cliffs. Its direction is S. by W. Four hours continued descent brought us into Wady Orta. The rocks here are granite, red porphyry, and grünstein, similar to what I had observed towards Akaba, at nearly the same elevation above the sea. At the end of six hours we left Wady Orta, which descends towards the sea, and turning to the right, entered a large plain called Mofassel el Korfa, in which we rode S.S.W. From the footsteps in the sand Ayd knew the individuals of the Mezeine, who had passed this way in the morning. The view here opened upon a high chain of mountains which extends from Sherm in the direction of the convent, and which I had passed on my return from Arabia, in going from Sherm to Tor. It is called Djebel Tarfa, and is inhabited principally by the Mezeine. At eight hours the plain widens; many beds of torrents coming from the Tarfa cross it in their way to the sea. This part is called El Akha, and excepting in the beds of the torrents, where some verdure is produced, it is an entirely barren tract. At nine hours we approached the Tarfa, between which and our road were low hills called Hodeybat el Noszara, i. e. the hump backs of the Christians. The waters which collect here in the winter flow into the sea at Wady Nabk. At ten hours the plain opens still wider, and declines gently eastwards to the sea. To the left, where the mountains terminate, a sandy plain extends to the water side. At eleven hours is an insulated chain of low hills, forming here, with the lowest range of the Tarfa, a valley, in which our road lay, and in which we halted, after a fatigueing day's journey of twelve hours. As there were only two camels for three of us, we rode by turns; and Ayd regretted his younger days, when, as he assured us, he had once walked from the convent to Cairo in four days. The hills near which we halted are called Roweysat Nimr, or the little heads of the tiger.

May 14th.—We descended among low hills, and after two hours reached the harbour of Sherm. This is the only harbour on the western coast of the gulf of Akaba, which affords safe anchorage for large ships, though, by lying close in shore. small vessels might, I believe, find shelter in several of the bays of this gulf. At Sherm there are two deep bays little distant from each other, but separated by high land, in both of which, ships may lie in perfect safety. On the shore of the southern bay stands the tomb of a Sheikh, held in veneration by the Bedouins and mariners: a small house has been built over it, the walls of which are thickly hung with various offerings by the Bedouins; and a few lamps suspended from the roof are sometimes lighted by sailors. Sherif Edrisi, in his geography, mentions these two bays of Sherm, and calls the one Sherm el Beit, or of the house, and the other Sherm el Bir, or of the well, thus accurately describing both; for near the shore of the northern bay are several copious wells of brackish water, deep, and lined with stones, and apparently an ancient work of considerable labour. The distance from Sherm to the Cape of Ras Abou Mohammed is four or five hours; on the way a mountain is passed, which comes down close to the sea, called Es-szafra, the point of which bears from Sherm S.W. by S.

Bedouins are always found at Sherm, waiting with their camels for ships coming from the Hedjaz, whose passengers often come on shore here, in order to proceed by land to Tor and Suez. The Arab tribes of Mezeine and Aleygat have the exclusive right of this transport. Shortly after we had alighted at the well, more than twenty Mezeine came down from the mountain with their camels; they claimed the right of conducting me from hence, and of supplying me with a third camel; and as both my camels belonged to Arabs of the tribe of Oulad Sayd, they insisted upon Hamd taking my baggage from his camel, and placing it upon one of theirs, that they might have the profits of hire. After breakfasting with them, a loud quarrel began, which lasted at least two hours. I told them that the moment any one laid his hands upon my baggage to remove it, I should consider it as carried off by force, and no longer my property, and that I should state to the governor of Suez that I had been robbed here. Although they could not all expect to share in the profits arising from my transport, every one of them was as vociferous as if it had been his exclusive affair, and it soon became evident that a trifle in money for each of them was all that was wanted to quiet them. They did not, however, succeed; I talked very boldly; told them that they were robbers, and that they should be punished for their conduct towards me. At last their principal man, seeing that nothing was to be got, told us that we might load and depart. He accompanied us to a short distance, and received a handful of coffee-beans, as a reward for his having been less clamorous than the others.

These people believed that my visit to Sherm was for the mere purpose of visiting the tomb of the saint. I had assigned this motive to Ayd, who was himself a Mezeine, telling him that I had made a vow to thank the saint for his protection in our encounter with the robbers; Ayd would otherwise have been much astonished at my proceeding to this distance without any plausible object. The nearest road from Sherm to the convent is at first the same way by which we came, and it branches off northward from Wady Orta; but as I was desirous of seeing as much as possible of the coast, I suggested to my guides, that if we proceeded by that route the Mezeine of Sherm might possibly ride after us, and excite another quarrel in the mountain, where we should find it more difficult to extricate ourselves. They consented therefore to take the circuitous route along the shore. Such stratagems are often necessary, in travelling with Bedouins, to make them yield to the traveller's wishes; for though they care little for fatigue in their own business, they are extremely averse to go out of their way, to gratify what they consider an absurd whim of their companion.

From Sherm we rode an hour and a quarter among low hills near the shore. Here I saw for the first and only time, in this peninsula, volcanic rocks. For a distance of about two miles the hills presented perpendicular cliffs, formed in half circles, and some of them nearly in circles, none of them being more than sixty to eighty feet in height; in other places there was an appearance of volcanic craters. The rock is black, with sometimes a slight red appearance, full of cavities, and of a rough surface; on the road lay a few stones which had separated themselves from above. The cliffs were covered by deep layers of sand, and the valleys at their feet were also overspread with it; it is possible that other rocks of the same kind may be found towards Ras Abou Mohammed, and hence may have arisen the term of black, applied to these mountains by the Greeks. It should be observed, however, that low sand hills intervene between the volcanic rocks and the sea, and that above them, towards the higher mountains, no traces of lava are found, which seems to shew that the volcanic matter is confined to this spot.

We issued from the low hills upon a wide plain, which extends as far as Nabk, and is intersected in several places by beds of torrents. Our direction was N.E. by N. The plain terminates three or four miles to the east, in rocks which line the shore. At the end of three hours and a half we halted under a rock, in the bed of one of the torrents. The whole plain appears to be alluvial; many petrified shells are found imbedded in the chalky and calcareous soil. In the afternoon we again passed several low water-courses in the plain, and, at the end of five hours Wady Szygha. At six hours and a half from Sherm we rested in the plain, in a spot where some bushes grew, amongst which we found a Bedouin woman and her daughter, living under a covering made of reeds and brush-wood. Her husband and son were absent fishing, but Ayd being well known to them, they gave us a hearty welcome, and milked a goat for me. After sunset they joined our party, and sitting down behind the bush where I had taken up my quarters, eat a dish of rice which I presented to them. The daughter was a very handsome girl of eighteen or nineteen, as graceful in her deportment and modest in her behaviour, as the best educated European female could be; indeed I have often had occasion to remark among the Bedouins, comparing them with the women of of the most polished parts of Europe, that grace and modesty are not less than beauty the gifts of nature. Among these Arabs the men consider it beneath them to take the flocks to pasture, and leave it to the women.

In front of our halting place lay an island called Djezyret Tyran: its length from N. to S. is from six to eight miles, and it lies about four miles from the shore. Half its length is a narrow promontory of sand, and its main body to the south consists of a barren mountain. It is not inhabited, but the Bedouins of Heteym sometimes come here from the eastern coast, to fish for pearls, and remain several weeks, bringing their provision of water from the spring of El Khereyde, on that coast, there being no sweet water in the island. Edrisi mentions a place on the western coast, where pearls are procured, a circumstance implied by the name of Maszdaf, which he gives to it. The name is now unknown here, but I think it probable that Edrisi spoke of this part of the coast. The quantity of pearls obtained is very small, but the Heteym pick up a good deal of mother-of-pearl, which they sell to great advantage at Moeleh, to the ships which anchor there.

May 15th.—We continued over the plain in a direction N. by E. and in two hours reached Wady Nabk, which, next to Dahab and Noweyba, is the principal station on this coast. Large plantations of date trees grow on the sea-shore, among which, as usual, is a well of brackish water. The plain which reaches from near Sherm to Nabk is the only one of any extent along the whole coast; at Nabk it contracts, the western chain approaches to within two miles of the shore, and farther northward this chain comes close to the sea. The promontory of Djebel Abou Ma bore from Wady Nabk N.N.E 1/2 E. From hence to Dahab, as the Arabs told me, is about six hours walk along the shore. The highest point of the mountain upon the island of Tyran bore S.E. by S.

The opposite part of the eastern coast is low, and the mountains are at a distance inland. Near Nabk are salt-pits, similar to those at Dahab. Except during the date harvest, Nabk is inhabited only by fishermen; they are the poorest individuals of their tribe, who have no flocks or camels, and are obliged to resort to this occupation to support themselves and families. We bought here for thirty-two paras, or about four-pence half-penny, thirty-two salted fish, each about two feet in length, and a measure of the dried shell-fish, Zorombat, which in this state the Arabs call Bussra. For the smaller kinds of fish the fishermen use hand-nets, which they throw into the sea from the shore; the larger species they kill with lances, one of which Ayd carried constantly with him as a weapon; there is not a single boat nor even a raft to be found on the whole of this coast, but the Bedouins of the eastern coast have a few boats, which may some-times be seen in the gulf. We saw here a great number of porpoises playing in the water close to the shore. I wished to shoot at one of them, but was prevented by my companions, who said that it was unlawful to kill them, as they are the friends of man, and never hurt any body. I saw parts of the skin of a large fish, killed on the coast, which was an inch in thickness, and is employed by these Arabs instead of leather for sandals.

We now turned from Nabk upwards to the convent, and in half an hour entered the chain of mountains along a broad valley called Wady Nabk, in which we ascended slightly, and rested at two hours and a quar-ter from Nabk under a large acacia tree. In the vicinity were three tents of Aleygat Arabs, the women of which approached the place where we had alighted, and told us that two men and a child were there ill of the plague, which they had caught from a relative of theirs, who had lately come from Egypt with the disease upon him, and who had died. At that time they were in a large encampment, but as soon as the infection shewed itself, their companions compelled them to quit the camp, and they had come to this place to await the termination of the disorder. My guides were as much afraid of the infection as I was, and made the women remain at a proper distance; they asked me for some rice, and sugar, which latter arti-cle they believe to be a sovereign remedy against diseases. I was glad to be able to gratify them, and I advised them to give the patients whey which is almost the only cooling draught the Arabs know; they conceive that almost all illnesses proceed from cold, and therefore usually attempt to cure them by heat, keeping the patient thickly covered with clothes, and feeding him upon the most nourishing food they can afford.

Not far from our halting place, on the ascent of the mountain, is a reservoir of rain water, where we filled our skins. The acacia trees of the valley were thickly covered with guin arabic. The Towara Arabs often bring to Cairo loads of it, which they collect in these mountains; but it is much less esteemed than that from Soudan. I found it of a somewhat sweet and rather agreeable taste. The Bedouins pretend, that upon journeys it is a preventive of thirst, and that the person who chews it may pass a whole day without feeling any inconvenience from the want of water. We set out in the afternoon, and at the end of three hours and a half from Wady Nabk, passed the Mofassel el Korfa, which I have already mentioned. At four hours and a quarter we crossed Wady el Orta, the direction of our road N.W. by N., and at the end of five hours and a quarter we halted in Wady Rahab. All these valleys resemble one another; the only difference of appearance which they afford, is that in some places the ground is parched up, while in others, where a torrent passes during the winter, the shrubs still retain some green leaves.

May 16th.—During the night we had a heavy shower of rain with thunder and lightning, which completely drenched both ourselves and our baggage. A beautiful morning succeeded, and the atmosphere, which during the last three days had been extremely hot, especially on the low coast, was now so much refreshed, that we seemed to have removed from a tropical to an alpine climate. We passed through several valleys emptying themselves into Wady Orta; the principal of these is called Wady Ertama. Route N.N.W. Although the rain had been heavy, the sands had so completely absorbed it, that we could scarcely find any traces of it. We started several Gazelles, the only game I have seen in the peninsula, except mountain-goats. Hares and wolves are found, but are not common, and the Bedouins sometimes kill leopards, of one of which I obtained a large skin at the convent. The Bedouins talk much of a beast of prey called Wober, which inhabits the most retired parts only of the peninsula; they describe it as being of the size of a large dog, with a pointed head like a hog; I heard also of another voracious animal, called Shyb, stated to be a breed between the leopard and the wolf. Of its existence little doubt can be entertained, though its pretended origin is probably fabulous, for the Arabs, and especially the Bedouins, are in the common practice of assigning to every animal that is seldom met with, parents of two different species of known animals. On the coast, and in the lower valleys, a kind of large lizard is seen, called Dhob, which has a scaly skin of a yellow colour; the largest are about eighteen inches in length, of which the tail measures about one-half. The Dhob is very common in the Arabian deserts, where the Arabs form tobacco purses of its skin. It lives in holes in the sand, which have generally two openings; it runs fast, but a dog easily catches it. Of birds I saw red-legged partridges in great numbers, pigeons, the Katta, but not in such large flocks as I have seen them in Syria, and the eagle Rakham. The Bedouins also mentioned an eagle whose outspread wings measure six feet across, and which carries off lambs.

After four hours and a half we reached Wady Kyd, and rested at its entrance under two immense blocks of granite, which had fallen down from the mountain; they form two spacious caverns, and serve as a place of shelter for the shepherdesses; we saw in them several articles of tent furniture and some cooking utensils. On the sides figures of goats are drawn with charcoal; but I saw no inscriptions cut in the rock. The blocks are split in several places as if by lightning. We followed the Wady Kyd, continuing on a gentle ascent from the time of our setting out in the morning. The windings of the valley led us, at the end of five hours and a half, to a small rivulet, two feet across, and six inches in depth, which is lost immediately below, in the sands of the Wady. It drips down a granite rock, which blocks up the valley, there only twenty paces in breadth, and forms at the foot of the rock a small pond, overshadowed by trees, with fine verdure on its banks. The rocks which overhang it on both sides almost meet, and give to the whole the appearance of a grotto, most delighful to the traveller after passing through these dreary valleys. It is in fact the most romantic spot I have seen in these mountains, and worthy of being frequented by other people than Arabs, upon whom the beauties of nature make a very faint impression. The camels passed over the rocks with great difficulty; beyond it we continued in the same narrow valley, along the rivulet, amidst groves of date, Nebek, and some tamarisk trees, until, at six hours, we reached the source of the rivulet, where we rested a little. This is one of the most noted date valleys of the Sinai Arabs; the contrast of its deep verdure with the glaring rocks by which it is closely hemmed in, is very striking, and shews that wherever water passes in these districts, however barren the ground, vegetation is invariably found. Within the enclosures of the date-groves I saw a few patches of onions, and of hemp; the latter is used for smoking; some of the small leaves which surround the hemp-seed being laid upon the tobacco in the pipe, produces a more intoxicating smoke. The same custom prevails in Egypt, where the hemp leaves as well as the plant itself are called Hashysh. In the branches of one of the date-trees several baskets and a gun were deposited, and some camels were feeding upon the grass near the rivulet, but not a soul was to be seen in the valley; these Bedouins being under no fear of robbers, leave their goods and allow their beasts to pasture without any one to watch them; when they want the camels they send to the springs in search of them, and if not found there, they trace their footsteps through the valleys, for every Bedouin knows the print of the foot of his own camel.

Notwithstanding its verdure, the Wady Kyd is an uncomfortable halting- place, on account of the great number of gnats and ticks with which it is infested. Beyond the source of the rivulet, which oozes out of the ground, the vegetation ceases, and the valley widens. We rode on, and at seven hours entered Wady Kheysy, a wild pass, in which the road is covered with rocks, and the sides of the mountains are shattered by tor-rents. We ascended through many windings, in the general direction of W.N.W. until we found the valley shut up by a high mountain, called Djebel Mordam. The rocks are granite and porphyry; in many parts of the valley grow wild fig-trees, called by the Arabs Hamad; here also grows the Aszef, a tree which I had already seen in several of the Wadys; it springs from the fissures in the rocks, and its crooked stem creeps up the mountain's side like a parasitic plant; it produces, according to the Arabs, a fruit of the size of a walnut, of a blackish colour, and very sweet to the taste. The bark of the tree is white, and the branches are thickly covered with small thorns; the leaves are heart-shaped, and of the same shade of green as those of the oak. This Wady, as well as the Kyd, is inhabited by Mezeine; but they all return in summer to the highest mountains of the peninsula, where the pasture is more abundant than in these lower valleys.

We ascended the Mordam with difficulty, and on the other side found a narrow valley, which brought us, at the end of eleven hours, to a spring called Tabakat, situated under a rock, which shuts up the valley. The spring is thickly overgrown with reeds and sometimes dries up in summer. Above the rock extends a plain or rather a country somewhat more open, intersected with hills, and bounded by high mountains. The district is called Fera el Adlial, and is a favourite pasturing place of the Arabs, their sheep being peculiarly fond of the little berries of the shrub Rethem, with which the whole plain is overspread. In order to take the nearest road to the convent, we ascended in a N. direction, the high moun-tain of Mohala, the top of which we reached at the end of eleven hours and three quarters; from hence the convent was pointed out to me N. b. E. On the other side we descended N.E. into a narrow valley on the declivity of the mountain, where we alighted, after a long day's march of twelve hours and a quarter. This mountain is entirely of granite; but at Tabakat beautiful porphyry is seen with large slabs of feldspath, traversed by lay-ers of white and rose-coloured quartz.

May 17th.—The night was so cold that we all lay down round the fire, and kept it lighted the whole night. Early in the morning we continued to descend the mountain, by a road called Nakb [A steep declivity is called by the Bedouins Nakb, the plural of which (Ankaba) is often used by them synonymously with Djebal, mountains.] Abou el Far, and in half an hour reached the Wady Ahmar, which, below, joins the Wady Kyd. Ascending again in this Wady, we came in an hour to the springs of Abou Tereyfa, oozing, like that of Tabakat, from below a rock which shuts up the narrow valley. On the declivity of the mountains, farther on, I saw many ruins of walls, and was informed by my guides, that fifty years ago this was one of the most fertile valleys of their country, full of date and other fruit trees; but that a violent flood tore up all the trees, and laid it waste in a few days, and that since that period it has been deserted. At the end of two hours and a half, we descended into a broad valley, or rather plain, called Haszfet el Ras, and perceived at its extremity an encampment, which we reached at three hours and a quarter, and alighted under the tent of the chief; he happened to be the same Bedouin who had conducted me last year from Tor to Cairo, and who had also brought the from Cairo to the convent. I knew that he was angry with me for having discharged him on my arrival at the latter place, and for having hired Hamd to conduct me to Akaba; he was already acquainted with my return, and that I had gone to Sherm, but little expected to see me here. He, however, gave me a good reception, killed a lamb for my dinner, and would not let me depart in the afternoon, another Arab having prepared a goat for our supper. We remained therefore the whole day with him, and, in the evening, joined in the dance and songs of the Mesámer, which were protracted till long after-midnight, and brought several other young men from the neighbouring encampments. The stranger not accustomed to Bedouin life can seldom hope to enjoy quiet sleep in these encampments. After the songs and dances are ended he must lie down in the tent of his host with a number of men, who think to honour him by keeping him company; but who, if the tent is not very large, lie so close as to impart to him a share of the vermin with which they are sure to be infested. To sleep in the open air before the tent is difficult, on account of the fierce dogs of the encampment, who have as great an aversion for townsmen as their masters have; the Bedouins too dislike this practice, because a sight of the female apartment may thus be obtained. I found the women here much more reserved than among other Bedouins; I could not induce any of them to converse with me, and soon perceived that both themselves and their husbands disliked their being noticed; a fastidiousness of manners for which they are no doubt indebted to the frequent visits of their husbands to the capital of Egypt.

We had another shower in the night; flying showers are frequent during the summer, but they are never sufficiently copious in that season to produce torrents.

May 18th left the tent before dawn, and proceeded along a Wady and then N.W. up an ascent, whose summit we reached in two hours. From thence a fine view opened upon a broad Wady called Sebaye, and towards the mountain of Tyh. We crossed Wady Sebaye, and then ascended the mountain which commands the convent on the south side, and descending again, reached the convent at the end of three hours and a half. Our march during the whole of this journey had been slow, except on the day of our flight from the robbers; for our camels were weak and tired, and one of us usually walked. There is a more northern road from Sherm to the convent, which branches off from that by which we came, at Wady Orta; it passes by the two watering places of Naszeb, and Ara- yne; the former, which is in a fruitful valley, where date- trees grow, must not be confounded with the western Naszeb, already mentioned.

Hamd, afraid of being liable to pay the fine of blood, if it should become known that the robber had fallen by his hand, had made us all give him our solemn promise not to mention any thing of the affair. When I discharged him and Ayd at the convent, I made them both some presents, which they had well deserved, particularly Hamd; this he was so imprudent as to mention to his uncle Szaleh, who was so vexed at not receiving a present, that he immediately divulged all the circumstances of our rencounter. Hamd in consequence was under the greatest apprehensions from the relations of the robber, and having accompanied me on my return to Cairo, he remained with me some time there, in anxious expectation of hearing whether the robber's blood was likely to be revenged. Not hearing any thing, he then returned to his mountain, four months after which a party of Omran, to whose tribe the men had belonged, came to the tent of the Sheikh of the Towara to demand the fine of blood. The man had died a few days after receiving the wound, and although he was a robber and the first aggressor, the Bedouin laws entitled his relations to the fine, if they waved the right of retaliation; Hamd was therefore glad to come to a compromise, and paid them two camels, (which the two principal Sheikhs of the Towara gave him for the purpose), and twenty dollars, which I thought myself bound to reimburse to him, when he afterwards called on me at Cairo. This was the third man Hamd had killed in skirmish; but he had paid no fine for the others, as it was never known who they were, nor to what tribe they belonged.

Had Hamd, whom every one knew to be the person who had stabbed the robber, refused to pay the fine, the Omran would sooner or later have retaliated upon himself or his relations, or perhaps upon some other individual of his tribe, according to the custom of these Bedouins, who have established among themselves the law of "striking sideways." [See my remarks on the customs of blood-revenge, in the description of Bedouin manners.]

The convent of Mount Sinai is situated in a valley so narrow, that one part of the building stands on the side of the western mountain, while a space of twenty paces only is left between its walls and the eastern mountain. The valley is open to the north, from whence approaches the road from Cairo; to the south, close behind the convent, it is shut up by a third mountain, less steep than the others, over which passes the road to Sherm. The convent is an irregular quadrangle of about one hundred and thirty paces, enclosed by high and solid walls built with blocks of granite, and fortified by several small towers. While the French were in Egypt, a part of the east wall which had fallen down was completely rebuilt by order of General Kleber, who sent workmen here for that purpose. The upper part of the walls in the interior is built of a mixture of granite-sand and gravel, cemented together by mud, which has acquired great hardness.

The convent contains eight or ten small court-yards, some of which are neatly laid out in beds of flowers and vegetables; a few date-trees and cypresses also grow there, and great numbers of vines. The distribution of the interior is very irregular, and could not be otherwise, considering the slope upon which the building stands; but the whole is very clean and neat. There are a great number of small rooms, in the lower and upper stories, most of which are at present unoccupied. The principal building in the interior is the great church, which, as well as the convent, was built by the Emperor Justinian, but it has subsequently undergone frequent repairs. The form of the church is an oblong square, the roof is supported by a double row of fine granite pillars, which have been covered with a coat of white plaster, perhaps because the natural colour of the stone was not agreeeble to the monks, who saw granite on every side of them. The capitals of the columns are of different designs; several of them bear a resemblance to palm branches, while others are a close but coarse imitation of the latest period of Egyptian sculpture, such as is seen at Philae, and in several temples in Nubia. The dome over the altar still remains as it was constructed by Justinian, whose portrait, together with that of his wife Theodora, may yet be distinguished on the dome, together with a large picture of the transfiguration, in honour of which event the convent was erected. An abundance of silver lamps, paintings, and portraits of saints adorn the walls round the altar; among the latter is a saint Christopher, with a dog's head. The floor of the church is finely paved with slabs of marble.

The church contains the coffin in which the bones of saint Catherine were collected from the neighbouring mountain of St. Catherine, where her corpse was transported after her death by the angels in the service of the monks. The silver lid of a sarcophagus likewise attracts attention; upon it is represented at full length the figure of the empress Anne of Russia, who entertained the idea of being interred in the sarcophagus, which she sent here; but the monks were disappointed of this honour. In a small chapel adjoining the church is shewn the place where the Lord is supposed to have appeared to Moses in the burning bush; it is called Alyka, and is considered as the most holy spot in Mount Sinai. Besides the great church, there are twenty-seven smaller churches or chapels dispersed over the convent, in many of which daily masses are read, and in all of them at least one every Sunday.

The convent formerly resembled in its establishment that of the Holy Sepulchre at Jerusalem, which contains churches of various sects of Christians. Every principal sect, except the Calvinists and Protestants, had its churches in the convent of Sinai. I was shewn the chapels belonging to the Syrians, Armenians, Copts, and Latins, but they have long been abandoned by their owners; the church of the Latins fell into ruins at the close or the seventeenth century, and has not been rebuilt. But what is more remarkable than the existence of so many churches, is that close by the great church stands a Mahometan mosque, spacious enough to contain two hundred people at prayers. The monks told me that it was built in the sixteenth century, to prevent the destruction of the convent. Their tradition is as follows: when Selim, the Othman Emperor, conquered Egypt, he took a great fancy to a young Greek priest, who falling ill, at the time that Selim was returning to Constantinople, was sent by him to this convent to recover his health; the young man died, upon which the Emperor, enraged at what he considered to be the work of the priests, gave orders to the governor of Egypt to destroy all the Christian establishments in the peninsula; of which there were several at that period. The priests of the great convent of Mount Sinai being informed of the preparations making in Egypt to carry these orders into execution, began immediately to build a mosque within their walls, hoping that for its sake their house would be spared; it is said that their project was successful and that ever since the mosque has been kept in repair.

This tradition, however, is contradicted by some old Arabic records kept by the prior, in which I read a circumstantial account how, in the year of the Hedjra 783, some straggling Turkish Hadjis, who had been cut off from the caravan, were brought by the Bedouins to the convent; and being found to be well educated, and originally from upper Egypt, were retained here, and a salary settled on them and their descendants, on condition of their becoming the servants of the mosque. The conquest of Egypt by Selim did not take place till A.H. 895. The mosque in the convent of Sinai appears therefore to have existed long before the time of Selim. The descendants of these Hadjis, now poor Bedouins, are called Retheny, they still continue to be the servants of the mosque, which they clean on Thursday evenings, and light the lamps; one of them is called the Imam. The mosque is sometimes visited by Moslim pilgrims, but it is only upon the occasion of the presence of some Mussulman of consequence that the call to prayers is made from the Minaret.

In the convent are two deep and copious wells of spring water; one of them is called the well of Moses, because it is said that he first drank of its water. Another was the work, as the monks say, of an English Lord, it bears the date 1760. There is also a reservoir for the reception of rain water.

None of the churches or chapels have steeples. There is a bell, which, I believe, is rung only on Sundays. The usual mode of calling the monks to morning prayers is by striking with a stick upon a long piece of granite, suspended from ropes, which produces a sound heard all over the convent; close by it hangs a piece of dry wood, which emits a different sound, and summons to vespers. A small tower is shewn which was built forty or fifty years ago for the residence of a Greek patriarch of Constantinople, who was exiled to this place by the orders of the Sultan, and who remained here till he died.

According to the credited tradition, the origin of the convent of Mount Sinai dates from the fourth century. Helena, the mother of Constantine, is said to have erected here a small church, in commemoration of the place where the Lord appeared to Moses in the burning bush, and in the garden of the convent a small tower is still shewn, the foundations of which are said to have been laid by her. The church of Helena drawing many visitors and monks to these mountains, several small convents were erected in different parts of the peninsula, in the course of the next century, but the ill treatment which the monks and hermits suffered from the Bedouins induced them at last to present a petition to the Emperor Justinian, entreating him to build a fortified convent capable of affording them protection against their oppressors. He granted the request, and sent workmen from Constantinople and Egypt, with orders to erect a large convent upon the top of the mountain of Moses; those however to whom the work was entrusted, observing the entire want of water in that spot, built it on the present site. They attempted in vain to cut away the mountain on each side of the building, with a view to prevent the Arabs from taking post there and throwing stones at the monks within. The building being completed, Justinian sent from Constantinople some slaves, natives of the shores of the Black sea, to officiate as servants in the convent, who established themselves with their families in the neighbouring valleys. The first prior was Doulas, whose name is still recorded upon a stone built into the wall of one of the buildings in the interior of the convent. The above history is taken from a document in Arabic, preserved by the monks. An Arabic inscription over the gate, in modern characters, says that Justinian built the convent in the thirtieth year of his reign, as a memorial of himself and his wife Theodora. It is curious to find a passage of the Koran introduced into this inscription; it was probably done by a Moslem sculptor, without the knowledge of the monks. A few years after the completion of the convent, one of the monks is said to have been informed in his sleep, that the corpse of St. Catherine, who suffered martyrdom at Alexandria, had been transported by angels to the summit of the highest peak of the surrounding mountains. The monks ascended the mountain in procession, found the bones, and deposited them in their church, which thus acquired an additional claim to the veneration of the Greeks. Monastic establishments seem soon after to have considerably increased throughout the peninsula. Small convents, chapels, and hermitages, the remains of many of which are still visible, were built in various parts of it. The prior told me that Justinian gave the whole peninsula in property to the convent, and that at the time of the Mohammedan conquest, six or seven thousand monks and hermits were dispersed over the mountains, the establishments of the peninsula of Sinai thus resembling those which still exist on the peninsula of Mount Athos. It is a favourite belief of the monks of Mount Sinai, that Mohammed himself, in one of his journeys, alighted under the walls of the convent, and that impressed with due veneration for the mountain of Moses, he presented to the convent a Firmahn, to secure to it the respect of all his followers. Ali is said to have written it, and Mohammed, who could not write, to have confirmed it by impressing his extended hand, blackened with ink, upon the parchment. This Firmahn, it is added, remained in the convent until Selim the First conquered Egypt, when hearing of the precious relic, he sent for it, and added it to the other relics of Mohammed in the imperial treasury at Constantinople; giving to the convent, in return, a copy of the original certified with his own cipher. I have seen the latter, which is kept in the Sinai convent at Cairo, but I do not believe it to be an authentic document. None of the historians of Mohammed, who have recorded the transactions of almost every day of his life, mention his having been at Mount Sinai, neither in his earlier youth, nor after he set up as a prophet, and it is to-tally contrary to history that he should have granted to any Christians such privileges as are mentioned in this Firmahn, one of which is that the Moslems are bound to aid the Christian monks in rebuilding their ruined churches. It is to be observed also that this document states itself to have been written by Ali, not at the convent, but in the mosque of the Prophet at Medina, in the second year of the Hedjra, and is addressed, not to the convent of Mount Sinai in particular, but to all the Christians and their priests. The names of twenty-two witnesses, followers of Mohammed, are subscribed to it; and in a note it is expressly stated that the original, writ-ten by Ali, was lost, and that the present was copied from a fourth successive copy taken from the original. Hence it appears that the relation of the priests is at variance with the document to which they refer, and I have little doubt therefore that the former is a fable and the latter a for-gery. Notwithstanding the difficulties to which the monks must have been exposed from the warlike and fanatical followers of the new faith in Syria, Arabia, Egypt, and the Desert, the convent continued uninjured, and defended itself successfully against all the surrounding tribes by the peculiar arms of its possessors, patience, meekness, and money. Accord-ing to the statement of the monks, their predecessors were made responsible by the Sultans of Egypt for the protection of the pilgrim cara-vans from Cairo to Mekka, on that part of the road which lay along the northern frontiers of their territory from Suez to Akaba. For this purpose they thought it necessary to invite several tribes, and particularly the Szowaleha and the Aleygat to settle in the fertile valleys of Sinai, in order to serve as protectors of this road. The Bedouins came, but their power increasing, while that of the monks declined, they in the course of time took possession of the whole peninsula, and confined the monks to their convent. It appears from the original copy of a compact between the monks and the above Bedouins, made in the year of the Hedjra 800, when Sultan Dhaher Bybars reigned in Egypt, that besides this convent, six others were still existing in the peninsula, exclusive of a number of chapels and hermitages; from a writing on parchment, dated in the

A.H.1053, we find that in that year all these minor establishments had been abandoned, and that the great convent, holding property at Feiran, Tor, and in other fruitful valleys, alone remained. The priests assured me, that they had documents to prove that all the date valleys and other fertile spots in the gulf of Akaba had been in their possession, and were confirmed to them by the Sultans of Egypt; but they either could not or would not shew me their archives in detail, without an order from the prior at Cairo; indeed all their papers appeared to be in great confusion.

Whenever a new Sultan ascends the throne of Constantinople, the convent is furnished with a new Firmahn, which is transmitted to the Pasha of Egypt; but as the neighbouring Bedouins, till within a few years, were completely independent of Egypt, the protection of the Pashas was of very little use to the monks, and their only dependance was upon their own resources, and their means of purchasing and conciliating the friendship, or of appeasing the animosity of the Arabs.

At present there are only twenty-three monks in the convent. They are under the presidence of a Wakyl or prior, but the Ikonómos, whom the Arabs call the Kolob, is the true head of the community, and manages all its affairs. The order of Sinai monks dispersed over the east is under the control of an Archbishop, in Arabic called the Reys. He is chosen by a council of delegates from Mount Sinai and from the affiliated convent at Cairo, and he is confirmed, pro forma, by the Greek patriarch of Jerusalem. The Archbishop can do nothing as to the appropriation of the funds without the unanimous vote of the council. Formerly he lived in the convent; but since its affairs have been on the decline, it has been found more expedient that he should reside abroad, his presence here entitling the Bedouins to great fees, particularly on his entrance into the convent. I was told that ten thousand dollars would be required, on such an occasion, to fulfil all the obligations to which the community is bound in its treaties with the Arabs. Hence it happens that no Archbishop has been here since the year 1760, when the Reys Kyrillos resided, and I believe died, in the convent. I was informed that the gate has remained walled up since the year 1709, but that if an Archbishop were to come, it must be again opened to admit him, and that all the Bedouin Sheiks then have a right to enter within the walls.

Besides the convent at Cairo, which contains a prior and about fifty monks, Mount Sinai has establishments and landed property in many other parts of the east, especially in the Archipelago, and at Candia: it has also a small church at Calcutta, and another at Surat.

The discipline of these monks, with regard to food and prayer, is very severe. They are obliged to attend mass twice in the day and twice in the night. The rule is that they shall taste no flesh whatever all the year round; and in their great fast they not only abstain from butter, and every kind of animal food and fish, but also from oil, and live four days in the week on bread and boiled vegetables, of which one small dish is all their dinner. They obtain their vegetables from a pleasant garden adjoining the building, into which there is a subterraneous passage; the soil is stony, but in this climate, wherever water is in plenty, the very rocks will produce vegetation. The fruit is of the finest quality; oranges, lemons, almonds, mulberries, apricots, peaches, pears, apples, olives, Nebek trees, and a few cypresses overshade the beds in which melons, beans, lettuces, onions, cucumbers, and all sorts of culinary and sweet-scented herbs are sown. The garden, however, is very seldom visited by the monks, except by the few whose business it is to keep it in order; for although surrounded by high walls, it is not inaccessible to the Bedouins, who for the three last years have been the sole gatherers of the fruits, leaving the vegetables only for the monks, who have thus been obliged to repurchase their own fruit from the pilferers, or to buy it in other parts of the peninsula.

The excellent air of the convent, and the simple fare of the inhabitants, render diseases rare. Many of the monks are very old men, in the full possession of their mental and bodily faculties. They have all taken to some profession, a mode of rendering themselves independent of Egypt, which was practised here even when the three hundred private chambers were occupied, which are now empty, though still ready for the accommodation of pious settlers. Among the twenty-three monks who now remain, there is a cook, a distiller, a baker, a shoemaker, a tailor, a carpenter, a smith, a mason, a gardener, a maker of candles, &c. &c. each of these has his work-shop, in the worn-out and rusty utensils of which are still to be seen the traces of the former riches and industry of the establishment. The rooms in which the provisions are kept are vaulted and built of granite with great solidity; each kind of provision has its purveyor. The bake-house and distillery are still kept up upon a large scale. The best bread is of the finest quality; but a second and third sort is made for the Bedouins who are fed by the convent. In the distillery they make brandy from dates, which is the only solace these recluses enjoy, and in this they are permitted to indulge even during the fasts.

Most of the monks are natives of the Greek islands; in general they do not remain more than four or five years, when they return to their own country, proud of having been sufferers among Bedouins; some, however, have been here forty years. A few of them only understood Arabic; but none of them write or read it. Being of the lower orders of society, and educated only in convents, they are extremely ignorant. Few of them read even the modern Greek fluently, excepting in their prayer-books, and I found but one who had any notion of the ancient Greek. They have a good library, but it is always shut up; it contains about fifteen hundred Greek volumes, and seven hundred Arabic manuscripts; the latter, which I examined volume after volume, consist entirely of books of prayer, copies of the Gospels, lives of saints, liturgies, &c.; a thick folio volume of the works of Lokman, edited, according to the Arab tradition, by Hormus, the ancient king of Egypt, was the only one worth attention. Its title in Arabic is. The prior would not permit it to be taken away, but he made me a present of a fine copy of the Aldine Odyssey and an equally fine one of the Anthology. In the room anciently the residence of the Archbishop, which is very elegantly paved with marble, and extremely well furnished, though at present unoccupied, is preserved a beautiful ancient manuscript of the Gospels in Greek, which I was told, was given to the convent by "an emperor called Theodosius." It is written in letters of gold upon vellum, and ornamented with portraits of the Apostles.

Notwithstanding the ignorance of these monks, they are fond of seeing strangers in their wilderness; and I met with a more cordial reception among them than I did in the convents of Libanus, which are in possession of all the luxuries of life. The monks of Sinai are even generous; three years ago they furnished a Servian adventurer, who styled himself a Knes, and pretended to be well known to the Russian government, with sixty dollars, to pay his journey back to Alexandria, on his informing them of his destitute circumstances.

At present the convent is seldom visited; a few Greeks from Cairo and Suez, and the inhabitants of Tor who repair here every summer, and encamp with their families in the garden, are the only persons who venture to undertake the journey through the desert. So late as the last century regular caravans of pilgrims used to come here from Cairo as well as from Jerusalem; a document preserved by the monks states the arrival in one day of eight hundred Armenians from Jerusalem; and at another time of five hundred Copts from Cairo. I believe that from sixty to eighty is the greatest number of visitors that can now be reckoned in a year. In the small but neat room which I occupied, and which is assigned to all strangers whom the prior receives with any marks of distinction, were the names of some of the latest European travellers who have visited the convent. The following inscriptions, written upon pieces of paper stuck against the walls, I thought worth the trouble of transcribing.

"Le quintidi, 5 Frimaire, l'an 9 de la République Française, 1800 de l'ère Chrétienne, et 3ème de la conquête de l'Egypte, les Citoyens Rozières et Coutelle, Membres de la Commission des Sciences et Arts, sont venus visiter les lieux saints, les ports de Tor, Ras Mohammed, et Charms, la mer de Suez et l'Accaba, l'extrémité de la presqu'île, toutes les chaines de montagnes, et toutes les tribus Arabes entre les deux golfes." (Seal of the French Republic.)

M. Rozières made great mineralogical researches in these mountains, but he and his companion did not succeed in visiting all the chains of mountains or all the tribes of Arabs. They never reached Akaba, nor traversed the northern ranges of the peninsula, nor visited the tribes of Tyaha, Heywat and Terabein. The following is the memorial left by M. Seetzen:

"Le 9 d'Avril, 1807. U.J. Seetzen, nommé Mousa, voyageur Allemand, M.D. et Assesseur de Collège de S. Majestè l'Empereur de toutes les Russies dans la Seigneurie de Jever en Allemagne, est venu visiter le Couvent de la Sainte Cathérine, les Monts d'Horeb, de Moise, et de la Sainte Catherine, &c. après avoir parcouru toutes les provinces orientales anciennes de la Palestine; savoir, Hauranitis, Trachonitis, Gaulonitis, Paneas, Batanea, Decapolis, Gileaditis, Ammonitis, Amorrhitis et Moabitis, jusqu'aux frontières de la Gebelene (Idumaea), et après avoir fait deux fois l'entour de la mer morte, et traversé le désert de l'Arabie Petrée, entre la ville d'Hebron et entre le Mont Sinai, par un chemin jusqu'à ce tems-là inconnu. Après un séjour de dix jours, il continuait son voyage pour la ville de Suez."

M. Seetzen has fallen into a mistake in calling the convent by the name of saint Catherine. It is dedicated to the transfiguration, or as the Greeks call it, the metamorphosis, and not to saint Catherine, whose relics only are preserved here. M. Seetzen visited the convent a second time, previous to his going to Arabia. He came then from Tor, and stopped only one day.

The visit of two English travellers, Messrs. Galley Knight and Fazakerly, is also recorded in a few lines dated February 13, 1811. The same room contained likewise several modern Arabic inscriptions, one of which says: "To this holy place came one who does not deserve that his name should be mentioned, so manifold are his sins. He came here with his family. May whoever reads this, beseech the Almighty to forgive him. June 28, 1796."

The only habitual visitors of the convent are the Bedouins. They have established the custom that whoever amongst them, whether man, woman, or child, comes here, is to receive bread for breakfast and supper, which is lowered down to them from the window, as no Bedouins, except the servants of the house, are ever admitted within the walls. Fortunately for the monks, there are no good pasturing places in their immediate neighbourhood; the Arab encampments are therefore always at some distance, and visitors are thus not so frequent as might be supposed; yet scarcely a day passes without their having to furnish bread to thirty or forty persons. In the last century the Bedouins enjoyed still greater privileges, and had a right to call for a dish of cooked meat at breakfast, and for another at supper; the monks could not have given a stronger proof of their address than by obtaining the abandonment of this right from men, in whose power they are so completely placed. The convent of Sinai at Cairo is subject to similar claims; all the Bedouins of the peninsula who repair to that city on their private business receive their daily meal, from the monks, who, not having the same excuses as their brethren of Mount Sinai, are obliged to supply a dish of cooked meat. The convent has its Ghafeirs, or protectors, twenty-four in number, among the tribes inhabiting the desert between Syria and the Red sea; but the more remote of them are entitled only to some annual presents in clothes and money, while the Towara Ghafeirs are continually hovering round the walls, to extort as much as they can. Of the Towara Arabs the tribes of Szowaleha and Aleygat only are considered as protectors; the Mezeine, who came in later times to the peninsula, have no claims; and of the Szowaleha tribe, the branches Oulad Said and Owareme are exclusively the protectors, while the Koreysh and Rahamy are not only excluded from the right of protection but also from the transport of passengers and loads. Of the Oulad Said each individual receives an annual gift of a dollar, and the Ghafeir of this branch of the Szowaleha is the convent's chief man of business in the desert. If a Sheikh or head man calls at the convent, he receives, in addition to his bread, some coffee beans, sugar, soap, sometimes a handkerchief, a little medicine, &c. &c.

Under such circumstances it may easily be conceived that disputes continually happen. If a Sheikh from the protecting tribes comes to the convent to demand coffee, sugar, or clothing, and is not well satisfied with what he receives, he immediately becomes the enemy of the monks, lays waste some of their gardens, and must at last be gained over by a present. The independent state of the Bedouins of Sinai had long prevented the monks from endeavouring to obtain protection from the government of Egypt, whose power in the peninsula being trifling, they would only by complaining have exasperated the Bedouins against them; their differences therefore had hitherto been accommodated by the mediation of other Sheikhs. It was not till 1816 that they solicited the protection of Mohammed Ali; this will secure them for the present against their neighbours; but it will, probably, as I told the monks, be detrimental to them in the end. Ten or twenty dollars were sufficient to pacify the fiercest Bedouin, but a Turkish governor will demand a thousand for any effectual protection.

The Arabs, when discontented, have sometimes seized a monk in the mountains and given him a severe beating, or have thrown stones or fired their musquets into the convent from the neighbouring heights; about twenty years ago a monk was killed by them. The monks, in their turn, have fired occasionally upon the Bedouins, for they have a well furnished armory, and two small cannon, but they take great care never to kill any one. And though they dislike such turbulent neighbours, and describe them to strangers as very devils, yet they have sense enough to perceive the advantages which they derive from the better traits in the Bedouin character, such as their general good faith, and their placability. "If our convent," as they have observed to me, "had been subject to the revolutions and oppressions of Egypt or Syria, it would long ago have been abandoned; but Providence has preserved us by giving us Bedouins for neighbours."

Notwithstanding the greediness of the Bedouins, I have reason to believe that the expenses of the convent are very moderate. Each monk is supplied annually with two coarse woollen cloaks, and no splendour is any where displayed except in the furniture of the great church, and that of the Archbishop's room. The supplies are drawn from Egypt; but the communication by caravans with Cairo is far from being regular, and the Ikonómos assured me that at the time I was there the house did not contain more than one month's provision.

The yearly consumption of corn is about one hundred and sixty Erdebs, or two thousand five hundred bushels, which is sufficient to cover all the demands of the Bedouins, and I believe that £1000. sterling, or 4000 dollars, is the utmost of the annual expenditure. The convent at Cairo expends perhaps two or three times that sum. The monks complain greatly of poverty; and the prior assured me that he sometimes has not a farthing left to pay for the corn that is brought to him, and is obliged to borrow money from the Bedouins at high interest; but an appearance of poverty is one of their great protections; and considering the possessions of this convent abroad, and the presents which it receives from pilgrims, I am much inclined to doubt the prior's assertion.

The Bedouins who occupy the peninsula of Mount Sinai are:

I. The Szowaleha. They are the principal tribe, and they boast of having been the first Bedouins who settled in these mountains, under their founder Ayd, two of whose sons, they say, emigrated with their families to the Hedjaz. The Szowaleha are divided into several branches: 1. The Oulad Said, whose Sheikh is at present the second Sheikh of the Towara Arabs. They are not so poor as the other tribes, and possess the best valleys of the mountains. 2. Korashy, or Koreysh, whose Sheikh, Szaleh Ibn Zoheyr, is at present the great Sheikh of the Towara, and transacts the public business with the government of Egypt. The Korashy are descendants of a few families of Beni Koreysh, who came here as fugitives from the Hedjaz, and settled with the Szowaleha, with whom they are now intimately intermixed. 3. Owareme, a subdivision of whom are the Beni Mohsen; in one of the families of which is the hereditary office of Agyd, or the commander of the Towara in their hostile expeditions. 4. Rahamy. The Szowaleha inhabit principally the country to the west of the convent, and their date valleys are, for the greater part, situated on that side. These valleys are the exclusive property of individuals, but the other pasturing places of the tribe are common to all its branches, although the latter usually remain somewhat separated from each other.

II. Aleygat. They are much weaker in number than the Szowaleha, and encamp usually with the Mezeine, and with them form a counterbalance to the power of the Szowaleha. A tribe of Aleygat is found in Nubia on the banks of the Nile about twenty miles north of Derr, where they occupy the district called Wady el Arab, of which Seboua makes a part. [See Journey towards Dongola, p. 26.] The Aleygat of Sinai are acquainted with this settlement of their brethren, and relate that in the time of the Mamelouks, one of them who had embarked with a Beg at Tor for Cosseir travelled afterwards towards Ibrim, and when he passed Seboua was delighted there to find the people of his own tribe. They treated him well, and presented him with a camel and a slave. I am ignorant by what chance the Aleygat settled in Nubia.

III. El Mezeine, who live principally to the eastward of the convent towards the gulf of Akaba.

IV. Oulad Soleiman, or Beni Selman, at present reduced to a few families only, who are settled at Tor, and in the neighbouring villages.

V. Beni Waszel, about fifteen families, who live with the Mezeine, and are usually found in the neighbourhood of Sherm. They are said to have come originally from Barbary. Some of their brethren are also settled in Upper Egypt.

These five tribes are comprised under the appellation Towara, or the Bedouins of Tor, and form a single body, whenever any foreign tribe of the northern Bedouins attacks any one of them; but sometimes, though not often, they have bloody quarrels among themselves. Their history, according to the reports of the best informed among them, founded upon tradition, is as follows: At the period of the Mohammedan conquest, or soon after, the peninsula of Mount Sinai was inhabited exclusively by the tribe of Oulad Soleiman, or Beni Selman, together with the monks. The Szowaleha, and Aleygat, the latter originally from the eastern Syrian desert, were then living on the borders of Egypt, and in the Sherkieh or eastern district of the Delta, from whence they were accustomed to make frequent inroads into this territory, in order to carry off the date-harvest, and other fruits. [Some encampments of Szowaleha are still found in the Sherkieh.] Whenever the inundation of the Nile failed, they repaired in great numbers to these mountains, and pastured their herds in the fertile valleys, the vegetation of which is much more nutritious for camels and sheep than the luxuriant but insipid pastures on the banks of the Nile. After long wars the Szowaleha and Aleygat succeeded in reducing the Oulad Soleiman; many of their families were exterminated, others fled, and their feeble remains now live near Tor, where they still pride themselves upon having been the former lords of this peninsula. The Szowaleha and Aleygat, however, did not agree, and had frequent disputes among themselves. At that period there arrived at Sherm four families of the Mezeine, a very potent tribe in the Hedjaz, east of Medina, where they are still found in large numbers, forming part of the great tribe of Beni Harb. They were flying from the effects of blood-revenge, and wishing to settle here, they applied to the Szowaleha, begging to be permitted to join them in their pastures. The Szowaleha consented, on condition of their paying a yearly tribute in sheep, in the same manner as the despised tribe of Heteym, on the opposite coast of the gulf of Akaba, does to all the surrounding Arabs.. The high spirited Mezeine however rejected the offer, as derogatory to their free born condition, and addressed themselves to the Aleygat, who readily admitted them to their brotherhood and all their pastures. Long and obstinate wars between the Szowaleha and Aleygat were the consequence of this compact. The two tribes fought, it is said, for forty years; and in the greatest and the last battle, which took place in Wady Barak, the Mezeine decided the contest in favour of the Aleygat. "So great," says the Bedouin tradition, "was the number of the Szowaleha killed in this engagement, that the nails of the slain were seen for many years after, the sport of the winds in the valleys around the field of battle." [No nation equals the Bedouins in numerical exaggeration. Ask a Bedouin who belongs to a tribe of three hundred tents, of the numbers of his brethren, and he will take a handful of sand, and cast it up in the air, or point to the stars, and tell you that they are as numberless. Much cross-questioning is therefore necessary even to arrive at an approximation to the truth.] A compromise now took place, the Szowaleha and Aleygat divided the fertile valleys of the country equally, and the Mezeine received one-third of their share from the latter. The Sheikh of the Szowaleha was, at the same time, acknowledged as Sheikh of the whole peninsula. At present the Mezeine are stronger than the Aleygat, and both together are about equal in number to the Szowaleha.

Besides the Towara tribes, three others inhabit the northern parts of the peninsula; viz. The Heywat, who live towards Akaba; the Tyaha, who extend from the chain of the mountain El Tyh northwards towards Ghaza and Hebron; and the Terabein, who occupy the north-west part of the peninsula, and extend from thence towards Ghaza and Hebron. These three tribes are together stronger than the Towara, with whom they are sometimes at war, and being all derived from one common stock, the ancient tribe of Beni Attye, they are always firmly united during hostilities. They have no right to the pasturages south of Djebel Tyh, but are permitted to encamp sometimes in that direction, if pasture is abundant. The pastures in their own territory, along the whole of the northern parts of Djebel Tyh, are said to be excellent, and to extend from one side of the peninsula to the other.

I believe that the population of the entire peninsula, south of a line from Akaba to Suez, as far as cape Abou Mohammed, does not exceed four thousand souls. In years of dearth, even this small number is sometimes at a loss to find pasturage for their cattle.

The Towara are some of the poorest of the Bedouin tribes, which is to be attributed principally to the scarcity of rain and the consequent want of pasturage. Their herds are scanty, and they have few camels; neither of their two Sheikhs, the richest individuals amongst them, possesses more than eight; few tents have more than two; it often happens that two or three persons are partners in one camel, and great numbers are without any. There are no horses even among the Sheikhs, who constantly ride on camels; but asses are common. Their means of subsistence are derived from their pastures, the transport trade between Suez and Cairo, the sale at the latter place of the charcoal which they burn in their mountains, of the gum arabic which they collect, and of their dates and other fruits. The produce of this trade is laid out by them at Cairo in purchasing clothing and provisions, particularly corn, for the supply of their families; and if any thing remains in hand, they buy with it a few sheep and goats at Tor or at Sherm, to which latter place they are brought by the Bedouins of the opposite coast of Arabia.

When Egypt was under the unsettled government of the Mamelouks the Towara Bedouins, who were then independent, were very formidable, and often at war with the Begs, as well as with the surrounding tribes. At present they have lost much of the profits which they derived from their traffic with Suez, and from the passage of caravans to Cairo; they are kept in awe by Mohammed Ali, and have taken to more peaceful habits, which, however, they are quite ready to abandon, on the first appearance of any change in the government of Egypt. Even now, they pay no duty whatever to the Pasha, who, on the contrary, makes their chief some annual presents; but they are obliged to submit to the rate of carriage which the Pasha chooses to fix for the transport of his goods. They live, of course, according to their means; the small sum of fifteen or twenty dollars pays the yearly expenses of many, perhaps of most of their families, and the daily and almost unvarying food of the greater part of them is bread, with a little butter or milk, for which salt alone is substituted when the dry season is set in, and their cattle no longer yield milk. The Mezeine appeared to me much hardier than the other tribes, owing probably to their being exposed to greater privations in the more barren district which they inhabit. They hold more intercourse with the neighbouring Bedouins to the north than the other Towaras, and in their language and manners approach more to the great eastern tribes than to the other Bedouins of the peninsula.

All the tribes of the Towara complain of the sterility of their wives; [They wish for children because their tribe is strengthened by it. But Providence seems to have wisely proportioned the fertility of their women to the barrenness of the country.] and though the Bedouin women in general are less fruitful than the stationary Arabs, the Towara are even below the other Bedouins in this respect, three children being a large family among them.

To the true Bedouin tribes above enumerated are to be added the advenae called Djebalye, or the mountaineers. I have stated that when Justinian built the convent, he sent a party of slaves, originally from the shores of the Black sea, as menial servants to the priests. These people came here with their wives, and were settled by the convent as guardians of the orchards and date plantations throughout the peninsula. Subsequently, when the Bedouins deprived the convent of many of its possessions, these slaves turned Moslems, and adopted the habits of Bedouins. Their descendants are the present Djebalye, who unanimously confess their descent from the Christian slaves, whence they are often called by the other Bedouins "the children of Christians." They are not to be distinguished, however, in features or manners, from other Bedouins, and they are now considered a branch of the Towara, although the latter still maintain the distinction, never giving their daughters in marriage to the Djebalye, nor taking any of theirs; thus the Djebalye intermarry only among themselves, and form a separate commmunity of about one hundred and twenty armed men. They are a very robust and hardy race, and their girls have the reputation of superior beauty over all others of the peninsula, a circumstance which often gives rise to unhappy attachments, and romantic love-tales, when their lovers happen to belong to other tribes. The Djebalye still remain the servants of the convent; parties of three attend in it by turns, and are the only Bedouins who are permitted to enter within the walls; but they are never allowed to sleep in the house, and pass the night in the garden. They provide fire-wood, collect dried herbage for the mule which turns the mill, bring milk, eggs, &c. and receive all the offals of the kitchen. Some of them encamp as Bedouins in the mountains surrounding the peaks of Moses and St. Catherine, but the greater part are settled in the gardens belonging to the convent, in those mountains. They engage to deliver one-half the fruit to the convent, but as these gardens produce the finest fruit in the peninsula, they are so beset by Bedouin guests at the time of gathering, that the convent's share is usually consumed in hospitality.

The Djebalye have formed a strict alliance with the Korashy, that branch of the Szowaleha which has no claims of protectorship upon the convent, and by these means they have maintained from ancient times, a certain balance of power against the other Szowaleha. They have no right to transport pilgrims to the convent, and are, in general, considered as pseudo-Arabs, although they have become Bedouins in every respect. They are divided into several smaller tribes, some of whom have become settlers; thus the Tebna are settled in the date valley of Feiran, in gardens nominally the property of the convent: the Bezya in the convent's gardens at Tor; and the Sattla in other parts, forming a few families, whom the true Bedouins stigmatize with the opprobrious name of Fellahs, or peasants. The monks told me that in the last century there still remained several families of Christian Bedouins who had not embraced Islamism; and that the last individual of this description, an old woman, died in 1750, and was buried in the garden of the convent. In this garden is the burial-ground of the monks, and in several adjoining vaulted chambers their remains are collected after the bodies have lain two years in the coffins underground. High piles of hands, shin bones, and sculls are placed separately in the different corners of these chambers, which the monks are with difficulty persuaded to open to strangers. In a row of wooden chests are deposited the bones of the Archbishops of the convent, which are regularly sent hither, wherever the Archbishops may die. In another small chest are shewn the sculls and some of the bones of two "Indian princes," who are said to have been shipwrecked on the coast of Tor, and having repaired to the convent, to have lived for many years as hermits in two small adjoining caves upon the mountain of Moses. In order to remain inseparable in this world, they bound two of their legs together with an iron chain, part of which, with a small piece of a coat of mail, which they wore under their cloaks, is still preserved. No one could tell me their names, nor the period at which they resided here. At the entrance of the charnel houses is the picture of the hoary St. Onuphrius. He is said to have been an Egyptian prince, and subsequently one of the first monks of Djebel Mousa, in which capacity he performed many miracles.

After two days repose in the convent and its delightful garden, I set out for the holy places around it, a pilgrimage which I had deferred making immediately on my first arrival, which is the usual practice, that the Arabs might not confound me with the common run of visitors, to whom they shew no great respect. The Djebalye enjoy the exclusive right of being guides to the holy places; my suite therefore consisted of two of them loaded with provisions, together with my servant and a young Greek. The latter had been a sailor in the Red sea, and appeared to have turned monk chiefly for the sake of getting his fill of brandy from the convent's cellar.

May 20th.—We were in motion before sunrise for the Djebel Mousa or Mountain of Moses, the road to which begins to ascend immediately behind the walls of the convent. Regular steps were formerly cut all the way up, but they are now either entirely destroyed, or so much damaged by the winter torrents as to be of very little use. After ascending for about twenty-five minutes, we breathed a short time under a large impending rock, close by which is a small well of water as cold as ice; at the end of three quarters of an hour's steep ascent we came to a small plain, the entrance to which from below is through a stone gateway, which in former times was probably closed; a little beneath it stands, amidst the rocks, a small church dedicated to the Virgin. On the plain is a larger building of rude construction, which bears the name of the convent of St. Elias; it was lately inhabited, but is now abandoned, the monks repairing here only at certain times of the year to read mass. Pilgrims usually halt on this spot, where a tall cypress tree grows by the side of a stone tank, which receives the winter rains.

On a large rock in the plain are several Arabic inscriptions, engraved by pilgrims three or four hundred years ago; I saw one also in the Syriac language.

According to the Koran and the Moslem traditions, it was in this part of the mountain, which is called Djebel Oreb, or Horeb, that Moses communicated with the Lord. From hence a still steeper ascent of half an hour, the steps of which are also in ruins, leads to the summit of Djebel Mousa, where stands the church which forms the principal object of the pilgrimage; it is built on the very peak of the mountain, the plane of which is at most sixty paces in circumference. The church, though strongly built with granite, is now greatly dilapidated by the unremitted attempts of the Arabs to destroy it; the door, roof, and walls are greatly injured. Szaleh, the present Sheikh of the Towara, with his tribe the Korashy, was the principal instrument in the work of destruction, because, not being entitled to any tribute from the convent, they are particularly hostile to the monks. Some ruins round the church indicate that a much larger and more solid building once stood here, and the rock appears to have been cut perpendicularly with great labour, to prevent any other approach to it than by the southern side. The view from this summit must be very grand, but a thick fog prevented me from seeing even the nearest mountains.

About thirty paces from the church, on a somewhat lower peak, stands a poor mosque, without any ornaments, held in great veneration by the Moslems, and the place of their pilgrimage. It is frequently visited by the Bedouins, who slaughter sheep in honour of Moses; and who make vows to him and intreat his intercession in heaven in their favour. There is a feast-day on which the Bedouins come hither in a mass, and offer their sacrifices. I was told that formerly they never approached the place without being dressed in the Ihram, or sacred mantle, with which the Moslems cover their naked bodies on visiting Mekka, and which then consisted only of a napkin tied round the middle; but this custom has been abandoned for the last forty years. Foreign Moslem pilgrims often repair to the spot, and even Mohammed Ali Pasha and his son Tousoun Pasha gave notice that they intended to visit it, but they did not keep their promise. Close by the footpath, in the ascent from St. Elias to this summit, and at a small distance from it, a place is shown in the rock, which somewhat resembles the print of the fore part of the foot; it is stated to have been made by Mohammed's foot when he visited the mountain. We found the adjacent part of the rock sprinkled with blood in consequence of an accident which happened a few days ago to a Turkish lady of rank who was on her way from Cairo to Mekka, with her son, and who had resided for some weeks in the convent, during which she made the tour of the sacred places, bare footed, although she was old and decrepid. In attempting to kiss the mark of Mohammed's foot, she fell, and wounded her head; but not so severely as to prevent her from pursuing her pilgrimage. Somewhat below the mosque is a fine reservoir cut very deep in the granite rock, for the reception of rain water.

The Arabs believe that the tables of the commandments are buried beneath the pavement of the church on Djebel Mousa, and they have made excavations on every side in the hope of finding them. They more particularly revere this spot from a belief that the rains which fall in the peninsula are under the immediate control of Moses; and they are persuaded that the priests of the convent are in possession of the Taourat, a book sent down to Moses from heaven, upon the opening and shutting of which depend the rains of the peninsula. The reputation, which the monks have thus obtained of having the dispensation of the rains in their hands has become very troublesome to them, but they have brought it on by their own measures for enhancing their credit with the Bedouins. In times of dearth they were accustomed to proceed in a body to Djebel Mousa, to pray for rain, and they encouraged the belief that the rain was due to their intercessions. By a natural inference, the Bedouins have concluded that if the monks could bring rain, they had it likewise in their power to withhold it, and the consequence is, that whenever a dearth happens they accuse the monks of malevolence, and often tumultuously assemble and compel them to repair to the mountain to pray. Some years since, soon after an occurrence of this kind, it happened that a violent flood burst over the peninsula, and destroyed many date trees; a Bedouin, whose camel and sheep had been swept away by the torrent, went in a fury to the convent, and fired his gun at it, and when asked the reason, exclaimed; "You have opened the book so much that we are all drowned!" He was pacified by presents; but on departing he begged that in future the monks would only half open the Taourat, in order that the rains might be more moderate.

The supposed influence of the monks is, however, sometimes attended with more fortunate results: the Sheikh Szaleh had never been father of a male child, and on being told that Providence had thus punished him for his enmity to the convent, he two years ago brought a load of butter to the monks, and entreated them to go to the mountain and pray that his newly-married wife, who was then pregnant, might be delivered of a son. The monks complied, and Szaleh soon after became the happy father of a fine boy; since that period he has been the friend of the convent, and has even partly repaired the church on Djebel Mousa. This summit was formerly inhabited by the monks, but, at present they visit it only in time of festivals. We returned to the convent of St. Elias, and then descended on the western side of the mountain for half an hour by another decayed flight of steps, into a valley where is a small convent called El Erbayn, or the forty; it is in good repair, and is at present inhabited by a family of Djebalye, who take care of the garden annexed to it, which affords a pleasing place of rest to those who descend from the barren mountains above. In its neighbourhood are extensive olive plantations, but I was told that for the last five summers the locusts had devoured both the fruit and foliage of these trees, upon which they alight in preference to all others. This insect is not less dreaded here than in Arabia, Syria, and Egypt, but the Bedouins of Mount Sinai, unlike those of Arabia, instead of eating them, hold them in great abhorrence.

We passed the mid-day hours at St. Elias, and towards evening ascended the mountain opposite to that of Mousa, which forms the western cliff of this narrow valley. After proceeding about an hour we stopped near a small well, where we found several huts of Djebalye, and cleared a place among the rocks, where our party encamped for the night. The well is called Bir Shonnar, from the circumstance of a monk who was wandering in these mountains, and nearly dying of thirst, having miraculously discovered it by seeing the bird Shonnar fly up from the spot; it is closely surrounded by rocks, and is not more than a foot in diameter and as much in depth. The Bedouins say that it never dries up, and that its water, even when exposed to the sun, is as cold as ice. Several trees grow near it, amongst others the Zarour, now almost in full bloom. Its fruit, of the size of a small cherry, with much of the flavour of a strawberry, is, I believe, not a native of Egypt, but is very common in Syria. I bought a lamb of the Bedouins, which we roasted among the rocks, and although there were only two women and one girl present, and the steep side of the mountain hardly permitted a person to stand up with firmness, and still less to wheel about, yet the greater part of the night was spent in the Mesámer, or national song and dance, to which several other neighbouring Djebalye were attracted. The air was delightfully cool and pure. While in the lower country, and particularly on the sea shore, I found the thermometer often at 102°—105°, and once even at 110°; in the convent it never stood higher than 75°. The Semoum wind never reaches these upper regions. In winter the whole of the upper Sinai is deeply covered with snow, which chokes up many of the passes, and often renders the mountains of Moses and St. Catherine inaccessible. The climate is so different from that of Egypt, that fruits are nearly two months later in ripening here than at Cairo; apricots, which begin to be in season there in the last days of April, are not fit to eat in Sinai till the middle of June.

May 21st.—We left our resting-place before sign-rise, and climbed up a steep ascent, where there had formerly been steps, which are now entirely destroyed. This side of Djebel Katerin or Mount St. Catherine, is noted for its excellent pasturage; herbs sprout up every where between the rocks, and as many of them are odoriferous, the scent early in the morning, when the dew falls, is delicious. The Zattar, Ocimum Zatarhendi, was particularly conspicuous, and is esteemed here the best possible food for sheep. In the month of June, when the herbs are in blossom, the monks are in the habit of repairing to this and the surrounding mountains, in order to collect various herbs, which they dry, and send to the convent at Cairo, from whence they are dispatched to the archbishop of Sinai at Constantinople, who distributes them to his friends and dependents; they are supposed to possess many virtues conducive to health. A botanist would find a rich harvest here, and it is much to be regretted that two mountains so easy of access, and so rich in vegetation, as Sinai and Libanus, should be still unexplored by men of science. The pretty red flower of the Noman plant, Euphorbia retusa of Forskal, abounds in al [l] the valleys of Sinai, and is seen also amongst the most barren granite rocks of the mountains.

As we approached the summit of the mountain we saw at a distance a small flock of mountain goats feeding among the rocks. One of our Arabs left us, and by a widely circuitous road endeavoured to get to leeward of them, and near enough to fire at them; he enjoined us to remain in sight of them, and to sit down in order not to alarm them. He had nearly reached a favourable spot behind a rock, when the goats suddenly took to flight. They could not have seen the Arab, but the wind changed, and thus they smelt him. The chase of the Beden, as the wild goat is called, resembles that of the chamois of the Alps, and requires as much enterprise and patience. The Arabs make long circuits to surprise them, and endeavour to come upon them early in the morning when they feed. The goats have a leader, who keeps watch, and on any suspicious smell, sound, or object, makes a noise which is a signal to the flock to make their escape. They have much decreased of late, if we may believe the Arabs, who say that, fifty years ago, if a stranger came to a tent and the owner of it had no sheep to kill, he took his gun and went in search of a Beden. They are however even now more common than in the Alps, or in the mountains to the east of the Red sea. I had three or four of them brought to me at the convent, which I bought at threefourths of a dollar each. The flesh is excellent, and has nearly the same flavour as that of the deer. The Bedouins make waterbags of their skins, and rings of their horns, which they wear on their thumbs. When the Beden is met with in the plains the dogs of the hunters easily catch him; but they cannot come up with him among the rocks, where he can make leaps of twenty feet.

The stout Bedouin youths are all hunters, and excellent marksmen; they hold it a great honour to bring game to their tents, in proof of their being hardy mountain runners, and good shots; and the epithet Bowardy yknos es-szeyd, "a marksman who hunts the game," is one of the most flattering that can be bestowed upon them. It appears, from an ancient picture preserved in the convent, which represents the arrival of an archbishop from Egypt, as well as from one of the written documents in the archives, that in the sixteenth century all the Arabs were armed with bows and arrows as well as with matchlocks; at present the former are no longer known, but almost every tent has its matchlock, which the men use with great address, notwithstanding its bad condition. I believe bows are no longer used as regular weapons by the Bedouins in any part of Arabia.

After a very slow ascent of two hours we reached the top of Mount St. Catherine, which, like the mountain of Moses, terminates in a sharp point; its highest part consists of a single immense block of granite, whose surface is so smooth, that it is very difficult to ascend it. Luxuriant vegetation reaches up to this rock, and the side of the mountain presented a verdure which, had it been of turf instead of shrubs and herbs, would have completed the resemblance between this mountain and some of the Alpine summits. There is nothing on the summit of the rock to attract attention, except a small church or chapel, hardly high enough within to allow a person to stand upright, and badly built of loose uncemented stones; the floor is the bare rock, in which, solid as it is, the body of St. Catherine is believed to have been miraculously buried by angels, after her martyrdom at Alexandria. I saw inscribed here the names of several European travellers, and among others that of the unfortunate M. Boutin, a French officer of engineers, who passed here in 1811. [M. Boutin came to Egypt from Zante; he first made a journey to the cataracts of Assouan, and then went to Bosseir, where he hired a ship for Mokha, but on reaching Yembo, Tousoun Pasha, the son of Mohammed Ali, would not permit him to proceed, he therefore returned to Suez, after visiting the convent of Sinai, and its neighbouring mountains. After his return to Cairo, he went to Siwah, to examine the remains of the temple of Jupiter Ammon, carrying with him a small boat built at Cairo, for the purpose of exploring the lake and the island in it, mentioned by Browne. He experienced great vexations from the inhabitants of Siwah; and the boat was of no use to him, owing to the shallowness of the lake, so that after a residence of three days at the Oasis, where he seems to have made no discoveries, he returned to Cairo in the company of some Augila merchants. On his way he passed the wood of petrified date trees discovered by Horneman; his route, I believe, was to the south of that of Horneman, and nearer the lesser Oasis. I had the pleasure of seeing him upon his return from Siwah, when I first arrived at Cairo. He remained two years in Egypt, and then continued his travels towards Syria, where he met with his death in 1816, in the mountainous district of the Nosayris, west of Hamah, having imprudently exposed himself with a great deal of baggage, in company only of his interpreter and servant, and without any native guide, to the robbers of that infamous tribe. He was a lover of truth, and a man of observation and enterprize; the public, therefore, and his own government, have to regret his death no less than his friends.] From this elevated peak a very extensive view opened before us, and the direction of the different surroundings chains of mountains could be distinctly traced. The upper nucleus of the Sinai, composed almost entirely of granite, forms a rocky wilderness of all irregular circular shape, intersected by many narrow valleys, and from thirty to forty miles in diameter. It contains the highest mountains of the peninsula, whose shaggy and pointed peaks and steep and shattered sides, render it clearly distinguishable from all the rest of the country in view. It is upon this highest region of the peninsula that the fertile valleys are found, which produce fruit trees; they are principally to the west and south-west of the convent at three or four hours distant.

Water too is always found in plenty in this district, on which account it is the place of refuge of all the Bedouins when the low country is parched up. I think it very probable that this upper country or wilderness is, exclusively, the desert of Sinai so often mentioned in the account of the wanderings of the Israelites. Mount St. Catherine appears to stand nearly in the centre of it. To the northward of this central region, and divided from it by the broad valley called Wady El Sheikh, and by several minor Wadys, begins a lower range of mountains, called Zebeir, which extends eastwards, having at one extremity the two peaks called El Djoze, above the plantations of Wady Feiran, and losing itself to the east in the more open country towards Wady Sal. Beyond the Zebeir northwards are sandy plains and valleys, which I crossed, towards the west, at Raml el Moral, and towards the east, about Hadhra.This part i [s] the most barren and destitute of water of the whole country. At its eastern extremity it is called El Birka. It borders to the north on the chain of El Tyh, which stretches in a regular line eastwards, parallel with the Zebeir, beginning at Sarbout el Djeinel. On reaching, in its eastern course, the somewhat higher mountain called El Odjme, it separates into two; one of its branches turns off in a right angle northward, and after continuing for about fifteen miles in that direction, again turns to the east, and extends parallel with the second and southern branch all across the peninsula, towards the eastern gulf. The northern branch, which is called El Dhelel, bounds the view from Mount St. Catherine. On turning to the east, I found that the mountains in this direction, beyond the high district of Sinai, run in a lower range towards the Wady Sal, and that the slope of the upper mountains is much less abrupt than on the opposite side. From Sal, east and north-east, the chains intersect each other in many irregular masses of inferior height, till they reach the gulf of Akaba, which I clearly distinguished when the sun was just rising over the mountains of the Arabian coast. Excepting the short extent from Noweyba to Dahab, the mountains bordering on the gulf are all of secondary height, but they rise to a considerable elevation between those two points. The country between Sherm, Nabk, and the convent, is occupied also by mountains of minor size, and the valleys, generally, are so narrow, that few of them can be distinguished from the point where I stood, the whole country, in that direction, appearing an uninterrupted wilderness of barren mountains. The highest points on that side appear to be above Wady Kyd, above the valley of Naszeb, and principally the peaks called Om Kheysyn and Masaoud.

The view to the south was bounded by the high mountain of Om Shomar, which forms a nucleus of itself, apparently unconnected with the upper Sinai, although bordering close upon it. To the right of this mountain I could distinguish the sea, in the neighbourhood of Tor, near which begins a low calcareous chain of mountains, called Djebel Hemam (i.e. death), not Hamam (or bath), extending along the gulf of Suez, and separated from the upper Sinai by a broad gravelly plain called El Kaa, across which the road from Tor to Suez passes. This plain terminates to the W.N.W. of Mount St. Catherine, and nearly in the direction of Djebel Serbal. Towards the Kaa, the central Sinai mountains are very abrupt, and leave no secondary intermediate chain between them and the plain at their feet. The mountain of Serbal, which I afterwards visited, is separated from the upper Sinai by some valleys, especially Wady Hebran, and it forms, with several neighbouring mountains, a separate cluster terminating in peaks, the highest of which appears to be as high as Mount St. Catherine. It borders on the Wady Feiran and the chain of Zebeir.

I took the following bearings, from the summit of Mount St. Catherine. These, together with those which I took from the peak of Om Shomar and from Serbal, and the distances and direction of my different routes, will serve to construct a map of the peninsula more detailed and accurate than any that has yet been published.

El Djoze, a rock distinguished by two peaks above that part of Wady Feiran where the date groves are, N.W. b. N.

Sarbout el Djemel, the beginning of Djebel Tyh, N.W. 1/4 N.

El Odjme, N. 1/2 E.

El Fereya, a high mountain of the upper Sinai region, N.N.E.

Zelka is in the same direction of N.N.E. It is a well, about one day's journey from the convent, on the upper route from the convent to Akaba, which traverses the chain of Tyh. The stations in that road, beyond Zelka, are, Ayn, Hossey, and Akaba. The bearing of Ayn was pointed out to me N.E. b. N.

The mountain over El Hadhra, a well which I passed on my road to Akaba, N.E. 1/2 E.

Senned, a secondary mountain between the upper Sinai and Hadhra, bordering upon Wady Sal; extends from E.N.E. to N.E.

Noweyba, E. We could not see the sea shore at Noweyba, but the high mountains over it were very conspicuous.

Wady Naszeb, on the northern road from Sherm to the convent, extended in a direction S.E. to E.S.E.

Dahab, on the eastern gulf, E.S.E.

Djebel Masaoud, a high mountain on the borders of the upper Sinai, S.E. b. E.

Wady Kyd, and the mountain over it, S.E.

The Island of Tyran, S S.E. 1/2 E.

Om Kheysyn, a high mountain between Sherm and the Sinai, S. 1/4 E.

The direction of Sherm was pointed out to me, a little to the eastward of south.

Djebel Thomman, a high peak, belonging to the mountains of Om Shomar, a little distant from the Sinai, S.

The peak of Om Shomar, S.S.W.

El Koly, a high peak of the upper Sinai, S.W. ½ S. At its foot passes the road from the convent to Tor.

The direction of Tor was pointed out to me S.W. The rocks of the upper Sinai, which constitute the borders of it in that direction, are called El Sheydek.

El Nedhadhyh, mountains likewise on the skirts of the upper Sinai, W. 1/4 S. Madscus, another peak of the upper Sinai, W. 1/4 N.

Serbal, N.W. 1/2 W. The well El Morkha, lying near the Birket Faraoun, in the common road from Tor to Suez, is in the same direction.

Om Dhad, N.W. This is the head of a Wady, called Wady Kebryt, on the outside of the Sinai chain.

Of the upper Sinai, the peaks of Djebel Mousa, of St. Catherine, of Om Thoman, of Koly, and of Fereya are the highest.

In making the preceding observations I was obliged to take out my compass and pencil, which greatly surprised the Arabs, who, seeing me in an Arab dress, and speaking their language, yet having the same pursuits as the Frank travellers whom they had seen here, were quite at a loss what to make of me. The suspicion was immediately excited, that I had ascended this mountain to practise some enchantment, and it was much increased by my further proceedings. The Bedouins supposed that I had come to carry off the rain, and my return to Cairo was, in consequence, much less agreeable than my journey from thence; indeed I might have been subjected to some unpleasant occurrences had not the faithful Hamd been by my side, who in the route back was of more service to me than all the Firmahns of the Pasha could have been.

We returned from Mount St. Catherine to the place where we had passed the night, and breakfasted with the Djebalye, for which payment was asked, and readily given. The conveying of pilgrims is one of the few modes of subsistence which these poor people possess, and at a place where strangers are continually passing, gratuitous hospitality is not to be expected from them, though they might be ready to afford it to the helpless traveller. The two days excursion to the holy places cost me about forty piastres, or five dollars.

Before mid-day we had again reached the convent El Erbayn, in the garden of which I passed a most agreeable afternoon. The verdure was so brilliant and the blossoms of the orange trees diffused so fine a perfume that I was transported in imagination from the barren cliffs of the wilderness to the luxurious groves of Antioch. It is surprising that the Europeans resident at Cairo do not prefer spending the season of the plague in these pleasant gardens, and this delightful climate, to remaining close prisoners in the infected city.

We returned in the evening to the convent, by following to the northward the valley in which the Erbayn stands. This valley is very narrow, and extremely stony, many large blocks having rolled from the mountains into it; it is called El Ledja, a name given to a similar rocky district, described by me, in the Haouran. At twenty minutes walk from the Erbayn we passed a block of granite, said to be the rock out of which the water issued when struck by the rod of Moses. It lies quite insulated by the side of the path, which is about ten feet higher than the lowest bottom of the valley. The rock is about twelve feet in height, of an irregular shape approaching to a cube. There are some apertures upon its surface, through which the water is said to have burst out; they are about twenty in number, and lie nearly in a straight line round the three sides of the stone. They are for the most part ten or twelve inches long, two or three inches broad, and from one to two inches deep, but a few of them are as deep as four inches. Every observer must be convinced, on the slightest examination, that most of these fissures are the work of art, but three or four perhaps are natural, and these may have first drawn the attention of the monks to the stone, and have induced them to call it the rock of the miraculous supply of water. Besides the marks of art evident in the holes themselves, the spaces between them have been chiselled, so as to make it appear as if the stone had been worn in those parts by the action of the water; though it cannot be doubted, that if water had flowed from the fissures it must generally have taken quite a different direction. One traveller saw on this stone twelve openings, answering to the number of the tribes of Israel; [Breydenbach.] another [Sicard, Mémoires des Missions.] describes the holes as a foot deep. They were probably told so by the monks, and believed what they heard rather than what they saw.

About one hundred and fifty paces farther on in the valley lies another piece of rock, upon which it seems that the work of deception was first begun, there being four or five apertures cut in it, similar to those on the other block, but in a less finished state; as it is somewhat smaller than the former, and lies in a less conspicuous part of the valley, removed from the public path, the monks probably thought proper in process of time to assign the miracle to the other. As the rock of Moses has been described by travellers of the fifteenth century, the deception must have originated among the monks of an earlier period. As to the present inhabitants of the convent and of the peninsula, they must be acquitted of any fraud respecting it, for they conscientiously believe that it is the very rock from whence the water gushed forth. In this part of the peninsula the Israelites could not have suffered from thirst: the upper Sinai is full of wells and springs, the greater part of which are perennial; and on whichever side the pretended rock of Moses is approached, copious sources are found within a quarter of an hour of it. The rock is greatly venerated by the Bedouins, who put grass into the fissures, as offerings to the memory of Moses, in the same manner as they place grass upon the tombs of their saints, because grass is to them the most precious gift of nature, and that upon which their existence chiefly depends. They also bring hither their female camels, for they believe that by making the animal couch down before the rock, while they recite some prayers, and by putting fresh grass into the fissures of the stone, the camels will become fertile, and yield an abundance of milk. The superstition is encouraged by the monks, who rejoice to see the infidel Bedouins venerating the same object with themselves.

Those who should attempt to weaken the faith of the monks and their visitors respecting this rock, would be now almost as blameable as the original authors of the imposture; for, such is the ignorance of the oriental Christians, and the impossibility of their obtaining any salutary instruction under the Turkish government, that were their faith in such miracles completely shaken, their religion would soon be entirely overthrown, and they would be left to wander in all the darkness of Atheism. It is curious to observe the blindness with which Christians as well as Turks believe in the pretended miracles of those who are interested in deceiving them. There is hardly a town in Syria or Egypt, where the Moslems have not a living saint, who works wonders, which the whole population is ready to attest as eye-witnesses. When I was at Damascus in 1812, some Christians returned thither from Jerusalem, where they had been to celebrate Easter. Some striking miracles said to have been performed by the Pope during his imprisonment at Savona, and which had been industriously propagated by the Latin priests in Syria, seem to have suggested to them the design of imitating his Holiness: the returning pilgrims unanimously declared, that when the Spanish priest of the convent of the Holy Sepulchre read the mass on Easter Sunday or Monday, upon the Mount of Olives, the whole assembled congregation saw him rise, while behind the altar, two or three feet in the air, and support himself in that position for several minutes, in giving the people his blessing. If any Christian of Damascus had expressed his doubts of the truth of this story, the monks of the convent there would have branded him with the epithet of Framasoun (Freemason), which among the Syrian Christians is synonymous with Atheist, and he would for ever have lost his character among his brethren.

A little farther down than the rock above described is shewn the seat of Moses, where it is said that he often sat; it is a small and apparently natural excavation in a granite rock, resembling a chair. Near this is the "petrified pot or kettle of Moses", a name given to a circular projecting knob in a rock, similar in size and shape to the lid of a kettle. The Arabs have in vain endeavoured to break this rock, which they suppose to contain great treasures.

As we proceeded from the rock of the miraculous supply of water along the valley El Ledja, I saw upon several blocks of granite, whose smooth sides were turned towards the path, inscriptions similar to those at Naszeb.

At forty minutes walk from Erbayn, where the valley El Ledja opens into the broad valley which leads eastwards to the convent, is a fine garden, with the ruins of a small convent, called El Bostan; water is conducted into it by a small channel from a spring in the Ledja. It was full of apricot trees, and roses in full blossom. A few Djebalye live here and take care of the garden. From hence to the convent is half an hour; in the way is shewn the head of the golden calf, which the Israelites worshipped, transmuted into stone. It is somewhat singular that both the monks and the Bedouins call it the cow's head (Ras el Bakar), and not the calf's, confounding it, perhaps, with the "red heifer," of which the Old Testament and the Koran speak. It is a stone half-buried in the ground, and bears some resemblance to the forehead of a cow. Some travellers have explained this stone to be the mould in which Aaron cast the calf, though it is not hollow but projecting; the Arabs and monks however gravely assured me that it was the "cow's" head itself. Beyond this object, towards the convent, a hill is pointed out to the left, called Djebel Haroun, because it is believed to be the spot where Aaron assembled the seventy elders of Israel. Both this and the cow's head have evidently received these denominations from the monks and Bedouins, in order that they may multiply the objects of veneration and curiosity within the pilgrim's tour round the convent.

On my return to the convent I could not help expressing to several of the monks my surprise at the metamorphosis of a calf into a cow, and of an idol of gold into stone; but I found that they were too little read in the books of Moses to understand even this simple question, and I therefore did not press the subject. I believe there is not a single individual amongst them, who has read the whole of the Old Testament; nor do I think that among eastern Christians in general there is one in a thousand, of those who can read, that has ever taken that trouble. They content themselves, in general, with their prayer-books, liturgies, and histories of saints; few of them read the gospels, though more do so in Syria than in Egypt; the reading of the whole of the scripture is discountenanced by the clergy; the wealthy seldom have the inclination to prosecute the study of the Holy writings, and no others are able to procure a manuscript copy of the Bible, or one printed in the two establishments in Mount Libanus. The well meant endeavours of the Bible Society in England to supply them with printed copies of the Scriptures in Arabic, if not better directed than they have hitherto been, will produce very little effect in these countries. The cost of such a copy, trifling as it may seem in England, is a matter of importance to the poor Christians of the east; the Society has, besides, chosen a version which is not current in the east, where the Roman translation alone is acknowledged by the Clergy, who easily make their flocks believe that the Scriptures have been interpolated by the Protestants. It would, perhaps, have been better if the Society, in the beginning at least, had furnished the eastern Christians with cheap copies of the Gospels and Psalms only, which being the books chiefly in use among them in manuscript, would have been not only useful to them, but more approved of by the directors of their consciences, than the entire Scripture. Upon Mohammedans, it is vain to expect that the reading of the present Arabic version of the Bible should make the slightest impression. If any of them were brought to conquer their inherent aversion to the book, they could not read a page in it without being tired and disgusted with its style. In the Koran they possess the purest and most elegant composition in their language, the rhythmical prose of which, exclusive of the sacred light in which they hold it, is alone sufficient to make a strong impression upon them. The Arabic of the greater part of the Bible, on the contrary, and especially that of the Gospels, is in the very worst style; the books of Moses and the Psalms are somewhat better. Grammatical rules, it is true, are observed, and chosen terms are sometimes employed; but the phraseology and whole construction is generally contrary to the spirit of the language, and so uncouth, harsh, affected, and full of foreign idioms, that no Musselman scholar would be tempted to prosecute the study of it, and a few only would thoroughly understand it. In style and phraseology it differs from the Koran more than the monkish Latin from the orations of Cicero.

I will not take upon me to declare how far the Roman and the Society's Arabic translation of the Old Testament are defective, being unable to read the original Hebrew text; but I can affirm that they both disagree, in many instances, from the English translation. The Christians of the East, who will seldom read any book written by a Moslem, and to whom an accurate knowledge of Arabic and of the best writers in that language are consequently unknown, are perfectly satisfied with the style of the Roman version which is in use among them; it is for the sake of perusing it that they undertake a grammatical study of the Arabic language, and their priests and learned men usually make it the model of their own style; they would be unwilling therefore to admit any other translation; and there is not, at present, either in Syria or in Egypt any Christian priest so bold and so learned as Bishop Germanus Ferhat of Aleppo, who openly expressed his dislike of this translation, and had declared his intention of altering it himself, for which, and other reasons, he was branded with the epithet of heretic. For Arab Christians, therefore, the Roman translation will not easily be superseded, and if Mussulmans are to be tempted to study the Scriptures, they must be clothed in more agreeable language, than that which has lately been presented to them, for they are the last people upon whom precepts conveyed in rude language will have any effect.

In the present state of western Asia, however, the conversion of Mohammedans is very difficult; I have heard only of one instance during the last century, and the convert was immediately shipped off to Europe. On the other hand, should an European power ever obtain a firm footing in Egypt, it is probable that many years would not elapse before thousands of Moslems would profess Christianity; not from the dictates of their conscience or judgment, but from views of worldly interest.

I was cordially greeted on my return to the convent, by the monks and the fatherly Ikonómos, one of the best-natured churchmen I have met with in the East. The safe return of pilgrims from the holy mountains is always a subject of gratulation, so great is their dread of the Arabs. I rested the following day in the convent, where several Greeks from Tor and Suez had arrived; being friends of the monks, they were invited in the evening to the private apartments of the latter, where they were plied so bountifully with brandy that they all retired tipsy to bed.

Several Bedouins had acquainted me that a thundering noise, like repeated discharges of heavy artillery, is heard at times in these mountains; and they all affirmed that it came from Om Shomar. The monks corroborated the story, and even positively asserted that they had heard the sound about mid-day, five years ago, describing it in the same manner as the Bedouins. The same noise had been heard in more remote times, and the Ikonómos, who has lived here forty years, told me that he remembered to have heard the noise at four or five separate periods. I enquired whether any shock of an earthquake had ever been felt on such occasions, but was answered in the negative. Wishing to ascertain the truth, I prepared to visit the mountain of Om Shomar.

As I had lost much of the confidence of the Bedouins by writing upon the mountains, and could not intimidate them by shewing a passport from the Pasha, I kept my intended journey secret, and concerting matters with Hamd and two Djebalye, I was let down from the window of the convent a little before midnight on the 23rd of May, and found my guides well armed and in readiness below. We proceeded by Wady Sebaye, the same road I had come from Sherm. In this Wady, tradition says, the Israelites gained the victory over the Amalekites, which was obtained by the holding up of the hands of Moses (Ex. xvii. 12.), but this battle was fought in Raphidim, where the water gushed out from the rock, a situation which appears to have been to the westward of the convent, on the approach from the gulf of Suez.

I was much disappointed at being able to trace so very few of the ancient Hebrew names of the Old Testament in the modern names of the peninsula; but it is evident that, with the exception of Sinai and a few others, they are all of Arabic derivation.

On a descent from the summit of Wady Sebaye, at an hour and a half from the convent, we turned to the right from the road to Sherm, and entered Wady Owasz, in a direction S. b. W. I found here a small chain of white and red sand-stone hills in the midst of granite. The morning was so very cold that we were obliged to stop and light a fire, round which we sat till sunrise; my feet and hands were absolutely benumbed, for neither gloves or stockings are in fashion among Bedouins. We continued in the valley, crossing several hills, till at four hours and a half we reached Wady Rahaba, in the lower parts of which we had passed a very rainy night on the 17th. Rahaba is one of the principal valleys on this side of the peninsula; it is broad, and affords good pasturage. We halted under a granite rock in the middle of it, close by about a dozen small buildings, which are called by the Bedouins Makhsen (magazines), and which serve them as a place of deposit for their provision, clothes, money, &c. As Bedouins are continually moving about, they find it inconvenient to carry with them what they do not constantly want; they therefore leave whatever they have not immediate need of in these magazines, to which they repair as occasion requires. Almost every Bedouin in easy circumstances has one of them; I have met with them in several parts of the mountains, always in clusters of ten or twenty together. They are at most ten feet high, generally about ten or twelve feet square, constructed with loose stones, covered with the trunks of date trees, and closed with a wooden door and lock. These buildings are altogether so slight, and the doors so insecure, that a stone would be sufficient to break them open; no watchmen are left to guard them, and they are in such solitary spots that they might easily be plundered in the night, without the thief being ever discovered. But such is the good faith of the Towara towards each other, that robberies of this kind are almost unheard of; and their Sheikh Szaleh, whose magazine is well known to contain fine dresses, shawls, and dollars, considers his property as safe there as it would be in the best secured building in a large town. The Towara are well entitled to pride themselves on this trait in their character; for I found nothing similar to it among other Bedouins. The only instance upon record of a magazine having been plundered among them, is that mentioned in page 475, for which the robber's own father inflicted the punishment of death.

We continued our route in a side branch of the Rababa, till at the end of five hours and a half, we ascended a mountain, and then descended into a narrow valley, or rather cleft, between the rocks, called Bereika. The camel which I rode not being able to proceed farther on account of the rocky road, I left it here in charge of one of the Djebalye. This part of Sinai was completely parched up, no rain having fallen in it during the last winter. W.S.W. from hence, on entering a narrow pass called Wady Zereigye, we found the ground moist, there being a small well, but almost dried up; it would have cost us some time to dig it up to obtain water, which no longer rose above the surface, though it still maintained some verdure around it. This defile was thickly overgrown with fennel, three or four feet high; the Bedouins eat the stalks raw, and pretend that it cools the blood. Farther down we came to two copious springs, most picturesquely situated among the rocks, being overshaded by large wild fig-trees, a great number of which grow in other parts of this district. We descended the Zereigye by windings, and at the end of eight hours reached its lowest extremity, where it joins a narrow valley extending along the foot of Om Shomar, the almost perpendicular cliffs of which now stood before us. The country around is the wildest I had yet seen in these mountains; the devastations of torrents are every where visible, the sides of the mountains being rent by them in numberless directions; the surface of the sharp rocks is blackened by the sun; all vegetation is dry and withered; and the whole scene presents nothing but utter desolation and hopeless barrenness.

We ascended S.E. in the valley of Shomar, winding round the foot of the mountain for about an hour, till we reached the well of Romhan, at nine hours from the convent, where we rested. This is a fine spring; high grass grows in the narrow pass near it, with several date-trees and a gigantic fig-tree. Just above the well, on the side of the mountain, are the ruins of a convent, called Deir Antous; it was inhabited in the beginning of the last century, and according to the monks, it was the last convent abandoned by them. I found it mentioned in records of the fifteenth century in the convent; it was then one of the principal settlements, and caravans of asses laden with corn and other provisions passed by this place regularly from the convent to Tor, for this is the nearest road to that harbour, though it is more difficult than the more western route, which is now usually followed. The convent consisted of a small solid building, constructed with blocks of granite. I was told that date plantations are found higher up in the valley of Romhan, and that the monks formerly had their gardens there, of which some of the fruit trees still remain.

May 24th.—Early this morning I took Hamd with me to climb the Om Shomar, while the other man went with his gun in pursuit of some mountain-goats which he had seen yesterday at sunset upon the summit of a neighbouring mountain; he was accompanied by another Djebalye, whom we had met by chance. I had promised them a good reward if they should kill a goat, for I did not wish to have them near me, when examining the rocks upon the mountain. It took me an hour and a half to reach the top of Shomar, and I employed three hours in visiting separately all the surrounding heights, but I could no where find the slightest traces of a volcano, or of any volcanic productions, which I have not observed in any part of the upper Sinai. Om Shomar consists of granite, the lower stratum is red, that at the top is almost white, so as to appear from a distance like chalk; this arises from the large proportion of white feldspath in it, and the smallness of the particles of hornblende and mica. In the middle of the mountain, between the granite rocks, I found broad strata of brittle black slate, mixed with layers of quartz and feldspath, and with micaceous schistus. The quartz includes thin strata of mica of the most brilliant white colour, which is quite dazzling in the sun, and forms a striking contrast with the blackened surface of the slate and red granite.

The mountain of Om Shomar rises to a sharp-pointed peak, the highest summit of which, it is, I believe, impossible to reach; the sides being almost perpendicular, and the rock so smooth, as to afford no hold to the foot. I halted at about two hundred feet below it, where a beautiful view opened upon the sea of Suez, and the neighbourhood of Tor, which place was distinctly visible; at our feet extended the wide plain El Kaa. The southern side of this mountain is very abrupt, and there is no secondary chain, like those on the descent from Sinai to the sea, in every other direction. I have already mentioned the low chain called Hemam, which separates the Kaa from the gulf of Suez. In this chain, about five hours from Tor, northward, is the Djebel Nakous, or mountain of the Bell. On its side next the sea a mass of very fine sand, which has collected there, rushes down at times, and occasions a hollow sound, of which the Bedouins relate many stories; they compare it to the ringing of bells, and a fable is repeated among them, that the bells belong to a convent buried under the sands. The wind and weather are not believed to have any effect upon the sound.

Bearings from Om Shomar.

Tor, W.1.S. The usual road to Tor from the upper Sinai lies through the valley of El Ghor, not far distant to the N.W. of Shomar; to the south of El Ghor extends the chain of Djed el Aali; and another valley called El Shedek, entered from the Ghor, leads towards the lower plain

Djebel Serbal, N. 1/4 W.

The Djoze, over Feiran, N. 1/2 W.

Om Dhad, N.N.W.

Fera Soweyd, a high mountain between Om Shomar and Mount St. Catherine, N. b. E. It forms one range with the peak of Koly, which branches of from hence, N.E. b. N.

Mountain of Masaoud, E.

Mountain over Wady Kyd, E. 1/4 S.

We took a breakfast after our return to Romhan, and then descended by the same way we had come. In re-ascending Wady Zereigye we heard the report of a gun, and were soon after gratified by seeing our huntsman arrive at the place where we had left our camel, with a fine mountain goat. Immediately on killing it he had skinned it, taken out the entrails, and then put the carcase again into the skin, carrying it on his back, with the skin of the legs tied across his breast. No butcher in Europe can surpass a Bedouin in skinning an animal quickly; I have seen them strip a camel in less than a quarter of an hour; the entrails are very seldom thrown away; if water is at hand, they are washed, if not, they are roasted over the fire without washing; the liver and lungs of all animals are usually eaten raw, and many of the hungry bystanders are seen swallowing raw pieces of flesh. After a hearty dinner we descended, by a different path from that we had ascended, into the upper part of Wady Rahaba, in which we continued N.E. b. E. for two or three hours, when we halted at a well called Merdoud, at a little distance from several plantations of fruit-trees.

My departure from the convent had roused the suspicions of the Bedouins; they had learnt that I was going to Om Shomar, and two of them set out this morning by different routes, in order to intercept my return, intending no doubt to excite a quarrel with me respecting my visits to their mountains, in the hope of extorting money from me. We met one of them at this well, and he talked as loud and was as boisterous as if I had killed some of his kindred, or robbed his tent. After allowing him to vent his rage for half an hour, I began to speak to him in a very lofty tone, of my own importance at Cairo, and of my friendship with the Pasha; concluding by telling him, that the next time he went to Cairo I would have his camel seized by the soldiers. When he found that he could not intimidate me, he accepted of my invitation to be our guest for the night, and went in search of a neighbouring friend of his, who brought us an earthen pot, in which we cooked the goat.

May 25th.—At one hour below Merdoud we again fell in with Wady Owasz, and returned by the former road to the convent. The monks were in the greatest anxiety about me, for the Bedouins who had gone in search of me, had sworn that they would shoot me; and had even refused a small present offered to them by the Ikonómos to pacify them, expecting, no doubt, to obtain much more from myself; but they now returned, and obliged him to give them what he had offered them, pretending that it was for his sake only that they had spared my life; nor would the monks believe me when I assured them that I had been in no danger on this occasion.

I passed the following four days in the convent, and in several gardens and settlements of Djebalye at a little distance from it. I took this opportunity to look over some of the records of the convent which are written in Arabic, and I extracted several interesting documents relative to the state of the Bedouins in former times, and their affrays with the monks. In one, of the last century, is a list of the Ghafeyrs of the convent, not belonging to the Towara. These are,

El Rebabein, a small tribe belonging to the great Djeheyne tribe of the Hedjaz; a few families of the Rebabein have settled at Moeleh on the Arabian coast, and in the small villages in the vicinity of Tor. They serve as pilots in that part of the Red sea, and protect the convent's property about Tor.

El Heywat, El Syayhe, are small tribes living east of Akaba, among the dwelling-places of the Omran. El Reteymat, a tribe about Ghaza and Hebron. El Omarein, or Omran. El Hokouk, the principal tribe of he Tyaha. El Mesayd, a small tribe of the Sherkieh province of Egypt. El Alowein, a strong tribe north of Akaba. El Sowareka, in the desert between Sinai and Ghaza. El Terabein. El Howeytat. Oulad el Fokora, the principal branch of the tribe of Wahydat near Ghaza. Individuals of all these tribes are entitled to small yearly stipends and some clothing, and are bound to recover the property of the monks, when seized by any persons of their respective tribes. In one of the manuscripts I found the name of a Ghafeyr called Shamoul (Samuel), a Hebrew name I had never before met with among Arabs.

On the 29th, I was visited by Hassan Ibn Amer, the Sheikh of the Oulad Said, who is also one of the two principal Sheiks of the Towara, and in whose tent I had slept one night in my way to the convent. He begged me to lend him twenty dollars, which he promised to repay me at Cairo, as he wished to buy some sheep to be killed on the following day in honour of the saint Sheikh Szaleh. I told him that I never lent money to any body, but would willingly have made him a present of the sum if I had possessed it. He then said in many words, that if it had not been for his interference, the Bedouins would have waylaid and killed me in returning from Djebel Katerin. I told him that he and his tribe would have been responsible to the Pasha of Egypt for such an act; and in short that I never paid any tribute in the Pasha's dominions. It ended by my giving him a few pounds of coffeebeans, wrapped up in a good handkerchief, a few squares of soap, and a loaf of sugar, to present to his women, and thus we parted good friends. In the evening his brother came and also received a few trifles. He had brought a fat sheep to kill in honour of El Khoudher (St. George), a saint of the first class among Bedouins, and to whose intercession he thought himself indebted for the recovery of the health of his young wife. In the convent, adjoining to the outer wall, is a chapel dedicated to St. George; the Bedouins, who are not permitted to enter the convent, address their vows and prayers to him on the outside, just below the chapel. I was invited to partake of the repast prepared by the brother of Sheikh Hassan, and much against the advice of the monks, I let myself down the rope from the window, and sat below for several hours with the Arabs.

I was invited also to the great feast of Sheikh Szaleh, in Wady Szaleh, which was to take place on the morrow, but as I knew that Szaleh, the great chief of the Towara, was to be there, and would no doubt press me hardly by his inquiries why I had come without the Pasha's Firmahn; and as the Arabs were greatly exasperated against me for my late excursion to Om Shomar in addition to other causes of displeasure, I thought it very probable that I might be insulted amongst them, and I therefore determined to seize the opportunity of this general assembly in Wady Szaleh to begin my journey to Cairo; by so doing, I should also escape the disagreeable necessity of having Bedouin guides forced upon me. I engaged Hamd and his brother with two camels, and left the convent before dawn on the 30th, after having taken a farewell of the monks, and especially of the worthy Ikonómos, who presented me at parting with a leopard's skin, which he had lately bought of the Bedouins; together with several fine specimens of rock crystals, and a few small pieces of native cinnabar. The crystals are collected by the Arabs in one of the mountains not far distant from the convent, but in which of them I did not learn; I have seen some six inches in length, and one and a half in breadth; the greater part are of a smoky colour, with pyramidal tops. The cinnabar is said, by the Bedouins, to be found in great quantities upon Djebel Sheyger, a few hours to the N.E. of Wady Osh, the valley in which I slept, at an Arab encampment, two nights before I arrived at the convent from Suez.

May 30th.—We issued from the narrow valley in which the convent stands, into a broader one, or rather a plain, called El Raha, leaving on our right the road by which I first reached the convent. We continued in El Raha N.N.W. for an hour and an half, when we came to an ascent called Nakb el Raha, the top of which we reached in two hours from the convent. I had chosen this route, which is the most southern from the convent to Suez, in order to see Wady Feiran, and to ascend from thence the mountain Serbal, which, with Mount Saint Catherine and Shomar, is the highest peak in the peninsula. I had mentioned my intention to Hamd, who it appears communicated it this morning to his brother, for the latter left us abruptly at Nakb el Raha, saying that he had forgot his gun, giving his camel in charge to Hamd, and promising to join us lower down, as his tent was not far distant. Instead, however, of going home, he ran straight to the Arabs assembled at Sheikh Szaleh, and acquainted them with my designs. Their chiefs immediately dispatched a messenger to Feiran to enjoin the people there to prevent me from ascending Serbal; but, fortunately, I was already on my way to the mountain when the messenger reached Feiran, and on my return I had only to encounter the clamorous and now fruitless expostulations of the Arabs at that place.

We began to descend from the top of Nakb el Raha, by a narrow chasm, the bed of a winter torrent; direction N.W. by N. At the end of two hours and a quarter we halted near a spring called Kanaytar. Upon several blocks near it I saw inscriptions in the same character as those which I had before seen, but they were so much effaced as to be no longer legible. I believe it was in these parts that Niebuhr copied the inscriptions given in plate 49 of his Voyage. From the spring the descent was steep; in many parts I found the road paved, which must have been a work of considerable labour, and I was told that it had been done in former times at the expense of the convent. This road is the only one passable for camels, with the exception of the defile in which is the seat of Moses, in the way from the upper Sinai towards Suez. At three hours and three quarters from the convent we reached the foot of this mountain, which is bordered by a broad, gravelly valley. This is the boundary of the upper mountains of Sinai on this side; they extended in an almost perpendicular range on our right towards Wady Szaleh, and on our left in the direction W.N.W. We now entered Wady Solaf, "the valley of wine," coming from the N. or N.E. which here separates the upper Sinai range from the lower. At five hours we passed, to our right, a Wady coming from the north, called Abou Taleb, at the upper extremity of which is the tomb of the saint Abou Taleb, which the Bedouins often visit, and where there is an annual festival, like that of Sheikh Szaleh, but less numerously attended. Our road continued through slightly descending, sandy valleys; at the end of five hours and a quarter, after having passed several encampments without stopping, we turned N. by W. where a lateral valley branches off towards the sea shore, and communicates with the valley of Hebran, which divides the upper Sinai from the Serbal chain. Wady Hebran contains considerable date- plantations and gardens, and this valley and Wady Feiran are the most abundant in water of all the Wadys of the lower country. A route from the convent to Tor passes through Wady Hebran, which is longer than the usual one, but easier for beasts of burthen.

At six hours and three quarters we halted in Wady Solaf, as I found myself somewhat feverish, and in want of repose. We saw great numbers of red-legged partridges this day; they run with astonishing celerity along the rocky sides of the mountains, and as the Bedouins do not like to expend a cartridge upon so small a bird, they are very bold. When we lighted our fire in the evening, I was startled by the cries of Hamd "to take care of the venemous animal!" I then saw him kill a reptile like a spider, to which the Bedouins give the name of Abou Hanakein, or the two-mouthed; hanak meaning, in their dialect, mouth. It was about four inches and a half in length, of which the body was three inches; it has five long legs on both sides, covered, like the body, with setae of a light yellow colour; the head is long and pointed, with large black eyes; the mouth is armed with two pairs of fangs one above the other, recurved, and extremely sharp. Hamd told me that it never makes its appearance but at night, and is principally attracted by fire; indeed I saw three others during this journey, and always near the evening fire. The Bedouins entertain the greatest dread of them; they say that their bite, if not always mortal, produces a great swelling, almost instant vomiting, and the most excruciating pains. I believe this to be the Galeode phalangiste, at least it exactly resembles the drawing of that animal, given by Olivier in his Travels, pl. 42-4.

May 31st.—A good night's rest completely removed my feverish symptoms. Fatigue and a check of perspiration often produce slight fevers in the desert, which I generally cured by lying down near the fire, and drawing my mantle over my head, as the Bedouins always do at night. The Bedouins, before they go to rest, usually undress themselves entirely, and lie down quite naked upon a sheep's skin, which they carry for the purpose; they then cover themselves with every garment which they happen to have with them. Even in the hottest season they always cover the head and face when sleeping, not only at night but also during the midday hours.

We continued in Wady Solaf, which was entirely parched up, for an hour and three quarters, and passed to the left a narrower valley called Wady Keyfa, coming from the Serbal mountains. At two hours we passed Wady Rymm, which also comes from the same chain, and joins the Solaf; from thence we issued, at three hours, into the Wady el Sheik, the great valley of the western Sinai, which collects the torrents of a great number of smaller Wadys. There is not the smallest opening into these mountains, nor the slightest projection from them, that has not its name; but these names are known only to the Bedouins who are in the habit of encamping in the neighbourhood, while the more distant Bedouins are acquainted only with the names of the principal mountains and valleys. I have already mentioned several times the Wady el Sheikh; I found it here of the same noble breadth as it is above, and in many parts it was thickly overgrown with the tamarisk or Tarfa; it is the only valley in the peninsula where this tree grows, at present, in any great quantity, though small bushes of it are here and there met with in other parts. It is from the Tarfa that the manna is obtained, and it is very strange that the fact should have remained unknown in Europe, till M. Seetzen mentioned it in a brief notice of his tour to Sinai, published in the Mines de l'Orient. This substance is called by the Bedouins, Mann, and accurately resembles the description of Manna given in the Scriptures. In the month of June it drops from the thorns of the tamarisk upon the fallen twigs, leaves, and thorns which always cover the ground beneath that tree in the natural state; the manna is collected before sunrise, when it is coagulated, but it dissolves as soon as the sun shines upon it. The Arabs clean away the leaves, dirt, &c. which adhere to it, boil it, strain it through a coarse piece of cloth, and put it into leathern skins; in this way they preserve it till the following year, and use it as they do honey, to pour over their unleavened bread, or to dip their bread into. I could not learn that they ever make it into cakes or loaves. The manna is found only in years when copious rains have fallen; sometimes it is not produced at all, as will probably happen this year. I saw none of it among the Arabs, but I obtained a small piece of last year's produce, in the convent; where having been kept in the cool shade and moderate temperature of that place, it had become quite solid, and formed a small cake; it became soft when kept sometime in the hand; if placed in the sun for five minutes it dissolved; but when restored to a cool place it became solid again in a quarter of an hour. In the season, at which the Arabs gather it, it never acquires that state of hardness which will allow of its being pounded, as the Israelites are said to have done in Numbers, xi. 8. Its colour is a dirty yellow, and the piece which I saw was still mixed with bits of tamarisk leaves: its taste is agreeable, somewhat aromatic, and as sweet as honey. If eaten in any considerable quantity it is said to be slightly purgative.

The quantity of manna collected at present, even in seasons when the most copious rains fall, is very trifling, perhaps not amounting to more than five or six hundred pounds. It is entirely consumed among the Bedouins, who consider it the greatest dainty which their country affords. The harvest is usually in June, and lasts for about six weeks; sometimes it begins in May. There are only particular parts of the Wady Sheikh that produce the tamarisk; but it is also said to grow in Wady Naszeb, the fertile valley to the S.E. of the convent, on the road from thence to Sherm.

In Nubia and in every part of Arabia the tamarisk is one of the most common trees; on the Euphrates, on the Astaboras, in all the valleys of the Hedjaz, and the Bedja, it grows in great plenty, but I never heard of its producing manna except in Mount Sinai; it is true I made no inquiries on the subject elsewhere, and should not, perhaps, have learnt the fact here, had I not asked repeated questions respecting the manna, with a view to an explanation of the Scriptures. The tamarisk abounds more in juices than any other tree of the desert, for it retains its vigour when every vegetable production around it is withered, and never loses its verdure till it dies. It has been remarked by Niebuhr, (who, with his accustomed candour and veracity says, that during his journey to Sinai he forgot to enquire after the manna), that in Mesopotamia manna is produced by several trees of the oak species; a similar fact was confirmed to me by the son of the Turkish lady, mentioned in a preceding page, who had passed the greater part of his youth at Erzerum in Asia Minor; he told me that at Moush, a town three or four days distant from Erzerum, a substance is collected from the tree which produces the galls, exactly similar to the manna of the peninsula, in taste and consistence, and that it is used by the inhabitants instead of honey. We descended the Wady el Sheikh N.W. by W. Upon several projecting rocks of the mountain I saw small stone huts, which Hamd told me were the work of infidels in ancient times; they were probably the cells of the hermits of Sinai. Their construction is similar to that of the magazines already mentioned, but the stones although uncemented, are more carefully placed in the walls, and have thus resisted the force of torrents. Upon the summits of three different mountains to the right were small ruined towers, originally perhaps, chapels, dependant on the episcopal see of Feiran. In descending the valley the mountains on both sides approach so near, that a defile of only fifteen or twenty feet across is left; beyond this they again diverge, when a range of the same hills of Tafel, or yellow pipe-clay are seen, which I observed in the higher parts of this Wady. At the end of four hours we entered the plantations of Wady Feiran, through a wood of tamarisks, and halted at a small date-garden belonging to my guide Hamd. Wady Feiran is a continuation of Wady el Sheikh, and is considered the finest valley in the whole peninsula. From the upper extremity, where we alighted, an uninterrupted row of gardens and date- plantations extends downwards for four miles. In almost every garden is a well, by means of which the grounds are irrigated the whole year round, exactly in the same manner as those in the Hedjaz above Szafra and Djedeyde. Among the date-trees are small huts where reside the Tebna Arabs, a branch of the Djebalye, who serve as gardeners to the Towara Bedouins, especially to the Szowaleha, who are the owners of the ground; they take one-third of the fruit for their labour. The owners seldom visit the place, except in the date harvest, when the valley is filled with people for a month or six weeks; at that season they erect huts of palm-branches, and pass their time in conviviality, receiving visits, and treating their guests with dates. The best species of these is called Djamya, of which the monks send large boxes annually to Constantinople as presents, after having taken out the stone of the date, and put an almond in its place. The Nebek (Rhamnus Lotus), the fruit of which is a favourite food of the Bedouins, grows also in considerable quantity at Wady Feiran. They grind the dried fruit together with the stone, and preserve the meal, called by them Bsyse, in leathern skins, in the same manner as the Nubian Bedouins do. It is an excellent provision for journeying in the desert, for it requires only the addition of butter-milk to make a most nourishing, agreeable, and refreshing diet.

The Tebna cultivators are very poor; they possess little or no landed property, and are continually annoyed by visits from the Bedouins, whom they are under the necessity of receiving with hospitality. Their only profitable branch of culture is tobacco, of which they raise considerable quantities; it is of the same species as that grown in the mountains of Arabia Petraea, about Wady Mousa and Kerek, which retains its green colour even when dry. It is very strong, and esteemed for this quality by the Towara Bedouins, who are all great consumers of tobacco, and who are chiefly supplied with it from Wady Feiran; they either smoke it, or chew it mixed with natron or with salt. Tobacco has acquired here such a currency in trade, that the Tebna buy and sell minor articles among themselves by the Mud or measure of tobacco. The other vegetable productions of the valley are cucumbers, gourds, melons, hemp for smoking, onions, a few Badendjans, and a few carob trees. As for apple, pear, or apricot trees, &c. they grow only in the elevated regions of the upper Sinai, where in different spots are about thirty or forty plantations of fruit trees; in a very few places wheat and barley are sown, but the crops are so thin that they hardly repay the labour of cultivation, although the cultivator has the full produce without any deduction. The soil is every where so stony, that it is impossible to make it produce corn sufficient for even the smallest Arab tribe.

The narrowness of the valley of Feiran, which is not more than an hundred paces across, the high mountains on each side, and the thick woods of date-trees, render the heat extremely oppressive, and the unhealthiness of the situation is increased by the badness of the water. The Tebna are far from being as robust and healthy as their neighbours, and in spring and summer dangerous fevers reign here. The few among them who have cattle, live during those seasons under tents in the mountains, leaving a few persons in care of the trees.

As Mount Serbal forms a very prominent feature in the topography of the peninsula, I was determined if possible to visit it, and Hamd having never been at the top of it, I was under the necessity of inquiring for a guide. None of the Tebna present knew the road, but I found a young man who guided us to the tent of a Djebalye, which was pitched in the lower heights of Serbal, and who being a great sportsman, was known to have often ascended the mountain. Leaving the servant with the camels, I set out in the evening on foot with Hamd and the guide, carrying nothing with us but some butter-milk in a small skin, together with some meal, and ground Nebek, enough to last us for two days. We ascended Wady el Sheikh for about three quarters of an hour, and then turned to the right, up a narrow valley called Wady Ertama in the higher part of which a few date-trees grow. In crossing over a steep ascent at its upper extremity, I met with several inscriptions on insulated blocks, consisting only of one line in the usual ancient character; but I did not copy them, being desirous to conceal from my new guide that I was a writing man, as it might have induced him to dissuade the Arabs in the mountains from accompanying me farther up. On the other side of this ascent we fell in with Wady Rymm, which I have already mentioned, and found here the ruins of a small village, the houses of which were built entirely with hewn stone, in a very solid manner. Some remains of the foundations of a large edifice are traceable; a little lower down in the valley are some date trees, with a well, which probably was the first cause of building a village in this deserted spot, for the whole country round is a wilderness of rocks, and the valley itself is not like those below, flat and sandy, but covered with large stones which have been washed down by torrents. From hence an ascent of half an hour brought us to the Djebalye Arab, who was of the Sattala tribe: he had pitched here two tents, in one of which lived his own, and in the other his son's family; he spent the whole day in hunting, while the women and younger children took care of the cattle, which found good pasturage among the rocks. It was near sunset when we arrived, and the man was rather startled at our visit, though he received us kindly, and soon brought us a plentiful supper. When I asked him if he would show me the way to the summit of the Serbal, which was now directly before us, he expressed great astonishment, and no doubt immediately conceived the notion that I had come to search for treasures, which appears the more probable to these Bedouins, as they know that the country was formerly inhabited by rich monks. Prepossessed with this idea, and knowing that nobody then present was acquainted with the road, except himself, he thought he might demand a most exorbitant sum from me. He declined making any immediate bargain, and said that he would settle it the next morning.

June 1st.—We rose before daylight, when the Djebalye made coffee, and then told me, that he could not think of accompanying me for less than sixty piastres. As the whole journey was to last only till the evening, and I knew that for one piastre any of these Bedouins will run about the mountains on messages for a whole day, I offered him three piastres, but he was inflexible, and replied, that were it not for his friendship for Hamd, he would not take less than a hundred piastres. I rose to eight piastres, but on his smiling, and shrugging up his shoulders at this, I rose, and declared that we would try our luck alone.

We took our guns and our provision sack, filled our water skin at a neighbouring well, called Ain Rymm, and began ascending the mountain straight before us. I soon began to wish that I had come to some terms with the Djebalye; we walked over sharp rocks without any path, till we came to the almost perpendicular side of the upper Serbal, which we ascended in a narrow difficult cleft. The day grew excessively hot, not a breath of wind was stirring, and it took us four hours to climb up to the lower summit of the mountain, where I arrived completely exhausted. Here is a small plain with some trees, and the ruins of a small stone reservoir for water. On several blocks of granite are inscriptions, but most of them are illegible; I copied the two following: [not included].

After reposing a little, I ascended the eastern peak, which was to our left hand, and reached its top in three quarters of an hour, after great exertions, for the rock is so smooth and slippery, as well as steep, that even barefooted as I was, I was obliged frequently to crawl upon my belly, to avoid being precipitated below; and had I not casually met with a few shrubs to grasp, I should probably have been obliged to abandon my attempt, or have rolled down the cliff. The summit of the eastern peak consists of one enormous mass of granite, the smoothness of which is broken only by a few partial fissures, presenting an appearance not unlike the ice-covered peaks of the Alps. The sides of the peak, at a few paces below its top, are formed of large insulated blocks twenty or thirty feet long, which appeared as if just suspended, in the act of rushing down the steep. Near the top I found steps regularly formed with large loose stones, which must have been brought from below, and so judiciously arranged along the declivity, that they have resisted the devastations of time, and may still serve for ascending. I was told afterwards that these steps are the continuation of a regular path from the bottom of the mountain; which is in several parts cut through the rock with great labour. If we had had the guide, we should have ascended by this road, which turns along the southern and eastern side of Serbal. The mountain has in all five peaks; the two highest are that to the east, which I ascended, and another immediately west of it; these rise like cones, and are distinguishable from a great distance, particularly on the road to Cairo.

The eastern peak, which from below looks as sharp as a needle, has a platform on its summit of about fifty paces in circumference. Here is a heap of small loose stones, about two feet high, forming a circle about twelve paces in diameter. Just below the top I found on every granite block that presented a smooth surface, inscriptions, the far greater part of which were illegible. I copied the three following, from different blocks; the characters of the first are a foot long.

There are small caverns large enough to shelter a few persons, between some of the masses of stone. On the sides of these caverns are numerous inscriptions similar to those given above.

As the eye is very apt to be deceived with regard to the relative heights of mountains, I will not give any positive opinion as to that of Mount Serbal; but it appeared to me to be higher than all the peaks, including Mount St. Catherine, and very little lower than Djebel Mousa.

The fact of so many inscriptions being found upon the rocks near the summit of this mountain, and also in the valley which leads from its foot to Feiran, as will presently be mentioned; together with the existence of the road leading up to the peak, afford strong reasons for presuming that the Serbal was an ancient place of devotion. It will be recollected that no inscriptions are found either on the mountain of Moses, or on Mount St. Catherine; and that those which are found in the Ledja valley at the foot of Djebel Katerin, are not to be traced above the rock, from which the water is said to have issued, and appear only to be the work of pilgrims, who visited that rock. From these circumstances, I am persuaded that Mount Serbal was at one period the chief place of pilgrimage in the peninsula: and that it was then considered the mountain where Moses received the tables of the law; though I am equally convinced, from a perusal of the Scriptures, that the Israelites encamped in the Upper Sinai, and that either Djebel Mousa or Mount St. Catherine is the real Horeb. It is not at all impossible that the proximity of Serbal to Egypt, may at one period have caused that mountain to be the Horeb of the pilgrims, and that the establishment of the convent in its present situation, which was probably chosen from motives of security, may have led to the transferring of

411

that honour to Djebel Mousa. At present neither the monks of Mount Sinai nor those of Cairo consider Mount Serbal as the scene of any of the events of sacred history: nor have the Bedouins any tradition among them respecting it; but it is possible that if the Byzantine writers were thoroughly examined, some mention might be found of this mountain, which I believe was never before visited by any European traveller.

The heat was so oppressive during the whole day, that I felt it even on the summit of the mountain; the air was motionless, and a thin mist pervaded the whole atmosphere, as always occurs in these climates, when the air is very much heated. I took from the peak the following bearings.

El Morkha, a well near Birket Faraoun on the road from Tor to Suez, N.W. b. W.

Wady Feiran, N.W.N.

Sarbout el Djemal, N.N.W.

El Djoze, just over Feiran, N.

Mountain Dhellel, N. b. E.-N.E. b. N.

Wady Akhdar, which I passed on my road from Suez to the convent, N.E. 1/2 E.

Wady el Sheikh, where it appears broadest, and near the place where I had entered it, in coming from Suez, E.N.E.

Sheikh Abou Taleb, the tomb of a saint mentioned above, E. 1/2 S.

Nakb el Raha, from whence the road from the convent to Feiran begins to descend from the upper Sinai, E.S.E.

Mount St. Catherine, S.E. 1/2 E.

Om Shomar, S.S.E.

Daghade,, a fertile valley in the mountains, issuing into the plain of Kaa, S.W.

The direction of Deir Sigillye was pointed out to me S. b. E. or S.S.E. This is a ruined convent on the S.E. side of Serbal, near the road which leads up to the summit of the mountain. It is said to be well built and spacious, and there is a copious well near it. It is four or five hours distant by the shortest road from Feiran, and lies in a very rocky district, at present uninhabited even by Bedouins.

I found great difficulty in descending. If I had had a plentiful supply of water, and any of us had known the road, we should have gone down by the steps; but our water was nearly exhausted, and in this hot season, even the hardy Bedouin is afraid to trust to the chance only of finding a path or a spring. I was therefore obliged to return by the same way which I had ascended and by crawling, rather than walking, we reached the lower platform of Serbal just about noon, and reposed under the shade of a rock. Here we finished our stock of milk and of water; and Hamd, who remembered to have heard once that a well was in this neighbourhood, went in search of it, but returned after an hour's absence, with the empty skin. I was afterwards informed, that in a cleft of the rock, not far from the stone tank, which I have already mentioned, there is a small source which never dries up. We had yet a long journey to make, Hamd, therefore, volunteered to set out before me, to fill the skin in the valley below, and to meet me with it at the foot of the cleft; by which we had entered the mountain. He departed, leaping down the mountain like a Gazelle, and after prolonging my siesta I leisurely followed him, with the other Arab. When we arrived, at the end of two hours and a half, at the point agreed upon, we found Hamd waiting for us with the water, which he had brought from a well at least five miles distant. A slight shower of rain which had fallen, instead of cooling the air appeared only to have made it hotter.

Instead of pursuing, from our second halting-place, the road by which we had ascended in the morning from Ain Rymm, we took a more western direction, to the left of the former, and reached by a less rapid descent, the Wady Aleyat, which leads to the lower parts of Wady Feiran. After a descent of an hour, we came to a less rocky country.

At the end of an hour and a half from the foot of Serbal, where Hamd had waited for us, we reached the well, situated among date-plantations, where he had filled the skins; its water is very good, much better than that of Feiran. The date-trees are not very thickly planted; amongst them I saw several Doum trees, some of which I had already observed in other parts of the peninsula. This valley is inhabited by Bedouins during the date-harvest, and here are many huts, built of stones, or of date-branches, which they then occupy.

In the evening we continued our route in the valley Aleyat, in the direction N.W. To our right was a mountain, upon the top of which is the tomb of a Sheikh, held in great veneration by the Bedouins, who frequently visit it, and there sacrifice sheep. It is called El Monadja. The custom among the Bedouins of burying their saints upon the summits of mountains accords with a similar practice of the Israelites; there are very few Bedouin tribes who have not one or more tombs of protecting saints (Makam), in whose honour they offer sacrifices; the custom probably originated in their ancient idolatrous worship, and was in some measure retained by the sacrifices enjoined by Mohammed in the great festivals of the Islam.

In many parts of this valley stand small buildings, ten or twelve feet square, and five feet high, with very narrow entrances. They are built with loose stones, but so well put together, that the greater part of them are yet entire, notwithstanding the annual rains. They are all quite empty. I at first supposed them to be magazines belonging to the Arabs, but my guides told me that their countrymen never entered them, because they were Kobour el Kofar, or tombs of infidels; perhaps of the early Christians of this peninsula. I did not, however, meet with any similar structures in other parts of the peninsula, unless those already mentioned in the upper part of Wady Feiran, are of the same class. At half an hour from the spring and date-trees, we passed to our left a valley coming from the southern mountains, called Wady Makta, and half an hour farther on, at sunset, we reached Wady Feiran, at the place where the date plantations terminate, and an hour's walk below the spot from whence we set out yesterday upon this excursion On many stones were drawings of goats and camels. This was once probably the main road to the top of Serbal, which continued along its foot, and turned by Deir Sigillye round its eastern side, thus passing the cleft and the road by which we had ascended, and which nowhere bears traces of having ever been a regular and frequented route.

After my departure in the morning for Mount Serbal, the messenger dispatched by the Arabs assembled in Sheikh Szaleh, arrived at Wady Feiran, and forbad the people from guiding me to the top of Serbal; the news of this order had spread along the whole valley, so that on our reaching the first habitations under the date-trees, where I intended to rest for the night, all the Arabs assembled, and became extremely clamorous as well against me, as against Hamd for having accompanied me. I cared but little for their insolent language, which I knew how to reply to, but I was under some apprehensions for my servant and baggage, and therefore determined to rejoin them immediately. We ascended the valley, by a gentle slope, and reached Hamd's garden late at night, greatly fatigued, for we had been almost the whole day upon our legs. We here met the Bedouins and their girls occupied in singing and dancing, which they kept up till near midnight.

June 2d.—When I awoke I found about thirty Arabs round me, ready to begin a new quarrel about my pursuits in their mountains. When they saw that I paid little attention to their remonstrances, and was packing up my effects, in order to proceed on my journey, they then asked me for some victuals and coffee. After having observed to them that I was more easily prevailed upon by civility than harshness, I distributed among the poorest such provisions as I should not want on my way back to Suez, together with some coffee-beans and soap. This immediately put them into good humour, and in return, they brought me some milk, cucumbers, and a quantity of Bsyse, or ground Nebek. I purchased from them a skinful of dates reduced to a paste, and one of them joined us for the sake of travelling in our company to Suez, where he intended to sell a load of charcoal; we then set out, leaving every body behind us well satisfied.

We followed the same road by which we had ascended last night, and halted again where the date trees terminate. Here the same Arabs whom we had found yesterday evening, having been informed that I had made some presents where I had slept, thought, no doubt, that by being vociferous they would obtain something. In this, however, they were mistaken, for I gave them nothing, telling them they might seize my baggage if they chose, but this they prudently declined to do. Ten years ago I should hardly have been able to extricate myself in this manner.

The valley of Feiran widens considerably where it is joined by the Wady Aleyat, and is about a quarter of an hour in breadth. Upon the mountains on both sides of the road stand the ruins of an ancient city. The houses are small, but built entirely of stones, some of which are hewn and some united with cement, but the greater part are piled up loosely. I counted the ruins of about two hundred houses. There are no traces of any large edifice on the north side; but on the southern mountain there is an extensive building, the lower part of which is of stone, and the upper part of earth. It is surrounded by private habitations, which are all in complete ruins. At the foot of the southern mountain are the remains of a small aqueduct. Upon several of the neighbouring hills are ruins of towers, and as we proceeded down the valley for about three quarters of an hour, I saw many small grottos in the rocks on both sides, hewn in the rudest manner, and without any regularity or symmetry; the greater part seemed to have been originally formed by nature, and afterwards widened by human labour. Some of the largest which were near the ruined city had, perhaps, once served as habitations, the others were evidently sepulchres; but few of them were large enough to hold three corpses, and they were not more than three or four feet high. I found no traces of antiquity in any of them.

At half an hour from the last date-trees of Feiran, I saw, to the right of the road, upon the side of the mountain, the ruins of a small town or village, the valley in the front of which is at present quite barren. It had been better built than the town above described, and contained one very good building of hewn stone, with two stories, each having five oblong windows in front. The roof has fallen in. The style of architecture of the whole strongly resembles that seen in the ruins of St. Simon, to the north of Aleppo, the mountains above which are also full of sepulchral grottos, like those near Feiran. The roofs of the houses appear to have been entirely of stone, like those in the ruined towns of the Haouran, but flat, and not arched. There were here about a hundred ruined houses.

Feiran was formerly the seat of a Bishopric. Theodosius was bishop during the Monothelite controversy. From documents of the fifteenth century, still existing in the convent of Mount Sinai, there appears at that time to have been an inhabited convent at Feiran. Makrizi, the excellent historian, and describer of Egypt; who wrote about the same time, gives the following account of Feiran, which he calls Faran. [The present Bedouins call it Fyran or Feiran, and thus it is spelt wherever it occurs in the Arabic documents in the convent. Niebuhr calls it Faran.]

"It is one of the towns of the Amalakites, situated near the borders of the sea of Kolzoum, upon a hill between two mountains; on each of which are numberless excavations, full of corpses. It is one day's journey distant [in a straight line] from the sea of Kolzoum, the shore of which is there called "the shore of the sea of Faran;" there it was that Pharaoh was drowned by the Almighty. Between the city of Faran and the Tyh are two days journey. It is said that Faran is the name of the mountains of Mekka, and that it is the name of other mountains in the Hedjaz, and that it is the place mentioned in the books of Moses. But the truth is, that Tor and Faran are two districts belonging to the southern parts of Egypt, and that it is not the same as the Faran (Paran) mentioned in the books of Moses. It is stated, that the mountains of Mekka derive their name from Faran Ibn Amr Ibn Amalyk. Some call them the mountains of Faran others Fyran. The city of Faran was one of the cities belonging to Midian, and remained so until the present times. There are plenty of palmtrees there, of the dates of which I have myself eaten. A large river flows by. The town is at present in ruins; Bedouins only pass there."

Makrizi is certainly right in supposing that the Faran or Paran mentioned in the Scriptures is not the same as Feiran; an opinion which has been entertained also by Niebuhr, and other travellers. From the passage in Numbers xiii. 26, it is evident that Paran was situated in the desert

416

of Kadesh, which was on the borders of the country of the Edomites, and which the Israelites reached after their departure from Mount Sinai, on their way towards the land of Edom. Paran must therefore be looked for in the desert west of Wady Mousa, and the tomb of Aaron which is shewn there. At present the people of Feiran bury their dead higher up in the valley, than the ancient ruins in the neighbourhood of Sheikh Abou Taleb. There is no rivulet, but in winter time the valley is completely flooded, and a large stream of water collected from all the lateral valleys of Wady el Sheikh empties itself through Wady Feiran into the gulf of Suez near the Birket Faraoun.

We rode for one hour from Feiran, and then stopped near some date trees called Hosseye, where are several Arab huts, and where good water is found. Here I remained the rest of the day, as I felt very much the effect of yesterday's exertions. In the evening all the females quitted the huts to join in the Mesámer, in which I also participated, and we kept it up till long after midnight. My servant [This was the same man who had accompanied me during my journey to Upper Egypt, as far as Assouan. I again engaged him in my service after my return fro [m] the Hedjaz.] attempted to join the party, but the proud Arabs told him that he was a Fellah, not of good breed, and would not permit him to mix in the dance. He met with the same repulse last night at Feiran.

June 3d.—We followed the valley by a slight slope through its windings W.N.W. and N.W. Many tamarisk trees grow here, and some manna is collected. The fertility of these valleys is owing chiefly to the alluvial soil brought down from the mountains by the torrents, and which soon acquires consistence in the bottom of the Wady; but if a year passes without rain these alluvia are reduced to dust, and dispersed by the winds over the mountains from whence they came. The surface was covered with a yellow clay in which a variety of herbs was growing. At two hours the valley, for the length of about an hour, bears the name of Wady el Beka, or the valley of weeping, from the circumstance, as it is related, of a Bedouin who wept because his dromedary fell here, during the pursuit of an enemy, and he was thus unable to follow his companions, who were galloping up the valley towards Feiran. The rock on the side of the road is mostly composed of gneiss. At three hours and a half we passed to our right Wady Romman. I was told that in the mountains from which it descends is a fine spring, and some date- trees about four hours distant. The road now turned N.W. b. W.; the granite finishes and sand-stone begins; among the latter rock-salt is found. At five hours we halted under a large impending sandstone rock, where the valley widens considerably, and continues in a W. direction down to the sea-side. Leaving this valley to the left, we rode in the afternoon N.W. b. W. ascending slightly over rocky ground, until we reached an upper plain at the end of six hours. The chain of granite mountains continued to our right, parallel with the road, which was overspread with silex, and farther on we met with a kind of basaltic tufa, forming low hills covered with sand. We then descended, and at six hours and a half entered the valley called Wady Mokatteb. The appellation of Djebel Mokatteb, which several travellers have applied to the neighbouring mountains, is not in use. To the north of the entrance of this valley near the foot of the higher chain, is a cluster of magazines of the Bedouins, at a spot called El Bedja.

The Wady Mokatteb extends for three hours march in the direction N.W.; in the upper part it is three miles across, having to the right high mountains, and to the left a chain of lower sandrocks. Half way down, it becomes narrower, and then takes the name of Seyh Szeder. In most places the sand-rocks present abrupt cliffs, twenty or thirty feet in height. Large masses have separated themselves from the cliffs and lie at their feet in the valley. These cliffs and rocks are thickly covered with inscriptions, which are continued with intervals of a few hundred paces only, for at least two hours and a half; similar inscriptions are found in the lower part of the Wady, where it narrows, upon the sand-stone rocks of the opposite, or north-eastern side of the valley. To copy all these inscriptions would occupy a skilful draughtsman six or eight days; they are all of the same description as those I have already mentioned, consisting of short lines, written from right to left, and with the singular character represented, invariably at the beginning of each. Some of them are on rocks at a height of twelve or fifteen feet, which must have required a ladder to ascend to them. They are in general cut deeper than those on the granite in the upper country, but in the same careless style. Amongst them are many in Greek; containing, probably, like the others, the names of those who passed here on their pilgrimage to the holy mountain. Some of the latter contain Jewish names in Greek characters. There is a vast number of drawings of mountain goats and of camels, the latter sometimes represented as loaded, and with riders on their backs. Crosses are also seen, indicating that the inscribers were Christians. It should be observed that the Mokatteb lies in the principal route to Sinai, and which is much easier and more frequented than the upper road by Naszeb, which I took in my way to the convent; the cliffs also are so situated as to afford a fine shade to travellers during the mid-day hours. To these circumstances may undoubtedly in great measure be attributed the numerous inscriptions found in this valley.

We rested for the night, after a day's march of nine hours and a quarter, near the lower extremity of the Seyh Szeder, and just beyond the last of the inscriptions. The bottom of the valley is here rocky, and as flat as if the rock had been levelled by art.

June 4th.—At a few hundred paces below the place where we had slept, the valley becomes very narrow, the mountains to the right approach, and a defile of granite rocks is entered in a direction W. by S. called Wady Kenna, where the tomb of a saint of the name of Wawa stands. I was told afterwards at Cairo, by some Sinai Bedouins, that lower down in Wady Kenna there is a very deep cavern in the rock. At three quarters of an hour we passed to the right of the defile, and turned N.W. into a valley called Badera. The valley of Badera consists of sand rock, and the ground is deeply covered with sand. We ascended gently in it, and in an hour and three quarters reached its summit, from whence we descended by a narrow difficult path, down a cliff called Nakb Badera, into an open plain between the mountains; we crossed the plain, and at two hours and a quarter entered Wady Shellal, so called from the number of cataracts which are formed in the rainy season, by the torrents descending from the mountains. A great number of acacia trees grow here, many of which were completely dried up; during the whole of our morning's journey not a green herb could be discovered. We here met several Bedouins on foot, on their way from Suez to Feiran. They had started from the well of Morkha early in the morning; and had ventured on the journey without water, or the hope of finding any till the following day in Wady Feiran. We gave them each a draught of water, and they went off in good spirits, purposing to pass the afternoon under some shady rock, and to continue their journey during the night. We descended the valley slowly, W.N.W. and at the end of four hours and a half reached its termination, opening upon a sandy plain on the sea- shore. Many bones of camels were here lying about, as is generally the case on the great roads through the desert; I have observed that these skeletons are found in greatest numbers where the sands are deepest; which arises from the loaded camels passing such places with difficulty, and often breaking down in them. It is an erroneous opinion that the camel delights in sandy ground; it is true that he crosses it with less difficulty than any other animal, but wherever the sands are deep, the weight of himself and his load makes his feet sink into the sand at every step, and he groans, and often sinks under his burthen. It is the hard gravelly ground of the desert which is most agreeable to this animal.

On the plain we fell in with the great road from Tor to Suez, but soon quitted it to the right, and turned to the north in search of a natural reservoir of rain, in which the Bedouins knew that some water was still remaining. At the end of five hours and a half, we reached a narrow cleft in the mountain, where we halted, and my guides went a mile up in it to fill the skins. This is called Wady el Dhafary; it is sometimes frequented by the Arabs, because it furnishes the only sweet water between Tor and Suez, though it is out of the direct road, and the well of Morkha is at no great distance. Some rain had fallen here in the winter, and water was therefore met with in several ponds among the rocks. This is the lowest part of the primitive chain of mountains, and, I believe, the only place, on the road between Tor and Suez, where they approach the sea, which is only three miles distant, with a stony plain ascending from it. A slave of a Towara Bedouin here partook of our breakfast; he had been sent to these mountains by his master several weeks ago, to collect wood and burn charcoal, which he was doing quite alone, with no other provision than a sack of meal. Charcoal, commonly called Fahm in Arabic, is by these Bedouins called Habesh, a term which I never heard given to it by any other Arabs; this word may perhaps be the origin of the name of Abyssinia, which may have been called Habesh by the Arabs from the colour of its inhabitants. Travellers will do well to enquire for the Dhafary, in their way to Feiran, as the water of the Morkha is of the very worst kind; this memorandum would be particularly useful to any person intending to copy the inscriptions of Wady Mokatteb.

We reached Morkha,, which bears from Dhafary N.W. b. N. in half an hour, the road leading over level but very rocky ground. Morkha is a small pond in the sand-stone rock, close to the foot of the mountains. Two date-trees grow near its margin. The bad taste of the water seems to be owing partly to the weeds, moss, and dirt, with which the pond is filled, but chiefly, no doubt, to the saline nature of the soil around it. Next to Ayoun Mousa, in the vicinity of Suez, and Gharendel, it is the principal station on this road. After watering our camels, which was our only motive for coming to the Morkha, we returned to the sea-shore, one hour distant N.W. We followed the shore for three quarters of an hour in a N.W. b. N. direction, and then halted close by the sea, where the maritime level is greatly contracted by a range of chalk hills which in some places approaches close to the water. Before us extended the large bay of Birket Faraoun, so called, from being, according to Arab and Egyptian tradition, the place where the Israelites crossed the sea, and where the returning waves overwhelmed Pharaoh and his host. There is an almost continual motion of the waters in this bay, which they say is occasioned by the spirits of the drowned still moving in the bottom of the sea; but which may also be ascribed to its being exposed on three sides to the sea, and to the sudden gusts of wind from the openings of the valleys. These circumstances, together with its shoals, render it very dangerous, and more ships have been wrecked in the Bay of Birket Faraoun than in any other part of the gulf of Tor, another proof, in the eyes of the Arabs, that spirits or demons dwell here.

This evening and night we had a violent Simoum. The air was so hot, that when I faced the current, the sensation was like that of sitting close to a large fire; the hot wind was accompanied, at intervals with gusts of cooler air. I did not find my respiration impeded for a moment during the continuance of the hot blast. The Simoum is frequent on this low coast, but the advantage of sea bathing renders it the less distressing.

June 5th.—We rode close by the shore, at the foot of sandy cliffs; but as the road was passable only at low water, we were obliged, as the tide set in, to take a circuitous route over the mountain. At the end of an hour we again reached the sea, and then proceeded north over a wide sandy plain. Towards the mountain is a tract of low grounds several miles in breadth, in which the shrubs Gharkad and Aszef were growing in great plenty. At the end of two hours and a half, having reached a very conspicuous promontory, of the mountain, over which lies the road to the Hammam Mousa, or hot-wells of Moses, we turned, on its south side, into a fine valley called Wady el Taybe, inclosed by abrupt rocks, and full of trees, among which were a few of the date, now completely withered. Want of rain is much more frequent in the lower ranges of the peninsula, than in the upper. At four hours and a half we passed Wady Shebeyke, reached soon afterwards the top of Wady Taybe, and then fell in with the road by which I had passed on my way to the convent from Suez. We rested in Wady Thale, under a rock, in the shade of which, at 2 P.M. the thermometer rose to 107°. After a march of eleven hours we halted in Wady Gharendel.

June 6th.—We continued in the road described at the beginning of this journal, and at six hours and a half reached Wady Wardan. Here we turned out of the great road to Suez, in a more western direction, towards the sea, in order to take in water at the well of Szoueyra, which we came to in three hours from Wardan. The lower parts of Wady Wardan, extending six or eight miles in breadth, consist of deep sand, which a strong north wind drove full in our faces, and caused such a mist that we several times went astray. Upon small sandy mounds in this plain tamarisk trees grow in great numbers, and in the midst of these lies the well of Szoueyra, which it is extremely difficult to find without a guide. It is about two miles from the sea. We here met many Terabein women occupied in watering their camels; I enquired of them whether they ever collected manna from the tamarisks; I understood from them that in this barren plain, the trees never yield that substance. In the evening we rode along a narrow path, parallel with the sea, for two hours and a half. The wind still continued, and obliged us to seek for shelter behind a hillock in the lower part of Wady Szeder, where we found protection against the driving sands.

June 7th.—In the morning we reached Ayoun Mousa. We found here, as we had previously done, in many places near the shore, the tracks of wheel- carriages, a very uncommon appearance in the east, and more particularly in deserts. It was by this road that Mohammed Ali's women passed last year from Tor to Suez in their elegant vehicles. Towards evening we entered Suez.

June 8th.—A caravan was to leave Suez this day, but its departure was delayed. As I knew that the plague had subsided at Cairo, and thought that the road was tolerably safe, I asked Hamd whether he would venture with me alone upon the journey; fear seemed to be quite unknown to this excellent young man, and he readily acquiesced in my proposal. We left Suez in the evening with some hopes of overtaking a caravan of Towaras, which we were informed had this day passed to the north of Suez, in their way to Cairo with charcoal. Towards sunset we came in sight of the castle of Adjeroud, when Hamd having descried from afar some Bedouins on foot, who, from the circumstance of their walking about in different directions in a place where no road passed, and where Bedouins never alight, appeared to him to be suspicious characters, we halted behind a hill till it was dark, and took our supper. After sunset we saw several fires at a distance, in the plain, which Hamd immediately concluded to be those of the Towara caravan. Taking advantage of the darkness, to avoid the observation of the suspected persons, we rode towards the fires, which, instead of being those of the Towara, proved to belong to a small party of Omran, encamped near the well in the Wady Emshash. Hamd was much alarmed when he perceived his mistake, for he was well acquainted with the bad character of the Omran, and he dreaded them the more on account of the Arab of their tribe whom he had killed near Akaba. They looked very greedily at my travelling sack, but as I pretended to belong to the Pasha's garrison at Suez, they did not make any attempt upon it. They told us that in coming here, they had found five Bedouins sitting near the well, who retired when they approached it, and who were probably the men we saw. As we thought it very likely that they would waylay us farther on, in the narrow pass of Montala, we deemed it prudent to retire to Adjeroud, and take shelter in the castle for the night. When we reached that place, it was with great difficulty that I persuaded the officer to open the gates and let us in; he was in no less fear of the robbers than ourselves; for two days they had driven back his people from the well of Emshash, where they were accustomed to fill their water skins, so that the garrison was reduced to great distress, as they had no provision of sweet water, and that of the castle well is scarcely drinkable. A Turkish officer, with his wife and son, and eight peasants from the Sherkieh, formed the whole garrison, and they trembled at the name and sight of the Bedouins as much as the monks of the Sinai convent.

June 9th.—This morning I proposed to the officer that we should go out in force and drive the robbers from the well, which was only half an hour distant; but this he refused to do, saying that he had no orders to leave the castle; he found it more convenient to seize my skins, which I had filled at Suez, and to make use of their contents for his family. Towards noon we saw several of the Bedouins hovering round the castle, no doubt expecting us to issue from it. In this difficulty, the Turkish officer having refused to lend his horse, I mounted Hamd in the evening upon the strongest of the camels, and told him to gallop to Suez, and acquaint the commander there with our situation, or else to hire some of his countrymen, who were there waiting for the departure of the caravan, and in their company to return to our relief, bringing with him a supply of water. He set out, but had not proceeded a mile before he saw the robbers running upon him from different quarters, and endeavouring to cut him off from the road. They fired at him, upon which he returned their fire, and gallopped back to the castle. The officer and his valiant garrison were now thrown into the greatest consternation, and could not devise any means of relief. I offered to ride to Suez, provided the officer would lend me his horse; but he appeared to be more afraid of losing the horse, than of dying from thirst. Being thus unable to effect any thing, I was under the necessity of waiting patiently till the great caravan from Suez should pass.

June 10th.—There was now not a drop of sweet water in the castle, and all that we could procure of the well-water of Adjeroud had been standing in the tank since it was filled from the well at the time of the last pilgrimage. The wheels of the well, which is two hundred and fifty feet in depth, are put in motion only at that time; during the rest of the year the building which encloses the well is shut up; and the person who keeps the key was now at Cairo. The water we were thus obliged to drink was saline, putrid, and of a yellow green colour, so that boiling produced no improvement in it, and our stomachs could not retain it.

June 11th.—A slight shower of rain fell, which the Turk ascribed to his prayers; but all the water we could collect in every vessel which the castle could furnish, scarcely afforded to each of us a draught. Hamd made a second attempt to night to go to Suez, but it being unfortunately moonlight, he was seen and again driven back.

June 12th.—After three days blockade, I had the pleasure of descrying the Suez caravan at a distance, on its way towards Cairo; we immediately got every thing ready, and when the caravan was opposite the castle, at about twenty minutes distance, Hamd and I hastily joined it. What became of the officer and his garrison, I never heard. I bought of the Bedouins of the caravan a supply of water, sufficient to last me to Cairo.

Although the passage of this desert is less dangerous than formerly, it is impossible to protect it effectually, without establishing a small body of horsemen or dromedaries at Adjeroud; and it is a discredit to the government of Egypt, that this is not done. The well of Emshash affords a seasonable supply of water to robbers, who lay in wait in the rocky country of Montala, where one of them stationed on the top of a hill gives notice of the approach of any enemy or object of plunder. The castle was undoubtedly intended as a look-out post against the Arabs. The French once had a garrison in it, and its walls have been repaired by Mohammed Ali Pasha, but the interior is in a very ruinous state, and few provisions are kept in the extensive store-houses within it.

On proceeding to Cairo, the caravan took, for the first stage from Adjeroud, a route somewhat to the southward of that by which I had gone to Sinai, and joined the latter at Dar el Hamra. Six hours and a half from Adjeroud we passed Wady Khoeyfera, the bed of a torrent, with trees growing in it, a very little below the level of the surrounding plain. Here I saw the ruins of a small stone reservoir, and to a considerable distance round it, ruins of walls, and several wells, some built with brick and others with stone. They appear to have been surrounded by a wall, which now forms a circular enclosure of mounds almost wholly covered with sands. The existence of these ruins, which I do not remember to have seen mentioned by any traveller, confirms my belief, that in the most ancient times regular stations were established on this road, to which we must also attribute the date trees now found in a petrified state.

A road, called Derb el Ban, leads from Adjeroud to Birket el Hadj, by the north side of the mountain El Oweybe; it is the most northern of all the routes to Suez, and is little frequented.

On the 13th of June, early in the morning, I entered Cairo; the plague had ceased, and had been less destructive, than it was last year.

APPENDICES

I. An Account of the Ryhanlu Turkmans.

Aleppo, May 12, 1810.

THE district inhabited by the Ryhanlu Turkmans begins at about seven hours distance from Aleppo, to the north-westward. The intermediate plain is stony and almost deserted, but it is in many parts susceptible of culture, and contains a great number of villages in ruins. At five hours march from Aleppo to the W.N.W. upon the ridge of a low hill are some plantations of olive and fig trees; on the other side of the hill lies a valley of an oval shape about eighteen miles in circuit, called Khalaka; at the foot of the low hills which surround it, are the following villages: Termine, Tellade, Hoesre, Tellekberoun, Bab, Dana, and some others. The Fellahs or inhabitants of these villages live in half ruined houses, which indicate the opulence of their ancient possessors. The soil of the plain is a fine red mould, almost without a stone. In March, when I visited the Ryhanlu, it was sown with wheat, but it produces in another season the finest cotton. The whole plain is the property of Abbas Effendi of Aleppo, the heir of Tshelebi Effendi, who was in his time the first grandee of Aleppo [.] Having crossed the plain of Khalaka, and the rocky calcareous hills which border it on the western side, a very tedious passage for camels, the first Turkman tents are met with at about six hours and a half or seven hours distance from Aleppo. The Turkmans, who prfer living on the hills, erect their tents on the declivities, and cultivate the valleys below them. These hills extend in a N.W. direction, above forty miles, the mountain of St. Simon, is in the midst of them. Their average breadth, including the numerous valleys which intersect them, may be estimated at fifteen or twenty miles. They lose themselves in the plain of Antioch, which is bounded on the opposite side by the chain of high mountains, extending along the southern coast of the gulf of Scanderoun. The river Afrin waters this plain; its course from the neighbourhood of Killis to where it empties itself into the lake of Antioch, is fifteen or twenty hours in length. At about seven hours above the lake, this river is about the size of the Cam near Cambridge; it regularly but moderately overflows in spring-time, and is full of carps and barbles; but the Turkmans have no implements of fishing. Besides the Afrin there are numerous smaller rivers and sources, which water the valleys. One of the must considerable of these is the river of Goul, which takes its rise near a Turkman encampment of the same name, about six hours distant from St. Simon, to the W. by N. in a small lake, about one mile and a half in circumference, and joins the waters of the Afrin, eight miles from its source. This beautiful little lake is so full of fish, that the boys of Goul kill them by throwing stones at them. The river turns several mills near Goul, and five or six more at six miles distance, at a place called Tahoun Kash, near a spot where the chieftain of the Ryhanlu, Mursal Oglu Hayder Aga, has built a house for his winter residence, and has planted a garden. On the right bank of the Afrin, about three quarters of an hour distant from it, and at three hours ride to the N.-westward of the tent of Mohammed Ali, my Turkman host, are two warm springs at half an hour's walk from each other. I only saw the southernmost, which is strongly impregnated with sulphur, and made my thermometer rise to 102°; it constantly bubbles from a bottom of coarse gravel, in the middle of the bason, which is about twenty feet in circumference, and four feet deep. The sulphureous smell begins to be sensible at a distance of twenty-five yards from it, and I was told that the northern spring was still more sulphureous. The Turkmans hold the medicinal powers of these springs, as baths, in great estimation: women as well as men use them for the cure of violent headaches, which are very prevalent amongst them. The fields of the Turkmans are sown with wheat, barley, and several kinds of pulse. Their wheat was sown only a fortnight before my arrival, viz, about the twentieth of February. As it is only a short time since they have become agriculturists, they have not yet any plantations of fruit trees, although the olive, pomegranate, and fig would certainly prosper in their valleys. Thirty years ago the hills which they now inhabit were partly covered with wood; the trade of firewood with Aleppo, however, has entirely consumed these forests. At present they cut the wood for the Aleppo market, in the mountains of the Kurds on the northern side of the Afrin, and when that shall fail, Aleppo must depend for its fuel upon the coast of Caramania, from whence Egypt is now supplied. The

Turkman hills are inhabited by vast numbers of jackals; wolves, and foxes are also numerous; and I saw flocks of Gazelles, to the number of twenty or thirty in each flock; among a great variety of birds is the Francoline, which the Syrian sportsmen esteem the choicest of all game. In the mountains of Badjazze, which borders on the Turkman plains, stags are sometimes killed. The Turkmans are passionately fond of hawking; they course the game with grey-hounds, or if in the plain, they run it down with their horses.

The population of the Ryhanlu Turkmans may be roughly calculated from the number of their tents, which amount to about three thousand; every tent contains from two or three to fifteen inmates. They can raise a military force of two or three thousand horsemen, and of as many infantry. They are divided into thirteen minor tribes: 1. The Serigialar, or tribe of the chief of the Ryhanlu Turkmans, Hayder Aga, has five hundred horsemen. 2. Coudanlut, six hundred. 3. Cheuslu, two hundred. 4. Leuklu, one hundred. 5. Kara Akhmetlu one hundred and fifty. 6. Kara Solimanlu, fifty. 7. Delikanlu, six hundred. 8. Toroun, sixty. 9. Bahaderlu, one hundred. 10. Hallalu, sixty. 11. Karken, twenty. 12. Aoutshar, twenty. 13. Okugu, fifty. The Serigialar derive their origin from Maaden, the Cheuslu from the neighbourhood of Badjazze, the Babaderli from the mountains of St. Simon, the Halalis from Barak. Each tribe has its own chief, whose rank in the Divan is determined by the strength his tribe; Hayder Aga presides amongst them whenever it is found necessary to call together a common council. His authority over the Ryhanlus seems to be almost absolute, as he sometimes carries his motions in the Divan even against the opinion and will of the assembled chiefs. He settles the disputes, which occur between these chiefs, and which are often accompanied by hostile incursions into one another's territory. The chiefs decide all disputes among their own followers according to the feeble knowledge which they possess of the Turkish laws; but appeals from their tribunal may be made to that of the grand chief. The whole Ryhanlu tribe is tributary to Tshapan Oglu, the powerful governor of the eastern part of Anatolia, who resides at Yuzgat. They pay him an annual tribute of six thousand two hundred and fifteen piastres, in horses, cattle, &c. He claims also the right of nominating to the vacant places of chieftains; but his influence over the Turkman Ryhanlu having of late much diminished, this right is at present merely nominal. The predecessors of Hayder Aga used to receive their Firmahn of nomination, or rather of confirmation, from the Porte. When the tribute for Tshapan Oglu is collected, Hayder Aga generally gives in an account of disbursements incurred during the preceding year for the public service, such as presents to officers of the Porte passing through the camp, expenses of entertaining strangers of rank, &c. &c. The tribute, as well as Hayder Aga's demands, are levied from the tribes according to the repartition of the minor Agas; and each chief takes that opportunity of adding to the sum to which his tribe is assessed, four or five hundred piastres, which make up his only income as chief. The Turkmans do not pay any Miri, or general land tax to the Grand Signor, for the ground they occupy. Families, if disgusted with their chief, often pass from one tribe to another without any one daring to prevent their departure.

The Ryhanlu, like most of the larger Turkman nations, are a no-made people. They appear in their winter quarters in the plain of Antioch at the end of September, and depart from thence towards the middle of April, when the flies of the plain begin to torment their horses and cattle. They then direct their march towards Marash, and remain in the neighbourhood of that place about one month; from thence they reach the mountains of Gurun and Albostan. The mountains which they occupy are called Keukduli, Sungulu, and Kara Dorouk, (upon Kara Dorouk, they say, are some fine ruins). Here they pass the hottest summer months; in autumn they repass the plains of Albostan, and return by the same route towards Antioch.

The winter habitations of the Turkmans in the hilly districts are, as I have mentioned before, erected on the declivity of the hills, so as to be by their position somewhat sheltered from the northerly winds. Sometimes five or six families live together on one spot in as many tents, but for the greater part tents of single families are met with at one or two miles distance from each other. In proportion to the arable land, which the hilly parts contain, these districts are better peopled than the plain, where a thousand tents are scattered over an extent, of the most fertile country, of at least five hundred square miles. The structure of the habitations of these nomades is of course extremely simple: an oblong square wall of loose stones, about four feet high, is covered over with a black cloth made of goats hair, which is supported by a dozen or more posts, so that in the middle of the tent the covering is elevated about nine feet from the ground. A stone partition is built across the tent, near the entrance: I found in every tent that the women had uniformly possession of the greater half to the left of the door; the smaller half to the right hand side is appropriated to the men, and there is also a partition at H [figure not included], which generally serves as a stable for a favourite horse of the master or of one of his sons. The rest of the horses and the cattle are kept in caverns, which abound in these calcareous hills, or in smaller huts built on purpose. Besides those who live in tents, many of the Turkmans, especially in the plain, live in large huts fifteen feet high, built and distributed like the tents, but having, instead of a tent covering, a roof of rushes, which grow in great abundance on the banks of the Afrin. The women's room serves also as the kitchen; there they work at their looms, and strangers never enter: unless, when, as I was told, the Turkmans meaning to do great honour to a guest, allow him a corner of the Harem to sleep in quiet among the women. The men's apartment is covered with carpets, which serve as beds to strangers and to the unmarried members of the family; the married people retire into the Harem. The Turkmans have also a kind of portable tent made of wood, like a round bird cage, which they cover with large carpets of white wool. The entrance may be shut up by a small door; it is the exclusive habitation of the ladies, and is only met with in families who are possessed of large property. The tent or hut of a Turkman is always surrounded by three or four others, in which the Fellah families live who cultivate his land. These Fellahs are the remaining peasants of abandoned villages, or some poor straggling Kurds. The Turkmans find the necessary seed, and receive in return half the produce, which is collected by a few of them who remain for this purpose in the winter quarters the whole year round. The Fellahs live wretchedly; whenever they are able to scrape together a small pittance, their masters take it from them under pretence of borrowing it; I was treated by several of them at dinner with the best dish they could afford: bad oil, with coarse bread; they never taste meat except when they kill a cow or an ox, disabled by sickness or age; the greater part of them live literally upon bread and water, neither fruits or vegetables being cultivated here; they are nevertheless, a cheerful good-natured people; the young men play, sing, and dance, every evening, and are infinitely better tempered than their haughty masters. My host, Mohammed Ali, began a few years ago to plant a small garden of fruit trees near his tents; his example will probably be generally followed, because the Ryhanlu families, at every returning season, pitch their tents on the same spot. It is only about ten years, that the Ryhanlu have cultivated the land; like the other Turkman hordes they had always preferred the wandering life of feeders of cattle. Agriculture was introduced among them by the persuasion of Hayder Aga, whose daughter having married a chief of the neighbouring Kurds, an alliance took place, which enabled the Turkmans to perceive the advantages, derived by the Kurds from the cultivation of the soil. The principal riches of the Turkmans however still consist in cattle. Their horses are inferior to those of the Arabs of the desert, but are well adapted for the mountains. Their necks are shorter and thicker than those of the Arab horses, the head

BURCKHARDT

larger, the whole frame more clumsy: the price of a good Turkman horse at Aleppo is four or five hundred piastres, while twice that sum or more is paid for an Arab horse of a generous breed. Contrary to the practice of the Arabs, the Turkmans ride males exclusively. The family of my host possessed four horses, three mares, about five hundred sheep, one hundred and fifty goats, six cows, and eight camels; he is looked upon as a man in easy circumstances; there are few families whose property does not amount to half as much, and there are many who have three or four times as many cattle. I have heard of some who are possessed of property in cattle and cash to the amount of one hundred and fifty thousand piastres. Such sums are gained by the trade with Aleppo and by usury amongst themselves.

At the time of their departure for Armenia the Ryhanlu buy up buffaloes and Arab camels, which they exchange in Armenia for a better breed of camels and for some other cattle, for the Aleppo market. The Armenian or Caramanian camel is taller and stronger than the Arab, its neck is more bent, and the neck and upper part of the thighs are covered with thick hair; the Arab camel, on the contrary, has very little hair. The common load of the latter is about six hundred weight, or one hundred and twenty rotolos, but the Armenian camel will carry one hundred and sixty rotolos, or eight hundred weight. The price of an Arabian camel is about two hundred and fifty piastres, that of an Armenian at Aleppo is twice as much.   This breed of camels is produced by a he-dromedary and a she- Arabian camel. The people of Anatolia keep these male dromedaries as stallions for the purpose of covering the females of the smaller Arabian breed, which the Turkmans, yearly bring to their market. If left to breed among themselves the Caramanian camels produce a puny race of little value. The Arabs use exclusively their smaller breed of camels, because they endure heat, thirst, and fatigue, infinitely better than the others, which are well suited to hilly districts. The camels of the Turkmans feed upon a kind of low bramble called in Turkish Kufan, which grows in abundance upon the hills; in the evening they descend the mountains and come trotting towards the tents, where each camel receives a ball of paste, made of barley meal and water, weighing about one pound. The expense of feeding these useful animals is therefore reduced to the cost of a handful of barley per day. The Turkmans do not milk their camels, but use them exclusively as beasts of burthen. Through their means they carry on a very profitable trade with Aleppo. They provide the town with firewood, which they cut in the mountains of the Kurds, distant about four hours to the N.W. of Mohammed Aga's tent; the Kurds themselves who inhabit those mountains have no camels, and are obliged to sell their wood and their labour in cutting it at a very trifling price. Besides wood the Turkmans carry to town the produce of their fields, together with sheep and lambs, wool, butter and cheese in the spring, and a variety of home made carpets. They transport the merchandize of the Frank merchants at Aleppo from Alexandretta to the city. The profits arising from the trade with Aleppo are almost entirely consumed by the demands of their families for cloth, coffee, sweetmeats, and various articles of eastern luxury; they seldom take back any cash to their tents.

The manner of living of the Turkmans is luxurious for a nomade people. Their tents are for the greater part clean, the floor in the men's room is furnished with a Divan or sophas, leaving only a space in the middle where a large fire is continually kept up to cheer the company and to make coffee, of which they consume a great quantity. Their coffee cups are three times the size of those commonly used in the Levant, or as large as an English coffee cup; whenever coffee is handed round, each person's cup is filled two or three times; when I was with them, I often drank twenty or more cups in the course of the day. The servants roast and pound the coffee immediately before it is drank. They pound it in large wooden mortars, and handle the pestle with so much address, that if two or three are pounding together they keep time, and made a kind of music which seemed to be very pleasing to their masters.

The Turkmans taste flesh only upon extraordinary occasions, such as a marriage or a circumcision, a nightly feast during the Ramazan, or the arrival of strangers. Their usual fare is Burgoul; this dish is made of wheat boiled, and afterwards dried in the sun in sufficient quantity for a year's consumption: the grain is re-boiled with butter or oil, and affords a very palateable nourishment; it is a favourite dish all over Syria. Besides Burgoul they eat rice, eggs, honey, dried fruit, and sour milk, called Leben. They have none but goats milk. Their bread is a thin unleavened cake, which the women bake immediately before dinner upon a hot iron plate, in less than a minute. Breakfast is served at eight o'clock in the morning, the principal meal takes place immediately after sunset. The Turkmans, are great coxcombs at table, in comparison with other Levantines; instead of simply using his fingers, the Turkman twists his thin bread very adroitly into a sort of spoon, which he swallows, together with the morsel which he has taken out of the dish with it. I remember sitting with a dozen of them round a bason of sour milk, which we dispatched in a few minutes without any person, except myself, having in the least soiled his fingers.

The Turkman women do not hide themselves, even before strangers, but the girls seldom enter the men's room, although they are permitted freely to talk with their father's guests. I was much struck with the elegance of their shapes and the regularity of their features. Their complexion is as fair as that of European women; as they advance in age the sun browns them a little. As to their morals, chastity becomes a necessary virtue where even a kiss, is punished with death by the father or brother of the unhappy offender. I could mention several instances of the extreme severity of the Turkmans upon this subject; but one may suffice. Three brothers taking a ride and passing through an insulated valley, met their sister receiving the innocent caresses of her lover. By a common impulse they all three discharged their fire-arms upon her, and left their fallen victim upon the ground, while the lover escaped unhurt; my host Mohammed Ali, upon being informed of the murder, sent his servant to bring the body to his tent, in order to prevent the jackals from devouring it: the women were undressing and washing the body to commit it to the grave, when a slight breathing convinced them that the vital spark was not yet extinguished; in short the girl recovered. She was no sooner out of immediate danger, than one of Ali's sons repaired to the tent of his friends, the three brothers, who sat sullen and silent round the fire, grieving over the loss of their sister. The young man entered, and saluted them, and said, "I come to ask you, in the name of my father, for the body of your sister; my family wishes to bury her." He had no sooner finished than the brothers rose, crying: "if she was dead you would not have asked for her, you would have taken the body without our permission." Then seizing their arms, they were hurrying out of the tent, in search of the still living victim; but Mohammed Ali's son opposed the authority of his father and his own reputation of courage to their brutal intentions; he swore that he would kill the first who should leave the tent, told them that they had already sufficiently revenged the received injury, and that if their sister was not dead it was the visible protection of the prophet that had saved her: and thus, he at last persuaded them to grant his request. The girl was nursed for three months in Mohammed Ali's family, and married after her complete recovery to the young man who had been the cause of her misfortune. Notwithstanding such severity the young Turkmans boast of their intrigues, and delight in all the dangers of secret courtship; and I have been assured, upon indisputable authority, that there are few men among them who have not enjoyed the favours of their mistresses before the consumnation of their nuptials. If the woman happens to become a mother, she destroys her illegitimate offspring as the only means of saving her own life and that of the father.

The Turkman ladies dress in the common style of Syrian women; their bonnet is adorned with strings of Venetian zequins, or other gold pieces. The dress of the men is that of the Turks of Anatolia. The horsemen wear wide riding pantaloons, or Sherwalls, of cloth; their head-dress consists of a red cap round which they twist a turban of cotton or silk stuff; the wealthy wear turbans of flowered stuffs, or even Persian shawls. Twenty years ago the national head-dress was a tall and narrow cap of white wool, in the shape of a sugar-loaf, since that time the Ryhanlu have left off wearing it, but I remember to have seen a headdress of this kind during my stay with the Turkmans near Tarsus. The Turkman women are very laborious; besides the care of housekeeping, they work the tent coverings of goats hair, and the woollen carpets, which are inferior only to those of Persian manufacture. Their looms are of primitive simplicity; they do not make use of the shuttle, but pass the woof with their hands. They seem to have made great progress in the art of dyeing; their colours are beauitful. Indigo and cochineal, which they purchase at Aleppo, give them their blue, and red dyes, but the ingredients of all the others, especially of a brilliant green, are herbs which they gather in the mountains of Armenia; the dyeing process is kept by them as a national secret. The wool of their carpets, is of the ordinary kind; the carpets are about seven feet long and three broad, and sell from fifteen to one hundred piastres a piece. While the females are employed in these labours the men pass their whole time in indolence; except at sunset, when they feed their horses and camels, they lounge about the whole day, without any useful employment, and without even refreshing their leisure by some trifling occupation. To smoke their pipes and drink coffee is to them the most agreeable pastime; they frequently visit each other, and collecting round the fire-place, they keep very late hours. I was told that there are some men amongst them, who play the tamboura, a sort of guitar, but I never heard any of them perform. If the young men would condescend to assist in agriculture, the wealth of the families would rapidly increase, and the whole of the plains of Antioch might in time be cultivated: at present, as far as I could observe, there are few families growing rich; most of them spend their whole income.

A Turkman never leaves his tent to take a ride in the neighbourhood without being armed with his gun, pistols, and sabre. I was astonished to see that they do not take the smallest care of their fire arms: a great number of them were shewn to me, to know whether they were of English manufacture; I found them covered with rust, and they complained of their often missing fire. They have no gunsmiths amongst them; nor any artizans at all, except some farriers, and a few makers of bridles and of horse accoutrements [.]

There are no lawyers or Ulemas among the Ryhanlu. Some families of consequence carry with them a Faqui or travelling Imam, to teach their children to read and to pray, and who in case of need performs likewise the duties of a menial servant, much like the young German baron's governor. These Faqui are for the greater part natives of Albostan, educated there in mosques: they follow the Turkmans to participate in the pious alms which the Koran prescribes. They are generally ignorant, even of the Turkish law: they are often consulted however by the chiefs, and their sentence is generally confirmed by the chief whenever there is no precedent or customary law in point to the contrary.

I did not see any books amongst the Turkmans, and I am certain that out of fifty hardly one knows how to read or write. Even few of them know the text of their prayers (which are throughout the Mohammedan countries in the sacred language, the Arabic), and therefore perform the prescribed prostrations silently and without the usual ejaculations. The married people, men as well as women, are tolerably exact in the performance of their devotions, but the young men never trouble themselves about them.

I did not stay long enough among the Turkmans to be able to judge correctly of their character, especially as I was ignorant of their language. I saw enough, however, to convince me that they possess most of the vices of nomade nations, without their good qualities. The Turkmans are, like the Arabs and Kurds, a people of robbers, that is to say, every thing which they can lay hold of in the open country is their lawful prize, provided it does not belong to their acknowledged friends. The Arabs make amends in some measure for their robberies by the hospitality and liberality with which they receive friends and strangers. In this respect I soon found that I had been led to form a very erroneous opinion of the Turkman character. I was introduced at Aleppo to Mohammed Ali Aga, a man of considerable influence amongst the Ryhanlu, as a physician who was travelling in search of herbs, and I succeeded in supporting my assumed character during near a fortnight's stay under his tent. Before my departure from Aleppo, I made him a present of coffee and sweetmeats, to the amount of sixty piastres, and I promised him another present, when he should have brought me back in safety to Aleppo. Notwithstanding these precautions, my reception in his tent was rather cool, and I soon found that I was among men who had no other idea than that of getting as much out of me as they could. They were not under the least restraint, but calculated in my presence how much my visit was worth to them, as I sufficiently understood, from their animated tone and gestures, added to the few Turkish words, which I learnt. To spare my dinner my host took me out a visiting almost every day, just before the dinner hour; and that he might know how far it would be prudent to incur expence on my account, he permitted one of his friends to search my pockets, and was cruelly disappointed when he found that my purse did not contain more than four or five piastres. My horse, for the maintenance of which I had agreed with my host, was fed with straw, until I told them that I should take care of it myself, when they were obliged to deliver its daily portion of barley into my own hands. Such was the liberality which I experienced in return for the medical advice and medicines which they received without hesitation from me upon demanding them. Their minds seemed intent only upon money, except among the lovers there was no other subject of conversation, and instead of the Arab virtues, of honour, frankness, and hospitality, there appeared to be no other motive of action among them than the pursuit of gain. The person of a Frank may be safe among them, but his baggage will be exposed to close search, and whatever strikes the fancy of a powerful man, will be asked of him in such a manner, that it is adviseable to give up the object at once. I had fortunately hidden my compass in my girdle, but a thermometer which they found in my pocket, attracted general notice; if I had explained to them the use I meant to make of it, it would have confirmed the suspicion already hinted to me by one of them, that I intended to poison their springs. I pretended that the thermometer was a surgical instrument, which being put into the blood of an open wound served to shew whether the wound was dangerous or not. It is not more from the behaviour of the Turkmans towards myself, that I formed my opinion of their character, than from their conduct towards each other. They are constantly upon their guard against robbers and thieves of their own tribe; they cheat each other in the most trifling affairs, and like most of the Aleppo merchants, make use of the most awful oaths and imprecations to conceal their falsehood. If they have one good quality it is their tolerance in religious matters, which proves, on the other hand, how little they care about them.

The men marry at fourteen or fifteen, the girls at thirteen. Excepting Hayder Aga, and some of his brothers, there are very few who have more than one wife. They celebrate their marriage feasts with great pomp. The young men play upon those occasions at a running game much resembling the "jeu de barre," known on the continent of Europe. Their music then consists in drums and trumpets, only, for the Turkmans, are not so fond of music as the Aleppines and the Arabs, nor did I ever meet among them with any of the story-tellers, who are so frequent amongst the Arabs of the desert. Whenever a son reaches the marriageable age, his father gives him, even before his marriage, a couple of camels and a horse to defray, by the profits of trade, his private expenses. At the death of the father, his property is divided amongst the family according to the Turkish law. The Ryhanlu bury their dead in the burying places which are found scattered among the ruins of deserted villages.

My observations were confined to the Ryhanlu. But they will probably in great measure apply to all the large Turkman tribes which inhabit the western parts of Asia Minor, and concerning which I obtained a few particulars.

In the level country between Badjazze and Adena lives a tribe which is tributary to the governors of these two places. They are called Jerid, and are more numerous than the Ryhanlu; they likewise leave their plains towards the approach of summer, and winter in the Armenian mountains, in the neighbourhood of the Ryhanlu. Like the latter they have one head, and several minor chiefs, and they are divided into six tribes: viz. Jerid (chief Shahen Beg), Tegir (chief Oglu Kiaya), Karegialar (chief Rustam Beg), Bozdagan (chief Kerem Oglu), Aoutshar (chief Hassan Beg), Leck (chief Agri Bayouk). The Lecks speak, besides the Turkish, a language of their own, which has no resemblance either to the Arabic, Turkish, Persian or Kurdine; "it sounds like the whistling of birds," said the Turkman from whom I obtained this information, and the same remark was confirmed by others. The name of the Leck, renders the supposition probable that they are descendants of the Lazi, a people inhabiting the coast of the Black sea, and who in the time of the great Justinian opposed his forces with some success. Chardin mentions having met descendants of the Lazi near Trebizond, whom he describes as a rude sea-faring people, with a peculiar language.

The Pehluvanlu are the most numerous tribe of the whole nation of Turkmans. They are governed by a chief, (Mahmoud Beg), who is tributary to Tshapan Oglu. A part of them have for a long period been cultivators, others are shepherds. They inhabit the country from Bosurk to near Constantinople, and pass the summer months at one day's journey distance from the Ryhanlu. They are in possession of a very profitable transport trade, and their camels form almost exclusively the caravans of Smyrna and of the interior of Anatolia. They drive their sheep for sale as far as Constantinople.

The Rishwans are more numerous than the Ryhanlu, but their tribe is not held in esteem among the Turkmans. They were formerly tributary to Rishwan Oglu, governor of Besna, which lies at one day's journey from Aintab; and they used then to winter in the neighbourhood of Djeboul, on the borders of a small salt lake, five hours to the S. E. of Aleppo. They are at present dependent on Tshapan Oglu, and winter in the plains near Haimani in Anatolia; they pass their summer months in the neighbourhood of the Ryhanlu. Their principal tribes are Deleyanli (chief Ali Beg Oglu), Omar Anli (chief Omar Beg), Mandolli (Omar Aga), Gelikanli (Hassan Beg Mor Oglu). The Rishwans are noted, even among robbers, for their want of faith.

The great tribes of the Turkmans are often at war with each other, as well as with the Kurds, with whom they are in contact in many places. These wars seldom cause the death of more than three or four individuals, after which peace is concluded. In a late war between the Ryhanlu and the Kurds, which lasted five or six months, and brought on several battles, the whole list of deaths was only six Kurds and four Turkmans. In the mountains, the Turkmans are accompanied in their military expeditions by foot soldiers, armed with muskets; these are men of the tribe who cannot afford to keep a horse. Neither the lance, nor the bow is used among them. Some tribes of Kurds, on the contrary, have never abandoned the use of the bow.

The Tar, or blood-revenge, is observed among the Turkman nations, as well among themselves, as with respect to foreigners. They have a particular species of Tar which I have never heard of among the Arabs. It attaches to their goods; the following incident will best explain it: a caravan of Turkman camels laden with wood was seized last winter, just before the gates of Aleppo, by a detachment of Karashukly (a mixt tribe of Turkmans and Arabs, who inhabit the banks of the Euphrates, in the vicinity of Bir). One of the Turkmans was wounded, the loads were thrown down, and fifty camels driven away, worth about five hundred piastres apiece. The Turkmans immediately dispatched an old Arab woman as ambassadress to their enemies, to treat for the restoration of their camels, and she succeeded in recovering them at the rate of one hundred and sixty piastres apiece, or eight thousand piastres, for the whole. "Thus," I was told by a Turkman chief, "the Tar between us will not be for the whole sum of twenty-five thousand piastres, the real value of the camels, but only for the sum of eight thousand piastres, for which we shall, on the first opportunity take our revenge."

There are no Sherif families, or families claiming a descent from the prophet, amongst the Ryhanlu. But family pride is not unknown among them. Descendants from ancient and renowned chiefs claim, though poor, some deference from wealthy upstarts. In one of their late battles with the Kurds, a young man of noble extraction, but poor, and without authority, was crying out in the heat of action: "Comrades, let us attack them on the left flank." Hayder Aga, who heard it, exclaimed: "Who are you? hold your tongue." After the victory the young man, was seen thoughtful and melancholy in the midst of the rejoicings of his brethren; Hayder Aga, as proud a man as ever sat upon a throne, to whom it was reported, sent for the young man, and when he entered the tent rose, and kissed his beard, begging him to forget whatever lie might have said in the heat of action, when he was not always master of himself.

Their ideas of decency appear singular, when compared with our own. A Turkman will talk before his wife, daughter, or sister upon subjects which are banished from our discourse; at the same time that he would be much offended if any friend should in the presence of his females speak in raptures or poetical terms of the charms of a beloved mistress.

Remains of Antiquity.

One of the principal motives of my visit to the Turkmans was my desire to visit some ruins near their encampments, particularly those of Deir Samaan, which at Aleppo I had heard compared to the temples at Baalbec. I therefore made it a condition with my Turkman host, that he should take me to Deir Samaan as well as to several other ruins whose names I had collected from different Aleppines. The day after my arrival under his tent, he set out with me towards the Deir, and we reached it after a ride of four hours over the rocky hills which encircle the mountain of St. Simon, called Djebel Samaan, or Sheikh Barekat. The Deir Samaan consists of the ruins of a church, monastery, or episcopal palace, built upon the top of an insulated hill, bearing from the top of the mountain of St. Simon, N. 20 E., about eight miles distant. It is now inhabited by several families of Kurds, who have their black goat hair tents pitched in the middle of the ruins. They received us with much hospitality; a sheep was immediately killed, and all the delicacies of the season were served up to us. After dinner and coffee, Tshay [FN#1] was served round, which the Aleppines and all Syrians esteem as one of the greatest dainties: it is a heating drink, made of ginger, cloves, rosewater, sugar and similar ingredients, boiled together to a thick syrup. Mursa Aga, the chief, a handsome young man, then took up his Tamboura or guitar, and the rest of the evening passed in music and singing.

The whole summit of the hill, which is six hundred paces in length and one hundred and seventy in breadth, was once covered with stately buildings. A thick wall of square hewn stones, is traceable all round. The principal ruins consist of two separate buildings, a palace, and a church, or monastery, which were separated from each other by a court-yard one hundred and ten paces in length. The palace, or perhaps the high priest's habitation, is not remarkable either for its size or elegance. I could not enter it because it was occupied by the Harem of Mursa Aga. A colonnade led from the palace to the church gate; the broken fragments only of the columns remain. Of the church most of the side walls are still standing, ornamented with pillars and arches worked in the walls; it is divided into two circular apartments of which the inner may have been the sanctuary. On the eastern side of the church is a dark vaulted room, which receives the daylight only from the door, and which appears to have been a sepulchre. A number of niches (if I recollect right, nine), not perpendicular like the Egyptian sepulchral niches, but horizontal, have been built around the wall. Into this chamber opens a subterraneous passage, which is said by the Kurds, to continue a long way under ground, in the direction of Antakia. I could not persuade any body to enter it with me. Adjacent to this sepulchre is another vaulted, open hall, which has been changed by its present proprietors into stables, and an apartment for receiving strangers in the heat of summer. The softness of the calcareous stone from the adjacent hills, with which the buildings are constructed, has caused all the ornaments of the arches and columns and even the shafts themselves to decay; enough remains however, of their clumsy and overcharged ornaments, to shew that the edifices are of an advanced period of the Greek empire. The columns are very small in proportion to the arches which they support, and I did not see any above eighteen or twenty feet high. The perishable nature of the stone has not left a single inscription visible, if there ever were any, with the exception of some names of Frenchmen from Aleppo, who visited the place eighty years ago. The sign of the cross is visible in several places. If these buildings were constructed in pious commemoration of the devout sufferings of St. Simon Stylites, who passed thirty-five years of his life upon a column, they are probably of the sixth century. St. Simon died towards the end of the fifth century, and in the seventh century Syria was conquered and converted to Islamism by the successors of Mohammed. The structures are certainly not of the date of the Crusades. On the eastern side of the building are the remains of an aqueduct, the continuation of which is again met with on the opposite hill. The Kurdine inhabitants of these ruins collect at present the rain water in cisterns.

Descending from the top of the hill on the western side, the remains of a broad paved causeway lead to an arch, which stands about ten minutes walk from the castle, and faces the ruins of a city, built at the foot of the hill, of which a number of buildings are still extant. These ruins, called Bokatur, are uninhabited, their circumference may be estimated at about one mile and a half. Amongst the many private houses a palace may be distinguished, surrounded by a low portico, at which terminates the causeway leading from the arch. At half an hour's distance to the S.W. of Bokatur, are ruins resembling the former in extent and structure. I saw several houses of which the front was supported by columns, of a smaller size than those of the palace at Bokatur. This place is now called Immature, at three quarters of an hour to the W. of it, are other similar ruins of a town called Filtire, which I did not see. The two latter places are now inhabited by some poor Kurdine families. The style of building which I observed in the houses of these ruined cities approaches more to the European than the Asiatic taste. The roofs are somewhat inclined, and the windows numerous, and large, instead of being few and small, as in Turkish houses. The walls, most of which are still remaining, are for the greatest part without ornament, from one foot to about one foot and a half thick, and built of calcareous squared stones, like Deir Samaan. The pillars which are still to be seen in some of the ruined buildings are none of them more than fifteen feet high. Their capitals, like those of the columns in the Deir Samaan, are rude and unfinished; if any order is discernible it is a corrupted Corinthian. The neighbourbood of these towns, at least for five miles round, presents nothing but an uneven plain, thickly covered with barren rocks, which rise to the height of two or three feet above the surface. A few herbs grow in the fissures of the rocks, which are scarcely sufficient to keep from starving half a dozen horses, the property of the present miserable inhabitants. There are several wells of good water in the neighbourhood of the ruins. To the S.S.E. of the Deir, at an hour and a half's distance, stands a single pillar about thirty-five feet high, the base and capital of which are like those of the Deir. No inscriptions are visible. At a few yards from the column is the entrance to a spacious subterraneous cavern. I passed this spot on my way to the Deir, and purposed to examine the contents of the cave on our return; I returned however by another route.

We left our friendly Kurds on the following day at noon. At taking my leave I told the chief that I should be happy to make him some acknowledgments for the hospitality shewn to me, whenever he should visit Aleppo. He excused himself for not having been able to treat us according to his wishes, and begged me to send him from Aleppo a few strings for his guitar; which I gladly promised. These Kurds have been for some time past at war with the Janissaries at Aleppo, which prevents them from going there.

On our road back to Mohammed Ali's tents, through Bokatur and Immature, we met halfway a poor gypsy, or as they are called here, Kurpadh; these Kurpadh are spread over the whole of Anatolia and Syria.

The Kurds have spread themselves over some parts of the plain which the Afrin waters, as well as some of the neighbouring mountains. They live in tents and in villages, are stationary, and are all occupied in agriculture and the rearing of cattle. They form four tribes, of which the Shum, who live in the plain, are the most considerable. The Kurds seem to be of a more lively disposition than the Turkmans; the Aleppines say that their word is less to be depended upon than that of the Turkmans. My hosts at Deir Samaan asked me many questions relative to European politics. I found the opinion prevalent among them which Buonaparte has taken such pains to impress upon the winds of the continental nations, that Great Britain is and ought to be merely a maritime power. This belief, however, proves very advantageous to English travellers in these countries. A Frenchman will every where be taken for a spy, as long as the French invasion of Egypt and Syria is in the memory of man, but it seems never to enter into the suspicions of these people that the English can have any wish to possess the countries of the Levant. I was astonished to find that all the Kurds spoke Arabic fluently, besides the Turkish and their own language, which latter is a corrupted mixture of Persian, Armenian, and Turkish. On the other hand, I only met three or four Turkmans who knew how to express themselves in Arabic, though both nations are alike in almost continual intercourse with Arab peasants and Aleppines.

Besides the ruins just described, there are many others dispersed over the Turkman territories; which, to judge from the prevailing architecture, are of the same date as those already mentioned. Tisin, Sulfa, Kalaa el [B]ent, Jub Abiad, and Mayshat, all of them at two or three hours distance from the tent of Mohammed Ali, are heaps of ruined buildings, with a few remains of houses. Kalaa el Bent and Jub Abiad contain each of them a square tower about sixty feet high. They have only one small projecting window near the top; the roof is flat. Tradition says that Kalaa el Bent or in Turkish Kislar Kalassi, (the castle of girls), was formerly a convent; probably of nuns. At Mayshat, a Turkman encampment on the top of a hill, at the foot of which is a large deep well, with a solid wall, I was shewn a subterraneous chamber, about twenty feet long and fifteen in breadth, hewn out of the rock, at the entrance to which are two columns;

there are two excavations in the bottom of it, like the sepulchral niches which I saw in the Deir Samaan. I have been told that near Telekberoun, a village situated at the foot of the hills which encircle the plain of Khalaka, there are remains of an ancient causeway elevated two or three feet from the ground, about fifteen feet broad, running in the direction from Aleppo to Antioch; it may be traced for the length of a quarter of an hour. In the plain of the Afrin, about three miles from Mursal Oglu's residence, and half an hour from the Afrin, stands an insulated hillock in the plain with the ruins of a Saracen castle, called Daoud Pasha; four miles to the N.E. of it is situated another similar hillock, with ruins of a castle, called Tshyie. The sight of these numerous ruins fills the minds of the Turkmans and Kurds with ideas of hidden treasures, and they relate a variety of traditionary tales of Moggrebyn Sheikhs, who have been once on the point of getting out the treasure, when they have been interrupted by the shrieks of a woman, &c. &c. Having provided myself at Aleppo with a small hammer to break off spesimens of rocks, the Turkmans could not be persuaded that this instrument was not for the purpose of searching for gold. Several Turkmans pressed me to do them the favour of working for a day in their behalf. I endeavoured to persuade them that the hammer was to assist me in procuring medicinal herbs.

[FN#1] Tshay is the Chinese word for tea; and our word is corrupted from it. The word Tshay is used all over Tartary and Turkey, where the dried herb, which is brought over land from China, is also well known. In Syria and Egypt, where the word is better known than the herb, real tea is generally distinguished by the name of Tshay Hindy (tea of India). Ed.

II. On the Political Division of Syria, and the recent Changes in the Government of Aleppo.

THE political division of Syria has not undergone any changes, since the time of Volney.

The Pashaliks are five in number. To the pashalik of Aleppo belongs the government of Aintab, Badjazze, Alexandretta, and Antakia. Damascus comprehends Hebron, Jerusalem, Nablous, Bostra, Hums, and Hama. The Pashalik of Tripoli extends along the seacoast from Djebail to Latikia; that of Seide or Akka, from Djebail nearly to Jaffa, including the mountains inhabited by the Druses. The Pasha of Gaza governs in Jaffa and Gaza, and in the adjacent plains. The present Pasha of Damascus is at the same time Pasha of Tripoli, and therefore in possession of the greater half of Syria. The Pashalik of Gaza is at present annexed to that of Akka.

Such is the nominal division of Syria. But the power of the Porte in this country has been so much upon the decline, particularly since the time of Djezzar Pasha of Akka, that a number of petty independent chiefs have sprung up, who defy their sovereign. Badjazze, Alexandretta, and Antakia have each an independent Aga. Aintab, to the north of Aleppo, Edlip and Shogre, on the way from Aleppo to Latikia, have their own chiefs, and it was but last year that the Pasha of Damascus succeeded in subduing Berber, a formidable rebel, who had fixed his seat at Tripoli, and had maintained himself there for the last six years. The Pashas themselves follow the same practice; it is true that neither the Pasha of Damascus nor that of Akka has yet dared openly to erect the standard of rebellion; they enjoy all the benefits of the protection of the supreme government, but depend much more upon their own strength, than on the caprice of the Sultan, or on their intrigues in the seraglio for the continuance of their power. The policy of the Porte is to flatter and load with honours those whom she cannot ruin, and to wait for some lucky accident by which she may regain her power; but, above all, to avoid a formal rupture, which would only serve to expose her own weakness and to familiarize the Pashas and their subjects with the ideas of rebellion. The Pashas of Damascus and of Akka continue to be dutiful subjects of the Grand Signior in appearance; and they even send considerable sums of money to Constantinople, to ensure the yearly renewal of their offices. (The Pashaliks all over the Turkish dominions are given for the term of one year only, and at the beginning of the Mohammedan year, the Pashas receive their confirmation or dismissal) The Agas of Aintab, Antakia, Alexandretta, Edlip, and Shogre, pay also for the renewal of their offices. There are a few chiefs who have completely thrown off the mask of subjection; Kutshuk Ali, the Lord of Badjazze openly declares his contempt of all orders from the Porte, plunders and insults the Sultan's officers, as well as all strangers passing through his mountains, and with a force of less than two hundred men, and a territory confined to the half ruined town of Badjazze, in the gulf of Alexandretta, and a few miles of the surrounding mountains, his father and himself have for the last thirty years defied all the attempts of the neighbouring Pashas to subdue them.

The inhabitants of Aleppo have been for several years past divided into two parties; the Sherifs (the real or pretended descendants of the Prophet), and the Janissaries. The former distinguish themselves by twisting a green turban round a small red cap, the latter wear high Barbary caps, with a turban of shawl, or white muslin, and a Khandjar, or long crooked knife in their girdles. There are few Turks in the city who have been able to keep aloof from both parties.

The Sherifs first showed their strength about forty years ago, during a tumult excited by their chiefs in consequence of a supposed insult received by Mr. Clarke, the then British Consul. Aleppo was governed by them in a disorderly manner for several years without a Pasha, until the Bey of Alexandretta, being appointed to the Pashalik, surprised the town and ordered all the chief Sherifs to be strangled [.] The Pasha however, found his authority greatly limited by the influence which Tshelebi Effendi, an independent Aleppine grandee, had gained over his countrymen. The immense property of Tshelebi's family added to his personal qualities, rendered his influence and power so great that during twenty years he obliged several Pashas who would not yield to his counsels and designs to quit the town.   He never would accept of the repeated offers made by the Porte to raise him to the Pashalik. His interests were in some measure supported by the corps of Janissaries; who in Aleppo, as in other

Turkish towns, constitute the regular military force of the Porte; but until that period their chiefs had been without the smallest weight in the management of public affairs. One of Tshelebi's household officers, Ibrahim Beg, had meanwhile been promoted, through the friends of his patron at Constantinople, to the first dignities in the town. He was made Mutsellim (vice governor), and Mohassel (chief custom house officer), and after the death of Tshelebi, his power devolved upon Ibrahim. This was in 1786.

Kussa Pasha, a man of probity and talents, was sent at that time as Pasha to Aleppo. Being naturally jealous of Ibrahim Beg's influence, he endeavoured to get possession of his person, by ordering him to be detained during a visit, made by Ibrahim to compliment the Pasha upon his arrival, for a debt which Ibrahim owed to a foreign merchant, who had preferred his complaints to the Pasha's tribunal. Ibrahim paid the debt, and was no sooner out of the Pasha's immediate reach, than he engaged Ahmed Aga (one of the present Janissary chiefs), to enter with him into a formal league against Kussa. The Janissaries, together with Ibrahim's party, attacked the Pasha's troops; who after several days fighting, were driven out of the town, and Ibrahim was soon afterwards named Pasha of three tails, and for the first time Pasha of Aleppo. From that period (1788-89) may be dated the power of the Janissaries. Ibrahim had been the cause of their rising into consideration, but he soon found that their party was acquiring too much strength; he therefore deemed it necessary to countenance the Sherifs, and being a man of great talents, he governed and plundered the town, by artfully opposing the two parties to each other. In the year 1789, Ibrahim was nominated to the Pashalik of Damascus. Sherif Pasha, a man of ordinary capacity, being sent to Aleppo, the Janissaries soon usurped the powers of government.

At the time of the French invasion of Egypt, the intrigues of Djezzar Pasha of Akka drove Ibrahim from his post at Damascus, and he was obliged to follow the Grand Vizir's army into Egypt. When after the campaign of Egypt the Grand Vizir with the remains of his army, was approaching Aleppo upon his return to Constantinople, Ibrahim conceived hopes of regaining his lost seat at Aleppo. Through the means of his son Mohammed Beg, then Mobassei, the Janissaries were persuaded that the Vizir had evil intentions against them, forged letters were produced to that effect, and the whole body of Janissaries left the town before the Vizir's arrival in its neighbourhood. Their flight gave Ibrahim the sought for opportunity to represent the fugitives to the Vizir as rebels afraid to meet their master's presence; they were shortly afterwards, by a Firmahn from the Porte, formally proscribed as rebels, and the killing of any of them who should enter the territory of Aleppo was declared lawful. They had retired to Damascus, Latikia, Tripoli, and the mountains of the Druses, and they spared no money to get the edict of their exile rescinded. After a tedious bargain for the price of their pardon, they succeeded at last in obtaining it, on condition of paying one hundred thousand piastres into the Sultan's treasury. Ibrahim Pasha, who had in the meanwhile regained the Pashalik of Aleppo, was to receive that sum from them, and he had so well played his game, that the Janissaries still thought him their secret friend. The principal chiefs, trusting to Ibrahim's assurances, came to the town for the purpose of paying down the money; they were a few days afterwards arrested, and it was generally believed that Ibrahim would order them the same night to be strangled. In Turkey however, there are always hopes as long as the purse is not exhausted. The prisoners engaged Mohammed, Ibrahim's beloved son, to intercede in their favour; they paid him for that service one thousand zequins in advance, and promised as much more: and he effectually extorted from his father a promise not to kill any of them. It is said that Ibrahim foretold his son that the time would come when he would repent of his intercession. A short time afterwards Ibrahim was nominated a second time to the Pashalik of Damascus, which became vacant by Djezzar's death, in 1804. His prisoners were obliged to follow him to Damascus; from whence they found means to open a correspondence with the Emir Beshir, the chief of the Druses, and to prevail upon him to use all his interest with Ibrahim to effect their deliverance. Ibrahim stood at that time in need of the Emir's friendship; he had received orders from the Porte to seize upon Djezzar's treasures at Akka, and to effect this the co-operation of the Druse chief was absolutely necessary. Upon the Emir's reiterated applications, the prisoners were at last liberated.

When Ibrahim Pasha removed to Damascus, he procured the Pashalik of Aleppo for his son Mohammed Pasha, a man who possesses in a high degree the qualification so necessary in a delegate of the Porte, of understanding how to plunder his subjects. The chief of a Sherif family, Ibn Hassan Aga Khalas (who has since entered into the corps of the Janissaries, and is now one of their principal men), was the first who resolved to oppose open force to his measures; he engaged at first only seven or eight other families to join him, and it was with this feeble force that the rebellion broke out which put an end to the Pasha's government. The confederates began by knocking down the Pasha's men in the streets wherever they met them, Janissaries soon assembled from all quarters to join Hassan's party; and between two or three hundred Deli Bashi or regular troops of the Pasha were massacred in the night in their own habitations, to which the rebels found access from the neighbouring terraces or flat roofs. Still the Pasha's troops would have subdued the insurgents had it not been for the desperate bravery of Hassan Aga. After several months daily fighting in the streets, in which the Pasha's troops had thrown up entrenchments, want of food began to be sensibly felt in the part of the city which his adherents occupied near the Serai, a very spacious building now in ruins. He came therefore to the resolution of abandoning the city. At Mohammed's request a Tartar was sent, from Constantinople, with orders enjoining him to march against Berber, governor of Tripoli, who had been declared a rebel. Having thus covered the disgrace of his defeat, he marched out of Aleppo in the end of 1804, but instead of proceeding to Tripoli, he established his head quarters at Sheikh Abou Beker, a monastery of Derwishes situated upon an elevation only at one mile's distance from Aleppo, where he recruited his troops and prepared himself to besiege the town. His affairs, however, took a more favourable turn upon the arrival of a Kapidgi Bashi or officer of the Porte from Constantinople, who carried with him the most positive orders that Mohammed Pasha should remain governor of Aleppo, and be acknowledged as such by the inhabitants, The Kapidgi's persuasions, as well as the Sultan's commands, which the Janissaries did not dare openly to disobey, brought on a compromise, in consequence of which the Pasha re-entered the city. So far he had gained his point, but he soon found himself in his palace without friends or influence; the Janissaries were heard to declare that every body who should visit him would be looked upon as a spy; on Fridays alone, the great people paid him their visit in a body. The place meanwhile was governed by the chiefs of the Janissaries and the Sherifs. At length the Pasha succeeded, by a secret nightly correspondence, to detach the latter from the Janissaries, who were gaining the ascendancy. The Sherifs are the natural supporters of government in this country; most of the villages round Aleppo were then in their possession, they command the landed interests, all the Aleppo grandees of ancient families, and all the Ulemas and Effendis belong to their body, and the generality of them have received some education, while out of one hundred Janissaries, there are scarcely five who know how to read or to write their own names. The civil war now broke out afresh, and Mohammed had again the worst of it. After remaining three months in the town, he returned to his former encampment at Sheikh Abou Beker, from whence he assisted his party in the town who had taken possession of the castle and several mosques. This warfare lasted nearly two years without any considerable losses on either side. The Sherifs were driven out of the mosques, but defended themselves in the castle.

Generally, the people of Aleppo, Janissaries as well as Sherifs, are a cowardly race. The former never ventured to meet the Pasha's troops on the outside of their walls, the latter did not once sally forth from the castle, but contented themselves with firing into the town, and principally against Bankousa, a quarter exclusively inhabited by Janissaries. The Pasha on his side would have ordered his Arnaouts to take the town by assault, had not his own party been jealous of his military power, and apprehensive of the fury of an assaulting army, for which reason they constantly endeavoured to prevent any vigorous attack, promising that they would alone bring the enemy to terms. After nearly two years fighting, during which time a considerable part of the town was laid in ruins, the Pasha with the Sherifs were on the point of succeeding, and compelling the Janissaries to surrender. The chiefs of the Janissaries had applied to the European Consuls for their mediation between them and the Pasha, the conditions of their surrender were already drawn up, and in a few days more their power in Aleppo would probably have been for ever annihilated by a treacherous infraction of the capitulation, when, by a fortunate mistake, a Tartar, sent from Constantinople to Mohammed, entered the town, instead of taking his packet to Sheikh Abou Beker; the Janissaries opened the dispatches, and found them to contain a Firmahn, by which Mohammed Pasha was recalled from his Pashalik of Aleppo. This put an end to the war; Mohammed dismissed the greater part of his troops and retired: the Janissaries came to a compromise with the Sherifs in the castle, and have since that time been absolute masters of the city.

I cannot omit mentioning that during the whole of the civil war, the persons and property of the Franks were rigidly respected. It sometimes happened that parties of Sherifs and Janissaries skirmishing in the Bazars, left off firing by common consent, when a Frank was seen passing, and that the firing from the Minarets ceased, when Franks passed over their flat roofs from one house to another. The Janissaries have this virtue in the eyes of the Franks, that they are not in the smallest degree fanatical; the character of a Sherif is quite the contrary, and whenever religious disputes happen, they are always excited and supported by some greenhead.

Since the removal of Mohammed Pasha the Porte has continued to nominate his successors; but the name of Pasha of Aleppo is now nothing more than a vain title. His first successor was Alla eddin Pasha, a near relation of Sultan Selim: then Waledin Pasha, Othman Pasha Darukly, Ibrahim Pasha, a third time, and the present governor Seruri Mohammed Pasha. Except the last, who is now in the Grand Vizir's camp near Constantinople they have all resided at Aleppo, but they occupied the Serai more like state prisoners than governors. They never were able to carry the most trifling orders into effect, without feeing in some way or other the chiefs of the Ja [n]issaries to grant their consent.

The corps of Janissaries, or the Odjak of Aleppo, was formerly divided, as in other Turkish towns, into companies or Ortas, but since the time of their getting into power, they have ceased to submit to any regular discipline: they form a disorderly body of from three to four thousand men, and daily increase their strength and number by recruits from the Sherifs. Those who possess the greatest riches, and whose family and friends are the most numerous, are looked upon as their chiefs, though they are unable to exercise any kind of discipline. Of these chiefs there are at present six principal ones, who have succeeded in sharing the most lucrative branches of the revenue, and what seems almost incredible, they have for the last six years preserved harmony amongst themselves; Hadji Ibrahim Ibn Herbely is at this moment the richest and most potent of them all.

The legal forms of Government have not been changed, and the Janissaries outwardly profess to be the dutiful subjects of the Porte. The civil administration is nominally in the hands of the Mutsellim, who is named by the Pasha and confirmed by the Porte. the Kadhi presides in the court of justice, and the Mohassel or chief custom house officer is [a]llowed to perform his functions in the name of his master, but the Mutsellim dares not enforce any orders from the Porte nor the Kadhi decide any law suit of importance, without being previously sure of the consent of some of the chief Janissaries. The revenue which the grand Signior receives at this moment from Aleppo is limited to the Miri, or general landtax, which the Janissaries themselves pay, the Kharatsh or tribute of the Christians and Jews, and the income of the custom house, which is now rented at the yearly rate of eighty thousand piastres. Besides these there are several civil appointments in the town, which are sold every year at Constantinople to the highest bidder: the Janissaries are in the possession of the most lucrative of them, and remit regularly to the Porte the purchase money. The outward decorum which the Janissaries have never ceased to observe towards the Porte is owing to their fear of offending public opinion, so as to endanger their own security. The Porte, on the other hand, has not the means of subduing these rebels, established as their power now is, without calling forth all her resources and ordering an army to march against them, from Constantinople. The expense of such an enterprize would hardly be counterbalanced by the profits of its success; for the Janissaries, pushed to extremities, would leave the town and find a secure retreat for themselves and their treasures in the mountains of the Druses: both parties therefore endeavour to avoid an open rupture; it is well known that the chief Janissaries send considerable presents to Constantinople to appease their master's anger, and provided the latter draws supplies for his pressing wants, no matter how or from whence, the insults offered to his supreme authority are easily overlooked.

The Janissaries chiefly exercise their power with a view to the filling of their purses. Every inhabitant of Aleppo, whether Turk or Christian, provided he be not himself a Janissary, is obliged to have a protector among them to whom he applies in case of need, to arrange his litigations, to enforce payment from his creditors, and to protect him from the vexations and exactions of other Janissaries. Each protector receives from his client a sum proportionate to the circumstances of the client's affairs. It varies from twenty to two thousand piastres a year, besides which, whenever the protector terminates an important business to the client's wishes, he expects some extraordinary reward. If two protectors happen to be opposed to each other on account of their clients, the more powerful of the two sometimes carries the point, or if they are equal in influence, they endeavour to settle the business by compromise, in such a way as to give to justice only half its due. Those Janissaries, who have the greatest number of clients are of course the richest, and command the greatest influence. But these are not the only means which the Janissaries employ to extort money. They monopolize the trade of most of the articles of consumption, (which have risen in consequence, to nearly double the price which they bore six years ago), as well as of several of the manufactures of Aleppo; upon others they levy heavy taxes; in short their power is despotic and oppressive; yet they have hitherto abstained from making, like the Pashas, avanies upon individuals by open force, and it is for that reason that the greater part of the Aleppines do not wish for the return of a Pasha. Though the Janissaries extort from the public, by direct and indirect means, more than the Pashas ever did by their avanies, each individual discharges the burthen imposed upon him more readily, because he is confident that it insures the remainder of his fortune; in the Pasha's time, living was cheaper, and regular taxes not oppressive; but the Pasha would upon the most frivolous pretexts order a man of property to be thrown into prison and demand the sacrifice of one fourth of his fortune to grant him his deliverance. Notwithstanding the immense income of the chief Janissaries, they live poorly, without indulging themselves in the usual luxuries of Turks-women and horses. Their gains are hoarded in gold coin, and it is easy to calculate, such is the publicity with which all sort of business is conducted, that the yearly income of several of them cannot amount to less than thirty or forty thousand pounds sterling.

It is necessary to have lived for some time among the Turks, and to have experienced the mildness and peacefulness of their character, and the sobriety and regularity of their habits, to conceive it possible that the inhabitants of a town like Aleppo, should continue to live for years without any legal master, or administration of justice, protected only by a miserable guard of police, and yet that the town should be a safe and quiet residence. No disorders, or nightly tumults occur; and instances of murder and robbery are extremely rare. If serious quarrels sometimes happen, it is chiefly among the young Janissaries heated with brandy and amorous passion, who after sunset fight their rivals at the door of some prostitute. This precarious security is however enjoyed only within the walls of the city; the whole neighbourhood of Aleppo is infested by obscure tribes of Arab and Kurdine robbers, who through the negligence of the Janissaries, acquire every day more insolence and more confidence in the success of their enterprises. Caravans of forty or fifty camels have in the course of last winter been several times attacked and plundered at five hundred yards from the city gate, not a week passes without somebody being ill-treated and stripped in the gardens near the town; and the robbers have even sometimes taken their night's rest in one of the suburbs of the city, and there sold their cheaply acquired booty. In the time of Ibrahim Pasha, the neighbourhood of Aleppo to the distance of four or five hours, was kept in perfect security from all hostile inroads of the Arabs, by the Pasha's cavalry guard of Deli Bashi. But the Janissaries are very averse from exposing themselves to danger; there is moreover no head among them to command, no common purse to pay the necessary expences, nor any individual to whose hands the public money might be trusted.

III. The Hadj Route from Damascus to Mekka.

IN later times the Hadj has been accustomed to leave Damascus on the 15th Shauwal. On the 26th or 27th it leaves Mezerib, and meets the new moon at Remtha or Fedhein.

The Hadj route from Damascus to Mekka has changed three different times; at first it passed on the eastern side of Djebel Haouran; the fear of the Arabs made the Pashas prefer afterwards the route through the Ledja and Boszra; about eighty years ago the present caravan route was established.

1st. day. The Emir el Hadj leaves the town about mid-day, and remains the night at Kubbet el Hadj el Azeli, an ancient mosque at a quarter of an hour from Bab Ullah or the southern gate of Damascus. Near the Kubbe lies the village of Kadem.

2. At four hours is the village of Kessoue, with a well provided Bazar. One hour Khan Denoun, situated on the river Aawadj, which comes from Hasbeia and empties itself into the Ghouta of Damascus. The Khan is in ruins. At a quarter of an hour to the S.E. from it lies the village of Khiara.

3. Four hours from Denoun is the village Ghebaib; it has a small Khan to the left of the Hadj route, to the right of it is a Birket or reservoir of water, which is supplied by the river Shak-heb, whose source, Ain Shak-heb, with a village called Shak-heb, lies to the N.W. of Ghebaib. In that source the barbers of Damascus collect leeches, The Shak-heb loses itself in the plain of the Haouran, after having watered the gardens and Dhourra fields of Ghebaib. Three hours farther the village Didy; one hour farther the ruins of a town and castle called Es-szanamein, where there are two towers built of black stone, still remaining. The Fellahs have a few houses there. An hour and a half farther a hill with a small Birket at its

foot, called El Fekia, containing a source which loses itself in the eastern plain. The Hadj passes the night sometimes here, and sometimes at Szannamein.

4. At four hours from Szannamein is a hill called the hill of Dilly, with a ruined village at the top. At its foot flows a river whose source is at Tel Serraia, a hill two hours W. of Dilly, likewise with a ruined village. The river works a mill near Dilly. In winter and spring time the district of Dilly is a deep bog; at four hours farther is a village called Shemskein, of considerable size, and in a prosperous state. Three hours farther is Tafs, a village, ruined by the Wahabis in June 1810. One hour farther is El Mezareib, with a castle of middling size, and the principal place in the Haouran next to Boszra.

5. At one hour from Mezareib is the Wady el Medan, which comes from the Djebel Haouran. In winter time the Hadjis were often embarrassed by it. Djezzar Pasha ordered a bridge to be built over it. The ground is a fine gravel; even in summer time, when the Wady is dry, water is found every where underground by digging to the depth of two or three ells. At three hours is the village El Remtha, inhabited by Fellahs, who have about ten cisterns of rain-water, and a small Birket in the neighbourhood of the village. Most of them live in caverns underground, which they arrange into habitations; the caverns are in a white rock. The Sheikh of Remtha is generally a Santon, that dignity being in the family of Ezzabi, who possesses there a mosque of the same name. On account of the sanctity of his family, the Pasha does not take any Miri from the Sheikh Ezzabi. The Hadjis sometimes sleep at Remtha, at other times they go as far as Fedhein, also called Mefrak, a castle four hours from Remtha, where the Pasha keeps a small garrison, under the orders of an Aga, or Odabashi. The Arabs of the Belka are in the habit of depositing in the castle of Fedhein their superfluous provisions of wheat and barley, which they retake the next year, or sell to the Hadj, after having paid to the Aga a certain retribution. From Fedhein runs a Wady E. which turns, after one day's journey towards the S. and is then called Wady Botun. The Djebel Heish, which continues its southerly course to the W. of the Hadj route, changes its name in the latitude of Fedhein into that of Djebel Belka. To the east of Fedhein the Djebel Haouran terminates, not far to the North of Boszra. At one day's journey from where the mountain finishes lies the village of Szalkhat. From Fedhein to the south-east the plain is uncultivated, and without habitations.

6. The castle of Zerka is at one day's journey from Fedhein. The Hadj rests here one day, during which the Hadjis amuse themselves with

hunting the wild boars which are found in great numbers on the reedy banks of Wady Zerka. The castle is built in a low Wady which forms in winter-time the bed of a river of considerable size, called Naher Ezzerka, whose waters collect to the south of Djebel Haouran. In summer time the Wady to the E. of the castle has no water in it, but to the west, where there are some sources, the river is never completely dried up. It then enters the Djebel Belka and empties itself into the Sheriat el Kebir. The Pasha of Damascus has an Aga in the castle, who is always an Arab of the tribe of Ehteim, part of whom live in tents round the castle and sow the ground. They have plenty of grapes, and sow Dhourra and wheat.

7. One day's journey is Kalaat el Belka. The name of Kalaat, or castle, is given on the Hadj route, and over the greater part of the desert, to any building walled in, and covered, and having, like a Khan, a large court-yard in its enclosure. The walls are sometimes of stone, but more commonly of earth, though even the latter are sufficient to withstand an attack of Arabs. The castle of Belka has a large Birket of rain-water. Its commander or Odabashi is always chosen from among the Janissaries of Damascus. It serves the Arabs of the Djebel Belka as a depot for their provisions. To the west of the castle the mountain of Belka terminates. The Arabs of Belka live in tents round the castle, and are Felahein or cultivators of the ground.

8. One day's journey from the latter is the Kalaat el Katrane, whose Odabashi is likewise a Janissary from Damascus. It has a Birket of rainwater. At one day's journey to the N.W. of it is the Kalaat Kerek, from whence the Arabs of Kerek bring wheat and barley for sale to the Odabashi of Katrane, who sells it again to advantage to the Hadjis.

9. One day's journey Kalaat el Hassa,, with a fine source, whose water is drawn up by means of a large wheel. The castle is built in the middle of a Wady running from E. to W.; in the winter a river runs through the Wady, which is dry in summer; but at a quarter of an hour W. from the castle, there are several springs of good water, which are never dry. They collect into a river which empties itself into the Jordan or Sheriat el Kebir at two days' journey from El Hassa. The Fellahs who live round the castle in the Wady, in several small villages, sow Dhourra and barley, those that live towards the western mountains, sow for their masters the El Hadjaia Arabs, and receive from them half of the harvest in return. To the S.E. of El Hassa, on the northern side of the Wady, about five hours distance from El Hassa, is a high hill, called Shehak, which is visible from Masn and Akaba. At the same distance due east from El Hassa is a watering place called Meshash el Rekban, where water is found

on digging to a small depth. To the S. of Wady el Hassa, in the Djebel Shera, is the town of Tafyle. South of it the Shera spreads into four or five branches, and embraces the whole country as far as Djebel Tor. At two days journey from Wady el Hassa, is a road leading along the summit of the mountain towards Gaza; this road is called Akaba, or more frequently Eddhohel; it is much frequented by the people of Tafyle and the Arabs Toueiha.

10. Half a day's journey is Kalaat Aeneze, with a Birket of rain-water.

11. Another half day's journey Kalaat Maan, where the Hadjis remain for two days. Maan has a large well of water. The town consists of about one hundred houses on both sides the Hadj route, which divides the town; the eastern part is called Shamie, the western Maan. The inhabitants cultivate figs, pomegranates, and plums in large quantities, but do not sow their fields. They purchase wheat from Kerek, which their women grind; and at the passage of the Hadj they sell the flour as well as their fruits to the pilgrims; which, is their means of subsistence. They purchase articles of dress and luxury from Ghaza and El Khalil.

12. A long day's journey to the castle of Akaba Esshamie, or the Syrian Akaba, so called in opposition to the Akaba el Masri or the Egyptian Akaba which is on the eastern branch of the Red-sea, at one day's journey from the Akaba Esshamie; here is a Birket of rain-water. The Hadj road, as far as Akaba, is a complete desert on both sides, yet not incapable of culture. The mountain chain continues at about ten hours to the west of the Hadj route. Akaba is in the hands of the Arabs el Howeytat, who are in communication with Cairo. From the foot of the castle walls the Hadj descends a deep chasm, and it takes half an hour to reach the plain below. The pilgrims fear that passage, and repeat this prayer before they descend; "May the Almighty God be merciful to them who descend into the belly of the dragon". The mountain consists of a red gray sand stone, which is used at Damascus for whetstones. There are many places where the stones are full of small holes. When the pilgrims reach the bottom of the descent they fire off their pistols for the sake of the echo. The mountain sinks gradually, and is lost at a great distance in the plain, which is very sandy. [FN#1]

13. Medawara, one day's journey, a castle with a Birket of rain-water.

14. Dzat Hadj, a castle surrounded by a great number of wells, which are easily found on digging two or three feet. It has likewise a

Birket of rainwater. At four hours from it is a descent, rendered difficult by the deep sand. It is called El Araie, or Halat Ammar; it was here that in the time of Daher el Omar, Pasha of Acre, and of Osman, Pasha of Damascus, the Arabs Beni Szakher plundered the Hadj in the year 1170 of the Hedjra (1757), the only example of such an event in the last century. From Halat Ammar the plain is no longer sandy, but covered with a white earth as far as Tebouk. The vicinity of Dzat Hadj is covered with palm trees: but the trees being male, they bear no fruit, and remain very low. The inhabitants sell the wood to the Hadj.

15. One day from Dzat Hadj is Tebouk, a castle, with a village of Felahein, of the tribe of Arabs Hammeide. There is a copious source of water, and gardens of fig and pomegranate trees, where Badintshaus (egg plant), onions, and ether vegetables are also cultivated. The Fellahs collect in the neighbouring desert the herb Beiteran (a species of milfoil), which the Hadjis buy up, and bring to Damascus. The castle is also surrounded by shrubs with long spines called Mehdab, which the Fellahs sell to the Hadj as food for the camels, and likewise two other herbs called Nassi and Muassal. They thus earn their livelihood. If the Hadj arrives in the neighbourhood of Tebouk at night, the bones of dead camels indicate the way to the castle. The Hadj rests here one day: and on its return is met by the Djerde, or provision caravan, headed by the Pasha of Tripoli, by which all the Syrian pilgrims, receive refreshments, sent by their families.

16. Akhdhar, a castle with a Birket of rainwater, upon a small ascent. Two or three hundred years ago, the Hadj went to the E. of the present route, and it is even now called the eastern road.

17. El Moadham, a very long day's march.

18. Dar el Hamra.

19. Medayn Szaleh, with a number of habitations hewn in the rock; and many sculptured figures of men and animals.

20. El Olla, a village of about two hundred and fifty houses, with a rivulet and agreeable gardens of fruit trees. Its inhabitants are all of barbaresque origin.

21. Biar el Ghanam, with many wells of fresh water.

22. Byr Zemerrod, a large well.

23. Byr Djedeyde.

24. Hedye, where the Hadj remains two days. It is a Ghadeir, or low Wady coming from Khaibar, which is four hours distant. The people of the caravan often go thither to buy fresh provisions.

25. El Fahletein; apes, and what the Arabs call tigers, are met with here. An ancient building of black stones is near it; it is called Stabel Antar.

26. Biar Naszeif, a number of wells in the sandy ground, which are every year newly digged up, because the wind covers them immediately after the caravan's departure. El Fahletein is the last castle. At all these stations small castles have been built, close to the basons in which the rain water is collected. If there are any wells, they are within the walls of the castle, and the water is drawn up by camels in order to fill the basons, on the arrival of the Hadj. The pilgrims, in order to lighten their loads, generally leave in every castle a small parcel of provisions, which they take on their return. These castles are garrisoned by four or five men of Damascus, who remain shut up there the whole year until they are relieved by the passage of the caravan. It often happens that only one man is left alive of the number; the others having been either killed by the Arabs, or having died from the effects of the confinement, for the fear of the Arabs seldom permits them to issue out of the castle. Each of these castles has a Meghaffer, or protector, among the neighbouring Arab tribes, to whom the Pasha pays a certain tribute. The office of these guardians, who are usually inhabitants of the Meidhan or suburb of Damascus, is very lucrative, on account of the presents and small contributions paid to them by the pilgrims. One of them has been known to remain for twenty-three years at Fahletein. Ibn Balousa, a man of the Meidhan of Damascus, is looked upon as the chief of all these castles, and resides generally at El Hassa.

27. El Medine, where the Hadj remains three days. There are two different roads leading from Medine to Mekke, the eastern and western. The principal men of the Arab tribes of both routes meet the Pasha at Medine, to learn which road the Hadj intends to take, and to treat with him about the passage duty. On the eastern route, the first station from Medine is:

28. (1) El Khona, a deep Wady with rain water.

29. (2) El Dereybe, a village with walls.

30. (3) Sefyne, a village.

31. (4) El Kobab, an assemblage of wells.

32. (5) Biar el Hedjar, wells.

33. (6) Set Zebeyde, a ruined village with a large Birket.

34. (7) El Makhrouka, wells.

35. (8) Wady Leimoun, a village with a rivulet.

36 (9) Byr el Baghle, wells.

37.(10) Mekke.

The western road, or as it is likewise called, the great road is the more usual, but Djezzar always used to take the other. The first station from Medine on this route is:

28. (1) Biar Aly, a village with wells and gardens.

29. (2) El Shohada, a spot in the plain, without any water.

30. (3) Djedeyde, and at a short distance before it the well called Byr Dzat el Aalem. Djedeyde is a considerable village on the sides of a rivulet. The Sheikh of the western route lives here. The year before the last Hadj caravan effected its passage, Abdullah Pasha of Damascus was attacked in a Wady near Djedeyde by the armed population of that village, who were Wahabi. They routed his army, and obliged him to pay forty thousand dollars for his passage. From Djedeyde the route leads through the villages of Esszafra, and El Hamra, to the second station, which is:

31. (4) The famous Beder, where Mohammed laid the foundation of his power by his victory over his combined enemies. It contains upwards of five hundred houses, with a rivulet. The Egyptian pilgrim caravan generally meets here the Syrian.

32. (5) El Kaa, a spot in the desert without any water. From thence a long march to

33. (6) El Akdyd, which is twenty-eight hours distant from Beder.

34. (7) Rabagh, a village. Between Rabagh and Khalysz, the Red sea is seen from the Hadj route. There are Wadys coming from the Red sea, which in times of high flood are filled with the sea water; it remains sometimes during the whole summer, at a distance of six and seven hours from the sea. The water brings with it a large quantity of fish. The camels and horses drink the water of these Wadys.

35. (8) Khalysz, a village with a rivulet.

36. (9) El Szafan, two wells.

37.(10) Wady Fatme, a rivulet, with a village and gardens.

38. Mekke.

APPENDICES

[FN#1] To the southward of Kerek all the women on the Hadj route wear the Egyptian face veil or Berkoa, which is not a Syrian fashion.

IV. Description of the Route from Boszra in the Haouran, to the Djebel Shammor

ON the western side of the Djebel Haouran, at a small distance from its southern extremity, lies Boszra. On the eastern foot and declivity of Djebel Haouran, are upwards of two hundred villages built of black stone in ruins, at a quarter or half an hour's distance from each other. The country beyond them is completely level and is called El Hammad. About five hours to the S. of the Djebel, lies the half ruined town of Szalkhat; it has a large castle, with strong walls, several cisterns and Birkets of rain-water. From that place begins the Wady Serhhan, which runs to the E.S.E. It is a low ground, with sloping sides; at every three or four hours a well is met with in the Wady, with a little grass round it, but even in winter there is no running stream; though water is found in many places at a small depth below the surface of the earth. The traveller frequently passes in that Wady small hills (Tels), which consist of thin layers of salt (about six inches thick), alternating with layers of earth of the same thickness. The Arabs sell the salt in the villages of the Haouran. Following the course of that Wady, which at length takes a more southerly direction, you arrive, after ten or eleven days journey (with camels about eight days), in the country called Djof. The Tels about Djof are called Kara. The Djof is a collection of seven or eight villages, built at a distance of ten minutes or a quarter of an hour from each other, in an easterly line. The ground is pure sand. These villages are called Souk (or markets), the principal of them are: Souk Ain Um Salim, Souk Eddourra, Souk Esseideiin, Souk Douma, Souk Mared. These villages are all built alike: the houses are built round the inside of a large square mud wall, which has but one entrance. This wall therefore serves as a common back wall to all the houses, which amount in some of the Souks to one hundred and twenty, in others from eighty to one hundred. The middle part of the enclosed square is empty. The roofs of the houses are made of palm wood, and their walls of bricks, called Leben, dried in the sun, which are about two feet square, and one foot thick. When strangers arrive, their camels remain in the middle of the Souk, and they themselves lodge at the different houses. Round the Souk are gardens of palm trees, which the inhabitants call Houta: in several of these are deep wells, the water from some of which is conducted by small canals into the gardens of those, who not having any wells are obliged to purchase water from their neighbours. She camels are employed to draw the water out of the wells; this is done by tying a rope round the camel, which walks away from the well till the bucket, which is fastened to the other end of the rope, is drawn up, and empties its contents into the canals. These she camels are called Sanie. Most of the inhabitants of the Djof are either petty merchants or artificers; they work in leather, wood, iron, and make boots, sword hilts, horse shoes, lance heads, &c. which they sell to the Arabs, together with the produce of their palm trees; in return they, take camels. They sow very little wheat; the small extent of ground which they cultivate is worked with the hand; for they have no ploughs. They eat very little bread, living upon dates, butter, and flesh meat. Besides the game which they hunt in the neighbourhood, they eat camels flesh almost daily, and they even devour the ostriches and wild dogs, the former of which are sold to them by the Arabs Sherarat. They preserve their dates in large earthen jars for the use of the great Arab tribes which often pass here; of these the Rowalla come almost every year: before the time of the Wahabi, the El Hessene and Beni Szakher likewise visited the Djof.

The Felahein of the Djof are called Karaune, a name which in the neighbourhood of Damascus is given to all Syrians or those who are presumed to be of Syrian origin. Although Fellahs, the people of the Djof intermarry with Arab girls, whence it happens that many Arabs of Shammor and Serhan have settled here and become Fellahs; and they continue notwithstanding, to be looked upon in their respective tribes by the heads of families, as proper husbands for their daughters. The workmen or artificers, on the contrary, never can marry Arab girls, nor even the daughters of the Fellahs, their immediate neighbours; they intermarry exclusively amongst themselves, or amongst the workmen who have settled in the Bedouin encampments.

Every Souk has a Sheikh or chief; the name of the present grand Sheikh is Ibn Deraa. It is about twenty years since they were converted to the Wahabi creed. Their grand Sheikh collects the tribute or Zika, for Ibn Saoud, and lodges it in a particular house; after taking from it the necessary expense for entertaining strangers, or for provisions for Wahabi corps which pass by, he sends the remainder to Saoud. The people of the Djof are all armed with firelocks; they have no horses.

At Souk Mared is an ancient tower of remarkable structure. Its height, I was told, is greater than the Minaret near my lodgings at Damascus, which I should compute at about forty-five feet. Its basis is square, it rises in steps and ends in a point; I had already heard at Aleppo from some travelling Turks, that there were in the desert, towards Deraye, pyramids like those of Cairo; by which they probably meant the Souk Mared. The door of the tower is about ten feet high and eight broad; but it is half filled up. The Kasr gate of Salamia, [FN#2] which is of wood with iron bars, has been transported here by the Arabs to serve as a gate for the tower. The inside is not paved. There are three floors, and staircases leading from one to the other. There are very small windows in the sides of the tower, which seem rather to have been destined for loop holes for musquetty. The walls of the tower are built of large square white stones, and are in good preservation. The two floors one over the other are not vaulted. On the top of the tower a watchman constantly resides, to give notice of the arrival of strangers. To the E. and somewhat to the S. from Djof, three hours, begins the plain called Eddhahi or Taous, a sandy desert full of small hills or Tels, from which it derives the name of. Although there is no water in the plain, a tree is very abundant which the Arabs call Ghada, about eight feet high; the people of Djof burn it as fire wood. Near the trees grows in spring a kind of grass, which in summer soon dries up, it is called Nassy, and resembles wheat. Wild cows are found here. My man told me that they resemble in every particular the domestic cow. The Arabs Sherarat kill them, eat them, and make of the leather targets, which are much esteemed. Of their horns the people of Djof make knife handles. Wild dogs, Derboun, of a black colour, are likewise met with here; the Arabs kill and eat them. It is principally in the Dhahy that ostriches breed, and great quantities of them are killed there. This desert is moreover inhabited by a large lizard called Dhab, of one foot and a half in length with a tail of half a foot, exactly resembling in shape the common lizard, but larger. The Arabs eat them in defiance of the laws of their prophet; the scaly skin serves them instead of a goat skin to preserve their butter in. These Arabs likewise eat all the eagles and crows which they can kill. The plain of Eddhahi continues for three days camel's march (with a caravan it would take six days), without any water, extending as far as the chain of mountains called Djebel Shammor which runs in an easterly direction five or six days journey. From where it ends to Deraye, the seat of Ibn Saoud, are ten days more. The Djebel Shammor is inhabited by the Arabs Shammor, many of whom have become Fellahs, and live in villages in these mountains. They are true and faithful Wahabis.

[FN#2] Salamia is a ruin eight or ten hours S.E. of Hamah.

V. A Route to the eastward of the Castle El Hassa.

FROM Kalaat el Hassa, towards E.S.E. continues the already mentioned Wady el Hassa. Passing the Tel Esshehak, two days journey from it, you meet with a great number of Tels, in the midst of which there is a well of good spring water called Byr Bair; near it is a tombstone, said to be the burial place of the son of Sultan Hassan. From Bair eastwards the Wady and its vicinity are called the district of Hudrush; it is without water, with the exception of the rain water which collects in the low grounds. The Hudrush extends for two days, as far as the country called Ettebig. From the beginning of Hudrush the Wady makes a bend to the N. and describing a half circle, again returns in the Tebig to its original direction. To the N. from Hudrush and Tebig the plain takes the name of Szauan, (i.e. flint) and extends for two days till it borders upon the Wady Serhhan. The plain Szauan is covered so thickly with small black flints, that the Arabs, whenever they are about to light a fire there, cover the ground with earth, which they carry with them, in order to prevent the splinters of the flint heated by the fire, from flying about and hurting them. There is but one spring in the Szauan: it is about two hours from Wady Serhhan, and at the same distance from Hudrush and Tebig, and is called Byr Naam el aatta Allah, in honour of a Christian travelling merchant, who about sixty years ago lying upon the flint, heard the noise of the water under his head, and thus discovered the spring. On the western side of the Szauan, nearer to the Wady Serhhan than to the Hudrush, is a castle called Kaszr Amera, and at a quarter of an hour from it, on the foot of a hill, the ruins of a village. Between the Kaszr and the village is a low ground where the rain water collects, and forms a small lake in winter half an hour in length. Before the castle is a well more than thirty feet deep, walled in by large stones, but without water. Over the well are four white marble columns, which support a vaulted roof or Kubbe, such as are often seen at wells in these countries. The castle is built of white square stones, which seem not to have been cemented together. Its dimensions are thirty-six or forty feet from W. to E. and twenty-five from S. to N. The entrance door, which is only about three feet high, is on the S. side, and leads into an apartment half the size of the whole building. In the middle of the western wall of this apartment is another door, as low as the former, leading to a second apartment of the same size as the former, except that one corner is partitioned off to form a third chamber. Each of the two latter have a window in the western wall. The roof of the apartments are vaulted below, and flat above. The walls which divide the apartments are two yards in thickness; in the two first rooms there is a stone pavement, in the small room the Arabs have taken up the pavement to dig for treasures; but they found nothing underneath, except small pieces of planks and some rusty iron. The ceiling of all the three apartments is chalked over, and looks quite new. In the small room it is painted all over with serpents, hares, gazelles, mares, and birds; there are neither human figures nor trees amongst the paintings. The colour of the paintings is red, green, and yellow, and they look as bright and well preserved, as if they had been done a short time ago. There are no kinds of niches, bas-reliefs, or inscriptions in the walls.

From Hudrush branches out a Wady towards Wady Serhhan, called Chadef. Four days beyond Tebig you arrive at a Byr called El Sheben or Szefan, situated upon a small ascent. According to my informant the Byr is two hundred yards in depth. To the north of that well the desert is called Beseita. For two days farther the earth is covered to the depth of six inches with small black gray stones, looking like flints. The plant Samah grows there, which is collected by the people of Djof. From the end of the Beseita to the Djof is one day's journey farther, and the Beseita ends in the Dhahi.

All the Arabs along this road from El Hassa, are Sherarat, the Aeneze do not come this way.

Between Tebig, Szauan, Hudrush, and to the S. of these places, are a quantity of wild asses, which the Arabs Sherarat hunt, and eat (secretly). Their skins and hoofs are sold to the wandering Christian pedlars, and in the towns of Syria. Of the hoofs rings are made, which the Fellahs of eastern Syria wear on the thumb, or tied with a thread round the armpit, to prevent, or to heal rheumatic complaints. I may here make a general remark that there is an infinity of names of places in the desert. Every Tel, every declivity, or, elevation in a Wady, every extent of plain ground, where a particular herb grows, has its name, well known to the Arabs. The Khabera, or places where the rain-water collects, winter-time, are generally distinguished by the name of some well known Sheikh who once pitched his tent near them; as Khabera Ibn Ghebein, the watering places of Ibn Ghebein.

The side of a Wady where the Arab descends is called by him Hadhera, the opposite side, where he re-ascends Sende.

A Ghadir is distinguished from a Wady, the two sides of the latter are hills which rise above the surface of the adjacent plain; the Ghadir on the contrary is only a hollow in the plain. The Wady is seen from afar, the Ghadir only on arriving near the descent.

V. Description of the Desert from the Neighbourhood of Damascus towards the Euphrates.

From the Wady Serhhan northward and north-eastward, the whole desert is called El Hammad, till it reaches the neighbourhood of the Euphrates, where the broad valley of the river is by the Arabs called Oerak (Irak). That name therefore is not exclusively applied to the Djezire or island between the Tigris and the Euphrates, but (in the Bedouin acceptation of the word at least), to the fertile country also between the desert and the river's right bank.

At the end of the Ghouta or Merdj of Damascus, begins the Djebel Haouran, [FN#3] which takes a south direction; to the north runs the Djebel Ruak (towards Tedmor). The intermediate plain, which is about a day and a half in breadth, is called Ard Esseikal, having journied for two days in this plain, the mountains to the S. are no more visible, and a waterless plain lies before the traveller, which according to the camels strength may be crossed in seven, eight, or ten days. Water is met with on the road, only in winter, when rainwater collects in the low grounds, and Ghadirs. There are no hills or Wadys. Small pipe heads, in the eastern fashion, and made of stone, are frequently found in the plain. The Arabs say that an ancient tribe called Beni Tamour fabricated them. At the end of the number of days above-mentioned, a high insulated hill is met with, which is visible all round to the distance of two days journey. The Arabs call it Djebel Laha. It consists of sandy earth: there are no springs near it. From the Djebel Laha run two Wadys towards the Euphrates, the one called Wady Haouran, begins on the hill's western side; the other Wady Tebbel, on its northern side. They run in a parallel direction, till they unite in the vicinity of the Euphrates. To the N.W. of the Laha, at one day's march, is another Wady, called Souan, which takes the same direction with the other two, and joins them, near their termination. In the middle of the Wady Tebbel is spring water. To the E. of Laha, about three days from it, is a low ground called Kaar (the general name given to such places), which is four or five days in circuit. It extends towards the Euphrates. The descent into it is two hundred or two hundred and fifty yards. There are two watering places in it, at a good day's march from each other; Rahh, with a number of springs, and Molassa. There is always some verdure in the Kaar, and when the Aeneze pass that way, the whole tribe encamps there. From Molass it is one day's journey to Gebesse, a poor village in a N.E. direction, from thence to Hit one. Hit, or Ith, is a well known station and village on the banks of the Euphrates.

The Djebel Ruak and the Djebel Abiad (which comes from the west) are united behind Tedmor with the Djebel Belaes which continues its course in a northerly direction, (somewhat to the E.) for two days. There is water in the Belaes but no villages. This mountain at the end of two days changes its name to Djebel Bishr, and terminates after one day's journey in the Zor, which is the name of the broad valley of the Euphrates, on its right bank, from Byr down to Aene and Hit. There are sources in the Bishr, and ruins of villages. It produces also a tree which is about eight feet high, and whose root has so little hold, that the smallest effort will throw it down.

London: Printed by W. Bulmer and W. Nicol, Cleveland-row, St. James's.

[FN#3] This northern part of the Djebel Haouran is called Es-Szaffa. On the eastern side of it is a pass called Bab es-Szaffa, where the mountain is entered by a deep clet in the perpendicular rock, about two yards broad. The passage is about one hundred yards long, it leads to a plain in the middle of the mountain, also called Szaffa, which has no other known entrance, and is two days in circuit. This pass and plain are famed among the Arabs, who often retire there, before the troops of the Pasha of Damascus. There is no water in the Szaffa, except the ponds formed by the winter-rains. The earth is fertile and is occasionally sown by he Arabs when they remain there a sufficient time.

Also from Benediction Books ...

Wandering Between Two Worlds: Essays on Faith and Art
Anita Mathias
Benediction Books, 2007
152 pages
ISBN: 0955373700

Available from www.amazon.com, www.amazon.co.uk
www.wanderingbetweentwoworlds.com

In these wide-ranging lyrical essays, Anita Mathias writes, in lush, lovely prose, of her naughty Catholic childhood in Jamshedpur, India; her large, eccentric family in Mangalore, a sea-coast town converted by the Portuguese in the sixteenth century; her rebellion and atheism as a teenager in her Himalayan boarding school, run by German missionary nuns, St. Mary's Convent, Nainital; and her abrupt religious conversion after which she entered Mother Teresa's convent in Calcutta as a novice. Later rich, elegant essays explore the dualities of her life as a writer, mother, and Christian in the United States-- Domesticity and Art, Writing and Prayer, and the experience of being "an alien and stranger" as an immigrant in America, sensing the need for roots.

About the Author

Anita Mathias was born in India, has a B.A. and M.A. in English from Somerville College, Oxford University and an M.A. in Creative Writing from the Ohio State University. Her essays have been published in The Washington Post, The London Magazine, The Virginia Quarterly Review, Commonweal, Notre Dame Magazine, America, The Christian Century, Religion Online, The Southwest Review, Contemporary Literary Criticism, New Letters, The Journal, and two of HarperSanFrancisco's The Best Spiritual Writing anthologies. Her non-fiction has won fellowships from The National Endowment for the Arts; The Minnesota State Arts Board; The Jerome Foundation, The Vermont Studio Center; The Virginia Centre for the Creative Arts, and the First Prize for the Best General Interest Article from the Catholic Press Association of the United States and Canada. Anita has taught Creative Writing at the College of William and Mary, and now lives and writes in Oxford, England.

"Yesterday's Treasures for Today's Readers"
Titles by Benediction Classics available from Amazon.co.uk

Religio Medici, Hydriotaphia, Letter to a Friend, Thomas Browne

Pseudodoxia Epidemica: Or, Enquiries into Commonly Presumed Truths, Thomas Browne

Urne Buriall and The Garden of Cyrus, Thomas Browne

The Maid's Tragedy, Beaumont and Fletcher

The Custom of the Country, Beaumont and Fletcher

Philaster Or Love Lies a Bleeding, Beaumont and Fletcher

A Treatise of Fishing with an Angle, Dame Juliana Berners.

Pamphilia to Amphilanthus, Lady Mary Wroth

The Compleat Angler, Izaak Walton

The Magnetic Lady, Ben Jonson

Every Man Out of His Humour, Ben Jonson

The Masque of Blacknesse. The Masque of Beauty,. Ben Jonson

The Life of St. Thomas More, William Roper

Pendennis, William Makepeace Thackeray

Salmacis and Hermaphroditus attributed to Francis Beaumont

Friar Bacon and Friar Bungay Robert Greene

Holy Wisdom, Augustine Baker

The Jew of Malta and the Massacre at Paris, Christopher Marlowe

Tamburlaine the Great, Parts 1 & 2 AND Massacre at Paris, Christopher Marlowe

All Ovids Elegies, Lucans First Booke, Dido Queene of Carthage, Hero and Leander, Christopher Marlowe

The Titan, Theodore Dreiser

Scapegoats of the Empire: The true story of the Bushveldt Carbineers, George Witton

All Hallows' Eve, Charles Williams

The Place of The Lion, Charles Williams

The Greater Trumps, Charles Williams

My Apprenticeship: Volumes I and II, Beatrice Webb

Last and First Men / Star Maker, Olaf Stapledon

Last and First Men, Olaf Stapledon

Darkness and the Light, Olaf Stapledon

The Worst Journey in the World, Apsley Cherry-Garrard

The Schoole of Abuse, Containing a Pleasaunt Invective Against Poets, Pipers, Plaiers, Iesters and Such Like Catepillers of the Commonwelth, Stephen Gosson

Russia in the Shadows, H. G. Wells

Wild Swans at Coole, W. B. Yeats

A hundreth good pointes of husbandrie, Thomas Tusser

The Collected Works of Nathanael West: "The Day of the Locust", "The Dream Life of Balso Snell", "Miss Lonelyhearts", "A Cool Million", Nathanael West

Miss Lonelyhearts & The Day of the Locust, Nathaniel West

The Worst Journey in the World, Apsley Cherry-Garrard

Scott's Last Expedition, V1, R. F. Scott

The Dream of Gerontius, John Henry Newman

The Brother of Daphne, Dornford Yates

The Downfall of Robert Earl of Huntington, Anthony Munday

Clayhanger, Arnold Bennett

The Regent, A Five Towns Story Of Adventure In London , Arnold Bennett

The Card, A Story Of Adventure In The Five Towns , Arnold Bennett

South: The Story of Shackleton's Last Expedition 1914-1917, Sir Ernest Shackketon

Greene's Groatsworth of Wit: Bought With a Million of Repentance, Robert Greene

Beau Sabreur, Percival Christopher Wren

The Hekatompathia, or Passionate Centurie of Love, Thomas Watson

The Art of Rhetoric, Thomas Wilson

Stepping Heavenward, Elizabeth Prentiss

Barker's Delight, or The Art of Angling, Thomas Barker

The Napoleon of Notting Hill, G.K. Chesterton

The Douay-Rheims Bible (The Challoner Revision)

Endimion - The Man in the Moone, John Lyly

Gallathea and Midas, John Lyly,

Mother Bombie, John Lyly

Manners, Custom and Dress During the Middle Ages and During the Renaissance Period, Paul Lacroix

Obedience of a Christian Man, William Tyndale

St. Patrick for Ireland, James Shirley

The Wrongs of Woman; Or Maria/Memoirs of the Author of a Vindication of the Rights of Woman, Mary Wollstonecraft and William Godwin

De Adhaerendo Deo. Of Cleaving to God, Albertus Magnus

Obedience of a Christian Man, William Tyndale

A Trick to Catch the Old One, Thomas Middleton

The Phoenix, Thomas Middleton

A Yorkshire Tragedy, Thomas Middleton (attrib.)

The Princely Pleasures at Kenelworth Castle, George Gascoigne

The Fair Maid of the West. Part I and Part II. Thomas Heywood

Proserpina, Volume I and Volume II. Studies of Wayside Flowers, John Ruskin

Our Fathers Have Told Us. Part I. The Bible of Amiens. John Ruskin

The Poetry of Architecture: Or the Architecture of the Nations of Europe Considered in Its Association with Natural Scenery and National Character, John Ruskin

The Endeavour Journal of Sir Joseph Banks. Sir Joseph Banks

Christ Legends: And Other Stories, Selma Lagerlof; (trans. Velma Swanston Howard)

Chamber Music, James Joyce

Blurt, Master Constable, Thomas Middleton, Thomas Dekker

Since Yesterday, Frederick Lewis Allen

The Scholemaster: Or, Plaine and Perfite Way of Teachyng Children the Latin Tong , Roger Ascham

The Wonderful Year, 1603, Thomas Dekker

Waverley, Sir Walter Scott

Guy Mannering, Sir Walter Scott

Old Mortality, Sir Walter Scott

The Knight of Malta, John Fletcher

The Double Marriage, John Fletcher and Philip Massinger

Space Prison, Tom Godwin

The Home of the Blizzard Being the Story of the Australasian Antarctic Expedition, 1911-1914, Douglas Mawson

Wild-goose Chase , John Fletcher

If You Know Not Me, You Know Nobody. Part I and Part II, Thomas Heywood

The Ragged Trousered Philanthropists, Robert Tressell

The Island of Sheep, John Buchan

Eyes of the Woods, Joseph Altsheler

The Club of Queer Trades, G. K. Chesterton

The Financier, Theodore Dreiser

Something of Myself, Rudyard Kipling

Law of Freedom in a Platform, or True Magistracy Restored, Gerrard Winstanley

Damon and Pithias, Richard Edwards

Dido Queen of Carthage: And, The Massacre at Paris, Christopher Marlowe

Cocoa and Chocolate: Their History from Plantation to Consumer, Arthur Knapp

Lady of Pleasure, James Shirley

The South Pole: An account of the Norwegian Antarctic expedition in the "Fram," 1910-12. Volume 1 and Volume 2, Roald Amundsen

A Yorkshire Tragedy, Thomas Middleton (attrib.)

The Tragedy of Soliman and Perseda, Thomas Kyd

The Rape of Lucrece. Thomas Heywood

Myths and Legends of Ancient Greece and Rome, E. M. Berens

In the Forbidden Land, Henry Savage Arnold Landor

Illustrated History of Furniture: From the Earliest to the Present Time, Frederick Litchfield

A Narrative of Some of the Lord's Dealings with George Müller Written by Himself (Parts I-IV, 1805-1856), George Müller

The Towneley Cycle Of The Mystery Plays (Or The Wakefield Cycle): Thirty-Two Pageants, Anonymous

The Insatiate Countesse, John Marston.

Spontaneous Activity in Education, Maria Montessori.

On the Art of Writing, Sir Arthur Quiller-Couch

The Well of the Saints, J. M. Synge

Bacon's Advancement Of Learning And The New Atlantis, Francis Bacon.

Catholic Tales And Christian Songs, Dorothy Sayers.

Two Little Savages: Being the Adventures of Two Boys who Lived as Indians and What they Learned, Ernest Thompson Seton

The Sadness of Christ, Thomas More

The Family of Love, Thomas Middleton

The Passing of the Aborigines: A Lifetime Spent Among the Natives of Australia, Daisy Bates

The Children, Edith Wharton

and many others…

Tell us what you would love to see in print again, at affordable prices!
Email: **benedictionbooks@btinternet.com**

www.ingramcontent.com/pod-product-compliance
Lightning Source LLC
Chambersburg PA
CBHW021538260326
41914CB00001B/62